Introduction to Marketing

Fourth Edition

Dr John Frain

INTERNATIONAL THOMSON BUSINESS PRESS

I Ⓣ P® An International Thomson Publishing Company

London • Bonn • Johannesburg • Madrid • Melbourne • Mexico City • New York • Paris
Singapore • Tokyo • Toronto • Albany, NY • Belmont, CA • Cincinnati, OH • Detroit, MI

Introduction to Marketing

Copyright © 1999 International Thomson Business Press

 A division of International Thomson Publishing
The ITP logo is a trademark under licence

British Library Cataloguing-in-Publication Data
A catalogue record for this book is available from the British Library

First edition published 1999 by International Thomson Business Press

Typeset by Columns Design Ltd, Reading, Berkshire
Printed in the UK by TJ International, Padstow, Cornwall

ISBN 1-86152-147-2

International Thomson Business Press
Berkshire House
168–173 High Holborn
London WC1V 7AA
UK

http://www.itbp.com

Contents

Abbreviations   vi

Preface   viiii

Chapter 1   Marketing:
Its Meaning and Significance   1

Chapter 2   Organizational Strategy   21

Chapter 3   Strategic Marketing:
Its Scope and Function   45

Chapter 4   Marketing in its Context, Part I:
Structure and Systems   75

Chapter 5   Marketing in its Context Part II:
Culture, Law and Ethics   93

Chapter 6   The Preparation Element, Part I:
Information as the Basis for Decision-Making   119

Chapter 7   The Preparation Element, Part II:
Customers and Customer Buying Behaviour   161

Chapter 8   The Strategic Formula, Element 2:
Products and Processes, Services and Ideas   193

Chapter 9   The Strategic Formula, Element 3:
Prices and Pricing Strategy   241

Chapter 10   The Strategic Formula, Element 4:
Distribution–Function and Strategy   263

Chapter 11   The Strategic Formula, Element 5:
Promotion–Function and Strategy   307

Chapter 12   The Strategic Formula, Element 6:
People   347

Chapter 13   The Broader Base of Marketing   371

Chapter 14   Thoughts on Forecasting and Marketing
Planning   393

Chapter 15   Marketing in the New Millennium   423

Bibliography   427

Index   437

Abbreviations

ABC	Audit Bureau of Circulations
ABSA	Association for Business Sponsorship of the Arts
ABMCR	Association of British Market Research Companies
AIDA	Attention, Interest, Desire, Action (model)
AMA	American Marketing Association
AMSO	Association of Market Survey Organisations
apcs	Additional Panel Classifications
ASA	Advertising Standards Authority
AT&T	Associated Telephone and Telegraph
ATR	awareness, trial, reinforcement (model)
BARB	Broadcasters' Audience Research Board Ltd.
BBC	British Broadcasting Corporation
BCG	Boston Consulting Group
BDHA	British Dental Health Association
BFA	British Franchise Association
BMRB	British Market Research Bureau
BPTO	brand/price trade-off model
BRAD	British Rate and Data
BSI	British Standards Institution
c.i.f.	cost, insurance and freight
c.k.d.	completely knocked down
CAB	Citizens' Advice Bureau
CAD/CAM	computer-aided design/computer-aided manufacturing
CAP	Committee of Advertising Practice
CAP	Common Agricultural Policy (EU)
CAPI	computer assisted personal interviewing
CATI	computer assisted telephone interviewing
CAVIAR	Cinema and Video Industry Audience Research
CBI	Confederation of British Industry
CEO	Chief Executive Officer
CIM	Chartered Institute of Marketing
CIM	computer-integrated manufacturing
CME	Chief Marketing Executive
CNG	Compressed natural gas
CSO	Central Statistical Office (until 1 April 1996)
CWS	Cooperative Wholesale Society
DAGMAR	Defining Advertising Goals for Measured Advertising Results (model)
DDP	delivery duty paid
DEC	Digital Equipment Corporation
DIY	do-it-yourself
DMU	decision-making unit
DSS	decision support systems
DTI	Department of Trade and Industry
EDI	electronic data interchange
EHO	environmental health officer
EIS	executive information system
EIU	Economist Intelligence Unit
EMU	European Monetary Union
EPOS	electronic point-of-sale
EU	European Union
f.o.b.	free on board
fmcg	fast moving consumer goods
GATT	General Agreement on Tariffs and Trade (see WTO)
GDP	gross domestic product
GUS	Great Universal Stores
HRM	human resource management
ICI	Imperial Chemical Industries

ILE	Inter-Linked Economy (of USA, Europe and Japan)
IMD	International Institute for Management Development
IMF	International Monetary Fund
IMRA	Industrial Marketing Research Association
IOCU	International Organization of Consumers' Unions
IPA	Institute of Practitioners in Advertising
IPR	Institute of Public Relations
ISBA	Incorporated Society of British Advertisers
ISIC	International Standard Industrial Classification
ISP	Institute of Sales Promotion
IT	information technology
ITC	Independent Television Commission
ITCA	Independent Television Companies Association
ITV	Independent Television
JIT	just-in-time
MBO	management by objectives
MIS	management information system
MKIS	marketing information system
MOPS	Mail Order Protection Scheme
MRS	Market Research Society
NAFTA	North American Free Trade Agreement
NHS	National Health Service
NRS	National Readership Surveys Ltd.
OFFER	Office of Electricity Regulations
OFGAS	Office of Gas Supply
OFT	Office of Fair Trading
OFTEL	Office of Telecommunications
OFWAT	Office of Water Supply
ONS	Office for National Statistics (from 1 April 1996)
OPSC	Office for Population Studies and Census (until 1 April 1996)
OSCAR	Outdoor Site Classification and Audience Research
OTS	opportunities to see
p.a.	per annum
p.k.d.	partially knocked down
PARC	Palo Alto Research Centre (Rank Xerox)
PC	personal computer
PIMS	profit impact of market strategy
PLC	public limited company
POUNC	Post Office Users' National Council
PR	public relations
PSM	price sensitivity measurement
RAJAR	Radio Joint Audience Research
RI	Research International Ltd
ROI	return on investment
RSA	Royal Society of Arts
SBU	strategic business unit
SIC	Standard Industrial Classification
SMA	Semiconductor Manufacturers' Association
SMEs	small to medium-sized enterprises
TDC	total distribution costs
TEC	Training and Enterprise Council
TGI	Target Group Index
TGRs	Target Group Ratings
TQM	total quality management
TSD	trading standards department
UNO	United Nations Organisation
USP	unique selling position
VMS	vertical marketing system
WTO	World Trade Organisation

Preface

It is very nearly twenty years since the first edition of this textbook was being prepared. Since then, marketing has evolved beyond its specialist focus and is far more strategic in its role. At the same time, its application has become more diffused and there are welcome signs that marketing is becoming established as a 'whole organization' concept and activity.

Since this fourth edition reflects these developments, it has become substantially different from previous editions. For example, in the past, like others, I have given the impression that the basic requirement for organizational success is to recognize the importance of marketing and plan accordingly. 'Making it happen' would then come about in some satisfactorily disembodied manner. This new text emphasizes that nothing ever happens unless *people* are committed to making it happen. There are countless references to this in the early parts of the book and a full chapter (Chapter 12) is substantially devoted to it.

Also, this edition makes a firm stand for ethical behaviour in all phases of an organization's operations and management. In *The World in 1999* (Economist Publications), Jim Wolfensohn, President of the World Bank has this to say:

> As the battered economies of the emerging markets piece themselves back together in 1999 one lesson will not be forgotten, rotten national economies spring from rotten corporations; if business life is not run on honest and open lines, there is little chance that the wider economy can be.

Given recent world-wide scandals, and the disregard for the planet and its population emanating from some organizations, it is an observation both necessary and overdue. Those engaged in marketing, the most public of organizational activities, need to keep it constantly in mind and, importantly, to act on it. I do not defend the fact that throughout this fourth edition they are constantly entreated to do so.

In keeping with the broadening of the book's objectives, the level of treatment of its subject matter has been raised so that, while still an introduction to the subject, it is aimed at first degree and MBA students, CIM and CAM students and practitioners wishing to keep abreast of developments in the subject.

As always, I am indebted to the many writers and researchers whose work I have drawn upon. I must also thank the large number of organizations who have so willingly sent original material for use in compiling the text. The following deserve special mention:

- A.C. NielsonCorporation
- A.C. Nielson•MEAL
- The Advertising Association
- The Advertising Standards Authority (ASA)
- Association of Market Survey Organisations (AMSO)

- Barclays Bank PLC
- British Market Research Bureau (BMRB International)
- CACI Limited
- The CAM Foundation
- The Chartered Institute of Marketing (CIM)
- The Committee of Advertising Practice (CAP)
- The Consumers' Association
- Cooperative Wholesale Society (CWS)
- Department of Trade and Industry (DTI)
- Economist Intelligence Unit Limited
- Euromonitor PLC
- Industrial Marketing Research Association (IMRA)
- Institute of Public Relations (IPR)
- The Market Research Society
- Mintel International Group Limited
- National Consumer Council
- The National Newspapers' Mail Order Protection Scheme Limited (MOPS)
- Office of Fair Trading
- Office for National Statistics (ONS)
- Research International Limited (RI)
- Taylor Nelson AGB PLC
- Verdict Research Limited

The text has a liberal sprinkling of extracts from articles in newspapers and magazines. I am grateful to the publishers and journalists concerned.

At the personal level, Paula Frain, LLB(Hons), Solicitor must again be thanked for her scrutiny of the material on the law and the ready assistance of Philip Spink and David Croft were also greatly appreciated. Sue Bioletti prepared my material for despatch to the publisher with her usual energy and good humour while Julian Thomas, Editorial Director at ITP, did much to mitigate the loneliness of the long-distance writer with his enthusiasm and support for the project. As ever, the understanding and encouragement of my wife Patricia was always in evidence. In one of his prefaces, J K Galbraith noted that all writers are more in debt to friends than they usually know. How true that was in this instance. Only errors and omissions have been perpetrated without assistance.

John Frain

Marketing: its meaning and significance

The significance of marketing

As this chapter was being written, the author turned to the appointments section of the UK national newspapers. As usual, there were a considerable number of advertisements for marketing executives. Here is just a sample:

- Marketing Director – business-to-business electronics
- Marketing Director – transport industry information systems
- Marketing Director – thick film membrane switches and touch panels
- Marketing Manager – confectionery (based Romania)
- Marketing Director – paper and print products
- Marketing Manager – business financial services
- Marketing Managers – fast moving consumer goods (based Moscow and St Petersburg)

Even this small list indicates the wide variety of posts available to the marketing professional and we can add to it, for two other advertisements appeared on that day:

- Marketing and Fundraising Director – The Royal Horticultural Society
- Marketing and Commercial Manager – Bath Rugby Club

On any day, in fact, skilled marketing personnel are in demand. The advertisements indicate that in addition to industrial and commercial organizations, charities, tourist boards, banks, business schools, libraries and football clubs seek marketing executives too. For its part, the academic press offers appointments to lectureships, readerships and professorships in marketing, while even towns and cities seem bent on marketing themselves. On this last point, the UK reader will be well aware of the City of Manchester's efforts to attract world sporting events while the organization responsible for the City of Birmingham's efforts to market itself has said: 'Birmingham is a product. It is capable of being branded just as Cadbury brands its chocolate products' (Aldersey-Williams, 1994).

The Isle of Man's campaign to become a world centre for financial services and the way in which numerous regions of the UK stress to potential investors their several competitive advantages are examples of what has come to be called 'place' marketing.

Recently, too, a newspaper headline declared:

Marketing practice far from perfect

1

This referred to the findings of a survey (Atchley, 1993) conducted within the accountancy profession, while in early 1996 *The Times* newspaper announced its fifth annual conference on 'Competitive Marketing for Accountants and Solicitors'. The conference programme, and its related workshop, included such topics as:

- niche marketing;
- changing the culture;
- targeting profitable work;
- developing an effective marketing strategy;
- how to do client surveys;
- database marketing.

Yet, not so many years ago, the idea of a learned profession marketing its services would have been greeted with doubt, uncertainty, hostility perhaps.

So, even the limited evidence provided up to this point clearly suggests that 'marketing' is a word of great current significance and here a further point must be made: reverting to the first in the list of advertisements above (Marketing Director – business to business electronics), part of its text read as follows:

> *We are looking for an outstanding Marketing Director with broadly based business skills to join the senior team and work closely with them, contributing original ideas and thoroughly researched plans. An understanding of the latest developments in the electronics industry and the ability to respond to challenges created by multiple businesses will be fundamental to your success.*
>
> *Using your excellent organisational and intuitive skills, you will take the lead in developing long-term strategic plans. This will include diversification into adjacent markets and products, prioritising the strengths of the existing business against available opportunities and leading the implementation of those plans.*

A dictionary definition of marketing usually employs such phrases as:

- to deal at a market;
- to put on the market;
- to buy and sell.

Yet the above advertisement suggests a much more extensive activity, seemingly central to the very existence of the company, as typified by references to:

- 'broadly based business skills' and
- 'long-term strategic plans'.

That the company is in earnest about the scope and responsibilities of the post is affirmed by the remuneration available ('£100,000 package') and the fact that the successful applicant will also become the 'Managing Director designate'.

It is worth adding that all the other advertisements listed at the beginning of this chapter, including those of The Royal Horticultural Society and the Bath Rugby Club, testify to a *broad*, *strategic role* for marketing, taking it well beyond a dictionary definition.

The significance of marketing appears to be clear enough but at this early stage in your study its precise scope and function are no doubt less certain. Defining marketing in its fullest and best sense is part of the purpose of this book. Let us now turn to it.

The meaning of marketing

Outside management and academic circles, most people asked to define marketing would lean heavily on the dictionary definition, suggesting it is really another name for selling. Some might also refer to its linkages with advertising and packaging. Of course it is correct to say that marketing is to do with selling and, as we shall come to understand the term 'marketing' in this book, we shall see that it emphasizes the vital role of selling. However, we shall also come to appreciate that it incorporates many other activities, including:

- marketing research;
- product design and development;
- forecasting and planning;
- related financial projections and control measures.

Beyond this, we shall see that marketing goes much further than even these activities and is also a guiding principle of how an organization should operate. This means we will have arrived at marketing of the *marketing concept*. It is this *concept* (note the emphasis), beyond its undoubtedly important sales function, which has given marketing a great deal of its present significance. It explains why thousands of organizations world-wide have either adopted marketing as both a guiding principle and an operational process, or are striving to do so.

Then finally, and as we noted in the job advertisements earlier, it will be clear to us that *marketing* has now become firmly linked with *strategy* so that *strategic* marketing has entered the vocabulary of organizations.

There are as many definitions of 'strategy' as there are authors in the field and it is difficult at this early stage to provide one which does not use words calling for further explanation. However, the following should be broadly understandable:

> Strategy defines where the organization wants to go to fulfil its purpose and achieve its mission. It provides the framework for guiding choices which determine the organization's nature and direction. These choices relate to the organization's products or services, markets, key capabilities, growth, return on capital and allocation of resources (Armstrong, 1993).

Figures 1.1–1.3 aim to provide an illustration of the development of marketing, from *function* to *concept* to *strategy*. The following section offers some words of explanation for these figures, then moves us towards a definition of marketing in its fullest and best sense.

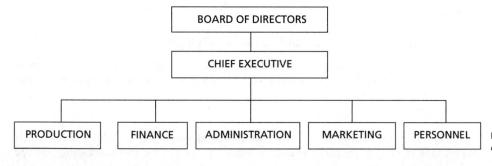

Figure. 1.1. *Marketing as an operating function*

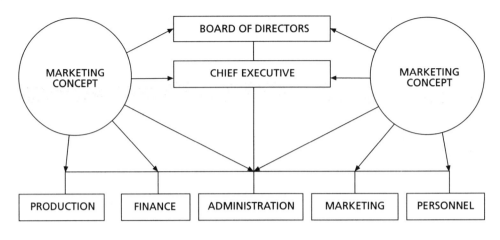

Figure. 1.2. *Marketing as philosophy and function*

Figure. 1.3. *Marketing in its strategic and functional roles*

Defining marketing: *function to concept to strategy*

Marketing as a function

Explanations under this heading need not detain us for long. The basic operations of an organization may be thought of as *functions*. For example, business organizations are usually structured around five basic functions. As Figure 1.1 indicates, these are:

● Production

● Finance

● Administration

● Marketing, and

● Personnel.

In smaller organizations, finance and administration functions are often combined.

The Figure 1.1 type of structure is a traditional one and, typically, a traditional view is taken of the marketing function – confining it to such activities as selling and advertising.

Marketing as a concept

A *concept* may be thought of as the fundamental principle, or philosophy which directs how the organization operates. As Figure 1.2 indicates, the *marketing concept* is not confined to the marketing function, it permeates the whole organization. We shall now spend a longer time defining the marketing concept and explaining why it has required its present importance.

First, let us look at two definitions which are grounded in the idea of marketing as an organizational way of life. These are linked, particularly, to business organizations:

> The simplest definition of marketing is that it is a process of matching the resources of a business with identified customer needs. In other words, marketing is concerned with customer satisfaction and with the focusing of the organisation's resources to ensure that the customer is satisfied – at a profit to the business (Christopher and McDonald, 1991).

and

> Marketing is the management process responsible for identifying, anticipating and satisfying customer requirements profitably (Chartered Institute of Marketing, n.d.).

These statements have much in common for they emphasize:

- the importance of the customer;
- the importance of profit;
- the importance of a managerial, organization-wide approach.

So when the marketing concept is applied to a business we can say it means at least three things:

- that every aspect of the firm's operations must be clearly based on the importance of the customer;
- that the firm must make an adequate 'profit' for its efforts (but more on this point below); and
- that all parts of the organization must co-operate enthusiastically in the marketing process.

Two eminent authorities wish to take a definition of marketing further and few, if any, would argue with them. They wonder whether:

> the pure marketing concept is adequate in an age of environmental problems, resource shortages, rapid population growth, world wide inflation and neglected social services (Kotler and Armstrong, 1990, p 14).

Their concern is that in satisfying individual wants, firms may not always be doing what is best for the consumers of their output or for society itself in the long run. They conclude that, in its basic form, the marketing concept overlooks possible conflicts between short-run consumer *wants* and long-run consumer *welfare*.

Hence their proposal for a *societal marketing concept*. The title is not particularly felicitous but the idea is logical and highly important to today's world. They define it as follows: 'A principle of enlightened marketing holding that a company should make marketing decisions by considering consumers' wants, the company's requirements, consumers' long-run interests and society's long-run interests' (Kotler and Armstrong, 1990, p 525).

Figure 1.4 attempts to depict the application of the societal marketing concept in a business firm and to summarize what has been said so far about marketing.

In concluding this short section on marketing as a concept we can say that it emphasizes:

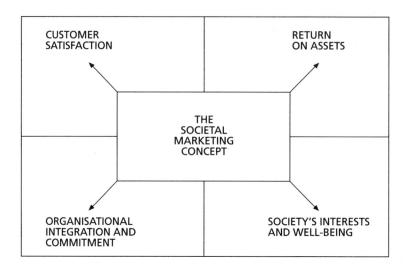

Figure. 1.4. *The societal marketing concept in a business firm*

- customer satisfaction;

- organizational commitment to the customer;

- the long-run welfare of the wider society

as key motive forces in attaining organizational objectives. Earlier, however, we identified profit as another component of effective performance. On this aspect, it is important to make some further points.

First, marketing in the business organization is very much to do with the generalized notion of *profit* and this is another reason why it should not be confused with selling, for as someone has wisely pointed out (Chisnall, 1989, p 8) selling can be accomplished and actually result in a loss, whereas marketing focuses on *profitable opportunities* suitable for the *resources* of a company. Sales growth may be linked to profitability which is why it is pursued by many companies, but this is not always the case. Also, customer satisfaction does not imply giving customers whatever they want but rather what can be provided with the resources, or assets, available to the company. This idea of *asset-based marketing* – the effective deployment of the firm's resources towards the most appropriate and profitable opportunities is the way to success through marketing. We shall be looking again at profit and profitability before the end of this chapter.

The second point to be made is that in examining what marketing entails we have so far considered only the business or profit organization. Yet a great deal of marketing is carried out by non-profit organizations. Government campaigns to support the privatization of the public utilities and to reduce drink-driving are conducted for non-profit motives as are, broadly, the marketing activities of charities, tourist boards, political parties, cities and geographical regions, libraries and museums.

The distinction between profit and non-profit is not a precise one because, as has been pointed out (Blois, 1987, p 405), what the term non-profit means in practice is that:

- some organizations may pursue profit-making activities but only in support of their prime (non-profit) objective; and that

- while other organizations do not seek profits as a primary goal, they do need to cover all their costs.

Moreover, to blur the distinction even further, we shall see in the next chapter that a business firm will typically set for itself a mixture of profit and non-profit objectives.

It seems reasonable therefore to substitute the word 'objectives' for 'profit' and 'non-profit' and this enables us to summarize what has been said so far in this chapter with the following short definition:

> The marketing concept emphasizes total organizational commitment to customer satisfaction and loyalty and to the long-run welfare of society as the motive forces for attaining organizational objectives.

Note that loyalty as well as satisfaction is now emphasized for, as we shall see later, *customer retention* should be the ultimate goal.

Marketing and strategy

You are invited to look back at the definition of strategy given on page 3. Words and phrases such as:

> 'to fulfil its purpose'; 'to achieve its mission'; 'the framework for guiding choices'; and 'the organization's nature and direction'

all indicate the fundamental importance of strategy to organizational existence and 'health'.

In all types of organization, there are issues so fundamentally important that they require the most competent judgement and decision-making of top management if these organizations are to survive. These are the *strategic issues* and among them are:

- consideration of the field in which the organization currently operates and other fields in which it might productively operate;
- the primary purpose of the organization (its mission);
- its short-term, medium-term and visionary objectives or goals;
- the framework of values within which the organization operates (its culture);
- the relationship between the organization and its environment (i.e. how it is influenced by the political, economic, social and technological forces which surround it and how it interacts with its customers, suppliers, competitors and society in general)
- the way in which it acquires, uses and renews its strategic inputs (i.e. information, people, finance, equipment and other scarce resources) and the nature of its output;
- the way in which the organization is structured so as to best utilize its resources and the mechanisms it uses for decision-making;
- the processes it employs to monitor and control the effectiveness of the way it uses its resources ('effectiveness' here being taken to mean 'doing the right things' as distinct from the lesser, though important, criterion of 'efficiency' which means 'doing things right');
- the way in which all effort is integrated and motivated in order to obtain the organization's objectives.

Strategy ultimately derives from *stratos*, the Greek word for army. It has been more widely interpreted as the 'art of generalship', i.e. how to use the resources at one's disposal to overcome an enemy. Interestingly, the link between management principles and military concepts is exemplified by language: marketing operations, for example, are frequently referred to as 'campaigns' or 'battles for market share' while the marketing process itself has been referred to, over-dramatically perhaps, as 'the art of civilized warfare'.

Such expressions as:

- asset-based marketing, and

- sustainable competitive advantage

which we shall meet quite often in this book are only a step or two away from the military expressions which the term strategy evokes.

There are countless instances of why the development of strategy is intrinsically important. The latest evidence is provided by a survey of 200 companies (Kelly, 1996), carried out by a dozen researchers working full-time for four months, and dealing with the gap between the information required by large investors in leading companies and the information published by those companies. The investors were based in the USA and five European countries. They had total assets under management of US $2500 billion (£1515 billion). The companies surveyed were located in twelve countries and represented a cross-section of leading industries.

An interesting discovery of the survey was that 'quality of management' was consistently stated as the main factor governing investment decisions. Investors try to evaluate this quality by examining six areas. In the order set out in a summary of the survey, these are:

- clarity of business strategy;

- performance (track record);

- ability to set and meet objectives;

- management experience;

- communication and presentation skills;

- credibility, consistency and integrity.

So strategic planning is more than a bureaucratic, intellectual exercise, as evidenced by this survey of 200 very large – mostly multinational – companies. Another survey (Kashani, 1996), conducted at the International Institute for Management Development (IMD), Lausanne, one of Europe's leading business schools, indicated that, of late, marketing has taken on a highly significant role in the *planning and development* of strategy.

More than 90 per cent of all the 220 manager-respondents to the survey reported that marketing had undergone major changes in their organizations as a result of which it had emerged larger in stature and with more influence on strategic decisions. Among these managers there was a surprising degree of uniformity both internationally and across a wide spectrum of sectors: raw materials, consumer and industrial goods, high technology products and low technology services. They stated that marketing has evolved to take on a far greater role than previously. The following extracts from a report of the survey substantiate this:

> *From specialist to strategic. With its more result-oriented scope, marketing has evolved beyond its traditional specialist focus … In its broader scope today's marketing is far more strategic than in its previous role as a specialist function – and with far more impact on results* (Kashani, 1996).

> *From isolated to widespread. As marketing has broadened in its scope, it has also become more diffused within the organization. That means marketing (or, more precisely, marketing orientation) is no longer an isolated concern of a few but has now become everyone's business – and for good reasons. … In short, marketing in its previous form has disappeared, only to return transformed and commanding a greater share of top management's attention* (Kashani, 1996).

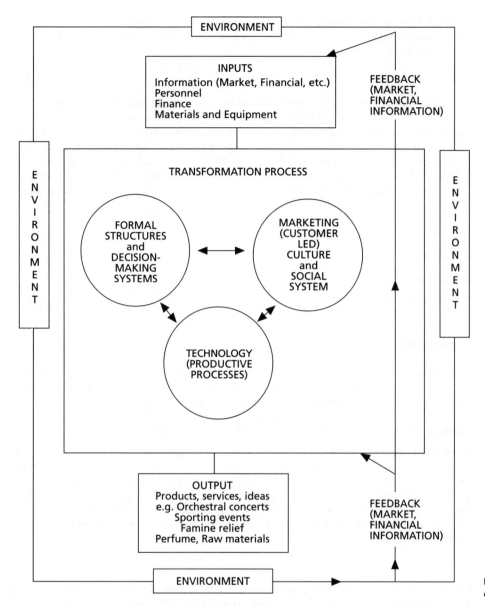

Figure. 1.5. *A market-led organisational system*

In the format of this book, the author has tried to reflect the changed and enlarged status of marketing, which is why Chapter 2 is completely taken up with the development of the organization's strategy. The nature of a marketing strategy to serve this broader organizational strategy is outlined in Chapter 3 and the context within which strategic marketing takes place is outlined in Chapters 4 and 5. The role of marketing research in providing information for managerial decision-making provides the context for Chapter 6. Only then does the book deal with the important but more specific areas of marketing activity – product development, pricing, distribution, selling, advertising, etc.

In the meantime, Figure 1.5 attempts to provide a simple outline of the strategic role of marketing in the operations of an organization, a notion introduced in Figure 1.3. Figure 1.5 is also meant to depict the findings of the IMD survey discussed above.

In order to understand fully the implications of Figure 1.5 it is important first to appreciate one or two concepts which have been adopted to analyse and explain how organizations operate. These concepts of *organizational behaviour* have been developed by social scientists from their studies of how organizations work. They have subsequently entered the vocabulary and the practice of managers. Let us look at some of these concepts.

Systems thinking

First, the repeated cycles of input, transformation, output and renewed input were identified. In its simplest form an organization can be thought of as a system involving an input, a transformation process and an output. Next, organizations do not stand alone, they are part of an economic and social fabric or *environment*. In other words, since they are part of a larger system, they can never be independent of external forces. They are affected by, and in turn, affect these external forces, so that at the boundaries of the production process there are several environmental influences at work:

- economic;
- political;
- demographic;
- technological;
- legal;
- competitive.

Central also to this type of systems thinking is the notion of the *feedback*, which provides the organization with knowledge of the environment, and particularly changes in it. The organization may therefore make adjustments to its structure and functions – at best to take full advantage of any opportunities provided by environmental change and at worst to avoid any threats posed by such change.

Monitoring the external forces which act on the organization is known as environmental scanning, a process in which the strengths and weaknesses of the organization are matched with the threats and opportunities posed by the environment. The technique employed, as we shall see more fully in Chapter 2, is known as SWOT analysis (strengths, weaknesses, opportunities, threats). It is an important feature of strategic decision-making. It should be noted that Figure 1.5 represents the environment in a simplified form.

Organizational culture

There has also been a growing realization, by both theorists and practitioners, that the strategy and operations of an organization are heavily influenced by its *culture* – that is the set of key values, beliefs, understandings and norms of behaviour which prevails within the organization.

For example, organizations in which the prevailing beliefs are essentially conservative, where low-risk strategies, secure markets and well-tried solutions are valued have been classified (Miles and Snow, 1978) as *defender-type* organizations. By contrast, organizations in which the dominant beliefs have more to do with innovation and breaking new ground, in which management is predisposed to higher-risk strategies and the quest for new opportunities, have been classified as *prospector-type* organizations.

Similarly, a *customer-led* culture exists when the prevailing belief is that the best way to manage the organization's affairs is for it to face *outwards* (i.e. towards the wants and needs of its customers) and not *inwards* (towards the organization itself and the way it has always operated).

This inward-looking culture, or orientation, often arises because the organization, instead of concentrating on its customers, is paying more attention to:

- its current methods of production;
- its current management experience;
- its existing raw materials and components;
- the current skills of its labour force.

In a highly competitive global economy, all of these things may be able to provide sought-after value for money, they may be key marketing assets. On the other hand, they may not. It all depends on the opinion of the customer. Since, as has been neatly expressed, marketing is about making what you can sell and not trying to sell what you like making, it is easy to see why marketing will thrive within a customer-led culture, within a customer orientation rather than a production orientation.

Figure 1.5 depicts a market-led organizational system. What is this meant to convey? These are the ideas central to such a system:

- the organization does not stand alone but exists within an environment, and by gaining constant feedback from the market (i.e. its customers) it maintains itself in being by adjusting its inputs and its methods of operation (its transformation process) if and when necessary;
- in addition to the way it is structured and the way in which it produces its output (i.e. its 'technology') its culture is also a key aspect of how it operates; and, this should be customer-led;

It can be seen from the examples of output that, in addition to business firms, all types of organizations (charities, sporting organizations, etc.) can and do adopt systems thinking in order to develop their strategies, based on a market- or customer-led approach. As the book proceeds, it will also become clear that the task of obtaining feedback, to monitor performance and make adjustments where necessary, is the central role of *marketing research*.

Marketing in practice

A definition of the marketing concept was proposed earlier, which was considered suitable for both profit and non-profit organizations:

> *The marketing concept emphasizes total organizational commitment to customer satisfaction and loyalty and to the long-run welfare of society as the motive forces for attaining organizational objectives.*

We can extract from this four factors underlying the unique nature of the concept:

- customer satisfaction and loyalty;
- organizational objectives;
- the long-run welfare of society;
- total organizational commitment.

In this section we shall be examining these factors in more detail, with practical examples of how they have been used to guide operations. As we proceed it will become clear that while these factors are being examined separately they complement and reinforce each other in powerful ways.

Customer satisfaction and loyalty

The word customer incorporates all the individuals and organizations being supplied. They may be end-users (consumers) or intermediaries (e.g. distributors). At this stage, we will make no distinction, though later in the book we shall see that their needs differ.

A good example of responsiveness to customer interests was provided by the conference organized by the UK Semiconductor Manufacturers' Association (SMA), in association with *The Times* newspaper. A large number of representatives of the electronic and electrical equipment industry were asked:

- *'Are we doing things right?'*
- *'Is what we do what customers want?'*
- *'How can we improve dialogue and the way we operate?'*

A spokesman for the SMA said: 'We as semiconductor manufacturers can only be as successful as our customers and we'd like to see them challenge us, push us harder' (Manners, 1993).

The key objective of the conference was to bring chip-makers and chip-users together to see how they could best use each others' skills and market their knowledge with the aim of advancing the electronics industry as a whole.

Another instance of the increasing focus on the customer was provided by the extensive survey of senior business opinion commissioned by the Digital Equipment Corporation (DEC) and the UK's Institute of Management. Here the primary aim was to discover what lessons British industry had learned from the economic recession of the late 1980s to early 1990s. When asked which steps taken to counter the recession had proven most effective, a major factor emerging was greater responsiveness to customers. More than 90 per cent of the executives interviewed agreed that customer focus and service were vital (though, sadly, it must be said that less than 50 per cent believed their own organizations were up to standard in this respect).

A third example comes from the Dell Computer Group. In the Spring of 1996 Dell, in its latest performance figures, reported a gratifying vindication of its direct-to-user sales strategy. Record sales of £3.5 billion had been achieved in the financial year ending 30 January 1995 – a 52 per cent increase on the previous year. Net profit had risen by 82 per cent to £180 million, strengthening the company's determination to build on the 58 per cent compound annual revenue growth of the previous five years.

The Dell Group considers the first principle of commerce to be that the 'customer is king' and bases this belief at the heart of its strategy. Its chairman and chief executive adds:

> Companies that fail to understand the way the market is going will pay for their lack of vision. In the year 2000 people will be able to create much larger enterprises faster – presenting a real challenge for companies hindered by their successes of the past (Dell, 1996).

Its customer focus has assisted the Dell Group to grow from very small beginnings to the present day, when it employs more than 8400 people and has 31 offices worldwide.

A fourth example of the benefits of customer orientation is provided by a very small company, again in the computing field. The 30 engineers of the Eden Group work in a disused chapel on the edge of the UK's Peak District National Park. They produce software to operate portable personal communicators, which can send and receive faxes and e-mail messages. It is likely to be some time before such communications become popular in the UK and therefore Eden's attention is directed to the markets of south-east Asia where, in the latest generation of consumer electronics, it competes with some of the largest names in US software.

The Eden salesforce consists of one person, the marketing director, but it has already sold its operating system to three hardware manufacturers including Hitachi. Since many companies in Asia have been angered by companies selling them technology that does not even exist, in practical terms, Eden have had to undertake a long process of gaining credibility. The managing director says: 'Our philosophy is to work in partnership with our clients. So we work with the silicon chip manufacturers to sell a complete solution to the companies producing the hardware' (quoted in Wolffe, 1996). Eden's sales are based on a series of licensing contracts which tailor the software to each customer. By means of a 'long courtship' with a wide range of contacts, Eden have concluded a series of contracts with such producers as Motorola, Philips and Hitachi. These organizations use their own sales teams to sell Eden software alongside their own processors.

It is interesting to note that a 'long courtship' strategy underlies Eden's marketing success, for such an approach epitomizes the increasingly important concept of *relationship marketing*. This is based on the belief that marketing in its fullest and best sense is to do with long-term, mutually satisfying relationships with customers, as opposed to a *transactional* approach where the relationship may not extend beyond a single contract. Reference will be made to the economic and other benefits of relationship marketing as the book proceeds. Here it might be useful to add that the concept, in its most complete form yet, is in evidence at the new assembly plant for Skoda, the VW subsidiary, at Mlada Boleslav, north of Prague.

The idea of co-ordinated production in motor manufacture is hardly revolutionary, producers in the West having followed the Japanese introduction of just-in-time (JIT) deliveries and other close-coupling techniques between supplier and customer for more than a decade. What is striking about the Mlada Boleslav development is that six important component suppliers have been allocated special zones adjacent to the production line in order to pre-assemble parts just before they are required for the manufacture of Skoda's Octavia saloon. The normally straight assembly line has been curved into a U-shape enabling the suppliers' zones to be located just where their parts have to be fitted to the Octavia. The curved production line also allows the suppliers' zones to be located along the exterior walls of the assembly area permitting direct truck access from outside the plant. This is a new dimension of what is meant by 'getting close to the customer' and since components account for approximately 60 per cent of total manufacturing costs of a new car, the economic benefits need no elaboration.

Keeping customers happy is of decided value to supplier and customer. Keeping happy customers is even more important as, in business organizations for example, it is being increasingly recognized that *customer retention* has a direct and significant impact on profitability.

An analysis by Bain & Co., management consultants, has disclosed that a 5 per cent increase in customer retention provides a marked increase in profitability – ranging from 25 per cent in bank deposits to as much as 85 per cent in car servicing (Murphy, 1966). A study by Price Waterhouse, accountants, demonstrates that a 2 per cent increase in customer retention has the same impact on profits as a 10 per cent reduction in overheads.

In most business organizations, acquiring customers usually entails disproportionately heavy expenditure at the primary stage – a process known as investment budgeting. Consequently, the return from each customer usually increases over time. Additionally, customer expenditure generally accelerates over time and buying behaviour becomes more efficient, resulting in cost savings for the supplier. Loyal customers also frequently recommend the supplier's service to others.

There is an important distinction between customer *satisfaction* and customer *loyalty*. US researchers Howe and Gaeddert (see Murphy, 1996) discovered that 40 per cent of customers who claimed to be satisfied subsequently switched suppliers. Similarly, consultants Bain & Co. reported that 60–80 per cent of customers who defected had informed interviewers immediately before defecting that they were 'satisfied' or 'very satisfied'. It would seem therefore that 'satisfaction' is a passive state – a willingness to stay until something better is offered whereas 'loyalty' denotes a positive inclination to stay.

The competition for customer loyalty is well illustrated in the UK's food retailing sector. It is estimated that two-thirds of UK adults have supermarket loyalty cards. While the companies concerned (Tesco, Sainsbury, Asda, Safeway, etc.) report increased sales beyond the level required to justify the additional promotion and administrative costs, the key value of loyalty schemes is the information obtained on customers. By November 1996, Tesco, for example, had conducted some 1300 different direct mail campaigns targeting vegetarians, diabetics, students, pensioners and others, utilizing information drawn from their database of 'Clubcard' holders.

Figure 1.6 illustrates some of the potential benefits to an organization which fosters long-term relationships with its customers. A final word on the importance of the customer can be left to the Chairman of Unilever, one of the world's largest companies:

> As anyone charged with corporate governance will attest, the public listed company survives and prospers to the extent that it meets and satisfies – in quantifiable and measured terms – the needs and requirements of a variety of stakeholders. ... The company answers those complex but interrelated challenges by one single means – by satisfying its customers ... with goods or services which they have agreed to purchase, at a price which demonstrates value added. Its ultimate stakeholder, therefore, is its customer, without whose approval the whole process is meaningless (Perry, 1996).

Organizational objectives

Organizations are established in order to achieve specific *objectives*. The attainment of these objectives is so crucial to the organization that if it fails to achieve them, the organization itself may be said to have failed.

If the primary objective of an organization is non-economic we refer to it as a non-profit organization. The British Red Cross, the Multiple Sclerosis Society and the Health and Safety Executive are all non-profit organizations and their primary objective is indicated by their title. As has been pointed out (Blois, 1987, p 405), such

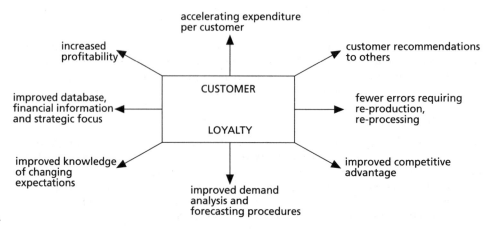

Figure 1.6. *Some potential benefits of fostering long-term customer relationships.*

organizations may undertake profit-making activities, for they must attract sufficient income to stay in existence to pursue their primary objective. Within its mix of objectives the non-profit organization may therefore pursue economic goals e.g.:

- *full cost recovery* – breaking even;
- *partial cost recovery* – minimizing the subsidies from other sources;
- *usage targeting* – ensuring the fixed resources available are fully utilised – as would a voluntary organization offering shelter to the homeless.

A business firm will also invariably have a mix of economic and non-economic objectives. Here are some non-economic objectives, linked to fields in which they would be particularly significant:

- leadership for innovation – computer software;
- quality leadership – expensive watches;
- leadership for financial security – banking;
- leadership for environmental concern – chemicals manufacture;
- leadership for safety – airline travel.

That said, 'the defining purpose of business is to maximise owner value over the long term by selling goods or services' (Sternberg, 1994, p 32). In other words unless the primary objective of a business is economic it is, simply, not a business. For the moment let us loosely call the primary objective the *profit objective*, although it has to be said that UK firms have been criticized for being too narrowly focused on short-term profit.

Indubitably, a business must make profit in order to:

- provide a return to investors which is better than alternative forms of investment;
- provide sufficient finance to cover the depreciation of its assets (e.g. buildings, machinery);
- provide sufficient funds for research and development to maintain and improve its competitive advantage.

An improvement in profit, or balance over costs, could be obtained by increasing sales revenue or by reducing costs. It is simple to see the contribution of marketing to increasing revenue but what is not so widely appreciated is how, with its sensitivity to the market, to the expectations of customers, marketing can *help to reduce costs*. The following example should make this clear.

In the early 1980s, Siemens of Germany was confronted by falling market prices for its medical equipment and by intense Japanese competition. The company had operated in a sellers' market for 20 years and had expensively customized its products for hospitals and other users. Study of the market revealed, however, that soaring costs were now making public health authorities more price conscious and customers were no longer prepared to pay for special features. Moreover, Toshiba and other Japanese companies were offering equipment which met users' needs without being too sophisticated. Manufacturers outside Japan, such as General Electric in the USA, were also competing aggressively.

In this situation, ironically, Siemens discovered that what had previously been regarded as a strength of German industry – engineering perfectionism – was now a brake on progress. Speaking of the danger of 'over-engineering' a spokesman for the firm said: 'The entry of the Japanese and slower growth [in the market] meant that our strength was no longer our strength but our weakness' (Fisher, 1994).

By the late 1980s Siemens had launched a radical programme to cut costs by streamlining its manufacturing operations, reducing development times and removing unnecessary frills from its products. This was no easy task, for Siemens' engineers had been educated very differently from their counterparts in Japan and the USA. They had been trained to produce a 'technical best' product whereas in the USA and Japan 'design to cost' had been emphasized throughout product development.

This brief illustration demonstrates how the closer attention to customer expectations implied by the market concept can be viewed as a means to improving profit performance. It is also a telling example of the dangers of production orientation, i.e. of looking inwards towards the firm and not outwards towards the market and, finally, it is the first of a number of examples in the book of how in marketing, as distinct from selling, cost-consciousness receives its requisite high level of attention.

The long-run welfare of society

The context in which organizations operate is undergoing significant change and there is an increasing call for business organizations, in particular, to be more accountable. First, despite the setbacks and frustrations of what has patronisingly been called 'the environmental lobby', organizations are being reminded of their responsibility to protect the world and its creatures from any harmful effects of their activities. Concern about the rate of depletion of scarce resources, about global warming, about the pollution of the air, seas and rivers, the safe disposal of radioactive waste, the extinction of rare species of birds and animals and the threat to the countryside posed by unbridled urban and motorway development, is clear and continuous.

At the same time, a number of financial scandals and incidences of fraud and 'insider dealings' have occurred in many countries, including the UK, within the last decade or so, and have led to mounting pressure on governments to legislate for the protection of investors, taxpayers, employees and others. The rewards obtained by some senior managers have also attracted strong criticism: customers of UK privatized water companies, for example, find it hard to reconcile the salaries and share options of their managers with the drought restrictions induced by the loss of as much as 30 per cent of supplies through lack of investment to curb leakages.

Finally, and not least, the unequal distribution of wealth and power within many societies and the contrast between the rich countries and those of the Third World are seen by some (Galbraith, 1996) as the most serious problems for society to confront at this time. There is a steadily widening demand for a total rejection of the 'greed is good' philosophy, which, from the late 1980s, has developed at both the individual and organizational level. During this period, governments of many countries in the West have reduced several of the regulatory 'burdens' on industry, have privatized many of their public sector activities and have decontrolled prices. These developments have been regarded by increasing numbers of electors not so much for their efficiency as for their social costs, including unemployment and the exploitation of workers.

Such views have not gone unchallenged and in Chapter 2, where the development of strategy at the organizational level is examined, both sides of the question will be considered. For now, let it be said that the view taken throughout this book reflects that of the economist (Kay, 1996b) who argues that the proposition that shareholders own the company is simply not true – they merely have certain specified claims upon it, as do others.

This book will seek to demonstrate how, as part of an organization's strategy, the marketing concept can help to contribute to the long-run welfare of society – that the 'good society' can become the achievable society with its assistance. The arguments and examples which follow support this claim.

First, the marketing concept recognizes that the faster and more cost-effective production techniques now in continuous development have the capacity to deliver either a higher standard of living or a mountain of waste, depending on whether or not the goods and services so produced are in phase with user needs. Since, through its marketing research function, marketers gather information on user needs before the cycle of production commences, it is evident that marketing as an organizing belief can assist society to make the most productive use of its scarce, often non-renewable, resources.

Next, and as noted earlier, it has been adopted by both profit and non-profit organizations. Campaigns to mitigate Third World hunger, to improve health care, to reduce drink-driving, to deter lawbreakers, etc., frequently employ the principles and practices of marketing.

Thirdly, the notion that ethics is not compatible with profit is false. Here note, for example, that in the UK by late 1996 there were 32 'ethical investment' funds with more than £1.1 billion under management – an increase of 50 per cent over the previous two years. The fund managers rigorously vet the companies in which they invest so as to exclude companies that damage the environment or operate in industries to which people have moral objections, for example, arms, tobacco, the fur trade, or countries which have repressive regimes.

The concept of ethical investment is already well established in the USA where the enormous sums controlled by churches and pension funds have had a marked impact on the activities of major corporations. In the UK such prominent names as Scottish Equitable, Abbey Life and Henderson Touche Remnant are active in this field. The largest and oldest UK fund is provided by Friends Provident, which introduced ethical investment to Britain in 1984 with its Stewardship Trust. The data on the performance of this fund (Table 1.1) substantiates the view expressed in this book that business ethics and business success are by no means mutually exclusive.

In 1995, Britain's Royal Society of Arts (RSA) conducted an enquiry into the foundations of long-term business success. It concluded that, in a changing world, a company must maintain five key relationships, these are with its:

- investors;
- employees;
- customers;
- suppliers;
- community.

The inquiry concluded that 'Whatever else changes, those relationships remain. The key to success in the future is to maximise the value of all of them' (Sir A. Cleaver in Caulkin, 1996b). As we shall presently see, this 'stakeholder' type of strategic management approach is a fundamental tenet of the marketing philosophy.

Again, it is interesting to note that in November 1996, linked to the RSA enquiry, Kleinwort Benson Investment Management launched its Tomorrow's Company investment fund and portfolio service. Kleinwort believed that the RSA report gave

Fund	Growth of each £100 invested (all figs. in £s)		
	1 year	3 years	5 years
Friends Provident Stewardship	113.6	133.72	179.05
Average U.K. growth unit trust	110.63	132.10	170.43

Table 1.1. *The comparative performance of an ethical investment*

Source: Money Mail (Daily Mail) 23.10.1996

the greatest possible clarity for investment analysis and claimed that a model share portfolio of such 'tomorrow's companies', backtested to 1992, would have substantially outperformed the all-share index. So it is now staking its professional reputation on its advice to investment fund managers that the portfolio of such companies will outperform similarly in the future.

This section concludes with two further illustrations of business ethics derived from looking outwards to customers and other stakeholders.

J. Sainsbury, plc

When cars are filled with petrol, a hazy mist escapes into the atmosphere. This is petrol vapour from the empty tank and is considered to be a health hazard if not for customers, at least for forecourt staff at operator-attended sites. Consequently, eight countries in the European Union have either legislated or announced legislation to curb the risk.

In 1994, the Sainsbury group completed a review of all its activities and their impact on air quality. As a result, by March 1996, eighteen months ahead of legal requirements, it had installed vapour recovery systems at 35 of its 180 petrol stations. The equipment is also being installed at all new sites and those undergoing major refurbishments. Tests subsequently showed a 40 per cent reduction in emissions at the pumps with reductions also measurable at a distance of 50 metres.

The group's environmental manager said:

'Our view is that, given this is a problem that faces everybody, if you can do something about it, then you should' (Austin in Baxter, 1996).

The Triodos Bank

In 1996 this small bank launched the first UK savings account which aims to mitigate Third World poverty. Its North–South account (a plan originally introduced in Holland in 1994) also provided a rate of interest for small savers better than that offered by most High Street banks. The underlying philosophy of the account is to give the Third World poor 'a hand up not a handout'. A loan of as little as £145, for example, was sufficient to purchase cloth and a sewing machine to start a business making children's clothes in Bogota, Colombia.

Total organizational commitment

We saw earlier in the chapter that the marketing approach signifies that all parts of the organization must co-operate enthusiastically in the marketing process. *Everyone* – production workers, accountants, designers, purchasing managers, etc., must be concerned, above all, with customer satisfaction and loyalty. Those parts of the organization nearest the customer, such as the marketing department, will have a distinctive part to play in this, but only a part because:

- customer satisfaction and loyalty,
- the attainment of organizational objectives, and
- the long-run welfare of society

are not the sole preserve of marketing personnel.

It is no easy matter to create a customer-led culture. The members of any organization do not constitute a monolithic group. In reality, most organizations consist of diverse individuals and groups, of multiple coalitions and alliances, with each of these striving to achieve its own goals and objectives.

So any assumption that an organization somehow exists apart from its members and that its goals are independent of the dominant groups or individuals within it is, at the least, hardly realistic. It has to be remembered that where individuals share power they frequently differ about what must be done and where these differences are of some consequence, decisions and actions will be the result of a *political process*. As one observer puts it: decisions and actions within organizations may be seen as the consequence of the pulling and hauling that is politics (Manghan, 1979, pp 16–17).

Of relevance here is the research project (Dearborn and Simon, 1968) which tested the idea of 'alternative perception' among a number of executives. The researchers concluded that even when executives are instructed to take a broad company-wide view of a problem, they tend to perceive only those aspects of a situation which relate specifically to the attitudes and goals of their own departments. The research discovered, for example, that a group of executives asked to designate the most important problems facing a company (depicted for them in a case study) differed markedly in their perceptions of the problems. For instance, 83 per cent of the sales executives identified 'sales' as the most important problem, whereas only 29 per cent of the other executives ascribed any importance to it.

Practitioners and theorists would agree that organizations consisting of a rag-bag of sub-cultures – a production sub-culture, R&D sub-culture, finance sub-culture, etc. – are already about to fail in today's highly competitive markets. A unified, customer-led culture is a minimum requirement, but in view of the difficulties outlined above, how is this to be achieved? How is the political equation to be solved? How, for example, can the notion be dispelled that 'customer focus' is only a convenient shorthand which conceals the 'empire-building' of the marketing executives?

Some years ago, when the author was a student, introductory textbooks would exhort the reader to remember that 'the standards in any organization are set by the people at the top'. Even today this is more than an apt truism, for it is certain that the customer-led culture will never take root unless senior management are determined it will. As this chapter closes, it might be useful to introduce some thoughts on how senior managers might do this, as a prelude to lengthier consideration in Chapters 2 and 3.

Communication is the starting point and and it may be helpful to consider the four purposes of communication suggested by Francis (1987, pp 5ff). He perceives these as being:

- *For sharing the compelling vision* – to give direction and sustain dynamism; to express corporate identity in ways that stir commitment.

- *For integrating the effort* – i.e. the efforts of different people to get complex things done with (i) administrative devices to integrate the work of specialists, (ii) geographical closeness, enabling informal integration to take place, and (iii) encouraging integration by effective downwards direction.

- *For sustaining a healthy community* – populated by willing, generally satisfied people who devote themselves to improvement within the system; the power structure is accepted, people are valued for their own sake, closeness and co-operation are always present.

- *For making intelligent decisions* – high quality decisions depend on accurate and speedy information, which is partly related to an effective communication system – important information must be detected and processed quickly.

With regard to this last point we shall see later how in a marketing-led organization the marketing information system, utilizing the techniques of marketing research, provides the basis for managerial decisions. It can be seen from the above outline that communication is about *doing things as well as saying things*. The two examples which follow illustrate how effective communication contributes to the development of a marketing culture.

Siemens of Germany

The cost and productivity gains achieved by Siemens were described on pages 15–16. Moves were also made to improve communication and hence the culture. At Siemens' new medical plant in Nuremberg, a glass partition is all that separates designers and marketing staff from the production line. Previously they would not have been in the same building, but currently all these hitherto separate functions work as a team to help speed up the whole chain of operations from design to delivery. This is a good example of how geographical closeness can assist the integration of effort.

Office for National Statistics (ONS)

The two branches of the UK Government's statistical service were merged on 1 April 1996. The Central Statistical Office (CSO) and the Office for Population Studies and Census (OPSC) were combined to form the new Office for National Statistics (ONS). The merger was intended to create more integration between the 'hard' economic data produced by the CSO and the social and health figures generated by the OPSC. It was also felt that the reorganization would help create more relevant management structures and a stronger awareness among employees of exactly why they were producing statistics, creating in them 'an idea of belonging – of vision and values'. The reorganization was seeking to replace the polite and hierarchical Whitehall culture with a greater focus on individual initiative and a 'customer' driven ethos (Tett and Bowley, 1996).

Organizational strategy

Introduction: *the purpose of this chapter*

In Chapter 1 we saw how marketing has been elevated from a function to a *whole-organization concept and commitment*. Integration of effort is the guiding principle, with everyone acquiring some responsibility for the quality of the marketing effort: everyone must see things through the eyes of the customer, as it were.

While it is one thing for production executives, designers and shop-floor workers to acquire a marketing outlook, it is clearly of equal importance that those employed in the marketing function itself acquire a whole-organization attitude. This is the reason why this chapter on organizational strategy is included in an introductory text on marketing, for it is increasingly important that the marketing executive takes a broad view of the organization's aspirations and activities and develops a keen sense of what the marketing function can contribute to them.

In the last quarter-century, the markets for most products and services have become *dynamic* – markets in which the needs, wants, tastes and fashions of customers are continually on the move. More recently the trend has intensified due to a number of factors, including:

- the dominance of technological and scientific development over the economic and social life of world populations;

- the emergence of world-scale industries and global markets, as an outcome of highly sophisticated transport systems, communications networks and production techniques;

- the deregulation by governments of industries and institutions in which competition was previously curbed and the transfer from the public to the private sector of many organizations formerly owned and operated by governments;

- the world-wide emergence of regional trade agreements, e.g. the European Union (EU), North American Free Trade Agreement (NAFTA), West African Economic and Monetary Union, South Asian Association for Regional Co-operation, etc., which, in some cases, may alter fundamentally the character of nation states;

- the cultivation of mixed economies by former socialist, i.e. 'command', economies as in Eastern Europe, and the emergence of new highly competitive economies on the world scene, e.g. Taiwan, Singapore, Hong Kong, South Korea, Malaysia;

- the increasing social concern about the physical environment, consumer rights, the widening gap between the world's rich and poor and the threat to stable employment in all economies.

These are six factors in a longer list so that the context, or *environment*, in which organizations operate is now highly complex and problematical (or turbulent). It is also apparent that in such a turbulent environment some organizations will excel, some will survive and some will die – and that past performance is no indication of future outcomes. Hence the need for some scheme, design or proposal which will enable the organization to make the most of opportunities offered by such profound changes and to avoid or at least minimize their threats. Such a scheme or design is known as a *strategy*, with the accompanying decision-making and actions being known as *strategic management*.

The literature on strategy and strategic management is vast. It contains a wealth of approaches, many of which are opposed to each other, and any number of techniques, some of which have proved to be of enduring value, and others which have been criticized for their lack of relevance and credibility in times of rapid change.

In a succinct and interesting way, Richard Koch (1995, pp 6–8) has identified six phases in strategic thinking. Table 2.1 is an attempt to provide the main strands of his summary.

---

1 1950s – early 1960s

Focus on planning for development of large multi-product firms.
Era of *classic strategic planning* at corporate centre.
Key objectives   – decentralization of organizations into large autonomous divisions
                 – diversification through acquisition of other (often unrelated) companies

2 1965–1975 approx
Period of *portfolio management*. Matrix of Boston Consulting Group (BCG) highly prominent.
Approaches highly prescriptive with following key emphases:
● focus on market leadership where possible/appropriate
● divest other businesses
● focus on cash rather than profit
● aim for lower costs than competitors
Large central planning departments in conglomerate organizations emergd.
Further diversification undertaken.

3 Mid to late 1970s
This phase 'one of intellectual exhaustion, corporate disillusion and a retreat into pragmatism on the part of the strategists' (Koch).

Micro-economic analytical techniques clearly powerful but used increasingly at *business unit level* rather than at corporate centre.
Results from huge central planning departments very disappointing and exacerbated by oil price rises, 1973 and stock market crash, 1974.
Attack on the BCG Matrix type of approach which went largely undefended at this stage.

4 1973 to the present
Reaction against excessive analytical orientation. Increased emphasis on intuitive, adaptive and creative aspects of strategy.
'Crafting strategy', associated with Mintzberg, emphasized using creative right-hand side of brain rather than logical left side.
During 1980s Ohmae drew attention to the intuitive creative leadership of Honda, Toyota, etc. who succeeded through market leadership, beating competition and satisfying customers.
In 1980–94 period other 'soft' strategists – Handy, Kanter, Peters, etc., also became influential.

5 1980s
In parallel with development of 'soft' strategy, emergence of scientific, rigorous approach of Porter who extended BCG framework of competitive advantage to include structural industry factors, e.g.
● threat from new entrants;
● bargaining power of customers/suppliers;
● threat from substitutes.
Porter's work also helped to re-emphasize the BCG philosophy of trying to find markets/'niches' firm could dominate and countering competition by low-cost or product differentiation strategies. He also developed a theory of competitive advantage.

6 The contemporary scene
Stategic focus built on organization's skills or competences and development of its sense of mission. Corporate centre stategy – creation of ambition and skills rather than allocation of resources.
Prominent writers e.g. Hamel, Prahalad, Goold, Campbell echo somewhat those mentioned in Phase 4 above.
Renewed integration of strategic focus with cost reduction (Business Process Re-engineering).
Time-Based Competition and the concept of Value Chain highlighted.
Competitive advantage emanating from specialization, business focus and segmentation, low-cost position and superior products and services.

Table 2.1. *Six phases in strategic thinking*

With acknowledgements to Koch (1995)

This historical survey is intended to assist us to appreciate what follows in this chapter, the content of which is central to an understanding of marketing as it is now developing. Occasionally, some of the terms used may be confusing to those new to the subject – if so, their meanings should have become clear before the end of the chapter. However, before leaving this introduction it might be helpful to illustrate what is meant by: corporate centre, strategic business unit (SBU) and the function/operations level of an organization.

Figure 2.1 is a simple diagram of the structure for strategic decision-making in a hypothetical firm we shall call Bursley Group PLC. Bursley is a well-established manufacturer of porcelain products. Porcelain is a very robust ceramic based on costly, good-quality ingredients and a high heat-treatment process. It is also highly adaptable to the needs of several markets and in Bursley's case there are three main markets:

- *the industrial market* – in which its porcelain insulators serve the needs of electricity generators/distributors world-wide;
- *the construction market* – in which its high-quality, durable porcelain tiles are especially suitable for the external cladding of buildings and internal architectural features;
- *the ornamental ware market* – in which its distinctive and exclusive figurines, jardinières and *objets d'art* enjoy world-wide popularity.

As we see from Figure 2.1 each of these aspects of Bursley's activity has been given divisional status and a strategic business unit (SBU) label. An SBU may be defined as: a unit of a company that has a separate mission and objectives and which can be planned independently from any other businesses within the company. Note here, however, that the phrase 'separate mission' needs to be qualified somewhat, because the SBU's mission is linked, at the very least, to the corporate centre mission (this point will become more clear as the book proceeds).

An SBU might be:

- an operating division within a company, as at the Bursley Group;
- a product range within a division (see Chapter 4, on product management, for example);
- a whole company within a large conglomerate organization of several companies;
- or even a single product or brand (see Chapter 8).

If some aspect of an organization's operations attracts different customers or competitors from its other aspects, there may well be a case for establishing it as an SBU.

The experience of the last 30 years has led to a world-wide recognition that, if left to itself, corporate centre strategy can be value-destroying rather than value-adding. Because managerial aspirations and rewards have inclined towards size, rather than the interests of customers, employees and shareholders, many organizations have become highly bureaucratic and overlarge. This has had a demotivating effect on their members who have felt remote and relatively powerless to influence performance. Coupled with a lack of flexibility in the face of rapidly changing markets this has led to some spectacular business failures and a cry for decentralization and for the delegation of responsibility and authority to those charged with obtaining the results.

Figure 2.1. *Bursley Group PLC: A framework for the development and implementation of strategy*

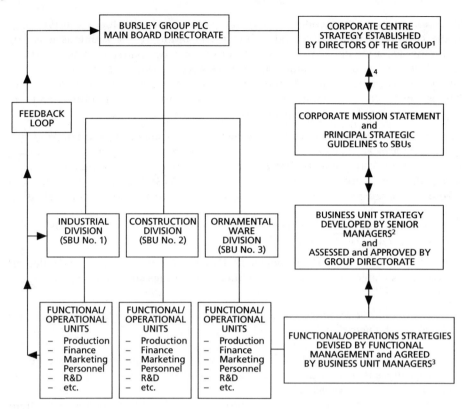

Notes:

1 *Corporate centre strategy* defines the overall 'mission', i.e. the fundamental purpose of the Group. It typically answers the important question 'what business are we in?' and provides policy guidelines on how the Group will develop, e.g. whether development will be by sales growth or acquisitions and, if the latter, which businesses will be acquired. It also determines how best the SBUs might be managed.

2 *Business unit strategy* is the heart of strategic activity and concerns itself with how each autonomous profit centre unit can create and sustain competitive advantage within the overall mission and values of the Group.

3 *Functional strategies* deal with the output, sales, budgetary targets, etc. for the achievement of each SBU strategy. The units are not completely self-contained: they share facilities for production, finance and R&D at Bursley.

4 The arrows on the diagram indicate the 'two-way' process of decision-making.

In this context, the following points have come to be generally accepted.

● Corporate centre strategy should provide little more than policy steering and oversight of the SBUs.

● Business unit strategy has great value, if done properly, and is best achieved through participation of everyone involved so that those responsible for achieving objectives feel that they 'own' the strategy and feel motivated to implement it.

● It is important to be pragmatic about the time and resources involved in strategic planning, especially since highly detailed plans can be counter-productive in these times of change and discontinuity. This will be discussed further but, in the meantime, it is hoped that the explanatory notes to Figure 2.1 help to clarify the difference between corporate centre and SBU strategy and provide an adequate preliminary picture of the strategic process.

The role of management

The work that managers do may be thought of in this way:

- Managers bring together *resources* (finance, information, personnel, etc.);

- so as to achieve *pre-set objectives*, both economic and non-economic (e.g. profit or usage targets, sales growth, full-cost recovery, a good health and safety record, ethical reputation);

- the whole process taking place within an *external environment*, in which a number of factors are at work (economic, political, technological, etc.).

In their strategic role, managers have five interrelated tasks. For example, in a business organization they must:

- establish what business the company will be in, develop a strategic vision of the direction in which it will proceed, inject a sense of appropriate purpose into the organization through the provision of long-term direction and a clear sense of mission;

- relate the strategic vision and the business mission to measurable objectives and clear performance indicators;

- develop (i.e. 'craft') a strategy to achieve the required results;

- implement the strategy by 'doing the right things', i.e. through *effectiveness* and by 'doing things right', through *efficiency*;

- monitor performance, review the emergence of new ideas, products, markets and environmental conditions, then adjust the long-term direction, strategy, objectives and performance indicators as necessary.

The strategic management process is represented in Figure 2.2. This depicts the strategy making, strategy implementation process guiding the use of scarce resources for the benefit of *stakeholders* with the whole process taking place within an *environment*, the various factors of which exert an influence on the process. Note in Figure 2.2 the arrows indicating feedback routes which enable the organization's performance to be monitored and, if necessary, adjusted. Some of the concepts encapsulated in Figure 2.2 are now explained.

The external environment

An organization's external environment is made up of all the elements outside its 'boundaries' which might affect it. The organization must monitor environmental conditions carefully and ensure it adapts to any changes in them where it is prudent to do so. The monitoring process best suited to the organization might be one of lesser or greater sophistication according to the methods used, for example:

- *the weak signal approach*: in which management attunes itself to pick up weak signals that indicate future change which might present opportunities or threats, the method's justification being that in situations where boundary conditions are so novel, projections from past experience are of little use in forecasting future events;

- *the QUEST approach*: (the Quick Environmental Scanning Technique) QUEST is a systematic and inexpensive way in which planners and executives can pool their knowledge and exchange views on those environmental trends and events which

Figure 2.2. *The strategic
management process*

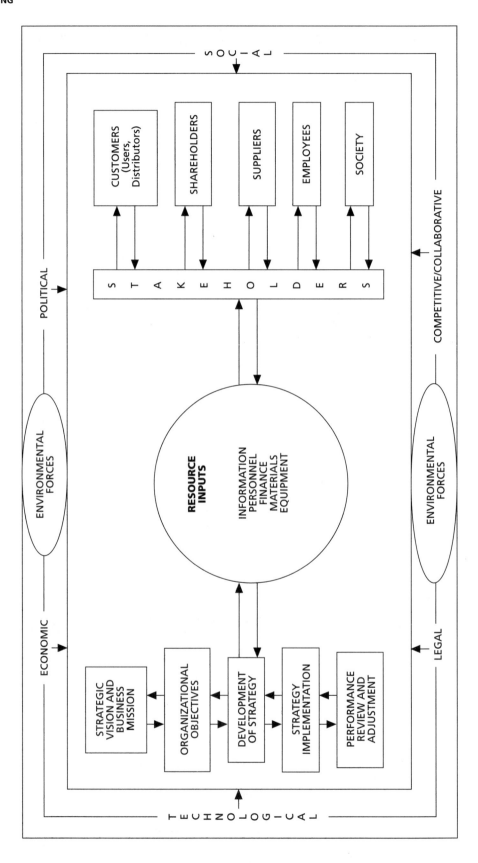

appear significant to the organization's strategies and objectives – although QUEST provides no more than a rudimentary and subjective picture, its systematic basis gives it an advantage over informal, unstructured methods;

- *environmental analysis*: the most formal, systematic approach which generates a comprehensive, current database on the environmental scene and disseminates this to decision makers on a planned, systematic, fully documented basis.

Since the methods are not mutually exclusive, they could be used in combination, time and resources permitting. Readers seeking a more detailed description of these approaches should refer to Baker (1996, pp 40–9).

The idea of an organization monitoring changes in its environment and adjusting to them is referred to as the *systems approach*. Its principles emanate from biology and the physical sciences. Our own bodies continually adjust to environmental changes – our eye pupils contract in bright light, the goosepimples which form as the temperature falls signal the flesh's effort to conserve body heat and our physical systems operate so that our blood sugar is maintained within the quite narrow tolerances necessary to aviod damage or death. Similarly, an organization must make appropriate responses to environmental change if it is to maintain itself in being or better yet, to grow and prosper.

Organizations operating thus are termed *open systems*. Organizations which are inward looking, slow to react to changing boundary conditions and resistant to making changes are described as *closed systems* and within such systems there is often a pathological condition known to marketing professionals as *production orientation*.

How best might an organization monitor environmental change? Our own bodies achieve this through a system of *feedback*. Our 'sensing devices' – the eyes, the skin, the nervous system – enable us to pick up the change and take corrective action. This feedback principle is also an important feature of the systems approach to the behaviour of organizations. Moreover, in Chapter 6 and subsequent parts of this book we shall see how a marketing information system, using the techniques of marketing research, is fundamentally important to the quality and speed of an organization's feedback. Obviously, when an organization's markets are undergoing rapid change the significance and value of marketing research only intensifies.

Organizational environments may be described according to their:

- stability;
- complexity;
- market diversity;
- 'hostility'.

Morris (1992, p 17), describing the environments of firms serving industrial markets, believes that, in general, these tend towards instability, increasing complexity and greater diversification in their customer bases with a number of hostile forces in evidence.

Morris cites the example of Digital Equipment Corporation (DEC), one of the largest American computer manufacturers, to support his thesis. From the mid-1980s onwards it found the pace and extent of technological change greatly affecting the *stability* of its environment. The demands of new high-growth development (e.g. computer-aided design and manufacturing, office automation) contributed to the *complexity* of that environment. The growth opportunities provided by the increase in small businesses and desktop workstations made its markets much more *diverse*. Strong traditional competitors, such as IBM, and the arrival on the scene of many new, aggressive small companies (e.g. Elxsi) have resulted in a more *hostile* environment.

To an increasing extent, such trends have affected most organizations and, as we near the year 2000, have intensified. Environments have become so turbulent in fact that one school of thought, prompted by the Darwinian concept of 'survival of the fittest', says 'why strategize?' for given the dynamism of competitive environments any short-term gains will be quickly eroded by the efficiency of markets. So let the environment do the selecting and not the strategic decision makers. (This, the evolutionary approach, is outlined, with other approaches – classical, processual, systematic – by Egan, 1995, pp 2–5). This seems a counsel of despair and, as the book proceeds, we shall come to appreciate that in such turbulent times a realistic and viable strategy is the best practical insurance for the firm's survival.

As will be seen from Figure 2.2, within the external environment there are a number of key influences at work. In nature, these are:

- economic;
- political;
- social;
- technological;
- legal;
- competitive/collaborative.

Although it is usual, and important, for these types of influence to be studied separately in the development of strategy, they are closely related, as will become apparent when we now consider each of them.

Economic influences

The state of a nation's economy has a profound bearing on the prospects for its organizations, which are significantly affected by its rate of growth, rate of inflation, employment levels, public sector borrowing requirement, etc. In 1992, for example, a survey (*Financial Times*, 1992) indicated that while the 1990s dawned amid hopes of a new era of prosperity, after the collapse of communism, the economic growth hoped for had not materialized, world output had stagnated, some countries were in lengthy recession and unemployment had risen sharply with many highly developed economies experiencing slow, if any, growth.

Since the early 1990s recovery has been patchy, at best, with clear recovery in the US economy, improvement in the UK – although consumer confidence and the 'feel good' factor are still fragile – but with slow growth and high unemployment in France and Germany and a depressed domestic market in Japan, where, at the time of writing, the stock market index continues to fall.

With the diffusion of high technology and the proliferation of regional trade agreements (EU, NAFTA, etc.) the creation of a 'borderless world' has been described by an influential writer who believes that organizations will be affected by the **Inter-Linked Economy (ILE)** of the USA, Europe and Japan/Asia based on the need to satisfy demanding consumers in these important regions (Ohmae, 1990).

Political influences

National and local governments also influence heavily the prospects for organizations and the way they operate. For example, despite deregulation and the withdrawal of governments from the ownership of companies and public utilities, governments are still large purchasers of goods and services, particularly in the defence and aerospace industries.

Government subsidies and policies have a great influence on the fortunes of firms and industries (note the EU Common Agricultural Policy and EU regulations on fishing rights). Where necessary, too, governments frequently bear much of the cost of the training and retraining of workers.

Government policies on trade, industry and investment have a direct effect on the operation of firms and markets. For example, as these words are being written, the UK government is being asked to note, and intervene on, the sustained growth of its currency exchange rate because the strength of the pound is having a marked effect on the exports of British goods, particularly those from price sensitive industries, notably metals, chemicals and textiles. In January 1997, for example, City analysts cut their profits forecast for British Steel by up to two-thirds due to the rise of sterling.

The political beliefs of the government (its ideology) will have, as a rule, a direct influence on the success or failure of firms. For example, the present UK government, perhaps fearing loss of national sovereignty, is reticent to join the first wave of entrants to the single currency proposal for European Monetary Union (EMU). Even so, unlike the Conservatives, new Labour do not seem averse to signing up to the EMU and the European social chapter, with its provisions for a national minimum wage and enhanced worker representation rights within organizations. The two parties are also diametrically opposed to each other on the principles of stakeholding, a concept explained later.

An example of how a political decision can lead to a market opportunity comes from the other side of the world. Recently, the Japanese government announced its intention to deregulate Tokyo's financial markets by the year 2001. Its commitment to this pledge was indicated in December 1996 with the signing of the US–Japan accord on insurance. This allows the direct marketing of motor policies. In the USA and the UK the method is enormously popular with motorists who, in the last ten years, have become used to 'shopping-around' by telephone for the keenest rates. The method is extremely rare in Japan but the accord has resulted in many foreign insurers moving into what is thought will prove to be an extremely lucrative sector of the Japanese market.

Technological influences

As has been pointed out by Jauch and Glueck (1988, p 94), organizations with effective strategies constantly monitor their environments for changes in technology which might affect their products, services, raw materials, production processes and distribution operations. Technology may, at worst, threaten a firm's existence but more usually, and if prudently 'strategized', it can offer major opportunities for sales growth.

Lasers, fibre optics, transistors and miniature integrated circuits have revolutionized life in the factory, home and office in the last quarter-century while the continued startling development of information technology and telecommunications have shrunk the world and made the prospect of a global economy more than a pipe-dream.

The intelligent organization need not look far for news of developments that might affect its future. This author's own analysis of press features during the writing of this section produced a wealth of news of technology's advance, including the items listed below.

- An 'intelligent' house is already under construction in Britain which will understand and obey telephoned instructions. On the homeward journey, the car phone can be used to order 'the house' to turn on the heating, start the oven, switch on the lights and open the garage doors.

- A flying catamaran that can take off vertically from the surface of the sea has been built by Russian scientists in a bid to create the world's most efficient form of transport, while in the USA a prototype 'aircar', which can also fly, has been built and tested.

- Rank Xerox is developing a photocopier which can translate documents into foreign languages and at its Palo Alto Research Centre (PARC) in California, their chief technologist, envisages a future in which computers can be carried in wallets and even key rings.

- Magnet technology, which was designed to propel satellites from a Star Wars type 'supergun' into orbit at 20 times the speed of sound, may soon be used to propel high-speed trains across America.

- Viewcall Europe, a small high-tech company has developed a system connecting a television with the Internet to provide online services such as home shopping, news, games and even inexpensive phone calls via a small black box similar to a satellite decoder – another example of the huge potential of the telemedia industry.

The influence of technology extends, of course, to processes as well as products, providing a marked competitive advantage to organizations that are alert and adaptable. Computer-aided design and manufacturing (CAD/CAM) are now well established features of the production process, but more recent developments have similar strategic importance: *rapid prototyping technology* has revolutionized conventional prototyping, in which a pattern maker translated two-dimensional drawings into a model in wood, often taking many weeks, by taking advantage of computerization to create a three-dimensional model within two hours and *optimized production* technology is another development reducing time-to-market, combining software with training so as to eliminate bottlenecks – an approach used successfully in a number of US and European engineering companies (e.g. General Electric in the USA, Lucas Industries in the UK) which manufacture complex products.

As with production, so with marketing. The World Wide Web is a software application which runs on the Internet and its multimedia capabilities enable customers to access a huge quantity of information about products and services within a maximum of two minutes (Sterne, 1995, p xvi). A number of large corporations, including IBM, Sun Microsystems and General Electric have already begun to use it as a marketing tool and the alert marketing executive must decide whether, and to what extent, it should be incorporated in his own plans for serving, communicating and transacting with customers.

We shall return to information technology later in this chapter, for certainly its use and applications now have immense implications for strategy and not only for individual organizations – the EU, for instance, has been criticized for supporting old and inefficient industries through its Common Agricultural Policy (CAP) whilst paying insufficient attention to the newer industries. According to a recent report (Kehoe, 1997), executives at several US high-tech companies believe that Europe is falling behind the USA and Asia in the use of information technology to an extent which threatens its future prosperity.

Social influences

First, the age profile of a nation has a significant effect on the type and volume of goods and services demanded in its markets. In common with other industrialized countries, the UK has an ageing population: female life expectancy is now 79 years and male expectancy 74 years. In 1901 the respective expectancies were 52 years and 49 years. Over 18 per cent of the population are over normal retirement age and when the increasing numbers of early retirers (often due to structural unemployment) are added to this proportion, the middle/old aged segment of the population is substantial. It is also commercially important, because a large proportion of the segment is relatively affluent and provides extensive demand not only for health care and long-term residential services but also for consumer durable goods, leisure services and travel to increasingly exotic locations.

In contrast, the proportion of young people (i.e. under 16) has fallen steadily in the UK in the recent past but, interestingly, based on research (Castells, 1996) from Europe, Asia, North and Latin America, it is clear that in the developed 'information' economies, productive worth is becoming increasingly concentrated in a young, highly educated, elite sector of the population, so that the portents are that society will become stratified by access to – and command of – information, another trend for the strategist to note.

Aside from demographics, important *socio-cultural* influences must be taken into account. The rise of *consumerism*, examined in some depth in Chapter 5, has expressed itself in a reaction against overpriced, inadequate and unsafe products. We have noted earlier (the societal marketing concept Chapter 1, the increasing concern for the physical environment and the depletion of natural resources. These mean that each individual organization must strive for cheaper, cleaner and most cost-effective methods of operation. It is notable too that, even allowing for the experienced 'activists' who are often involved, the population in general is increasingly prepared to forgo the political process and make its views known more directly, whether the issues involved are road improvements, by-pass construction, airport extension or animal rights.

An equally notable socio-cultural development is the call for organizations to search for a new moral dimension in defining their objectives. The recent spate of frauds, scandals and 'fat-cat' pay deals in Britain and other countries has intensified this call. Boardrooms are perceived to be too biased towards the interests of shareholders and senior executives. In the Spring of 1996, for example, the behaviour of America's largest corporations and the distribution of rewards produced by the free-enterprise system of the USA was fundamentally challenged. It emanated both from the populist political right (Pat Buchanan) and the Democratic centre-left (President Clinton).

It seemed that stock market prices and corporate redundancies were soaring together, indeed that they were 'both sides of the same coin' (Stelzer, 1996) for when Associated Telephone and Telegraph (AT&T) fired 40,000 employees its share price rose and when the US government announced that more than 700,000 new jobs had been created (February 1996), the stock market tumbled. 'Has capitalism failed?' was the question, when it was observed that downsizing drove up share prices and that higher share prices increased the value of stock options and raised executive rewards.

Organizational environments are changing because consumers are no longer content to buy blindly the products put before them, since a growing consciousness of the presence, or absence, of corporate ethics is having repercussions in firms, industries and whole economies. With economic power increasingly in the hands of the business community, governments are seeking concessions from it, hence the UK's new Labour party's call for a 'stakeholder society'. The idea of stakeholding (discussed later), though challenged in some quarters, seems an idea of more than temporary goodwill.

A strategy informed by a value system based on ethical principles has less to do with saving whales or funding the arts than with running all phases of the organization in its environment with a proper sense of ethical concern. The supporters of 'business ethics' hold that business can be true to its definitive objective of maximizing long-term owner value and still be fully ethical.

Legal influences

Though these are closely related to political and social influences, the influence of the law on organizations is extensive and profound so that a full understanding of the environment's influence cannot be provided without examining the legal aspects, if only in outline.

The period since 1945 has been one of ever-increasing legislation. In Britain, for example, this has affected all aspects of the nation's affairs, not least its industry and commerce. Legislation concerning trade descriptions; consumer protection and consumer credit; terms of contracts; hire purchase; pricing and price marking; monopolies and restrictive practices; and patents and trade marks; must all be mentioned here. Moreover, the tide of legislation does not slacken in the UK, for example following the winding up of the Titan Business Club new restrictions on pyramid selling and similar 'get-rich-quick' schemes became law in February 1997, with a maximum penalty of two years' imprisonment and/or a £5000 fine.

Other legal provisions are designed to ensure that employers take adequate steps to protect the health and safety of workers, that business organizations operate within the requirements of company law and that, as employers, they observe the labour law relating to contracts of employment, equal pay, racial and sexual discrimination, trade union membership, redundancy payments, etc.

The law can ultimately determine:

- the location of a factory or warehouse;
- its discharges into the atmosphere, the sea and rivers;
- the noise levels produced by its processes and products;
- the way in which it advertises and promotes the sales of its output.

Nor is UK organization bound only by Parliamentary legislation (Acts of Parliament) for the common law, that is the law originally developed and administered by the royal justices, which stands alongside statute, or parliamentary law, also imposes obligations, for example the duty of care owed by an organization for the safety of visitors to its premises is a fundamental concept of the common law of negligence. *Delegated legislation* (that delegated by Parliament to public corporations and boards, local authorities and other bodies) also influences what an organization can and cannot do: an organization may be required to take steps to improve its effects on the physical environment by the power of a local authority by-law.

Firms marketing internationally face a multitude of legal influences. First, the laws of the countries with which they trade must be observed, that is to say the rule and principles of international law (unless, of course, there is some alternative provision in the contract of sale, for example that the contract will be governed by UK law). Secondly, a nation's law might be subject to the law of an international organization of which it is a member. Since the UK is a member of the European Community, the *law of the Community* as expressed through the treaties, and the *delegated legislation*, stemming from Community institutions (the Council, the Commission, the European Court of Justice) are also important influences, direct and indirect, on the operations of individual UK organizations. The Regulations are laws made by the Council of Ministers, or more rarely by the Commission, which are binding on Member States. They override national law and can create important rights for individuals which can then be enforced against offending parties (employers, for instance) in the individuals' national courts.

Competitive/collaborative influences

Competition

In Chapter 1 we noted that strategy has been widely interpreted as 'the art of generalship', that is to say how to use the resources at one's disposal to overcome an enemy. To pursue the military analogy further, the general typically moves his army only when satisfied about the location of the enemy, the strength of his forces, arms and ammunition, and his probable counter-moves when the general's own intentions become clear.

Competition is a fundamental aspect of the free enterprise system. The development of the global market together with the move of many governments to open up their public sectors to competition mean that strategic decisions, in nearly all fields, must confront competition, which forever intensifies.

'Know thine enemy' has long been a dictum basic to Japanese business, as Ohmae has indicated:

> In the real world of business, 'perfect' strategies are not called for. What counts, as we have seen, is not performance in absolute terms but performance relative to competitors. A good business strategy, then, is one by which a company can gain significant ground on its competitors at an acceptable cost to itself. Finding a way of doing this is the real task of the strategist (Ohmae, 1982, pp 37–8).

In the West, historically, 'know thine enemy' has been restricted to an amalgam of glimpses from trade statistics and gossip from the salesforce, of the 'XYZ has lowered prices!' variety.

Of late, however, this has changed somewhat, in favour of what is defined as 'strategic competition' and in this development, competitive intelligence has an important function. Jain, for example, believes that: 'Competitive, or business, intelligence is a powerful new management tool that enhances a corporation's ability to succeed in today's highly competitive global markets' (Jain, 1993, p 90). This is a formal approach designed to provide early warning intelligence and a framework for the better interpretation of, and retaliation to, competitors' activities. Writing in 1993, Jain quoted a 'recent survey' which indicated that over 300 US firms were involved, or interested, in running their own competitive intelligence system. No doubt many European firms have adopted the same approach as part of their environmental scanning.

The increased emphasis on contending with competition as a key element in formulating strategy owes much to the writings of Michael E. Porter (1991). Porter's central tenet is that it is easy to perceive competition too narrowly, and pessimistically. He believes it amounts to more than the activities of the other 'players' in the market. For Porter, the state of competition in an industry depends on five basic forces which go 'well beyond the established combatants in a particular industry'. These forces are:

- the threat of new entrants to the industry;
- the bargaining power of suppliers;
- the bargaining power of customers;
- the threat of substitute products or services;
- the jockeying for position among current competitors in the industry.

He believes that the strategist must look in depth at the sources of each of these, searching for the answers to such important questions as: 'what makes this industry so open to new entrants?' and 'what underlies the bargaining power of these suppliers?' The answers provide the strategic *agenda* and assist in the identification of the organization's *strengths and weaknesses*, how it should be *positioned* in the industry, the areas where strategic *changes* may yield most *benefit* and the extent to which observed trends provide *opportunities or threats*.

Figure 2.3 is intended to convey how competitive intelligence helps the organization to attain sustainable advantage. There are two segments to the intelligence process:

1 *industry analysis* – which considers the changing characteristics of each industry, e.g. its trends in volume, costs, price and return on investment, its ability to raise capital, the relationship between current/future demand and its manufacturing capacity, and the effect on profits, etc;

2 *competitor analysis* – which sets out to discover how each competitor is likely to perform, given the structure revealed by the industry analysis.

Collaboration

Whilst Ohmae's (1982) dictum on the centrality of competitive strength seems self-evident, the question of *how* to achieve strength is now being more broadly interpreted. The current business environment has become so risky and unpredictable that many organizations see *strategic alliances* as their preferred method of dealing with this uncertainty. Moreover, the partners they choose are frequently from former key competitors.

Consider the following:

- the increased need to compete effectively in 'the global market', where the major players are the ones that achieve significant economies in scale and scope;

- the need to maintain competitive advantage in the national market while developing it for a variety of international markets;

- the high cost and the 'perishability' of technological development, precipitating the need to share R&D knowledge and expenditure;

- the need to combine sophisticated technology with sophisticated marketing to produce the sophisticated 'packages' of product benefits now demanded by increasingly sophisticated consumers.

These are some of the factors underlying the dramatic escalation of strategic alliances which are now being seen as the way to achieve growth while coping with substantial discontinuity. As Egan (1995, p 152) points out, these alliances occur in many different industries, between firms of different sizes and for numerous purposes. Egan cites research, based on a study of 839 agreements, which produced the following profile of the industries involved:

automobiles	24%
aerospace	19%
telecommunications	17%
computers	14%
other electrical industries	13%

This research revealed that the largest share of the agreements were in joint product development (38 per cent) and *nearly three-quarters of agreements were formed between rivals* (this author's italics). On this latter point, one is reminded of the recent words of Sir Peter Bonfield, chief executive of British Telecommunications: 'You are talking to companies who are competitors one day, collaborators the next and partners the next. Until recently, this has not been common in the telephone business' (Bonfield, 1996).

It is clear that not all strategic alliances are sustainable or successful, but it is equally clear there is now a world-wide appreciation of their potential contribution to organizational advantage, as these recent examples indicate:

- the decision of British Petroleum to place its European petrol stations, refineries and lubricants businesses into a partnership with the US oil giant Mobil, to produce an impressive 'market player' with assets of $5 billion and sales of $20 billion;

- the decision by Kawasaki Heavy Industries to acquire a 6 per cent stake in Rolls Royce's Trent 900 programme, as an important element of its strategy to remain present in the global aerospace market;

- the likely further expansion of the Nedcar joint venture facility in the Netherlands (Volvo/Mitsubishi) for the manufacture of a third model at the end of this decade as an important element of Mitsubishi's expansion plans in Europe.

So collaboration can be seen, through alliances and networks, as the reverse side of the coin of competition – a strategic outcome perhaps as a result of shrewd and purposeful environmental scanning. That it is not the preserve of industrial giants is illustrated by the Commission on Public Policy and British Business which in its 1997 report (Campbell, 1997) recommends that in order to develop world class small and medium-sized enterprises (SMEs) the UK government should investigate how best to encourage networks and provide an information campaign to promote them. A collaborative network in an extended and sophisticated form is the European Airbus project, which we shall be looking at later.

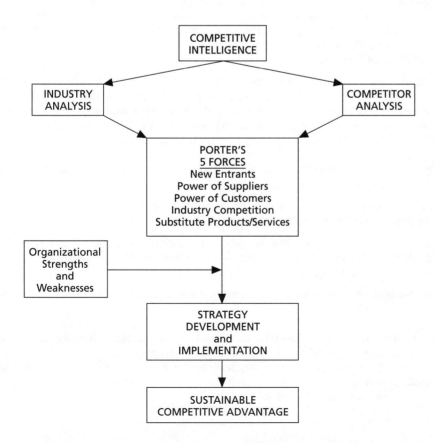

Figure 2.3. *Sustainable advantage through strategic competition*

The learning organization

The manner in which the organization minimises the threats and maximises the opportunities posed by the external environment is by a process of adaptation depending on these crucial qualities:

- the possession of systems for continuous monitoring of the environment to detect significant change;
- the ability to relate this information to the principles or 'norms' guiding current operations;
- the ability to detect significant variations from current norms;
- the ability to align the organization with environmental change through appropriate corrective action.

As Morgan (1986, pp 86–7) indicates, the implementation of strategy is a concept based on a theory of communication and learning derived from cybernetics. It has found favour with practitioners and academics, establishing 'the learning organization' as an important feature of management thinking.

However, the idea of such self-regulating behaviour requires an important qualification when the environment becomes so turbulent and discontinuous that the existing operating standards, or norms, are no longer appropriate. Here it is helpful to distinguish between what cyberneticians term the *process of learning* and the process of *learning to learn*, between 'single-loop' and 'double-loop' learning (see Figure 2.4).

The distinction between single- and double-loop learning is similar to that between the speedometer of a motor vehicle and its driver. The speedometer can only register the speed at a given point in time. It is the brain of the driver which sets the new desirable norm (e.g. by lowering the speed when the environment is threatening, such as heavy traffic conditions or a sudden storm, or by increasing the speed when road conditions improve).

This then leads to the issue of whether organizations can *learn to learn*, i.e. whether it is possible to consider *organizations as brains*. Morgan believes that with an adequate philosophy of management it *is* possible and offers four guidelines as to how 'this learning approach to organization and management can be developed' (Morgan, 1986, pp 91–5). These may be broadly summarized as follows:

- the organization should openly accept that error and uncertainty are facts of life in complex and changing environments;
- the analysis and solution of complex problems can best be approached through the exploration of different viewpoints;
- over-prescriptive approaches to planning should be avoided because more double-loop learning can be developed through a bottom-up, participative approach to planning;
- organizational structures and processes should be created to help implement these principles.

Space is not available for a lengthier treatment of organizational learning in an introductory work of this kind, but manifestations of its importance and value will occur throughout the book, including its implications for management style which we shall be noting shortly. (For a more detailed description of organizational learning see Figure 2.4 and Morgan (1986, ch 4).)

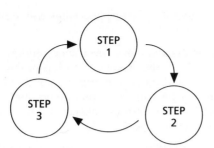

Figure 2.4. *Single- and double-loop learning.*

(*Source*: Morgan, 1986)

Step 1: the process of sensing, scanning and monitoring the environment

Step 2: the comparison of this information against operating norms (e.g. financial budgets, targets of output, sales, profits, etc.)

Step 3: the process of initiating appropriate action

Single-loop learning is based on the ability to detect and correct error in relation to a given set of operating norms

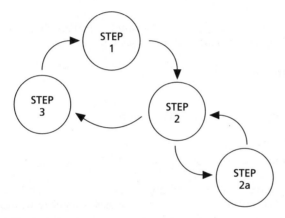

Step 2a: the process of questioning whether existing norms are appropriate

Double-loop learning – taking a 'double look' and questioning the relevance of operating norms

The stakeholder concept

This concept suggests that the objectives of an organization should not stem from the organization exclusively but from the claims upon it of its various stakeholders – its customers, shareholders, employees, suppliers, distributors, the general public, central and local government – all the parties who have a stake in its well-being and are affected by its operations. The strategic objectives proposed should constitute a *reasonable balance* of all their claims upon the organization.

The underlying theory is that the organization has an ethical duty towards all the above constituents and unless it takes these into account it is not behaving ethically. This is not the traditional view which holds that the business organization exists only to make a profit and that by a trickle-down economic process it will therefore automatically benefit its workers through the employment it provides and the community through the taxes it pays. Moreover the traditionalist view still has very many adherents who denounce stakeholding as 'socialism'.

This is an unfortunate misconception, for those who propagate stakeholding do not hold that an organization should be *managed* by these constituents but that their interests should *influence* its operations. Here the notion of 'reasonable balance' (see above) is important, for some of these various claims will inevitably conflict with each other.

More importantly, there is evidence that, even when judged from the narrow viewpoint of return on investment, the stakeholding business is often more successful. Here, the British economist and influential writer, John Kay, has this to say: 'Indeed it was the realisation from my own research that a very high proportion of the most effective businesses were founded and run on stakeholder lines that led me to understand the importance of this issue' (Kay, 1996a).

Philip Kotler, arguably the world's principal contributor to the literature of marketing, writes in a similar vein (Kotler, 1994, p 64).) when he speaks of 'the dynamic relationship connecting stakeholder groups'. He points out that the progressive company, creating a high level of employee satisfaction, will actually lead employees to work on continuous improvements as well as breakthrough innovations. These will result in higher quality products and services and hence high customer satisfaction, which leads to higher growth and profits and thus high shareholder satisfaction. In this, Kotler is really affirming the basic ideas of his *societal marketing concept* (see Chapter 1).

Professor Kay has suggested (quoted in Caulkin, 1996a) there are five interests of companies that directors should at all times seek to advance:

1   returns to shareholders;

2   employee skills;

3   stable employment and trading relationships;

4   good quality for customers;

5   enhanced reputation and business standards.

It is, of course, management and not constituent groups which is responsible for the success of the organization. Management also has a legal obligation to maximize a company's value on a sustainable basis, but there is nothing in law to prevent managers paying attention to other relationships which have an impact upon its operations and are, in turn, influenced by them. Moreover it is wrong to assume that stakeholding assumes greater formal powers for these constituents. Nor should it be equated with higher costs. Minimally, stakeholders should be seen as an important variable in the strategic equation for, as research from the USA indicates (Collins and Porras in Caulkin, 1996a), companies that ranked shareholders' interests as only one priority among others provided greater shareholder returns than companies which explicitly put shareholders first.

Implementing strategy

Earlier in this chapter we noted that having crafted a strategy, a key role of management is to implement it by 'doing the right things' (i.e. through effectiveness) and by 'doing things right' (i.e. through efficiency). Here we shall consider some introductory thoughts on this.

Given the highly fluid nature of technologies, products and markets, for most organizations implementing strategy can be accurately thought of as *managing change*. This means they must first examine the *context* in which strategic change might be brought about. In their work for consultants McKinsey & Co, Waterman, Peters and Phillips (1991, pp 309–14) devised a framework useful for the analysis of organizations and concerned with the factors they considered necessary for the successful implementation of strategy. Figure 2.5 is a highly stylized version of the McKinsey 7-S Framework. This framework was proposed as a diagnostic approach to the description or 'personality' of an organization and to serve as an aid to the successful implementation of strategic change.

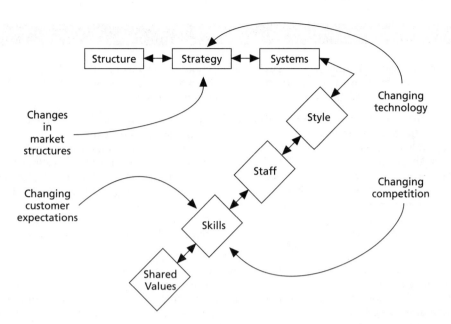

Figure 2.5. *A framework for effective strategic change*

(Adapted from Waterman, Peters and Phillips, 1981.)

In short, the framework perceived strategic success as being rooted in the effective alignment of seven variables:

- *structure* – the way in which the organization is structured (by divisions, functions, matrices, SBUs, etc.);

- *strategy* – the overall design or action plan by which scarce resources are to be utilized over a given period of time to achieve economic and non-economic objectives;

- *systems* – the 'technical' procedures, formal and informal, by which operations are performed, e.g. within accounts, budgeting, manufacturing, marketing, training, etc.;

- *style* – the style of management (e.g. task-centred, people-centred) and the organization's symbolic behaviour (e.g. to what organizational level does R&D report? how consistently is research funded?);

- *staff* – the people of the organization, including its management – 'a pool of resources to be nurtured, developed, guarded and allocated' (Waterman *et al.*, 1991, p 313) (author's note: here it would be useful to include the important element of organizational culture);

- *skills* – the distinctive competences of personnel and of the organization as a whole – the dominant features of its capability and its strategic 'thrust';

- *shared values, superordinate goals* – the overriding philosophy, values and aspirations around which the organization operates and which senior management seeks to infuse throughout the organization (e.g. a 'customer-led' ideal, a passion for 'excellence', a quest for quality leadership).

Figure 2.5 is intended to convey that the threats and opportunities of a turbulent environment – of which change is the only unchanging feature – can best be addressed through a preparatory framework, such as the 7-S. Its authors claim that productive change is not simply a matter of structure, nor of strategy, though both of these are critically important. For them, it depends on the relationship between the seven variables set out in the framework. It is offered here as an example of a number of approaches to implementation currently in vogue.

Concluding comments

Since marketing is now best regarded as a 'whole organization' effort, it seemed prudent to provide an early chapter which took a whole organization standpoint, which considered organizational strategy before marketing strategy.

Of course, the literature on organizational strategy is so copious that this chapter has inevitably been an exercise in selection and compression. Moreover, it is a field which abounds in different schools of thought, many of which are opposed to each other. To take an illustration: based on his study of major US corporations (1850–1920) American economic historian Alfred Chandler emphasized that firms should first determine their strategy, then their structure (see Chandler, 1962). Koch (1995, p 135) reports Peters' view that Chandler 'got it exactly wrong'; he adds that the question of which comes first is still very much a live issue and suggests: 'The truth is probably that Chandler was more right than wrong when he wrote, and that Peters is [right] now' (Koch, 1995, p135).

It is also the case that such is the continuing development of the subject that a chapter of this kind can be no more than one still in a moving picture. For example, the 1960s were dominated by the traditional approach to strategy, of which centralized planning was a feature and in which such writers as Ansoff and Andrews were prominent. In the 1980s the failure of the traditional approach was emphasized and its weakness (the separation of planning from implementation) highlighted. Also, since plans are more likely to be successful if the people responsible for making them work are involved in their development, operational managers began to acquire more status in the process than planners, for 'ownership' of the strategy was important.

At the same time, it became recognized that an organization is not a blank slate on which a strategy can be written – a structure is already in place, as are the people with their capacities, limitations and culture. Change cannot therefore begin tomorrow, when the plan is brought forth, better to let it emerge gradually over time. This, the *logical incrementalism* approach to strategic decision-making, has found favour with many managers who sense its closer approximation to the 'real world'.

However, since neither the traditional approach nor the emergent strategy approach provide sufficient guidance for those managing in turbulent times (the traditional approach assumes the future is predictable, the incremental approach is insufficiently proactive), strategists now find the insights becoming available from *complexity theory* to have some promise. Our present theorizing about organizations is based on linear logic, in which cause and effect are closely linked. Complexity theory utilizes non-linear approaches and is grounded in the belief that our ability to forecast the future is essentially limited for 'quite minor changes in apparently isolated phenomena can provoke major changes in the total system' (Turner, 1997, p 8). Whether non-linear logic provides the touchstone all strategists seek or whether it will also be discarded in a fashion-conscious field remains to be seen – a case of 'watch this space'.

Given the difficulties, this author has offered some concepts of relevance and value that seem to him durable and non-controversial, though recognizing at the same time that it is a claim open to challenge. If the chapter has done no more than provide some appreciation of the complexity and importance of 'whole organization' strategy, as a prelude to a description of marketing's contribution to the process, it will have amply served its purpose.

Before moving to the next chapter, however, where marketing strategy is examined in some depth, the following examples of *strategy in action* will serve to support perhaps what has been said in this chapter on the significance of the strategic process.

SP Engineering/Camber International

This example illustrates the use of *diversification* as a strategic choice. SP Engineering, in the UK Midlands, had operated historically as a subcontractor making parts for excavators and machine tools. However, it had long been an ambition, in the words of one of the joint owners, to 'make our own products, rather than turning out a bag of bits for other companies'.

In 1989, the company made a bold move to diversify by purchasing Camber International, a struggling company in Leicester manufacturing knitting machinery. The purchase coincided with the recession, which followed the boom years of the 1980s, and in which many UK manufacturers ceased operations. Moreover, although the UK had been a world leader in knitting machinery up to the 1960s, globally it was now barely represented in this sector.

Despite these unpromising beginnings, the diversification strategy appears to have been successful, for Camber International is now a successful supplier to the world's textile industries, despite intense competition from large Japanese and German companies. By December 1996, Camber's annual sales had doubled to approximately £11 million and output per employee had quadrupled. This progress had been helped by a programme of product development and the acquisition of some notable export business. The prospects seem particularly good for a new range of electronic machines developed with partners in the Italian and Japanese industries.

Airbus Industrie (the European Airbus Project)

One of the best illustrations of the *value of alliances and networks* in strategic management is provided by the Airbus project. Figure 2.6 attempts to give some idea of the complexities involved. If the full framework were depicted (see footnote to Figure 2.6), the unique and venturesome nature of this project would become even more apparent.

Like all strategies, and particularly those based on collaboration, the planning has been easier than the implementation. Since the project was founded in 1970, agreement between the partners has at times been difficult to achieve – as one observer noted, their debates have been 'like European monetary union without the passion' (Skapinker, 1997).

Notwithstanding the difficulties, the achievements of the project have been impressive:

- Airbus has consistently obtained one-third of the world's civil aircraft market, whilst some competitors (e.g. Lockheed, McDonnell Douglas) have faded from the scene;

- in 1994, Airbus obtained more orders than Boeing (the first time in the jet age that the US group had lost its leading position);

- in 1996, based on the number of contracts signed by airlines, Airbus estimates that it secured 42 per cent of the world market;

- not least, and significantly from a strategic standpoint, the project has enabled four countries to retain a presence in aircraft construction and to avoid destructive 'internal' competition.

As competition intensifies (e.g. Boeing's projected acquisition of McDonnell Douglas) it has been announced that Airbus will become a limited company in 1999.

Credit Suisse

In Chapter 8, we shall see that the term 'brand' and the activity of 'branding' are important facets of marketing strategy since a brand is devised for a product or service to provide identity, ownership and differentiation from the competition.

CS Holdings, now renamed Credit Suisse, is one of the world's largest organizations in the financial services sector. In 1996 to counter increasing global competition, the

Figure 2.6. *Airbus Industrie: A simplified framework*

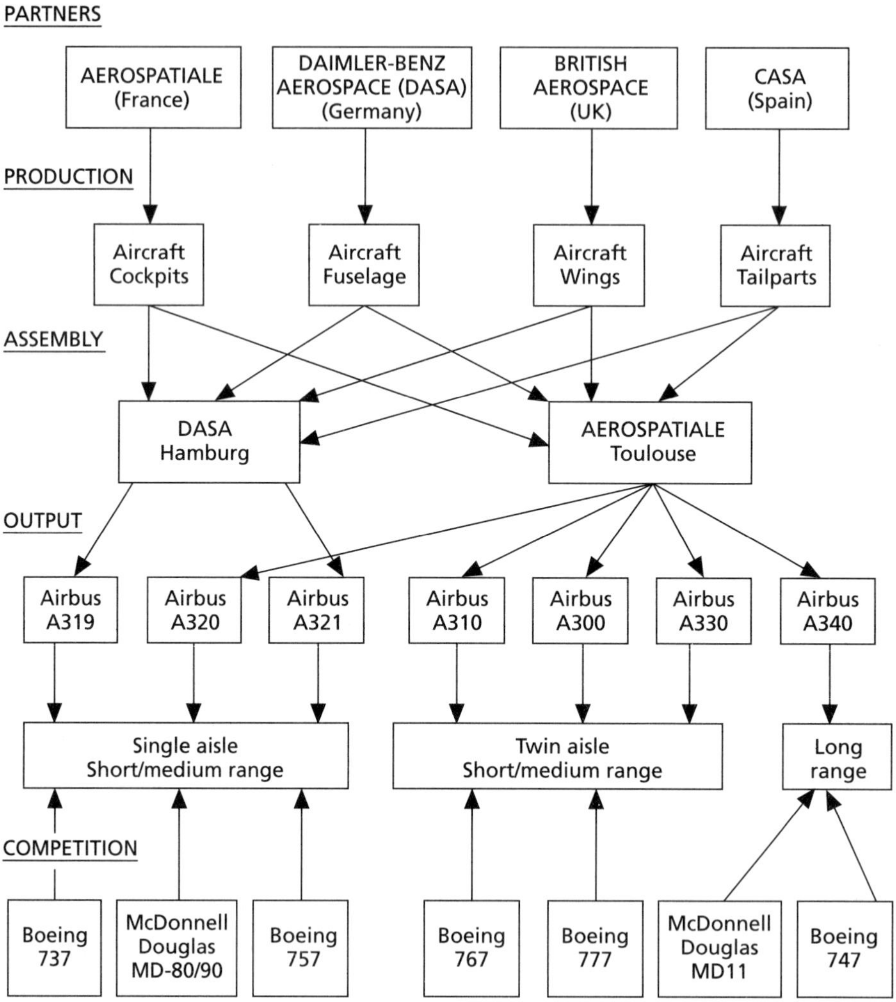

PARTNERS

| AEROSPATIALE (France) | DAIMLER-BENZ AEROSPACE (DASA) (Germany) | BRITISH AEROSPACE (UK) | CASA (Spain) |

PRODUCTION

| Aircraft Cockpits | Aircraft Fuselage | Aircraft Wings | Aircraft Tailparts |

ASSEMBLY

| DASA Hamburg | AEROSPATIALE Toulouse |

OUTPUT

| Airbus A319 | Airbus A320 | Airbus A321 | Airbus A310 | Airbus A300 | Airbus A330 | Airbus A340 |

| Single aisle Short/medium range | Twin aisle Short/medium range | Long range |

COMPETITION

| Boeing 737 | McDonnell Douglas MD-80/90 | Boeing 757 | Boeing 767 | Boeing 777 | McDonnell Douglas MD11 | Boeing 747 |

N.b. This diagram concentrates on the contribution of the four partners to the project. It takes no account of the work of contracted suppliers, e.g. General Electric, Pratt & Whitney, Rolls Royce, Belairbus, etc. for engines and instrumentation, etc.

group underwent major restructuring and in early 1997 it announced its intention to build a strong corporate brand so that its institutional image reflected the significance of this restructuring.

Credit Suisse consists of four main businesses: corporate and investment banking; asset management; private banking; and Swiss retail banking. Its restructuring and rebranding strategy is rooted in the belief that within a few years global markets for financial services will be dominated by just a small number of international banks. In this regard, Credit Suisse feels it vital to change its image from a Swiss bank with international activities to an international financial institution which happens to have its headquarters and some of its core businesses in Switzerland.

At the heart of the marketing strategy for the rebranding objective was the decision to commit approximately £10 million, above the normal annual advertising expenditures of its businesses, to finance an appropriate advertising campaign. The move is similar to that of other large banks (e.g. Deutsche Bank of Germany) to provide uniformity for their international subsidiaries.

Prior market research was used to determine that Credit Suisse had to be the brand needed for an international identity, despite strong internal competition from the brands of the other CS businesses (e.g. the CS First Boston subsidiary was a strong brand but according to the research (Smith, 1997), was perceived as clever but also as a 'local' North American bank lacking critical mass). Even so, adopting an international, rather than a Swiss, identity meant removing the Swiss cross from the logotype (i.e. the brand symbol).

Credit Suisse provides an example of:

- the increasing significance of the global market for strategy;
- the link between corporate strategy and marketing strategy;
- the nature of strategic decision-making at the corporate level.

Strategic marketing:

its scope and function

In Chapter 1 we noted:

- the meaning and significance of marketing;
- its essential character as a whole organization activity;
- its more recent development for the planning and development of strategy;
- its acquisition of general as well as specialist significance;
- its move from an isolated to a widespread function.

Chapter 2 examined, at a basic level:

- organizational strategy: some concepts of relevance and value;
- the characteristics of organizational, business unit and functional strategy;
- some ideas on the implementation of strategy (e.g. via the 7-S Framework).

This chapter, and Chapter 4 which follows, will be taking a closer look at the following:

- some fundamental precepts of marketing strategy;
- how these serve the aims of the whole organization;
- how marketing strategy is closely linked to an organization's structure, culture and ethics.

We begin this chapter with an outline of the typical *levels and types* of strategy to be found in organizations. As we saw in Chapter 2, when the organization is large, containing perhaps a number of strategic business units, the development and implementation of strategy will take place on at least three levels:

- at the corporate centre;
- at the SBU level;
- at the functional/operational level.

Our focus in this and the following chapter is to examine, primarily, marketing strategy at the SBU level. There are two reasons for this:

- it is at the SBU level that *detailed* marketing strategy is generally to be found;
- not all organizations are large and diversified.

On this second point, note that while multinational corporations are a powerful influence on the world scene, so are the smaller businesses. In the UK, for instance, small firms employ 35 per cent of the private sector workforce and produce 17 per cent of the nation's turnover. In Germany, two-thirds of total employment, half the gross national product and four-fifths of professional apprenticeships are created by its small and medium-sized enterprises (SMEs). Now in the preponderance of small firms and many medium-sized firms, what is termed 'SBU strategy' is the strategy of the whole firm. Hence our focus on strategy at the SBU level.

That said, it is important to pay some attention to *corporate centre strategy* and logical, therefore, that we begin at this first level.

Corporate centre strategy

Though its role and responsibilities will vary with the size and type of the organization, the *corporate centre* or 'head office' will be intrinsically involved with the following aspects of strategy:

- the determination of the overall *mission* of the group, i.e. its fundamental purpose, and the development of its *corporate values*;
- the development of policy guidelines on how the group will develop (e.g. by sales growth, by acquisitions (with clarification of what type of organizations should be acquired) by divestment of under-performing SBUs, by a combination of these strategies, etc.);
- the determination of how best the SBUs might be managed – which will include the selection and recruitment of chief executives for the SBUs and the development of an appropriate management style for the corporate centre, e.g. a centralization or decentralization strategy, an 'intervene as appropriate' strategy, a 'finance centralized, the rest decentralized' strategy, etc.;
- a positive, supportive role in the development of *synergy* in the group (i.e. the development of a group performance which is greater that the sum of the performances by the individual SBUs);
- the review, revision and unification of the major strategic approaches proposed by the SBUs;
- not least, to make available to the SBUs the necessary financial and other resources, and then to monitor the use and productivity of these resources.

The central focus of the corporate centre is to build a collection of high performing business units and to add value to their efforts through challenge and insight. Its emphasis here should be on assisting the SBUs to develop *competence* and a *culture* appropriate to the mission and values of the group and to ensure that the synergy developed across the SBUs can be employed to competitive advantage. Although the strategic emphasis at the centre should be essentially long-range and visionary, it can be seen from the above that it has an important role in leading the SBUs, reviewing their performances, relating these to the needs of the stakeholders and adjusting strategy where necessary. Fundamental though the functions are, experience across the world in the last two decades suggests that, ideally, the corporate centre should be 'wise, cheap and very small'.

The difficulty with management language is that it can obscure rather than clarify, so some of the terms and concepts used so far in this section will now be explained.

Organizational vision and mission

The views and aspirations of senior management as to what activities the organization intends to pursue and the nature of the direction it will take in the long term may be thought of as their *strategic vision*. As Thompson and Strickland put it: 'A strategic vision provides a big picture of who we are, what we do and where we are headed.' (Thompson and Strickland, 1996, pp 22–3). This vision constitutes the first step on the way to effective management, for without it the strategist lacks a fundamental concept of the business itself, what activities it should, or should not, pursue and what kind of strategic position it should adopt with regard to customers, other stake-holders and competitors.

Sometimes 'vision' and 'mission' are used interchangeably but vision is essentially long-term, whereas 'mission' is essentially concerned with the present. A convenient way to remember the place of the 'mission' within the scope and process of strategic planning is through the acronym MOST, formed from the initial letters of the words:

Mission

Objectives

Strategy

Tactics

The broad, written expression of the organization's mission is its *mission statement*. Here is an imaginary example:

> The mission of Acme Computers is to provide products and services of such quality that our customers receive the best possible value, our employees and business partners share in our success and our shareholders receive a sustained, superior return on their investment.
>
> We strive to achieve our mission through the design, development, production, marketing and servicing of microprocessor-based personal computers in the European Community and other markets.
>
> At all times, our mission also incorporates care and concern for the physical environment and for the larger society in which we exist and operate.

There are a number of points to note about this mission statement:

- it serves the primary purpose of all mission statements, for it is a response to the question 'what business are we in?' and is therefore quite precise about the activities to which resources will be committed (i.e. PCs and no other types of computer);

- it declares itself to be a customer-focused organization;

- through this, other 'stakeholders' in the business – employees, shareholders, suppliers, etc. – will benefit;

- the company is mindful of its wider obligations – to society and the environment;

- the extent of its operations is made clear – it is international in scope.

Returning to the MOST acronym, the *objectives*, or 'goals', of the organization are the ends it will strive for in trying to achieve its mission. The *strategies* are the directions in which the organization will move in order to achieve its objectives and because they often have major resource implications they are similarly broad in scope. The *tactics* are the detailed operations that follow from the key strategic decisions which have been made. We shall be looking at the MOST sequence in more detail later in the chapter under the heading SBU strategy.

According to Thompson and Strickland (1996, p 23) there are 'three distinct aspects involved in forming a well-conceived strategic vision and expressing it in a company mission statement:

- 'Understanding what business a company is really in.
- Communicating the vision and mission in ways that are clear, exciting, and inspiring.
- Deciding when to alter the company's strategic course and change its business mission.'

As we shall also see later, mission statements for business units and functions (e.g. marketing, finance, etc.) are derived from the corporate mission statement.

Corporate values

These may be defined as 'the relatively few important beliefs and convictions held to be crucial for the success of a given organization and which substantially drive the behaviour of people of that organization'. This particular definition has been adapted from the report of Humble, Jackson and Thomson (1994, pp 28–42) on the 1992 study of corporate values undertaken in the UK and sponsored by DEC.

These authors indicate that 429 managers participated in the study and that they were drawn from a wide range of manufacturing and service businesses. Two of the key findings of the study were that:

- 80 per cent of the organizations had written values statements, and that
- 89 per cent expected values to be more important for organizational success in the immediate future.

A statement of corporate values is a formal recording of the importance of the key factors in an organization's success and the commitment of the organization to developing and sustaining these.

In the DEC study, for instance, the managers were asked to rank in order the following values according to their perceived importance:

- *people* (i.e. staff) as a crucial asset for success;
- dedication to meeting *customer* needs;
- commitment to the delivery of the highest *quality* standards;
- total *social responsibility* in dealings and relationships;
- commitment to outperforming *competition*;
- constant increase in the *productivity* of organizational resources;
- the importance of simple, non-bureaucratic *systems*;
- the commitment to *innovation* throughout the organization;
- the significance, for survival, of *short-term profitability*.

What is interesting about the response of managers to this checklist is that while all factors were seen to be important, people, customers, quality and social responsibility received the highest ratings (97 per cent or above) and *short-term profitability* the lowest (79 per cent).

On this last point, the managers felt, none the less, that properly implemented corporate values contribute to profitability. Moreover, staff *need* the stability and guidance of clear corporate values in periods of rapid change.

The development of a statement of such values rests in the first instance with top management for unless there is clarity and commitment at the corporate level there is little chance that a values statement will be developed and acted upon at the SBU and functional levels. Also, as with the mission statement, minimizing the distance between the rhetoric and the reality has much to do with the quality of management at all levels. The last word here may safely be left to Humble, Jackson and Thomson:

> Sometimes, a corporate values statement is purely cosmetic, mixing platitudes with good intentions. The staff see through such public relations exercises immediately. Cynicism is strengthened. The real values continue to be what people on the whole really believe, not what is on the poster or in the video (Humble *et al.*, 1994, p 35).

Synergy

Corporate management must constantly be looking for ways in which combined or co-ordinated action between parts of the organization may produce better results than would the parts working separately. This is the achievement of *synergy* based on the idea that 2 + 2 can equal 5, rather than 4, or even 3 (known as negative synergy).

Sometimes this can be done by *acquisition* – for example of a supplier, a distributive network, or a manufacturer in a related field, thus widening the product range and improving the product–market posture of the whole organization (an example here would be the acquisition of a cutlery manufacturer and/or a glass manufacturer, by a group producing ceramic tableware). *Joint ventures* and *strategic alliances* are also typically undertaken to achieve *sustainable competitive advantage* through synergy – the Airbus Industrie project outlined in Chapter 2 provides an excellent example here.

Additionally, top management must constantly be looking for ways in which the component parts of the existing organization can, by cross-bracing each other's efforts, provide an increased return on resources. Figure 3.1 aims to illustrate how such an objective may be realized in practice. It reintroduces us to Bursley Group PLC, the imaginary organization we met in Chapter 2 when examining the concepts of corporate centre strategy and the strategic business unit (see Figure 2.1). As a reminder:

- SBU No. 1 serves the industrial market, producing insulators and other items of electro-ceramics;

- SBU No. 2 serves the architectural/construction market with its porcelain tiles;

- SBU No. 3 serves world-wide ornamental ware markets with its distinctive and exclusive figurines, jardinières, etc.

As Figure 3.1 indicates, these operate as a cohesive organization guided and orchestrated by a corporate centre HQ (labelled 'Head Office'). As the diagram indicates, the industrial division (SBU No. 1) has introduced rapid prototyping technology in the process of developing new products. Replacing the lengthy, time consuming process of modelling prototypes in clay, wood or metal by computer-assisted three-dimensional modelling, the division has substantially reduced the time required to bring new products to the market. Encouraged by Head Office, the technology has been made available to the other two divisions.

Figure 3.1. *Bursley Group PLC: Sustainable competitive advantage through synergy*

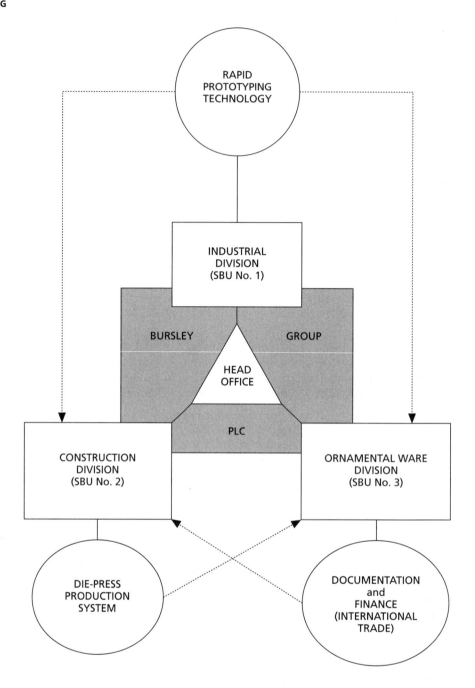

Similarly the production system used for producing tiles in the construction division (SBU No. 2), based on die-pressing the powdered raw material has been successfully adapted for the production of giftware by the ornamental ware division (SBU No. 3). Faster production times and consequent increased output has enabled this division to introduce a new lower priced range to increasingly competitive international markets, complementing the traditionally produced, high quality products favoured by its more affluent customers.

In the process of building its global network of outlets, the ornamental ware division has accumulated considerable skills in the documentary and financial processes involved in international trade. With the deregulation of markets world-wide, the construction division is making efforts to expand the geographical base of its activities. In doing this, it is calling on the considerable experience and skills of the ornamental ware division.

It is easy to see how the synergies attained by the supportive, collaborative atmosphere engendered by Head Office redounds to the benefit of Bursley Group as a whole.

Core competences

As Thompson and Strickland (1996, p 42) indicate, strategy is powerful if it produces a sizeable and sustainable competitive advantage and weak if it results in competitive disadvantage. The corporate centre's role here is to stimulate and monitor the actions taken by SBUs to develop the skills and capabilities required for competitive advantage. In the 1990s, the concept of building *competences* in one or more *core activities* to achieve strategic advantage over rivals has gained substantial credibility.

Prahalad and Hamel (1990, pp 79–91) have contributed notably to such thinking, drawing attention to the success of Japanese companies in this respect. Honda's powerful competence in designing, manufacturing and improving engines has been the basis of its success with a wide range of products, including motor cycles and cars, lawnmowers, power tillers and outboard motors. Canon's undoubted competences in microelectronics, precision mechanics and optics have been at the root of its success with copying machines, video cameras, printers, etc.

As noted earlier, the long-term direction of the organization is governed by the strategic vision of corporate centre management. Prahalad and Hamel draw attention to the commitment of Japanese management to:

- cradle and progress towards a vision of a desired future;
- use this vision to integrate the efforts of the whole organization for a common purpose;
- through this common purpose, identify and develop the core competences necessary to achieve the vision.

A *core competence* is something an organization does especially well in relation to competitors. It is often based on some specialized skill, experience or expertise that competitors do not possess and, importantly, cannot readily develop. Such competence may derive from *specialized knowledge and skill* (e.g. of raw materials, research and development, technology, markets) or *capability* (e.g. of management, manufacturing, marketing, finance, customer service) – indeed any attribute which will result in sustainable competitive advantage for an organization's products or services.

Though he uses the term 'distinctive capability' for 'core competence', British writer John Kay supports the concept and points out that reputations are created in specific markets. He concludes that: 'The value of a competitive advantage will depend on the strength of the firm's distinctive capability, the size of the market, and the overall profitability of the industry' (Kay, 1996b, p 47).

As we shall see later in this chapter, the idea of competitive advantage through core competence is closely related to such maxims of marketing as *market segmentation* and *product positioning*.

It is most important to bear in mind that a significant function of the corporate centre derives from its responsibility for *corporate marketing*. We will not be looking at this in any detail here for it is logical to do so in Chapter 13 (the broader base of marketing). Suffice it to say here that whatever the number of SBUs, products, services and brands within the organization they will benefit from the projection of a clear and powerful corporate image based on the over-arching objectives established at the corporate centre. In other words, in addition to its output, the organization itself must be marketed. More of this later.

Implementing corporate centre strategy

For many experienced managers, the real problem lies not so much in creating strategy as in implementing it. The short case studies in this section provide examples of Head Office strategy in action. Hopefully, they will substantiate the claim that, properly conducted, such strategy is very much more than a once-a-year theoretical exercise.

Rover Cars

The following outline provides an example of how the major strategic approach of an SBU is directed by the corporate centre.

In 1994, the German manufacturer BMW purchased the UK's Rover Group for £800 million from British Aerospace. The retail franchises for Rover Cars were separated from those of the strong and successful Land Rover range and it was initially thought that Rover Cars would concentrate on the volume market whilst benefiting from the institutional image of the BMW 'luxury' brand.

Due to intense competition from the mass production plants of Europe and Asia it has been decided to develop Rover Cars as an 'upmarket twin' to BMW, with its share of the UK market reducing from 12 per cent to perhaps 7–10 per cent in the long term, accompanied by a significant increase in world-wide sales. In line with this strategic shift, Rover has committed extensive expenditure to the retraining of its sales staff (along the lines of the Daewoo passive 'consultant' approach).

The marketing strategy will be to provide vehicles and servicing to fit the lifestyle of target consumer groups – for example, the latest edition of Rover's Mini (the Equinox) is being advertised in the fashion press. Selling individual brands such as the Mini through boutique type retail shops is another option which is being considered. This move to develop a quality image is also being extended through increased marketing effort for the MG range and a possible resurrection of the prestigious Austin Healey brand.

Further evidence of Rover's drive for increased quality is provided by the partnership arrangement at its Longbridge site with the German firm Durr, a world leader in installing painting systems for car plants. The contract with Durr provided not only for a £45 million new paint facility but also for the indefinite location of a Durr team at Longbridge to ensure its smooth operation. Thanks to this strategic partnership approach, since the facility began operations in 1995, the number of cars having no paint defects is between 85–90 per cent, compared to the 70–80 per cent which is reckoned to be the accepted level in installations of this type.

Keppel Corporation

The last decade has seen the breaking up or rationalization of many large 'conglomerate' corporations. Despite this, Singapore provides an interesting case study in successful diversification, proving that there is no 'one best way' in corporate strategy.

Keppel began operations in 1968 as a single shipyard. Like many organizations its existence was severely threatened by the recession of the 1980s. In addition, a storm hit the shipyard in 1982. Also, because of the depressed oil market, shipowners were not particularly keen to repair their vessels and yards were competing intensively for the reduced business. Competitive advantage was nevertheless being stifled by high labour costs and the earnings of the industry as a whole were in decline.

Despite divesting itself of non-core operations and writing down the value of non-performing vessels, Keppel announced a loss in 1984 of $173.9 million. In 1985, for the first time since independence, the economy of Singapore experienced a downturn (1.8 per cent). Because all sectors of its business had collapsed and its level of debt was very high a further round of severe reductions was necessary, including the cutting of the shipyard labour force from 3800 to 2300.

It was at this stage that the overall strategy of the group was switched to one of:

● rationalization in Singapore of existing operations;

● prudent diversification in Singapore and overseas.

Today what was once a single shipyard has become a broadly-based group with assets of $16 billion and ten listed subsidiaries operating in such diverse fields as banking, property, stockbroking, mobile phones, engineering and insurance. In 1995, pre-tax profits reached a record level ($445 million). Ship repair and shipbuilding accounted for a mere 12 per cent of this while banking, financial services and property made up 70 per cent of the group's profits. Straits Settlement Land, Keppel's property arm, active in Singapore, China, Vietnam, Indonesia and the Philippines increased its profit by over 50 per cent to a record $138 million.

It is now planned that the group's shipyard headquarters at Telok Blangah will be completely replaced by an extensive waterfront residential and commercial development organized by its own property subsidiary.

Business strategy and the contribution of marketing

In this section, we shall consider the development and implication of strategy for *one specific line* of organizational activity. These last few words are carefully chosen, for they are intended to encompass non-profit as well as profit activity even though we are dealing here with what is termed business (or business unit) strategy.

Bear in mind, too, that business strategy can mean the strategy of a business unit in a large corporation or simply, the strategy of an autonomous, single-business company (e.g. an SME). In the latter case, corporate strategy and business strategy are one and the same, as noted earlier.

At the heart of the business-level strategy there is a primary objective: the development and reinforcement of sustainable competitive advantage in the market place. This building and strengthening of the long-term competitive position is the responsibility of the chief executive (who may be the head of a division in a large, diversified corporation, the managing director of a single business, or even a product or brand manager responsible for the fortunes of one or more products (see Chapter 4)). Figure 3.2 is an attempt to depict many of the duties incorporated in this overall responsibility; they provide the basis for assessing the effectiveness of the chief executive. Hopefully, the diagram explains itself but an additional word or two may be helpful.

As we see from the top centre and bottom centre of the diagram, sustainable competitive advantage results from:

● the *development* of an effective strategy;

● its *implementation* and *continuing development* (e.g. through adjustments to changed environmental conditions, or to the development of technology or to the activities of competitors).

Figure 3.2. *Business strategy: responsibilities of the chief executive*

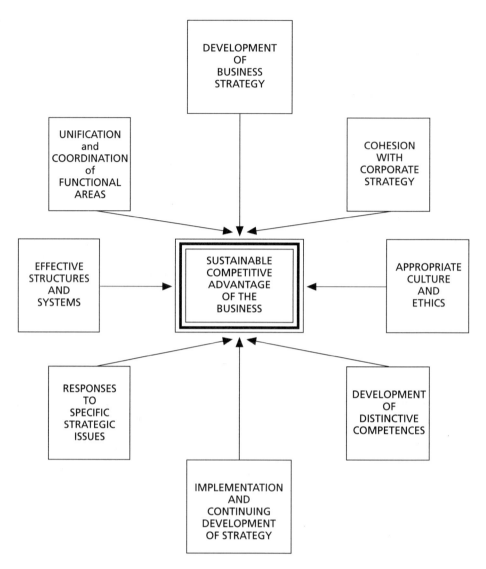

Flanking these responsibilities, six equally important aspects of strategy are highlighted:

- the connection between business unit and corporate strategy – the vision, mission and values of each must cohere;

- similarly, the strategies for each functional area (marketing, production, finance, etc.) must support the overall business strategy;

- effective strategy can only be fostered if the organizational climate is right, i.e. through a customer-led culture and a wholly legal and adequately ethical framework;

- effective structures and systems must be devised and operated (discussed in more detail in Chapter 4);

- as mentioned earlier, the achievement of strategic advantage through the concept of developing distinctive competences has now gained credibility and support by both practitioners and theorists – the chief executive must ensure the skills and capabilities required for competitive advantage are developed and nurtured;

- effective implementation of strategy can, and frequently does depend on speedy action to resolve specific issues, e.g.

  – upgrading of plant and equipment;

  – increase in marketing expenditure;

  – improvement of the cash flow situation.

It is the chief executive who is responsible, ultimately, for the resolution of such issues.

Finally, the successful development and implementation of strategy depends on a *two-way process* of communication and involvement at all levels – corporate, business and functional.

Developing competitive advantage

When we consider how the business can develop competitive advantage the significance of marketing, at the strategic and functional level, immediately becomes clear: the creation of such advantage is essentially a *marketing problem* requiring *marketing thought* and a *marketing approach* for its solution.

Given the particular scale of financial and other assets available and its distinctive competences there are at least *three* decisions required for a strategy to provide sustainable competitive advantage for the business:

- where best the advantage may be won – i.e. which markets?
- how best the advantage may be won – i.e. what product or service attributes are required?
- how best to overcome the efforts of competitors.

Approaching strategy may be, for example, a matter of pursuing:

- *price leadership* – aiming for a cost-based competitive edge over rivals through being the lowest-cost producer in the industry, or
- *differentiation* – securing advantage through the specification, performance, output, durability, service or design of what is being offered, or
- *focus* – identifying a niche in the market which provides an opportunity to outdo the competition by providing a better service to the particular needs of the buyers in this niche (this approach often explains why small firms exist profitably in an industry alongside much larger competitors and is known to practitioners as a process of 'sliding down the cracks').

Based on his painstaking research on how companies actually operate, these are three ways by which companies can gain competitive advantage according to Michael Porter (1985) whose work was mentioned in Chapter 2. (Although Porter has attracted some criticism for reducing his ideas and extensive theorizing to such a simple list of headings, as Crainer (1996, p 94) points out, the fact that his views are so influential 'is a triumph for Porter's abilities of dissection and logic'.)

The first of Porter's headings, *price leadership*, seems clear enough and need not detain us, but *differentiation* and *focus* should be explained further, giving rise as they do to the important collateral concepts of *segmentation* and *positioning* which are now examined.

Market segmentation

A market can be defined in terms of a *place* where a product is sold, in terms of a specific *product or service* (the insurance market, the leisure market, the money market) or in terms of the *customer*. Not surprisingly, in marketing as we understand it, the last approach is favoured, as in the following definition by Kotler:

> *A market consists of all the potential customers sharing a particular need or want who might be willing and able to engage in exchange to satisfy that need or want.*
>
> *Thus the size of the market depends upon the number of persons [or organizations] who exhibit the need, have resources that interest others, and are willing to exchange these resources in exchange for what they want* (Kotler, 1994, p 11).

Sometimes, a business will direct its marketing efforts to the total population of potential customers for its particular products or services. This is the process of *undifferentiated marketing* and would be appropriate where:

- the market was a very small one;
- where heavy users of the product constituted such a considerable proportion of the market that the obvious strategy would be to direct all effort towards these heavy users;
- where the organization's product (its brand) so dominated the market that its appeal was *total*, i.e. to all sections of the market.

Such cases are more the exception than the rule and generally marketers are more concerned to direct their efforts not so much to the total population of potential buyers as to certain types, or classifications, of buyer. This is the strategy of *market segmentation* and where efforts and assets are directed towards a single market segment the process is referred to as *concentrated marketing*.

Segmentation recognizes that, typically, a product is not bought by everyone, but rather by some specific sub-group. A high-priced, exclusive type of perfume, packaged and advertised with restraint and dignity, will not be bought by the same population sub-group as a perfume which is low-priced, mass-produced, packaged and advertised so as to appeal to the less wealthy. The young adult market for sports goods is rather different from the middle-aged market for sports goods.

By adopting a key group as its target market, the whole marketing effort becomes more manageable and productive in that products can be developed through close attention to the needs of a more homogeneous group of buyers. Once that group is identified it should also be easier to communicate with it (through advertising, etc.) – thus reducing wastage in promotional budgets, which occurs when the advertising overlaps groups which have neither the means nor the propensity to buy. Here we can discern two facets of *asset-based marketing* – the first, to develop the products or services which make the best use of the core competences of the business and the second, to make the most productive use of its resources.

Predictably, while it is one thing to aim for precision, it is another to achieve it. Even so, though not always easy, the identification of appropriate sub-groups as target markets is an important exercise and one to which organizations, frequently through market researchers, pay a great deal of attention. The key questions are:

- Who buys?
- Why do they buy?
- How are their needs being satisfied?
- How do we reach them?

They are the starting point to the identification of the 'target' market, or appropriate segment.

Although market segmentation is widely used in the consumer field (e.g. food, fashion, tourism) it is also valuable in industrial marketing (e.g. raw materials, capital equipment, factory maintenance services). F.E. Webster, a noted author in the industrial marketing field, writes clearly and forcefully on the strategic importance of segmentation. He describes carefully selected customers as:

> *those that stand to benefit most from what the supplier has to offer, those whose needs and buying practices best fit the supplier's capability. They will ask the firm to do things that it can do well and that are consistent with its strategy. They will value the resources that the firm commits to solving their problems, and they will be willing to pay for them* (Webster, 1991, p 97).

Through the process of segmentation, concentrated marketing effort is applied to a target market. The classifications used for particular types of individuals and organizations are referred to as *segmentation variables*. We shall be looking at these variables in some detail in Chapter 6.

Positioning

Authors Zikmund and d'Amico (1993) suggest that there are six major stages in the strategic marketing process. Their framework suits this stage of our study quite well and so Figure 3.3 depicts it in outline.

The first element in the process is one of analysing marketing opportunities and this has two facets:

- an analysis of the external environment to clarify how change might offer either opportunities or threats to the organization, and

- an analysis of the organization itself to clarify its strength and weaknesses, matching these against the environmental opportunities and threats as a first stage in planning strategy.

This procedure, known as SWOT analysis (strengths, weaknesses, opportunities, threats) is the basis for the analysis of marketing opportunity, although, of course, if the environment were sufficiently threatening, the strategy might be more defensive than opportunistic, so as to minimize those threats.

Segmentation analysis, Stage 2 in the process, has already been outlined and Stages 4, 5 and 6 will be described in detail later in the text. At this point it is Stage 3, positioning strategy, which we must briefly examine.

Positioning signifies the market, or competitive, position of a product or service and it is governed by the way in which its customers perceive that product or service in relation to the competition. The essence of a positioning strategy is to establish clearly the competitive advantage of the product and this is typically done by stressing the particular characteristics, features or benefits which differentiate the product from the competition.

The concept of positioning is linked, as a rule, with the technique of *branding* in that an organization will employ a particular name, term, stylized form of lettering, symbol, picture, colour, or some combination of these in order to identify its product or service and to establish its ownership of that brand. Also, the position occupied by the brand in the market is not only a function of the product itself but also of its price level, of where it may be bought (its distribution) and of where and how it is advertised (its promotion).

Thus, as Figure 3.3 indicates, positioning strategy includes the development of an appropriate 'mix' (product, price, place (i.e. distribution) and promotion). It is not

Figure 3.3. *Stages in the strategic marketing process (Adapted from: Zikmund and d'Amico, 1993, p 47).*

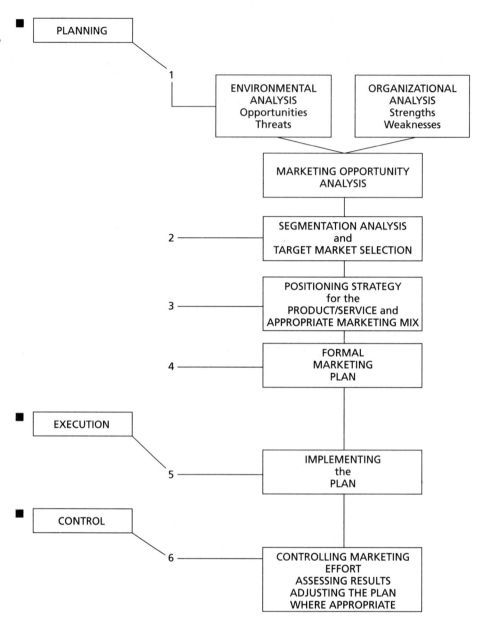

solely a question of positioning the product – it would make no sense to develop a high quality, exclusive product and distribute it to retail outlets specializing in low-cost goods or advertise it in newspapers circulating mainly to the poorer sections of the population. It should be noted that the *marketing mix* is usually considered to comprise four elements: *product* (or service), *price*, *place* (distribution) and *promotion* – but in this text, a broader view of 'the mix' is taken, as we shall see later.

Marketing research has an important role in positioning strategy for it can clearly identify how customers perceive the organization's product (its *brand image*) compared with their perceptions of competing products. This will assist the development of a *positioning map* which signifies the location of each product in relation to particular dimensions (price, quality, etc.). A void on the map (i.e. a space between clusters of products) may indicate room for a new product and, where research is conducted to assess customers' perception of the ideal brand, the individual organization may set out to develop such a product or to modify its existing product so as to move it towards the ideal. The technique will become clearer in Chapter 8, where mapping is used in the development of a new national newspaper.

In this short introduction to positioning, a final point must be made. On the one hand, the way in which positioning supports a *differentiation* strategy can clearly be seen. By marketing what is new, exclusive, lowest-priced, etc. we can differentiate ourselves from the competition. In a sense, this is *avoidance behaviour* – we are avoiding a direct comparison with competition. On the other hand, however, the particular assets of the organization may justify *confronting* competitors on their own terms – a strategy known as *head-to-head positioning*. Using a military analogy, in this instance we decide to engage the enemy rather than avoid him. Figure 3.4 illustrates these strategic approaches and indicates how they emanate from the particular assets and skills of the two imaginary organizations involved.

Suppose there are two firms producing a similar quality of ceramic tableware. The first of these (Firm A) conducts an audit of its assets and skills and finds the following factors especially significant to its competitive position:

- it has a sophisticated mass-production system which provides it with the capacity for long production runs of standardized products;

- its equipment is kept constantly abreast of technological development;

- because of the scale of its production (e.g. resulting in low overheads per unit of output) it is highly cost competitive;

- thanks to surpluses from current operations, its ability to use debt and equity financing and the willingness of its parent company to support its needs, it has ready access to capital;

- because of the scale of the investment and risk involved it has become particularly proficient at forecasting demand for its products and budgeting its expenditure in accordance with flows of revenue;

- in many of the markets it serves it has become a high share supplier;

- its sales representatives have become experienced and skilled in the negotiation of large contracts (e.g. with hospital trusts, universities, and other institutional users);

- due in part to the stability of employment it offers, its workforce is highly motivated and extremely loyal (turnover is very low and strikes are unheard of).

As a result of this audit, Firm A has decided that in all its markets, even those to which it is a newcomer, it will meet the competition head-to-head with a supporting marketing message of 'value for money'.

By contrast, Firm B's audit produces this profile of its distinguishing characteristics:

- comparatively, it is a large spender on R & D and has a well developed new product capability;

- its use of flexible manufacturing systems means it is extremely well placed to meet the growing sophistication of demand in an era of global competition, in which customers increasingly seek a specialized product at or near a mass production price;

- its world-wide experience of dealing with customer firms large and small has helped it to become adept at credit management and the financial procedures required for international trade;

Figure 3.4. *Distinctive competences and positioning strategies.*

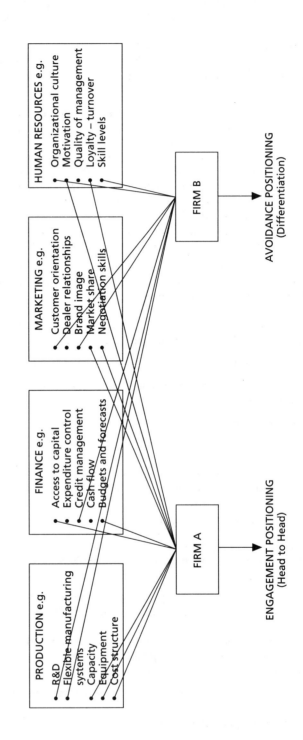

- in all phases of its operations and management it is customer-led and it understands and acts upon the impact on profitability of customer retention;

- because of its reputation for innovation and flexibility its brand image is that of a reputable supplier of appealing tableware, often of novel and intriguing design;

- an organizational culture has been built up which minimizes internal conflict, is dedicated to meeting customer needs and is based on a highly skilled and adaptable workforce.

Firm B has decided that its positioning strategy will invariably be based on avoidance of direct comparison with competitors. Its target markets will consist of affluent, discriminating users who are prepared to pay a premium for what is novel and distinctive. The firm has decided that in all its advertising and packaging, a caption will accompany its trade mark which reads: 'the badge of exclusivity'.

In addition to clarifying the meaning of 'engagement' and 'avoidance' positioning, it is hoped that these imaginary examples will also demonstrate why a strategy is not necessarily right or wrong, but only right or wrong for a particular organization.

Strategic marketing: *some relevant techniques*

This chapter continues with a brief review of some of the concepts which are deemed relevant and valuable for developing marketing strategy. Again, we must remember that the management process is still more art than science and that the complexities of managing in turbulent times and the pace of change are such as to raise the question of whether 'scientific management' will ever be possible. Nevertheless, influential writers such as John Kay (1996b, pp 26–31) believe that the task of turning management from a subject based on the assertions of gurus to one which reproduces the structure of concepts, hypotheses and empirical tests characteristic of the natural sciences is not a hopeless one.

What follows therefore is a description of some of the approaches which have been found *useful* in structuring strategic thinking and *helpful* in implementing strategy. More of these concepts will appear as the book proceeds.

The marketing mix

Developing an idea of Professor James Culliton (1948) who, in a study of manufacturers' marketing costs, once described the business executive as a 'mixer of ingredients', Neil H. Borden writing in 1964, reflected on how, 15 years earlier, he had liked Culliton's idea of calling a marketing executive: 'a mixer of ingredients, one who is constantly engaged in fashioning creatively a mix of marketing procedures and policies in his efforts to produce a profitable enterprise'. From the time of Culliton's study and assisted by Borden's advocacy, the term 'marketing mix' has caught and held the attention of marketing people. It has developed wide usage because it has helped managers to conceptualize more clearly the processes in which they were engaged, and which had formerly been described in duller language.

The concept suggests that there are four key variables in marketing operations:

- the *product*
- its *price*
- its *place* element (i.e. its distribution)
- its *promotion*

Borden pointed out that these, the 4Ps, might be thought of as the ingredients in a mixture, a recipe for marketing success. Though not a profound notion, it caught the popular imagination to the extent that when practitioners speak of planning and programming of marketing effort, they invariably refer to the 'marketing mix'.

There are a number of points to emphasize in relation to the concept:

● The *nature of the product itself will influence the balance of ingredients* thus, products with a high fashion content, e.g. clothes for young adults, will require substantial attention to product development and design and extensive promotion. Considerations of price and methods of distribution (place) are not so fundamental perhaps. On the other hand, staple commodities in consistent demand, e.g. canned baked beans, may require emphasis on price and accessibility (i.e. place) with product development and promotion playing a lesser role.

● The *concept of a 'mix' captures the idea that the blend of ingredients may be varied from time to time in order to achieve objectives* – the following questions, typical of marketing mix development, might clarify this statement:

– To what extent might an increase in the number of distributive outlets increase sales above the increase in distribution costs and hence increase profitability?
– To what extent would the increased costs of improved product quality and performance be offset by an increase in market share (with some expenditure being offset, possibly, by a decrease in advertising expenditure)?
– To what extent would an increase in price, making available an increased budget for promotion, improve return on investment?

● *The marketing strategy is devised with a view to securing objectives at minimum cost* – based on the idea of marketing as the income generating function, management must review alternative blends of the ingredients in the marketing mix with attention to the costs of alternative blends and their effects on profitability. The ideal is to plan for maximum effectiveness at minimum cost.

● *The marketing strategy cannot be static, it must respond to changes in the organization's environment* – in the short term, the blend of elements is fixed; in the longer term, however, increased competitive activity, the appearance of substitute products, changes in legal requirements, customer needs, government policies, etc., may force a reappraisal of strategy and an alteration in the mix. *Marketing research must therefore be a continuous process so that the organization can take advantage of, and not be threatened by, environmental change.*

The case for an enlarged marketing mix
Note that the last sentence above has been emphasized. The importance of marketing research is so fundamental to customer-led operations it has led this writer to question whether it is wise to separate it from the marketing mix. Successful products and services are not developed in a vacuum, they generally emerge as a result of painstaking enquiry into the needs of customers. The emergence of global markets and the dynamic rate of change in those markets only serve to underline the importance of this, the marketing research process. It must be, whether formal or informal, a *continuous* process, to monitor change and to assist organizational adjustment to change. To use it in an *ad hoc* or episodic manner, or when 'we have run out of ideas' is to misunderstand its purpose and value. This author believes its fundamental strategic importance is best safeguarded if we regard it as an element in the marketing mix and if it is sensible to preserve the convenient shorthand of the letter 'P' alliteration, why not label its particular function P for *preparation*?

Again, the author's experience of marketing management, spanning more than four decades, suggests that the difference between success and failure in marketing plans invariably depends on the *people* involved. Is it, therefore, correct to resonate on the central significance of skilled, well trained, highly motivated people and yet exclude them from the strategic formula, i.e. the marketing mix? People are not an additive to the marketing plan. They constitute the core on which it is constructed. What hope for the plan if the organizational culture runs counter to it? Hence the plea for a sixth element in the mix, P for *people*.

In the next chapter, we shall be looking at the context, or background, against which marketing strategy takes place – the organization's structure, systems, culture and ethics and in succeeding chapters we shall be considering in more detail these six elements of the strategic formula (or enlarged marketing mix);

- preparation (marketing research);
- product;
- price;
- place (distribution);
- promotion;
- people.

In the meantime, it is hoped that Figure 3.5 will clarify the function of the strategic formula within the marketing planning process.

Gap analysis

The value of some planning tools derives from their ability to depict the complexities of the planning task in relatively simple form, for this will help to highlight the areas or types of development requiring particular attention. This explains the appeal of *gap analysis* in forward planning, the fundamental idea of which is illustrated in Figure 3.6.

Bennett Engineering, another imaginary company, manufactures and distributes high quality steel components for a limited number of industries. Led by the chief executive, the management team of this medium-sized, successful organization takes on the task of setting itself an objective in quantitative terms to be achieved within the next three year cycle. Note that the objective could be expressed in a number of ways – for example an increase in the firm's market share or its rate of return on investment, etc. Here it is expressed in financial terms, to increase annual sales revenue from its present level of £10 million to £13 million.

This seemingly formidable objective is considered by the Bennett team to be wholly realistic. The steps in its thinking, outlined in a report, are as follows:

- *Suppose we do nothing other than maintain our present course?*
  Answer: given the highly competitive nature of our markets, we would do little more than maintain our present revenue level.

- *What if we aim to increase the productivity of our present operations?*
  Answer: this is a promising prospect, for example we can improve the training and the efficiency of our sales force; we can increase our prices to reflect more realistically the quality we offer (with no detriment to sales) and we can reduce our distribution costs. These measures would improve the revenue forecast by as much as £1 million.

- *What can we achieve with the introduction of new products?*
  Answer: again, an increase in £1 million p.a. by the end of the planning period – the prototypes shown to selected customers have been very well received and we

Figure 3.5. *The function of the strategic formula in the marketing planning process*

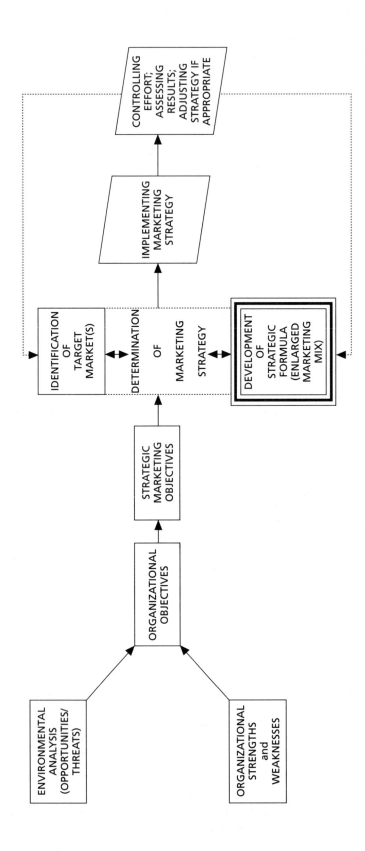

are at an advanced stage of negotiating a number of new contracts for purpose-made components.

- *What are the prospects for cultivating new markets?*

  Answer: for us, this means, essentially, new geographical markets and it is a 'must': too much of our revenue comes from the UK. At the first stage, we could do far more in the EU, increasing yearly revenue, at a conservative estimate, by £0.5 million.

- *What other options are open to us?*

  Answer: from the details given separately it can be seen that a measure of low-risk diversification plus the acquisition of two small but quite successful engineering businesses would be a very prudent move resulting in a further annual addition of £0.5 million by Year 3.

Perhaps Figure 3.6 and the above, extremely simplified outline, will help to convey the gist of the gap analysis approach. Here, we have been concerned with planning for the organization in the round, as it were, but the approach is equally valuable for the development of sub-strategies, for example for the product range or for *cash flow* (What is our present flow level? What level will we need to sustain our general objective? What is the gap? How can we improve present flows through payment incentive schemes – through reinvestment of earnings, through loans, through share flotations?).

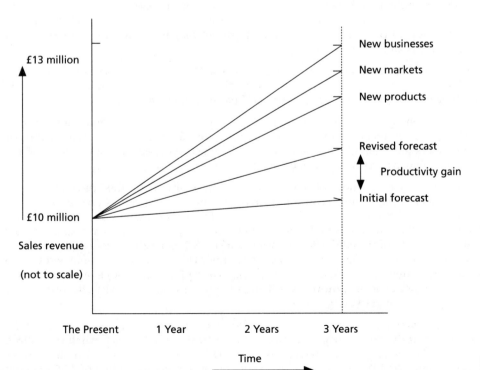

Figure. 3.6. *Bennett Engineering: gap analysis*

Pareto analysis (the '80/20' rule)

The *Pareto principle* (named after a nineteenth-century Italian economist) or the '80/20' rule, as it is more generally called by management practitioners and theorists, states that:

> If the components of a distribution are ranked by cumulative value, approximately 80 per cent of the value of the distribution would be derived from 20 per cent of the components of that distribution.

Behind this seemingly dry-as-dust expression lies a concept of immense practical value, so much so that Richard Koch, writer on strategy, concludes: 'One of the most glorious insights about life, the Universe and everything, is the EIGHTY/TWENTY (80/20) RULE' (Koch, 1995, p 17). Certainly, experience suggests that in a wide range of industries, product groups and markets, within plus or minus a few percentage points, the principle holds good.

One of the key applications of Pareto in marketing relates to the management of the product range (product portfolio). Here, the key issue relates to the breadth (number of products) and depth (number of types, sizes, designs per product) of the range.

In business operations, there is an almost insistent pressure for the range to expand, with salesmen, distributors and customers encouraging the production of 'another size', 'another quality', 'another tolerance'. This is all to the good provided the return in sales volume and/or profitability justifies the extra resources involved. Frequently, however, the result is not to expand sales but to extend a static sales volume over an increased product range, with a consequent reduction in average sales per product. When this happens, costs inevitably increase through uneconomical production runs, and possibly split deliveries to customers, as the firm attempts to cope with out of stock situations.

The position can become chronic enough for a large proportion of output to be responsible for a small part only of sales/profits, while a relatively small proportion of output is responsible for most of the sales/profits. Hence the shorthand description '80/20', for 20 per cent of the product portfolio may be bringing in 80 per cent of sales/profits and vice versa.

When this happens, management has to ask itself: 'is there a sound case for rationalizing the range?', which will entail dispensing with the unprofitable and/or slow selling products and marketing a 'leaner' but more effective range.

Pressure on space will allow only one other illustration of this important concept. The 80/20 tendency is not confined to products, for it frequently holds good for customers and markets. Consider Table 3.1, which resulted from an analysis of the marketing database of an actual company.

Due to the magnitude of the actual numbers involved, this particular firm's customers, sales volume, costs and profits have been expressed as profiles adding to 100. On the basis of its marketing cost analysis, thoroughly conceptualized and executed, the firm discovered that 51.8 per cent of its customers were responsible for 87.5 per cent of its sales. On the other hand, 48.2 per cent of its customers were adding a mere 12.5 per cent to its sales volume. However, this marginal addition to its sales volume was responsible for no less than 44.7 per cent of its marketing costs. The 87.5 per cent of turnover was being obtained much more cost effectively (only 55.3 per cent of marketing costs).

In effect, when the firm set out to explore its database for any signs of an 80/20 tendency, it discovered what was virtually a 90/10 situation! In fact, when its realized net profit figure was expressed as 100, 51.8 per cent of its customers were responsible for 143.5 per cent of that profit because there was a loss of 43.5 per cent as a result of the firm's dealings with 48.2 per cent of its customers.

	All customers	Profitable customers	Unprofitable customers
Number of customers	100	51.8	48.2
Sales volume (£)	100	87.5	12.5
Gross profit (£)	100	88.1	11.9
Marketing costs (£)	100	55.3	44.7
Net profit before interest and taxation	100	143.5	−43.5

Table 3.1. *Marketing cost analysis (profitable/ unprofitable customers)*

Sadly, this is not an isolated case for, in the absence of adequate marketing cost analysis, many organizations *do not know* the actual cost of servicing each of their customers. Unsurprisingly, we shall be returning to the 80/20 rule as the book proceeds.

Strategic cost analysis (the value chain)

According to Norman and Ramirez (1993) the principal role of strategy is 'the art of creating value'. They believe that if the direction determined by strategy is customer-oriented, strategy can provide the energy to create and deliver value to customers.

A key aspect of delivering value is to assess whether the organization's costs are competitive with rivals and to take appropriate action where necessary. This is certainly vital if a *price leadership* strategy is being pursued with the object of achieving a cost-based competitive edge over rivals. And even where a differentiation strategy is the choice, an organization must at least keep its costs in line with rivals and take care that any added costs it incurs create added value in the perception of the buyer.

What is clear is that organizations may, and frequently do, incur different patterns of cost in supplying similar products to target markets. Disparities can arise from a number of factors, including differences in:

- the prices paid to suppliers for raw materials, components, power supplies, etc.;
- the technologies employed and the age of plant and equipment;
- operating costs as a result of organizational size, the skills and training of workers, structures and systems, etc.;
- marketing and selling costs;
- inward and outward physical distribution costs;
- the costs and profit margins of the agents and distributors (e.g. wholesalers, retailers) employed to transfer the product from the point of manufacture to the final user.

In his work on competitive advantage, Michael E. Porter (1985) has provided a framework, the *value chain*, which breaks down an organization's activities into strategically relevant activities and processes. He suggests that the approach provides a better understanding of cost structures and identification of the major elements of costs. Better control and improvement of costs should then follow. Porter's concept is reproduced in Figure 3.7.

Porter's chain of value creation consists of a number of primary and support activities and *value chain analysis* is the process of assessing the activities, costs and assets associated with these. A very brief description of these headings is as follows:

Figure 3.7. *The value chain*

Source: Porter, Michael E. *Competitive Advantage*. New York: The Free Press, 1985.

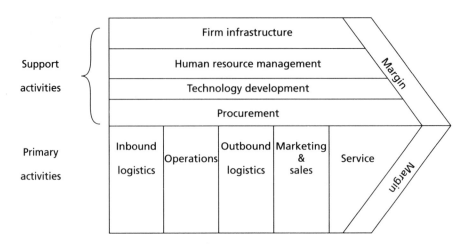

Primary activities

- *Inbound logistics* – reception, warehousing, inspection and (stock) control of inputs from suppliers.

- *Operations* – the conversion of inputs into the final product.

- *Outbound logistics* – the distribution of the product to buyers.

- *Marketing and sales* – the functional aspects of marketing, including market research, advertising, selling and dealer support.

- *Service* – the after sales service associated with the product, e.g. installation, maintenance and repairs, information and complaint procedures.

Support activities

- *Procurement* – the processes of purchasing inputs and assets – raw materials, capital equipment, consultancy services, etc.

- *Technology development* – research and development on products, processes and systems and the applications of technology (including information technology).

- *Human resource management* – recruitment, selection, training of personnel and the design of employment conditions and rewards.

- *Firm infrastructure* – this relates to matters of management style, processes of strategic planning, corporate affairs, etc.

Margin

- The element added to costs as a reward for organizational effort, to reflect the value created.

The concept requires an activity-based cost accounting approach as opposed to the traditional cost accounting/departmental budget procedures but among the advantages claimed for value chain analysis is that the *linkages* between independent activities and their potential contribution to competitive advantage are sharply focused. Thus, the way that one activity is performed may affect the cost or effectiveness of another activity. Also, close attention to these linkages often reveals the possibility of competitive advantage through *trade-offs* – for example more costly product design or raw materials may lead to more than commensurate savings in after sales service; a modification to packaging may increase the pay-load of containers and reduce the cost of outbound distribution.

Also, as Thompson and Strickland (1996, p 101) report, the most important application of value chain analysis is to clarify how a particular firm's cost position compares with that of its competitors. Since cost advantage/disadvantage may vary from product to product, customer to customer and market to market, estimating the organization's position against rivals is no easy task (Thompson and Strickland describe it as 'an advanced art in competitive intelligence').

That said, it is clear that many organizations *are*, in fact, *benchmarking* the costs of performing a given activity either against competitors' costs or against a non-competitor considered to be achieving 'best practice' for the performance of a highly similar activity. It may be the case that benchmarking can be achieved by indirect means, e.g. by reference to published reports, trade associations, industry groups, suppliers, customers and independent consultants. The partners in a joint venture may also be able to exchange mutually beneficial information for similar products and processes. Often, though, it may be necessary to undertake fieldwork to observe operations in other organizations and to exchange key data (on aspects of raw materials preparation, production times, staffing levels, technology applications, etc.).

It may be advantageous to extend the scope of benchmarking beyond the immediate industry. The Xerox Corporation, which pioneered its use and has applied it for 20 years, extended its survey work to any organization regarded as 'world class' in performing any activity relevant to Xerox's operations. Similarly, it is reported (Thompson and Strickland, 1996, p 104) that a car manufacturer developed its 'just-in-time' deliveries policy (see Chapter 10) based on its examination of stock replenishment in supermarkets, while an airline improved its turnaround times through studying procedures employed for car racing pit stops.

The value system

The second aspect of Porter's value chain concept is, if anything, even more important to the marketing executive. Porter draws attention to the undoubted fact that, even if the organization's own costs for its own activities are competitive, the activities performed by its suppliers and/or its distributors may not be so and this will adversely affect the competitive position of the organization itself.

By perceiving itself as part of a larger system (see Figure 3.8) the individual organization can best protect its own competitive position. The art of creating value for end-users of consumer and industrial products and services does not rest with the organization alone. Much also depends on what happens 'upstream' and 'downstream' in the overall system. The organization must concern itself with what these relevant third parties take out of the total transaction for the value they add to it. Where necessary the organization may need to switch to more efficient and cost-effective suppliers and distributors or ones content with a lower balance-over-costs.

Porter's observation, made explicit in Figure 3.8 may seem no more than the organization of common sense. 'Haven't marketing executives always known this?' seems a reasonable enquiry. While the answer is 'yes' it is improbable that it was always acted upon expeditiously. Now, such current developments as the single-sourcing of supplies, just-in-time programmes and *relational marketing*, whose objective is customer retention through close and continuing attention to customer needs, only seem to reinforce the relevance of the *value system* notion to structured thinking.

Like many management ideas, value chain analysis is not without its critics. Norman and Ramirez (1993), for example, are not enamoured of its 'old assembly line' mode of conceptualization adding that global competition, changing markets and new technologies are opening qualitatively new ways of creating value.

Figure 3.8. *The value system*

Source: Porter, Michael E.
Competitive Advantage. New York:
The Free Press, 1985.

Upstream value chain	Organization's value chain	Downstream value chain	
Operations, costs and profit margin of suppliers	'Internal' operations, costs and profit margins	Operations, costs and profit margins of agents and distributors	Consumer/ buyer value chain

While this may be true, this writer's experience of markets and marketing leads him to the belief that a proper appreciation of costs and cost structures inevitably increases marketing effectiveness. Accordingly, the following comment from Thompson and Strickland has much to commend it:

> With rare exceptions, a firm's products or services are not a basis for sustainable competitive advantage – it is too easy for a resourceful company to clone, improve on, or find an effective substitute for them. Rather, a company's competitive edge is usually grounded in its skills and capabilities relative to rivals, and, more specifically, in the scope of its ability to perform competitively crucial activities along the value chain better than rivals (Thompson and Strickland, 1996, p 107).

The PIMS (profit impact of market strategy) database

In developing its strategy, the prudent organization will seek to discover the key variables affecting its profit performance. A number of studies of firms' performance suggest that *profitability is related to market share*. Obviously, several clear advantages accrue to the one with the largest market share, frequently including:

- advantages of large-scale production, high recognition of the company's brand, dominance in the distribution channel, and high leverage in bargaining with customers and suppliers;

- lower unit costs and technological improvements and beneficial product modification and re-design as a result of accumulating experience faster than competitors (the *experience curve* effect);

- as indicated above, the significance of market share for profitability.

With regard to this last point, influential evidence for this emanates from the profit impact of market strategy (PIMS) database project. The project began in the early 1960s as an internal study by the General Electric Company in the USA. It was anxious to discover the reasons underlying the differences in profitability of its SBUs. By the 1970s it was extended to other companies and from 1975 onwards, under the aegis of the Strategic Planning Institute, an independent non-profit organization, the database extended to many markets and industries in the USA and Europe (writing in 1995, Aaker (1995, p 160) reported that it contained data from over 3000 SBUs, representing more than 450 firms, with some of the SBUs having been in the database since 1970).

One of the key PIMS findings is the link between return on investment (ROI) and market share (see Table 3.2). The PIMS data revealed that, on average, a difference of 10 per cent in market share is accompanied by a difference of approximately 5 per cent in return on investment before taxation. Also, analysis of the database has demonstrated that very nearly 80 per cent of the variations in ROI can be accounted for by a combination of 37 variables. Lest this should seem staggering in its potential

Market share percentage	Average pre-tax return-on-investment (%)
less than 10	13.2
10–20	18.0
20–30	23.6
30–40	24.4
more than 40	32.3

Table 3.2. *PIMS project: relationship between market share and pre-tax return on investment*

Number of businesses: 2,000 approx.
Source: adapted from Aaker, 1995.

complexity it should quickly be noted that the following five variables emerge as the most weighty for planning purposes:

- market share;
- the ratio of investment to sales (investment intensity);
- the growth rate of the market;
- the stage in the life-cycle (explained later in the text);
- the ratio of marketing expenditure to sales.

PIMS may be thought of as a form of continuous research for those businesses that can subscribe to the project. They would decide to do so if they felt that their planning could be improved by PIMS data which purports to indicate the current profitability of particular types of business, the likely outcome of the subscriber's current strategy, and what revision of strategy is needed to improve results. In addition to the direct costs of subscription there are the indirect costs of preparing information on the business's markets, competition, finance and costs and its sales and strategy projection. For that reason, its use is usually restricted to the larger firm and the SBUs of the multi-divisional organization.

Apart from considerations of costs and time, the project has attracted some criticism, e.g. two factors moving in the same direction (market share and profitability) do not establish a cause–effect relationship and since the data are historical, how useful are they for planning strategy in dynamic markets, etc. On the other hand, John Kay (1996b, p 6), who has been described as 'the best management theorist in Britain', has pointed out that the most substantial body of empirical research to be found under the heading of strategy is based on the PIMS database. As Lancaster and Massingham (1993, p 91) conclude, PIMS is a useful aid to managerial judgement and 'even for the non-subscribing company, the general and published findings of PIMS regarding key determinants of return on investment have proved to be a useful guide to strategic marketing planning decisions.' More information on the project than can be provided here can be found in the works of these authors and of Aaker .

The balanced scorecard

There is a saying among managers that 'what gets measured gets managed'. Unfortunately, what gets measured is often what is *easy* to measure and is often too restricted to be of real value for the implementation and adjustment of strategy. Traditionally, measures of financial performance have been used as an all-encompassing assessment that the strategy is on track and working well. Yet Robert Kaplan, a professor of accounting, and David Norton, president of an information technology consultancy, consider that while this approach worked well in its own time, it is ill-suited to conditions of dynamic markets and the global competition of today. Indeed, we can perceive ourselves how defective it would be to assess the success of a stakeholder strategy solely on financial measures.

Kaplan and Norton (1992) point out that a pilot flying an aircraft and relying on one instrument is on the way to fatality: he needs information on many aspects – airspeed, fuel, altitude, bearing, conditions at the destination, etc. They also indicate that some managers have ignored financial measures in the short run and have concentrated on improving operational measures, such as production and delivery cycle times, defect rates, etc., in the hope that satisfactory financial results would follow.

To this, they respond 'why choose between operational and financial measures?'. Since no single measure can provide a clear performance target or bring critical areas of the business into proper focus, why not opt for a balanced presentation of both financial and operational measures?

Accordingly, Kaplan and Norton conducted a year-long research project with twelve companies, which they describe as being 'at the leading edge of performance measurement'. As a result, they have devised the concept of a *balanced scorecard* to provide managers with speedy but comprehensive information on the organization's progress. On this aspect of *comprehensiveness*, of course, the business must guard against measuring too much too often in case it has to be rescued from bureaucratic nightmare.

Kaplan and Norton propose that use of the balanced scorecard minimizes information overload, for it is based on the answers to just four questions:

- How do customers see us? – customer perspective.
- What must we excel at? – internal perspective.
- Can we continue to improve and create value? – innovation and learning perspective.
- How do we look to shareholders? – financial perspective.

To operate the balanced scorecard, each organization must devise one of its own, based on these four perspectives, laying down clear goals within each perspective and translating these goals into specific measures. The following are some examples of specific measures:

- *Financial perspective*: cash flow, sales and income growth, return on equity, return on total assets.
- *Customer perspective*: on-time delivery, customer retention, single-source supply contracts, percentage of sales from new products, market share.
- *Internal perspective*: manufacturing cycle time, unit costs, output rates, design efficiency, employee satisfaction and turnover.
- *Innovation and learning perspective*: product and process introduction, improvement in operating efficiencies, applications of new technology.

Kaplan and Norton emphasize the importance of numbers in making the strategy explicit at all levels of the organization, thus increasing employee involvement and motivation. Moreover, the numbers should be generated as objectively as possible, through customer and employee surveys and the benchmarking of best practice.

According to Leadbetter (1997, p 17) the *balanced scorecard* has a growing band of business advocates. He reports Norton's comment that 60 per cent of large US corporations use some form of the approach and adds that in Europe, companies as diverse as Skandia, the Swedish insurance company; BP Chemicals; Xerox Corporation and Renfe, the Spanish railway company, are among its adherents.

Business strategy at work

Differentiation strategies in the home insurance market

There is intense competition in the British home insurance market and this goes beyond the price factor. It is reported (Pratt, 1996) that many insurers are now providing additional services in order to differentiate themselves from rivals. For their 'over 50s' clients, Cornhill Direct's household policy now offers to pay up to £500 towards the cost of professional counselling. The company has perceived a clear need for this facility because claims often result from burglary, fire, storm or a similar traumatic event. The severe psychological effects, particularly upon older people, can often be mitigated with professional help, hence Cornhill's move in this direction.

Where a burglary is 'aggravated', e.g. accompanied by a violent attack on member(s) of the household, the trauma may be so severe that the insured cannot bear to live any longer in the property involved. The Cotswold policy of the Cox insurance company will provide up to £5000 as a contribution to moving expenses where this is the case. This same company believes it is important to recognize the needs of customers and, where appropriate, to offer help to meet them. Where appropriate, it has provided financial assistance towards the installation of a burglar alarm system and the provision of a safe for jewellery storage.

These developments are a logical extension of the helpline facilities provided by insurers in the first wave of differentiating their services and as the process intensifies, there is pressure to supply added facilities of specific relevance to other target markets. For example, B&Q, a major DIY (do-it-yourself) retailer in Britain, offers a household policy to members of its Over-60s Club. Members of this club can claim a 10 per cent discount on purchases made on Wednesdays (which helps, of course, to reduce weekend pressure on the stores).

The company recognizes that many Over 60s buy their gardening equipment and supplies from B&Q and also realizes that gardening is an especially important pastime for this sector of the population. Unfortunately, it is also the sector where a sudden and unexpected admission to hospital may be necessary. The B&Q Over 60s household policy will pay £100 towards the cost of a gardener if this occurs.

Segmentation in the personal computer market

Bresnahan, Stern and Trajtenberg (n.d.) have provided an interesting case study of the personal computer (PC) market in the late 1980s, which has been published in the US by the National Bureau of Economic Research.

The market at that time had low barriers to entry, a high degree of price competition and clear differences between products, based on technology and brands. As a result of the launch of the 386 chip by Intel, building a new generation of PCs to exploit it required considerable technical skill and resulted in a much more expensive product than the one based on its predecessor, the 286 chip. As the authors put it, there was a clear market distinction between those machines with frontier technology and the rest and this enabled the two generations of machines to co-exist for a while.

Bresnahan *et al.* also discovered another important division in the market, based on the distinction between branded and non-branded PCs. A nationally publicized brand virtually guaranteed buyers reliability, service and support and although branding has now become more commonplace, the authors judged that in the late 1980s only IBM, Compaq, AT.&T and Hewlett Packard had brand status.

These two basic distinctions, frontier technology and branding, created four market clusters:

- *Branded/frontier* – e.g. the 386 PCs made by Compaq and IBM, selling in 1988 at an average price of $7577 ($4620).

- *Non-branded/frontier* – e.g. the '386s' made by small high-tech manufacturers and selling at an average price of $5130.

- *Branded/non-frontier* – such as the '286' machines produced by AT.&T and Hewlett Packard and selling, on average, at $2924.

- *Non-branded/non-frontier* – produced by small companies manufacturing what were known as 'clones', selling at an average of $2574.

This 'clusters' profile indicates the price premium chargeable to technology and branding, which decays as these advantages disappear.

Based on their sophisticated statistical analysis of the sales of more than 120 models of PC in the years 1987 and 1988, Bresnahan *et al.* came to two main conclusions:

- competition in PCs was 'largely localised within clusters', i.e. new entrants were likely to take market share within the cluster they were targeting, but would not make much headway in other clusters;

- 'having a brand name conferred a large advantage in the sense of shifting out the demand function, whereas being early at the technological frontier did not.'

Martin (1996, p 18) concludes from these findings that, although they apply to a particular market at a particular point in time, then, as long as expenditure on technology is sufficient to allow a company to compete at all, incremental expenditure might be better spent on branding than on technological research (and this in a high-tech market!).

Marketing in its context: Part I:

Structure and systems

Organization design and management

In Chapter 2 we noted the 7-S Framework, devised by Waterman, Peters and Phillips (1991) as a tool for the successful implementation of strategy and strategic change. *Organizational structure* is featured as one of the key elements in that framework. Also mentioned briefly, at the end of Chapter 2, was the hoary issue of 'which comes first, strategy or structure?' Suffice it to say here experience teaches that, in the long run at least, structure follows strategy (Piercy, 1992, p 141). In the short run, most organizations adapt strategies to 'fit' existing personnel and existing structures. Only when inefficiencies and operating problems emerge does a new strategy give rise to a wholly new structure. An exception to this is the introduction in the 1990s of *business process re-engineering* which returns organizations to first principles, and a blank sheet of paper, for the design of their structures. From all that has been researched and written, it would seem that an ideal approach to design is first to ask whether a proposed strategy is viable within an existing structure, however approximate the fit. If it is not viable, then either the strategy must be changed or the structure must be changed.

Fundamentally, the design and management of organization structures entails:

- identifying the tasks necessary to implement strategy;
- grouping these tasks into organizational units (e.g. departments, SBUs, etc.);
- allocating resources to these units.

These are the first steps in developing a viable structure for:

- the assignment of responsibility;
- communication within and between units;
- the coordination of effort;
- assessment of results and adjustments, if necessary, to strategy and/or structure.

For fitting structure to strategy, Thompson and Strickland (1996, pp 247–8) offer four guidelines which may be summarized as follows:

- identify the activities and tasks in the value chain which are fundamental to the successful implementation of strategy and make these the building blocks of the structure;
- where all aspects of a strategy-related activity cannot be placed under one manager, bridge departmental lines in some way to achieve the necessary co-ordination;

- establish the degrees of authority necessary to manage each organizational unit and strike a balance between the advantages of centralization and decentralization;

- determine which activities can be more effectively performed by 'outsourcing' than by internal operations.

To these guidelines we need to add an important rider, namely, that market opportunity may, increasingly, best be exploited through the use of networks and the formation of strategic alliances, as described in Chapter 2 (Airbus Industrie q.v.) The design of structures may therefore need to provide for the successful implementation of strategy by more than one organization and to provide for quite complex collaborative effort. Doyle explains the trend very clearly:

> Not only do core capabilities have to be shared within a large organization, but strategic alliances increasingly require sharing skills across quite separate organizations. Pressures to accelerate innovation, the speed of change in markets and technology and the high cost of developing new products and new markets are encouraging firms to share skills. Co-operative research, product licensing, co-marketing arrangements and joint ventures are all rapidly growing. Structures are now created to facilitate the organization's learning of new marketing and technical skills (Doyle, 1994, p 29).

So far, we have been looking at organizations 'in the round' whereas the key purpose of the early sections of this chapter is to examine the structures employed for marketing. Nevertheless, before we proceed to these it is important to make some further general points.

The first point can safely be regarded as an eternal truth and it is: *there is no one best way to structure an organization*. The examples of structures found in textbooks are indicative of what has been found viable for particular organizations, at particular points in time in relation to particular strategies. Some of these types of structure have been both popular and effective but this is a long way from saying they have general applicability even for similar types of organization in similar contexts. A viable structure is one that makes for functional effectiveness and, as Sandra Dawson (1992, p xix), a leading writer on organizations, points out, the way an organization functions depends on the nature of, and the linkages between, six key characteristics:

- its people, and their attitudes and values;

- its strategies and tactics;

- the technology or 'hardware' of its production processes, plant machinery, materials and products;

- the external environment in which it operates;

- the roles and relationships expressed in its organization charts and its control systems and administrative procedures;

- the pattern of shared values and beliefs which are the basis of the organization's 'culture'.

Although these characteristics seem of particular relevance to manufacturing organizations, the terms used can be broadened to 'fit' service organizations. Also, technology has a profound influence on administration as well as production and is highly relevant to structure as we shall see later. In the meantime, Dawson's list helps to emphasize the danger of a 'cook book' approach to developing structures. Each organization is unique and this must be recognized from the outset.

The second point to bear in mind is that as a result of the emergence of the global economy; of increased competition; of the continuing, almost fearsome, rate of technological development and of the pressure to innovate, etc., the bundle of 'rules' for the design of structures is constantly being re-examined.

For example, until recently, it was invariably the case that organizations would be structured and would operate according to well-established 'principles', for example

- that every individual had a clearly defined role and a clear understanding of how her/his role related to other roles, as depicted in an organization chart;
- that each individual knew the exact extent of her/his responsibility and authority, her/his working relationships with subordinates and superiors, with each individual being responsible to one immediate superior (the principle of 'unity of command');
- that all operations systems and techniques were highly prescriptive and, ideally, were set out in detail in manuals of procedure.

It could be argued that such principles still have much relevance and value, but not necessarily so, because of the pressures of competition, technology and markets mentioned above. This has called for greater flexibility from organizations, and for improvements in the speed and nature of response to customers. In turn, this has had considerable implications for the ways in which organizations are structured and the relationships between managers and employees.

Traditionally, organizations have been structured on the lines of a hierarchy, with senior management at the top of a pyramid, shop-floor workers at its base, and a number of levels of responsibility in between. The management style has been one of 'command and control' where the major decisions were taken at the top and relayed for implementation down the 'chain of command'. This strategy of *centralization* held good for the relationships between head office and the subsidiaries and business units in the large, diversified corporations and for top management and the less exalted in the individual, smaller firm.

In the last ten years, the hierarchy has come under great pressure for change, for these reasons:

- many organizations have become too large and complex to be managed 'from the top';
- in highly competitive, rapidly changing markets the hierarchy often impedes timely and flexible response;
- the hierarchy has become costly – with more than ten tiers in the pyramids of some companies;
- information technology has drastically reduced the cost of automated information processing and transfer, making it possible for top management to communicate directly with the shop floor, thus rendering many middle management jobs seemingly obsolete;
- the pressure for speedier response, forcing companies to cut the amount of vertical communication, has seen whole tiers of high level management committees replaced, usually at much lower levels, by *task forces* and *project teams* spanning departmental boundaries. This *cross-functional* drive has been accompanied, typically, by a trend towards *empowerment*, which provides employees lower down the traditional hierarchy – and who, incidentally, are closer to customers and markets – with more responsibility and authority, enabling them to by-pass tiers of middle managers;
- all the above trends and influences have been reinforced by the economic recessions which affected many industrialized countries in the late 1980s and early 1990s.

This context for change provides us with a backdrop against which to review the ways in which the marketing effort may be organized in order to implement marketing strategy. At the end of this introduction it is useful to remind ourselves of the major premises which have emerged, namely that:

- each organization is different and there is no structural approach of universal applicability;

- technology and the importance of the customer are powerful influences on structural design – the traditional structure may be effective still but it should be tested against the needs of the customer and the benefits that technology makes possible.

Organization for marketing

In this section we shall examine some of the established approaches to organizing marketing effort, bearing in mind that throughout the world structures are being re-examined to achieve sustainable competitive advantage in the face of the trends and influences which have just been described.

Functional organization

Let us first look at an organization in the most rudimentary, general sense. Figure 4.1 is a simple representation of an organization with a *functional* structure – an approach still adopted by very many firms, particularly of small or medium size. This type of structure is also frequently adopted whether the 'production' involved is of goods or services and whether the organization operates for profit or otherwise. It is also clear how effort is co-ordinated as the organization pursues its objectives, i.e. through senior/middle managers at the head of each function reporting to a chief executive, or 'managing director' who is in turn answerable to a board of directors.

The chief executive and the management team must bring together the efforts of everyone so that the whole organization is working towards its strategic objectives. In a marketing-orientated organization this is done by focusing everyone's attention on the customer. To say this is one thing and to bring it about is quite another. To create a marketing culture is hard going, not least because of the background, training and instincts of people employed in functions other than marketing. How it might be achieved is outlined in the section on Culture, in Chapter 5.

The marketing department – functional organization

Where a separate marketing department exists, which is more usually the case in medium-to-large sized organizations, roles and responsibilities within it might also be grouped together by functions (see Figure 4.2).

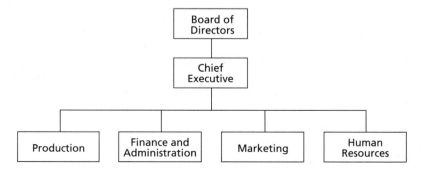

Figure 4.1. *An organization with a functional structure*

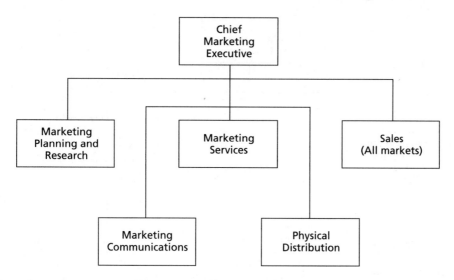

Figure 4.2. *A marketing department – functionally organized*

(Note: Where a separate marketing department exists, it will not *invariably* contain all the above posts. Purely for purposes of illustration, an integrated full-service marketing department is depicted here.)

It may be helpful to make one or two comments concerning Figure 4.2. It is envisaged that the Planning and Research Section incorporates product policy and planning; 'Marketing Services' incorporates marketing administration and the selection, recruitment and training of staff. The Marketing Communications Section is responsible for the conduct of the organization's advertising, sales promotion and public relations operations and since this organization considers that warehousing and transport have a significant influence on the effectiveness of marketing (for reasons which will become clear in Chapter 10) the Marketing Department incorporates a Physical Distribution Section. These notes may help to explain why the structure in Figure 4.2 is described as that of an integrated, full-service marketing department.

It will be seen from Figure 4.2 that the *span of control* of the Chief Marketing Executive (CME) is five, since he (or she) has to coordinate the work of five sections through their executives. Such a structure will free him of a great deal of detail, leaving time for forward planning and integrating the work of the marketing department with other departments (finance, production, etc.). Most importantly, it also allows the CME to play his full part in organizing overall corporate/strategic planning, supported by his own Planning and Research Section.

The structure in Figure 4.2 might be adequate where products and markets are relatively few in number. However, as the organization develops, its problems increase and become more complex. At the next stage of development, therefore, the sections may be grouped together for better coordination and this will mean adding further managers, as in Figure 4.3. Note that the CME's span of control has now been reduced from five (Figure 4.2) to two (Figure 4.3) and this will obviously free him from a large measure of day-to-day detail, increasing the time for strategic thought and planning. Note also that the sales function, previously managed by the CME, now has its own manager (Marketing Operations) and that this function is divided between UK and overseas markets, reflecting the importance of the latter as the organization's international trade develops.

We can see that the revised structure is now based on a division into two principal areas – 'Planning and Services' and 'Operations'. However, while the span of control of the chief executive has been reduced from five to two, it is clear that the levels of management in the hierarchy have been increased from two (Figure 4.2) to three (Figure 4.3) or four if the heads of the UK and Overseas Sales Sections are given managerial status.

Figure 4.3. *A marketing department – functional organization (stage 2)*

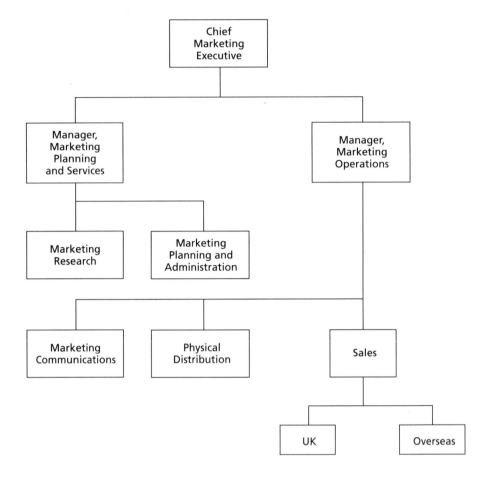

Figure 4.3 is an illustration of the basic fact that reducing the span of control increases the levels in the hierarchy and thus lengthens the process of 'going through channels'. Achieving a satisfactory balance between levels in the hierarchy and the span of control is a key factor in organizational design, made even more important due to the trends and influences mentioned earlier in this chapter. Where success is grounded in flexibility and speed of response to the market, decision-making cannot depend on a lengthy process of 'going through channels' – hence the tendency for organizations to become 'leaner and meaner'.

Brand/product structure

Growth and development are often achieved by adding products to the range already being marketed. This is logical and sustainable as a strategy unless the range becomes so sizeable that planning is hideously complex, the time and attention given to individual products has to be reduced and profitability per product becomes a clouded issue. Even if the organization structure has been further developed, as in Figure 4.3, it may not be robust or flexible enough to withstand the pressures that growth, development and increasing competition bring with them.

In such a situation, the *brand/product management* type of structure has found favour with some organizations, particularly large organizations producing an extensive range of rapid-turnover consumer products (e.g. food, detergents, cosmetics, patent medicines). In addition, the concept has been applied successfully in the industrial products field and in financial services. Usually, the terms 'brand' and 'product' are used interchangeably for consumer products, whereas for industrial goods, the approach is known as *product management*. While it is said that this type of structure originated almost a century ago, its genesis has always been closely linked with the Procter and Gamble company who first adopted the idea in 1927.

Brand/product management is based on the idea of dividing the range into sections which are logical from a marketing standpoint and allocating responsibility for each of these to a specialist manager who is also linked operationally to management colleagues in marketing and other functional areas (see Figure 4.4). Depending on their sales volume and strategic importance, some product sections may consist of a single brand, others of a cohesive group of products, as Figure 4.4 indicates.

In this *matrix* form of organization each brand manager would have the following responsibilities for her/his brand or group of brands:

- assessing market, competition, business/economic trends, etc.;

- recommending strategic plans to achieve appropriate targets of sales volume and profitability within appropriate budgets;

- negotiating tactical programmes for achieving these plans;

- cooperating effectively with colleagues within and beyond the marketing department to implement these plans and programmes;

- recommending monitoring procedures for sales, budgets, profitability;

- developing contingency plans and negotiating for their adoption where necessary.

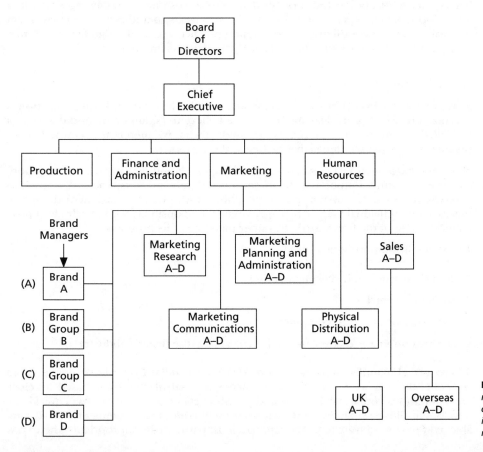

Figure 4.4. *Brand management in a functionally organized firm with an integrated full service marketing department*

Because of the necessity of working effectively with so many others, a key attribute of the brand manager has been described as 'the ability to cross organizational lines without making the organization cross'. The other side of this particular coin is the complaint from brand managers that they are too often given responsibility without commensurate authority. Note in Figure 4.4, for instance, that while the brand manager may be in close operational contact with the heads of production and finance it is not on the basis of status or equality, for their peer in this respect is the chief marketing executive. Note also that such words as 'negotiating' and 'recommending' are chosen carefully in describing the brand manager's duties, but where he/she is given full authority to achieve agreed objectives then such words as 'developing' and 'implementing' would appear more frequently.

Where due authority does accompany full responsibility for profit performance as well as sales targets, he/she will 'buy' the time of the salesforce and of the marketing research department from within his/her approved budgets and work closely with marketing communications to determine appropriate expenditure; to allocate this, when approved, to various methods of advertising and sales promotion and to assess the effectiveness of such communications campaigns.

From this brief outline, it will be apparent why brand management roles have, in the past, proved to be an excellent form of organization for the development of senior managers. Today, for some of the reasons outlined earlier, organizations are a little more circumspect about its adoption. One drawback is that with the accretion of senior (e.g. group brand managers) and junior (e.g. assistant brand managers) posts, the system can lose its flexibility through generating its own hierarchy. The 'healthy competition' for resources between brand managers which is thought to contribute to organizational drive can, at worst, become bitter and counterproductive, though this may be due more to senior managers' lack of hold on the situation than to the approach itself. Finally, and perhaps more significantly, the brand manager may become more fixated on the product than on the customer, leading, at worst, to a product-orientated organization. Despite these caveats, brand/product management has made a telling contribution to marketing practice and to the significance of marketing itself. In one form or other, it is likely to retain its importance.

Market structure

Piercy (1992, pp 141–2) has wisely remarked that the way the marketing operation is organized reveals a great deal about what we believe to be important and that one of the critical things in what we *do*, as opposed to what we merely *say*, is whether we organize to do well the things that matter to the customer.

Market management is a customer-focused approach and it is particularly appropriate where a firm's output is sold in several different markets, each of which has specialized needs. The system has some affinity with brand management though in this case the individual market manager is given responsibility for the sales and profitability of one of the firm's markets, rather than one of its products.

To give an illustration, steel is used:

- for construction and civil engineering;
- for motor vehicles;
- for domestic electrical equipment;
- for institutional and governmental markets (e.g. the defence industry).

Where a steel manufacturer adopts a market management approach, it derives from the belief that expert knowledge of the needs of particular markets, based on close and continuous contact with actual and potential client organizations, will quickly be developed. Close proximity to the customer will contribute prominently to sustainable competitive advantage. The approach is particularly appropriate where raw materials are marketed on a large scale and Figure 4.5 illustrates its application for a producer of china clay, which has important applications in several industries.

Where the total demand is the sum of the demands from a number of types of user, and where serving each of those types of user requires a close and expert attention to their needs, perhaps with skilled after sales service, there may be distinct advantage in adopting the market management structure.

An important version of the approach is based on *geographic division* where structure is determined by the number, location and business potential of customers. Head office functions may be partly decentralized to regions, which may also possess spares, stockholding and showroom facilities. The system applies to services as well as products, e.g. the branch networks of banks, retail organizations and fast-food outlets (although information technology, providing opportunities for direct-to-customer services, is making inroads into the banking branch network structures). In international trade, an example is the *global area structure* adopted by some multinationals in which geographic divisions are responsible for all manufacturing and marketing in their respective areas.

Composite (product/market) structure

Product structures and market structures are not mutually exclusive. The product manager specializes in a narrow range of products and must develop knowledge of the needs of several, perhaps highly divergent, markets. The market manager specializes in one or a few markets and in addition to detailed knowledge of markets must commission knowledge of the many, perhaps highly divergent, products bought by those markets. Where a single organization is producing multiple products for multiple markets it may be an advantage to combine the two concepts by developing a *composite product/market structure*.

Imagine a manufacturing organization specializing in polymer engineering and called Peerless Plastics. It produces four grades (gauges) of plastics and these can be used in a number of different markets.

- *industrial* – for capital equipment and commercial motor vehicles;
- *construction* – e.g. for pipes, sanitary fittings, windows, downspouts;
- *consumer durables* – e.g. for refrigerators, washing machines, television and video equipment;
- *leisure* – e.g. for toys and games, inexpensive sports equipment.

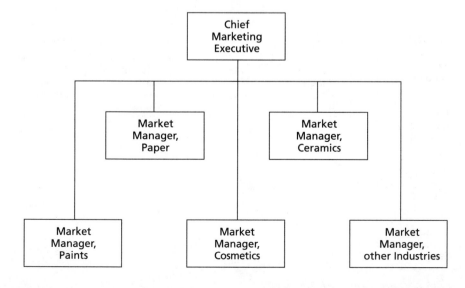

Figure 4.5. *China clay producer : market management organization*

83

Peerless Plastics decides to adopt a composite product/market structure as depicted in Figure 4.6. The four product managers have sales and profit responsibility for their respective grades of material. They will plan for the use of their material in each of the four existing markets plus any others that may be developed by the Peerless organization. Their key points of reference for planning purposes will be the individual market managers and the total sales forecast for each grade of plastic will comprise the estimate of sales made in consultation with each market manager based on *their* respective demand analyses.

The market managers will be primarily concerned with the changing composition of user needs in their respective markets, the development of products appropriate to those needs and the profitability for Peerless of the market for which they are responsible. The development of sales for specific grades of plastic is not their first consideration but they will liaise closely with each product manager on matters of prices and output capabilities.

Given that Peerless is entirely self-supporting in the matter of materials supply, the total sales forecasts of the market managers should correspond closely with those of the product managers. The planning horizon of the market managers will necessarily be more extended than that of the product managers, because the monitoring and evaluation of medium- and long-term trends affecting the use of plastics and the importance of these for product development will be a significant part of their role.

Task force structures

At the beginning of this chapter the pressures on hierarchical structures and the forces making change necessary were outlined. The trend towards 'flatter' organizations is now well advanced internationally and a parallel trend is the move towards *task force management*. This concept, also called 'Liberation Management' by writer Tom Peters (1992) and others, entails breaking down organizations into the smallest possible independent units. Key objectives here are to give employees a sense of 'empowerment', by expanding the discretionary component of their work, and a strong sense of revenue–cost–profit relationships.

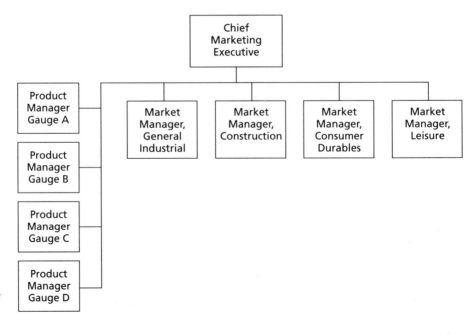

Figure 4.6. *Peerless Plastics: product/market management structure*

It is claimed that performance in 'task forces' outstrips that in more formal hierarchical structures because:

- team members focus more clearly on tasks and keep to deadlines;
- team members are motivated not to let down colleagues;
- the team is usually close to customers;
- the team obtains constant feedback on its performance.

Despite the powerful latter-day publicity for the idea, it is not new. Thirty years ago, Burns and Stalker (1968) investigated the almost complete failure of traditional Scottish firms to absorb research and development engineers in electronics into their organizations despite the pressure on these organizations to innovate in highly competitive markets.

They concluded it was wrong ('pathological') for organizations to try to cope with the problems of change, innovation and uncertainty while sticking to formal bureaucratic structures. They classified such organizations as 'mechanistic' and contrasted them with 'organic' organizations which adapt to unstable conditions by continually redefining and adjusting individual tasks, with the *contributive* rather than the *restrictive* nature of specialist knowledge being emphasized. So it seems that the 'organic' approach, 'liberation management' and 'task force management' amount to much the same thing.

The development of a new product provides a good setting to illustrate the task force approach. The team might consist of a number of specialists – in R&D, finance, production and not least, in marketing research and marketing. The team would be given a brief, a budget and, most importantly, a specific timetable for the completion of its work. These specialists could be drawn from different levels in a formal organization structure. So a relatively junior person might exercise considerable influence in the task force because of the value of his or her specialist knowledge in that specific situation.

The task force, having completed its mission, is then disbanded and the specialists revert to their traditional roles in the organization until they are called upon to join another task force. Of course, in what Peters terms 'liberation management' such small teams may have a lengthier, or indeed permanent, existence.

Clearly, such organizational arrangements enable a firm to develop speedier, more flexible responses to the market. At the same time, however, coordination and control of an organization consisting of a number of small teams require senior management skills of a high order – for one thing it is the ideal in this approach for each task force to have direct access to top management, so the opportunities for misunderstandings and conflict need no elaboration.

Even so, when thinking about ways of organizing effort, the reader should bear in mind the current influence of the small group approach.

The use of external agencies

Earlier in the chapter Figures 4.2 to 4.4 indicated marketing departments containing areas such as 'marketing research', 'marketing communications' and 'physical distribution' within their frameworks. From this, it could be assumed that each of these functions will be operated by fully staffed departments containing an appropriate range of specialist personnel. This is not the case for the vast majority of small and medium-sized organizations and even in the largest organizations where such in-house departments exist, because of recent trends to become 'leaner and meaner' there has been an increasing tendency to 'outsource', that is to contract out, certain functions to specialist external agencies.

Therefore, although an employee may have the job title 'marketing research manager' or 'advertising manager' it is typically the case that rather than managing a fully-fledged functional department, he or she, supported perhaps by a colleague or two, is responsible for co-ordinating the organization's efforts with the services of an agency. Two of these, the *marketing research organization* and the *advertising agency* are particularly important and we shall be looking at the services they provide in later chapters.

Settling the structure

The two short examples which follow aim to provide illustrations of some of the issues examined so far in this chapter.

TLG Lighting, UK

This Hertfordshire based organization which manufactures lighting equipment has recently reorganized its structure because, contrary to the views of Euro-sceptics, it has found standards and tastes converging across Europe.

In the early 1990s it discovered that due to this convergence, in both product characteristics and installation methods, it was becoming increasingly difficult to persist with a country by country approach. By 1991 a matrix system was adopted by which regional executives assumed certain responsibilities for the whole of Europe, for example:

- the UK marketing director was also responsible for architectural projects lighting for the whole of Europe;
- the marketing director for France also acquired Europe-wide responsibility – in that case, for outdoor lighting.

By early 1996 it was clear that this structural change was not adequate to meet the needs of wholesale and retail customers who were themselves thinking increasingly in Europe-wide terms and wishing to deal with one company throughout Europe.

Assisted by consultants Ernst and Young, by 1997 TLG had developed a new management structure. Among the options considered, and discarded, was the traditional function approach which would have provided manufacturing, technical and marketing directors each with responsibility for operations throughout Europe. Because of the disparity in production methods between the different types of lighting it was felt more appropriate to group the manufacturing, product development and marketing functions by *product type*.

The consultants advised that the product range and TLG's European factory network be rationalized. Accordingly, three 'centres of excellence' have been established in Europe based on the core ranges: indoor commercial lighting, indoor architectural lighting and outdoor lighting. Each of these divisions is headed by a managing director with responsibility for the whole of Europe. Even more interestingly, a European commercial director has been appointed to manage the existing sales forces, which continue to be organized by country. This is based on the desire for the point of contact with customers to remain unchanged.

This last point illustrates that there are no right and wrong ways to structure activities, but only right and wrong ways for a particular company, which can be as idiosyncratic as it wishes in pursuit of satisfactory results.

The Unilever organization

The 'globalization versus localization' debate has assumed great significance recently, with many companies pondering whether the development of a standardized product suitably priced for world-wide markets might fail because of its lack of suitability for local needs.

In this regard, the recent reorganization of Unilever, one of the world's largest companies, is instructive. Essentially, it has replaced its previous management structure by one with only two tiers of responsibility. The first of these consists of a seven-strong executive committee responsible for global strategy. The second tier comprises fourteen operational groups, each with a president responsible for business performance.

Product category divisions have been established for Europe and North America while the rest of the world has been divided into regions. This approach acknowledges the difference between advanced and emerging markets in that, in the former, the keynote strategy is *consolidation* to meet the increased competition emanating from new trading blocs, faster communications and the advantage of information technology, whereas in the developing world strategies must capitalize on the opportunity for *strong growth*.

Essentially, Unilever has reorganized to establish the decision-making structures it believes are essential for effective product management and competitive advantage. Also, while the organization is planning strategy globally, due to the differences in markets, very few of its products have been globalized. It does believe, however, in *regionalization* and its reorganization assists it in seeking opportunities to standardize across a number of countries wherever this is possible.

Systems

The word 'system' has a dull and pedestrian ring to it and this is a pity for the quality of an organization's systems are as significant to it as is the central nervous system to each individual. Jain (1993, p 302), for example, warns that systems provide ample opportunity for strategies to fail while Waterman, Peters and Phillips (1991, pp 311–12), describing the 7-S Framework, suggest that to discover how one organization really does, or doesn't get things done, one should look at the systems. Reassuringly, they add: 'Yet it is astonishing how powerfully systems changes can enhance organizational effectiveness – without the disruptive side effects that so often ensue from tinkering with structure.'

The *formally organized procedures* that permeate all organizational activities are referred to as *systems* and they can be broadly classified under three headings:

- *Operational systems*: basic to the organization's day-to-day existence and covering all the primary and support activities in the value chain – supplies must be purchased and received, production must be undertaken, orders must be obtained and despatched, invoices must be mailed, payments must be received, employees must be recruited and paid – underlying each of these activities, and countless others, there has to be a *system* or chaos will soon ensue.

- *Monitoring and control systems*: which are designed to assist management to steer the organization towards its objectives and consist of four basic steps:

    – setting standards and establishing methods to measure performance;
    – measuring performance;
    – comparing performance with the set standards;
    – where necessary, taking corrective action or adjusting the standards.

Again, these systems pervade every aspect of the organization and provide management with vital information on such matters as amount and quality of output, levels of expenditure, cash flow, sales and revenues, labour turnover and training, etc.

- *Developmental systems*: which is this author's description of those systems developed in order to obtain strategic, competitive advantage. Unlike operational and control systems which are used to implement existing strategy, developmental systems can be used to create new strategy. Their function will become clearer as this section proceeds and examples are given in the short case studies at the end of the section.

There is the danger that top management, having negotiated a strategy, ascribes a lower-order value to the systems which support it and this must be avoided for as Jain (1993, p 303) points out, integrating all systems with strategy requires great vision and the ability to see the organization as an organic whole. While top management will not be occupied with the fine detail it must include systems in its strategic thinking. It has been said that 'what gets measured gets managed' and once the factors for strategic success have been identified and translated into targets and budgets it is vital that all the appropriate measurements, quantitative and otherwise, are set via adequate systems. With this involvement at the top, two of the common pitfalls with systems can be avoided – namely, measuring what is easy to measure and measuring factors which no longer serve current strategy.

Although their relative importance will vary with the particular organization and its present situation it is fair to say that dependable and effective systems possess certain positive characteristics. These are now briefly summarized.

The characteristics of effective systems

- *Customer-centred*. This must come at the top of the list. The key question should be 'how does this system benefit the customer?' The benefits may be direct or indirect. Systems which improve delivery times or help to reduce prices are self-evident, but systems which assist in the development of a marketing culture or which improve knowledge of market trends, though of indirect benefit, are of vital importance to the customer too.

- *Connected to strategy*. Here is where influence 'from the top' is important. It is not sufficient, and may in fact be harmful, to measure what was measured in the past or merely to concentrate on current strategy. The systems should reflect where the organization is going, as projected by *strategic intent*. The focus should be on the key areas that govern success and should be forward looking.

- *Acceptable to organization members*. Any targets set by the system should, by agreement, be realistic and achievable. The rules governing the system should be clear and comprehensible to those who operate it and their views should be sought in its design and revision. People denied 'ownership' of the system may find it easy to subvert its objectives.

- *Economically viable*. Unless carefully controlled, systems tend towards expansion and increasing complexity. The economic question is an important one to ask, e.g. what is the value of particular information? what is the cost of obtaining it? and are the systems proposed suited to the resources of the organization? The systems framework should be frequently re-visited, preferably with a 'do we really need this?' approach.

- *Fitted to the organization*. This is another aspect of the costs–benefits issue and requires a realistic assessment of the organization's work flow and the skills and aptitudes of its members. The disruption caused by the introduction of a system may be beneficial, where it helps to create necessary change, but it could be counterproductive. Where this seems likely, more may be required than a system – e.g. a training programme or an adjustment to the work flow.

● *Accurate*. Needless to say this is a 'make or break' characteristic and sound managerial judgement is required to assess whether the system is accurately measuring what it purports to measure. There is more to this than the innate quality of the system itself. If fear pervades the organization, reporting may become distorted and the recipient may be told what he or she wants to hear. So accuracy is as much to do with culture and management style as it is with methodology.

● *Timely*. The system must provide information in good time for appropriate action to be taken where necessary. Systems that are simple to understand and to operate score highly in this regard. This characteristic has become even more important now that 'time to market' is becoming at least as important as price and quality. The timeliness and reach of systems have been vastly improved by information technology which we shall be examining shortly.

● *Flexible*. Systems which cannot respond to change have short life-cycles. It is no easy task to design systems that are flexible enough to respond to the dynamic nature of technology and markets but in present conditions a system's adaptability is a decisive criterion for its success.

● *Objective and subjective basis*. We pay an exaggerated respect to anything expressed in numerical form, forgetting perhaps that it is as easy to produce quantitative, as it is to produce qualitative, rubbish. Often the hard data on orders received, expenditure incurred, reject rates, production 'down time', etc. brook no argument. That said, a balanced system of performance indicators combines *managerial judgement* with numbers – a combination of soft and hard data.

Data, derived from the Latin verb 'dare', to give, means 'facts given' or, more eloquently, given facts. When the given facts originally collected (frequently called the 'raw data') are treated methodically, usually by statistical processes, conclusions can be drawn from them. In their treated form these data will yield 'information' which is then used as the basis for management decisions. For example a firm collects data on thousands of sales transactions. When these are processed by an appropriate system, they yield valuable information on sales per product, per region, per type of outlet, per month, per salesman, per country, etc. to assist planning and decision-making. In the last few decades, the whole process of gathering, analysing and using information has been transformed by the computer. Although the impact of the 'information revolution' on organizational systems would merit a textbook of its own, we can at least allow ourselves a brief look at the phenomenon.

Information technology (IT)

Computers were originally introduced into organizations for narrowly focused purposes, usually to do with accounting and invoicing functions. At the next stage, it became clear that computing could be extended beyond the routine processing of large volumes of standard data – it could be used for the production of a *management information system* (MIS). Such a system would yield accurate, timely and relevant information comprehensive enough for planning and strategic, as well as control, purposes.

The initial management information systems emanated from a mainframe computer located in its own special department and were usually based on standardized report forms. With the advent of the personal microcomputer (PC), managers have been able to gain 'online' access to the databases in the main management information system. In fact, through the 'workstation' on his desk, which has now become the norm, the individual manager is able to create his own database and electronically manipulate it in support of decision-making. Such *decision support systems* (DSS) make possible specialized and speedy decision interventions whenever necessary, and augment the monitoring of ongoing activity by the general MIS.

Beyond this, the use of *artificial intelligence*, which simulates the process of human thought, is being used by some organizations for strategic purposes. Artificial intelligence techniques are employed to develop *expert systems*. These systems diagnose problems, recommend solutions and justify their recommendations. They are particularly useful in unstructured situations, acting like a human expert to guide the user and are more tolerant of errors and imperfect knowledge than are conventional programs. Also, in a given time, the amount of data that can be evaluated by an expert system is far beyond the capacity of the human expert. To illustrate its application: in the marketing field, from the information fed to it, an expert system might make recommendations on the closing of a warehouse or the development of a new product.

The personal computer has also made possible the system of *networking*, which is the linking together of people and departments within an organization, or between organizations, provided the systems used are compatible. Within an organization, for example, a PC network might enable several employees to share information on every phase of developing a new product, from designing and testing prototypes to factory layout for full-scale production.

Electronic data interchange (EDI) is the term used for the linking of networks *between* organizations. Perhaps the best example here, from a marketing standpoint, is the linking of the retail supermarket chain with its suppliers, eliminating a huge volume of paperwork and speeding the processes of buying, reordering and invoicing.

Similarly, a car manufacturer may establish an EDI network extending from its plants to the showrooms of its distributors. Through the network the distributor can check immediately on the delivery position of a proposed order which specifies model, engine size, colour and other options. When the car order is confirmed, the network will automatically order the parts used from suppliers, issue instructions for building the car, invoice the dealer and pay suppliers through the EDI linkage to the manufacturer's bank.

These two examples demonstrate how information technology enables systems to be used 'developmentally', for strategic, competitive advantage. More generally, its contribution to competitive performance can be summarized under a number of headings, for example:

- through increased operational performance and lower costs;
- through increased management efficiency, particularly in decision-making and control;
- through improvements in organizational flexibility and coordination – an EDI network, for example, can be used to develop the task force approach, skirting departmental barriers (the task force, linked electronically, come together for a specific project, then disband);
- through its impact on the hierarchy: increasing the span of control and reducing the number of levels in the hierarchy makes possible a smaller management structure, freeing resources that can be used elsewhere.

The impact of IT based systems on marketing is far-reaching and profound. In Chapter 1, the strategic importance of customer loyalty and retention was summarized (see Figure 1.6, for instance). EDI networks make possible *relationship marketing strategies*. Customers are, in a sense, 'locked in' to these networks and cannot speedily and conveniently switch to other suppliers.

IT systems provide the capacity for the generation, storage and retrieval of vast amounts of data. Customer databases are at the heart of *direct marketing* strategies, that is of strategies by which suppliers promote and sell products and services direct to end-users – an increasingly significant method of distribution as we shall see in Chapter 10.

Databases on the competition, economic indicators and other environmental factors increase the quality and quantity of research information available about markets, with portable PCs increasing the speed and flexibility of research information despatched by investigators in the field.

And finally, only time will tell, but it may well be that an organization's presence on the Internet and the World Wide Web may exert the most profound influence yet on its marketing and sales strategies.

Systems for strategic advantage

Each year, organizations throughout the world demonstrate that attention to their systems improves their competitive strength. This is particularly so where the advantages of information technology are recognized and acted upon. The following two examples, from the UK, are evidence of this.

PPP Healthcare

The organization is one of the leading providers of health care services. In 1995, deciding that its mainframe computer was not providing information speedily enough for the efficiency of the business, it concluded that what was required was a system which users within PPP could interrogate for themselves. Answers to queries using the mainframe system could take months to produce and often depended upon a team of programmers producing a new application. What PPP users required was a system which produced answers in minutes, or hours at most. With the assistance of IT specialists, Sequent, in an advisory role, workshops were held in which PPP's potential users discussed the information they sought by IT operation and delivery. This was followed by a 12 week prototyping programming operation to demonstrate to the users what could be achieved.

It was reported (Black, 1997) in March 1997, that the new 'data warehousing' system adopted had been operating successfully for a year. Containing information on claims, income and customers, the system had mainly been used by PPP's hospital contracts division, but take-up was being extended as other departments recognized its value. PPP Healthcare can now examine closely its working relationships with the hospitals and specialists providing services to its customers. It is also much clearer about the nature of its costs, an especially important factor since four-fifths of its £500 million p.a. income is absorbed by hospitals and specialists.

In an increasingly competitive field, PPP is now able to tailor its provision to the most cost-effective services in the UK and its marketing efficiency is further improved by its newly developed ability to offer insurance policies linked to a particular hospital.

The mainframe computer has been retained, mainly for routine processing and PPP believes that the £1 million required for the new 'data warehousing' system has been recovered in the first year thanks to increased efficiency.

Do-It-All

As we saw in Chapter 3 the balanced scorecard approach is based on the view that no single measure, operational or financial, can provide a clear performance target or bring critical areas of business into proper focus. In this chapter, the value of management information systems (MIS) has been outlined. By providing key performance data about each department, these systems enable an organization to develop an up-to-date rolling profile of its progress. They also allow marketing managers, for example, to look beyond mere summaries of data and into fine levels of detail about particular products, customers and markets.

According to Couldwell (1996, p 23), the DIY retail chain Do-It-All has now used its Windows Executive Information System (EIS), to create a balanced scorecard enabling the organization to use its EIS as a learning mechanism. In this way, Do-It-All expected (August 1996) to be better placed to determine which areas of business were not making a satisfactory return, how the number of retail outlets might be reduced and how the outlets retained might become more profitable.

Marketing in its context: Part II:

Culture, law and ethics

Culture

Marketing executives attach at least two meanings to the word 'culture'. One of these relates to buying behaviour and the factors that influence it. We shall be looking at this subject in the next chapter (Marketing research). At this point, we are concerned with the second meaning of culture in the organizational setting, as outlined in Chapter 1, as *the set of key values, beliefs, understandings and norms of behaviour which prevails within the organization.*

'Culture' in this sense has a decisive influence on the fortunes of the organization affecting, as Johnson and Scholes (1989, p 38) point out, its strategy, structure, the types of people who hold power, its control systems and the way it operates. The most elegant and soundly conceived plans will come to nothing if applied in a setting in which 'the way we do things around here', the organizational 'climate', militates against them.

We noted in Figure 3.2 that to achieve sustainable competitive advantage, one of the responsibilities of the chief executive is to lead the organization in the development of an appropriate culture. 'Appropriate' here means wholly fitted to the corporate values of the organization which its owners and senior managers have determined as its driving force and which may be summarized through some key objectives, for example:

- a customer-led ideal;

- a passion for 'excellence';

- a quest for quality leadership.

It is clear that currently attaining such objectives entails fitting the organization to an external environment undergoing rapid economic, political and technological change on a global scale: an environment so demanding that reducing the lead time of getting products and services to the market is frequently more effective than reducing prices. It is an environment in which only nimble organizations and nimble management will succeed.

To minimize the threats and maximize the opportunities of such a turbulent external environment it is necessary to ensure that the 'internal environment', the culture, is wholly suited to that purpose. The evidence for this is extensive. To give just one example: to test the belief of Dale and Kennedy (1982) that culture has a major effect on the success of a business, Baker (1996) and Hart analysed a matched sample of successful and less successful firms within a cross-section of growth ('sunrise') and declining ('sunset') industries. Contrary to the belief that success is determined by certain critical factors (e.g. entrepreneurship, simple structures, 'lean' staff, etc.) they discovered that many of the attributes of successful firms were also present in less successful firms and so could not be used to differentiate between them. They added: 'Consequently we were driven to the conclusion that success is not so much a matter of what you do but of how well you do it. In other words, culture and commitment are vital to organizational performance' (Baker, 1996, p 57).

Given its importance, how should the CEO manage the culture? At the first stage, through careful observation, the nature of the present culture must be resolved:

- is it *functional*? (i.e. does it support current objectives?), or

- *disfunctional*? (i.e. does it obstruct current objectives?), and

- if *currently* functional will it support future intended objectives?

Also, as Armstrong (1993, p 37) puts it: 'Culture management is about reinforcing or embedding an existing functional culture or changing a disfunctional culture ... a matter of analysis and diagnosis followed by the application of appropriate reinforcement or change levers.'

Imagine a situation where the culture is disfunctional and the chief executive and his board believe that the best route to their objectives is via the development of a customer-led culture. Experience suggests that however charismatic the CEO – and charismatic leadership has a part to play in changing the culture – a few inspirational speeches will achieve nothing. We have all had experience of organizations which have followed the fashion in developing their 'customer charter', 'student's charter', 'patient's charter', etc., but in their actual operations have changed very little.

The benefits of customer loyalty, as outlined in Chapter 1 (see Figure 1.6) may be clear, but changing the culture in favour of fostering long-term customer relationships proves typically to be a long and arduous process strewn with disappointments and frustrations. Why should this be?

One general reason why the long established and deeply felt attitudes and beliefs at the root of culture are so resistant to change derives from our psychological make-up. Kurt Lewin's concept of 'force-field theory' is useful here (see Cole, 1994). Lewin suggests that all behaviour is based on the 'driving forces' and 'restraining forces' in our psyche. The driving forces in us push for change; the restraining forces, favouring the status quo, inhibit change. Behaviour is at the equilibrium point between these opposing forces.

Discussing Lewin's theory, Cole (1994, p 145) points out that individuals seeking to bring about change generally prefer to use driving forces, attempting to win a kind of mental victory over those who oppose them. Lewin's view accounts for the failure of so many change programmes administered in this way in that the more the agent for change exerts pressure the more those opposing change resist it, resulting in deadlock. The better starting point for change would thus appear to be not 'how can we convince them *we* are right to seek change?' but 'what are *their* worries and concerns about change and how best can we allay them?' As Cole indicates, writers on change now advocate that reducing the opposition to change, rather than pressurizing for change, is the better way. So the 'how' question of bringing about change is fundamental.

A more particular issue arises when the objective is to develop a customer-led culture. Mistakenly, customer interests are regarded as the sole province of the marketing department and sadly, in many organizations, a pronounced psychological distance separates marketing from the other departments, hindering co-operation. Figure 5.1 is an attempt to illustrate this.

In interpreting Figure 5.1 it is important to remember that these are opposing viewpoints or tendencies. It is useful to think of them as orientations rather than as implacable opposites. No responsible marketing executive would insist on 'market prices' if these resulted in a financially threatening situation. Nor would the conscientious production manager insist on long runs of few models if this led to calamitous levels of unsold stock. Nevertheless Figure 5.1 has enough import to indicate why, because of their different experience, training and background, some departments may regard the development of a customer-led culture as a thinly-veiled power-play emanating from the marketing department.

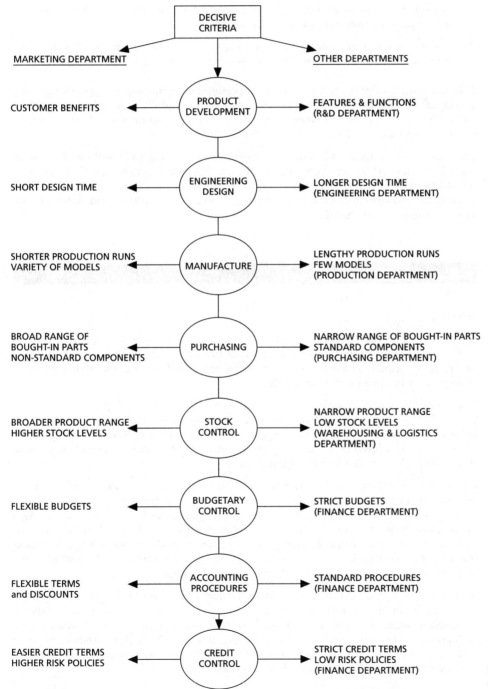

Figure 5.1. *Tendencies to departmental conflict*

Evidence of this lack of a shared commitment between departments is provided by Thomas Masiello, and reported by Piercy (1992, p 366). After studying a range of different industries in the USA, Masiello concluded:

- Most functional areas do not understand the concept of being driven by customer needs, and if marketing plans exist they are not told about what is in them or what they mean.

- Consequently, most employees do not see how their jobs have anything to do with customers or customer needs.

- Most functional areas do not really understand the roles of the other functions in the company, so they have no basis for co-operation.

- Most functional areas have little or no meaningful input to the marketing direction of the company (and this includes service engineers and R&D executives).

This is a world away from the idea of marketing as a philosophy permeating every aspect of an organization's operations and Piercy rightly concludes that before addressing the interests of external customers, 'we need to do something about the internal customers of all kinds' (Piercy, 1992, p 366).

The most finely judged and immensely elaborate marketing plan will come to nothing if it is imposed on an alien culture. Hence this author's view that 'P for people' should be part of an enlarged marketing mix. For this reason, Chapter 12 is earmarked for thoughts on the development of a marketing culture and how commitment to it might be fostered.

Creating the culture

Goetze Components

A central task of the organization is to develop a culture wholly appropriate to its external environment and its objectives. That this is no fanciful notion is confirmed by the many examples of successful culture change and development. Typical of these examples are the ones which now follow.

Goetze of Burscheid, Germany, a well-known manufacturer of piston rings, had endured three years of mounting financial losses before it was acquired by T&N, the British components and specialist engineering group. T&N believed the acquisition of Goetze would provide it with a significant share of the German market for piston rings, a key component in engine manufacture.

Mr Ian Darke, brought in by T&N to supervise the acquisition and work with the German management remembers that: 'They were a formidable competitor in Europe, with half the market. But ... had the trappings of being rich and having a bloated overhead structure' (Burt, 1996). As an illustration of this, Darke discovered that the firm had ten layers of management and seven grades of secretary. It was clear that a change in attitudes was also needed for there was a 'culture of hierarchy', emanating from the previous owners, which prevented change.

As a result of restructuring, some rationalization of the workforce and the closing down of inefficient production lines, costs were sharply reduced and Goetze returned to profit in 1994, a result partly due 'to more aggressive marketing as well as increased demand'. This is a considerable distance from the situation in 1992 when the firm 'had not adapted to new technology, and was arrogant with its customers ... deciding who deserved to be supplied'.

Klaus Junge and Stefan Prigge, recruited from BMW to revive the fortunes of Goetze, believe that the improved fortunes of the company are due to the efforts of the German management and were not simply imposed by the British, for the Germans already knew what needed to be done and were allowed to pursue the required course. They consider, however, that the T&N acquisition was the mechanism which released Goetze from its inertia. A footnote to the change in culture is the comment from Stefan Prigge that the idea of creating shareholder value should not permeate the whole of a company and especially not in research and development (see Darke, 1996).

DHL Delivery Service

Fennell (1996, p 43) has remarked that in the UK the human dimension remains the blind spot in discussions about business success. However, he cites DHL, the global delivery service, as an exception here for the company 'is convinced that the critical element in retaining customer loyalty is the skills and disposition of its workforce'.

In 1996, after a two year process of refining the way in which the organization was managed, DHL was recognized as having met the UK's Investors in People Standard. The Standard, in its sixth year when this book was being written, is an award given to organizations which have demonstrated commitment to the training and development of all their employees. The organization which upholds, promotes and renews the Standard is Investors in People UK. According to its advertisements:

> To meet the Investor in People Standard, an organization should create an environment where everyone knows how they fit in. And by setting up personal objectives and individual training programmes it should give everyone a chance to get where they want to be.
>
> In this way, no-one will feel they're leading an aimless existence, getting nowhere. And apart from a sense of direction, everyone will have a sense of satisfaction (see Fennell, 1996).

The Director of Human Resources at DHL says:

> We see our people as being the 'added value' in what we offer to our clients and we are very keen that individuals should have a better understanding of their role in the organization. The method we've used to achieve this objective is Investors in People (see Fennell, 1996).

DHL did not undertake the exercise in order to achieve the award but to attain improvements in the management of the business – to achieve consistently what it had been doing sporadically in the past. It has also helped DHL managers to appreciate their own responsibilities for the development of their staff.

Law and ethics

In this section we shall be looking at the influences of law and ethics on the context within which organizations operate. 'Law' describes those actions which the organization is mandated to do, for it has no option other than to operate on legal lines. Beyond such stipulation, 'ethics' describes those actions and attitudes which it chooses to adopt as its way of doing business. Let us now consider each of these in turn.

Marketing within the legal framework

As we saw in Chapter 2, the law is one of the most potent influences in the organization's environment, affecting every aspect of its operations. It might be helpful to re-read pp 31–2, which provide a brief glimpse of the effects of common, statute and international law, and delegated legislation, before proceeding further.

What now follows is an outline of how the law affects marketing operations. The legislative examples it provides are taken from English law as it stood in May 1997. If you are resident outside the UK you should read the outline for purposes of illustration and discover what parallel provision exists in your own country.

The law of contract

All organizations, profit or non-profit, enter into commercial transactions and these are regulated by the *law of contract*.

The basis of the contract between buyers and sellers of goods and services had historically been grounded in the *common law*, the general meaning of which is to be found in Curzon's (1978, p 9) definition: 'the body of law judicially evolved from the general custom of the realm'. The basic elements of English common law emanate from:

- the legal systems of the Anglo Saxons enforced in the medieval Shire Courts and Hundred Courts, and

- the rules of customary law, based on rights established by long usage and general consent.

Historically, Parliament was reluctant to interfere with commercial transactions and left the parties free to contract on whatever terms they chose. If a buyer was careless of his own interests, he had only himself to blame – the law would not intervene (the age-old legal maxim of *caveat emptor* – let the buyer beware).

In the last century or so, the situation changed. The development of the law of contract, the remedies supplied by *equity* (a system of legal doctrines and procedures which developed alongside the common law and evolved to remedy some of its defects) and such legislation as the Sale of Goods Act 1893 decidedly improved the position of the buyer. However, in the last few decades, and reflecting general wishes and opinion, the law has rallied emphatically to the buyer's cause. Significant Acts of Parliament in this period include those now briefly described.

Trade Descriptions Act 1968–1972

This Act established a far more powerful code of conduct than the Merchandise Marks Acts of 1862, 1887 and 1953 which it replaced. Its main purpose is to ensure, as far as possible, that when sellers state or imply certain important facts about their goods, prices and services, what they say is true. Under the Act, it is an offence:

- to apply a false trade description to any goods; or

- to supply or offer to supply any goods to which a false trade description is applied.

Goods must be as they are described – whether the description be on the package, on point-of-sale material, or consist of a verbal description given by the seller. It would be an offence, for example, to describe a book covered with a plastic derivative as leather bound.

Fair Trading Act 1973

This Act provided for the appointment of a Director General of Fair Trading who, in the public interest, investigates monopolies and mergers, collects information on unfair consumer trading practices and is a prime mover in the development of consumer legislation. Consumer trading practices include the terms and conditions relating to the supply of goods or services, the manner in which these are communicated, the promotion or methods of salesmanship, the packaging of goods and the methods for securing payment for the supply of goods and services.

Among the duties and powers of the Director General, implemented through the Office of Fair Trading, are the following:

- to keep under review the carrying on of commercial activities in the UK which relate to goods supplied to consumers;

- to collate evidence of practices which may affect the economic interests or the health and safety of consumers;

- where there is evidence of a particular consumer trade practice which is likely to mislead or to adversely affect consumers to refer it to the Consumer Protection Advisory Committee with a recommendation and proposal that the Secretary of State exercise powers to control the practice by an order under the Act;

- the encouragement of publication of codes of practice relating to consumers;

- action against those persisting in conduct detrimental to consumers;

- the supervision of enforcement of the provisions of the Consumer Credit Act.

In its time, the Sale of Goods Act 1893 was a great turning point in the direction of consumer protection stipulating certain implied terms into contracts of sale (although as we shall see the parties were still free to exclude them). The Fair Trading Act 1973 is thought by many to be of equal, if not greater, significance.

Consumer Credit Act 1974

The objectives of this Act were to provide a uniform system of statutory control with regard to the granting of credit and the protection of consumers through a system of licensing of persons offering credit facilities. The Act relates to consumer credit, consumer hire and credit token agreements (i.e. involving stamps, cards, etc.). Such agreements, defined for the purposes of the Act as *regulated agreements*, must be in writing and signed by the debtor and by, or on behalf of, all other parties to the agreement.

Goods are deemed as 'protected' under the Act where, though the property in the goods remains with the creditor, the debtor has paid or tendered at least one-third of the total price of the goods and has not terminated the agreement. Unless the debtor so agrees, protected goods may be recovered only by Court Order.

In certain situations the debtor is allowed a 'cooling off' period whereby he or she may cancel the agreement. This applies where the agreement was signed off trade premises, for example at the debtor's home, and is thus designed to combat the practice of 'doorstep selling' whereby the salesperson might employ 'heavy pressure' sales techniques.

Unfair Contract Terms Act 1977

Prior to this Act it was possible for a trader to limit his own legal liability, arising out of his business, for death or injury in any contract by way of an *exclusion clause*, for example 'The company or any of its agents shall not be liable for any injury or damage to person or property caused by or in connection with the article.' The Act prevents a party being able to exempt himself from liability for death or injury caused by his negligence.

In addition, in consumer contracts, a party cannot:

- exclude or restrict liability for his own breach of contract;
- claim to be entitled to render a contractual performance which is substantially different to that reasonably expected; or
- render no performance at all,

except in so far as the exclusion clause satisfies the requirement of reasonableness, i.e. whether the contract term was fair or reasonable having regard to all the circumstances of the case which were, or ought reasonably to have been, known when the contract was made.

Other consumer legislation

Some other important aspects of recent consumer legislation have provided the following rights, and collateral duties:

- In advertisements for credit where a creditor requires security for the loan by way of a mortgage over the debtor's home, the advertisement must contain the following statement: 'Your home is at risk if you do not keep up repayments on a mortgage or other loan secured on it' (The Consumer Credit (Advertisement) Regulations 1989).
- The Unsolicited Goods and Services Acts 1971–1975 preclude a demand for payment for unsolicited goods sent to a person otherwise than for the purposes of his business. The recipient may retain the goods without payment if they are not collected by the supplier within the time limit prescribed by the Act.
- The right to be given due weight, due measure (where goods are sold by weight or measure) and an adequate number of items where goods are sold by number (Weights and Measures Act 1985).

Also, the Consumer Protection Act 1987 makes it a criminal offence for a person in the course of a business to give to consumers an indication which is misleading as to any price at which goods, services, accommodation or facilities are available.

The Sale of Goods Act 1893 was consolidated by the Sale of Goods Act 1979 and subsequently amended by the Sale and Supply of Goods Act 1994 as a result of which the rights of the consumer have been further strengthened. The rights are 'implied' in that they do not have to be mentioned by the buyer, either orally or in writing, whenever goods are bought. They relate to such matters as:

- the seller's proper title to the goods (i.e. the right to sell);
- the entitlement of the buyer to be supplied with goods which 'correspond with description';
- satisfactory quality (taking into account such things as freedom from minor defects, safety and durability);
- fitness for all the purposes for which such goods are commonly supplied.

The Sales of Goods (Implied Terms) Act 1973 implies similar terms into contracts for hire purchase and the Supply of Goods and Services Act 1982 into contracts for the supply of services.

The Sale of Goods Act 1893 enabled parties to a contract for the sale of goods to agree in the contract that these rights should not operate. This could result in exploitation of the following types:

- that in some instances the consumer could only buy goods if he/she were willing to give up his/her rights; and

- that in business, as distinct from consumer transactions, small firms might have no option other than to forfeit these rights in order to obtain goods from organizations dominating the supply side of the market.

Until the Supply of Goods (Implied Terms) Act 1973 it was possible to exclude the implied term as to title. This is no longer possible in either consumer or trade contracts and following the Unfair Contract Terms Act 1977 the other implied terms cannot be excluded at all where a person acting in the course of his/her business supplies goods to a consumer. The display or publication of such a clause is now not only void but is also a criminal offence. In business to business sales, such terms may only be excluded if they satisfy the test of reasonableness.

Influence of European Community law

The Maastricht Treaty on European Union, negotiated in November 1991 and effective from November 1993, will contribute to the attainment of a high level of consumer protection. This includes specific action which supports and supplements the policy pursued by Member States to protect the 'economic interests of consumers' and to provide 'adequate information to consumers'. In the UK and other Member States, a further significant increase in the enactment of legislation designed to protect consumers therefore seems most likely.

The Unfair Terms in Consumer Contracts Regulations 1994 which were enacted in order to implement an EC Directive into UK law introduce for the first time a requirement of good faith in consumer contracts which have not been individually negotiated, i.e. are subject to the standard written terms of a business, and require that such terms should be drafted in plain intelligible English. The Director General of Fair Trading has the power to consider complaints and to seek injunctions to prevent the continued use of unfair terms.

The organized effort to develop the rights and powers of consumers in the face of the increasing dominance of large public and private organizations is a world-wide phenomenon which began in the late 1950s. The UK legislation just described was heavily influenced by this development. In addition to the force of legislation there are now many organizations and agencies active in the field of consumer protection. Some of these are now briefly described.

Consumerism: organizations and agencies

A significant element in the development of consumerism was President Kennedy's 1962 'Consumer Bill of Rights' which, while not acquiring the force of law, none the less widely influenced thinking on consumer protection. Some of the tenets of that Bill provided ethical markers for organizations in business and government, for example:

- *The right to safety* – to be protected against the marketing of goods hazardous to life and health.

- *The right to be informed* – to be protected against fraudulent, deceitful or grossly misleading information, advertising, labelling or other practices, and to be given the facts needed to make an informed choice.

- *The right to choose* – to be assured, whenever possible, of access to a variety of products and services at competitive prices, and in those industries in which competition is not workable and government regulation is substituted, to be assured satisfactory quality and service at fair prices.

- *The right to be heard* – to be assured that consumer interests will receive full and sympathetic consideration in the formulation of government policy, and fair and expeditious treatment in its administrative tribunals.

The improved attitude to the rights of consumers which began to develop world-wide from the time of the Kennedy Bill resulted in extensive legislation, as we have seen from the outline of British experience. Also, the 'consumer movement', developing in ways ancillary to and outside of the law, showed that it was capable of quite powerful organization and commitment. Staying with the British experience, some organizations, agencies and general outcomes are listed below.

The Consumers' Association

The Consumers' Association was formed in Bethnal Green, London as long ago as March 1957. The contemporary Molony Report on Consumer Protection had said that:

> The business of making and selling is highly organised, often in large units, and calls to its aid at every step complex, highly expert skills. The business of buying is conducted by the smallest unit, the individual consumer, relying on the guidance afforded by experience if he possesses it, and if not, on instinctive but not always rational thought processes.

The Consumers' Association, which modelled itself on its counterpart, the Consumers' Union of the United States, came into being to help balance the power of the seller and that of the buyer. Its work has been to provide independent and technically based guidance on the ever-increasing variety of goods and services available to the consumer and then to publish the results within its magazines. The first and best known of these, *Which?*, was launched in October 1957. Published monthly, *Which?* issues reports on a wide variety of products and services, including:

- domestic appliances;
- money matters (e.g. mortgages, tax, investment, insurance);
- legal rights;
- motoring (e.g. new and used cars, accessories, garage servicing, car security);
- leisure products (e.g. stereo systems, cameras, video recorders);
- food and health (e.g. food and drink, dietary issues, stress, smoking);
- home maintenance and improvements (e.g. tools and DIY materials, fuel conservation, security);
- public and private sector services (e.g. telephone services, Royal Mail, rail services, medical GPs, opticians, solicitors).

Five thousand copies of the first issue of *Which?* were printed and an extra 5000 had to be produced to meet the demand. Today it has around 700,000 subscribers. The cornerstone of its operations is the expert testing of products in its own laboratories and in user trials and the testing and researching of services through experienced researchers, specialists and professional surveys conducted on the needs and experiences of *Which?* subscribers.

The Association is, and takes care to be seen to be, independent of all interests other than those of the consumer. It accepts no money from government, trade or industry (other than for specific services rendered which could not compromise its independence) and it takes no advertising in any of its publications.

In addition to the provision of information to assist consumers in making wise, value-for-money choices, the Association devotes a great deal of campaigning effort to persuading suppliers to improve safety, performance and quality and encouraging the government to enact laws to protect consumers against exploitation. It has been responsible for important Acts of Parliament in this regard, for example, the Unfair

Contract Terms Act 1977 and the Consumer Agreements Arbitration Act 1988. Hence its claim that it campaigns on behalf of all consumers and not just the subscribers to its magazines. The Association also works closely with international aid agencies, such as UNICEF and the World Health Organization, on a number of projects of special significance to the Third World.

Within Europe there are many consumer organizations which undertake comparative testing and publish magazines in much the same manner as the UK's Consumer Association. These include: Association des Consommateurs (Belgium), Union Federale des Consommateurs (France), Stiftung Warentest (Germany), Consumenten-bond (The Netherlands) and Federation Romande des Consommatrices (Switzerland).

National Consumer Council

The National Consumer Council was set up by the UK Government in 1975 to give an independent voice to the nation's consumers. It does not deal directly with individual consumers nor does it test individual products. Its main focus is to ensure that 'the consumer view is heard, and heeded, by all who take decisions that affect consumers' (National Consumer Council, 1996) – that is those in the UK government and civil service, the European Union, local councils, regulatory and professional bodies and trade associations.

The scope of the Council's activities is broad, for in addition to general consumer products and services it is closely concerned with such public organizations as hospitals, schools and the recently privatized utilities supplying gas, water and electricity, where competition, hence consumer choice, is limited. The Council has a special brief to represent consumers with special needs – for example the elderly, the disabled and those on low incomes.

Its efforts to promote and safeguard the interests of UK consumers consist of:

- *research* into their experiences and concerns;
- the development of *policies* to improve the consumer's interests;
- *campaigns* devised to ensure these policies are acted upon;
- *support* for the work of other consumer representatives.

British Standards Institution (BSI)

The main task of the British Standards Institution is to establish performance and safety standards. It provides tests for performance and safety, issues specifications relating to products and may also recommend the way in which goods should be used and maintained by consumers. When a manufacturer attains compliance with a British Standard, the product can be marked 'BS', followed by a number. The number indicates the particular standard for that product.

A 'Kitemark' or 'Safety Mark' on a product indicates that BSI has had samples of it independently tested against the appropriate standard and that the standard has been complied with in every respect. Continued quality is assured through the monitoring of a quality system agreed between BSI and the manufacturer concerned. Complete sets of British Standards are kept for reference at most central public libraries throughout the UK.

In a marketing context, it is also important to note the Institution's BS5750 standard which was first published in 1979 as the quality assurance standard for engineering and other manufacturing industries. Its revision in 1987 enabled it to be harmonised with the ISO9000 and EN29000 series standards and it is now applicable to a variety of industries. Hence, an organization accredited under BS5750 is also automatically accredited under the ISO9000 series and therefore recognized internationally as meeting quality standards.

The significance of BS5750 for marketers is that, as Wille (1992, p 120) points out, increasingly accreditation under this standard is being insisted upon as a condition of being accepted as a supplier by many of the most reputable firms. More of quality assurance when, in Chapter 8 the philosophy of *total quality management* (TQM) is considered.

The UK is typical of many advanced industrial countries in having a number of other organizations which serve consumer interests. The following outline, short though it is, indicates their extent and variety.

Trading standards departments (TSDs)

Part of the local community, regional or borough councils, the principal function of trading standards departments is to enforce consumer protection legislation at all levels of trade so as to ensure product safety, correct descriptions and prices, accurate weights and measures, food of proper quality and fairness of contracts for credit transactions. They can also act against anyone who knowingly or recklessly gives a false description about the services they provide.

TSDs can prosecute traders who sell short measures and test the weighing machines and equipment used in shops for accuracy. Similarly, they can prosecute anyone who sells goods which are in breach of safety regulations. Some TSDs operate *consumer advice centres* near main shopping areas. Advice and information is available to shoppers and traders, and problems and complaints may be dealt with.

Environmental health departments

Environmental health officers (EHOs) also work, as a rule, in the local district, borough or city council. Their job is to deal with food safety as well as to protect and improve the environment.

Selling food which is unfit for human consumption is a criminal offence and alongside TSDs, EHOs have a key role in ensuring food is safe and is prepared in hygienic conditions. They inspect places where food is handled, such as markets, food shops and restaurants, to check on the level of hygiene and ensure that the food is not contaminated.

Citizens' Advice Bureaux

For nearly sixty years, the Citizens' Advice Bureaux (CABs) of the UK have provided advice and information, given freely and in complete confidence. Of the very large volume of enquiries handled by these bureaux each year, those for consumer and debt issues are very prominent.

The National Association of Citizens' Advice Bureaux, which by the early 1990s had more than 1300 outlets, including main bureaux, extension bureaux and advice sessions, offers advice and practical help on most consumer problems. Having monitored people's problems, it ensures that these are brought to the attention of policy makers at both the local and national level. In a recent year, approximately 23,000 people were working in the CAB service and, interestingly, 90 per cent of these were volunteers.

Trade associations

The idea of going beyond basic legal requirements to ensure a high level of customer service is reflected in those trade associations which have established collective *codes of practice*.

Trade associations comprise business organizations involved in the manufacture and distribution of particular products or product groups or in the provision of particular services. In the UK, a number of these associations have issued guidelines for members on standards of customer service and often they have arbitration or conciliation schemes for handling complaints. Their codes of practice, frequently produced in consultation with the Office of Fair Trading, are voluntary and have no legal weight but they do extend considerable extra protection to customers. Some of the fields covered by these codes of practice are:

- mail order trading;
- laundering and dry cleaning;
- electrical goods (and their servicing);
- 'package' holidays;
- shoes and shoe repairs.

Organizations belonging to a trade association usually display the association's symbol and title in their premises and advertisements and on their letterheads.

Users' associations and consultative councils

For a number of products and services (including those provided by public utilities) there are consumer or consultative councils or regulators. They monitor operations within their field and help with consumer problems and complaints. They also provide information to business organizations and government on consumer advisory services, consumer legislation and improvement of voluntary codes of practice.

Among these associations and councils the following are prominent:

- OFTEL (Office of Telecommunications),
- OFFER (Office of Electricity Regulations),
- OFGAS (Office of Gas Supply),
- OFWAT (Office of Water Supply),
- POUNC (Post Office Users' National Council),
- Air Transport Users' Committee.

Complaints concerning banking, building society and insurance services can be referred to the *ombudsman* established for each of these sectors, whilst the Finance and Leasing Association and the Consumer Credit Trade Association deal with complaints concerning credit companies.

The influence of government

In addition to the legislation described earlier, the influence of the UK government in many of the consumer organizations and concepts just described can be discerned. It is also useful to mention that in the summer of 1991, the then Conservative government announced its *Citizens' Charter*, intended to make the country's public services more responsive to customer needs and to bring about cultural changes in government departments.

Since that time, many aspects of the public services, including health, education, transport, housing and environmental services have been scrutinized and new performance indicators have been established. Clearly, if such initiatives did succeed in the long run they would play a part in developing a more customer-oriented outlook in business as well as government but, sadly, with many such statements of intent there is too frequently a gap between the rhetoric and the results.

As has been mentioned, government's influence in respect of monopolies, mergers and the public interest is also apparent through the functions of the Office of Fair Trading (OFT). Lack of competition in business may be detrimental to the public and the OFT is charged with keeping a watch on monopolies, mergers and trade practices that may be restrictive or anti-competitive. In some cases, such an issue is referred to the Monopolies and Mergers Commission for more detailed investigation. Interestingly, as this chapter was being written, the President of the Board of Trade of the UK Labour government elected in May 1997 announced sweeping new proposals in competition law, with firms facing fines of up to 10 per cent of their UK turnover, if found to be in breach of it. 'Present competition is not working well', said the President, 'Its reform is long overdue' (Beckett, 1997).

The proposals, based on European legislation and replacing laws passed in the last 25 years, include the replacement of the Monopolies and Mergers Commission by a Competition Commission and envisage increased government supervision of the public utilities (gas, water, electricity, etc.). The new legislation, set to be enacted by October 1999 will, for the first time, enable customers and competitors damaged by anti-competitive behaviour to seek damages.

Reverting to European legislation, since the UK is a member of the EU it is, of course, subject to the provisions of Article 85 of the Treaty of Rome which prohibits all agreements between business organizations which prevent, restrict or distort competition within the EU, and to the provisions of Article 86 which declares that the abuse of a dominant position in the market structure is incompatible with the objectives of the EU. Both Articles aim, ultimately, to prevent developments inimical to the interests of consumers and it can be perceived that the proposals for new UK legislation, as described above, seek to increase the fusion process between the two systems.

On the international scene, and to conclude this outline of some agencies of consumer protection, the work of the International Organization of Consumers' Unions (IOCU) should be noted. It was founded in 1960 to represent the interests of consumers world-wide. It supports the growth of consumer organizations in developing countries, arranges seminars and conferences and represents consumer views to international policy makers (e.g. the United Nations). There are 170 member organizations and three offices (for Europe and North America; Latin America and the Caribbean; Asia and the Pacific). Recently, it has been looking at ways of helping consumer representation develop in Africa, Eastern Europe and India.

Voluntary codes of practice and conduct

It was the late Lord Maugham (1977, p 37) who said: 'No profession attains any standing in the eyes of the public until it takes proper steps to discipline itself.' The last two words of his dictum are especially significant for this section in which we shall review elements of the voluntary codes of practice and conduct developed by some British marketing bodies.

The codes are voluntary in the sense that they are completely self-imposed. They are designed:

- to extend professional standards beyond legal minimum standards;

- to provide guidance on standards where no legal standards exist.

The Committee of Advertising Practice (CAP) and The Advertising Standards Authority (ASA)
CAP is the self-regulatory body which devises and enforces The British Codes of Advertising and Sales Promotion. In the latest editions of the Codes (published 1 February 1995), CAP's membership comprised 22 major organizations in the fields of advertising, sales promotion and advertising media.

ASA is the independent body responsible for ensuring that the system works in the public interest. The ASA's activities include investigating complaints and conducting research.

The Codes apply to:

- advertisements in newspapers, magazines, brochures, leaflets, circulars, mailings, catalogues and other printed publications, facsimile transmissions, posters and aerial announcements;
- cinema and video commercials;
- advertisements in non-broadcast electronic media such as computer games;
- viewdata services;
- mailing lists, except for business-to-business lists;
- sales promotions;
- advertisement promotions;
- advertisement promotions covered by the Cigarette Code.

It should be briefly noted here that *advertising* consists of the purchase and use of space or time in communications media (e.g. newspapers, magazines, outdoor locations, radio, etc.) by an identified sponsor (the advertiser) for the promotion of goods, services or ideas. *Sales promotion* usually complements an organization's advertising and other selling operations and includes those activities designed to:

- encourage user-purchase at point-of-sale, and
- increase dealer effectiveness.

Examples of these activities are in-store displays, demonstrations and exhibitions. Expenditure on 'special offers', competitions, etc. is usually included under this term. The concepts will be dealt with in more detail in Chapter 11.

There are a number of aspects of marketing activity to which these particular Codes do *not* apply including, for example:

- broadcast commercials, which are the responsibility of the Independent Television Commission (see below) or the Radio Authority;
- the contents of premium rate telephone calls, which are the responsibility of the Independent Committee for the Supervision of Standards of Telephone Information Services;
- advertisements in foreign media;
- health-related claims in advertisements and promotions addressed only to the medical and allied professions;
- private correspondence;
- press releases and other public relations material;
- packages, wrappers, labels and tickets unless they advertise a sales promotion or are visible in an advertisement.

The principles of the Advertising Code include the stipulations that all advertisements should be 'legal, decent, honest and truthful', should be prepared with a sense of responsibility to consumers and to society, should accept the principles of fair competition generally accepted in business, should not bring advertising into disrepute and must conform with the Codes. The principles of the Sales Promotion Code have the added proviso that all sales promotions 'should be conducted equitably, promptly and efficiently and should be seen to deal fairly and honourably with consumers. Promoters should avoid causing unnecessary disappointment'. Both Codes are applied in the spirit as well as the letter.

Details of how this self-regulatory system actually works can be found in the latest version of the Codes, obtainable from the Committee of Advertising Practice, 2 Torrington Place, London, WC1E 7HW (Tel. 0171–580–5555).

Independent Television Commission (ITC)

The ITC is the public body responsible for licensing and regulating commercially funded television services provided in and from the UK, including Channel 3 (ITV), Channel 4, public teletext and a range of cable, local delivery and satellite services. Its responsibilities do not include the services provided by the BBC or by S4C, the fourth channel in Wales. The ITC is concerned with television services only, the regulation of the independent radio services being the responsibility of the Radio Authority.

While the work of the ITC has been incorporated in this section of the chapter on 'Voluntary codes of practice and conduct', it should be noted that the Commission is required to draw up and enforce a Code of Advertising Standards and Practice by the Broadcasting Act, 1950. Its duty to consider complaints about television advertisements which are alleged to be misleading derives from the Control of Misleading Advertisements Regulations 1988. Its regulatory tasks are achieved by:

- setting standards;
- ensuring compliance;
- investigating complaints.

With regard to *standards*, the main objectives of the ITC Code are to ensure that television advertising:

- is not misleading;
- does not encourage or condone harmful behaviour;
- does not cause widespread or exceptional offence.

In addition to general rules concerning all advertising, the Code has more detailed rules on particular categories, for example alcoholic drinks, financial services, medical products, advertising to children and advertising by religious or charitable groups.

Although long established elsewhere, programme sponsorship which rewards sponsors for their financial contribution by a credit associating them with a particular programme, has only been permitted in the UK since 1991. The main purpose of the rules contained in the ITC's Code of Programme Sponsorship is to ensure 'that sponsors do not exert influence on the editorial content of programmes and that sponsorships are made clear to viewers'.

The National Newspapers' Mail Order Protection Scheme Ltd. (MOPS)

In addition to the protection provided by the British Codes of Advertising and Sales Promotion, UK consumers also benefit from the efforts of organizations which maintain their own specific advertising codes to deal with the detailed protection often desirable in a particular area of business. A good example of such a code is the Mail Order Protection Scheme organized by the 22 major national daily and Sunday newspapers in the UK. This scheme exists to ensure that, in addition to their statutory rights, newspaper readers enjoy the fullest possible protection of their money in relation to 'cash with order' advertisements.

While most mail order traders are well-established, with substantial experience of selling by post, they have a special responsibility to the public because their potential customers cannot see or examine goods before ordering. They must also assume that the mail order company concerned is operating with complete integrity.

An extract from the MOPS *Guide for the Shopper* (1996 edition) reads as follows:

> In 1975 the Mail Order Protection Scheme was formed in consultation with the Office of Fair Trading and under an agreement between the National Newspapers, the Institute of Practitioners in Advertising and the Incorporated Society of British Advertisers, the prime concern being to ensure that postal shoppers are protected when placing their orders.
>
> Its function is to reimburse readers who might otherwise lose money if the goods which have been ordered fail to be delivered as a result of an advertiser going into liquidation or bankruptcy or ceasing to trade. It also covers readers who have returned goods and not received a refund from a failed advertiser.
>
> This gives you, the shopper, peace of mind in the knowledge that your money is secure.
>
> The administrators of the scheme also protect the public by demanding a formal application from each new Mail Order advertiser. This ensures that the applicant is in all respects suitable before recommending that their advertising is accepted by the National Newspapers in the Scheme. Even then, it does not automatically follow that the advertising will be published as the final decision rests with the National Newspaper concerned.

The *Guide for the Shopper* (there is also a *Guide for Advertisers*) makes it clear that the scheme has been extraordinarily successful in protecting readers' interests and that in relation to the volume of sales involved, 'claims for compensation have been negligible'.

From time to time, MOPS' own advertisements can be seen in the national press. These inform members of the public about the scheme and outline the action they should take in the event of a query about any mail order national press advertisement.

The Chartered Institute of Marketing

The Chartered Institute of Marketing is the largest professional body in the UK marketing field and, for more than four decades it has provided an invaluable service in propagating the importance of the marketing concept. Also, its education and training programmes have done a great deal to develop the professional skills of practitioners.

It has had a long-established code of professional conduct and, in accordance with its Royal Charter, it published on 2 December 1992 its *General Regulations for the Provision of Professional Standards and Disciplinary Procedures*. The Chartered Institute requires all members to adhere to the Code of Professional Standards, set out in the General Regulations, as a condition of membership.

One of the objects of the Institute, set out in Article 2 of its Royal Charter, is: 'To promote and maintain for the benefit of the public high standards of professional skill, ability and integrity among persons engaged in marketing products and services.'

The Code of Professional Standards, set out in accordance with Royal Charter by-laws 16–19 includes the following requirements of the Institute in respect of its members:

- that members' integrity be upheld at all times and the honour and dignity of the profession be preserved;
- avoidance of unfair or unprofessional practices;

- honesty at all times in dealing with customers and clients (actual and potential), employers and employees;

- avoidance of knowingly or recklessly disseminating false or misleading information;

- the obligations that the member and his employees keep abreast of current marketing practice in their field and always act competently and diligently;

- avoidance of any conflict of interest between himself and any business in which he may be involved with prior voluntary and full disclosure of all matters that may give rise to such conflict;

- the obligation of the member concerning confidentiality of information of a customer's, a client's or an employer's business except as required by law or with the authorization of the employer and the obligation not to use any such information to his own profit or advantage;

- the obligation of the member not to promote or seek to obtain business in an unprofessional or unethical way.

Other sections of the by-laws describe the roles of the Institute's Ethics Committee, its Disciplinary Committee, the Procedure for Complaints, the Processing of Disciplinary Complaints, Inquiries Before and Hearings of the Disciplinary Committee and the Publication of Decisions.

The Market Research Society (MRS)

This Society is the representative body of individuals in the UK engaged in marketing research and social research. Its aim is to ensure that professional standards are maintained in these types of research, that knowledge of such research is communicated among practitioners (its conferences and published papers are authoritative and well regarded) and that the value of research is appreciated by the business community and the public at large. An extract from the January 1997 edition of the *Code of Conduct* reads as follows:

> This Code of Conduct was agreed by the Market Research Society to be operative from January 1994. It is an amended version of a self-regulatory code that has been in existence since 1954.
>
> The Code of Conduct is designed to support all those engaged in marketing or social research in maintaining professional standards throughout the industry. It applies to all members of the Market Research Society, whether they are engaged in consumer, business to business, social, opinion or any other type of confidential survey research. It applies to quantitative and qualitative methods as well as to mystery shopping and other techniques for data gathering. Assurance that research is conducted in an ethical manner is needed to create confidence in, and to encourage cooperation among the business community, the general public and others.

The key principles of the Code relate to the responsibilities of professional market research to:

- *informants*: e.g. non-disclosure of identity without consent, identity not used other than for research purposes; freedom from coercion or unwelcome intrusion; no child under 14 to be interviewed without parental consent;

- *responsibilities to general public and business community*: e.g. other activities (such as selling) under no circumstances to be represented as market research which shall also be honest and objective with neither research methods or findings used to mislead;

- *responsibilities to clients*: e.g. except by consent, client's identity, business information and the commissioned research data to remain confidential; full methodological details of the research must be supplied to the client;

- *general responsibilities*: e.g. all written and verbal assurances must be factually correct and honoured; everyone subject to the Code must adhere to its full provisions.

The Society also has guidelines for handling databases, following extensive consultation with members and the Data Protection Registrar, so as to ensure that research is conducted in accordance with the principles of the Data Protection Act.

Marketing within the ethical framework

The form of the heading to the section we have just concluded, 'Marketing within the legal framework', was chosen after some thought. It is meant to denote the belief that over and above marketing operations there is a governing structure which determines whether every decision and action is right or wrong in the fundamental matter of legality. Alternative headings such as 'Marketing and the law' or 'Law in the marketing framework' seemed to this author much more partial and dilute.

The form of the above heading makes a similar claim to authority on behalf of ethics, that *it is over and above marketing operations, governing each decision and action*. Such phrases as: 'to some degree', or 'it all depends' have no place here. Quite simply, if an action is unethical, it is not 'marketing', as the word is being interpreted in this textbook.

'What ought I to do?' and 'How ought I to live?' are the fundamental practical questions of ethics and the theories that attempt to answer them constitute the more abstract portion of *normative ethics* i.e. the part concerned with guiding action.

As Green (1994, p 47) points out, 'ethics' is derived from the Greek word 'ethos', meaning the character or custom of a people. 'Morality' derives from the Latin word 'mos' which is also linked to the customs and practices of a social group. Since both words relate to the expected behaviour of a group and thus, its individual members, 'ethics' and 'morality' describe what society believes to be right or wrong. We derive our value judgements of what is right and wrong from formative influences which may, in origin, be religious, secular or both, for example:

- for many, the Christian ethic, with its golden rule 'do unto others as you would have them do unto you', is an important guide to behaviour;

- a more secular attitude to ethical actions is grounded in the moral philosophy known as *utilitarianism*, which emanates from the objective of 'the greatest good for the greatest number' and which judges actions on the consequences for all the parties affected by those actions (note our term 'stakeholders' in this connection).

Too often, while we may as private persons exhibit qualities that are recognized and honoured in most human societies – stemming from a sense of justice, loyalty, compassion, generosity, sensitivity and the like – how we behave in an organizational setting may be markedly at odds with our private personality. For instance, the dictionary definition (*Chambers Twentieth Century Dictionary*, 1982) of the word 'oxymoron is 'a figure of speech by means of which contradictory terms are combined' and, among the disbelieving, the concept of 'business ethics' is just such an oxymoron.

As Solomon (1993, p 354) points out, 'greed' is often cited as the sole engine of business life and the ethical view of business for most of history has been almost wholly negative – Cicero, a great practical thinker, paid careful attention to the question of fairness in ordinary business transactions, while Aristotle denounced 'chrematisike' (trade for profit), declaring such activity wholly devoid of virtue and calling those who acted from such purely selfish motives 'parasites'. Such Christian moralists as St Paul, Thomas Aquinas and Martin Luther have expressed similar views on what we today term 'the business world'.

Despite what stands on the broad, historical canvas and despite the continuing fear and mistrust of the 'slick' salesman and a residual, healthy scepticism about the fairness of capitalism, the business enterprise has now come to be generally regarded as a central, respectable feature of modern society. However, as we saw in Chapter 1 the disgraces, scandals and disasters of the recent past have been widely regarded as evidence of the corporate world at its worst and most irresponsible, with 'greed is good' firmly back on its agenda.

Three of the most general concerns expressed of late have been based on:

- the fact that greed of gain increasingly treats human resources as wholly expendable, irrespective of the social tragedies and dangers this generates;

- the fact that economic growth seems inescapably related to environmental damage and urban pollution;

- the fact that the relationship of the business world to the Third World appears too frequently to be exploitative and uncaring.

In addition to concerns of a general nature, the following are of special significance for marketers:

- concern that product development should take total account of health and safety factors;

- concern that the quality of products often leaves much to be desired;

- concern that the level of after sales service should, at the least, be adequate;

- concern that prices should constitute good value and that pricing techniques should aim to assist and not to exploit;

- concern that the concentration of retail buying power into fewer and larger hands is leaving some sections of society, particularly the poor and those without private transport, with reduced access to, and choice of, necessary goods (recently, Dutch visitors to a large housing estate in Glasgow were astonished that they were unable to find a single retail shop);

- concern that advertising should be honest and genuinely informative, that user guarantees should be free from ambiguity and that personal selling techniques should be objective and honourable.

In their text, *The Ethical Organisation*, Kitson and Campbell (1996, p 172) report the views of Ferrell and Gresham (1985) that three elements, with attendant variables, are likely to influence the ethical status of either or both of:

- the marketer's intentions;

- the marketing 'output'.

Figure 5.2 is this author's attempt to present these views diagrammatically. As the diagram indicates, Ferrell and Gresham suggest that from an ethical standpoint any particular marketing decision will be the outcome of the effect of the ethical issue mediated by the three areas of influence:

- *the marketer's own value system*, which in turn has been influenced by family, education and the wider cultural context;

- *'significant others'* i.e. reference groups within the organization whose influence is a function of their social distance from the marketer, the organizational climate of ethical/unethical behaviour, and the visibility of top management – highly significant in that the more remote management are, the more their power to influence will be taken over by peer groups;

- *opportunity* – in that increased opportunity for unethical marketing behaviour will increase its occurrence: companies and professions promoting and enforcing ethical codes will raise standards of behaviour, whereas reduction of punishment and higher rewards for unethical behaviour will tend to increase it.

Kitson and Campbell (1996) outline other studies which support the Ferrell and Gresham reasoning. This affirms what may be expressed as the 'common-sense' observation that no matter what influences the individual or society (i.e. the wider cultural context) bring to bear, the ethical status of marketing behaviour is significantly governed by the organization itself. Two additional points are worth making here:

- as we have seen earlier in this text, if marketing is a 'whole organization' activity then all personnel are marketers – the production operative who relaxes a product's safety inspection in order to boost output rates is as much at fault in marketing ethics as the salesman who misrepresents the price of that product;

- if, as we have also seen (Chapter 2), marketing is increasingly based on collaboration, then proper concern for ethical standards must extend *beyond* the organization – e.g. to its suppliers and to collaborators in its own marketing network.

If in ethics, as in so many other aspects of organizational life, the standards are set 'at the top' then this underscores the importance of acting upon the *values statement*

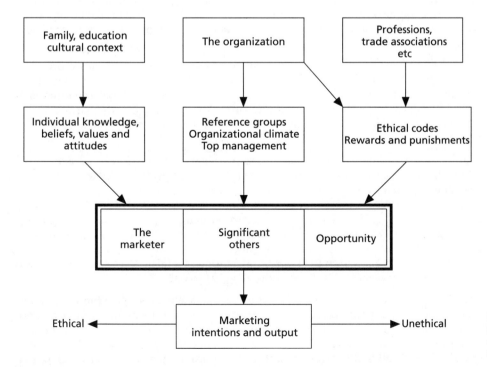

Figure 5.2. *Influences on the ethical status of marketing intentions and output after Ferrell and Gresham.*

(see Chapter 3) by devising and implementing a *code of ethics*. Here, the views of Dibb *et al.* are useful:

> It is difficult for employees to determine what is acceptable behaviour within an organisation if the organisation does not have uniform policies and standards. Without standards of behaviour, employees will generally make decisions based on their observations of how their peers and managers behave. Codes of ethics are formalised rules and standards that describe what the company expects of its employees. Codes of ethics *encourage ethical behaviour by eliminating opportunities for unethical behaviour: the company's employees know both what is expected of them and what the punishment is for violating the rules* (Dibb et al., 1991, p 632).

Note in the closing words of this extract the importance of management *action* and recall the views of other authors that cosmetic exercises, mixing platitudes with good intentions, fool no one and only strengthen cynicism.

A lengthier treatment of marketing ethics and ethical issues, though fundamentally important, is beyond the scope of this work, though one or two other observations before closing the chapter are quite vital.

First, the development of a code of ethics must be preceded by adequate analysis – an *ethical audit*. Such an exercise can reveal discrepancies between the values the organization thinks it holds and those values which its actions demonstrate it really holds. It may also indicate differences between the values held and those it *ought* to hold.

Secondly, talk of ethics, codes and audits *may* suggest a flight from reality in which the power of competition is ignored. Might striving for some ideal impair achieving an adequate return on assets? Would sharing ethical objectives with suppliers and within marketing networks be seen as a patronizing attempt to 'put the world right'? Fortunately, the evidence now runs counter to these fears.

Earlier in this book, we noted the increase in ethical investments and saw that the comparative performance of well-managed 'ethical' organizations leaves nothing to be desired. We also noted, from the DEC study that the manager-respondents rated social responsibility as among the most important factors, while short-term profitability received the lowest rating.

Every day, society's wish for organizations to behave ethically becomes more clear and insistent. Notwithstanding this, as Sternberg (1994, p 20–2) observes, many businessmen are contemptuous of business ethics, rejecting conventional applications of ethical standards to business as irrelevant or anti-business. She adds that the 'moral muteness' of managers is renowned and explains much of their reluctance to raise ethical concerns.

Fear of being thought disloyal and unbusinesslike, and the forces of conformity within organizations ('good employees don't rock the boat') help to explain the reluctance of managers to raise ethical concerns. It stems, moreover, from a misjudgement of what business ethics 'is all about'. Entreaties for business to support charitable causes, and to foster social welfare in many aspects, have nothing to do with business ethics, however worthy such causes may be. An *ethical issue*, handily defined by Dibb *et al.* is: 'an identifiable problem, situation or opportunity requiring an individual or organisation to choose from among several actions that must be evaluated as right or wrong, ethical or unethical' (1991, p 625).

Such issues pervade every aspect of an organization's activities: selection and recruitment of personnel, choosing suppliers, relations with customers, fixing prices, establishing strategic objectives, allocating resources, determining dividend distribution, monitoring and controlling workers, planning schedules, awarding contracts, etc. – and all raise ethical issues. They constitute the ethical framework within which organizations operate and several things may be said of such issues, namely that they are frequent, complex, of infinite variety and, in many cases, novel. Sternberg (1994, p 19) is clear that many of the most dramatic business failures and the most significant business losses of the last decade have been the result of unethical conduct. In short 'bad ethics is bad business', for short-term gains won by unethical conduct seldom pay in the end. She writes with conviction on the costs of being unethical:

> Many standard business problems have unsuspected ethical elements, which businesses without a proper moral framework typically fail to recognise. High fault levels, high 'shrinkage', high turnover of staff and suppliers, employee illness, anxiety and absenteeism, low productivity and low repeat business are among the many business difficulties that typically result from unethical business conduct; unsatisfactory behaviour by stakeholders often results from unethical treatment of them. When the underlying ethical questions are ignored, it is usually not the problems, but the business that goes away (Sternberg, 1994, pp 19–20).

Given the salience and complexity of ethical issues even an organization anxious to operate ethically is hardly likely to succeed if the resolution of such issues is left entirely to managers judged to have been 'nicely brought up', who can be 'relied upon to be fair'. The development and implementation of a code of ethics is fundamentally important, but its setting within a robust conceptual framework is no less important. Elaine Sternberg, whose doctorate in philosophy and extensive experience as an investment banker in London, New York and Paris lend authority to her views, sounds a warning note in this connection. She finds that most commentaries on business ethics have no theoretical foundation or else rely on inadequate, often incoherent philosophical doctrines, adding that theories which cannot accommodate human action have little hope of making sense of ethics or of business. She offers: 'a sustained argument to demonstrate that business can be true to its definitive objective of maximising long-term owner value and still be fully ethical' (Sternberg, 1994, p 5), and has developed an Ethical Decision Model based on her belief that, since being ethical in business consists of maximizing long-term owner value subject only to distributive justice and ordinary decency, it is entirely plausible that 'good ethics is good business' in markets the world over.

It would seem prudent for organizations developing codes of ethics to familiarize themselves with models such as Sternberg's or the NORM methodology of Green (1994).

Implementing the law

Reports of decided cases in the national press provide many examples of how the law operates to protect buyers and users of goods and services. Below are extracts taken from a recent bulletin issued by the Office of Fair Trading. They provide examples of action on unfair contract terms, taken by the Unfair Contract Terms Unit of that Office.

- Following a complaint by a Trading Standards Department, a company carrying on a wall-coating business had to amend its contracts in several respects. For example, the Unit found that, having regard to appropriate legislation, a payment term which could be understood to require full payment on completion of the work with no right for the consumer to hold back the balance of the contract price if the work had not been completed to a satisfactory standard or as promised, was seen to be potentially unfair. The revised term now requires payment only if the work is *satisfactorily* completed.

- A supermarket chain provides facilities for its customers. The conditions printed on the ticket issued to consumers on entering the car park stated: 'All persons using this Car Park do so entirely at their own risk and no liability will be accepted for loss, damage or injury to persons or vehicles including contents however such loss, damage or injury be caused.' The term had potential for unfairness as it could have had the effect of excluding or limiting the legal liability of the company in the event of death or personal injury or damage to or loss of property caused by negligence. The source of the complaint was a consumer and the company concerned informed the Office of Fair Trading that by the end of January 1997 the term would be removed from all tickets issued to consumers and all customer notices displayed in the company's car parks.

- A Trading Standards Department complained about the conditions being imposed by a company operating a holiday caravan park. One broadly framed clause gave the company the right to refuse entry to the park without reason. The Unit found this was potentially unfair because it could enable the company to dishonour any booking made. The company agreed to amend the clause.

Implementing the ethical code

In this chapter, the claim has been made that a business can be true to its definitive objective of maximizing long-term owner value and still be fully ethical and any belief that the opposite is the case is misconceived.

Newspapers, magazines, radio and television are now providing a notable and ever-increasing volume of evidence that:

- stakeholding, for example, now goes well beyond academic theory, political philosophy, or the faint aspirations of well-meaning executives – it is a social reality which managers cannot avoid;

- shareholders themselves are now becoming increasingly vocal in their aim to improve the environmental and ethical performance of the businesses they finance.

The examples below provide a glimpse into the extensive material accumulated by this author which demonstrates that economic objectives and ethical conduct are not mutually exclusive.

The Queen's Awards for Environmental Achievement, 1997
The seven products/processes receiving the award, in the words of Leyla Boulton (1997), 'provide ample support for the thesis that helping the environment can help company profits too' and rebut the widespread view, particularly among smaller businesses, that environmental concern means greater expenditure.

On the contrary, 'green' policies can often produce cost savings. Waste reduction provides an excellent opportunity for savings, particularly now its disposal is becoming increasingly expensive. The pressure for firms to either change production methods or find alternative uses for by-products has intensified in the UK since October 1996, when a new tax was imposed on waste sent to landfill sites.

The absorbents division of Laporte, Cheshire won an award for Ferral, a water purification coagulant made from a clay processing waste product. Ferral is used to coalesce impurities in raw water being processed for drinking supplies. The development of this process, now patented, avoids waste disposal to landfill and also provides a cost-effective solution to problems of the water industry.

H. & R. Johnson Tiles, Stoke-on-Trent provides a similar example. The firm obtained the award for a method of turning scrap from twelve pottery tableware manufacturers into high quality ceramic tiles. As a result, the firm is able to recycle each year 3500 tonnes of scrap pottery with its own waste. This not only diverts a large volume of waste from landfill sites, it also reduces the amount of raw material H. & R. Johnson needs to bring by road from south-west England.

Reducing expenditure is one way of improving profit performance and another is increasing revenues from sales. An interesting instance here is provided by the Industrial and Marine Gas Turbines division of Rolls-Royce, Anstey, Coventry. Its dry low emissions system is used on a range of its industrial gas engines and has 'dramatically' reduced emissions of nitrous oxide and carbon monoxide. Marketed after a four-year development programme, to April 1997, the system had won nearly £100 million in new business.

The preparation element:
Part I:

Information as the basis for decision-making

Information as a basis for decision-making

A manager, not least a marketing manager, spends most of his time making decisions. The analysis, evaluation and utilization of information is part and parcel of the decision-making process. In fact, the quality of the decision is crucially influenced by the quality of the information which precedes it.

An understanding of past performance, a sound interpretation of current performance and robust predictions as to future performance do a great deal to reduce risk and uncertainty in decision-making. A customer-led culture depends on adequate knowledge of customers and why they buy. When that knowledge is developed and refined continuously it assists customer retention and hence, as we have seen, profitability. Information gained as a result of environmental scanning enables the organization to align itself creatively with changes in that environment – changes which may signal new opportunities for products and markets or sound a warning note about the organization's present course.

Timely and relevant information can contribute to the long-run welfare of society (e.g. through assisting the development of ecologically sound products and processes), can help to foster total organizational commitment to operating ethically and can provide important insights into the needs and expectations of stakeholders. Pertinent information enables each manager to deal with every threat and every opportunity *objectively*. Guesswork, undue optimism and prejudice have always threatened good decision-making. In the face of ever-increasing global competition and the pressing need to reduce 'time to market' they spell doom.

The significance of marketing information was once handily summarized by the executive who remarked to the author: 'I would back a genius against formal input of data any day – the trouble is, I don't know how many geniuses there are about.'

Figure 6.1 aims to convey the idea of the permanent place of marketing information in the continuous cycle of determining and adjusting strategy. Reading clockwise:

- the first element is *consumer needs and expectations* – are these stable or changing?

- the appropriate signals of threat and opportunity are monitored by the *marketing information system*, which provides the first preparatory step for strategic change, if this is necessary;

- the new information is matched with the *core competences* of the organization;

- this assists strategic decisions on *new markets/market segments* (see Chapter 7) and what *positioning* approach should be adopted – 'head to head' (engagement) or 'avoidance' (differentiation);

Figure 6.1. *The preparation element in the cycle of strategic review and development.*

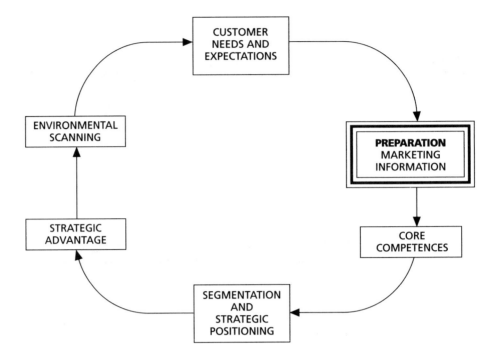

- the objective of these decisions is the attainment of *strategic advantage*;

- in the meantime, the external environment and the organization's markets may be dynamic and turbulent – now more the rule than the exception;

- in turn this may generate *revised and additional customer needs and expectations* – even more threats or opportunities;

- it is important that the marketing information element remains in place to track such signals and, if necessary, to point the way to consequential adjustments to strategy.

Strategic decision-making is an iterative process, a repeated cycle of analysis, adjustment and renewed implementation. Hence the case for *preparation* (Marketing information) as an element in the enlarged marketing mix, introduced in Chapter 3.

The marketing information system

Accelerated by the rapid and continuing progress of information technology, for organizations throughout the world, planning and implementing strategy has become a process of decision-making based on the acquisition and use of up-to-date, relevant information. Consequently, a *management information system* (MIS) serving corporate needs, and all functional areas in turn – finance, marketing, production, personnel, etc. – has become an established feature of organizational life. Our purpose in this section is to look at the form and purpose of a major component of the overall information system, the *marketing information system* (MKIS).

Philip Kotler has been a leading advocate for the development and use of such a system. He feels that the planning, execution and control of marketing operations are best served by a marketing information system which: 'consists of people, equipment, and procedures to gather, sort, analyse, evaluate and distribute needed, timely, and accurate information to marketing decision makers' (Kotler, 1997, p 110). Kotler's concept of such a system as being made up of four sub-systems has also become widely accepted, so that the overall system is generally perceived to comprise:

- The *internal records system* which provides management with current reports on costs, stocks, cash flow, customers' accounts and sales by products, product group, area, region and market, etc.

- The *marketing intelligence system* which keeps management abreast of developments in the external environment and entails the scrutiny of newspapers, journals, research papers, trade publications, reports from customers, distributors, suppliers, etc; the purchase of information from specialist sources, public and private; and ideally, the establishment of a mechanism to collect and distribute such intelligence.

- The *marketing research system* which enables management to commission specific studies on marketing issues and opportunities, resulting in reports to assist decision-making.

- The *marketing decision support system* which has been described as 'a coordinated collection of data, systems, tools and techniques with supporting software and hardware by which an organization gathers and interprets relevant information from business and environment and turns it into a basis for marketing action' (Little, 1979, p 11).

Figure 6.2 indicates how the marketing information system operates. Within the overall system are the two major sub-systems – *data collection* and *decision support*. The three elements of the data collection sub-system – internal records, marketing intelligence and marketing research provide the raw material on which the *marketing database* is established. The database will contain two types of data:

- *Primary data* – assembled for a specific objective and usually resulting from a particular *marketing research* project, for example a survey among users of a product in order to evaluate its acceptability or brand image.

- *Secondary data* – previously assembled for some purpose other than the context in which it is now being utilized, for example data on economic trends, supplied by the UK's Office for National Statistics (ONS), fed into the database via a firm's *marketing intelligence system* for use in that firm's *demand analysis*.

Note also the *interactive processing element* within the decision support system. In hands-on mode, and utilizing appropriate user-friendly software, marketing executives are able to interrogate and manipulate the database, applying suitable models and analytical procedures in the quest for outcomes to assist decision-making.

It might now be productive to add a little more detail to each of the four components of the marketing information system.

The internal records system

Data on sales (volume and revenues) by product, sales territory, region and market; expenditure on distribution and advertising; product manufacturing costs; costs per order; cost per enquiry, etc., all assist the marketing department to assess its progress to sales and profit objectives and to monitor its effectiveness in managing its allocated budgets. Beyond the department, such data are important inputs to calculations at an organizational level on return on investment, liquidity, financial strength, corporate valuation, investment ratios and shareholder value added.

As noted in Chapter 4, where a system of networking based on the personal computer operates, the links between people and departments augment this system

Figure 6.2. *The structure of a marketing information system (MKIS)*

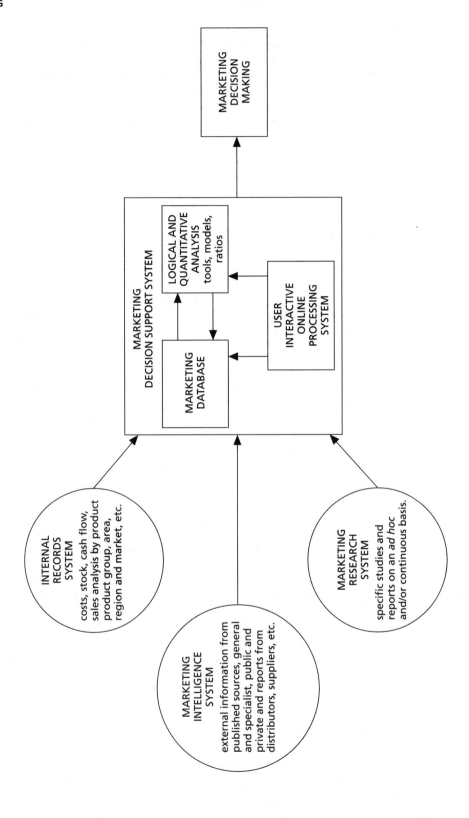

and make it even more productive. For instance, data on reduced production costs as a result of changes to factory layout or improvements in productivity emanating from new selection and training programmes are facts which can be translated to marketing advantage. Most significantly, electronic data interchange (EDI), linking networks between organizations, dramatically increases the prospects of augmenting the internal records system. Data from suppliers and customers have great value in this respect.

The marketing intelligence system

Such is the abundance of secondary data from the departments of domestic and international governments, the United Nations, the World Bank, trade associations, the trade press, professional and academic journals, TECs, chambers of commerce, universities, commercial research organizations, etc., that often the issue is not what to include but what to leave out in the attempt to monitor an organization's performance and to forecast its future.

The task of monitoring performance is illustrated by the thumb-nail sketch in Figure 6.3. The lower curve depicts the rate of increase in volume of sales (percentage per annum) achieved by an individual firm in the recent past. The firm's marketing staff may be induced to relax in the comfort of a curve which is rising until, that is, data are obtained on the rate of increase for the total market. The firm's increase (2 per cent over a 4 year period) lags markedly behind the rate of increase for the total market (over 6 per cent for the same period). This indicates better progress by competitors and a brake on further increases in sales by the firm in question particularly if competitors use the economic benefits of their increases in output to lower their prices. Background information which relates performance to some appropriate context is vital for monitoring purposes, as it is for analysing demand and forecasting sales for a region, a country or a market.

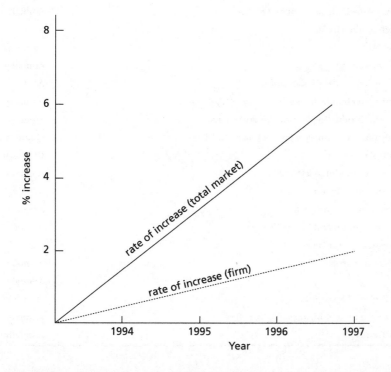

Figure. 6.3. *Performance monitoring*

Table 6.1 provides a mere glimpse of the types of data available from UK government sources. Readers outside the UK are advised to survey the range available from their own official sources. The growing 'internationalization' of statistical sources should also be noted: under the aegis of Eurostat, for instance, the Member States of the European Union are establishing a network of Data Shops, to provide Eurostat publications as well as predefined, standard and fixed output statistical products to users. Specifically tailored data, closer to users' individual needs in electronic or 'hard copy' formats will also be available.

On this last point it is interesting to note how the delivery of data by electronic media, for importing into users' own IT systems, is constantly being extended. The Navidata 2 system at the UK's ONS utilizes the Windows™ 3.x/95 software, enabling subscribers to be much more flexible in their use of up to 50 years' worth of economic data. Time series information (e.g. for forecasting purposes – see Chapter 14) can be analysed to create new data comparisons.

Title	Published
UK National Accounts (The Blue Book)	Annually
UK Balance of Payments (The Pink Book)	Annually
Economic Trends	Monthly
Producer Price Indices (MM22)	Monthly
Retail Prices Index (MM23)	Monthly
Consumer Trends	Quarterly
Overseas Trade – by Industries (MQ10)	Quarterly
Review of External Trade Statistics (MM24)	Monthly
Overseas Direct Investment (MA4)	Annually
The Health of Adult Britain	Ad-hoc
Occupational Health	Decennial
Key Health Statistics from General Practice	Annually
Food Safety in the Home	Ad-hoc
Labour Market Trends	Monthly
New Earnings Survey	Annually
Standard Occupational Classification	Ad-hoc
UK Directory of Manufacturing Businesses (CD-ROM)	Annually
Motor vehicle production and new registrations	Monthly
Manufacturing and primary – Product Sales and Trade	Quarterly/Annual
Population Trends	Quarterly
Key Population and Vital Statistics	Annually
Looking Towards the 2001 Census	Ad-hoc
National Population Projections	Annually
Housing Deprivation and Social Change	Ad-hoc
Annual Abstract of Statistics	Annually
UK Business in Europe	Ad-hoc
Key data	Annually
Monthly Digest of Statistics	Monthly
Size Analysis of the UK Businesses (PA 1003)	Annually
Regional Trends	Annually

Table 6.1. *Examples of data available from the UK Office for National Statistics (ONS)*

Extracted from: 'The Source', Office for National Statistics, 1997 catalogue

Although the distinction between public and private sector organizations in the marketing intelligence field is not always valid (the ONS, for example, also operates on commercial lines) 'commercial organizations' is the term still used to describe those suppliers who have traditionally operated on a fee-earning basis. There is a vast number of these but the very limited list below provides an interesting glimpse of the provision available:

● Mintel International Group Ltd. publishes about 120 reports each year in its Marketing Intelligence series. All published reports include analyses of market factors, market trends and sizes, distribution channels, supply structures, promotional strategies, the consumer, future opportunities and weaknesses, market value/size forecasts. Mintel's Index of Reports, produced since 1995, covers a vast range of products and services from Abrasives to Zinc carbon batteries.

● Verdict Research Ltd. analyses each year the main retail sectors and the companies operating within them in a well-established series of reports. Each sector covered examines leading retailers in terms of trading performance, competitive positioning, market shares, product offers, marketing strategies, future prospects, etc. Verdict also provides a 5 year forecast of retail sales by sector (Retailing 2000) a forecast of sales for nearly 80 product markets (Retail Demand 2000) and an analysis of future growth in retail floorspace and sales densities (Space 2000).

● Euromonitor plc has created global databases of market information and provides market analysis reports on industries in any country, research into buyer–supplier relations and trade attitudes, corporate research and competitive analysis, strategic analysis and market entry evaluations, etc.

● A.C. Nielsen has, for over 70 years, been a global leader in providing business information, analysis and insights to consumer packaged goods companies in 88 countries world-wide. Beginning its global drive more than 50 years ago, it has created and built a prestigious and extensive overseas business in decision support information. In the UK its capabilities span continuous market information, advertising expenditure measurement, advertising media, decision and solution systems, market modelling and analytics, and merchandising.

● The Economist Intelligence Unit Ltd. (EIU) publishes quarterly reports on over 180 countries. The EIU Country Reports provide objective and timely intelligence and insights on each country's prospects for short-term growth, the challenges facing companies doing business there, long-term developments, the political influences affecting foreign companies, political stability, economic priorities (growth, inflation, trade and investment), commitment to international cooperation and fair trade, GDP performance and the outlook for specific sectors of the economy, developments in foreign trade, etc.

As the book proceeds there are a number of other examples of the marketing intelligence industry and its providers. In the meantime, it should be clear that no organization, in the developed world at least, should be hampered in its efforts for lack of basic marketing intelligence. Before committing resources to any market, even the smallest company, with its time and finances at a premium, can obtain sound basic intelligence from the daily and weekly news media, business journals, directories and the reference section at the local library. With regard to the news media, publications such as *Business Week* and *The Economist* provide perceptive summaries of the challenges of the global market place as well as weekly briefings on issues in world regions, economic prospects, corporate strategies, etc. The *Financial Times* continually provides reports on industries and markets in both its newspaper format and its newsletters. Its newsletter on East European Markets, for example, provides fortnightly news, analysis and comment on business investment, banking, business trends, industry, technology and new legislation in that region. Finally, directories such as *The Hambro Company Guide* will provide intelligence on the financial standing, operations and performance of prospective client organizations.

Warning note

The value of marketing intelligence is clear, in fact it is hard to understand how marketing, in its fullest and best sense, could be implemented without it. It is also easy to visualize how an adequately staffed bureau, or office, specializing in the collection, analysis and dissemination of appropriate data could easily recover its costs in a large, multi-product corporation. But what of the small firm employing perhaps 200 personnel and three or four managers, or indeed, the one-man business?

Judgement is required as to where along the marketing intelligence continuum the individual organization should position itself, the opposite poles of the continuum being, in this case, the sole trader whose marketing intelligence system is largely in his head and the sophisticated bureau with access to a wide field of data sources through utilizing such technology as the computer, electronic mail, fax facilities, the Internet and the CD-ROM. There is a great merit in establishing an intelligence system that will 'just do', for elaboration beyond this point inevitably means diminishing returns.

Marketing is about speed and flexibility. It abhors bureaucracy. Calm analysis is one thing, a fetish for figures quite another. Because the marketing executive has to deal with so many imponderables, the receipt of data, any data, reduces his anxiety. This carries the danger of paralysis by analysis and can actually inhibit timely decision-making ('we can't act until we've got all the facts'). Often, by the time all the facts are known, the market has changed anyhow. Peter Drucker doubtless had such an issue in mind when he suggested that firms don't optimize, they *satisfice*. Marketing intelligence can point the way to opportunity but too much of it can delay decisions.

Marketing research

Marketing research is the third element in the overall MKIS. Although the terms 'market research' and 'marketing research' are frequently used interchangeably this is not strictly accurate. Baker's (1996, p 230) explanation is helpful here, for he states that while 'market research' is concerned with the measurement and analysis of markets (e.g. the size and nature of the market in terms of the age, sex and social status of consumers; the geographical location of potential consumers; etc.), the scope of 'marketing research' is much broader and is concerned with all those factors which impinge on the marketing of goods and services and so includes such issues as the study of advertising effectiveness, distributive channels, competitive products, marketing policies and the whole field of consumer and organizational behaviour. 'Market research' is therefore a constituent part of the wider process of 'marketing research'. One of the definitions of marketing research emanating from the American Marketing Association (AMA) indicates not only *what* this research process is, but *how* it achieves its purpose. The AMA, for example, has defined marketing research as the:

> function which links the consumer, customer and public to the marketer through information – information used to identify and define marketing opportunities and problems; generate, refine and evaluate marketing actions; monitor marketing performance and improve understanding of marketing as a process. Marketing research specifies the information required to address these issues; designs the method for collecting information; manages and implements the data collection process; analyzes the results; and communicates the findings and their implications.

The latter part of the definition describes a number of the key stages of research activity, a topic we return to later in the chapter. Although marketing research information can sometimes be obtained by the use of a standardized procedure (e.g. the purchase of question units in an omnibus survey, also explained later) much marketing research consists of the design and implementation of a research project carried out by a specialist research organization (or agency) and tailored closely to the client organization's needs.

To appreciate the scope of marketing research, it is useful to consider first the broad markets in which client organizations operate, that is consumer markets and industrial markets.

Consumer markets

Consumer markets cover:

- *fast moving consumer goods (fmcg)* – manufactured for direct immediate use, bought regularly and having a limited life, e.g. food, drink, confectionery, health and beauty products;
- *durable consumer goods* – manufactured for direct immediate use, but bought less frequently and having a much longer life, e.g. television and radio sets, washing machines, video cassette recorders, personal computers, motor cars;
- *consumer services* – e.g. banking, insurance, hairdressing and travel services.

Industrial markets

Industrial markets cover:

- *industrial 'consumption' goods* – manufactured for use or transformation in a process of further production and which, because of their consequent limited life, have a frequent purchase pattern, e.g. chemicals, lubricants, cement, clay, sheet steel, plastics moulding powder;
- *industrial durable goods* – the machinery and equipment used in the production of further goods, e.g. lathes, furnaces, presses, grinding and milling machinery;
- *industrial services* – e.g. facilitating services (finance, storage, transport, insurance, waste disposal, factory maintenance) and advisory/consultancy services.

It is clear that these classifications are not descriptively watertight but they do serve as a convenient shorthand to handle the analysis of marketing activity.

The scope of research into consumer markets is very broad and typically seeks to find answers to one or more of the following questions: how many actual/potential consumers of this product/service are there? where are they situated? how may they be broadly classified (e.g. in terms of age, sex, social-economic status, etc.)? what motivates them to buy? where do they buy? how satisfied are they with our products/prices? what are the main competitive products and prices? how best can our products be promoted (media/message)? what scope is there for introducing new products? what short-/long-term trends are in evidence in this market? and so on.

The information obtained assists more efficient decision-making on such elements of the marketing mix as product/service offer, price, distribution, advertising and, on occasions, on how the organization itself may improve its image in the market place.

With regard to industrial markets, the UK's Industrial Marketing Research Association (IMRA) has published the results of its own inquiries to identify the principal characteristics of 'industrial' firms using marketing research and the reasons why they were doing so (Pearce, n.d.).

Marketing research applications were found to extend over several industries but the following, ranked in order, were among the major users:

- chemical and allied industries;
- vehicles;
- engineering and electrical goods;
- construction;
- metal manufacture.

Companies using marketing research tended to be characterized more by financial and capital intensity than by number of employees. The ten principal functions of marketing research in those industries surveyed were found to be as follows:

Functions	Percentage conducting regular research
Sales forecasting	76
Analysis of market size	70
Trends in market size	61
Estimating demand for new products	51
Comparing competitive position of products	48
Determining characteristics of markets	43
Determining present uses of existing products	41
Study of economic factors affecting sales volume	38
General business forecasting	30
Evaluation of proposed new products/services	30

Much of the rest of this chapter is devoted to the principles and practice of marketing research but one of its most important aspects, *sales forecasting*, is deferred until Chapter 14, where its contribution to the strategic marketing process is considered.

The marketing decision support system

As we can see from Figure 6.2 the decision support system (DSS) comprises three components:

- the database;
- the analytical models system;
- the user interaction system.

The *database* will contain a mass of facts and figures arranged in a logical and systematic manner for computer storage and processing. The names, addresses, postal codes and the types and volume of purchases will almost certainly be recorded for each customer. Environmental data on population, incomes, social grade composition for each TV region, county, postal code, etc. will also be recorded. For industrial marketing, the size, structure and geographic dispersion of appropriate industries would be at the heart of the database. Internal records relating to costs, sales, shipments, budgets, etc. form another important part of the database. More general environmental data, for example economic and industrial statistics, news of technological/industry developments, overseas trade news, etc., may be imported into the database via telecommunications links with specialist organizations which assemble and market databases of a specialized or general nature.

The *analytical model systems* can typically draw upon a number of *statistical tools* (e.g. regression, factor, cluster analysis), *models* (e.g. probability, product pre-test and sales response) and *optimization routines* (e.g. differential calculus, mathematical programming, decision theory, game theory). It will utilize statistical software systems, spreadsheet software and decision models to analyse and restructure data, identify relationships between data, estimate the strength and influence of variables, classify customers, firms and industries into appropriate categories and much, much more.

The third DSS component, the *interaction system* manages the interface between the user and the overall system and must be so user-friendly that people with no expert knowledge of computers can use the system and, at the same time, control its output in a manner which will be effective for analysis, review of choices and decision-making.

In many instances, the marketing manager can now access the DSS through the workstation on his desk. As he uses an appropriate model to assemble and analyse the relevant data, and employs a specialized software program to determine an optimal course of action, he closely resembles a pilot on the flight deck of an aircraft. Imagine the activity on that flight deck as the aircraft comes in to land. Information is being received from traffic control at the airport about the aircraft's present position in relation to the runway which has been allocated to it, about the surface conditions on the runway and about the direction and speed of the prevailing winds. The pilot and his crew are acting on this information by altering their approach speed and rate of descent, by adjusting the attitude of the aircraft or its aerodynamic shape (e.g. by bringing down the flaps so that they act as airbrakes). It is not too fanciful to suggest that, as with the pilot so with the marketing manager, who is 'flying' the organization towards its objectives through the numerical columns, colour charts, graphs and maps which appear on the screen of his workstation, generated by the DSS.

A simple example of how the DSS can assist the development of strategy is the case where an organization has a list of all its customers within its central database. Appropriate software enables the organization to assemble a new file, listing high-volume customers only. Further analytical procedure enables it to classify these customers in terms of their socio-economic status and area code. This then enables the firm to develop a customer-retention strategy in the shape of loyalty incentives, special offers, revised advertising and so on.

There are now a considerable number of software programs to support decisions on analysing and segmenting markets, setting prices, fixing advertising budgets, selecting advertising media, structuring and managing salesforce activities and many other aspects of marketing operations. The developments continue to come at an unabated pace. Mention has already been made of the use of artificial intelligence (expert systems) in this connection (Chapter 4). *Neural networking software*, which simulates the pattern of cells in the human brain and can actually 'learn' from large sets of data, does not, in most instances, require large and expensive computing power. This means that the marketing manager can access the knowledge of experts, by simple routines, via his own personal computer. In fact, the following comment is very revealing: 'By the beginning of the twenty-first century, it is widely believed, expert systems will be the primary force in segmenting, targeting, and making marketing and sales more efficient' (Kotler, 1997, p 130).

Marketing research revisited ⋮

In this section we shall be taking a longer look at that part of the marketing information system labelled 'Marketing research' which, as already noted, is concerned in the main with the commissioning of specific studies on marketing issues and opportunities, resulting in reports to assist decision-making. In this case, the data on which these reports are based are referred to as *primary data*, as noted above, that is to say data assembled for a specific purpose, usually resulting from a particular marketing research project.

Before we move on, since this area of marketing is perhaps the one containing the largest amount of specialist terminology, it might be helpful to be crystal clear on the distinction between 'data' and 'information'. 'Data' derives from the Latin verb *dare*, to give, and means *given facts*. It is from these given facts that other facts may be deduced because, by using statistical processes, the data originally collected (frequently called the 'raw data') can often be treated methodically so that conclusions can be drawn from them. In their treated form, these processed data will yield 'information', which is then used at the basis for management decisions. For example, if you look back at the thumb-nail sketch in Figure 6.3, its curves were constructed from a mass of statistics on sales volume. The statistics constitute the *data* used for the curves. Only when these data have been processed as the sketch depicts, is the management of the firm in possession of the *information* that the trend of its own sales is noticeably lagging behind that of the total market and that it is time to make some decisions to remedy the situation. As Drucker (1991b, p 30) puts it, with his usual attractive simplicity: 'Information is data endowed with relevance and purpose.'

The significance of marketing research

Organizations world-wide now regard marketing research as a vital part of their operations. Its significance in the UK, for instance, is illustrated by Figure 6.4. The companies which are members of the Association of Market Survey Organizations (AMSO) represent the major part of the UK's research industry. These companies earned £446 million in 1996, the last year for which data was available when this chapter was being written. This represents growth of 11.6 per cent on 1995, or 9.1 per cent in real terms, allowing for a UK (non-housing) inflation rate of 2.5 per cent. Figure 6.4 shows the marked upward trend in earnings in the period since 1993, the figures for each year exceeding by a wide margin the prevailing rates of inflation.

Apart from AMSO members, some UK research organizations are members of the Association of British Market Research Companies (ABMRC) and, in this connection, the following extract from AMSO's Annual Report 1997 is helpful:

> The total size of the commercially-available market for research is hard to assess precisely. This year AMSO and AMBRC have combined their turnovers to arrive at a joint estimate of £600m for 1996. When estimates are added for agencies and suppliers that are members of neither trade association, the total for the industry as a whole is estimated at around £750m. It is also clear that agencies are growing, on average, at above 10 per cent in real terms right across the size range, since the growth rate in AMBRC was the same as in AMSO.

A £750 million turnover emphasizes the importance accorded to the research function by client organizations in the UK and Figure 6.5, reproduced from AMSO sources, reveals that in 1996 research by UK organizations into foreign markets represented 29 per cent of AMSO members' turnover.

While domestic growth was strong, international growth was stronger. In fact, although domestic research grew at over three times the rate of UK inflation for the fifth successive year among AMSO members, international research was the source of the fastest growth – evidence for the statements made earlier in this text on the growing globalization of markets.

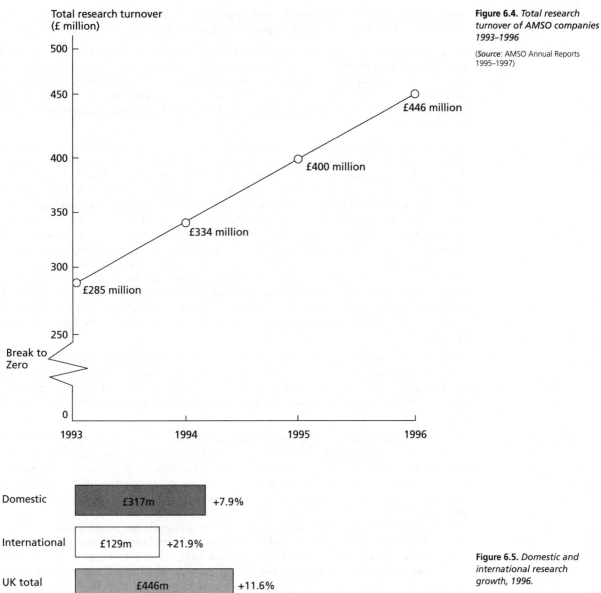

Total research turnover
(£ million)

Figure 6.4. *Total research turnover of AMSO companies 1993–1996*

(*Source*: AMSO Annual Reports 1995–1997)

£446 million

£400 million

£334 million

£285 million

Break to Zero

1993   1994   1995   1996

Domestic	£317m	+7.9%
International	£129m	+21.9%
UK total	£446m	+11.6%

Figure 6.5. *Domestic and international research growth, 1996.*

(*Source*: AMSO Annual Report 1997)

Scientific method and the research project

A number of definitions of 'science' are readily to hand, for example. 'any systematic field of study or body of knowledge that aims, through experiment, observation and deduction, to produce reliable explanation of phenomena, with reference to the material and physical world' (Lafferty and Rowe, 1994, p 523).

In essence, 'science' (Latin *scientia*, knowledge) can be taken to mean an *objective* investigation of empirical phenomena, that is of the observations which derive from our experience. It is also true to say that whenever a branch of supposed factual knowledge is rejected by science, it is invariably on the basis of its methodology. In science itself, scientific method is based on the belief that experimentation and observation, properly understood and applied, can avoid the influence of cultural and social values and so build up a picture of a reality independent of the observer.

It is important to adopt this type of 'scientific' approach to interpret marketing phenomena because sound decision-making must be based on *facts* – on the truth of a situation – and not on the prejudices of the researcher or the rationalizations of the marketing executive. The word objective has been emphasized in the preceding paragraph for, unless the investigation is objective, the outcome of the research will be worthless.

Marketing, of course, is not so much about the material and physical world as it is about *people* and the way they behave in the market place. For this reason it is not as easy to apply scientific method in a social context as it is in a physical context. For one thing, our knowledge of human behaviour is nowhere near as well developed as we might wish it to be. In attempting to understand behaviour in the market place and to classify types of consumer, for example, there has been a traditional reliance on theoretical insights imported from psychology, sociology, anthropology and economics. More recently, as we shall see in the next chapter, attempts have been made to derive a new understanding and new classifications by actually studying what happens in markets rather than relying on insights from the social sciences. Even so, this is far from establishing an interpretive theory of consumer behaviour and many of those who subscribe to the 'marketing is an art not a science' school would say that such an objective is illusory. There is substantial evidence in their favour.

Another point advanced in defence of the 'intuitive' school of management is that, given the dynamic rate of change of most markets, the time and expense incurred by the scientific method can hardly be justified. By the time we know the true facts, the market will have changed anyway, so why bother? We will return to this issue later in this chapter.

Despite these concerns, the prolific growth in the value of commissioned research in the UK, as instanced in the AMSO Annual Reports (see Figure 6.4) demonstrates the confidence which an increasing number of organizations place in the marketing research industry. To justify such confidence it is important that research is undertaken with thoroughness and care. In this respect it was claimed some time ago (Farbridge, 1982, p 47) that standards in Britain were 'higher than anywhere else in the world'. AMSO appears to indicate that these standards are being maintained for, in its 1997 Annual Report, it indicated that its member companies achieved a turnover of £84.1 million in 1996 for services performed for clients overseas. This was an increase of 16 per cent on the 1995 turnover, which itself was an increase of no less than 40 per cent on 1994. AMSO concluded that this reinforces the UK marketing research industry's fast-growing success as an international operator, strengthening its position as a centre for coordinating international research.

That said, it is important for anyone commissioning research and interpreting results that the data provided are as valid and objective as possible in accordance with the canons of scientific method. David Schwartz (1981, pp 57–8) reminds us that scientific method has four basic characteristics:

- *rationality* – in all stages of the research process rationality, not emotionalism, must be the keynote, with theories, hypotheses and proposed solutions to problems being rigorously tested;

- *objectivity* – the search for data must not be conditioned by the desire to keep prejudices warm or to substantiate pre-judgements but to discover the situation as it really is – which in turn implies a willingness to discover and face up to unpalatable findings, if necessary; bias must not affect either the design/conduct of the research or the interpretation of its results;

- *precision* – the research must be executed thoroughly, the acquisition of accurate data should be the aim and the results should be stated with clarity and exactitude;

- *honest interpretation* – this is an important characteristic of scientific method: it is often said that if four managers read the same research report they will interpret it in ways which support what they 'always believed' – even though this results in four different interpretations; the threat this poses for sound decision-making is self-evident.

Arnold Tableware: a 'research project'

Perhaps the best way to illustrate scientific method within a marketing research project is to outline its application to the problems of an imaginary company.

PCB Arnold Ltd. is a medium-sized, hitherto successful company, manufacturing ceramic tableware. Recently, its sales have declined with gathering momentum – so much so that management has decided to commission a research survey to discover why. It might be the price, the quality of the product, its packaging or distribution, competition from imports, a combination of all these factors, or a different reason entirely. Everyone has a pet 'theory', but no one is really sure.

The marketing research company awarded the contract conducted the project along the following lines:

1 Initially, at what can be termed the *observation stage* discussions took place with in-store purchasers, small groups of housewives and others found from previous data to be typical users of this grade of tableware.

2 This enabled the researchers, at the second stage, to formulate a hypothesis that the designs and colours currently available from Arnold were felt by many (and particularly the younger, first-time buyers) to be too traditional, making the tableware difficult to coordinate with contemporary tastes in furnishings and interior decor.

   The research organization then moved to establish a significant quantitative basis for this tentative hypothesis, in this case by the use of a questionnaire with a sample of users – a sample sufficiently large and representative to validly reflect the opinions of the total population of actual and potential users of such types of tableware (i.e. 'the market').

3 The survey confirmed the hypothesis to such an extent that the researchers felt safe in settling for it and in its report to Arnold cited the evidence for their view, both statistical and otherwise. At this third stage the researchers suggested that if the tableware range was redesigned along contemporary lines this would improve sales prospects, adding that there was no way of verifying the prediction other than in the market place.

4 Arnold and the agency agreed that the safest way commercially to test the prediction was to pilot-test a limited-quantity production of re-designed tableware. The agency indicated that two common ways of arranging the experiment were by

   – a limited area try-out (a 'test' market);
   – enlisting the cooperation of a 'key account'.

5 Arnold chose the second of these methods, selecting a distributor with a national network of retail outlets. Through computer analysis of its own sales and the use of mathematical modelling the distributor was able to forecast, from the sales of the trial range through selected branches:

– eventual sales through its national network for at least one year;

– a reasonably robust estimate of likely sales in at least one subsequent year.

The distributor had a sophisticated DSS and EDI links with a number of its leading suppliers. Arnold's judgement was that knowing the proportion of its existing sales taken up by this distributor would enable it to estimate what its own initial sales of the new range might be – certainly to a degree which would lift the venture from the plane of a gamble to one of legitimate business risk.

6   Arnold have gone ahead with the experiment, taking care not to alienate its other distributors, who might otherwise have reacted against the apparent 'preferential treatment' of one of their competitors, by explaining to them that the limited distribution trial was being undertaken for the purposes of marketing research, which would ultimately benefit all distributors. In this way, misunderstanding and ill-will were avoided.

The above outline of a research project, although necessarily simplified and abbreviated, illustrates the scientific approach to making marketing decisions, the method being based upon a sequence of steps, namely:

1   *observation* – to ascertain the facts of a situation in an objective way, leading to a clear definition of the problem;

2   *hypothesis formulation* – which at the first stage may be tentative and require verification, perhaps by quantitative examination of a larger and more representative sample of users, the data so acquired being rigorously tested for its validity;

3   the *prediction of some outcome* – based on this hypothesis, if certain action is taken ('if you re-design the tableware along contemporary lines, this will improve your chances of arresting the decline in sales');

4   the *testing of the hypothesis* – again, as rigorously as possible, in this case under conditions made to represent, as far as possible, the opportunities and pitfalls of full-scale marketing.

Clearly, the project just outlined is a great distance away from the precision of the physical sciences, where we can say that by adding type X acid to type Y solid we will generate type Z gas. However, we are also some distance away from a 'method' of approaching marketing problems guided only by prejudice and 'experience', which is notoriously fallible, especially in changing markets.

As a footnote, the author has used the selected distributor/EDI approach in testing markets for new products and has found it a low-cost, helpful aid to decision-making.

Typical purposes of marketing research

Other examples of the purposes for which marketing research is typically undertaken, in both the consumer and industrial goods fields, have been described earlier. Figure 6.6 depicts how the research process can be linked to decision-making:

● for elements of the strategic formula (including the people element);

● at the level of the organization itself.

Examples have also been given above of ways in which marketing research can be related to the more traditional elements of the strategic formula – the product or service, its price and so on. The questions listed on the 'marketing planning' side of Figure 6.6 give a further indication of some of the issues typically involved. However,

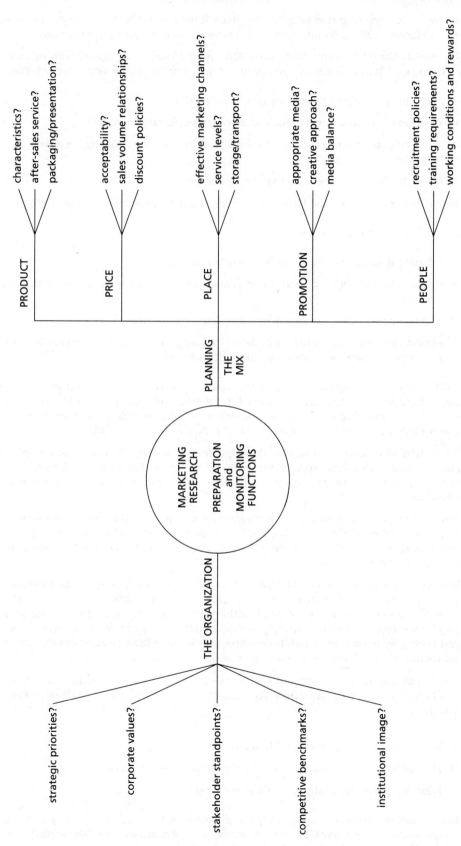

Figure 6.6. *Marketing research and some typical issues at the organizational and marketing planning levels.*

in this text, marketing research has not been linked so far with the *people* element, the key factor in all marketing activity. A few words here might be appropriate.

The British Market Research Bureau (BMRB International) is an agency with extensive experience in *human resource management research*. Its recruitment research can:

- help identify the best targets for recruitment effort;
- show how a profession is perceived among specific target groups;
- measure perceptions of individual firms within a sector, allowing comparisons to be made;
- highlight the key factors affecting career choice;
- identify and evaluate the favoured sources of information affecting career choice.

Its *staff retention research* can:

- evaluate staff attitudes from an independent standpoint;
- explore knowledge of, and identification with, management objectives and strategy;
- evaluate communication practices within an organization;
- identify and evaluate factors relating to job satisfaction, such as appraisals, career progression, training needs and working conditions.

BMRB International has carried out this type of research for a wide range of public and private sector clients and for the UK's Training and Enterprise Councils (TECs), signalling the growing and long overdue realization that people are the most valuable asset of any organization – a theme we shall return to in Chapter 12.

What then of research applied to the organization itself? The organization side of Figure 6.6 indicates some typical questions for which marketing research would be a useful way to find answers and, again, the idea might best be illustrated with practical examples.

Note, for instance, that an organization-level issue exemplified by Figure 6.6 is that of *corporate values*, defined in Chapter 3 as comprising the relatively few important beliefs and convictions crucial for an organization's success and a substantial driver of its personnel's behaviour.

Research International is another large and well-known marketing research organization in the UK. One of its divisions, RI Specialist Units Ltd., offers a Corporate Values Programme to clients. A typical study within the Programme would start with an in-depth investigation among carefully selected staff, conducted on a one-to-one basis and lasting up to one and a half hours. From these interviews researchers identify the values thought to characterize the organization.

The values are then incorporated into a self-completion questionnaire which is sent to all staff within the organization. For each of the identified values, staff are asked to assess:

- where the organization currently stands;
- at what level, ideally, they would like the organization to perform;
- how important each value is to them personally.

In this way, the research can identify the *priorities* staff place on different corporate values and also any *gaps* in the organization's performance on those very same values. Moreover, while the analyses can be aggregated over the staff as a whole, it is possible to look closely at the responses of particular groups of staff. Thus research can ensure that the corporate values statement is no mere cosmetic exercise 'mixing platitudes with good intentions' (a danger referred to in Chapter 3). Such a 'health audit' strengthens the glue that holds the different parts of the organization together and is particularly useful in introducing programmes, such as total quality management, designed to improve performance in the market place.

There would be little point in a firm advertising its products extensively and being resolute in providing good value, if the organization itself were to remain unknown in the public perception or were to be seen as 'colourless and ordinary' or worse, 'aloof and uncaring'. Moreover, and particularly in the services sector, the organization itself may logically be viewed as 'the offer'. This has given rise to *corporate marketing*, a process taken up enthusiastically by the retail trade. It has been reported (AMSO, 1997), in fact, that while total turnover among AMSO members grew by 11.6 per cent in 1996, there was a very large year on year increase (40 per cent) in research spending by retailers.

For this type of client, researchers are now being asked to provide data aimed to revamp all or part of the 'corporate package' from store design to product range, type and level of services and advertising.

Gordon Simmons Research has used attitudinal data, together with conjoint analysis (see Chapter 8) and demographics (Chapter 7) to develop customer profiles for clients and to identify how their stores are perceived.

Research International has developed its Locator model which aims to clarify the influence of image attributes on customer perceptions. Locator has been used by the Sears Group subsidiary, Adams Childrenswear, to reposition, in marketing terms, stores perceived to have 'lost their edge' in a market sector where discounting was taking hold.

It is hoped that these examples, together with Figure 6.6 and information earlier in the chapter, will help to indicate the value of marketing research and its increasing scope.

Types of data

The distinction between primary and secondary data having already been made, in this section we shall be looking at other classifications of data generated by the various processes of marketing research.

Internal and external data

Internal data are drawn from the organization's own records and typically include details of sales by products, sales by territories, sales per time period, sales trends over previous time periods, profitability of products, selling and administrative expenses per product, and data on cash flows, raw materials usage, production costs, human resource costs, etc. – all the data, in fact, held within the *internal records subsystem* of the MKIS described earlier in this chapter. When combined with and compared to *external data* (see below) it can be used to monitor progress to marketing/profit objectives and to make forecasts of future performance.

It is also worth re-stating that where the organization operates a system of networking, based on the personal computer, links between personnel and departments help to augment the system so as to make it even more productive: hitherto undisclosed data (e.g. on new production processes or reduced production costs) can often lead to marketing advantage.

External data are data other than internal data and can comprise:

- primary data – from a specific, specially commissioned research project;
- secondary data – from published sources;
- a combination of both.

To illustrate this last point, an analysis of secondary data on the volume, value and type of products being imported into an international market might suggest to an organization that opportunities exist there for its own output. It might accordingly decide to undertake a research survey among users in that country so as to obtain primary data on whether and how its products should be adapted for maximum acceptability there.

Ad hoc and continuous data

When specific research is commissioned on some particular aspect of marketing operations (Figure 6.6 gives some examples), it is described as *ad hoc* research and the data it generates are labelled *ad hoc* data. Such data are highly specific and self-contained. Each *ad hoc* research project calls for careful consideration of the research tools available, the way these might be deployed most productively, the time and finance available and the way in which results might be presented to the client. Such research accounts for a high proportion of total research expenditure.

Quite separate from such 'one-off' research, or often complementary to it, a client organization may require a stream of continuous data on product performance in the market place and how this relates to the performance of its competitors. Although a number of examples of continuous research will be found later, perhaps the best illustration at this point is provided by the dealer audit research of the A.C. Nielsen Corporation. With over 9000 clients Nielsen is a global leader in the marketing research field, operating in more than 90 countries.

The success of dealer audit research stems from the realization that sales from the factory and sales from the retailer do not keep pace with each other. At its worst, when sales to the user might be slowing down, the manufacturer might be undertaking more production. Consequently, it has long been recognized that the most reliable and comprehensive data on questions of market size, market trends, market share, product performance and the performance of competitors can best be found in the shop itself. Nielsen's Retail Index databases measure the market at point-of-sale and provide clients who are contracted to purchase the data with details of the success or failure of their own products, comparative data on competing products and data on current dealer and consumer sales promotions as well as on advertising, packaging and retail prices.

This continuous picture of the actual market place is provided by regular visits to shops from the Nielsen auditors. In essence, they check and record stock levels as well as noting prices, displays and other details important to clients. They also establish the actual sales made by the retailer since the last audit by the simple formula:

Retail sales (this period) = Stock at previous audit + purchases since

previous audit − stock at current audit

In addition to informing the manufacturers about the performance of their own products and of competing products, Nielsen is able to provide an up-to-date picture of new products which may be having a detrimental effect on the client's sales, the 'shelf availability' of the client's product(s), and the manner in which the total market for the particular product group is developing for different sizes of the product, in both different geographical areas and different types of outlet.

The development of electronic point-of-sale (EPOS) systems has been one of the key drivers of change in the retail trade, for it has not only revolutionized the management of the retail store but has also heralded a new era of information systems – the channel marketing information systems – which the supplier can 'tap' into to service his own needs for data retrieval.

The Nielsen organization has pioneered the development of EPOS sales data to create a database suited to the needs of today's intensely competitive grocery market. Its SCANTRACK service was the first UK continuous monitor of sales through scanning stores – providing speedy, actionable information across a wide range of product areas. See Figure 6.7 for an indication of the phenomenal growth of grocery scanning in the period 1985–95.

Such a precise analysis of weekly movements provides the marketing organization not only with a clear understanding of the sales performance of products but also with insights into the effects of advertising, sales promotions, pricing changes and competitive activity.

Nielsen offers a complete portfolio of sample and census-based information services across the food, health and beauty care, durables, confectionery and beverage industries covering all the key trade channels:

- supermarkets;
- independent food stores;
- convenience stores;
- petrol stations/forecourts;
- pharmacies and drug stores;
- liquor stores;
- confectioners and tobacconists.

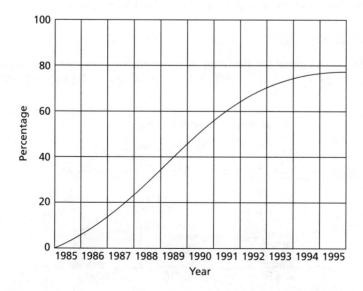

Figure 6.7. *Development of grocery scanning – percentage of grocery sales across scanners.*

Source: AC Nielsen

Its tracking services provide invaluable insights since they enable organizations to:

- track overall sales performance and the effectiveness of marketing and sales strategies;
- forecast future trends and meet production needs efficiently;
- understand the immediate impact of influential 'external' factors, e.g. major weather change;
- evaluate the effectiveness of tactical marketing and sales campaigns;
- evaluate the impact of new product launches and range extensions;
- speedily and effectively monitor short-term pricing activity;
- monitor the state and positioning of product(s) in store.

In addition to providing standardized data to contracted clients, this type of continuous research can be tailored to specific strategic needs and for any element of the marketing mix. Figure 6.8, reproduced by kind permission of A.C. Nielsen illustrates this point with regard to sales promotion strategy. The development of future strategy will be assisted by precise measurements of how different activities have worked in the past.

- Is a 10 per cent discount more effective than an extra free quantity of the product? ('extra fill').
- Does a discount for a multiple purchase (e.g. a 'threepack') appeal to consumers of this product? ('multibuy').
- How best should the offer be communicated in-store:
    - by product display only? ('unsupported')
    - by a promotional sticker at the edge of the display? ('shelf talker')
    - by a separate display at a high-visibility location in the store? ('secondary display')

As Figure 6.8 indicates, in this particular case, all promotional activities generated significant sales increases but communication of the offer is a critical factor – with secondary displays markedly enhancing consumer uptake.

Although this concludes our introduction to continuous data, a number of examples of this type of research provision will be found later in the book.

Quantitative and qualitative data

It is not difficult to grasp the meaning of *quantitative data*. Sometimes called 'hard data', they comprise all the research findings expressed in the form of numbers. For

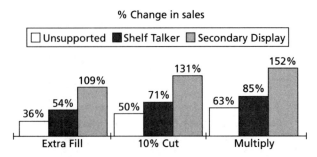

Figure 6.8. *Optimizing the sales promotion strategy* Source : AC Nielsen

example, the marketing manager of a national newspaper, having commissioned a survey on the readership of particular papers will obtain from it extensive quantitative data on the number of people reading these papers, their age, sex, occupations, neighbourhood types, ownership of consumer durables, foreign travel, the length of time they have been buying particular papers, the average time spent reading each issue, the manner in which they obtain their papers (collection, delivery) and so on. All of these data would probably be obtained by means of a *questionnaire*.

Prior to the use of this questionnaire, however, it is quite possible that some *discussion groups* were conducted among newspaper readers to explore their attitudes towards national newspapers. Also, to obtain clear expressions of such attitudes for use in the questionnaire, so as to discover whether such attitudes were generally held by readers – this is another illustration of the scientific method procedure: hypothesis formulation and a subsequent attempt at its verification. The expressions obtained from the readers are *qualitative data* and are often required as 'soft' data, but note that the word 'soft' is not to be thought of as denoting data of poorer quality and lesser value. On the contrary, in dynamic markets where projections from past numerical data become less useful in forecasting future demand, qualitative data become ever more valuable, hence the steadily widening quest for these forms of data in advanced economies.

While quantitative data depict *what people do*, qualitative data assist researchers to describe *why they do it*, through the exploration of the attitudes and motivations of informants. For its methodology, qualitative research draws on the techniques of applied behavioural science. These techniques typically include depth interviews, sentence completion tests, word association tests, attitude scaling techniques, role playing and, to a lesser extent, what are called 'psycho-physical' measures, for example galvanic skin response, eye blink rate measurement. The two main techniques used in qualitative research are *in-depth interviews* with individual informants and *group discussions* conducted by a moderator with about eight people. Variants of this include *paired interviews* in which, prompted by the moderator, two informants have a dialogue and *mini-groups* of three or four informants. Where it seems clear that the research areas are too complex to yield to the more straightforward techniques then the techniques of the behavioural science laboratory are more appropriate. As McPhee (1996, p XIII) points out, these might call for moderator/interviewer skills in neuro-linguistic programming, projective and enabling techniques, transactional analysis, role playing or psycho-drama.

According to the Gordon Simmons Research Group, applications of qualitative research include:

- generating ideas on new product development, packaging, design, product strategy, branding or image;
- in advertising, the examination of strategy and its implementation and the pre-testing of advertisements;
- exploration of the processes of purchase decisions;
- exploratory studies prior to quantitative research;
- depth studies subsequent to quantitative research.

In its objective of shedding light on to the impressions, expectations and prejudices of consumers, as Cobb (Cobb, 1996) observes, qualitative research may confirm a marketing organization's beliefs or confound them. Either way, it contributes to the quality of decision-making and may even stimulate the *lateral thinking*, which runs counter to vertical, or traditional logical thinking and can be used in a deliberate manner in order to achieve creativity. Here, de Bono's dictum (1990, p 2) that creativity is concerned not only with bringing about new ideas but also updating old ones is particularly pertinent when the markets for so many goods and services exhibit accelerating rates of change.

Although historically there were doubts and concerns among marketing practitioners about the value of qualitative research, mainly centred on the small samples typically involved and the fact that 'attitude' is not a synonym for 'behaviour', such research does now play a significant part in assisting decisions. Apart from its corporate contribution, qualitative data can help consumers derive greater satisfaction from products and services. Moreover since behaviour in the market place is an aspect of human behaviour neglected by social scientists in the past, this type of research can also assist them to develop more robust and rounded interpretive theories of how and why people behave as they do.

Methods of data collection

As we have noted, two basic types of data may be obtained from research surveys: primary (obtained from what is termed 'field research') and secondary (obtained from what is termed 'desk research').

Basically, there are three methods of collecting primary data:

- observation;
- experimentation;
- surveys, using questionnaires, administered by personal interview, by telephone or by post.

Secondary data may be collected:

- from within the organization (e.g. from reports and records);
- from external sources.

Since much has already been said about the collection of secondary data, in this section we shall consider some of the main ways in which primary data can be collected.

Observation may consist, for example, of monitoring the movement and behaviour of shoppers in a supermarket leading to suggestions on how its layout may be improved or how the package design of a product may be changed to increase its visibility and impact. The study of workers operating complex tools and equipment in order to discover whether there is a need for a new type of equipment or for modification of existing equipment is an example of the use of observation for product development. As we shall see later, observation may also be used with other methods of data collection, for example discussion groups. A distinct advantage of observation is that it is an *unobtrusive research measure*, that is since there is no interviewer participation, bias and behaviourism can be avoided and objectivity can be maximized.

As its name suggests *experimentation* borrows heavily from the scientific method concept. In a *controlled experiment*, for instance, let us say for the development of a new patent medicine, an experimental group, carefully selected on relevant and precise classifications, for example age, occupational grouping, medical history, etc. will be treated with the medicine for a given period. In addition, a control group will be assembled comprising an identical number of people of exactly the same classifications. Over the same period, the condition of their health will be monitored, although in their case they may be given no medicine at all, or the medicine that is most closely competitive to the one being administered to the experimental group.

In addition, such external influential factors as climatic conditions, type of residential location, etc. will be matched carefully for both groups. In this way the effectiveness of the proposed new product can be assessed objectively.

Test marketing is one of the main methods of experimentation used in commercial operations. Prior to full-scale marketing of a proposed new product, for example, the product may be given a limited area try-out. The geographical area chosen will bear a very high degree of similarity to the full-scale market in terms of such factors as economic prosperity, population profile, urban/rural balance, retail distribution network, media availability, etc. Experiments may also be conducted to test the effect on sales of some change in marketing tactics, for example in methods of sales promotion, special offers, credit facilities, etc. Here again, in the best traditions of scientific method, great care must be taken that the experimental area and the marketing effort within it are matched as closely as possible with the 'control' area (where no tactical change is taking place) and the scale of *its* marketing effort. At all times, the quest must be for objectivity in the cause of accurate assessment.

The use of *questionnaires* is widespread – in fact, for most people, the term 'marketing research' conjures up the image of an interviewer with a clipboard, on a street or in a shopping centre, taking an informant through a questionnaire form. It should be noted here that the recent rapid extension of CAPI – Computer Assisted Personal Interviewing – is making pen, paper and the clipboard outdated. More will be said on the technology of research later in the chapter.

In addition to personal interviewing, the use of questionnaires enables research to be conducted by mail and by telephone. Although there are drawbacks to postal surveys, particularly low response and the possible unrepresentativeness of that response when compared with the general profile of the total market, there seems to be no reduction in its popularity as a method of data collection. All of us are now increasingly used to receiving postal questionnaires – from banks, travel companies, car manufacturers, the privatized utilities, etc. – all seeking responses on various aspects of their products, services or general customer care. To curb low response rates, small gifts or competition entries are frequently offered to induce completion and return of the questionnaires. Quite high response rates have been recorded when the subject of the survey is of special interest to respondents, for example the improvement of manufacturing performance, crop yields, or labour saving in the garden.

Questionnaire design calls for much knowledge and skill. To be an efficient research tool, Morton-Williams (1986, p 114) suggests that a questionnaire should fulfil six functions:

- the maintenance of the informant's cooperation and involvement;
- effective communication to the informant;
- assisting the informant to work out his or her answers;
- the avoidance of bias (i.e. error or inaccuracy), which can arise from a variety of causes unless the research is of the necessary high quality;
- making the interviewer's task easy;
- providing a basis for data processing.

Maintaining the informant's cooperation is more probable if the questionnaire is easy to complete and does not require the informant to perform arduous mental tasks or prodigious feats of memory. Completion is easier when most questions can be answered with a simple 'tick in a box' response.

Usually, three types of question are employed:

1 *dichotomous* (literally, 'cut in two')

Yes	
No	

2 *multiple choice*, e.g. 'On those days when you are pressed for time, which parts of your newspaper do you read? (Just tick a box, please)'

Headlines

Front page

Sports page

Editorial comment/leader

Readers' opinions/letters

Business/finance section

etc.

3 *open-ended* – these are frequently the 'why' questions. They force the informant to think and to take a stand. Although they are often the most difficult for coding and analysis of answers, they usually produce data of much richness and variety. Often, they follow on from an earlier response, for example the respondent may have indicated that he or she does not think Brand X is good value for money. The interviewer then asks 'why?' and a significant amount of space is left on the questionnaire form for the answer:

Why? _____

_____

_____

_____

Before the questionnaire is used for full-scale research it is invariably pilot-tested on a small group of respondents which is carefully matched with the profile of the target-group for full-scale research. This will help to ensure that the questionnaire will elicit relevant answers and is free from ambiguity, unfamiliar words, difficult and abstract concepts and does not overload the respondent's memory with too many instructions.

In the remainder of this section we shall be looking at some of the other main procedures by which research data can be collected.

Group discussions

These are frequently used in qualitative research, as we have already seen, and in Chapter 8 we shall return to them in the context of *concept testing* and *product testing*. Their use in exploratory studies prior to quantitative research has also been noted and here, an illustration is their use in obtaining the 'item pool' from which questions can be constructed for the questionnaire to be used in a fieldwork survey. This is again in line with the precepts of scientific method in that the marketer and even the researcher may believe they know what the underlying issues are for the situation they are to research. As a result of the group discussion, they discover, quite often, that the *real* issues are somewhat different.

In such a situation, the group discussion enables researchers to explore the origins and complexities of the attitude areas in question – perhaps towards a product or an advertising campaign – in order to decide precisely what it is they wish to measure. Also, the discussion may enable them to obtain clear expressions of such attitudes in a form appropriate for use as statements in attitude or rating scales within a questionnaire.

With regard to qualitative research, Chisnall (1986, p 148) makes the additional point that the group discussion is very useful for people who find the fact-to-face interview difficult. He indicates that in the group, influenced by the psychological atmosphere generated, such people seem to become much more frank and talkative. In fact, the way in which people react to each other in the group and influence each other's attitudes may often be of great significance for the research.

To safeguard the quality of the research it is important that the researcher leading the group should be skilled and experienced in this type of work, encouraging discussion but not letting this stray from the objectives of the research and being especially careful not to impose his or her own views. Objective observation of the group and video/audio recording of the discussion are important for subsequent analysis.

Group discussions might take place in hotel rooms or even in the living room of the moderator if a homely atmosphere is thought to add value to the process. Cobb (1996, p xiv) reports that there has been an increase in the number of purpose-built suites which, though more expensive to hire, include such facilities as video recorders and one-way mirrors, behind which the client sponsoring the research can observe the discussion.

As Cobb points out, whether a client should observe discussions and whether the participants should be told when this is happening is under debate in the UK since it is an ethic of professional research that individual respondents will not be identified. The issue is whether this rule is being skirted when clients observe the proceedings. The general practice is that groups are told there is a one-way mirror or video, but the identity of viewers is not disclosed as this might affect the discussion. The client is not told the names of the participants and does not have access to their recruitment questionnaires. Where a video recording is involved, the research agency will either arrange for a restricted viewing or require undertakings to limit its use.

It is easy to visualize the use of group discussions in consumer research, for example an enquiry into shopping habits, but their value in industrial marketing should also be noted. Pointing out that British Oxygen use the group discussion method to get a better understanding of markets, to solve problems and to stimulate action from managers, Chisnall (1989, p 126) adds that in technical markets a group discussion among engineers, for example, can bring out areas of interest which the sponsor of the research did not even know existed. Such a discussion among production managers may well generate ideas for the modification and development of, perhaps even the introduction of, new capital equipment.

As was indicated above, the group usually consists of a few people. Whilst broadly representative of the market in question, the level of accuracy typically found in sampling procedures for large-scale quantitative fieldwork is not necessary. Because the discussion invariably *focuses* on some particular research objective, or issue, the group is often termed a *focus group*.

Consumer panels

A key method of obtaining continuous research data is by means of the *panel*. For example, the retail stores providing the basic data for the A.C. Nielsen services described earlier constitute, in marketing research terms, a panel.

However it is among consumers that the panel procedure has its most extensive applications. Groups of consumers, carefully selected to represent some particular market and continuously monitored on such aspects as purchase behaviour and product usage are described as *consumer panels*. These panels are available to measure consumer behaviour in a variety of fields, including:

- the purchase of household products;
- television viewing;
- radio listening;
- the preparation and consumption of food and drink in the home.

Among communications media organizations, the British Broadcasting Corporation (BBC) has always been at the forefront in its use of panel data to assess the appeal of its current programme schedules and to develop future programme schedules.

Superpanel, launched by Taylor Nelson AGB in January 1991 is the most comprehensive continuous consumer panel available within Great Britain. It consists of a panel of 10,000 households (out of a total population of 22.5 million households) and collects detailed information on products purchased, prices paid and special offer details as well as identifying the retail outlet where the product was purchased and the person making the purchase.

The households are selected to represent the profile of the population as a whole on such key classifications as telephone ownership (a must), ITV region, household size, socio-economic status, age of housewife, employment status of housewife, and presence of children.

All household members, including children, record details of their purchases and the individual stores visited, by scanning on-pack bar-codes using a specially designed, computerized scanner together with a code-book. For non bar-coded fresh food products, the special code-book has pre-printed bar-codes to ensure the collection of the necessary product details. The scanning equipment in each household is kept in a modem directly linked to the power supply and a telephone socket. The reporting week runs from Monday to Sunday and the speed at which results can be reported back to client organizations is indicated by the fact that data capture from households is by overnight polling.

Some idea of the scope and value of the panel method of collecting data can be gauged from the other types of panel operated by Taylor Nelson AGB. These include:

- *The Family Food Panel* – the largest database on food and drink consumption habits and practices in the UK (11,000 households).
- *The European Toiletries and Cosmetics Database* – which makes possible comparison of the consumption of cosmetics and toiletries in Britain, France, Germany, Italy and Spain (an international panel of 7000 consumers).
- *The Personal Care Panel* – which tracks the consumption of cosmetics, toiletries and feminine hygiene products in the UK and provides a source of behavioural data for evaluating and developing new product opportunities.
- *The Eating Out of Home Monitor* – a continuous measurement of the eating out market based on a random sample of 70,000 face-to-face interviews per annum.

- *Specialist Panels* – which are large tailor-made panel projects established to answer specific client problems and conducted for periods ranging from 6 to 18 months.

Till-roll analysis is a method of collecting continuous data linked somewhat to the consumer panel concept. Its use in framing distribution channel policy will be outlined in Chapter 10.

Omnibus surveys

Although large and complex projects do feature in marketing research activity, they are by no means the exclusive preserve of organizations with substantial budgets. A great deal of research has to take place within tight timetables and restricted budgets. In this context, price competitive data collection methods such as omnibus surveys and by telephone research are popular.

A single omnibus survey can be used to obtain data on a wide variety of products and services on behalf of a large number of client organizations. Charges are made by the research agency on the basis of 'question units' (e.g. one question with six possible pre-coded answers) with discounts available to clients who require only a minority sample of the survey's total informants being interviewed (and here it will be appreciated that even a large organization may occasionally wish to investigate only a single issue with a few people).

The omnibus services provided by the British Market Research Bureau (BMRB) provide good examples of this method of data collection. The Bureau's ACCESS Face to Face omnibus consists of 2000 interviews per week with a nationally representative sample of adults (aged 15 years or over) across Great Britain. Its ACCESS to Youth omnibus provides 1000 interviews with 7–19 year olds every month and its ACCESS by Telephone omnibus conducts 1000 interviews per weekend.

The ACCESS Face to Face and the ACCESS to Youth services consist of home interviews conducted by a Computer Assisted Personal Interviewing (CAPI) system. Interviewers use portable laptop computers for recording information. Both services employ a type of random location sampling to ensure that every household has an equal chance of selection. The ACCESS by Telephone omnibus, which uses a form of random digit dialling to select its sample, employs a Computer Assisted Telephone Interviewing (CATI) system for data collection and all interviews are conducted from the BMRB's central location telephone unit.

The need for speedy retrieval of information, given the dynamic nature of markets, has been indicated earlier in this text. It is worth mentioning therefore that the electronic data capture utilized by the BMRB enables results to be made available the day after fieldwork ends.

An interesting development in omnibus provision is the Business Line service of Taylor Nelson AGB. This is a small business sector omnibus and it surveys 2000 'small businesses' (i.e. firms with less than 50 employees) each quarter. The small businesses in the UK and other developed countries are often described as the 'engine room' of future economic prosperity. They are certainly a most important target sector for suppliers of industrial goods and services.

Taylor Nelson AGB considers that its Business Line service can assist the suppliers in many critical decisions including:

- reactions to new products and services;
- tracking the effects of advertising and promotional campaigns;
- determining the size and potential of the small business market for a specific product or service;

- pinpointing the current perception of the supplier and his output;

- analysing how competitive products and services are used and regarded.

Selection of an appropriate 'omnibus' can yield important information at a fraction of the cost of a tailor-made research project, particularly where the answers to one or a few questions are sufficient for decision-making.

Hall tests

Quite often, a consumer walking along a street or through a shopping centre will be asked a few preliminary questions by a market research interviewer and then asked if he or she can spare a few minutes in a nearby hall or some other central location – hence the name 'hall tests'. Assuming agreement, the respondent either individually, or in a group, is then taken through a more intensive research process. The testing of new products, or concepts for products, feature prominently in this type of survey work and it may also be used for the pre-testing and impact testing of advertisements (see Chapter 11). Moreover, hall tests are a good preliminary method of assessing how an organization and its products are regarded *vis-à-vis* the competition.

The questions asked outside the hall are to establish whether or not the person approached would be an appropriate respondent for the subject under test. Where expensive equipment is being assembled in the hall (e.g. electronic equipment for hands-on testing or demonstration), respondents are frequently pre-recruited by telephone.

The hall-test is a very good method of formulating a hypothesis – that the idea for a new product has apparent validity perhaps – for subsequent quantification in a large-scale survey.

Mystery shopping

In this method of data collection, the research fieldworker, called an *evaluator*, assumes the guise of an ordinary shopper and reports back to the client on the topic being investigated. Imagine, for example, that a car manufacturer wishes to assess the standards within his dealerships. The answers to the following questions would be helpful:

- was the showroom clean and well-kept?

- was there an adequate range of vehicles on display with sufficient supporting literature?

- was the salesman friendly, courteous and knowledgeable?

- were all questions answered satisfactorily?

- were financial documents produced and adequately explained?

- was the whole experience satisfactory?

Similarly, a retail organization with a national network of outlets might commission a mystery shopping survey to evaluate store layout, customer care, checkout speeds, etc. at an appropriate sample of its branches.

There are, of course, certain checks and balances to be employed in this type of research. Is it, for instance, wholly ethical to take up too much time of a salesman who is paid on a commission only basis? Also, there is the view that, without disclosing too many details, the staff concerned should be told of any proposed mystery shopping survey. Against this, one could ask whether in that case one was measuring what one purported to measure or a set of conditions not typical of ordinary standards and practice. It is notable that, in this regard, the UK's Market

Research Society published in March 1997 a set of guidelines for clients and agencies utilizing mystery shopping methods.

This concludes our outline of the main methods of data collection, though it should be noted that the objective of this type of introductory text precludes a detailed description of the techniques of applied behavioural science and the psycho-physical measures typically employed in what are classified as 'depth interviews'.

Table 6.2 gives an indication of the comparative importance of the various methods of data collection, based on an analysis of the 1996 turnover of members of AMSO.

The design and implementation of research

As Chisnall (1986, p 23) indicates, whether research is being conducted in the consumer, industrial or public service fields, five logical steps can be identified in the process of organizing a research project:

- the *research brief* – in which the problem is defined;
- the *research proposal* – which includes the methods to be adopted and an estimate of the time and costs involved;
- *data collection* – the heart of the survey in which the research plan is put into operation;
- *data analysis and evaluation* – in which the data collected have to be processed, analysed and interpreted;
- the *research report* – in which the findings of the research have to be prepared and presented.

In addition, in order to select the most appropriate organization to conduct the research, on which more later, the client's part in securing the high quality and value of the research entails obligations for adequately briefing the agency and subsequently an objective evaluation and, hopefully, implementation of the research findings. Figure 6.9 is an attempt to depict the total process and in this section we shall briefly review each of the stages in that process but with particular emphasis on the responsibilities of the client.

Method	Value (%)
Personal interview	43.1
Telephone interview	18.3
Hall test	11.2
Group discussion	9.9
Self completion/Post	8.0
Depth interviews	4.0
Street interviews	2.6
Mystery shopping	2.2

Table 6.2. Interviewing methods by value

Source: Annual Report 1997, AMSO

Figure 6.9. *The design and implementation of the research process*

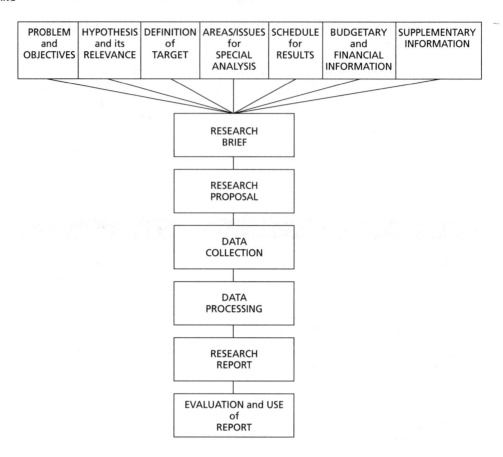

The research brief

Figure 6.9 indicates the key elements of the brief. In introducing the reasons for the project the client must be clear about why it should be conducted. Defining the problem and outlining research objectives is not always easy. Sometimes exploratory research will have pointed the way but, more often, what is called for is an honest *situation analysis* of the firm, its strategy, performance and aspirations.

Reviewing market image, market share, etc. should lead to the statement of some hypothesis, for example that a new product or a new market might be successful, that a change in pricing or 'channel' policy might improve revenues and profitability. Again, prior small-scale research may have pointed the way.

In so far as the client is able, the market should be clearly defined, for example in terms of types and size of client companies, consumer classifications or geographical area: the 'domestic market' might mean the north-west of England to the client and the European Union to the agency. Precision is essential and the agency will help if necessary.

Areas or issues for special analysis should be highlighted – the client may need to know, for instance, whether its poor image or its dealerships, rather than its products, might be constraining sales.

The schedule for publication of the results should be realistic. Today the emphasis is understandably on speed and technology. This is making faster results possible but impatience can impair quality.

The budgetary or financial provision being made for the project should be stated at the outset and finally, any supplementary information on the client's history, strategic objectives, organization structure, size, type, numbers employed, products and services will assist the agency in its assessment of what the research should set out to accomplish.

Two extracts from Market Research Society (MRS, n.d.) guidelines on briefing a research agency are worth adding here:

> Whether approaching a number of consultancies on a competitive basis or briefing your chosen company, the quality of your initial instructions can make all the difference between a successful project or a wasted exercise, . . . A short brief reflects a lack of knowledge in undertaking research by the commissioning company and is often a tell-tale sign that not enough discussion has taken place internally as to what it is meant to achieve.

The research proposal

With an adequate briefing and a clear statement of the timing and finance factors, the agency can now plan the research design. The project may entail a study of secondary data only, a study of primary data or a combination of both. Whether the data should be gathered on an *ad hoc* or continuous basis, or again whether there is a place for data of both types will also be specified. With regard to continuous or secondary data, the agency will indicate whether it is within its own scope to supply this or whether a syndicated research service from a third party agency (e.g. Mintel, Nielsen, as described earlier) should be utilized.

As noted above, the collection of primary data will be by way of observation or experimental studies or by survey methods. Note once more, however, that these methods are not mutually exclusive. With respect to surveys, an early decision has to be made on the number and types of individuals or organizations to be interviewed. Where the population under investigation is small it might be possible, within the budget available, to interview all its members i.e. to conduct a *census* of that population. For example a manufacturer of filtration equipment for the ceramic industry, wishing to know the sales potential of a newly developed process in the UK market might be able to conduct a census of users since there are relatively few factories producing ceramics in the UK. A survey among distributors may similarly be carried out by census. But even in the industrial field, a census survey may be impractical. A manufacturer of compressors attempting to survey all actual and potential users in the UK would find the costs and time involved formidable. As a general rule, therefore, whenever a marketing organization wishes to learn something about a large group – termed a 'population' or 'universe' – all actual and potential users of compressors, all soccer fans, all UK housewives, etc., it will look carefully at a small part of it, a *sample*. The process of sampling is now briefly described.

The sampling process

As just noted, for most products and markets, conducting a census is impracticable because of the costs involved. These would be far in excess of the value to the marketer of doing so. Delay occasioned by the time it would take is also important given the speed of change in most product/markets. Moreover, the information gained from a representative group of the 'population' under study, a sample, can be obtained more quickly and economically. It can also be highly reliable as the survey can be conducted more thoroughly than if the available resources were used to conduct a census.

However, we have to bear in mind that any measurement based upon a sample can never be totally accurate – it can only provide an *estimate*, which may be more or less close to the true situation in the 'population' but is unlikely to be strictly precise. To understand why this is so, we must think a little about the issue of *error* in research surveys.

The types of error to which survey work gives rise can be classified, for simplicity, as *sampling* and *non-sampling error*. The second of these relates to flaws in the operation of the research process itself which cause any results to be unrepresentative of the population under study. Here are some ways non-sampling error may occur:

- there may be non-response from some sections of the sample;
- the fieldworkers conducting the survey may take insufficient care in questioning the respondents, or they may bias the results by the way in which the questions are put or the answers are recorded;
- the questions on the survey prompt list or questionnaire may be ambiguous and may thus lead to inaccurate answers.

Non-sampling error can be avoided or minimized by careful selection of the organization conducting the research and by adequate supervision of the total research process.

Sampling error is itself of two types: *administrative error* and *random error*. Administrative error results from flaws in the design and development of the sample itself which cause it to be unrepresentative of the population under study. Again, this error can be avoided or minimized by strict supervision of population definition and design of the sampling process. Random sampling error is endemic to the sampling process itself and is due to chance and cannot be avoided. It derives from the fact that every time we sample we lose something. No sample is likely to be exactly representative of the population from which it is drawn and no two samples, independently drawn from the same population, can be expected to be exactly alike. The likely error of this type in a sample estimate is given the special name *standard error* (it is the standard error of the estimate). It can be reduced by increasing the sample size i.e. the larger the sample we devise and use, the smaller will be the standard error, but to halve the standard error we would need to increase the sample to four times its original size (since the standard error varies inversely with the square root of the sample size).

In this last respect, the question of costs:benefits or, more precisely, costs:increments in accuracy is an important factor in marketing research and exercises the minds of sponsors and researchers in ways we shall discuss towards the end of the chapter. A further important point is that for *probability samples* (described below) the standard error of the estimate can be calculated and allowed for in subsequent decision-making (see the Appendix to this chapter).

Types of sample

In selecting the sampling approach to be adopted there is a choice between *probability* and *non-probability* samples.

The *simple random sample* is regarded as a probability sample in its purest form. In this type of sample every element of the population under investigation has a known and equal chance, or probability of being selected into the sample. The valid theoretical basis of probability sampling makes possible the use of the mathematics of probability, for example for the calculation of the standard error referred to earlier.

Random sampling necessitates access to a comprehensive and up-to-date listing of the population involved for the *sampling frame* from which the actual sample is drawn. This is by no means easy. In consumer research, the Electoral Register might be used for the sampling frame but it becomes out of date from the day of every revised compilation. Membership lists of professional bodies, clubs and societies are perhaps less perishable in this regard, but the danger is still there.

Each member of the sample is selected by the application of random numbers to the sampling frame, using either a computer or a table of random numbers. Of course, the very randomness of the selection method means that the chosen respondents in a simple random sample may be geographically scattered, entailing perhaps a number of 'calls-back' before the respondent is finally available for face-to-face interview. The fact that the quantitative validity of the estimates made possible by this method increases the confidence with which survey results can be accepted has to be set against its costs, of course.

In this context, two points are noteworthy. First, where the survey can be conducted by telephone, simple random sampling has been used successfully through the use of *random digit dialling*. Secondly, *systematic sampling* produces samples that are virtually identical to those derived from simple random procedures. The advantage here is that it is 'often simpler, less time consuming and less expensive to use' (McDaniel and Gates, 1993, p 479) and, of course, the standard error can be calculated as previously.

A complete and up-to-date listing is again required for the sampling frame but here members of the sample are chosen by the equal (or 'skip') interval method. This interval is calculated by dividing the number of required respondents into the total number of elements in the sampling frame. Where, for example, it is proposed to interview 2000 members of a professional body containing 30,000 current members, each 15th member would be selected, since 30,000/2000 = 15.

The *quota sample* provides a good example of the non-probability approach to sampling. Whereas in the random sample, the interviewer is given the details of the prospective interviewees, with the quota sample the interviewer is provided with a checklist of interviewee characteristics and instructed to interview a specified number of people with those characteristics (in industrial marketing research, the characteristics would generally relate to organizations rather than individuals). Proportions for filling the quota will be laid down for the sample structure. These will reflect the relevant proportions in the population as a whole or the proportions known from previous data to be significant for the product or market under survey.

An example may make this last point clearer and yet again we will return to our hypothetical example of PCB Arnold Ltd. and their tableware problem. A quota sample is to be used and let us say that Arnold, or their research specialists, know that the purchase of this class of tableware is markedly correlated with socio-economic status ('social grade') and with age. Moreover, they know that very young homemakers do not figure prominently in this market nor do those of lower social status and that females have a decisive influence on the purchase decision. So an analysis of current data may thus lead to each individual interviewer being asked to interview 100 women in accordance with the following classifications:

Age group	Social grade	Numbers		
15–24	ABC_1	10	15	
	C_2DE	5		
25–44	ABC_1	25	45	100
	C_2DE	20		
45–65+	ABC_1	25	40	
	C_2DE	15		

The advantages of this method of sampling are that surveys can be conducted more quickly and economically than with random sampling and there are no costly 'calls-back'. Also, it is possible to use the method when a suitable frame for a random sample does not exist. Against this, since the selection of respondents is left to the interviewer the method is open to bias in that the more enthusiastic and articulate may be favoured for selection leaving the final quota of interviews slanted in favour of this sub-population, with certain other key groups under-represented. Again however, it is a danger which can be overcome by adequate investigator briefing and supervision. However, with non-probability sampling it is not theoretically admissible, strictly speaking, to estimate the standard error (in accordance with the approach outlined in the Appendix to this chapter). However, as Collins (1986, p 103) points out, while virtually all academic and public sector surveys, and many large commercial surveys, use random or probability sampling methods, the majority of commercial surveys do not, instead they use quota sampling.

'What price scientific method?' might be the response here but the following points are important:

- experience tends to demonstrate that the greater sources of opportunity for error occur more at the interviewer stage, or through ambiguous questions, or in faulty processing of data, than in sampling error – therefore, the advantages of quota sampling often outweigh the disadvantages;

- since, as has been said, most marketing research work deals in broad trends, aggregates, averages, etc. a high level of statistical accuracy is not usually the objective.

Based on his extensive experience of survey work, Collins suggests that the standard error of a typical quota sample estimate may well be about one and a half times as large as that of a multi-stage random sample estimate, using the same sample size – higher if the quota controls are not rigorous, lower if they are. This is a margin most marketing research activity can accommodate.

The subject of sampling has been treated at some length in this section because it is at the root of many facets of marketing research. Even so, only the barest outline has been provided and a deeper knowledge can be gained from reading any of the specialized texts now so widely available.

Before leaving this topic three further points are worthy of note:

- Quota sampling is sometimes alternatively described as *stratified sampling*, in that the sample is built up in strata (e.g. men/women) which are known from previous experience to be fundamentally important to the sample design.

- *Stratified random samples* are used quite frequently in marketing research and here, having divided the total sample into its appropriate strata, respondents within each of these sub-samples are then chosen at random. Stratified, rather than simple random samples are used because of their potential for greater statistical efficiency (smaller sampling error).

- Recourse is often made to *weighting* certain sub-groups of a sample so that the number of interviews is increased in these sub-groups in accordance with particular survey objectives.

Concluding comments

Marketing research is no panacea. It will not guarantee success. It is a well-established tool to assist managerial decisions for it has been demonstrated that better decisions are made with marketing research in support. The growth in commissioned research in the UK and across the world is testimony to this claim.

The balance between costs and an adequate level of accuracy calls for fine judgement. The choice of agency is an important factor here. The Organisations Book published by the Market Research Society (UK) and the appropriate international research directories are of immense help in making a sound preliminary assessment. They also provide compelling evidence of the extent of the sophisticated resources engaged in research operations.

The second important factor is that of research design. As with the overall marketing information system itself, so with marketing research – the method that will 'just do' has much to commend it, never forgetting that speed of data retrieval gains steadily in importance.

In stating that the net value to be realized from any research project is the marginal increase in the expected value of the decision less the cost of the research, Jolson (1978, p 220) adds that it can be expressed mathematically as follows:

$$V_o = (V_r - V_{\bar{r}}) - C_r$$

where V_o = the net value of the research project;

V_r = the expected value of the marketing decision when made with the aid of research;

$V_{\bar{r}}$ = the expected value of the marketing decision when made either without the benefit of research or with the benefit of secondary data only;

C_r = the cost of research.

Although the formula assumes that V_r and $V_{\bar{r}}$ can be quantified, usually in money terms, Jolson's formula is included here since it expresses the issue of costs versus benefits much more eloquently than words or phrases. When the student-reader of this text becomes a practitioner he will understand fully why the issue is so significant.

In the chapters which now follow, the application of research techniques for identifying and understanding the customer, for the development of the marketing mix and for determining the potential of international markets will be described.

Finally, the Appendix to this chapter is an attempt to describe, in the simplest terms, some of the quantitative method that relates to sampling activity. Technical terminology has either been either replaced or explained, as far as this is possible. Understanding the Appendix content calls for little more than the ability to add, subtract and divide numbers and to appreciate that the square root of a number, n ($\sqrt{n}$) is the value which, when multiplied by itself results in the original number, n: thus $\sqrt{4} = 2$ for $2 \times 2 = 4$.

Appendix: *Some quantitative concepts relating to sampling theory*

It is difficult, perhaps, to appreciate that the likely behaviour of thousands of people can be estimated from small samples of a few hundred or so of those people. Yet by making use of some concepts of what is known as *classical statistical inference*, such behaviour can, in fact, be estimated. In this Appendix, some of these concepts and their relation to sampling theory are outlined. A deeper treatment of them and their underlying theory can be found in a number of works on the subject – see in particular Hague and Harris, 1993; Ehrenberg, 1991; Webb, 1992; and Worcester and Downham, 1986.

Measures of central tendency

One way in which the marketer can grasp the significance of the huge amount of data typically available, even by sampling, is to calculate some single number typical of all the values involved. In everyday language, these single numbers, or *measures of central tendency* are called *averages*.

One such average is known as the *arithmetic mean*. Supposing we asked five people to estimate how many hours per week they spent watching television, and if we obtained the following answers:

$$3 \qquad 10 \qquad 16 \qquad 20 \qquad 31$$

we can calculate the arithmetic mean quite easily, by adding these values and dividing the result by the number of values, thus

$$\begin{array}{l} \text{arithmetic mean} = \dfrac{80}{5} = 16 \text{ hours.} \\ \text{(TV viewing)} \end{array}$$

In statistical notation, the arithmetic mean is referred to as 'x bar' and is represented as $\bar{x}$. Therefore,

$$\bar{x} = \frac{\sum x}{n}$$

where $\sum$ is the sum of all the values of x ($x_1, x_2, x_3, x_4,$ etc.) and n is the number of values.

The disadvantage of the arithmetic mean is that it is very much affected by extreme values. Thus, the mean value for the five TV viewers is 16 hours per week but their estimated viewing times range from as little as 3 hours to as much as 31 hours. So the arithmetic mean gives a distorted picture of reality. To overcome the distortion, two other types of measure are helpful. The *median*, is at the middle of a set of values when all the values are arranged in order of magnitude. Therefore, one half of this range of numbers will be larger and the other half will be smaller than the median.

The median value is calculated by the formula $(n + 1)/2$ where n is the total number of values. Of course n might be an even number and so there would appear to be no 'middle' value, but the formula resolves this for us. So, if numbers for the weekly beer consumption (pints) of eight men are arranged as follows:

$$2 \qquad 5 \qquad 6 \qquad 9 \qquad 10 \qquad 12 \qquad 15 \qquad 18$$

the median is the $(n + 1)/2$th measurement i.e. $9/2 = 4.5$th measurement

or the mid point between the 4th and 5th values = 9.5 pints.

The *mode* is also a measure which helps to insulate calculations from extreme and untypical values. It is the measure which occurs most often in a range of values. Imagine 50 students are asked to record the number of visits per month to the computer suite in their Department. Their recorded results are then grouped into a frequency distribution as follows:

	No. of visits	No. of students
	6	2
	10	7
	12	12
mode	16 ←——→	18
	20	6
	24	5

The *modal value* in this distribution is 16 visits since this is the one which occurs most often (18 students recording it).

The standard deviation

Although such *measures of central tendency* are of some help to marketers and researchers when a mass of data is being scrutinized, their help is rather limited. For instance, an average might tell them where most of the numbers are bunched but nothing about the clustering or the dispersion of those numbers around their average value.

Fortunately, it is possible to calculate a single value to indicate the dispersion of a set of values around their average. The most important *measure of variability* used in marketing research is the *standard deviation*, which provides a measurement of how closely individual numbers are grouped around their arithmetic mean.

The standard deviation is calculated by the following formula:

$$\text{Standard deviation} = \sqrt{\frac{\sum (x - \bar{x})^2}{n}}$$

where x = the value of each measurement;

$\bar{x}$ = the mean value of all measurements;

$\sum$ = the summation mark;

n = the total number of measurements.

Again, let us look at a simple illustration. Imagine that in a group discussion ten women are asked how many times per month they purchase ready-made meals from retail outlets. Their individual estimates are shown below (heading x). The standard deviation is then calculated from these figures.

x (ready made meals)	$x - \bar{x}$	$(x - \bar{x})^2$
8	+3 (8 − 5)	9
6	+1 etc.	1
3	−2	4
7	+2	4
2	−3	9
8	+3	9
1	−4	16
4	−1	1
6	+1	1
5	0	0

$\sum x$ $\underline{50} \therefore \bar{x} = \dfrac{50}{10} = 5.$ $\underline{54} = \sum (x - \bar{x})^2$

(n.b. obviously the minus signs disappear when the numbers are squared.)

$$\text{Standard deviation} = \sqrt{\frac{54}{10}} = \sqrt{5.4} = 2.32.$$

So this figure (2.32) gives us a measure of how closely these figures of product purchase are clustered around the mean measurement(s) – the more concentrated the cluster, the smaller is the standard deviation and the more dispersed about the mean, the larger the standard deviation.

Another important point to note is that in marketing research the standard deviation has an important function in relation to estimates resulting from the sampling process – more of this later.

Binomial distribution and the standard error

We discussed earlier the use of dichotomous questions in survey work. Much research is taken up with allocating the answers of respondents into one of two categories, for example buyer/non-buyer of a product or service. Data of this type are said to follow a *binomial distribution* (consisting, that is, of two classes – the event and its non-occurrence).

In sampling activity, the standard deviation is termed the *standard error* and this error is fundamentally important for assessing the precision of an arithmetic mean resulting from a sample. It is calculated by dividing the square root of the sample size into the standard deviation, as in the following sample:

400 UK motorists report their weekly purchases of petrol and the following results are obtained

Mean ($\bar{x}$) = 10 gallons (45 litres)

Standard deviation = 4 litres

Sample size = 400

$\therefore$ Standard error $\bar{x} = \dfrac{4}{\sqrt{400}} = \dfrac{4}{20} = 0.2$ litres.

Incidentally, note that the divisor is not the sample size but the square root of the sample size which means that if the research sponsor wished to halve the standard error he would need to commission a fourfold increase in the sample size – a key consideration in survey costs, obviously.

When sample survey data follow a binomial distribution (e.g. buyers/non-buyers) we can regard the arithmetic mean of the sample as the proportion (i.e. percentage) of the sample possessing the attribute in question (i.e. buyers of the product).

The standard error of the proportion (percentage) is calculated by the following formula:

$$\text{Standard error } (p\%) = \sqrt{\dfrac{p\% \times (100 - p\%)}{n}}$$

The value 'q' is used to denote the percentage not having the attribute in question and is therefore $100 - p\%$ so that the formula becomes

$$\text{Standard error } (p\%) = \sqrt{\dfrac{p \times q}{n}}$$

(or as researchers say, 'root pq over n').

Going back to the hypothetical example of PCB Arnold Ltd. and the re-design of their tableware, imagine their new design has been tested on a random sample of 600 housewives and not a quota sample as described and 60 per cent of them have stated their liking for it.

Since $p\% = 60$, $q\% = 40$ $(100 - 60)$ and the standard error of $p\%$

$$= \sqrt{\dfrac{60 \times 40}{600}} = \sqrt{\dfrac{2400}{600}} = \sqrt{4} = 2.$$

The standard error of this proportion is 2 and at the end of the next section we shall show how knowing this will assist PCB Arnold to come to a 'go/no go' decision on the production and marketing of the new design.

The curve of normal distribution

One of the concepts fundamentally important to statistical inference is that of *normal distribution*. If, for example we were to measure the heights of say, 400 students and plot the range of their heights against their frequency of occurrence, the graphed result would take the form of a *curve of normal distribution* (see Figure 6.10). Some of the key characteristics of the *normal curve* are these:

● it is bell shaped and its mean lies at the peak of the curve;

● it has only one mode (i.e. the particular value which occurs most frequently) – a bimodal (i.e. two mode) distribution would have two peaks;

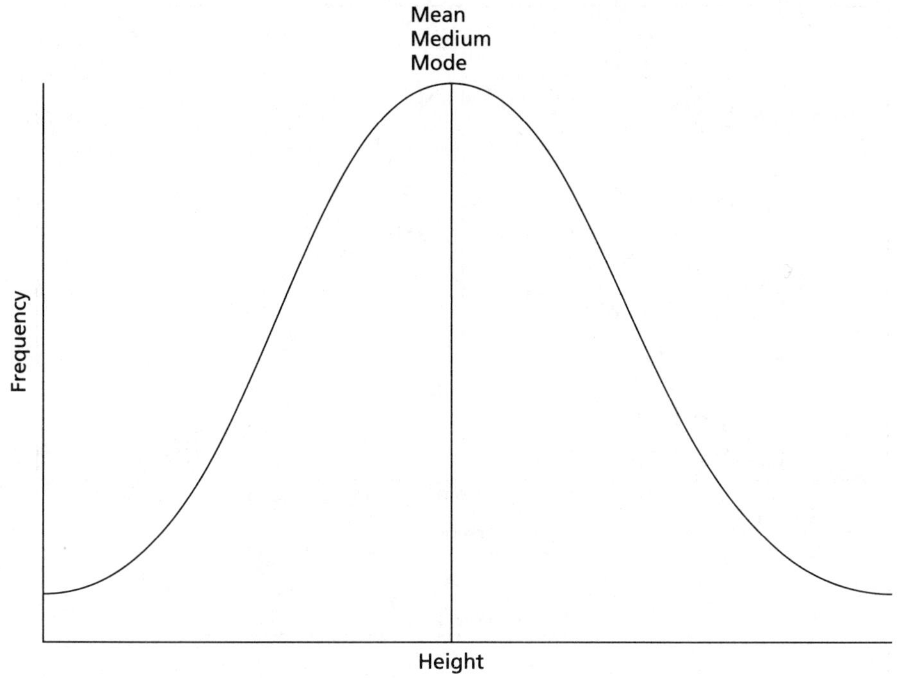

Mean
Medium
Mode

Figure 6.10. *Student heights: the curve of normal distribution*

Frequency

Height

- the normal distribution is symmetrical about its mean, which means that it is not skewed and all three measures of central tendency are equal to the same value;

- a particular normal distribution is uniquely defined by its mean and standard deviation;

- the total area under a normal curve is equal to one, meaning that it takes in all observations;

- the two tails of the curve never actually touch the horizontal axis although they continuously approach it.

A further key characteristic which provides the basis for much of the statistical inference especially significant for marketing research is the *proportional property* of the normal distribution. For instance the area between the mean and plus or minus one standard deviation (standard error) takes in approximately 68 per cent of the area under the curve, that is, 68 per cent of the observations upon which the curve is constructed.

The area between the mean and plus or minus 2 standard deviations accounts for approximately 95 per cent of the observations, and the area between the mean and plus or minus 3 standard deviations accounts for approximately 99.7 per cent of the observations. Figure 6.11 illustrates this important characteristic.

The significance of the normal curve for marketing research

For large samples ($n > 100$), distributions approximate to this normal curve, particularly those relating to human characteristics, for example height, weight, personality, intelligence. Moreover, many variables of significance to marketers have probability distributions that are close to the normal distribution, for example, number of glasses consumed by soft drink users, number of times people who eat at fast food restaurants visit them in an average month, average number of hours per week spent watching TV.

Figure 6.11. *The proportional property of the curve of normal distribution*

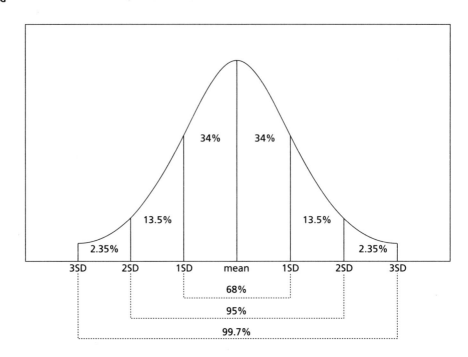

The symmetrical distribution of sampling characteristics allows researchers to make certain statements about the population being surveyed. As already noted, it is possible to use the standard error to qualify the sample estimate with regard to its probable accuracy. Also, since the distribution of many results from probability samples takes the form of a normal curve it is possible for the researcher to make a statement about the *limits of confidence* that can be applied to a single sample result when determining its precision.

Confidence limit (%)	Qualification of sample result
68.0	sample result ± 1 standard error
95.0	sample result ± 2 standard errors
99.7	sample result ± 3 standard errors

Now as we saw above, the standard error of the estimate in the PCB Arnold Ltd. research was ± 2. Applying limits of confidence to this, researchers will report to Arnold that if the new design is launched nationally they can be:

● 68 per cent confident that the favourability of the new design in the total market is estimated to be between 58 per cent and 62 per cent (60 ± 2);

● 95 per cent confident that its favourability will be between 56 per cent and 64 per cent (60 ± 4);

● 99.7 per cent confident that its favourability will be between 54 per cent and 66 per cent (60 ± 6).

In looking at its 'worst case scenario', Arnold Ltd. will probably settle for a 95 per cent confidence limit (± twice the standard error). Minus twice the standard error is 56 per cent (60 per cent − 4). The firm will now ask itself whether a design which appeals to little more than half its target market is sufficient to lift the idea of a national launch from the plane of a gamble to one of legitimate business risk – probably not and it becomes a case of 'back to the drawing board'. Marketing research may not have delivered the message Arnold Ltd. wanted to hear but it may well have prevented costly failure.

The preparation element: Part II:

Customers and customer buying behaviour

Customers: consumers and organizations

Often, we speak of the 'customer' (the buyer of a product or service) and the 'consumer' (the user of the product or service) as meaning the same thing. This is frequently the case, but not always so. So let us begin by clarifying the difference. First let us distinguish between *ultimate customers*, that is individuals or organizations who will actually use the goods and services they buy and *intermediate* or *trade customers*, those dealers who purchase for resale.

The ultimate customers for consumer goods and services are well enough understood – they 'consume', for example, food, clothing, confectionery and entertainment for their own needs and satisfactions. The ultimate customers for 'industrial' goods and services – manufacturing firms, departments of central and local government, educational institutions, hospitals and other types of organizations – use up the goods and services they purchase either within their operations (as with stationery, heating, lighting and lubricants) or by incorporating them within their own finished products (e.g. computers, cranes and motor vehicles). Strictly speaking, these organizations are consumers too, since they 'consume' products and services but in common parlance we refer to them simply as 'customers', 'industrial customers' or, more untidily 'business to business customers' – never as 'consumers'.

So much for the ultimate customers – but what of the intermediate customers – the dealers or, in marketing language, 'the trade'? The role of dealers is discussed in Chapter 10 (the *place* element) but, to appreciate customer-buying behaviour more fully, some explanation is necessary at this point.

The justification for dealers in the distribution chain is that they provide:

- *utilities of form* – the individual consumer will wish to purchase the product singly or in small quantities and not in the large consignments the manufacturer needs to deliver;

- *utilities of place* – the consumer will wish to purchase at a convenient location – not at the manufacturer's premises or at some distant depot;

- *utilities of time* – the product must be available *when* it is required, not when it is convenient to the manufacturer to produce and deliver it: so time utility also incorporates a *storage* function.

As we shall see in Chapter 10, the requirement of ensuring that the right product is in the right place at the right time is the responsibility of the physical distribution function. It is a function which *adds value* to the product or service, for if a consumer, for example, were to undertake the function he would incur costs. Not only is the function concerned with judicious choice of a location where the consumer may conveniently buy the product, it is also concerned with storage, handling and transportation – all the processes involved in moving the product from the end of the production line to the hands of the user.

An important part of an organization's marketing activity is the arrangement of a method of distribution which is both cost-effective and convenient for its customers. Figure 7.1 will be helpful in making some other points about distribution.

In Figure 7.1, a flow line labelled 'push' strategy extends from the manufacturer to the wholesaler and the retailer (whose specific roles will be described in Chapter 10). This strategy is sometimes described as 'trade loading' and is intended to ensure that the product is readily available when the consumer asks for it. Often the push strategy involves offering dealers an incentive (e.g. a low introductory price or a free additional quantity of the product) to induce them to 'stock up'. This is often the case with a new product, the extra costs involved being absorbed by the manufacturer as part of an 'investment budget' strategy to launch the product.

In Figure 7.1 a flow line labelled 'pull' strategy extends from the manufacturer direct to the user. Here the manufacturer is communicating to the consumer, usually by way of an advertising campaign, the merits of the product, its novel aspects, its value for money, etc. – all the reasons why it should be bought in preference to competing products. In this case, by creating a 'back-demand' on the dealers, the manufacturer is said to be 'pulling' his product through the chain of distribution – he is, in effect, selling *through* the dealers rather than *to* them.

In practice, a great deal of the marketing of consumer products utilizes 'push' and 'pull' strategies in combination. Indeed, it is often the case that the organization will not succeed in its push strategy to the dealers unless it shows them evidence of a substantial pull strategy (e.g. in the shape of an extensive advertising/sales promotion campaign) to assist them to sell their stocks at an adequate rate.

Now that the terms 'customer' and 'consumer' have been distinguished, it is important to consider why customers buy, to consider some of the influences and motivations generally thought to lead to purchase decisions. The early pages of the review will focus on the consumer and later, some insights into organizational buying behaviour will be outlined.

The reasons transactions take place

The explanation accompanying Figure 7.1 provides some information as to how, when and where exchange transactions take place. We will now consider the exchange process more fully with especial emphasis on *why* it takes place.

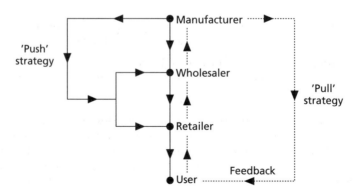

Figure 7.1. *The distribution of a consumer product*

162

Lanigan (1992, p 386) describes a potential customer as an individual or an organization with a need or a problem which can be alleviated or removed by a product or service purchased from one of the businesses in the market place. With regard to customers, however, he adds two other important criteria:

- they must be able to pay a price which allows the supplier to make an adequate profit, and
- they must be willing to pay that price.

Lanigan's criteria are a useful start. His second criterion is an *economic* one – either people have the ability to pay or they have not. In analysing the economic factors underlying consumer demand, Morden (1989, p 115) indicates that these comprise:

- the real disposable income available to people for expenditure on consumer goods and services;
- the prices of the available products and services;
- personal perceptions of what constitutes good value for money;
- relative prices of substitute products;
- relative prices of complementary products (a basic camera is inexpensive, not so colour films and processing).

So far so good – which leaves us with the first and third of Lanigan's criteria to consider:

- customer needs or problems and how these arise, and
- customer willingness to pay the price.

Now these do not rest on economic considerations; often they are *psychological* in nature and stem from inner drives, motives, feelings and aspirations, i.e. they are *behavioural*.

Thus, the demand for products and services is said to be influenced by both economic and behavioural factors. It is the behavioural factors, which help us to understand why people need or want particular products and services, that we shall be considering in the early part of this chapter.

Boone and Kurtz (1980, p 105) have expressed the belief that consumer behaviour (B) is a function (f) of the interaction of the personal influences of consumers (P) and the influences of environmental forces (E). Thus their equation:

$$B = f(P \times E)$$

Some of the conventional ideas about the factors in the equation are now examined.

Consumer buying behaviour

In the ninth edition of his work *Marketing Management – Analysis, Planning, Implementation and Control*, Philip Kotler (1997, p 172) summarizes his perceptions of consumer buying behaviour with a model which depicts linkages and interactions among four elements of an overall framework. These elements, or sub-systems, comprise:

- the external influences shaping buying behaviour and the context, or environment in which they operate;

- the personal characteristics of the buyer which interact with these stimuli;

- the steps in the buying decision process collateral to these two sub-systems and which are, in turn, influenced by them;

- the outcome of this decision process in terms of consumer choice.

The Kotler model provides a useful schema for the examination of consumer buying behaviour and Figure 7.2. is an outline of it in basic form. This section's description of the buying process is aligned with the sub-systems of the model.

External influences on buying behaviour

As we see from the first section of the model (Figure 7.2 top left), the external influences can be divided into:

- stimuli from marketing activity;

- factors in the external business environment.

With regard to the first of these, as we have seen earlier, strategic marketing consists of the manipulation of six elements in a *strategic formula* (preparation; product; price; place; promotion and people) the resultant mix being offered to the market by a *strategic process*, that is the actions necessary to bring the mix to the market place. From the standpoint of the individual organization the marketing stimuli thus produced will be mediated by the various factors in the organization's *external environment*. Some of these may stimulate and reinforce the stimuli, others may weaken them. Below are the factors described at length in Chapter 2 and, to remind ourselves of the nature of their influences, a brief example or two accompanies the factors:

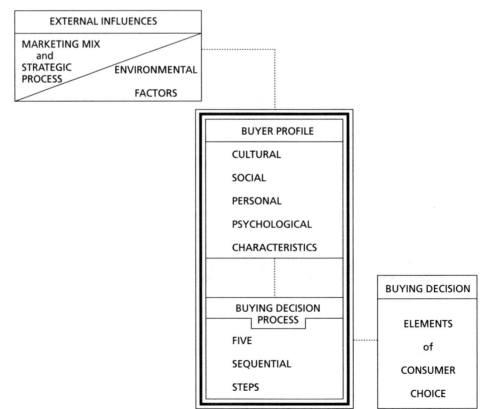

Figure 7.2. *A model of consumer buying behaviour (adapted from P. Kotler, Marketing Management, 9th Edn., p 172)*

- *economic influences* – e.g. rate of growth, interest rates, employment levels;

- *political influences* – e.g. government regulation/deregulation, action on exchange rates, policies on the physical environment;

- *technological influences* – e.g. inventions, new materials, continuing development of information technology and telecommunications;

- *social influences* – e.g. changes in population profile, further developments in consumerism, increased calls for ethical conduct in organizational behaviour;

- *legal influences* – e.g. credit and pricing legislation, health and safety considerations, new regulations on product descriptions and labelling;

- *competitive/collaborative influences* – e.g. direct or indirect competition either from individual organizations or from organizations acting in collaboration.

Buyer profile

We can see that the heart of the model is a 'black box' comprising two sub-systems: the characteristics of the individual buyer and the decision process of that buyer. Both of these will be influenced by the stimuli they receive from the strategic marketing process and the external business environment. In turn, from the standpoint of the individual organization, they will affect the outcome of its stimuli, positively or negatively.

Some aspects of the characteristics of the buyer, again with brief examples, are now described.

Culture and sub-culture

We are influenced in our values, perceptions and behaviour by the cultural institutions which surround us. The culture of a sophisticated economy is one in which health, well-being, comfort, success, efficiency and individualism are highly evident. In turn this will generate a demand for health and beauty products and services, leisure products and services, 'high-tech' products, etc. On the other hand a Third World country, most of whose people exist on the lowest levels of subsistence, will possess a culture preoccupied with the necessities of life – one in which 'high-tech' products have little or no meaning.

Within the general culture there will be smaller sub-cultures based on race, religion, geography, age, etc. which provide a framework for even closer identification and which generally have a marked influence on buying behaviour.

Social class is another aspect of cultural influence. It is determined by an amalgam of variables, including occupation, income, terminal educational age, location of residence, and exercises a great deal of influence on the acquisition and use of products and services – homes, investments, clothing, transport, holidays, leisure activities, etc. Mobility between social classes and hence changes in purchase behaviour depend on economic opportunity and the rigidity or otherwise of the class structure.

Social factors

The groups we belong to – the family especially, the work group, the professional group, the student group, the friendship/leisure group – all have their socially sanctioned rules of conduct (their 'norms of behaviour'), which represent the values held by the group and which the group itself enforces in a direct or indirect way.

These are referred to as an individual's *reference groups*. An important point here, also, is that membership is not a pre-condition for reference group influence but we may so aspire towards it that it becomes a standard, a *reference point* for our goals and behaviour. 'Pop' stars, international athletes, successful entrepreneurs, the caring professions, etc. may all constitute reference groups for different types of individuals. The purchase of a technologically sophisticated and expensive motor vehicle might fit our idealized perception of a particular reference group. Advertising of cosmetics and designer-label fashion very often draws upon reference group influence – the 'glamorous', the 'jet set' and so on.

Roles and statuses within groups also influence buying behaviour. Our roles as husband, father, company accountant, housewife, mother, magistrate, etc. all confer a particular type or level of status. We tend to purchase products and services which identify and reinforce our status. In fact, some exclusive products are referred to as 'status symbols'.

Personal factors

The theory of how people see themselves – their self-concept – is a useful starting point here. Self-concept theory offers a number of classifications, for example:

- the *real self* – the objective view of what the individual is really like;
- the *self image* – which is how the individual sees himself and which is likely to contain some element of distortion, since 'no man can be a judge in his own case';
- the *mirror self* – which is how individuals think others see them;
- the *ideal-self* – which is how the individual would like to be.

The parts of the 'ideal-self' image serve as a set of behavioural objectives, since we are all striving towards the attainment of the ideal self. Thus, a young woman will buy the types of dress in keeping with her ideal-self image. The boy who hopes to be a professional footballer one day will plague his parents to buy him the type of kit which fosters his concept of an ideal-self.

We noted that *social class* has an influence on buying behaviour and two of its key determinants, *occupation* and *income grouping* can also be classified as personal characteristics. Our occupation often determines the type of clothes we wear (the clothes for the executive suite are different from the clothes for the production line), the way we travel to work (e.g. by car or by public transport) and even our spare-time activities (i.e. the skilled manual worker may enjoy angling; the aspiring young manager may spend many hours each week studying to improve his qualifications). The type of products and services we seek are influenced by our level of *income*. This has a number of aspects – obviously the nature, quality and range of our purchases are influenced by the income itself but this in turn affects our ability to obtain bank loans and other forms of credit, thereby affecting our purchasing power. Income also affects our propensity and ability to save and invest, again influencing the composition of our buying – a worker on very low pay is hardly likely to be seeking the services of a financial adviser.

Life-style is another personal characteristic useful in classifying buying behaviour and it may succeed in doing this when other characteristics (e.g. socio-economic status) prove blunter instruments. Determining life-style groupings is based on responses to questions on *activities*, *interest* and *opinions* (AIO). A typical survey, known to the writer, used some 230 life-style statements for male respondents and a slightly larger number for females. Each research interviewer sought agreement or otherwise with particular statements, which ranged typically over such topics as: likes, fashion, home, housework (for women), men's interests, food, health/hygiene products, religion, social issues, attitudes to other countries, etc. Within the interview, data were collected concerning the press readership, cinema going, radio listening and television viewing of the informants. Product usage data were also obtained from informants, who, in addition, were analysed by such established classifications as age, sex, social grade, education, etc.

What results from such research is an extremely large bank of data which is subjected to sophisticated analytic techniques using computers. These *data reduction techniques*, such as *cluster analysis*, are used to group informants so that each group or 'cluster' contains people who are similar to each other and different from the people in the other groups on the behavioural components measured (AIO).

The life-style classifications, for example 'social resisters', 'experimentalists', 'achievers/ conspicuous consumers', 'belongers', 'survivors', etc. are a useful supplement to standard data for the purposes of product planning and the design of advertising campaigns. The marketing department will seek to establish relationships between their products and particular life-style classifications. 'High achievers', for example may be clearly correlated to the purchase of PCs and other sophisticated equipment.

Age and stage in the life-cycle are prominent factors in the classification of consumers. Age has an important bearing on the purchase of products and services. The young adult market has a heavy emphasis on the purchase of designer label clothing, pop music, video cassettes and cinema admissions. The retired, elderly market has a high level of demand for health care products, chiropody and other medical support services. An important qualification here, however, is that in Western society, earlier retirement and increased life expectancy have made the retired market a significant one for home improvement merchandise, consumer durables and leisure and recreation services, including foreign travel.

The influence of the *family* on buying behaviour has been mentioned very briefly in the description of social factors (reference groups). It is important to mention here that, in spite of the latter-day pressures upon it, the family is still the basic unit in our population structure. Obviously, the market for many products and services will be related to such factors as the number of dependants in the family (family size) and the stage reached in family formation (family life-cycle).

We shall return to the family and household composition in the section on 'Market segmentation' later in this chapter. Also included in that section is the recent and significant classification which clusters consumers by their *residential neighbourhoods* which has demonstrated its importance as a factor in purchase behaviour.

Psychological factors

Because marketing is all to do with the satisfaction of human needs, it is not surprising that the *nature of needs* has provided another focus for the examination of buyer behaviour. More specifically, the *motivation* to take action in order to relieve the tension arising from the need has been the subject of study. A number of theories of motivation have been examined, including those of Freud and of Herzberg. Both of these writers provide insights of some value to marketers. Freud's theory is based on the assumption that the psychological forces shaping behaviour reside largely in the unconscious. In short, the buyer is not fully aware of his or her motivations. She or he may tell the researcher the fax machine was purchased to increase his or her efficiency whereas she or he may well have been drawn to it for the status it was believed to confer.

Herzberg's 'two-factor theory' distinguishes motivational 'dissatisfiers' from 'satisfiers'. The absence of dissatisfiers (factors that cause dissatisfaction – the 'hygiene' factors in Herzberg's terminology) while important, will not motivate behaviour; the satisfiers will. The service interval on a medium-priced family car might be 12,000 miles. If this were the case, generally, a smaller service interval would be a dissatisfier. Where the 12,000 mile interval applies, such a potential dissatisfier is absent. This is a point in the car's favour but would not necessarily turn the purchaser towards it.

What would do so perhaps would be such satisfiers as fuel consumption and rear-seat roominess (a key attribute for the buyer with a growing family).

Maslow's *hierarchy of pre-potent needs* has also received a lot of attention from the marketing fraternity. Maslow proposed five distinct categories of need (see Figure 7.3). Maslow's categories can be described as follows:

- *Physiological* – the need to satisfy hunger, to obtain shelter and clothing.
- *Safety* – the need to protect oneself from physical harm, to obtain security and safety from accident and similar unexpected dangers.
- *Love and belongingness* – the social needs centred on the desire for acceptance and affiliation.
- *Esteem* – the need for status, for a sense of achievement, for recognition and respect.
- *Self-actualization* – the need to realize one's full potential, to ensure one's skills are being totally utilized.

Maslow argues that these needs are arranged in order of importance from the lowest order needs – physiological – to highest order needs – self-actualization, adding that satisfied needs provide no motivation.

Also, 'pre-potent' means that needs at the base of the pyramid (Figure 7.3) must at least be partially satisfied before the next higher-level need becomes important and a motivator of action – and so on up the scale. Obviously the starving beggar will hardly be concerned with matters of self-esteem and self-actualization preoccupied as he or she is with satisfying his or her dire physiological needs.

It is easy to discern how marketing and advertising operations have been influenced by these ideas. For example, promotional campaigns for:

- food, gas and electricity frequently relate to physiological needs;
- the purchase of retirement investment plans relate to safety needs;
- computer dating and social group membership relate to love and belongingness needs;
- professional societies and university courses relate to self-esteem needs;
- 'learning to draw' and 'writing that novel' relate to self-actualization needs.

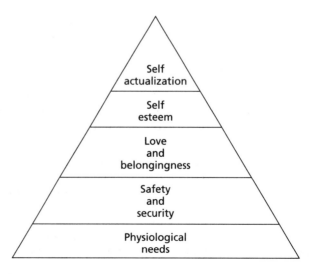

Figure 7.3. *Maslow's hierarchy of pre-potent needs.*

Although Maslow's hierarchy has not been well supported by studies of its validity, and although it may be naïve to expect 'a direct causal relationship between motive and behaviour' (Oliver, 1980, p 31), his ideas have achieved some popularity among marketing executives none the less, perhaps because they have an 'organized common sense' look about them. Certainly they are significant enough to be mentioned in any review of buyer behaviour.

Perception

In studies of consumer behaviour, the process of *perception* has also come in for scrutiny. In the context of marketing communications campaigns, obviously we perceive through our sense organs – seeing, hearing, touching, etc. This is how we process information about a *stimulus object* – usually a representation of the product and an accompanying promotional message.

An important aspect of this processing for marketers is the realization that the mind is not a *tabula rasa* (blank slate) on which advertisers are free to make impressions. The individual brings to the act of perceiving a complex mixture of past experiences, aspirations, motivations and so forth which intervene in the message being transmitted. Because of this process of intervention, people will have quite different impressions of the same product or message.

A consequence of this is that through a process of *selective perception* people perceive only what they want to perceive and interpret information in a way which supports rather than challenges their own beliefs. Because of this, marketing executives employ a variety of techniques to penetrate the consumer's *perceptual screen* and increase the attention-getting value of their advertisements, for example colour in an otherwise black-and-white newspaper, humour on an outdoor billboard, an advertisement in which the reader must rearrange the words for it to make sense, the surprise opening seconds of a TV commercial.

Attitude research and measurement

Many studies of consumer behaviour are based on the concept of *information processing* – the consumer gathers information from advertisements, brochures and other promotional material which is then processed for the purpose of decision-making. The process is one of evaluating the gathered information through the consumer's own system of beliefs and attitudes. *Attitude research and measurement* has consequently become an important part of marketing research and operations. An organization wishing to measure attitudes to its products or services will become involved in:

- *identifying attitude dimensions* – usually by informal interviewing and/or group discussions, sometimes aided by projective images or pictures, the interviews and discussions being tape-recorded and subjected to a thorough content analysis;

- *developing suitable measuring instruments* – and here, attitude scaling methods are important.

The *semantic differential*, developed by Osgood *et al.* (1957) is an attitude scaling method with a long history of use in marketing research. It consists of a number of seven-point rating scales, with each extreme point of the scale being defined by an adjective or descriptive phrase. Thus, the scales used for product image testing of a newspaper might be similar to those given in Figure 7.4.

The informant rates the newspaper on each dimension by marking one of the seven boxes which lie between the two extremes. A profile of that newspaper *for that informant* can then be produced by linking the ratings so obtained. The averaged rankings for all informants then become the generalized profile of the newspaper, which

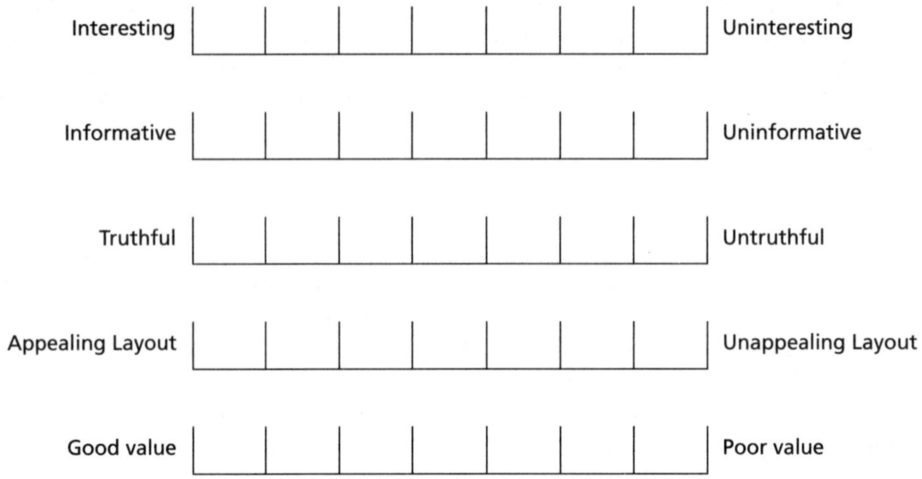

Figure 7.4. *The semantic differential – image testing of a newspaper*

Interesting								Uninteresting

Informative								Uninformative

Truthful								Untruthful

Appealing Layout								Unappealing Layout

Good value								Poor value

can subsequently be compared to the profiles produced for competing newspapers and for the 'ideal' newspaper (also determined by research).

While establishing the link between attitudes and behaviour is more elusive (e.g. such attitude-to-object research, while clearly helpful towards product modification and development, does not disclose the consumer's attitude to the act of *buying* a particular newspaper), research continues in this regard. Oliver (1980, p 26), for example, reports that financial constraints, demographic and socio-economic factors, expected stock levels at distributive outlets and the influence of people significant to the buyer are all interrelated pressures which combine with attitudes to influence buying behaviour.

Learning

The *theory of learning* has also been examined for its value by interpreters of consumer behaviour. Research has entailed examination of:

- the *drives* (or impulses) towards purchase decisions – hunger, fear, the urge to compete, etc.;

- the *environmental cues* directly related to response – advertising, point-of-sale displays, etc.;

- the *responses of the individual* to such cues and drives.

Note that, in this context, 'cue' can perhaps be described simply as the stimulus object used to guide response and a 'drive' as the impulse prompting the individual to act in the desired manner.

A basic tenet of the theory of learning may be described as the modification of a response following upon or emanating from experience of results. Since response depends upon cues, drives and on whether or not existing behaviour has become a habit, then to a greater or lesser degree, learning theory may provide valuable information on brand preference and brand loyalty.

Another important aspect here is the *expectation* of the outcome arising from a particular response ('If I buy this brand it may not be as nourishing as the one I usually buy'). Any organization will obviously benefit from knowledge of the expectations which surround the possible purchase of its products.

Cognitive dissonance

In this brief review of the psychological aspects of consumer behaviour, we have concentrated on influences *prior* to purchase. Marketing activity must also take note of a post purchase influence – that of *cognitive dissonance*, for although attitudes are significantly resistant to change, they sometimes change significantly after the purchase!

Through their research, Leon Festinger and his colleagues (1962, pp 93–102) have established the importance of suppliers staying concerned with the attitude of users in the post-purchase stage because of the possible development of cognitive dissonance – a state of doubt, uncertainty or anxiety as to whether the correct purchase decision has in fact been made. Such dissonance typically accompanies major purchase decisions, such as a house or a car, and is accentuated if faults are discovered, however minor, or if the attraction of alternatives is emphasized to the buyer (perhaps by a 'knowing friend').

Comprehensive and reliable after sales service is a powerful antidote to cognitive dissonance (as we shall see in Chapter 8) as is a well-established system for the speedy and fair treatment of complaints. Setting up a complaints procedure is a key indicator of whether an organization's declaration of being 'customer-driven' is any more than mere rhetoric. *Reassurance advertising* in which the quality of the product, its economies, significant features, etc. are again emphasized is also important for reducing dissonance.

Before leaving this glimpse into the psychology of consumer behaviour it is worth adding that the amount of work undertaken by marketing research agencies to interpret this behaviour would justify a lengthy textbook of its own. Perhaps just one example will suffice for our purposes.

As Research International (RI), one of the world's leading agencies has indicated, *usage and attitude studies* provide the basic building blocks for consumer marketing activity since they are conducted to provide an understanding of the market in which a particular brand is, or is planned to be, sold.

This type of research sets out to provide a description of the market *from the consumer's point of view*, in order to identify market opportunities, optimize brand/product positioning or identify target markets. The RI approach to usage and attitude studies, Conceptor, recognizes the need to look at actual product usage occasions. Conceptor provides a quantification of usage and of attitudes towards products or brands. In addition to this it provides an integrated database which permits the influence of attitudes and needs on usership to be assessed (by looking at needs on a particular occasion and how far they are met by the product chosen) and by allowing the segmentation of the market to be examined in the context of particular occasions ('segmentation' will be explained later in this chapter).

Decision-making units and the decision making process :

Reverting to Figure 7.2, we must now move to the second part of the 'black-box', in the centre of the model, that is the *actual process of consumer buying*. Before considering the process itself, however, we must give some thought to a key issue in marketing strategy, which is *who makes the decision to buy?* In marketing language, the question is: what is the composition of the decision-making unit (the DMU)?

Very often, it is safe to say that the DMU is an individual consumer, making a decision based on the interaction of the personal and environmental influences depicted in the Figure 7.2 model. A young adult male or female buying a book or a compact disc purely for the purposes of his or her own entertainment might seem to fit that category although even here, the individual is not the free agent he or she might suppose, being influenced perhaps, however unconsciously, by some reference group.

Similarly, we might conclude that in the purchase of everyday household products the housewife is the decision-making unit but we know, on reflection, that with respect to food items in particular she may be heavily influenced by her children. It is no accident that much television advertising for food products centres upon the likes and dislikes of the children in the family.

The family itself is clearly the appropriate DMU for many products and services especially the house, the car and expensive household appliances. We can easily recognize that the cultural norms established in our original family have a marked influence on our attitudes, beliefs and therefore on our behaviour as consumers. Subsequently, marriage provides the opportunity for many of us to form a new family and as it goes through the stages of the family life cycle – from the 'full nest' stage of the young married couple with a number of dependent children to the empty nest' stage of the older married couple, or of an individual living alone – changes occur in the demand for products and services, including housing itself and domestic equipment.

As in any human group, family roles and role relationships exert their influence and *role specialization* is clearly related to the pattern of household decision-making. In this respect, Engel, Blackwell and Kollatt (1978, p 152) have distinguished four categories of role and structure:

- the *autonomic* – in which decisions are made individually by one or other of the married partners (e.g. on alcoholic beverages, certain types of tools and equipment);

- the *husband dominant* – e.g. on life insurance, car accessories, garden tools;

- the *wife dominant* – e.g. on food, children's clothing, kitchen ware, cleaning products;

- the *syncratic* – in which decisions are made jointly by the married partners e.g. on housing, schooling, furniture, holiday plans and outside entertainment.

So family structures are one of the broad categories which assist organizations to direct marketing, and particularly promotional, effort. Of course within society generally there are significant strands of continuing change which affect the family itself and roles within it – the increase in cohabitation, in the number of working wives and the widening of career opportunities for women, the marked increase in single parent families and the growing number of single person households resulting from increased life expectancy and other trends. The marketing executive and the researcher have to keep a close and continuing watch on such changes if buying behaviour is to be interpreted and, hopefully, understood.

The decision-making process

Even for a relatively simple consumer product, the structure of the decision-making unit can be quite complex: Kotler (1997, p 190), for example, distinguishes five roles people might play in a buying decision – initiator, influencer, decider (on any component of the decision) buyer and user (who may not be the same person as the buyer). To the list we might add the role of financier (as in the case of a fond parent!).

Notwithstanding the important secondary roles, the steps in the decision process of the actual buyer have long interested marketing professionals because of their implications for marketing action. With regard to consumer buying, it might serve our purposes best to consider a relatively simple model such as that also proposed by Kotler (1991, p 182). Figure 7.5 provides an illustration of this and the following explanatory notes describe the implications for marketers at each stage of the process.

- *The buyer first recognizes a problem or need*. This may come from within, be stimulated by environmental factors or it may come about as a result of the marketer's promotional activity. The 'musts' for the marketer here are to be sensitive to environmental changes which may give rise to consumer needs and to ensure that promotional campaigns awaken interest in change and are educational as well as informative.

● At the *information search* stage, the marketer now has a clear opportunity to influence the consumer towards his product or service. Promotional campaigns that are genuinely informative and helpful, which are consumer oriented in that they are based on solving users' problems or fulfilling their needs, are important. Since some of the information will come from other people (e.g. the peer group, the family) the marketer must remember that satisfied users are often the best advertisement. At this stage too, the marketer must *differentiate* his product from the competition (see Chapter 11) – emphasizing the characteristics, performance, value or other attributes that make it different from, and preferably superior to, the competition.

● At the *evaluation* stage the consumer is making an assessment of what is on offer and weighing the alternatives. The marketer must ensure that his product or service is on that list of alternatives – the consumer must be aware of his product. Secondly, the reasoned selling argument he has advanced for it must kindle the buyer's interest so that he or she becomes convinced of its *suitability*. All of this presupposes that the marketer has arranged for adequate distribution of the product so that it is really *accessible* to the consumer.

● At the *purchase decision* stage, the consumer will have decided which attributes are important for the fulfilment of his or her needs and accorded each of them a level of importance. The ideal product will have all the attributes being sought and to the required degree. When the decision to purchase is made, the product judged to be at or nearest to the ideal will be chosen. The marketer must have done everything to ensure that his is the 'ideal' product.

● Earlier in this chapter, the psychological state of *cognitive dissonance* was outlined. Post purchase fears and uncertainty can be countered by reassurance advertising but most importantly there must be no gap between the expectations

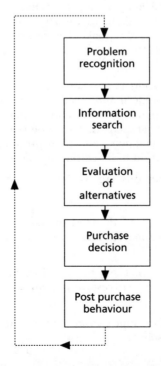

Figure 7.5. *A model of purchasing behaviour (Kotler)*

created and product performance. Where repeat buying of the product is appropriate this will take place only if the consumer is fully satisfied with the original purchase. In the event of dissatisfaction, the whole decision-making process must begin again (see the broken line in Figure 7.5).

Organizational buying behaviour

Because industrial markets are made up of organizations which buy many of the same products and services used by individuals and families – e.g. paper products, automobiles, PCs, tools and transportation services – Webster (1991, p 9) believes that industrial marketing is distinguished from consumer marketing *more by the nature of the customer than by the nature of the product*. Some observations on this might therefore be helpful.

Industrial customers can be classified as follows:

- *manufacturing and processing firms* – with the latter category including food, chemical and petroleum processors;

- *distributors* – who purchase and re-sell to other industrial and institutional users;

- *OEMs (original equipment manufacturers)* – a special type of manufacturer, making equipment which incorporates the components of other manufacturers.

- *institutional customers* – including health care and educational organizations;

- *governmental customers* – operating at the municipal, regional and national level and often constituting for many firms their largest single source of demand.

For convenience, we shall use the term 'industrial marketing' to apply to all three major categories of customer – industrial, institutional, governmental. Note again, however, that some writers refer to industrial marketing as 'business marketing' or 'business to business marketing'.

The nature of demand for industrial products and services stems from the obvious fact that organizations require land, labour, raw material, machines and other 'inputs' to produce their 'output'. The demand for any input depends therefore on the demand for the products it is used to make. Hence we say that the demand for industrial products and services is *derived demand*, meaning that it is derived ultimately from consumer demand.

'Industrial' customers buy products and services to produce products and services for their own customers. Writing in 1989, Semich (pp 43–7) pointed out that at that time Apple Computer was spending more than 60 per cent of each sales dollar on purchased materials. Virtually all the parts and components that made up its computers were designed by Apple engineers and then produced to their specifications by other firms, a carefully chosen set of industrial suppliers.

A number of general observations are used in describing industrial/organizational markets:

- that because demand is *derived*, demand analysis requires a close scrutiny of user industries and should also incorporate a very careful consideration of economic forecasts;

- that though a particular market may be large in value terms it is typically *concentrated*, with relatively few buyers responsible for a large amount of its purchasing power;

- that the products are often much more complex than consumer products and therefore require expert selling;

- that frequently there are a large number of influences at work in reaching purchase decisions – buying being very much a *group* process;

- that after sales service usually assumes much greater importance than in the selling of consumer goods;

- that the buying process is thought to be more rational, being based on economic and technological criteria (but see below);

- that the unit price is generally high, as is the average value of an order, with a typically lengthy negotiation period, and that finance facilities, arrangements for leasing, etc. are therefore very important.

There are one or two points to note here. First, Baker (1979, p 134) emphasizes that the differences between the marketing of consumer and industrial goods are of degree, rather than kind, and he adds: 'undue emphasis of differences may be harmful if it induces practitioners in either field to neglect thought and practice in the other.'

The second point relates to the supposed rationality of the buying process. There has been much discussion as to whether this is really the case. Some writers point out that the *culture* of the organization is important in this context, that is, the buying process will be influenced by whether it is risk oriented, technology oriented or customer oriented.

Group dynamics and interpersonal factors also enter into the process. The buying group (or 'centre') typically includes a number of participants and each affects, and is affected by, the others. Nor does the participant with the highest rank always have the most influence.

Similarly, each participant brings to the buying process personal motives, perceptions and preferences. These individual factors are affected by age, income, education, professional identification, personality and attitudes towards risk. Buyers also have different buying styles. Younger, professionally educated buyers may make 'in-depth' analyses of competitive proposals aided by information technology. Older buyers may be adept at pitting suppliers against each other in order to obtain the best possible quotation.

Finally, the list of choice criteria provided by John O'Shaughnessy (1988, pp 97–8) provides very useful guidance as to the how, why, when and where of organizational buying. The list is based on an investigation of the attributes sought in the choice of suppliers and is as follows:

- *Economic criteria* – the relative cost outlays associated with the purchase of the product and related support services: price, delivered cost, total life costs, credit terms, operating costs, salvage value, warranties, maintenance, etc.

- *Overall technical performance criteria* – suitability of the product (and related services) to the application involved, that is performance characteristics, operating features, composition/quality of the material used, convenience in use, ancillary functions.

- *Supplier/buyer relationship criteria* – willingness and desire of the supplier to:

  – offer technical services and operator training, if needed;
  – be customer oriented and flexible;
  – provide credible personnel in relation to customer requirements.

- *Adaptive (supplier capability) criteria* – where there is uncertainty over whether suppliers can supply to time and/or specification, buyers may adapt to this uncertainty by ensuring that the reasons for favouring one supplier over another include relative assessments of:

– capability of delivery in accordance with the buying schedule;

– production capability to supply consistently to specification;

– quality of after sales service.

● *Legal criteria* –

– government regulation (safety, pollution, purchasing from specified sources etc.);

– company buying policies (e.g. reciprocal trading, embargoes on purchasing from particular organizations).

Decision-making units (DMUs)

Compared to consumer decision-making, industrial buying behaviour is characterized by the participation of many persons interacting with each other within an organizational framework – designers, production managers, financial controllers, purchasing officers, etc. The buying process typically takes longer and may be more highly structured, though not necessarily more rational, as has been hinted earlier.

The possible complexity of the organizational DMU can perhaps best be understood if we examine the BUYGRID model initially developed by Robinson et al. (Morris, 1992, pp 114–16). See Figure 7.6.

This somewhat simple model was based on extensive research by the Marketing Science Institute of America and was subsequently adopted by that Institute.

Robinson and his colleagues concluded that the buying process is an eight-stage model which, though broadly sequential, may well have two or three of the stages occurring simultaneously. In addition to these *buyphases*, there are within the model three categories of buying decision, termed *buyclasses*, namely:

● *new task classes* – the most complex and difficult, usually with several influences and decision-makers involved;

● *modified rebuy classes* – which are somewhat more routine;

● *straight rebuy classes* – in which decisions are relatively automatic.

Buyphases	Buyclasses		
	New task	Modified rebuy	Straight buy
1. Anticipation or recognition of a problem.			
2. Determination of characteristics and quantity of needed item.			
3. Description of characteristics and quantity of needed item.			
4. Search for and qualification of potential sources.			
5. Acquisition and analysis of proposals			
6. Evaluation of proposals and selection of supplier(s).			
7. Selection of an order routine.			
8. Performance feedback and evaluation.			

Figure 7.6. *The BUYGRID model of buying behaviour*

(Source : Marketing Science Institute)

The most complex buying situations occur in the upper left portion of the BUYGRID frame and involve the largest number of buying influences and decision-makers. Engineers and production managers might play the major role in the early stages of the new task and modified rebuy situations, while the purchasing manager may be a factor of far less influence. Research indicates that purchasing personnel exert less influence in the early stages of purchases involving the more technical product with which the organization has had little experience.

Conversely, the purchasing department may be of key importance throughout the stages of a *straight rebuy* decision. Other research has found, more generally, that engineers play a dominant role in product selection and purchasing managers in supplier selection. The point also needs to be made that, as decision-making develops through the various buyphases, so there is a diminishing prospect of other suppliers entering the negotiations. In this regard and in his appraisal of the buyphases, Gordon Brand (Frain, 1990, p 177) writes: 'The suppliers who are involved at the early problem stage and who assist the purchasing organisation's technical staff in making up their minds can provide a far more persuasive quotation.'

The decision-making process

Figure 7.7 is a very simple adaptation of an industrial buying model developed by J.N. Sheth. To some extent it adds weight to what has been said earlier about industrial buying behaviour. Readers preparing for examinations might find it useful to commit the framework to memory when revising.

The factors which determine the expectations (Element 1) include the background and psychological characteristics of members of the decision-making unit; the sources and amounts of information available on suppliers and their products; the

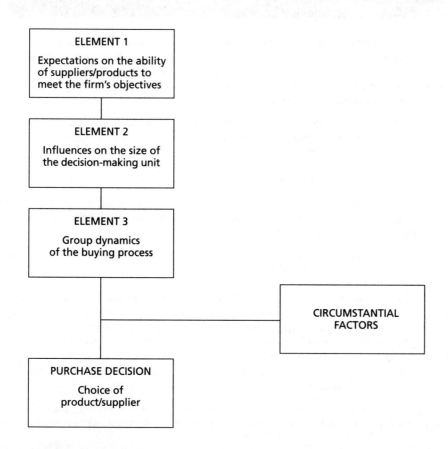

Figure 7.7. *Industrial buying behaviour : elements of a purchasing decision*

(Adapted from J.N. Sheth : A Model of Industrial Buyer Behaviour)

way in which that information is interpreted; and the satisfaction of the firm with past purchases.

The size of the decision-making unit or 'buying centre' (Element 2) will depend on the time available for the decision; the risk involved (e.g. a first-time purchase of a major item of capital equipment will probably involve a large number of people); the culture or orientation of the organization (risk oriented, technology oriented, customer oriented) which may concentrate responsibility in certain areas of operations – production, marketing, etc.; and the extent to which authority has been centralized or delegated.

Element 3 (group dynamics of the buying process) has much to do with the interpersonal influences at work, for each participant affects, and is affected by, other participants – this is the pulling and hauling of organizational politics. Again, bear in mind that the participant with the highest rank does not necessarily have the most influence.

Finally, note that Sheth's framework allows for the fact that circumstantial (or 'situational') factors may sometimes exercise a great deal of influence on a purchase decision. Such circumstances occur quite separately from the other three elements of the framework and may include, for instance:

● an unexpected strike which prevents deliveries from a key supplier;

● a sudden glut or shortage in the world supply of some particular raw material;

● a take-over or merger between firms which has a direct influence on the choice of suppliers.

Market segmentation

Now that we know something of the customer's buying process we move on to consider the ways in which customers are more precisely described or 'classified' – an important process because of its relationship to buying behaviour and because it facilitates market targeting or 'segmentation'. Let us begin by returning to the word *segmentation*, introduced in Chapter 3.

Occasionally, an organization will direct its marketing effort to the *total population* of potential buyers for its particular class of products or services. Again, it is worth pointing out that this would apply where:

● the market was a very small one; or

● where 'heavy' users of the product constituted such a considerable portion of the market that the obvious strategy would be to concentrate on developing products for, and communicating with, these heavy users; or

● where the organization's product (i.e. its 'brand') so dominated the market that its appeal was 'total', i.e. to all segments of the market.

In most cases, however, and usually marketing practitioners are more concerned to direct products not so much to the total population of potential buyers as to certain *types*, or *classifications*, of buyer. This strategy of *market segmentation* recognizes that a particular type of product will not be bought by everyone, but rather by some specific sub-group. The active elderly may constitute an important market for motor vehicles, as do the affluent young, but their product choices usually differ markedly. The same could be said, as a rule, of the holiday choices.

By adopting one key group as the target market, the whole marketing effort becomes more manageable in that products can be developed which pay closer attention to the needs of a more homogeneous group of likely buyers. Once the 'target' group is identified it will prove easier to communicate with them through advertising, etc. while at the same time reducing waste of promotional budgets – which occurs when the advertising overlaps those groups which are not true 'prospects' for the product in that they lack the means and/or the intention to buy.

Again, it is one thing to aim for precision, another to achieve it. Though it may prove difficult, the identification of appropriate sub-groups as target markets is a fundamentally important exercise and one to which researchers pay a great deal of attention on behalf of client organizations. Who buys? Why do they buy? and How are their needs being satisfied? are the questions which precede the planning of marketing operations and they point the way to identification of the target market – the appropriate market segment.

In Chapter 3 we noted how Webster championed the cause of segmentation in industrial marketing. He also has this to say:

> *Ideally, customer selection strategy is based on careful analysis of markets and company capabilities. Just as a good purchasing strategy, guided by careful statement of objectives, leads to a reasonable choice among competing suppliers and the development of effective suppliers, so should marketers develop statements of objectives for selecting among potential customers and developing effective long-term customer relationships. (Webster, 1991, p 98)*

Webster goes on to explain that, in practice, customer selection is often opportunistic, unplanned and short-term oriented rather than strategic. The result is that weaknesses may appear in the form of customer dissatisfaction, unrealistically low prices, product failure, distribution inefficiencies, high marketing costs and a high rate of turnover in the customer list. As a description of how segmentation assists an organization to make the most productive use of strategic resources, the views of Webster can hardly be bettered.

To conclude this outline of segmentation it is important to note that a 'viable' segment, that is one of practical and economic value, must be:

- capable of being clearly identified and measured;
- relevant to the purchase and use of the product or service;
- of sufficient potential to deliver an adequate return on any investment allocated to it;
- accessible through promotional and distributive channels.

The sections which follow describe some of the various classifications used for identifying target markets. In marketing terminology, these are *segmentation variables*.

Demographic classifications

Classification by the following factors has traditionally been an important first-stage exercise in consumer research:

- *age* (15–24 years; 25–34; 35–44; 45–54; 55–64; 65 and over);
- *sex* (male; female [and housewives]);
- *social (socio-economic) grouping*;
- *family size*.

The socio-economic element of this *demographic classification* has historically been based upon the occupation of the head of the household. These social classifications are the ones widely used in UK marketing and derive from its *National Readership Survey*, conducted under the auspices of National Readership Surveys Ltd (NRS), formerly the Joint Industry Committee for National Readership Surveys (JICNARS) – more about this survey in Chapter 11. Table 7.1 provides a profile of the UK population (aged 15 and over) derived from these classifications.

Clearly, the *age* of users is an important classifier of purchase behaviour. The young adult market with its emphasis on CDs, soft drinks, mobile phones and cinema admissions is a world away from the retired, elderly market with its high level of demand for health care products, chiropody and other medical services. While it is true that the interests and life-style of men and women are becoming less divergent, many products and services have a *gender* factor of high significance, women for example show a propensity to purchase feminine hygiene products, slimming plans, beauty products and homemaker journals while men are more likely to buy angling and car maintenance products, DIY and beer. Within the female heading, it is usual to incorporate the sub-division housewives – that is, those primarily responsible for household cleaning and catering. The significance of this segment for the marketing of food products, domestic cleaning products and other 'family budget' items is obvious.

Although the social grade classification, based as it is on the occupation of the head of the household, is thought to be of less value than it once was, these groupings do tell us something about disposable income (we would expect that, in large proportion, the ABs (see below) would constitute the market for luxury goods, for instance) and disposable income sets the framework for what is to be bought.

Family life-cycle

Of course, people brought together in the same income groups, based on broadly the same occupations, may differ widely in their life-styles, an important determination of which are the size and composition of their families. Consequently, *family size* becomes an important segmentation variable.

Social grade	Social status	Occupation of head of household	Population (000s)	Approximate percentage
A	Upper middle class	Higher managerial, administrative or professional	1,415	3
B	Middle class	Intermediate managerial, administrative or professional	8,348	18
C_1	Lower middle class	Supervisory or clerical and junior managerial administrative or professional	12,837	28
C_2	Skilled working class	Skilled manual workers	10,350	22
D	Working class	Semi-skilled and unskilled manual workers	7,843	17
E	Those at the lowest levels of subsistence	State pensioners or widows (no other earners), casual or lowest grade workers	5,357	12

Table 7.1. *Social classification (UK population aged 15 and over)*

Source: NRS (Fieldwork period July 1996 – June 1997)

Since the market for many products and services will not only be related to the number of dependants in the family (i.e. its size) but also the stage reached in family formation (its life-cycle), the following classifications are also used in relation to buying behaviour since their relevance and value is clear:

Young single	Young couple, no children	Young couple, youngest child under 6	Young couple, youngest child 6 or more	Older couple, with children 18+ at home	Older couple, no children at home	Older, single

Geographical classifications

An extension to the demographic classifications just described is that of *geographical location*. In the UK, for example and at the most basic level, data produced by the Office for National Statistics (ONS) reveals that despite the population movements of the recent past, the south-east region still provides the greatest proportion of regional demand for goods and services.

Beyond this basic picture, however, the regional statistics of many countries will often reveal important differences, region by region, in:

- productivity;
- employment;
- average gross weekly earnings;
- percentage of dwellings, owner occupied;
- average dwelling price, etc.

These and other data are of great significance for marketing organizations which invariably incorporate geographical data of some form or other into their planning processes. As a starting point in their planning, for instance, they will take heed of statistics on population, recent changes in population and forecasted future population changes.

Through a number of syndicated and other research services the marketing executives in many 'Western' style countries can also obtain important geographical data on distribution outlets for particular product groups and on patterns of consumer expenditure, newspaper readership and television viewership (see Chapter 11). Since it obviously makes sense to plan operations in alignment with the way in which marketing research data are available, it may well be the case that a firm will plan its marketing effort via a country's commercial television regions if the contractor companies provide valuable data on markets within the regions they serve.

An example of the sophisticated geographical data now available to UK marketers is that of CACI's Area Data service. This is a massive consumer database which holds the UK 1991 census data (the national census being conducted at 10 year intervals), the current Electoral Roll and market research data from leading UK research organizations.

Therefore, whatever specific catchment area is being studied (e.g. drivetime, radius, Local Authority, sales or franchise area) Area Data can provide information on the catchment population such as age/sex, housing type, employment, social grade, income, car ownership, life-styles and consumption and expenditure habits by products and services – vital information for planning purposes. These data can be presented by paper reports, diskettes and maps – the formats supplied being compatible with most PCs and spreadsheet packages.

Geodemographic classifications

In 1978 an important refinement of geographic segmentation was launched and it has now become a key profiling and 'target' market classification system. *Geodemographics*, as the system is known, has provided for the first time a scientific link between geography and demographics. It can identify the consumer demographics for a given location and, conversely, the geographic profile of a particular consumer characteristic.

The world's first geodemographic classification system was developed by CACI Ltd. of London. This system, *ACORN, which stands for 'A Classification of Residential Neighbourhoods', is founded on the premise that people who live in similar neighbourhoods are likely to have similar behavioural, purchasing and life-style habits. To give an example of the value of the *ACORN classification, a comparison of two neighbourhoods on an 'AB social grade index' gave comparative scores of 233:200. These same neighbourhoods, on a 'Wine-heavy usage index' achieved comparative scores of 367:142, showing the discriminatory power of segmentation by neighbourhood type.

CACI's *ACORN classification system consists of six categories, 17 groups and 54 neighbourhood types. The six categories are:

- A – thriving;
- B – expanding;
- C – rising;
- D – settling;
- E – aspiring;
- F – striving.

The 17 groups are as follows:

- Category A
  1. Wealthy achievers, suburban areas
  2. Affluent greys, rural communities
  3. Prosperous pensioners, retirement areas

- Category B
  4. Affluent executives, family areas
  5. Well-off workers, family areas

- Category C
  6. Affluent urbanites, town and city areas
  7. Prosperous professionals, metropolitan areas
  8. Better-off executives, inner city areas

- Category D
  9. Comfortable middle-agers, mature home owning areas
  10. Skilled workers, home owning areas

- Category E
  11. New home owners, mature communities
  12. White collar workers, better-off multi-ethnic areas

- Category F
  13. Older people, less prosperous areas
  14. Council estate residents, better-off homes
  15. Council estate residents, high unemployment
  16. Council estate residents, greatest hardship
  17. People in multi-ethnic, low income areas

To give some idea of the whole classification system, Table 7.2 reproduces the details of two of the *ACORN Categories A – Thriving and F – Striving together with the groups and neighbourhood types for these categories. These data are reproduced by kind permission of CACI Limited.

*ACORN Categories	*ACORN Groups	*ACORN Types		% of Households in Great Britain	Corresponding social grades
A **THRIVING**	1. Wealthy Achievers, Suburban Areas	1.1	Wealthy suburbs, Large Detached Houses	2.2	AB
		1.2	Villages with Wealthy Commuters	2.8	AB
		1.3	Mature Affluent Home Owning Areas	2.7	ABC_1
		1.4	Affluent Suburbs, Older Families	3.4	ABC_1
		1.5	Mature, Well-Off Suburbs	2.9	ABC_1
	2. Affluent Greys, Rural Communities	2.6	Agricultural Villages, Home Based Workers	1.5	ABC_2D
		2.7	Holiday Retreats, Older People Home Based Workers	0.7	ABC_2D
	3. Prosperous Pensioners Retirement Areas	3.8	Home Owning Areas, Well-Off Older Residents	1.5	ABC_1
		3.9	Private Flats, Elderly People	1.3	ABC_1
F **STRIVING**	13. Older People Less Prosperous Areas	13.39	Home Owners, Small Council Flats, Single Pensioners	2.3	C_2DE
		13.40	Council Areas Older People, Health Problems	2.1	C_2DE
	14. Council Estate Residents Better-Off Homes	14.41	Better-Off Council Areas New Home Owners	2.0	C_2DE
		14.42	Council Areas, Young Families, Some New Home Owners	2.7	C_2DE
		14.43	Council Areas, Young Families, Many Lone Parents	1.6	C_2DE
		14.44	Multi-Occupied Terraces, Multi-Ethnic Areas	0.7	C_2DE
		14.45	Low Rise Council Housing, Less Well-Off Families	1.8	C_2DE
		14.46	Council Areas, Residents with Health Problems	2.1	C_2DE
	15. Council Estate Residents High Unemployment	15.47	Estates with High Unemployment	1.3	DE
		15.48	Council Flats, Elderly People Health Problems	1.1	C_2DE
		15.49	Council Flats Very High Unemployment, Singles	1.2	DE
	16. Council Estate Residents, Greatest Hardship	16.50	Council Areas, High Unemployment, Lone Parents	1.5	DE
		16.51	Council Flats, Greatest Hardship Many Lone Parents	0.9	DE
	17. People in Multi-Ethnic, Low-Income Areas	17.52	Multi-Ethnic, Large Families, Overcrowding,	0.5	DE
		17.53	Multi-Ethnic, Severe Unemployment, Lone Parents	1.0	DE
		17.54	Multi-Ethnic, High Unemployment, Overcrowding	0.3	DE

Table 7.2. *A description of some *ACORN categories, groups and types*

(Reproduced by kind permission of CACI Limited.)

An example of the value of the *ACORN classification when interlaced with product usage data, either from the marketing organization's own data stream or from such sources as the Target Group Index (described in Chapter 11), was provided by the wine-heavy usage index mentioned above.

While the main *ACORN classification serves as a natural starting point for many marketing planning exercises, the increasing complexity and fragmentation of many consumer markets frequently generates a demand for even more specialized targeting. To meet this demand, CACI has created a family of classifications for sharper analysis of the consumer bases related to different products and markets. These classifications make use of UK Census data together with other data sources and an outline of them is provided below together with some examples of their practical application.

- Investor *ACORN – A luxury goods manufacturer or a financial services organization may wish to target people with high disposable income. Investor *ACORN uses a mix of census data and a share ownership database which identifies areas of high disposable income and people most likely to buy high value products.

- Change *ACORN – A discount food retailer or a 'budget' mail order clothing company may wish to identify areas where there is low consumer confidence and cautious spending. The Change *ACORN classification analyses changes over a decade to enable such clients to pinpoint areas where consumer confidence is depressed.

- Household *ACORN – Uses Electoral Roll data to target households for direct mail.

- Scottish *ACORN – Identifies consumer types which are distinctive to Scotland.

- Financial *ACORN – This targets people according to the financial products they are likely to purchase.

- Custom *ACORN – Uses the customer's own sales data in order to build targeting classifications specific to his or her organization.

This is a necessarily cursory look at various approaches to segmentation but before we leave it, it is very important to say something about some of the other main methods of classifying potential customers.

Benefit segmentation

The issue of discovering the *causes* of buying behaviour, rather than merely describing consumers, has led to the concept of *benefit segmentation*. Pioneered by Russell Haley (1968, pp 30–5) the concept is founded on the basis that it is wrong to assume all consumers seek the same thing from a product. Haley's research into the toothpaste market discovered that:

- one segment bought the product for its flavour;

- another segment for its effectiveness in preventing decay;

- yet another for its power in brightening teeth.

The 'benefits' approach is favoured by a growing number of researchers since it produces reasons why certain 'brands' (see Chapter 8) are favoured, which is a considerable improvement on the description of only the members of the segment buying the brand.

British writer Michael Thomas (1980, p 26) has reported that studies have shown benefit segmentation to be a better determinant of consumer behaviour than several of the other approaches used to segment a market. The evaluation of brands is discovered by research into consumer attitudes. Respondents are asked for their agreement or disagreement with statements concerning various characteristics of a product group and the benefits being sought. Their replies enable them to be 'clustered' into segments which relate to the benefits they are seeking.

National classifications

Despite the importance of multinational corporations, which frequently conduct advertising campaigns for a standardized product in several countries at the same time, and despite the emergence of international associations of retail organizations promoting their international 'own brands', attitudes and preferences still persist that are essentially *national* in character. Consequently, although a product or service can sometimes be discovered to have a general appeal across a number of national boundaries, for many products and services a particular nation state will constitute a particular market. This is because within a particular nation, in addition to a cluster of user preferences, based as they often are on social, tribal, ethnic, religious and cultural factors, there will be economic, legal and political systems in place which all play a part in fashioning a specific type of demand. We shall be considering this further in Chapter 13 when we review the factors involved in mapping a market.

These comments would seem to be at variance with those earlier in the book on 'global markets' and 'the global economy', so a few words of explanation would be prudent here. While it is true that, as Koch (1995, p 226) has pointed out, globalization is a reality for most of the world's largest companies, in the sense that they think and operate with a global perspective on customers, technology, costs, sourcing, strategic alliances and competitors, *few real global products exist* (this writer's emphasis). This is doubtless what one of the world's noted authors, Kenichi Ohmae (1990) has in mind when he persuasively argues the case for inevitable and beneficent globalization, based however on *local globalization* rather than universal products.

There are countless examples of how products often have to be modified or completely re-styled in order to appeal to particular foreign markets:

● the Swedes prefer a four-bladed lawnmower rather than the conventional five-bladed models used in other markets;

● whereas the British taste for the finish of furniture is to let the grain and tone of the wood speak for itself, for acceptability in some Central European countries, the wood may have to be sprayed with a dense gun-metal grey finish;

● the manufacturer of shock absorbers may have to carry out extensive tests under varying road conditions before he can be sure he has a product that will withstand the rough terrain of some foreign countries – Poland is a case in point;

● in some countries, clothing suppliers must pay particular attention to the 'fashion' element of their output; in other countries (e.g. Germany) the primary emphasis will be on durability and value for money.

National classifications are clearly the most broad of the segmentation variables but, as an organization moves beyond its domestic market, they are of great significance.

Ethnic and religious classifications

Like other forms of classification, the analysis of markets by spatial, geographic, area or regional classification is a handy and efficient method of division particularly for the purposes of strategy – for example for the phased introduction of products, for the territorial allocation of sales representatives, and for the monitoring of marketing revenues pro rata to marketing costs.

It is also true that there are some well-established differences in buying and consuming behaviour on this dimension: in the USA, for example, biscuits and particular types of footwear enjoy greater popularity in the South, whilst Mexican food is considered a great treat in the south-west. The people on the west coast are accounted to be rather more friendly and 'open' than those in the east. They are also prepared to travel great distances, which has had some influence on the location of retail stores. We have just been examining classifications by nation state and must also be conscious of important differences within nation states – of markets within a market, as it were.

Dawson (1979, p 113) is broadly correct, though, when he says that regional segmentation of purchasing behaviour is essentially a 'coarse sieve'. At the other end of the scale, however, it is possible to define, with a great degree of accuracy, groups which represent quite distinct markets for certain products and services and which, even if they may be small, none the less constitute important segments within the total marketing area.

In the UK, for example, such ethnic minorities as the Jews, the Irish and the immigrants from India, Pakistan, the West Indies and other parts of the world are important and interesting sub-groups. Many of these groups have their own news media, their own retail outlets and entertainment facilities, their own dietary laws and cultural patterns and these are of significance for marketing organizations. Williamson (1979, p 18), for instance, points out that many Asians are afflicted by vitamin D deficiency, brought about by cultural and religious restrictions on such products as fish and margarine. Vegetable oil margarine is not so restricted, however, and Van den Berghs have actively promoted their Blue Band margarine to the Asian communities, emphasizing its vitamin D content.

Whilst some of these purchasing differences are linked to religious and cultural ideologies, other differences, though often significant, are difficult to explain. African-American families in the USA, for instance, buy substantially more cooked cereals, corn meal, household insecticides, cream, rice, spaghetti and frozen vegetables than their white counterparts, according to Van Tassel (1969, p 303). He also points out that the average African-American male is likely to buy 77 per cent more pairs of shoes during his lifetime than the average white male, and is prepared to pay more for them.

Nor do these differences remain with purchasing habits: Dawson (1979, p 114) points out that the shopping patterns of Catholic and Protestant religious groups in Belfast are different in terms of the shops they each patronize. Reporting Murdie, Dawson (1979, p 114) adds that the patterns of travel to retail outlets in south-western Ontario differ between Mennonites and the majority culture. Those differences that are grounded in religious belief very often account for regional differences – the 'Protestant ethic' doubtless exercises some influence on attitudes to products and the marketing campaigns that accompany them: the regional differences in Germany, for example, have some of their roots in religion.

If the cow is holy to the adherents of one religion and the pig is an unclean animal to another, this will have an impact not only on products but also on the packaging, advertising and on the symbols used in promoting the products. Colour is an important element in this context too. Many ethnic groups prefer brighter colours than may be used in selling to the main market and as most marketing students already know, from the frequency with which it appears in examinations answers, whilst white is generally a popular colour, suitable for many occasions in most European markets, it signifies mourning in many Eastern markets.

These examples may help to convey how data related to ethnic and religious factors can be used to identify differences in buying behaviour – not only for marketing in those overseas countries where such factors predominate, but also for marketing to appropriate minority segments within 'home' markets.

Industrial segmentation

As noted earlier, a substantial proportion of the demand in industrial markets is derived. A product, a component part, a sub-assembly or a service is often required as a result of the demand for some other product or service. In order to classify markets by segments and to estimate demand, the industrial goods producer will survey *user industries* carefully. Of course, some products and services do not pre-select particular segments. Office equipment and supplies, industrial cleaning equipment, the installation and maintenance of information technology, etc. can quite logically be marketed to industries and organizations of all types. However, for most industrial products 'the market' is not a huge undifferentiated one but a cluster of segments, some of which may be quite small. The concept of segmentation is therefore as relevant here as it is in the consumer field, although it is not always as straightforward to apply.

As can be noted from information earlier in this text, there is a great deal of secondary research data available on industrial markets. The UK's Office for National Statistics provides, in published form and via electronic media, a vast amount of data on the economy, the manufacturing and primary sectors, the labour market, the service sector, etc. In addition its Sector Reviews and its Product Sales and Trade series provide each quarter a range of valuable statistics, from a broad manufacturing overview right down to data on individual products.

In addition to government sources, some of the specialized information available from the Economist Intelligence Unit, the *Financial Times*, Dun and Bradstreet and numerous professional, technical and marketing research organizations is of great assistance in identifying how best to segment markets.

One basis on which to approach the task is, of course, by *area (geographical) segmentation*. Although this was well-marked in the days of the heavy industries, such as coal, steel, shipbuilding and textiles, the lighter, more 'high-tech' industries of today are more geographically dispersed. Even so, geography is frequently an important segmentation variable. In the UK, for instance, anyone interested in selling to producers of cars and commercial vehicles, cutlery, ceramics, electronics, etc. will find that *locality* is an important first stage in establishing a segmentation framework.

As a frequent and key step in industrial segmentation is the analysis of secondary data, particularly from government sources, a key to locating the sources of relevant data is the Standard Industrial Classification (SIC) which provides a framework for the collection, tabulation, presentation and analysis of data about economic activities. Its use ensures that the data collected and disseminated by UK government departments and agencies have a uniform basis.

The SIC (92) incorporates the latest revision of this classification and was designed to align it with the classification of economic activities employed by the European Union. The framework provided by SIC 1992 comprises 17 sections, 14 sub-sections, 60 divisions, 222 groups, 503 classes and 142 subclasses. An organization interested in data relating to the manufacture of soft furnishings, for example, would find its way to these data via the following approach:

Section D	Manufacturing (comprising divisions 15 to 37)
Subsection DB	Manufacturing of textiles and textile products (comprising divisions 17 and 18)
Division 17	Manufacture of textiles
Group 17.4	Manufacture of made-up textile articles, except apparel
Class 17.40	Manufacture of made-up textile articles, except apparel
Subclass 17.40/1	Manufacture of soft furnishings.

What may seem a daunting task in this example becomes easier through repetition, of course, and ensures that only highly relevant data are being scrutinized for the purposes of segmentation and demand analysis. Mention should also be made here of the International Standard Industrial Classification (ISIC) which was devised by the United Nations Organisation (UNO), its objective being to standardize statistics between nations so as to facilitate comparisons – an important issue in the international marketing of industrial products.

Some years ago, Peter Fitzroy (1976, pp 125–7) suggested that industrial segmentation could be approached in two stages and this approach retains much of its value. It is outlined below.

Stage 1 The identification of macrosegments, based on such characteristics as:

- size of customer;
- customer usage rate;
- application of the product;
- SIC category of customer;
- customer organizational structure;
- geographical location of customer.

Note that these bases, either singly or in combination, are common forms of industrial segmentation.

Stage 2 The sub-division of each macrosegment in terms of:

- the structure, authority and methods of the buying centre;
- perceived importance of the purchase;
- whether first purchase or repeat purchase;
- relative importance of the determinants of the buying decision;
- loyalty and attitudes towards vendors.

The adoption of new products, services, concepts

Before closing this chapter it might be useful to comment on another aspect of buyer behaviour which is of significant interest to marketers – the manner in which new products, concepts and ideas are taken up or 'adopted'.

In his classic work on the 'diffusion of innovations' Everett Rogers (and Shoemaker, 1971) has suggested that customers can be classified according to 'adoption categories' (see Figure 7.8). He suggests that a typical population of users has the following percentage distribution:

2.5%	innovators
13.5%	early adopters
34.0%	early majority
34.0%	late majority
16.0%	laggards.

As Figure 7.8 indicates, these percentages produce a curve of normal distribution.

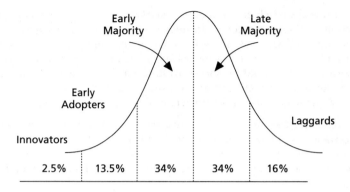

Figure 7.8. *Adoption categories (based on elapsed time of adoption of innovations)*

(*Source*: Everett M. Rogers, *Diffusion of Innovations*)

The *innovators* are willing to take risks, to try something new – a new product, a new concept. They are usually to be found in the higher income, higher social groups. The *early adopters* are almost in the same category as the innovators and are the main opinion leaders in their community. The *early majority* show some willingness to take risks but this is not as developed as in the previous two adoption categories and they show less potential for opinion leadership. The *late majority* are imitators, but rather cautious – they will adopt products and ideas when these are well and truly tried and tested, while the *laggards* are generally change resistant and lacking in imagination.

Obviously, when a product launch is being undertaken and particularly when this is based on an entirely new or revolutionary concept, the marketer will be particularly interested in reaching and persuading the first two of these categories.

In a similar vein to Rogers' outline of diffusion theory, Katz and Lazarsfeld (1955, p 325) suggest that within each human group there is a minority of trend setters or *opinion leaders*. Marketing information flows from the organization to the opinion leaders and from these leaders to the rest of the market. The opinion leaders obtain their self-fulfilment by being 'first in the field', for example with such contemporary significant products as cable television, the personal computer, the mobile telephone, etc. This group of people is therefore important to the marketing organization, not only at the launch stage of a new product but also for their influence as opinion formers and word of mouth advocates. The views of opinion leaders carry much weight with the rest of the population and their advice is often sought.

These ideas on innovation and opinion leadership are obviously interesting, even though they stand in need of further investigation and development. In this regard, the work of the UK researcher, J.A. Lunn (1968, p 413), although also reported some time ago, is still worthy of mention. His basic idea was not to fit the consumer to a pre-determined set of psychological or sociological classifications (e.g. introversion–extroversion) in the hope that these would relate in some way to buying behaviour, but to derive new classifications from the study of the consumer as a consumer.

Lunn's *criterion group* approach began by identifying groups with known different purchasing patterns. Next, his research method sought to discover the psychological characteristics that differentiate such groups. He then established a number of consumer personality scales each of proven value in a number of the product fields that were under examination. Some of the more general classifications which emerged included:

- thrift;

- experimentalism;

- traditionalism.

The significance of this approach is that if *experimentation* emerged as a key variable for a particular product then a marketing strategy would be devised to appeal to this section of the population. Samples of informants for marketing research purposes (e.g. for product and advertisement testing) would be mainly drawn from this priority group. If experimentalists could be shown to have particular viewing and reading habits (such data having been collected in the same research) then the planning of promotional campaigns would take this into account.

It is noteworthy that since the time of Lunn's research and, as a result of media owners' research into their own markets, the coverage of some media has been described in terms of 'economic venturesomeness' and 'economy-mindedness' as well as by the more general classifications, many of which have been described in this chapter.

Customer screening in practice

1   Sampling is used in marketing research because the alternative, to conduct a census, is both costly and time-consuming. However, one UK census of significant interest to marketers is the UK census of the national population, conducted by the Office for National Statistics at ten year intervals. The next of these, the first of the new millennium, will take place in the year 2001.

Organizations have always acknowledged the value of the national census as a marketing tool. As Garrett (1996, p 2) points out, with 96 per cent of households taking part, it provides an unrivalled snapshot of the nation's living conditions and consumer-habits, broken down area by area, enabling organizations to target areas where their products and services would be most likely to sell. An indication of its value is the fact that up to November 1996 the 1991 census had earned the ONS £4.6 million from the sale of its data.

That said, one of the weaknesses of the census for targeting purposes was the omission of the respondents' incomes. Traditionally, the census authorities had been reluctant to include an appropriate question on the grounds that it might deter people from completing the census forms, fearing perhaps that the information might be used for increased taxation or the withdrawal of benefits. Nevertheless, a trial conducted in 1997, and outlined by Garrett, will among other things, enable the ONS to improve its competitive edge against the life-style surveys which have for some time now been successfully asking questions about income. The trial, which took place with a sample of 104,000 households across Britain, posed a number of new questions including religious affiliation, voluntary care provided to relatives and friends, access to a garden and qualifications gained after school. It also asked respondents to indicate which of seven bands from 'nil' to '£25,000 or over' fitted their income.

Historically, research companies have derived an indication of affluence from questions relating to the occupation of the head of the household and from such questions, included in the census, as the number of rooms in the house, the number of cars people own and the newspapers they read.

Thus, although the primary objective of the national census is to assist HM Government in its own activities, this brief example demonstrates the supplementary commercial value of the data it generates and how these must be successively refined for competitive purposes.

2   The Single Person Households survey produced by the Mintel research agency and available to marketers in Spring 1996 provides another example of the commercial significance of changes in population profiles and life-styles.

Diane Summers (1996, p 7) draws attention to a number of important points from the survey:

- the number of people living alone is set to rise to 8 million by the end of the century, from 6.8 million in 1995;

- younger, single home-makers – increasingly likely to be owner-occupiers – will be interested in cheap ways of brightening their homes;

- convenience foods, home security devices and services linked to socializing are likely to have extra market potential;

- single person households made up 24 per cent in 1985 and 28 per cent in 1995; by the year 2000 the figure will have grown to 30 per cent;

- the rising divorce rate and the tendency towards later marriage partly account for this trend among younger age groups, whilst steadily increasing life expectancy has contributed to the growth in numbers of older single person households;

- although nearly 50 per cent of people who live alone are aged 65 or over, it is the non-pensioner groups which have shown the highest rate of growth in recent years;

- the proportion of single person households belonging to the socio-economic group ABC_1 (professional and non-manual) has increased to 45 per cent, from 38 per cent in 1990. It is noteworthy, however, that this is still smaller than for the population as a whole, where the ABC_1 classification accounts for 49 per cent of households;

- single people have more leisure time than other groups – an additional eight hours per week for those under 55 – the implications for the leisure industry are clear.

The strategic formula: Element 2:

Products and processes, services and ideas

Products, processes and the marketing mix

The notion of a *marketing mix* was described in Chapter 3 where the case for its enlargement was outlined. In its enlarged form it comprises the following six elements:

- preparation (marketing research);
- product;
- price;
- place (distribution);
- promotion;
- people.

The traditional elements (the 4Ps): *product*, *price*, *place* and *promotion* in positions 2–4 (above) will be dealt with in this chapter and in the three chapters which follow. The *preparation* element we have reviewed in Chapters 6 and 7 and the *people* element will be considered in Chapter 12, with some emphasis upon:

- the development of organizational commitment to marketing and marketing objectives;
- the management of change.

In this chapter, then, we shall be looking specifically at the *product* element (or ingredient) in the mix, emphasizing that the term *product* is broadly interpreted to include *processes*, *services* and *ideas* as well as *physical products* designed for consumer and industrial use.

Before moving on to our review of products and product development it would be useful to remind ourselves of what was said, at greater length, about the marketing mix in Chapter 3, namely that:

- the nature of the product will influence the balance of the ingredients in the mix;
- the concept of a 'mix' reflects the idea that the blend of its ingredients may be varied, from time to time, in order to achieve objectives;
- the marketing strategy, and hence the mix, is devised with a view to attaining objectives cost-effectively;
- the marketing strategy, and mix, cannot be static – they must respond to changes in the organization's environment.

This means that, although the mix is the main instrument through which strategies are implemented, its recipe must be continually adjusted in the light of pressure from organizational strengths and weaknesses, customers, competitors and economic and other forces in the general external environment.

Defining the product

The product is the basic ingredient upon which the marketing mix is constructed – without it there is no need for the other ingredients. Segmentation strategy, positioning strategy ('engagement' or 'avoidance'), indeed, the whole current performance of the organization and its resilience over the longer term are all based upon performance of its product. The product is, in fact, the key factor enabling an organization to adapt to its environment in order to survive.

Since we become involved with hundreds of products in our daily lives, we might seemingly have no difficulty in providing a definition – for example a physical object which is *produced*, hence the term *product*. Then, along the lines of this definition we can begin to classify products.

Consumer products

- *convenience products*, which are low-cost, repeatedly bought and readily accessible, e.g. bread, milk and newspapers.

- *shopping products*, which are more highly priced, bought less frequently and after some thought and effort, e.g. furniture, domestic electrical equipment, personal computers.

- *speciality products* which are similar to shopping products in terms of purchasing patterns though more exclusive and highly priced because of the distinctive features they possess, e.g. a vintage car or furniture by an 'old master' – products essentially 'minority market'.

Industrial products

Industrial products range from capital equipment, accessories and components, raw materials, etc., to the consumable supplies which facilitate production and administrative operations.

However, a definition of 'product' as a physical object takes us only so far and for the sake of completeness and accuracy we need to bear in mind the points that are listed below.

In marketing the word product is defined very broadly

For some time now, following the lead of the American Marketing Association, marketers have held to the view that 'product' includes not only physical objects but services, systems, personalities, organizations, geographical locations and even specific, desirable objectives.

Therefore, a 'product' could be entertainment at a local theatre, a parliamentary candidate, a region or city wishing to attract inward investment or a desirable objective such as awakening interest in the plight of the world's wildlife. At the bottom line, these are all products to be marketed.

This broader approach to a definition has gained substantial acceptance with the result that insurance policies and financial investment plans are now referred to by the organizations marketing them as their 'products', although traditionally we have regarded the insurance and financial sectors as providing 'services'.

The Times newspaper (Askham, 1992, p 22) once contained an article on how a specialist in history, archaeology, fell walking and road tours had discovered, by market research carried out in Europe and North America, a need for in-country specialists to compile tailor-made itineraries for those tourists seeking something more individualistic than a packaged holiday. The product, on which a business has subsequently been successfully built was, in essence, *information*.

The product is rarely a simple concept

The product is often much more than a collection of component parts or the result of fusing together various raw materials. It can include, for instance:

- accessories;
- an installation service;
- an operating manual;
- a package;
- a brand name or trade mark;
- a user guarantee;
- after sales service.

Even the simplest consumer product is typically much more than a physical object or a given quantity of material, for at least a package and a brand name will be added. It is because the value-offer which we call a 'product' can be quite complex that the phrase 'total product' will sometimes be used in this text. The concept underlying the phrase has important implications for marketing success as we shall see later.

Products are bought not so much for what they are as for what they will do

The physical specification of the product is important only in so far as it satisfies the needs of the user. We must always bear in mind that 'the sale takes place in the mind of the buyer' and that any work or effort with a product that does not begin and end with the satisfaction of the user is production orientation and not market orientation.

Lanigan (1992, pp 344–5), for example, in the context of industrial products, suggests that the evaluation of a product-offer involves at least six attributes:

- *quality* – the degree to which the objective and subjective features of the product meet the customer requirements;
- *conformability* – the degree to which it initially meets its declared quality specification;
- *availability* – the degree to which the product maintains its declared quality specification throughout its useful life;
- *delivery time* – which can range from virtually nothing for simple products 'off the shelf' to many years for complex products;
- *confidence* – an attribute which depends on the consequences of failure to the customer and depends upon customer perception of the supplier as well as of the product;
- *price* – which is not only the initial purchase price but the *price of ownership* which comprises the initial price plus product operating costs, repair and maintenance costs and any net disposal cost when its useful life has expired.

Lanigan (1992, p 345) explains that aggregated together, the first five attributes – quality, conformability, availability, delivery time and confidence – constitute '*product value*, as it is perceived by the potential customer in the particular circumstances which apply to that customer'. He then underscores the salience of customer benefits by adding that the product *benefit ratio* is determined by the equation:

$$\text{Benefit ratio} = \frac{\text{product value}}{\text{product price}}$$

and it is this ratio which is a measure of the *competitiveness* of a product.

Christopher and McDonald (1995, pp 128–32) similarly emphasize the importance of benefits to the customer adding that 'it will be his perception of these benefits that will influence his decision to buy or not'. They formalize the matching procedure between the benefits of products and selected market segments through the use of a *benefit analysis worksheet*. These authors found that there were a number of sources of potential benefits to customers but that, in reality, they would not all be equally attractive. Accordingly, for the worksheet approach they adopted the classifications of major benefits, secondary benefits and lesser benefits allotting a maximum possible points score to each classification for use in the evaluation of individual products. In this way, the technique enables an organization to assess, and improve, its output in terms of the benefits it provides.

The success of the product is not to be measured solely by concrete satisfactions

Economy, durability, speed, rate of output, ease of application – these are all concrete and important satisfactions which may have been promised by a supplier in the value offer and, once promised, they must be delivered for they are vital to the product's success. Yet, as we saw in Chapter 7, psychological and social satisfactions are important too. Demand is driven by behavioural as well as economic influences.

For instance, people may buy a product because it relates satisfactorily to their self-image. Buying this newspaper or that motor car may confer status and move the individual nearer to his or her ideal-self. Again, where products are bought with social influences to the fore, it is because they relate to the norms of some group which is significant to the user —the family, young adults, sporting heroes, the legal profession, etc.

Nor are such psychological and social satisfactions related only to the purchasers of consumer products. They may also be significant to organizational buyers. Note, for instance, that Lanigan (1992, p 344) referred to product quality as encompassing subjective as well as objective factors. In their textbook *Business Marketing Management*, Hutt and Speh (1992, p 273) point out that a product is all of the value satisfactions that a customer derives at both an organizational and a personal level. They add that a purchase of cold rolled steel, for example, is buying:

- physical specifications (thickness, chemical composition);
- technical advice;
- delivery reliability;

but, in addition, the seller may be able to satisfy more personal needs of the buyer by reducing risk and improving the buyer's status within the organization. Here it should also be noted that often the market standing of bought-in components will confer status on the organization using them in their own products – witness the fact that in the advertisements of personal computer suppliers, the Intel Pentium processor is usually well to the fore.

Summarizing what has been said above then, we can classify the characteristics of a product under three headings:

- *physical* – shape, style, colour, size, weight, etc.;

- *functional* – its performance in use;
- *symbolic* – based on the psychological and social satisfactions it delivers.

It is also clear that *all* these characteristics have a great bearing on the product's success or failure.

The significance of the process

Whilst we acknowledge the salience of the product for marketing success, we must not neglect the importance of the *process* by which it is brought into being. It is as important to be customer-led in the design, development and operation of the process as it is of the product. An example of an engineering process might make this clear. Consider the manufacturing area of machining. As one observer (Burman, 1993, pp 48ff) has pointed out, suppliers are aiming continuously to improve methods as well as products because today's customers will no longer accept that a percentage of products will be sub-standard or that their price must rise on a regular basis.

If we take the case of tolerances in machining, these are now typically being determined by automated assembly systems, which means that the need to hold to close limits is paramount. Nevertheless, the cost factor is obviously a key issue and, in the customer oriented firm, the design/production engineering team is expected to be fully aware of the implications of any tolerances they set for, as Figure 8.1 indicates, tightening tolerances means sharply rising costs. It thus becomes quite vital to develop new methods and apply techniques which will lead to higher standards without increasing costs.

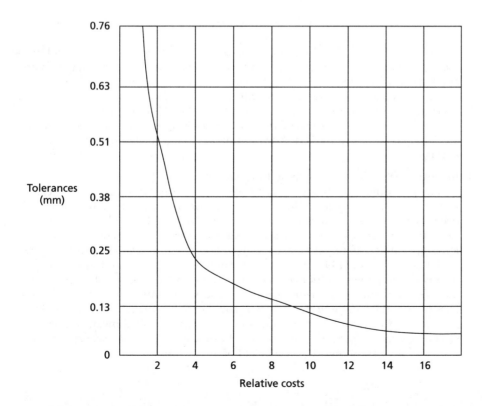

Figure 8.1. *Effects of typical machining tolerances on cost*

(Acknowledgements to SME Tool and Manufacturing Engineers Handbook and Automotive Engineer).

Also, in order to be flexible in the face of market demand and to keep close control of inventories, the machining process must be set up to cope with a wide variety of products, frequent change-overs and small batch quantities. At the same time, however, all change-overs are costly. Even so, costs can be minimized by careful planning both initially, for example when designing production facilities for a new product, and subsequently for example when preparing its production schedules.

Machining tolerances, designing production facilities and preparing production schedules may seem far away from the world of the marketing executive – but this is not so. 'Total organizational commitment' and 'a unified customer-led culture', phrases we met in Chapter 1, have immense practical implications. Where they are in place, design and production people will automatically bear 'the market' in mind as they conceive and plan. Marketing people will bear in mind the significance of process as well as product in developing competitive strength. Where such techniques as *simultaneous engineering* are adopted, which provide for the voices of marketing research and sales to be heard at the earliest stages, the task becomes easier.

In their reference to *computer-integrated manufacturing* (CIM) Christopher and McDonald (1995) help to bring out the importance of *process* for marketing success. They point out that using traditional investment appraisal techniques CIM often appears to be uneconomic in terms of the cost reduction it promises, but they go on to say:

> However, the major benefits of CIM, as the Japanese are demonstrating, exist primarily not in terms of reduced costs but rather in the greater manufacturing flexibility it provides, the shorter throughput times and the reduction in working capital. This translates into direct marketing benefits to the manufacturing company. For example, companies using this technology can respond more rapidly to customer needs; they can produce greater variety with little or no cost penalty; they can reduce inventories and thus boost return on investment (ROI) (Christopher and McDonald, 1995, p 8).

Among the practical examples of the significance of the process are these:

- In early 1997 Siebe, the UK engineering group, announced that it was adopting the 'six-sigma' programme, a ferociously demanding approach to quality control which entails reducing defects in a process to just over three per million. The programme is both costly and time consuming but has been adopted by such leading US companies as Motorola and General Electric. Siebe's move has been described 'an application to join a world elite of super-efficient manufacturers' (Jackson, 1997, p 11). More will be said about 'six-sigma' in the section on techniques later in this chapter.

- In November 1996, a report based on data assembled by McKinsey, the US management consultants, disclosed that Britain led Europe in terms of the quality of its motor parts production. The report, based on an exhaustive study of automotive component production throughout the world, indicated that the international car manufacturer customers of UK companies made 512 complaints about quality for every million parts, compared with 1050 for Germany and 780 for France. According to Marsh (1996, p 13), the research broke new ground in assessing the quality of companies' output by examining not only the volume of defective parts but also the less quantifiable area of 'process quality'. This was defined by McKinsey as the summing up of a company's ability to manufacture and deliver a product to the specification agreed with the customer. This meant the research took account of a company's ability to be flexible and, as one McKinsey consultant put it: 'to perform somersaults on behalf of its customer'.

The planning and introduction of new products

Innovation

From what we have read so far in this text, it is clear that because of the rate of change in their respective environments, there is within many organizations great pressure to *innovate* – derived from the idea that to do nothing is to go backwards. Doyle provides us with a handy definition of innovation:

> For a manager, innovation should be defined as developing and delivering products or services that offer benefits which customers perceive as new and superior. Opportunities for innovation are created by environmental changes which generate new customer needs or make possible better solutions to current needs (Doyle, 1994, p 189).

Rather like the sale then, innovation is caught up with what happens in the mind of the buyer. Unfortunately, when compared to some countries, the UK appears not to have a good track record in innovation. Details of a survey of manufacturing innovation (Cassell, 1996, p 9), which appeared in 1996 and was conducted among 3500 manufacturing companies, highlighted the extent of the British failure to innovate.

For the six co-authors of the report, product innovation is essentially a business process embracing many stages but primarily related to the market application of existing knowledge; it may, or may not, be linked to significant technological advance. In the three countries surveyed, the UK, Germany and Ireland, the research findings point to a 'strong and overwhelmingly positive link' between innovation and sales growth. In the UK, for example, companies strong on innovation achieved an annual sales rise of 7 per cent compared to the 5 per cent rise of companies less innovation-minded. Similar results were evident in the growth of both employment and export sales.

However, while innovation was regarded as important in all three countries, fewer UK companies introduced new products compared with their competitors in Germany and Ireland. Among the factors impeding innovation in the U.K. were these:

- skill shortages;
- the inferior quality of education and training;
- concern over low levels of return on investment;
- the 'riskiness' of innovation and lack of suitable finance.

Obviously, if innovation is so important, the UK's problem needs to be addressed – by its government and its financial institutions as well as its businesses.

The 'new' product

How might we define those 'new' products that are clearly so important? Guiltinan, Gordon and Madden (1997, pp 193–4) suggest that 'newness' is a matter of degree and that a product may be:

- new to the market (i.e. never produced or marketed before) or
- new to the firm.

Combining these types of newness with degree of newness they produce the following six classifications of a 'new product':

- *new to the world products* – which create entirely new markets, with completely new product life-cycles and have no direct competition when first launched, e.g. the Sony Walkman;

- *new product lines* – product entries into existing markets which are new to the firm, e.g. printer manufacturer Hewlett-Packard's entry into the personal computer market;

- *additions to existing lines* – new products which offer different kinds or levels of benefit to the market currently being served, e.g. the development of a tartar control toothpaste for the Crest brand;

- *improvements to existing products* – i.e. products which offer enhanced performance or greater perceived value, e.g. annual model changes of car manufacturers, 'new and improved' versions of Windows 95 software;

- *product repositionings* – very modest developments that allow a product to offer new applications and serve new needs, e.g. the repositioning of prescription ulcer medicines such as Tagamet and Pepcid as over-the-counter stomach-acid blockers;

- *cost reductions* – versions of existing products which provide comparable performance at lower cost – though not really new from a marketing perspective they can improve competitiveness – the continuous price reductions of the standard versions of well-established brands of personal computer being an example.

Systematic new product planning

Despite its clear importance, the history of product innovation is one of high failure rates. Quoting research findings, for instance, Majaro (1993, p 83) indicates that for roughly every 20 products brought to the market, only one is likely to be a complete success. In counselling against despair, Baker (1981, pp 145–6) points out that there is no universal definition of failure and what may be a failure to one organization, for example, failure to achieve a target rate of return on investment, may well be a success to another. Even so, Baker also makes the perceptive comment that the pressure to innovate comes at a time when the increasing costs of innovation and high failure rates may prove ruinous. It is not hard to find evidence in support of this comment: a clear illustration of the escalating cost of innovation was the development of Ford's Mondeo. Using an international design team to develop this 'car for the world' (the meaning of the name) took six years of the company's time and cost £3 billion.

Not all companies have a world-wide reach, of course, but whatever the size of company or the scale of its investment, innovation cannot conceivably be free from risk and all organizations would be happy to reduce it. Having examined the various studies made of product failure rates and the views of various writers on the topic, Figure 8.2 is an attempt to summarize the major underlying reasons for the problem. Two points are worth making with regard to the aspect on the inadequacy of distribution:

- with some fast moving consumer goods, particularly food products, failure to interest the large retail multiple organizations that dominate the sector may prove ruinous to prospects for a new product;

- related to timing, if the new product is introduced during economic recession, distributors may be cautious about taking even a trial quantity.

With regard to the annotation on development costs being higher than projected, it is worth adding Peter Kraushar's observation that a project for a new product often 'generates a momentum within a company which is difficult to stop and it is then looked at with rose-tinted spectacles' (1981, p 132).

It is not altogether straightforward to suggest the best way for new products to be planned and introduced. Stanton (1981, p 173), for example, believes that some turn-around in the size of the risks involved would be achieved if more organizations:

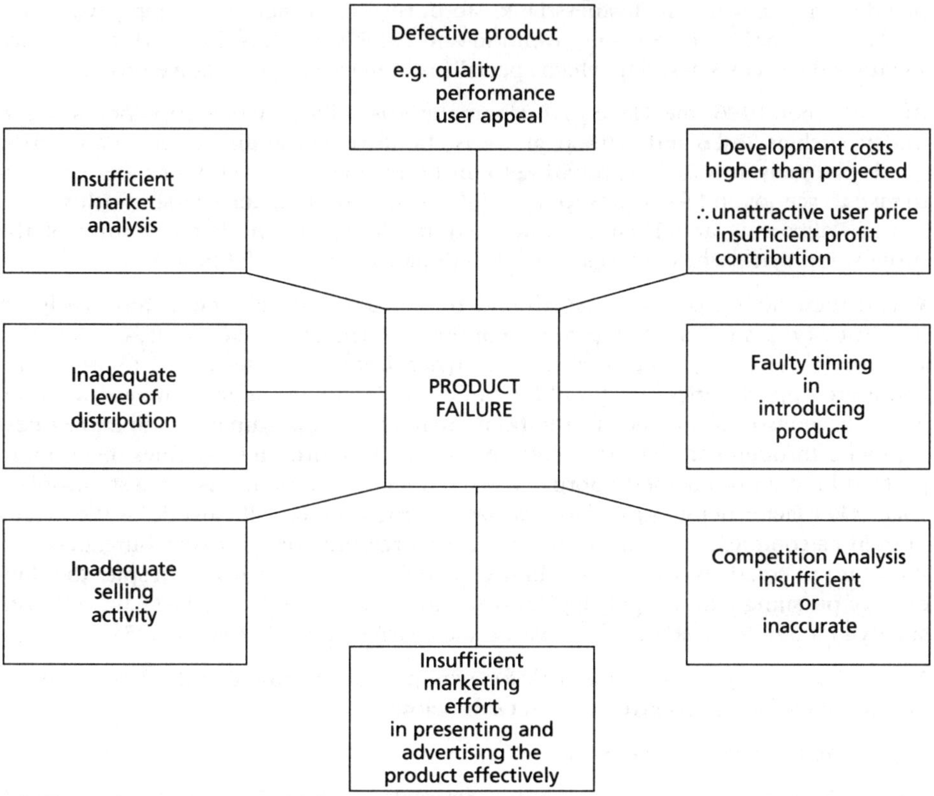

Figure 8.2. *The anatomy of product failue*

```
                         ┌─────────────────────┐
                         │  Defective product  │
                         │                     │
                         │  e.g. quality       │
                         │       performance   │
                         │       user appeal   │
                         └─────────────────────┘
┌──────────────┐                                    ┌──────────────────────┐
│ Insufficient │                                    │ Development costs     │
│ market       │                                    │ higher than projected │
│ analysis     │                                    │                       │
│              │                                    │ ∴ unattractive user   │
└──────────────┘                                    │   price               │
                                                    │   insufficient profit │
                                                    │   contribution        │
                                                    └──────────────────────┘
┌──────────────┐         ┌─────────────┐            ┌──────────────┐
│ Inadequate   │         │  PRODUCT    │            │ Faulty timing│
│ level of     │─────────│  FAILURE    │────────────│    in        │
│ distribution │         │             │            │ introducing  │
│              │         └─────────────┘            │   product    │
└──────────────┘                                    └──────────────┘
┌──────────────┐                                    ┌──────────────────┐
│ Inadequate   │                                    │ Competition      │
│ selling      │                                    │ Analysis         │
│ activity     │                                    │ insufficient     │
│              │                                    │      or          │
└──────────────┘                                    │ inaccurate       │
                         ┌─────────────────────┐    └──────────────────┘
                         │ Insufficient        │
                         │ marketing           │
                         │ effort              │
                         │ in presenting and   │
                         │ advertising the     │
                         │ product effectively │
                         └─────────────────────┘
```

- took practical steps to systematize their new product planning;
- made better use of marketing research in order to assess market needs and opportunities properly;
- perfected methods to screen and evaluate products and ideas for products.

Peter Drucker (1991, p 3) echoes Stanton's belief, declaring that most of what happens in successful innovations is not the happy occurrence of a blinding flash of insight but, rather, the careful implementation of an unspectacular but systematic management discipline. Greenhalgh (1986, p 425), on the other hand, takes the view that it would be convenient if new products were developed by a logical step-by-step approach so that such development could be 'learned by rote'. He believes, however, that the facts are quite the opposite and that the majority of new products are developed by a series of fairly unordered steps, the order and the degree of attention paid to each varying from company to company and from project to project.

Again, while Drucker's views always deserve attention, it is not difficult to find numerous examples of successful products which have emerged as a result of the 'blinding flash of insight' he finds such a rarity. For example, Mandy Haberman first realized the need for a self-sealing drinking cup when she saw the agility required by a friend's sister to supervise her child's efforts to drink. The result was Haberman's Anyway Cup, a spill-proof device with a valve in its spout that seals between sips. This means that liquid emerges from the cup only when the child is drinking and not when the cup is dropped, shaken or turned upside down. This not only demonstrates that blinding flashes of insight do happen but that product development is not the sole preserve of the large organization with sophisticated R&D facilities – for when Haberman hit upon her solution, Houlder (1996, p 16) reports that she employed consultants to work on the tooling and build a prototype, enlisted the help of a design counsellor at Business Link, Hertfordshire, to help her comply with standards, raise finance, patent the invention and exhibit it, whilst for marketing advice she turned to V&A Marketing which specializes in marketing innovative products.

By November 1996, the Haberman Company was selling 10,000 cups per week to outlets such as Tesco and Safeway and was about to license the design to a US baby goods company. It was also preparing to introduce the Gojo, a cup for older children to take to school and for adults to use while playing sports. James Dyson with his Sea Truck, Ballbarrow and Dual Cyclone vacuum cleaner is another examplar of the proposition that flashes of insight can, and do, lead to successful products.

Where then does that leave us? Should new product development rely solely on insight or on a structured step-by-step approach? The view taken in this text is that structure is necessary, and even more so when information technology raises more and more opportunities which call for *collaboration* between departments of a firm. As we have also seen earlier in the book, marketing opportunity is sometimes best exploited through *collaboration between firms*. Structure thus becomes much more preferable to an unplanned approach. What degree of structure is a question of balance, a key factor being organizational size. A structure that will 'just do' is the ideal – both in its complexity and its formality, never forgetting that excessive bureaucracy is the death of creativity. Greenhalgh himself concludes: 'Nevertheless, despite the difficulty of pursuing a thoroughly logical structure, in practice it is well to have one constantly in mind, to avoid going too far off the charted course' (1986, p 425).

Figure 8.3 is a suggested framework for new product planning and a brief explanation of each of the steps involved is set out below.

Step 1   Scan sources of innovation

Newspapers, television, radio, journals, technical publications, research papers, the organization's own research and development department, employees, inventors, customers (including their complaints), distributors and government departments are just some of the host of sources which can be scanned for innovation possibilities.

Step 2   Generate ideas for new products

Creative, imaginative handling of Step 1 sources should yield ideas but no source of new ideas should be discounted for no organization can have too many. Boone and Kurtz (1980, p 170), for example, quote one survey which established that following tests for commercial viability and other screening devices, 58 ideas resulted in only one successful product.

Andrall E. Pearson (1991, p 9) of the Harvard Business School believes that organizations should be structured to permit innovative ideas to rise above the demands of running a business (see also Chapter 12 – People).

Step 3   Screen ideas for feasibility

Does an idea 'fit' with short- and long-term strategic objectives, profit and non profit? and with institutional image?

Is it compatible with existing technical expertise? with existing skills of workers? with existing equipment and raw material? Is the technology available to develop the product?

What investment would be required, particularly where the answer to any of these questions is 'no'? How does the projected price relate to direct and indirect competition? Questions for this step are legion.

Step 4   Concept testing

Concept tests can provide guidance on:

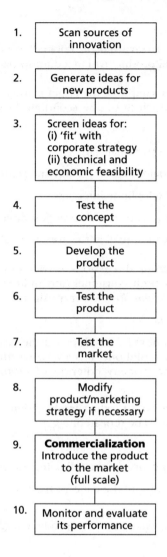

Figure 8.3. *Systematic new product planning (ten steps)*

- the product ideas that seem most promising, justifying further time and attention;

- the ways in which they can be developed further;

- the segments of the market that are the apparent 'targets'.

These tests set out to discover whether the idea will deliver *customer benefits* and, with consumer products for example, the expression of the concepts to be tested might range from:

- simple oral statements (sometimes tape recorded, for uniformity from interview to interview)

to:

- written statements (words on a card)

- 'line' drawings

- dummy packs

- mock advertisements (e.g. for press or television)

or:

- if no heavy investment is involved, a 'cribbed' product (a prototype or close approximation to the real product within a dummy pack).

The test is administered to a sample of the target market and, depending on the type and quantity of test material which can be economically made available, the test can take place:

- in-home (by interviewer's personal call);

- by post (with a questionnaire for completion and return);

- by post, with 'follow-up' telephone interview;

- exclusively by telephone (e.g. testing an oral description of the concept);

- by testing in a central location (e.g. in theatres, test halls or mobile test vans).

Concept tests often utilize group discussions, carried out in locations suitable for the numbers in the group. For both consumer and industrial products, such developments as *rapid prototyping technology* are very valuable.

Step 5 Product development

A trial product can now be developed if the concept test confirms that the original idea seems a valid one. It is always worth repeating that testing must take place with the primary criterion of *customer benefits* constantly in mind.

Where the concept test calls for a product modification, a study of its economic and technical feasibility may have to be repeated.

Step 6 Product testing

This can provide guidance on the following issues:

- whether the promise of the concept has been confirmed by the trial product;

- whether and in what ways the product might be further improved or developed;

- what further investment of time and resources will be required, if this seems necessary;

- which of any alternative specifications/designs of the product appear to be most promising.

Again, the testing will be conducted with a representative cross-section of the target market and, of course, by the time of the product test the marketing team will be more informed about which group of people, or organizations, make up the product's target market.

With nearly all industrial products and many consumer products, the product is tested 'in use'. For consumer products, the home is often the most appropriate place for a test. In which case the product is placed with the informant by a researcher who then calls back or telephones to re-interview. Where the product and the process of obtaining information are relatively straightforward an in-use product test can be conducted by post, if necessary.

If costly promotional material (e.g. a mock TV advertisement) is used in conjunction with the test, the first stage takes place with a group of informants in a central location, such as a test hall. Re-call interviews can then be conducted by either home visit or telephone call after the product has been used. Sometimes the testing, as well as the 'placement', occurs in a test room within the central location so that follow-up interviews are not required. Quite often 'panels' of informants are organized and kept on record in order to test products. Again, the testing process can be accompanied by personal call for re-interview or, if appropriate, the whole process can be conducted by post.

Where the product is tested alongside another product (e.g. the leading product in the field) the process is known as a 'paired comparison' test – an experimental design found frequently in market research. Where the identity of the products, and/or their producers, are unknown to the informant the process is known as 'blind-product testing', as opposed to 'branded testing', where such information is known.

In countries with advanced marketing systems there are a considerable number of specialist research organizations strong in the areas of product testing, usage and attitude studies, promotional development (e.g. TV advertising) and brand image research. In the UK for instance the Pre-Max system of BMRB International aims to provide actionable information in the minimum possible time on such key issues as to whether the product meets customer needs, whether and how it can be improved and whether potential sales justify the cost of additional development and refinement.

In the current competitive climate, small differences between products can be critical. Pre-Max is a well-validated technique for predicting both trial and repeat purchase rates through 'intelligent modelling'. According to BMRB, Pre-Max will:

- identify the attributes of the new product that will encourage trial;

- identify the attributes that encourage repeat purchasing;

- produce estimates of sales volume and value;

- diagnose areas of strength and weakness in the proposed new brand;

- provide data that is at all times clear, accurate and actionable.

Figure 8.4 is an example of how Pre-Max provides information for the client.

Step 7   Testing the market

This is the stage for marketing analysis and perhaps test marketing. Distribution through selected outlets, perhaps utilizing the computer models of key distributors or limited area 'try-outs' (test marketing) may be appropriate here. The objective now is to obtain a detailed quantitative assessment of user acceptability and potential return on investment of the proposed new product.

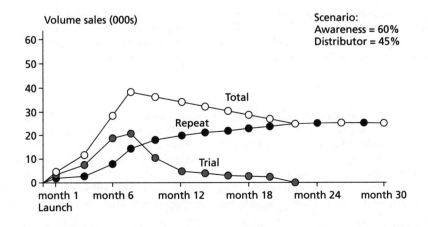

Figure 8.4. *The Pre-Max System : information for the client organization*

Source: BMRB International, London W5.

The product and the marketing strategy, that is all the elements in the marketing mix, are now under examination. Another approach is that of *pilot marketing* where a paired comparison methodology is typically employed. For example, the product's price may be varied in one of two identical test markets, with all other factors held constant. When test marketing is employed, the time taken to complete the exercise and the uniqueness of the product need careful prior consideration in case competitors, having noted the new product, quickly duplicate it and move to full-scale marketing before the originator does.

Step 8   Strategic product/marketing review

The product's design, its technical and economic elements and the marketing strategy are then reviewed in the light of what has been learned in Step 7. The feasibility of the entire plan is considered and necessary changes are made to the product, its production schedules and marketing plan, if market testing and subsequent analysis indicate the necessity for this. It is now 'crunch' time and the final decision has to be taken on whether to market the product on a commercial scale.

Step 9   Commercialization

The full-scale marketing process is now put into effect. This entails the planning of the launch strategy including the timing of the product's introduction, the settling of the final budgets for the entire project and the coordination of all the programmes (introductory pricing, selling, advertising, promotion and distribution) supporting the strategy.

Step 10   Monitoring and evaluation

The performance of the product and the entire marketing programme are continuously monitored and adjusted where necessary, and if possible. It is only at this stage that the ultimate future of the product and its contribution to organizational objectives can be assessed. Where an *investment budget* procedure has been adopted (i.e. disproportionately high early promotion expenditure is undertaken to launch the product with its later recoupment planned as sales build up), this will be carefully monitored. Consequential adjustments to the marketing strategy may also be needed as a result of the reactions of competitors. First steps for the longer-term management of the product are now considered.

Techniques for product development and management

For many organizations, new products form part of what is termed the *product mix*, that is to say the full range of products offered for sale. The development and maintenance of a competitive product mix is the process of *product management*. In this section we shall be looking at some of the techniques and concepts found useful in both new product development and product management. Later in the chapter we shall review some of the issues involved in managing the product mix.

The product life-cycle

Analysis of the sales performance of many products shows they follow a *life-cycle*, not unlike the human life-cycle (though not as precisely defined in actuarial terms!). After its development, when the product is first introduced, sales progress relatively slowly. In the *growth* stage, as the product becomes established in the market, sales increase rapidly. The rate of sales growth slackens during the *maturity* stage, which precedes the *decline* stage where, as newer and perhaps more competitive products appear, sales volume falls off at a highly significant rate. Figure 8.5 illustrates the concept.

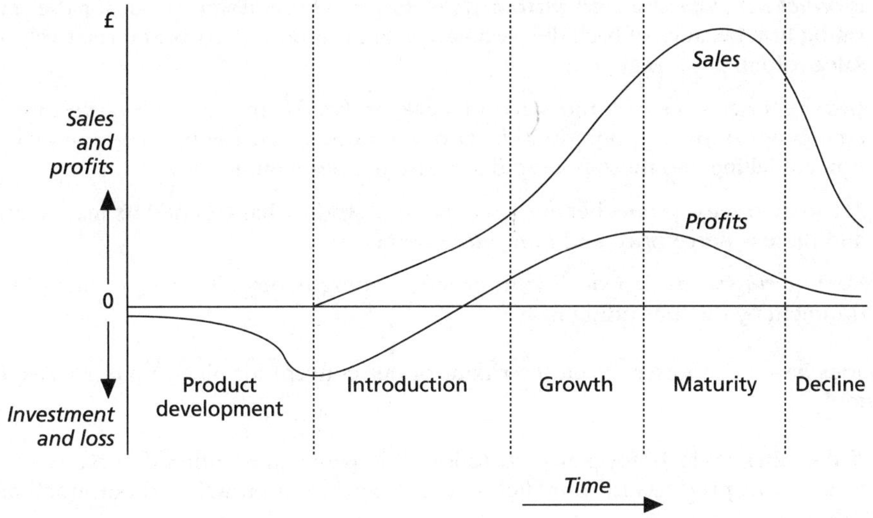

Figure 8.5. *The product life-cycle*

As Doyle (1994, p 131) succinctly points out, the organization's strategic objective will alter as the product moves through its life-cycle thus:

Stage in the life-cycle

	Introduction	Growth	Maturity	Decline
Strategic objective	Aggressive entry	Maximise share	Boost profits	Milk product

His point concerning strategy can be illustrated by reference to the promotion policy (i.e. for advertising, etc.) related to the new product. Expenditure here will not be at some standard rate throughout the life-cycle. At the introduction stage, particularly in highly competitive markets, a disproportionately heavy expenditure is typically undertaken in order to launch the product – 'aggressive entry' is Doyle's phrase. This *investment budget* technique may extend over a considerable period with profit 'pay-back' only being realized when the product has become established and promotional support has been adjusted to more normal levels. At the decline stage it may be sound planning policy to withdraw promotion altogether, thus killing off the product more quickly in order to assist the introduction of new and improved replacement products. In the short run, withdrawal of promotional expenditure will produce greater profitability – a strategy, as Doyle puts it, of 'milking the product'.

The following may prove to be the *price history* of the product through the time period of the sales curve:

- *Introduction stage* – price may be experimental: there may be wide variations between the product's price and those of competitors;

- *Growth stage* – price differences may still be significant but settling down to a pattern determined by market leaders;

- *Maturity stage* – price differences minimal;

- *Decline stage* – price competition may be renewed as firms fight to retain market share (except for those products being 'killed off', of course).

Profit performance at these stages, as indicated by the lagged curve indicated in Figure 8.5, generally follows this pattern:

- *Product development and introduction stages* – little, if any, profit for the innovating firm because of high development and promotional costs and relatively low sales volume;

- *Growth stage* – usually the stage of peak profits for the innovators despite the emergence of price competition from new entrants, because unit costs of production are falling and there is a rapid increase in sales volume;

- *Maturity stage* – profits begin to decline: the product has reached its mass market and there is fierce price and non-price competition;

- *Decline stage* – further decline in profits, leading perhaps to the product's abandonment by the innovating firm.

Queries have been raised about the rigour of this concept for planning purposes. For example:

- If the sales cycle is supposed to follow this generalized normal curve, why do well-known products in some fields sustain long-term growth without much difficulty?

- At what level are we attempting to describe the sales cycle:

  – product class, e.g. 'ceramic tableware'?
  – product form, e.g. 'teaware'?
  – individual brand?

- What is meant by 'time' in this context? for time will vary, of course, from a few months for fashion goods to a much longer period for basic raw material in consistent demand.

On this last point, it is up to the individual firm, through its marketing information system and the development of an adequate database, to determine what is meant by 'time' and what the shape of the curves might be in its case – normal? reverse J shaped? hump-back skew shaped?

Later in this chapter we shall see how, even if taken as no more than a statement of general tendency, the life-cycle concept can be used to assist planning. Illustrations of its practical value and application are readily to hand. Waters (1996, p 22), for example, recently remarked on how the showrooms of car dealers in the USA were 'bulging' with the latest stylings and engine technology. He noted that with the US and European automotive markets under strain the financial consequences of these new model launches had been painful but drew attention to the view of consultants Arthur D. Little that: 'Product life cycles are coming down and changeovers are going to happen more frequently', who then added that carmakers must: 'learn how to do them more quickly and at lower cost' (see Waters, 1996).

Test marketing

Test marketing might best be termed a 'process', rather than a 'technique' but semantics aside, it is logical to include it here. The idea of test marketing was introduced in this text as part of the framework for new product planning, but some further points need to be made.

Firstly, Dibb *et al.* (1991, p 251) make the point that test marketing is not an extension of the product development stage but 'a sample launching of the entire marketing mix'. This is not to say, of course, that if test marketing discloses some weakness in the product itself this is some sort of bonus, for each variable in the mix is being tested as well as the variables in combination. In effect, test marketing is based on the undoubted fact that, with so many variables at work in the marketing of a product, the only way to obtain some indication of its acceptance and its likely performance with regard to sales volume and profitability is to test it as a component part of a projected marketing mix.

With fast-moving consumer goods the ability of test marketing to provide concrete information on repeat purchasing is a clear advantage. If a seemingly successful product is not re-bought, the risk of further investment by the manufacturer and the distributors can be fully identified and consequential adjustments made to the product, the mix or both.

The 'limited area try-out', as it is sometimes called, may take place in a town, city or commercial TV region – broadly speaking, the idea is to select a defined geographical area for its close similarity to the main market in terms of level of competition, availability of advertising media, distributive structure, characteristics of user population, adequacy of research facilities, etc. and then to launch a marketing campaign scaled down to allow for the proportionate significance of the chosen area in terms of total market potential. Figure 8.6 is an attempt to illustrate some of the key issues involved in the choice of a test area.

Since the methodology is to plan the scale of effort in the test market, on all dimensions of marketing activity, in proportion to the planned marketing effort in the main marketing region when this is subsequently undertaken, it is hoped that in addition to product favourability, some forecast, however tentative, of sales volume and return on investment after full-scale marketing might also be provided. Such results, however cautiously interpreted, clearly have some value, though an absence of any information on how the competition will react in subsequent full-scale marketing has to be borne in mind.

Just as great care is needed in the selection of the test market, the controls to be applied in this form of *experimental marketing* must also be chosen judiciously. For example, matching the scale of local promotional effort to that of the projected full-scale effort is no easy task and requires thoughtful analysis of data if the results are not to be skewed in some way.

As Cannon (1980, p 172) has pointed out, test marketing has not been adopted in the UK with quite the same enthusiasm as in the USA where 'the complexity of the market, its size and the costs involved have created an environment in which the savings usually outweigh the risks'. One of the risks Cannon refers to, already mentioned in this chapter, is where the technology gap between products and organizations is so small that the competition may introduce a new brand based, at least in part, on information obtained as a result of the innovator's test market.

Another risk is that of 'competitive jamming' where test results are invalidated due to the increased advertising, reduced prices or special incentives of competitors. In addition to the *costs* of the experiment, in an environment where speed of market entry is increasingly important, the *time* involved in test marketing must be long enough to gauge the rate of repeat purchasing.

These time, cost and risk factors do nothing to reduce the desirability of test marketing for decision-making, hence the development of *simulated test marketing*. A simple version of the approach is one in which consumers at shopping centres are shown an advertisement for a new product and are given a free sample to take home for trial. They are subsequently interviewed by telephone and asked for their assessment of the product. Scanner-based technology is also employed for simulated test marketing purposes. Many market research agencies are able to assist clients in this regard, for example the A.C. Nielsen Company and Research International with its Micro-Test model.

Three basic types of simulated test are these:

- *mini-test markets* – in which a permanent consumer panel is serviced by a retail system operated by the research agency;

Figure 8.6. *Testing the test area*

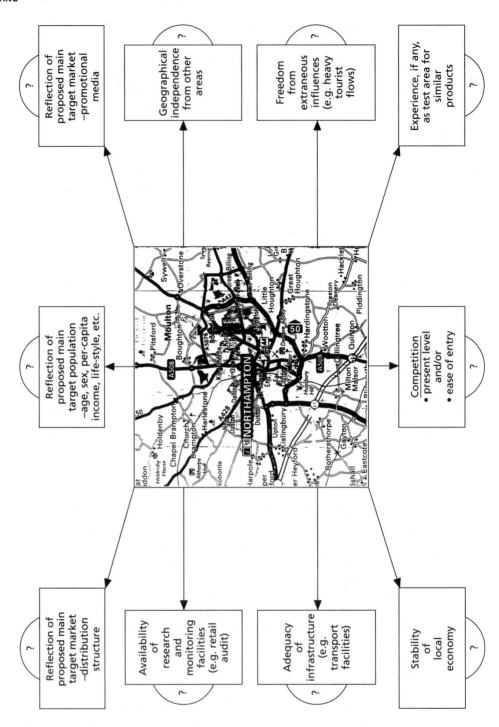

- *laboratory test markets* – in which the consumer choice situation is simulated by mock store/display units and choice and repeat buying factors are estimated by computer modelling;

- *calibrated tests* – in which answers to purchase-related questions are converted to trial, repeat and volume predictions using empirically derived weighting factors.

BASES, ASSESSOR, LITMUS and DESIGNOR are some of the models employed to provide the cost reductions and improved security of simulated test marketing for client organizations.

Portfolio models

While it is important to consider carefully the concepts and principles linked to the development of the individual product, in many instances, the organization markets more than a single product. Consequently, product strategy invariably calls for the management of a *range* of products – usually termed the *product mix* or the *portfolio* of products.

Next, as Segev (1995, p 3) points out, since many corporations are multi-industry or multi-product/market units, that is multi-unit business concerns, they do not compete directly in the market place, but do so through their business units. In Chapter 2 we defined the strategic business unit (SBU) and saw that it might have various manifestations, from an operating division to a single product.

To assist in developing strategy at the corporate level and to assist in the corporate review of business units, a number of matrices, or models, have been developed for use in the process of *portfolio analysis and management*. Since this is a section on techniques we will restrict ourselves to some thoughts on the actual models involved, leaving other general issues of portfolio management until later in the chapter.

The SBU – a unit of a company that has a separate mission and objectives and that can be planned independently from any other business within the company – is the common feature of all models for portfolio planning. Segev is clear about the significance of its identity:

> All too often managers who wish to implement portfolio planning in their companies focus too much of their attention upon the question of choice of analytic technique and not enough upon the identification and definition of the strategic business units. This first step is the most critical. The accurate designation of SBUs is crucial to the quality of portfolio analysis (Segev, 1995, p 7).

The first corporate portfolio matrix, a two dimensional model of business unit positions, had in Segev's phrase: 'an immediate and profound effect on corporate strategy making in the U.S.A. and the world'. This was the BCG (Boston Consulting Group) matrix or 'Boston Box', in popular parlance, and its fundamental tenet was that SBU. performance was determined by *market growth rate* and *relative market share*.

The concept of the matrix was based on the product life-cycle concept and the Boston Consulting Group's own work on *experience-curve effects*, which indicate that every time 'production experience' – accumulated volume – is doubled the variable cost per unit of production decreases by 10–30 per cent.

On the vertical axis of the matrix (see Figure 8.7) *market growth rate* provides a measure of the attractiveness of the market to the organization, especially its rate of growth and stage of market development (i.e. stage in its life-cycle). On the horizontal axis, *relative market share* represents the share of the market held by an organization when compared with the shares held by other organizations. It serves as a

Figure 8.7. *The Boston Consulting Group (BCG) growth share matrix*

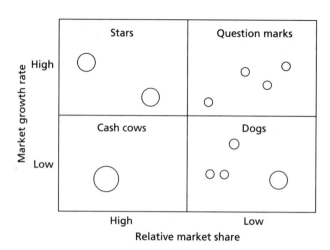

measure of the organization's competitive position in that market and especially its share of the market compared with the share of its largest competitor.

The SBUs (businesses or products) can now be classified into four types, with 'colourful' labels which have helped to popularize the Boston Box matrix among marketing practitioners. These are:

- *Stars* – which are high growth, high market share businesses or products. To finance their rapid growth they often require considerable resources. As their growth slows down, they will turn into 'cash cows'.

- *Cash cows* – these are low growth, high market share businesses or products. Because they are well-established they need less investment to hold their market share. The company can therefore use them to meet its financial obligations and, importantly, to provide investment for other SBUs in need of it.

- *Question marks* – also called 'problem children', these are businesses or products in high growth markets but with low share. Just to maintain their market share, let alone improve it, they require considerable resources. Management must consider carefully whether to phase any of these out, and if so which, or whether to divert resources to them in order, hopefully, to build them into 'stars'.

- *Dogs* – these are the low growth businesses/products with low market share. They may generate sufficient income to maintain their own existence but they are not likely to provide income in large amounts.

Obviously, the outcome of such an approach is a method of allocating resources based primarily on the income generating/income using needs of various combinations of businesses or products/markets.

To illustrate this with an imaginary example, note the various circles in the four quadrants of Figure 8.7. These represent the eleven products which currently make up a firm's portfolio. The area of each circle is proportionate to the amount of sales generated (in £ sterling, US dollars, etc.). It will be noted that the company has two Stars, neither of which is particularly well developed. It has no fewer than four Dogs and four Question Marks. All of the latter are insignificant from a sales standpoint. Thankfully, it does have a sizeable Cash Cow, but only one, which has thus become the sole support for the whole of the present portfolio. Clearly, some product decisions need to be made very soon!

The BCG model has subsequently attracted criticism, for its imprecise definition of the market, and therefore of market share; its overemphasis on market share's contribution to cash flow, profits and competitive advantage relative to other variables; the lessening effect of the experience curve with the move from high volume markets; and the fact that high growth rate is only one measure of the attractiveness of a market. However, as Segev notes, this is a hazard of being first in the field. Perhaps we should note that criticism might also stem from over-enthusiastic use of the BCG matrix as the predominant weapon for strategy formulation whereas, like any other technique, it is only one item in the armoury.

The 'Boston Box' has also had value in generating more sophisticated portfolio approaches to strategic planning and by the early 1980s the matrix developed by General Electric and McKinsey & Co. had become the most popular. This is a two-dimensional, nine-cell presentation of SBU positioning and because it entails the quantification of subjective factors and their inclusion in the analysis it is said to yield more decision-relevant information. The two axes of the matrix – *relative market dominance* (or *business strength*), which signifies the X axis and *market attractiveness* – the Y axis, require values to be assigned for the variables set out in Table 8.1.

In an introductory work of this nature, though it is tempting, it is not practical to say more about portfolio models. The interested reader is referred to Segev's (1995) excellent work on these.

Value management

Value analysis is a technique which applies the approaches of method study to the design of products. It scrutinizes all the elements of cost of an existing product in order to determine:

- whether elements of cost can be reduced, or eliminated, without impairment of functional and quality requirements, or
- whether functional and quality requirements can be improved at the existing level of costs.

The originator of the approach, Lawrence D. Miles, was a US engineer working on aero engine components during the Second World War. The intensive demands of the war and a host of supply and production difficulties led him to study ways to overcome bottlenecks. To do so, he veered towards components, and what they were designed to do, and away somewhat from the product itself. As he examined other ways of achieving a component's purpose he was often able to cut costs in the process and as he developed his approach, by drawing on established management techniques, he christened it *value analysis*. Soon he was able to report that when

Business strength variables (X axis)	Market attractiveness variables (Y axis)
Relative market share	Market growth rate
Market share growth	Product differentiation
Distribution network coverage	Characteristics of competition
Distribution network effectiveness	Relative industry profitability
Calibre of personnel	Customer value
Customer loyalty	Customer brand loyalty
Technology skills	
Patents	
Marketing skills and strength	
Flexibility	

Table 8.1. *The GE/McKinsey model*

Source: Segev, 1995

applied, reductions of 15–25 per cent in manufacturing costs were quite commonly being achieved.

Apocryphal or otherwise, there is the story that when Miles' idea was enthusiastically applied by the US Navy, not having a budget line for 'analysis', they allocated it to the heading 'engineering' which is how the technique came to be called 'value engineering', a title still retained in America. In the UK, on the other hand, this comparison of costs with functions became quite generally referred to as 'value analysis' when applied to the development or prototype stage of new products. Today, when the approach has come to be applied throughout the world, it is commonly labelled 'value management', the term adopted in this text.

In comparing costs with functions to determine whether

- performance can be enhanced at the existing level of costs, or
- whether the same performance can be achieved at lower cost,

function is deemed to have four facets:

- *use function* – i.e. the performance standard of the product or service;
- *esteem function* – an assessment of its appearance;
- *exchange function* – based on its trade-in capability; and
- *cost function* – based on the 'value for money' it currently offers.

Figure 8.8 is an attempt to depict a typical value management procedure.

After its enthusiastic reception in the 1960s, the success rate for value management was such that its use became obligatory for many government contracts, particularly in the USA. Today, it has to be remembered that, even where the cost/value quotient has been rigorously attended to in the original design, the constant development of new materials and new processes of production and assembly provide untold opportunities for the application of value management.

When the technical representative of a supplier is drawn into a team from the cost accounting, production, design, purchasing and marketing functions of a customer organization it enables that representative to act virtually as an assistant buyer for the customer organization. The possibility of the supplier obtaining business is thus considerably strengthened. So commitment to, and expertise in, value management becomes an important marketing tool for the supplier.

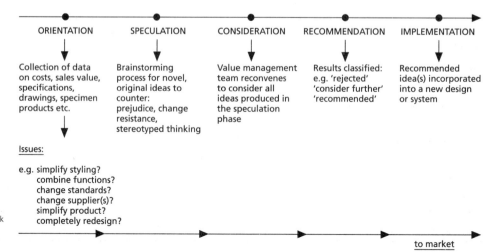

Figure 8.8. *Phases in the Value Management process*

Adapted from The Gower Handbook of Management (Lock and Farrow eds)

Not surprisingly, this procedure – which objectively examines the function of products, materials, components, sub-assemblies, etc., considers their cost, derives alternatives and evaluates these – has historically, had its greatest application in the mass production of standardized items, where a fractional saving per unit of output may result in very large total savings.

In the industrial field, for example, an organization supplying ceramics manufacturers with production or drying equipment might, through the application of value management, devise a product with an increased life-span or which minimizes energy costs in use. In the consumer goods field, a supplier might produce a consumer durable with brazed, rather than soldered assemblies, thereby reducing the price to the consumer whilst maintaining performance standards.

Services as well as products can benefit from a value management approach. For example, in 1994 the Edinburgh Healthcare NHS Trust began to look for ways in which costs could be reduced and services improved. It set up value analysis groups to examine catering, portering and laundry services. In January 1997, it was reported (Clayton, 1997, p 39) that the Trust had improved a number of aspects of its services and achieved a saving of £400,000 on a £5 million budget. Subsequently, the Trust has developed the approach into a more long-term policy in order to make it part of its management process.

The 'take-up' of value management has been significant in the UK public sector and includes the Ministry of Defence, the Scottish Office, the Highways Agency and the NHS (National Health Service). The Audit Commission has been encouraging local authorities to incorporate value management approaches in their operations so as to obtain better value for money for council tax payers. The European Union has also set up a value management programme to assist European industries to become more competitive.

Marketing executives in all fields should fully recognize the benefit of value management, not only in terms of cost reduction and improved performance of products and services, but also because it is an ideal tool for challenging old ideas, stimulating innovation and promoting teamwork and cooperation between departments.

Gap analysis

In Chapter 3, the concept of *gap analysis* was introduced in the context of forward planning at the organizational level and the setting of objectives in quantitative terms – see Figure 3.6. In marketing parlance, the term has more than one meaning and in this section we shall be looking at gap analysis as a concept in the development of new products.

In the last chapter the subject of attitude research and measurement, for the study of consumer behaviour, was outlined. Mention was made of Osgood's *semantic differential*, an attitude scaling method which has been used extensively for measuring brand, product or company images. As Figure 7.4 indicated, certain attributes were employed for the image testing of a newspaper, for example 'truthful', 'untruthful', 'appealing layout' – 'unappealing layout', etc. It is dangerous, of course, for the researcher to assume he knows what attributes are relevant in a given situation and how best to express them. Usually, therefore, they are elicited from prior unstructured, exploratory interviews but the problems emanating from psychological, language and social barriers have long been recognized as a threat to the accuracy of interview responses.

Because traditional exploratory research interviews have been criticized, from a subjectivity standpoint and for their occasional failure to obtain responses in the 'true language of the consumer' (Sampson, 1986, p 37), attitude research has been supplemented by such 'tightening' techniques as the *repertory grid*. Strictly, it is much more than a technique and historically it emerged as a testing procedure attached to a highly developed and formal theoretical framework called *personal construct theory*, published by an American psychologist, G.A. Kelly. Since Kelly's personal construct theory is based on a fundamental postulate and eleven corollaries it would be outside the scope of this text to discuss Kelly's theory, even if there were space to do so. Let us just say that Kelly's actual definition of a construct is as follows: 'a construct is a way in which two things are alike and by the same token different from a third' (Kelly, 1955).

This provides the basis for the 'triads' technique which is used in a highly structured test situation and employs a strict stimulus–response procedure. As Sampson (1986, p 37) outlines, a wide variety of different types of stimuli may be used. In a research project on beverages, for example, they might take the form of:

- the actual products, e.g. tea, coffee, milk, drinking chocolate;
- product brands e.g. Typhoo, Brooke Bond, Twinings;
- concept statements, e.g. 'slow-roasted coffee granules'.

Word labels, written statements, drawings, photographs, advertisements, products and/or their packages are some of the ways in which stimuli may be presented.

Let us consider an imaginary example, staying in the field of newspapers. First, the 'brand names' of newspapers are presented to respondents in sets of three with the question 'in what important way are any two of these alike and in that way different from the third?' Now mention has already been made of this approach to objectively determine relevant attributes for use with the semantic differential technique and it could also be used in the gap analysis approach. A single repertory grid sheet would tell a researcher very little, but content analysis of up to say 50 of these, which is usual, would yield important information for scales in attitude research. The information may also be computer analysed using one of the multivariate statistical techniques which, as their terminology suggests, can be used to evaluate the many variables and the ways they interrelate in the typical marketing mix.

The grid would be used on a sample of newspaper readers, in research parlance, 'to establish the dimensions of the product'. The attributes thus evolved would be subjected to multivariate analysis using, typically, the technique of factor analysis and then matched against existing, new or even imaginary ('ideal') newspapers by means of a brand/attitude survey. The information emerging could then be used to construct a multi-dimensional model which relates both attributes and brands. Figure 8.9 is a simple example of such a model.

According to the accompanying sales figures, Paper A has a quite considerable market. As the model demonstrates, it has a great deal of light reading, quite a lot of 'hard news' and relatively little sport in its editorial make-up. Paper B is also a significant seller and has an editorial policy slanted towards 'heavy' reading, although not so much 'hard news' (as distinct from news comment) and not very much sport. Meanwhile, there appears to be a market for Paper X, a heavy, with not so much hard news as Paper A but with rather more sport than either Paper A or Paper B.

Such an approach can be very useful for charting attitudinal constructs. Finding market gaps by such a method could be helpful both for *testing* new product ideas and for *generating* new product ideas in areas of unfulfilled needs.

It should be noted that the attributes in the model are merely for purposes of illustration and are purely speculative. The writer has no particular grounds for believing that they are important, or even relevant, as characteristics which satisfy the requirements of newspaper readers.

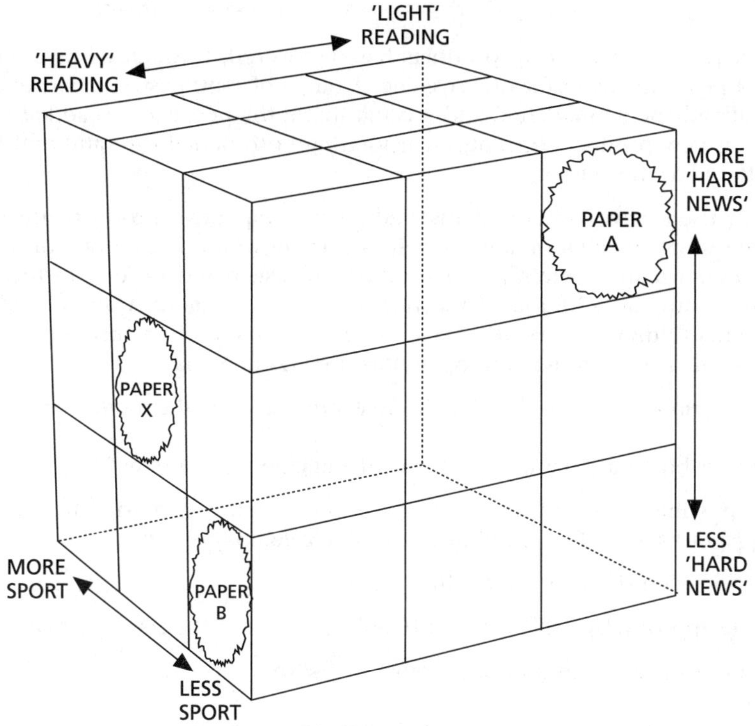

Figure 8.9. *Gap analysis: newspapers*

Conjoint analysis

Writing in 1993 on the US contemporary scene in marketing research, McDaniel and Gates had this to say:

> 'In a relatively short period of time conjoint analysis has become a popular analytical technique in marketing. Conjoint applications have appeared in virtually all major product and service categories, ranging from highly complex industrial products to consumer nondurable goods and services (McDaniel and Gates, 1993, p 645).

In fact, the technique has been used in fields as diverse as hotel design, motor vehicle styling, ethical pharmaceuticals, travel services and credit card operations and it is now being utilized in Europe. Through marketing research procedures, the users are often asked to identify their 'ideal' product or service and *rating scales*, such as the semantic differential, are used for this purpose. Now here there is a practical difficulty, for the user will plump for the ideal on *all* the product's attributes – for example, the ideal car will be fast, powerful, economical on fuel, extremely stylish, highly reliable and safe, and, not least, low in price – attributes strewn with contradictions.

As we know, in a world that is not ideal the user must make 'trade-offs' between product attributes, trading-off power against fuel consumption, styling against price and so on. Unfortunately, the basic rating scales lack the capacity to measure these trade-offs. This is the reason for the emergence of *conjoint analysis*, a set of techniques designed to measure:

- the importance users attach to each attribute of a product or service, and

- their degree of preference for each *level* of each attribute.

The use of conjoint analysis might best be illustrated if, again, we look at an imaginary example.

Example: The development of a new toothpaste product

A manufacturer of dental care products has discovered, through its pharmaceutical division, a powerful agent for oral hygiene. A range of toothpastes, incorporating fluoride, is already being marketed and it is felt that if the new agent is added to one of these that a new product concept, incorporating both dental care and oral hygiene, can be offered to the market.

Trials with users have confirmed that although competitive products are available which are said to 'freshen breath' as well as prevent tooth decay, none of these is as effective as the manufacturer's own product on test, based on one of the fluoride toothpastes with the addition of the new oral hygiene agent. Consequently it has been decided to move to the next stage, the development of an appropriate product strategy as a first stage in the development of a marketing mix.

The elements now to be considered in the final formulation of the product are as follows:

- three possible brand names ('Dencare', 'Dengiene', 'Fluorgiene')
- three possible types of container (A – tube with screw top; B – tube with pump/spout action; C – round tin with solid 'cake' of product)
- three possible prices (£0.99; £1.10; £1.20)
- possible approval by British Dental Health Association (BDHA) (Yes/No)
- possible offer of a money-back guarantee (Yes/No).

If all possible combinations of these attributes were to be tested, there would be 108 concepts in total ($3 \times 3 \times 3 \times 2 \times 2$). Apart from the time and cost involved, research informant fatigue would be quite an issue here. In fact, even a quarter of the total (27 concepts) might be too many for an informant to handle, but perhaps one sixth (18 concepts) might well be manageable.

Fortunately, an experimental design can be used to simplify the 108 concepts situation. This utilizes a *fractional factorial orthogonal array* approach which produces a design in which the combinations to be tested are selected so as to ensure that the independent contributions of all the five factors in question are *balanced* and in this case, only 18 of the total possible combinations (108) are required. Accordingly, 18 concept cards are then presented to each informant who is asked to rank them in order of preference. An example of a concept card is shown in Figure 8.10.

Table 8.2 is an extract from one consumer's ranking of the 18 stimulus combinations. It can be seen that the second of the options assessed (Card 6) obtains the highest rank. It is important to remember that what is being ranked is the *overall offer*, comprising the product and its brand name, packaging, price, etc. The informant does not make a separate evaluation of the individual attributes and prior to the assessment the informant is given careful guidance on how to provide the assessment data. In addition to the *ranking*, in some research projects, the informant may be asked to rate the combinations on a relevant dimension such as likelihood of purchase.

There are a number of statistical programs available for the analysis of conjoint data. According to Tull and Hawkins (1990, p 365) regression is the most widely used analytical approach. Details of the other approaches can be found in their work (Tull and Hawkins, 1990). Compilation and analysis of an individual consumer's responses will reveal the *utility functions* of the attributes being tested, *for that consumer*. Figure 8.11 is a graphic display of the consumer's attribute utilities for the toothpaste, based on analysis of the full (18) combinations under test.

The utilities are measured on a scale from 0 to 1 and the higher the score on the utility scale, the greater the preference for that level of the attribute. Thus we see that for this consumer, Dengiene has by far the greatest utility as a brand name and the price of 0.99, not surprisingly, scores highest (see Figure 8.11).

Figure 8.10. *Concept card*

Card no.	Brand name	Packaging	Price	Approval	Money-back Guarantee	Rank number
2	Dencare	A	£1.10	No	No	14
6	Dengiene	B	£0.99	Yes	Yes	1
16	Fluorgiene	C	£1.20	No	No	18

Table 8.2. *An extract from one consumer's ranking of attribute combinations for the evaluation of a new toothpaste*

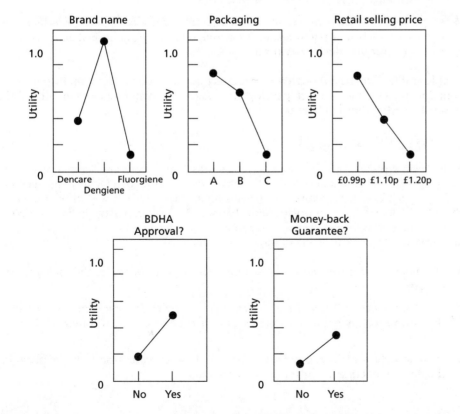

Fig. 8.11. *Conjoint Analysis : graphic display of attribute utilities for a new toothpaste*

Let us imagine that data are collected from a large sample of the target market for toothpaste and after statistical processing they reveal an identical pattern of preferences, namely:

- Brand name : Dengiene
- Packaging : Type A (tube with screw top)
- Price : £0.99
- BDHA approval : Yes
- Money back guarantee : Yes

The relative importance of each attribute can also be assessed by comparing their scores. In this case, the brand name and, to a lesser extent, the packaging and the price are the most important attributes, with the approval and the money-back guarantee lagging behind. Thus it can be seen why the utilities of the attributes are referred to in market research terminology as their *part worths*.

From a product strategy standpoint, if the details in Figure 8.11. are broadly valid for all informants, several points emerge, namely:

- the case for the brand name (Dengiene) and the packaging (tube with screw top) is well made – both attributes are important and the choices are clear;

- price is important but the utility of the £0.99 price is not significantly greater than the £1.10 price – for return on investment purposes, or in order to generate a larger budget for advertising, the £1.10 price may therefore be adopted. Certainly, the case for 'educational' advertising in respect of the new powerful agent for oral hygiene is a strong one;

- although the case for seeking BDHA approval is not so important, the results obtained might make it worthwhile to do this;

- surprisingly, the offer of a money-back guarantee for a quite novel product does not have much utility and again, for profitability or promotional purposes, the manufacturer may decide against it.

Simple and hypothetical though it is, perhaps this case study will exemplify the use of conjoint analysis for product development and for greater understanding of the trade-off mechanisms in buyer behaviour.

Total quality management

If, in Levitt's phrase, 'the purpose of a business is to create and keep a customer' (1986, p 19) then all marketing should be conversant with Total Quality Management (TQM) which has been defined by Armstrong as: 'a systematic way of guaranteeing that all activities within an organization happen the way they have been planned in order to meet the defined needs of customers and clients' (1993, p 199). Armstrong summarizes TQM as consisting of three basic concepts:

- *customer satisfaction*: it being the only real measure of the quality of a product or service;

- the *significance of internal customers*: meaning that everyone within an organization who receives goods or services from a colleague is a customer of that colleague;

- *total quality*: which requires *all* employees in an organization to be involved *all* the time in meeting *all* customer requirements.

From this it will be gathered that TQM is not a technique so much as an *organizational philosophy* driven by top management and utilizing an array of techniques. In effect it is a *strategic approach* to generating customer satisfaction through the provision of the best possible product or service. One might say 'product *and* service' here for it is bound up with all aspects of contact with the customer including order taking, credit provision, product/service delivery, invoicing and after sale service. Organizing for TQM means creating an appropriate culture in which TQM can thrive. Culture change will be discussed further in Chapter 12 Element 6: *People*, but here it can be said that the philosophy entails everyone at every organizational level having a steadfast belief in quality and a commitment to achieve it in practice. It is influenced in part by Japanese management practices which, in the absence of a Japanese word for quality utilize the word *kaizen* which implies improvement that is never ending and is dependent on the actions of everyone.

Atkinson (1990, pp 14–18), a UK consultant in organization development, indicates some of the quality initiatives which can be incorporated within the TQM philosophy. These are briefly described below.

- *Quality circles* – basically a 'bottom up' change strategy. Quality circles are groups of people, often basically standard work-groups with their supervisor. They meet voluntarily to discuss 'improvements' – in productivity, quality, working methods, etc – and make recommendations to management. Ideally, circle members will have had some training in problem solving.

- *Customer care programmes* – used by British Airways and many other service organizations in the UK, Atkinson says these can be a 'great boon' and are often successful. Emphasis should be on the internal functioning of the organization and the programmes stress that meeting the requirements of the internal customer is as vital as meeting those of the external customer.

- *Quality assurance systems* – which are designed to confirm that every effort is being made to ensure that output conforms to the specifications formally established. Though it is based on inspection procedures, the best systems provide for both inspection of output and the development of systems by the inspectors to *prevent* a breakdown in quality.

- *Taguchi methodology* – adopted by many companies in Japan and the USA, the methods of Dr Genichi Taguchi for improving quality engineering at low cost are now gaining a foothold in Europe. The approach focuses on the design of products and uses analytical and experimental techniques which will ultimately quantify the loss which occurs due to deviations from quality and performance standards.

- *Statistical process control* – based on the axiom that 'what gets measured gets managed'. Measurement charts record deviations from agreed tolerances, performance standards and product specifications. The charts thus provide an early warning system that a problem is arising and allow corrective action to be taken. Atkinson (1990) believes that: 'SPC works marvellously – even in service areas. To be successful it requires total commitment and someone who can explain the use of statistics simply'.

- *Just-in-time* – the aims of which are to minimize inventory and its associated costs, meet the requirements of each external and internal customer immediately on demand, achieve a continuous flow of production without delay or waste and ensure totally reliable delivery of required parts and material on time. While its apparent objective is to minimize excessive inventory through the closest possible attention to the needs of the customer, this is only part of the picture, for the full benefits of just-in-time (JIT) will not be realized unless use is made of analytical techniques (e.g. the *kanban* system) to correct problems within the production process.

Earlier in this chapter, mention was made of Siebe, the UK engineering group, which was adopting a 'ferociously demanding approach to quality control'. It would be useful now to say something of the technique underlying Siebe's approach.

The *'Six sigma' programme* – is, in a sense, part of the group of techniques incorporated in statistical process control. It deserves some words of its own, however. In the Appendix to Chapter 6, the importance in marketing research of the standard deviation as a measure of variability was outlined. Sigma (σ) is the symbol for the standard deviation. As we saw when looking at the curve of normal distribution, 2 standard deviations (2 sigma) account for 95 per cent the observations upon which such a curve is constructed.

As a basic statistical concept, the standard deviation has many applications, for example in production as well as in marketing research and countless other business operations. Jackson (1997, p 11) outlines its application in quality control with an example of the manufacture of tin plate 1 mm thick. The firm's customers state their satisfaction with a variation of ± 0.1 mm. Imagine that on checking the proportion of output which falls within this range, the manufacturer discovers this to be 95.5 per cent (i.e. 2 sigma). At first glance a 2 sigma performance seems pretty commendable but it would actually mean 45,000 defects per million. On the other hand, a 6 sigma performance would result in a reduction of defects to 3.4 per million.

A 6 sigma target represents an enormous improvement in quality levels and implies a tightening of tolerance on processes to virtually incredible levels. The word 'processes' should be noted here for companies operating six sigma programmes aim to control the relevant processes at the outset rather than measure quality by checking the final product. Applying this concept entails two preparatory steps:

- gathering information on what customers want – usually done through surveys, and

- analysing exactly the make-up of the firm's output, which involves breaking down its work into discrete processes and then measuring the defect rate of each of these.

Companies such as General Electric and Motorola were pioneers in applying the approach which can be applied to administrative as well as manufacturing operations. According to the Six Sigma Academy of Phoenix, Arizona, the average company operates to around 4 sigma. In which case, the cost of fixing defects, internal and external, is approximately 10 per cent of turnover.

This concludes the review of some of the techniques and approaches for the development and management of products and services. Apart from the obvious relevance and value of the techniques for marketing operations, the review has been included here for two reasons:

- to support the statement that marketing has now become a 'whole organization' concern and operation, and

- while there is a consequent need for all management functions to take on the mantle of marketing, it is important for the marketing function to understand and support ways in which the other functions can best satisfy the customer.

One most important technique not featured here is that of *break-even analysis*. It seemed more appropriate to incorporate this in the next chapter because of its close relationship with pricing policy.

The total product

Earlier in the chapter when the total product concept was being outlined, the package of benefits being offered to the user in exchange for the price was seen to include elements other than the product or service, for example:

- a brand name;
- a package;
- a user guarantee;
- a level of after sales service, etc.

We shall now consider some of these elements at greater length.

The development of product/brand identities

The American Marketing Association provides the following definition of a *brand*:

> *A BRAND is a name, term, sign, symbol or design, or a combination of them, intended to identify the goods or services of one seller or group of sellers and to differentiate them from those of competitors.*

Leading writer Philip Kotler (1997, p 443) believes that the most distinctive skill of professional marketers may well be their ability to create, maintain, protect and enhance brands. Kotler also suggests that marketers in general hold the view that 'branding is the art and cornerstone of marketing'. Certainly, branding is no simple, self-contained action consisting merely of attaching a name to a product. Rather it is a *process* on which the organization can sharpen its strategic skills, entailing a consideration of the organization's patents, processes, history and experience, knowledge of raw materials, the skills of its labour force and, not least, the segments of the market in which it will operate.

On this last point, we saw earlier in the text that segmentation is a strategy in which products are directed at certain types or classifications of buyer. Chanel No. 5 perfume will be bought by a different sub-group from one that buys a cheaper type, while the 'market' for a BMW 3 Series Convertible is distinctly different from that of the Nissan Micra. These are very simple examples of how markets can be delineated by the products being offered to them and leads us to a fuller point, namely that the individual motor manufacturer, for instance, does not set out to expand the market for motor cars in general, but only for the vehicles he produces. And, unless the producer decides that his output will be traded as a *commodity* without a distinct identity, as are many raw materials, then the process of branding is evident for most products – be they marmalades, seat belts or earth-moving equipment.

The significance of branding will be evident if we look beyond products. Below are some examples based on recent UK experience.

- The Royal Society for Mentally Handicapped Children and Adults (Mencap) relaunched itself in an attempt to improve its campaigning image and the status of mentally handicapped people in society. Its former brand-image was based on 'little Stephen', a logo of a weepy-looking little boy. This was felt to be embarrassing by people with learning difficulties and thought to convey a sad, pathetic 'begging bowl' image, to the detriment of the charity. A new brand-image was designed based on photographs of mentally handicapped people looking cheerful and decidedly 'positive'.

- One of the key lectures at a national conference for the marketing of legal services was 'the role of the brand in professional practice'. The lecture dealt with

(i) identifying a legal practice's competitive advantages, (ii) positioning the practice in the market place and (iii) developing and protecting the practice's brand against competition.

● The Whitbread brewery, restaurant and hotel company reported a pre-tax profit increase of 11.6 per cent in the six month period to end August 1997. It related this to its strategic focus of developing its branded outlets – its Dôme cafés, Beefeater restaurants and Hogshead pubs. This had entailed an investment of £226 million, expected to more than double during the full business year. Whitbread was opening a new restaurant every four days and a new hotel every ten days within an industry in which one thousand unbranded pubs close each year.

● By March 1996, it was being reported (Mitchell, 1996, p 23) that the brand image of Britain itself might well have become boring and outdated, based as it was on 'tradition' and 'heritage'. In effect, Britain's image was impeding the promotion of British assets. Certainly, Britain's role as a leader in scientific research and as a world finance, media and communications centre belied the image it too often projected of post-imperial decline. While it was important not to overlook Britain's past achievements it was difficult to sell technologically advanced products on this basis, as well as its pop music, films, fashion and design and its vibrant youth culture. British Airways, British Gas and British Telecom were, in fact, having to grapple with the thorny issue of whether to keep the word 'British' in their brand name. The chief executive of a leading brand identity firm declared: 'Our image has been left in a time warp. There is a need, if Britain is not to become the world's "Ye Olde Gifte Shoppe", to inject a sense of dynamism and modernity'.

The value of the branding process was demonstrated by statistics available from Datastream and the *Financial Times* in December 1997 which showed that, for the period January 1982 to December 1986, the UK shares index indicated that companies with 'heavily branded products' had achieved markedly better share performance than 'unbranded' companies. The fact that so much strategic effort is now devoted to developing *brand reputation* and *brand integrity* is underlined by the work of the UK's Accounting Standards Board on how brands can be accorded a value for viewing in a balance sheet.

Brand integrity as an objective means that the image being projected of the organization, its products or services must be more than superficial or 'skin deep'. It must reflect truly held attitudes and values. A recent paper from Mercer Management Consulting contained the following comment:

> Given its importance in the marketplace, a company's brand should be analysed and managed every bit as rigorously as any other major corporate asset. Unfortunately, this is not generally happening to-day ... Few have a clear brand strategy or an effective brand management process (see Trapp, 1997, p 9).

This consultancy team believes firmly in the importance of *brand equity* which is 'the total value of all qualities and attributes implied by the brand name that impact (upon) actual customer choices. It translates into monetary terms a brand's power in convincing a customer to purchase the company's product instead of competing offerings'. The improvement and maintenance of brand equity rests squarely on the shoulders of management. So, let us now turn to the practicalities of managing brands and the branding process.

Brand management

Yet again, sound decision-making will only emerge as a result of a careful assessment of the market. All considerations must focus on customer satisfaction. If time and finance allow formal research to be done, so much the better. Key questions to contemplate include:

- Can the market be segmented and, if so, in which segment(s) should we operate?
- Based on our core competences and adequate assessment of customer needs and wants, what service values should distinguish our offer, e.g. quality, value for money, aesthetic appeal, novelty, effectiveness, or some combination of attributes?
- Is it logical to brand our product or should it be sold merely as a *generic* (e.g. 'soda ash') in which only the type of product is identified?
- Would it be more productive to market our product under a distributor's 'own brand'?
- If we are to brand our own products, should this be done individually by *brand family*, using the firm's name for example or by *individual brands* within a family brand?
- Should the brand(s) be legally protected?
- Can an existing brand be repositioned in some way in order to increase market share?

Two important connotations arise from the term 'brand':

- *identity* – slaves, thieves and army deserters were often branded in order to identify them – stark but telling examples of this connotation;
- *ownership* – cattle were branded so as to signify that they belonged to a particular ranch.

Although branding is employed in less gruesome contexts nowadays the connotations of *identity* and *ownership* still apply. An organization brands its product by using a name, term, stylized form of lettering, symbol, picture or some combination of these to identify that product and to establish its ownership. With regard to ownership, although the law may vary slightly from country to country, a brand is legally protected if it is listed in a register maintained by an appropriate department of government – for example comptroller-general of patents, designs and trademarks. This registration gives the proprietor the exclusive use of the trade mark in connection with the goods in respect of which it is registered, and any invasion of this, as by another using a mark which is the same or so similar as to be likely to confuse, is an infringement actionable for an injunction, damages or an account of profits. Thus the term 'trade mark' is, in essence, a legal term and denotes a brand which, through registration has been given legal protection. Unregistered brands, if and where they exist, are not protected against infringement although an action for 'passing off' is usually available to the injured party.

Examples of *individual brands* are legion – 'Ariel', 'Surcare', 'Tide' and 'Bold' are just some in the detergent field, for instance. Heinz, Kelloggs and Cadbury are powerful *family brands* and here the advantage is that each product in the family benefits from the promotion of, and goodwill attaching to, other products. In some instances, the family brand, for example Marks and Spencer's 'St. Michael' label, is the sole distinguishing mark of a whole range of products. In other instances, a family brand and a product brand are used in combination, for example Renault's 'Clio', 'Megane' and 'Laguna'. Vauxhall's 'Astra', 'Corsa', 'Frontera' and 'Tigra'.

The development of brand names would merit a whole textbook. Here perhaps it might be helpful to provide some examples of effectiveness in this regard. 'Electrolux' is a very suitable name for high quality electrical products as is 'Hardura' for heavy duty floor covering. 'Limmits' conveys the concept of control, as in a calorie controlled diet, while 'Ready Brek' and 'Instant Whip' convey the message of their producers in unmistakable terms. The ultimate goal for the brand owner is for the brand name to become so institutionalized that it emerges as a substitute word for the product in use – as with 'Hoovering' for the process of vacuum cleaning.

Throughout world markets technology is forcing the standardization of products so that there are few, if any, material differences between competing items. Hence the need for the individual organization to invest its product with an 'image' or 'personality' for the purposes of identification and ownership. Marketing communication has a significant role in brand management and it can be perceived in the choice of a brand name, the typographical design for the brand name, the choice of colours and the design of the package, the symbol or the mascot figure appearing on the package and in the 'what', 'where' and 'how' of the promotional activity involved ('what' being the type of message', 'where' the choice of advertising media and 'how' the method of transmitting the message – be it factual or figurative, frivolous or serious, earnest or escapist).

Some impression of the scale of advertising expenditure required for the management of a leading brand is provided by Table 8.3.

Once the required identity for the product has been defined, every element, in every advertisement, in every advertising campaign, must develop that identity with a cumulative, repetitive force, so that the product's buying public can be in no doubt about it and can mistake no other product for it. If a single word can be employed to summarise the ideals of brand management, that word has to be *cohesion*.

To give another example, English high-quality cut-glass of traditional design will be advertised using words absolutely suited to the purpose, printed with typographical good taste and using appropriate borders, rules and ornaments for the framework of the advertisement so that the reader immediately absorbs a clear conception of product quality. The message itself and where it appears (perhaps in magazines for the affluent) will be based on a carefully considered:

- communications policy;
- which is part of a marketing policy designed to develop sustainable competitive advantage for the brand;
- which stems from the organization's general strategic objectives;
- which are derived from overall corporate objectives.

An imaginative attempt to define the word 'brand' has been made by Cox (in Greenslade, 1992), who says:

> A brand is the summation of everything you come to understand about the product, the physical, the emotional, the rational and also the irrational. You build up a picture from impressions gained through, say, packaging and advertising. From these complex communications grow a set of values. Those values represent the brand.

Table 8.3. *The top 10 confectionery products (12 months ending December 1995)*

Source: A.C. Nielsen for *Marketing* magazine, 4 July 1996.

Brand	Owner	£m sales	Advertising expenditure (£000s)
1. Kit Kat	Nestlé	Over 125 m	6920.3
2. Mars Bar	Mars	100 – 105	3814.2
3. Cadbury's Dairy Milk	Cadbury	80 – 85	2472.1
4. Galaxy	Mars	75 – 80	5374.6
5. Cadbury's Roses	Cadbury	65 – 70	727.3
6. Twix	Mars	60 – 65	2964.1
7. Quality Street	Nestlé	55 – 60	2604.6
8. Snickers	Mars	50 – 55	3204.7
9. Maltesers	Mars	45 – 50	2149.7
10. Fruit'n'Nut	Cadbury	35 – 40	662.4

There is an abundance of empirical evidence to demonstrate that 'a successful brand invariably results in superior profit and market performance (PIMS)' (Christopher and McDonald, 1995, p 173), but this can only come about if the brand, having been fittingly creatively conceived, is nurtured and developed through the sound commercial processes of effective brand management.

The objective of brand management is to build *brand integrity* and thus *brand loyalty*. To do this, the product must be everything the promotion claimed for it or otherwise the brand's owner will be cursed by the phenomenon of *brand switching*. Having clearly identified its product, an organization becomes closely bound up with its success or failure. So it cannot afford to relax quality standards or provide less value for money than it promised in its advertising. It cannot hide any sub-standard output in the general flow of goods to its markets. The product is no longer anonymous – the brand name and often the organization's name appears on the package and in the advertisement. Distributors and users will know where to look if the product fails to deliver what its brand management promised.

Packaging

In relation to a product, a *package* is its immediate outer container which may take one of several forms – box, bottle, jar, can, drum or tube. It should be distinguished from a *pack* – which is an outer container, for example a large carton or a wooden pallet with a sealed plastic cover, designed to hold a considerable number of packages.

The package really came into its own as the mass production of products developed, for part of its physical function is to contain a product which has been pre-measured, pre-weighed or pre-sorted before it is *packaged* – the final stage in the mass production process. The package also has a *protective* function, shielding the product against breakage, corrosion, leakage, dampness or other atmospheric or climatic hazards. Other functional requirements of the package are these:

- it must be easy for the user to handle, open, close, store, dispense from and dispose of;

- it should be of an appropriate weight and shape for it to be carried and, if possible, allow its contents to be seen;

- it should allow its advertising message to be seen for as long as the product is being used;

- it should identify the brand/product so precisely that other brands/products cannot be substituted for it;

- its shape, colour, size, materials and general design should powerfully project the brand/product image the supplier is trying to convey, be this an image of beauty, quality, economy, dignity, happiness or whatever – and in the role of developing brand identity the package must be carefully integrated with other marketing efforts (e.g. advertising);

- the package must also be integrated with the needs of the distribution function – easy to stock and display and economical with space – and where self-service and self-selection are being used, the package design must take account of the impact it makes *en masse* in shelf displays and in relation to competitors' packaging;

- where the product is perishable, any appropriate date stamping, e.g. 'use before' or 'sell by' dates must be clearly conveyed;

- where appropriate, details of the product's composition and instructions for its use must be set out clearly;

- there is an added advantage to the user and the supplier if the package can be re-used in some way, for storage.

In addition to its functional and promotional roles, the package may have important *legal* functions to perform. Some points have been made above concerning product composition and instructions for use. In this respect there may be strict legal requirements in relation to the health and safety of users, which may stipulate what information the package should contain. Similar legal requirements may extend to trade descriptions, weights and measures and price marking.

Although the benefits of packaging to the producer and the user are readily apparent, it is also an area of marketing which attracts much criticism. A major concern is that it uses up too great a proportion of our natural resources. According to one report (Sharpe and Morgan, 1992, p 19), a shopping expedition for £75 worth of goods included expenditure of more than £10 on cling-wrap, polystyrene, cardboard, paper, plastic and other assorted wrappings. This concern is intensified when other reports indicate too frequent use of over-sized packaging to mislead consumers about the amount of the contents.

Apart from ethical/legal considerations can excess packaging be justified when we note that non-biodegradable plastic is made from the earth's non-renewable oil reserves, that 140 species of tree are under threat of extinction from intensive forestry in Sweden and that our passion for aluminium cans has left large areas of disfigured land in Queensland and Brazil due to extensive bauxite mining?

The situation is serious enough for governments to intervene. In June 1992, for example, the European Commission approved a draft Directive which would, within ten years, require all EC countries to dump no more that 10 per cent of their packaging waste. Two-thirds of the 90 per cent recovered had to be recycled; the rest could be incinerated for power. The Commission also wished to see product labelling which indicated how its container should be recycled.

Aside from these understandable concerns, it is not part of a genuine 'marketing' approach, as we have come to understand it:

- to use up too big a proportion of our scarce resources;

- to spend an amount on the package which is not proportional to the intrinsic value of the product itself;

- to use packaging to deceive the customer by suggesting the package's contents are greater in amount than they really are;

- to use a type of packaging that is dangerous or an environmental hazard.

In fact, one sign of how effective marketing can be is the measure of balance it applies to the costs of packaging bearing in mind the functional, legal and promotional benefits and requirements which have been outlined. An indication of marketing's awareness of its responsibilities is provided by Nutting (1996, p 17). He believes that the design of a cold-drink can is as demanding as the design of 'an aircraft's wing' and points out that the technique of converting aluminium or tin-plate sheet into cans is extremely sophisticated, for the side-wall of the can is just four thousandths of an inch thick, yet the can must support a load of more than 200 lb during the processes of filling it and fixing its top.

Despite this, the drive for cost reductions from the leading drinks companies – Coca Cola used almost 30 per cent of the 190 billion cans made in 1995 – has reduced the weight of the average aluminium can from 18 gm to less than 11 gm. This means that US industry, for instance, has 'saved' more than 6 millions tons of aluminium in the past three decades. On the promotional side, Nutting points out that despite the drive towards cost reduction, Coca Cola is exploring the use of shaped cans to emulate the distinctive curves of its famous glass bottle. This move follows the tremendous success of its 20 oz plastic bottles which followed the contours of the glass bottle, first launched in 1916 and registered as a US trademark in 1977.

The 'competitive' aspects of packaging performance were mentioned earlier, in relation to massed displays of products in retail outlets. Here it is interesting to note the report of Baxter (in Nutting, 1996, p 17) on a development by VR Solutions of Salford, UK. This organization has launched a virtual reality system which gives packaging designers and fillers the opportunity to see what their package will look like on a supermarket shelf without having to produce an expensive physical model. The system was designed for British Steel Tinplate who were investigating how prototype steel cans might be 'built' in a virtual environment. The VR Solutions approach enables customers to view and change designs using any Intel-based PC or workstation. Thus, products can be displayed in a virtual warehouse or supermarket enabling such issues as labelling, stackability, shelf impact and design feasibility to be dealt with, without the actual packaging having ever existed.

The packaging of services

We have seen how in marketing the word 'product' is broadly defined. The same holds good for packaging.

When an insurance company decides that the opaque jargon of its policies will be replaced by easy-to-understand, 'user friendly' language it is improving the 'packaging' and presentation of its 'product'. No doubt the increased interest in marketing now being taken by solicitors and accountants will result in the improved packaging of their services too.

A very good illustration of the packaging of services comes from the British banking sector. A few years ago, the National Westminster Bank launched an initiative to build the bank of the future and to enhance the public perception of its service. Through a plan, codenamed Project Fame, the bank aimed to rebuild completely most of its 2,700 branches to enable it to meet customer demands more effectively.

The core objective of Project Fame (Furnishing and Merchandising Experiment) was to remove all administrative paperwork from the branches and to place it in 90 specialized service centres throughout the UK. This would allow the bank to free the large amount of space in its branches hitherto reserved for processing cheques and payments. The traditional branch has 80 per cent of its space reserved for staff and 20 per cent for customers. In the new branches of its 're-packaged' service these proportions would be reversed.

Labelling

The word 'label' is somewhat dated, for the stick-on label is now often incorporated into the package design, particularly on plastic containers. The label is that part of the package providing details of the brand name, manufacturer's name and address, size of the product or amount of contents and, where appropriate, details of the product's composition and instructions for its use. As stated earlier, when the product is perishable, date stamping is also frequently incorporated in the label.

The design of the label must be fully in phase with the desired image of the product; in fact, it is the part of the package which carries the identification/promotion functions described earlier. The organization must also pay close attention to the legal requirements relating to the contents of the label. In many countries, statutes are in force concerning false trade descriptions, weights and measures and price marking. Even then, the situation is far from ideal. In November 1997, Britain's Co-op retail organization and its wholesale arm, CWS, published a report which claimed that food manufacturers were misleading shoppers.

The report stated that while shoppers believed in food labels, thinking them governed by strict regulations, the rules were weak and the food industry ignored the spirit of the law to make packaged products appear bigger and better than they are. According to Cowe (1997, p 9) it was possible to identify seven ways in which shoppers were misled. Six came from poor labelling – a product called 'mince and onions', for example, had mechanically recovered chicken as its main ingredient. Meaningless adjectives such as 'premium', 'wholesome' or 'traditional' were frequently used; '90 per cent fat free' obscured the fact that the product contained 10 per cent fat; 'free from preservatives' made a virtue out of a normal attribute of food. The seventh way of misleading shoppers derived from the image conveyed. Many illustrations on packaging either used small plates to make the food look bigger or were re-touched.

The CWS has produced a code which would eliminate misleading illustrations, product names and claims and has called on the UK government to adopt it as part of its drive to improve food standards. This report, and the issues which give rise to it, provide another example of the fact that what sometimes masquerades as 'marketing' in effect runs counter to it.

User guarantees

We have noted that the act of 'branding' a product provides some assurance that the manufacturer will maintain necessary standards of quality and efficiency. If his efforts slacken, only his product will suffer for he has given it a distinctive identity, and as W.H. Thomas (1979, p 153) indicates many manufacturers go beyond this and issue a *guarantee* to the user. This is an even more decisive act of standing behind the product. However, what bothers Thomas, a leading writer on consumer law, is that too often the consumer is placed in a confusing position if the product goes wrong.

Imprecise wording in the guarantee may allow the dealer to try to avoid responsibility, referring the user to the manufacturer. The manufacturer, in turn, may insist that repairs can only be carried out provided the user 'registered' the purchase with him (e.g. by return of a section of the guarantee card) and that, even then, the user must return the product at his own expense, and also be responsible for the labour charges involved.

Thomas points out that although some manufacturers do provide considerably more support for their products than the legal minimum, there are others who, at best, make it expensive and time-consuming for the user to obtain adequate service and, at worst, prevent the user from obtaining fair treatment. Because of this, and as in the UK, governments will often intervene on behalf of the user, legally banning clauses in guarantees which limit or avoid the rights of the buyer under contracts for the sale of goods and rendering as void any term in a consumer guarantee which excludes or limits liability for loss or damage caused by defective goods and resulting from negligence in their manufacture or distribution.

What then can we conclude on the functions of guarantees as elements in the marketing mix, if we take 'marketing' to imply:

- mutually satisfactory relationships with users, and

- based on this, an adequate return on investment for the producer?

Clearly, a user guarantee which, in the event, merely leads the user through a tangled skein of obstacles resulting in frustration, disappointment, anger even, has no place in a mix allegedly based on the marketing philosophy. Customer satisfaction means guarantees that are *clear and free from ambiguity* – that are not misleading or unfair. A firm oriented to the market recognizes that the user is vulnerable in this respect since he or she often does not know the terms of the guarantee until the sale is made. Such a firm will be anxious to provide a guarantee:

- adequate in all respects for the type of product or service;

- which is clear in its terms; and

- is gladly given and willingly executed if required.

So much for the firm's attitude to the customer, but what of its own return on investment? McCarthy (1978, p 239) is helpful here, reminding practitioners that while it is important to clarify what is being offered and for what length of time it is being offered, this is not the same as providing something overlong or overgenerous. Costs are proportionate to the length and nature of the guarantee, so a balance must be struck. The axiom is – provide what is adequate, that is to say offer a *total product* which constitutes *good value for money*.

Williamson (1979, p 84) is also pertinent when he counsels us to 'be clear what we mean by price', which is not the amount of money paid to obtain a product but to obtain a *total product*, including guarantees, installation, after sales service, etc. The implication here is that marketing communications must convey exactly what is being offered for what is being asked. He instances a report from the Confederation of British Industry (CBI) which suggests the country's exporters sometimes miss opportunities due to lack of emphasis on what is being offered for the prices quoted.

Although a marketing-oriented firm will often go beyond legal minima in the cause of the customer, some other legal points are worth mentioning. A contract for the sale of goods is, in essence, an exchange of promises between the parties involved. Where these promises are so basic to the intentions of the parties that they represent essential terms of the contract, they are classified as *conditions*. Breach of a condition gives rise to a right to treat the contract as repudiated. Other stipulations, although important, do not go to the root of the contract but are collateral to its main purpose. Such stipulations are called *warranties*. Breach of these gives rise to a claim for damages though not a right to reject the products in question or to treat the contract as repudiated. So an organization must be very clear, and ensure the customer is clear about the nature and extent of its undertakings in respect of the 'total product' it provides.

Next, whether the parties to a contract of sale have called its various stipulations 'conditions' or 'warranties' is one thing, but what the law considers them to be may be quite another. To determine this, a court of law will examine the contract as a whole. It is worth repeating again that the essential consideration is an adequate balance of customer satisfaction, affordable cost and, hence, a respectable return on investment.

For our third legal point we return to guarantees. These are usually provided by makers to cover the early life of their products, but any *maker's* guarantee does not extinguish the rights of the customer against the *seller*. In effect, the customer has the choice of bringing any grievance to the notice of the maker or the seller. Moreover, no matter what the guarantee may say, the maker cannot use it in such a way as to limit his liability for damage or loss resulting from a defect in the product caused by his neglect. The onus is on the seller to deal with customer grievances of course.

The notion of going beyond basic legal requirements to ensure the best possible level of service is exemplified by those *trade associations* which have established collective *codes of practice*. These were described in Chapter 5, but it might be useful for you to look at this again.

After sales service

The efficiency of a supplier's repair and maintenance operations and his or her spare parts provision is often as powerful an influence in obtaining business as the quality and value of the product itself. This is certainly true in the industrial field and is increasingly so in consumer markets.

In industry, particularly where mass production techniques or process technologies are being operated, 'downtime' – periods of enforced inactivity due to production breakdown – must be avoided or kept to an absolute minimum. Even when spare plant capacity can be utilized to fill the gap, setting-up time and the diverting of materials and labour will be costly for the customer.

From the industrial customer's standpoint, some alternatives are possible. He (or she) may feel it so important to avoid 'downtime' that he employs his own maintenance specialists. Or, he may demand such a high level of reliability from the products that they are virtually maintenance-free – and for this reliability he may be willing to pay a premium price. A third option is that a separate contract for repairs and maintenance to be carried out on a routine, repetitive basis can be agreed with the supplier, subsequent, possibly, to a 'free' maintenance period. These alternatives remind us of Rose's (1965, p 128) view that after sales service can be a potent factor in marketing though again, 'this depends ultimately on clear thinking about the place of service in the price structure of the product'.

From the seller's standpoint where there is an adequate financial return on maintenance and repair activity, its provision can usefully be marketed in addition to the organization's products. Sometimes it is a point of strategic marketing policy to supply the main equipment at an especially low price, or hiring rate, in order to obtain a high return from materials and other supplies. Photocopier contracts provide a good illustration of this policy but a word of warning here – the ethics of some particular schemes have been called into question.

After sales service is likely to increase in importance. As products become increasingly automatic ('Just point and shoot for a perfect picture – the camera makes all the adjustments') their internal mechanisms become more complex and the linkages between their sub-systems more extended. This means more things to go wrong and increased reliance by customers on the provision of systems to put them right. Thus not only industrial goods, but also consumer durables, have an ever increasing need for effective after sales service. This was recently brought home to a manufacturer of personal computers selling direct to the public. Customers became increasingly frustrated because of the long delays in getting through on the manufacturer's 'help-lines'. Following complaints to the media, an increased number of help-lines had to be provided. Also, as is evident from the advertising campaigns of motor manufacturers, which often attempt to outbid each other with details of generous and lengthy warranty cover, it is clear that each car buyer is purchasing, in effect, a *composite of product and service*.

Repair and maintenance is only one aspect of after sales service, of course. 'Service' in a general sense is also important and retail organizations, particularly, ignore this at their peril. Speedy and just complaints procedures play a vital role in shaping the corporate image. The success in the UK of the Marks and Spencer organization is based, among other things, on the speedy and trouble-free way in which garments purchased at one branch can, given a reasonable explanation, be exchanged at any other.

It should also be noted that any circumstances which bring the manufacturer into direct contact with the user has its own added value. Guarantee cards incorporating a simple questionnaire can be an important extra source of marketing research, for instance. An organization which is truly customer-led will be as concerned with the customers' satisfaction after the sale (i.e. in the 'after-market') as before it. This outline of the importance of after sales service may have provided some thoughts on how best this concern should be implemented.

Product strategy and management

In this chapter we have considered some of the concepts and techniques relevant to the development of an individual product. In the vast majority of cases, however, the organization or the SBU markets more than a single product. Consequently, product strategy invariably calls for the development and management of a *range* of products, in marketing language termed the *product mix* or *portfolio*. We took a glimpse into this process earlier in the text when we looked at *positioning strategy* (Chapter 3) while in this chapter we have considered some relevant techniques including the *product life-cycle*, *portfolio analysis* and *branding*. In this section we shall be looking at it in a more rounded fashion so it might be useful to skim the earlier discussions just mentioned before we proceed.

While it may be tiresome to repeat the point yet again, it has to be said that product strategy must emanate from an organizational strategy and the development of general objectives emanating from an examination of

- the business the organization is in;
- its strengths and weaknesses;
- a clear perception of the threats and opportunities it faces.

To put it succinctly, *product strategy* begins with *corporate strategy*.

Product/market strategy

In the first instance, corporate planning should lead to decisions based upon:

- the target markets, or segments, in which the organization will operate;
- the products/services it will offer to those markets; and from this
- the attainment of defined objectives.

An approach to clarify thinking here is the Ansoff 2 × 2 matrix (see Figure 8.12). In one of the earliest and most notable works on corporate strategy, Ansoff (1968, p 99) suggested that strategic analysis should seek 'to identify particular properties of individual product-markets which will give the firm a strong competitive position'. He illustrated his thinking with the 2 × 2 matrix represented in Figure 8.12. Over 30 years after its appearance planners still find it relevant and useful. The simple schematic to the right of the matrix is this author's representation of the level of risk perceived by Ansoff as accompanying the strategies implied by the labels of the four cells in the matrix. The word 'theoretical' is added by this author on the basis of life's capacity to surprise us. Below is a brief outline of the various strategic options.

Market penetration
The organization opts for a strategy of retaining existing customers and developing new customers in its existing market. It should know this external environment well

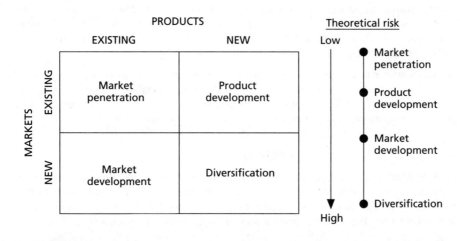

Figure 8.12. *The Ansoff matrix. Source: Ansoff (1968, p 99)*

enough and, while competitive pricing and energetic promotion will probably be important, the level of theoretical risk should be low.

Product development

Here, guided by customer needs and wants in the existing market(s) the strategy is to modify existing products and develop new ones. Given the failure rate of new products, this is a slightly more risky option. Strengths to which the organization can play here might include speedy access to new technology and the superior skills of its workforce.

Market development

Seeking to sell existing products to new markets adds yet another increment of risk in that the geographical base might have to be widened. Foreign markets present new environments and being a global player means being supremely well prepared. Developed skills in marketing research and operations might point to this path.

Diversification

The combination of new products for new markets produces the highest risk strategic option but the organization might, after careful analysis and evaluation, prove itself right by choosing to diversify. Mergers, acquisitions and 'breakthrough' concepts are usually in evidence here.

In any organization, decisions on major resource allocation to create future revenue streams are among the most important and the most complex. To structure thinking on this major issue, the Ansoff matrix has some simple but clear organizing power.

Another broad framework for decision-making in the product/market context relates to *marketing strategy*. For example, an organization might decide to pursue an *undifferentiated* marketing strategy which means it ignores the differences between various market segments and markets a single product to all possible customers, utilizing a single marketing mix. Such an approach generally calls for mass distribution and mass advertising based on a broad general promotional appeal.

A *differentiated* marketing strategy, by contrast, targets several market segments and designs a separate marketing mix, including the product, for each of these. This strategy is clearly the one employed by most of the world's car manufacturers. The central objective is to achieve higher sales and a stronger position within each segment through differentiation.

Another possible strategy, appealing particularly where the organization is relatively small, or its resources are limited, is that of *concentrated marketing*. In marketing language, this is sometimes referred to as *niche* marketing, or by this author as 'sliding down the cracks'. Here the organization's total marketing activity is focused upon a single segment or, at most, a very few segments. Concentrated marketing often assists small manufacturers to exist profitably alongside larger companies in the same product field.

Let us now turn to some of the considerations attaching to the product portfolio itself. Some of the considerations involved were described earlier in the chapter when the use of portfolio models was outlined. Below we shall look briefly at some of the other considerations pertinent to managing a range of products.

Cost:volume:profit relationships

Each product must be considered, not only on its own merits but for its relationship with, and effect upon, the other products in the range. The first step here is to analyse the *cost:volume:profit relationships* of all the products. Sometimes it may be necessary to manage the range as a mix of 'high yield', 'break-even' and 'loss leader' products. A 'high yield' product, for example, might have its price, and therefore its projected profitability, set at a higher level than its costs would warrant because it is required to produce higher than average profits in order for the organization to achieve its overall target rate of return on investment. This will become clearer in the next chapter (on pricing) when the use of a *product estimation chart* is explained.

Range rationalization

One of the primary aspects of product management concerns the 'breadth' and 'depth' of the range. 'Breadth' refers to the number of products in the range and 'depth' to the number of styles, sizes or types of *each* product. There is an almost insistent pressure for the range to expand: sales representatives, and even distributors, may encourage production of another colour, another size, another quality.

As noted in Chapter 3, this is all to the good provided the return in volume and/or profitability justifies the expenditure involved. Frequently, however, the result is not to expand sales but to extend a static sales volume over an increased product range, with consequent reduction in average sales per product. When this happens, costs increase through uneconomic production runs, and possibly 'split' deliveries to customers, as the firm attempts to cope with recurring out of stock situations.

It is worth saying again that the outcome can become chronic enough for a large proportion of output to be responsible for only a small part of sales, profits or both, while a relatively small proportion of output is responsible for most of the sales/profits. As we know from our look at Pareto analysis earlier, this is known as the 80/20 tendency because 20 per cent of the product portfolio may be bringing in 80 per cent of the sales/profits, and vice versa. When this is happening, management may adopt a strategy of *range rationalization*, dispensing with the unprofitable or slow selling products and marketing a 'leaner' but more effective range.

Range extension

Earlier in this chapter we noted the concept of the product life-cycle which, though not a fixed and perpetual law can still usefully be thought of as a statement of general tendency. Where an 80/20 situation does not apply, and there seems to be a good case for range extension, one way an individual organization might be able to do this is by developing alternative formulations of its basic product. For example, a manufacturer of industrial porcelain (e.g textile thread guides, shuttle eyes) faced with a decline in demand may, by modifying the output, enter the electro-ceramic (insulators) and architectural ceramic (tiles) fields.

As Figure. 8.13 indicates the life-cycle of the basic product is enlarged in this way and the traditional shape of the life-cycle curve is altered for, throughout the extended time period, a series of loops is being added on to it.

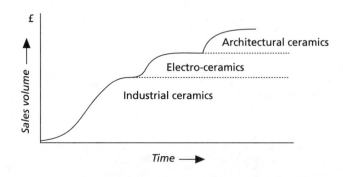

Figure 8.13. *Extending the life-cycle : industrial porcelain*

With regard to the life-cycle concept itself, mention was made earlier in the chapter of the criticism it has attracted for its lack of 'rigour'. We should not be overly concerned with this for the model has some value for planning purposes. For example, it focuses the attention of management on the importance of innovation for business performance and helps to ensure sufficient new products are being developed to sustain growth (see Figure 8.14.).

As Mercer remarks, the concept also often brings to the attention of management a most important message concerning cash flow, because:

> The model offers a clear reminder, if needed (and it often is), that the launch of new brand requires significant investment, and that this can last right through from its launch to the end of the growth phase – a longer period than most organizations allow for (Mercer, 1992, p 314).

'Own-label' products

The last 35 years have seen a marked concentration of retailer buying power, as we shall see in Chapter 10 on distribution. In the UK, for example, such organizations as Sainsbury, Tesco and Marks and Spencer by imposing a standard assortment of products on their branch networks and concentrating the buying power of these networks, have been able to secure the lowest possible prices from suppliers. Passing some of their savings on in the form of lower consumer prices has been a prime factor in their phenomenal growth.

From this position, it has been a logical step for these organizations to develop 'own label' products. This has enabled manufacturers to obtain the economies of large-scale production without having to bear heavy promotional costs for launching or sustaining products in mass markets – a daunting expense, particularly for small/medium-sized organizations. Larger manufacturers have usually found it possible and profitable to adopt a composite policy of product management, with some of their output being marketed under their established brands whilst also providing for the retailers' 'own-label' market.

A situation has thus emerged in which a large number of manufacturers have been directing some or all of their production to the market under the Marks and Spencer 'St. Michael' brand, or the family brands of Sainsbury, Tesco and Asda, etc. Initial consumer appeal was through prices lower than manufacturers' nationally advertised brands. At the onset, some of the buying public may have been doubtful about the quality of own-label products but user experience, coupled with the market-standing of the firms typically offering own-label products, have long since dispelled such fears.

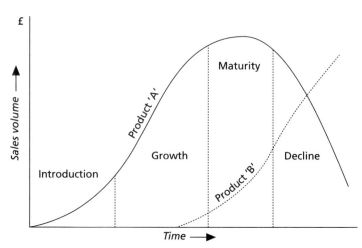

Figure 8.14. *The product life-cycle concept as an aid to planning*

In the recent past, however, a significant trend has emerged in the packaged grocery field which has marked implications for product management. This is the development of supermarkets' 'budget' own-label products which have emerged as the fastest growing sector of the UK's £22 billion market for packaged groceries. The sector, which was incorporated in Sainsbury's 'Essentials' campaign and includes Tesco's 'Value' lines, hardly existed in 1994. By March 1996 it had grown by 500 per cent and then accounted for £814 million worth of sales. This has meant that heavily advertised manufacturers' brands have to fight extremely hard to keep customers, as Table 8.4. demonstrates.

In the field of fast moving consumer goods, a sequence of salient questions might be:

- to brand or not to brand?
- to produce for distributors' 'own-labels'?
- to produce for distributors' budget labels?

Concluding comments

At the beginning of this chapter, the point was made that 'the product' is the key factor enabling an organization to adapt to its environment in order to survive. The length of this chapter gives some indication of the salience of 'the product'. The fact that the word 'product' is broadly interpreted in marketing was another early point and before closing the chapter, we must say something about two other manifestations of 'the product', namely *services* and *ideas*.

The marketing of services

Economic well-being, rising standards of living, increased leisure time and technological progress all generate a phenomenal growth in the demand for services. *Personal services* – hairdressing, tailoring, counselling; *professional services* – legal, commercial, medical; *general services* – entertainment, travel, sport, information and *business services* – plant repair and maintenance, commercial transport, cleaning, consultancy, etc., all benefit from this rapid increase in demand.

If the suppliers of services are to trade profitably and to withstand the competition that buoyant markets inevitably attract, then their need for *market analysis* is just as pronounced as it is with tangible products. The role of marketing research in minimizing risk at the development stage and monitoring performance at the implementation stage should be well to the fore. Providers of services need to understand how trends in the population profile and in incomes affect demand. They need to determine what market segments they can best cultivate, what user needs and expectations they should aim to satisfy, the price/value assessment typically employed by

Product	Market share 1995 (%)	Increase/decrease 1993–95 (%)	Price comparison (Market average = 100)
Brand leaders (Top two brands)	40.3	−1.8%	120
Supermarket own label	30.3	+0.8%	94
Budget brands	7.9	−1.9	77
Supermarket budget label	3.7	+2.1	55
Other brands	17.8	−0.7	123

Table 8.4. *UK packaged grocery market*

Source: *Financial Mail on Sunday,* 3 March 1996

their customers and what influences – personality, peer group or whatever – motivate buying behaviour.

In addition, the development of new services and the improvement of existing services is just as vital as in any other field. The service organization must decide upon:

- the characteristics of the service to be offered;
- the 'width' and 'depth' of the services mix;
- the positioning of its own service in relation to direct and indirect competition;
- (and not least) what support the service will be given in relation to promotion, branding, warranties, etc.

Yet beyond these points of general importance, as Helen Woodruffe (1995, pp 18–19) indicates, services can be distinguished by some key characteristics of special relevance to marketing. For instance:

- because they are *intangible*, there may be lack of confidence on the part of the customer who may therefore search for evidence of quality in the nature of the premises or the qualifications of the provider;
- since services are *inseparable*, for they are produced and consumed at the same time, the service provider is a key part of the service itself, hence the importance of the waitress in the restaurant and the clerk in the travel bureau for example;
- services are both *heterogeneous* and *variable* for an act of service is unique, i.e. it can never be exactly repeated, mainly because people comprise part of the service offering – which underlines the importance of staff training and the monitoring of customer satisfaction;
- services are *perishable* – an empty seat in a theatre or a medical centre is a marketing opportunity lost forever, for services cannot be stored.

It should be easy to discern from these characteristics how vital it is to establish a whole-organization commitment to the customer. In fact, some intriguing lessons can be learned from the application of marketing to the field of services. With regard to the planning of services, for instance, the point was made above that the organization must decide on the *positioning* of its service. How might this be done? Kotler (1997, p 289) provides an excellent outline of how services provision might be differentiated from competition. For instance, an organization might improve the way in which orders can be placed. He cites the instance of the healthcare company in the USA which provided its customers with computer terminals to increase their *ease of ordering*. The speed, accuracy and care with which the service is *delivered* can be a strong differentiator as can excellent *installation*, *consultancy* and *customer training* provision. Readers seeking a clear and comprehensive treatment of services marketing will find the Woodruffe (1997) text helpful.

The marketing of ideas

One of the ways in which marketing contributes to the well-being of society is in the propagation of ideas. To do this, marketing campaigns are conducted to galvanize opinion concerning some pressing problem of the day. For example, public concern in the UK has been raised in the recent past on such issues as drink-driving, healthy eating, protection of the environment, home security ('Beat the burglar'), child immunization, and the benefits of screening for life-threatening diseases. As these words are being written, a campaign is being conducted by the National Consumer Council to warn against the possible threat to food safety, and hence public health, as a result of the use of antibiotics in animal feed and the increased use of pesticides in arable farming.

The most widespread and sustained marketing of ideas probably occurs in the field of politics and Britain has recently provided an example of how all elements of the strategic marketing formula can be employed in favour of a political idea.

'New Labour'

Commenting in October 1997 on a report by the Henley Centre consultancy, Winston Fletcher (1997) pointed out its finding that *far more people now have faith in famous product brands than in many British public institutions*, including the monarchy, the police, parliament and the press. In Fletcher's own words: 'Kellogg's and Marks & Spencer are up to eight times more trusted than parliament (and about a dozen times more trusted than journalists)' (1997, p 19).

As Chairman of the Bozell advertising and marketing group, Fletcher considers that the establishment of New Labour as a trustworthy brand name 'was a textbook marketing operation'. He outlines key factors adopted in the strategy as follows:

- *reformulation of the product* – 'old Clause 4 ditched, old policies emasculated';
- *up-dating of the brand name* – 'NEW – one of the most powerful words in marketing';
- *market surveys* – 'particularly focus group discussions were constantly used to check the acceptability of every policy, every message, every idea';
- *competition* – its 'strengths and weaknesses' were 'assiduously analysed';
- *target market* – 'middle of the road wobbly Tories';
- *communications* – 'coordinated and unified to maximise impact'.

Fletcher suggests that New Labour's successful 1997 election campaign was based on the principles of integrated marketing and it would be very difficult to disagree. New Labour's campaign echoed the activities and processes of organizations developing the integrity of their brand(s). He also makes the acute point that while brands help companies to build and protect their sales, 'their real strength and appeal comes from their power to simplify and define'. And, just as the brand helps the consumer to cope with the information overload generated by the 35,000 different items in the average supermarket, so New Labour's campaign helped the elector make an informed choice between complex, significant and opposed political ideas.

One final point – in this section we have been considering ideas in a general sense. There are, of course, other ideas specific to the individual organization and usually related to the development of new products, processes and services. Many such ideas are revolutionary and important enough to be patentable. In commercial language they are usually referred to as '*intellectual property*', another marketable 'product' which is dealt with separately in Chapter 13 in the section on international trade.

The strategic formula: Element 3:

C·H·A·P·T·E·R

NINE

Prices and pricing strategy

Introduction: *prices and pricing strategy*

Income generation is one of the key tasks of the marketing executive. Income must be generated which 'Production' and 'Personnel' will utilise and which 'Finance' will administer but which 'Marketing' must obtain. Moreover, it must be obtained:

- in the required volume;
- at an adequate rate of flow per time period; and
- at an acceptable level of cost.

Kotler and Armstrong (1990) remind us that *price* is the only element in the marketing mix which produces revenue and that all the other elements represent costs. Given the fundamental nature of income generation, it might be supposed that marketing executives would have become quite skilled at the pricing process. Kotler and Armstrong have a different view:

> Yet many companies do not handle pricing well. The most common mistakes are: pricing that is too cost-oriented; prices that are not revised often enough to reflect market changes; pricing that does not take the rest of the marketing mix into account; and prices that are not varied enough for different product items and market segments (Kotler and Armstrong, 1990, p 283).

Robert J. Dolan (1995, pp 174–83) Professor of Business Administration at the Harvard Business School echoes this sentiment: 'Pricing is managers' biggest marketing headache. It's where they feel the most pressure to perform and the least certain that they are doing a good job'.

Michael Morris (1992, p 364), a leading writer on industrial marketing, believes that the potential of the price variable is not fully realized in many 'industrial' firms, adding that price is a complex decision area that management too often tries to over-simplify. He points out that the price of a product is a valuable marketing tool that can be used in a number of ways to accomplish a variety of objectives.

Some of the consequences of setting an inappropriate price for a product or service are indicated in Figure 9.1 and need no elaboration. Economists speak of an *equilibrium price* in which supply and demand are exactly in balance, enabling the supplier to sell all of his output profitably without any unsatisfied customers. This is

Figure 9.1. *Equilibrium price: balancing supply and demand*

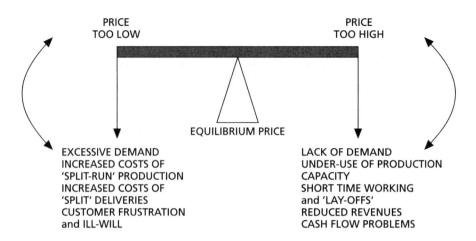

fine, as far as it goes, provided 'profit', however loosely defined, is the *pricing objective*, but Table 9.1 lists ten other possible objectives from an even longer list.

The list in Table 9.1 illustrates what is meant by 'the potential of the price variable' and explains why Baker (1979, pp 230–1), for example, in supporting the views of Kotler and others, laments the too frequent lack of a 'creative pricing policy' which takes sufficient account of external as well as internal variables and which is clearly and logically linked to attaining the organization's overall objectives. Rudimentary formulae based on 'rule of thumb' approaches lead to 'mechanical' pricing decisions which fail to take account of the dynamic nature of markets and the opportunities that this dynamism provides.

In this introduction to prices and pricing strategy, one other point needs to be made, that is that pricing is becoming more, rather than less, important. Price has, historically, been the major determinant of customer choice. This is still true in many markets, for example in Third World markets, commodity markets and in the poorer segments of otherwise prosperous markets. And even in the prosperous markets of the West, where non-price factors have become increasingly important in recent decades, global competition is restoring the pre-eminence of the price element in many product/markets.

Given the importance of pricing strategy, how best might it be developed? In the next section, we shall consider some of the indicators of best practice.

1.	Sales growth
2.	Entry to a new market
3.	Provide support to distributors
4.	Establish a particular institutional image
5.	Early recovery of research and development costs
6.	Promote sales of other products/services
7.	Deter new entrants to the market
8.	Improve cash flow
9.	Generate interest in a 'breakthrough' concept
10.	Discourage competitors from reducing prices

Table 9.1. *Ten possible pricing objectives*

Pointers to pricing strategies

Briefly, the more significant of these may be summarized as follows:

- Prices must be related to overall corporate policy, including the institutional 'image' the organization wishes to develop and maintain, its philosophy toward price competition, etc.

- Decisions on products and services, distribution, promotion, administration are all affected by decisions on price – cause and effect relationships within marketing objectives and 'mix' strategies must therefore be carefully studied.

- Price has a key influence on demand and therefore the market's perception of price and its implications for cost:volume:profit relationships must be closely examined.

- Pricing strategy must take sufficient account of external constraints – for example, government economic measures (on inflation), price regulation and monopolies legislation, and the reactions of distributors, competitors, suppliers, etc. which may all act as important determinants on prices.

- The life-cycle concept has significant implications for the pricing of products.

- In most cases, price must be related to the requirements of the total product portfolio and hence to overall marketing objectives.

- In developing strategy, *future* trends in costs, demand and competition must be carefully considered and policies on adapting prices to changed market conditions must be devised.

- Most markets are in a constant state of change which heightens the risks of price decisions – wherever possible and, however informal, marketing research and any other relevant techniques should be employed in developing pricing strategy.

The ideas underlying these 'precepts' might now be usefully considered.

Price and corporate policy

As outlined earlier in the text, the organization has legal obligations with regard to its pricing policies. The values and mission statements should reinforce its commitment to acting legally in all phases of its operations and management, including its pricing activities. Beyond this the obligation to act ethically must also be fixed, defined, published and acted upon. 'Fair value' should condition the approach to price planning and administration. Misleading pricing, apart from its illegality, has no place in the customer-led firm.

If the organization wishes to cultivate a 'value for money' image, the emphasis may be on pricing its products or services lower than the competition (hence the claims to be 'never knowingly undersold'). On the other hand, an organization might pursue the objective of being regarded as the one which leads on product quality. Here strategy may demand a high-level pricing approach – to cover the costs of extensive research and development, high quality raw materials and highly skilled labour.

Price as a component of the marketing mix

Clearly, the specifications of the product, its characteristics, quality, performance standards, etc., will be greatly influenced by the price being set for it – the higher the price, the better the possible specification. Also, the price must 'fit' with the market position at which the product is being aimed and enough has been said on segmentation and positioning for this point to be understood. It is also important to remember that user attitudes to the product may be influenced by psychological as well as physical attributes. This is why many organizations use the *perceived value* approach to pricing strategy. This approach is discussed later in the chapter.

The *total product* concept will stand repetition under this heading for it is important that the user appreciates what is being offered at the price in addition to the product itself – for example guarantees, installation and after sales service, etc. Only in this way can the value of the offer be judged. Mention was made in the last chapter of how organizations laying greater stress on their total product might make more headway in international markets. The alternative which presents itself here is to 'unbundle' the offer and charge separately for installation and after sales service operations. Customer attitudes and the policies of competitors are important factors in this equation.

The links between price and the elements in the 'mix' other than the product are evident enough and need not delay us. For example, the higher the price the greater the possibility of increasing distributors' margins, quantity discounts, etc., and hence distributive support. The higher the price, the greater the possibility of increased budgets for advertising, publicity, sales promotion and salespeople's commissions.

Price–demand relationships and the market

First, the *nature of the market* will markedly influence prices and pricing strategies. It is possible to distinguish four broad types of market, namely:

- markets of perfect competition;
- monopoly markets;
- markets of monopolistic competition;
- oligopoly markets.

Under *perfect competition* the individual organization has no discretion concerning pricing strategy. It has to be a *price taker*, which is to say that it must accept the prevailing market price as its own price, if it wishes to survive. In a perfectly competitive market there are many buyers and sellers and the individual firm's product is indistinguishable from all other products and is therefore traded as a commodity. In fact, the world's commodity markets for tin, copper, wheat, etc. provide good examples of perfect competition.

As its name suggests, there is a single seller in a pure *monopoly market* who is therefore a *price maker*, having significant discretion on fixing the market price. The pricing strategy adopted may be, for example, to maximize sales so as to deter competitors from entering the market (*entry-limit pricing*) or to maximize profits. Some qualifications now need to be added. First, it may well be in the public interest for the supplier to be a monopolist, as where a government controls the nation's postal service. Secondly, governments are sensitive to the abuse of monopoly power and may regulate its prices on the basis of a 'fair return' or slow down consumption of the monopolist's output (e.g. power supply). Demand is also influenced by *price elasticity* of the monopoly output, as will be explained later.

Markets in which perfect competition or pure monopoly prevail are rare, for in practice most markets are characterized by *monopolistic competition*. This is to say that while competition is plainly evident, each organization is the 'monopoly supplier' of its own output. Hence, since most products in such markets are highly substitutable, the individual organization attempts to differentiate itself from the competition, for example through branding. Since competition prevails, firms do not have total control over their prices and segmentation and positioning strategies are well to the fore, as is the marketing approach in general.

In a condition of *oligopoly*, the market is dominated by a small number of sellers. Competition is plainly evident, with each seller being highly sensitive to the policies and practices of competitors and each seller considering carefully the likely reaction of competition to its own moves. For example, if one firm raises its price, will the others follow suit? Where one organization emerges as *price leader* then its competitors may have little option other than to trail the leader's strategy. Since pricing tensions and uncertainties could be reduced through collusion between the suppliers to fix prices, governments are watchful in case *cartels* are formed to the detriment of customer interests.

The second point to make in this section is that prices and pricing policies are also influenced by the *nature of demand*, as well as by the *nature of the market*. First, a word on demand in general.

If we look at the curves depicted in Figure 9.2 (i) and (ii) we observe that, in both cases, demand extends as price falls or, conversely, contracts as price rises. This tendency can be expressed as follows:

> In general there is a central law of demand *which states that there is an inverse relationship between the price of a good and the quantity demanded* assuming all other factors that might influence demand are held constant (Nellis and Parker, 1997, p 23).

Since both curves are downward sloping they uphold this central law of demand but we can observe that in the case of Figure 9.2 (ii), a fall in price is accompanied by a much larger increase in demand than is the case with Figure 9.2.(i). Assessing the responsiveness of demand to changes in price is an important task for managers and is referred to as *the measurement of price elasticity*. Where a change in price results in a less than proportional change in quantity sold, demand is said to be *inelastic* (see the curve in Figure 9.2 (i)). Where a change in price results in a more than proportional change in sales volume, demand is said to be *elastic* (as in the curve in Figure 9.2 (ii)).

When demand is elastic, pricing will be an important area for management decision-making and a great deal of prior thought must be given to price changes. To obtain a foothold in highly competitive markets, an *investment-budget approach*, incorporating low prices, may be necessary, with prices being revised as, hopefully, brand loyalty develops. When demand is inelastic, *product differentiation* and other forms of *non-price competition* become more appropriate.

Where different, even dissimilar, substitutes can be seen to compete against the product in question – toughened glass, plastics and even paper compete with

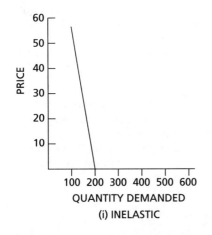

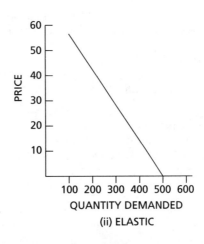

Figure 9.2 (i) and (ii). *Price elasticity of demand*

ceramics in the tableware market, for instance – there is said to be *cross-elasticity of demand* and assessing this entails measuring the responsiveness of the quantity of a specific product demanded to changes in the prices of other products, complements as well as substitutes.

The decision maker will also be interested in any evidence for *income elasticity of demand*, the measure of how demand responds to any changes in the real incomes of consumers. Rising real incomes can have a significant effect on the demand for luxury goods and professional services for instance, as well as for home ownership.

For each of these types of elasticity, a *coefficient* can be calculated in accordance with the simple general formula:

$$\text{Coefficient of elasticity} = \frac{\text{Percentage change in quantity demanded}}{\text{Percentage change in the relevant variable}}$$

Prices and external constraints

The role of government, and supra-national organizations such as the European Union, provides a significant example under this heading. Aspects of a government's economic management, its attitudes and policies to prices and incomes, to monopolies and mergers and to any price-fixing agreements deemed contrary to the public interest, all act as important influences on management decision-making in this area. Increased government intervention in the performance of products and aspects of health and safety constitute similar constraints. The influence of foreign governments on pricing strategy in international markets will be referred to later in the text.

The strategy and tactics of competitors must be monitored closely and where the organization is not the price-leader, the value or quality of its offer may perhaps be emphasized. One of the best examples of such an approach known to the author was in the field of optical equipment. Competitive products were thoroughly examined and sales personnel were issued with technical information sheets on them, enabling the value of the organization's own products to be emphasized during negotiations.

The support of distributors has to be safeguarded. For example, a price reduction to meet competition may leave them with large stocks bought at a higher price – how best can the loyalty and motivation of distributors be retained in this situation? Similarly, suppliers may be asked to reduce their prices to counter competition but they can hardly be expected to forgo an adequate return. Finally, the general business environment may operate as a constraint against some projected pricing strategy, for example depressed economic conditions.

Price and the product life-cycle

As we have seen earlier, the price history of a product may indicate significant changes as it moves through the stages of its life-cycle. As will be explained later in this chapter, an approach to pricing may be adopted in which the producer adds a percentage mark-up to the sum of his own costs so as to arrive at the final selling price of his product. The point here is that this mark-up need not be rigidly fixed throughout the life-cycle.

Imagine the product is at the introduction stage, that demand is elastic and an investment-budget strategy is being pursued. Here, market share may be preferred to profitability and therefore the customary mark-up may be reduced. Conversely, if the product is well into its maturity stage, a mark-up policy may be pursued which yields the largest balance over cost in order to assist the launching of other products – even if this means an earlier demise for the already mature product.

Price and the product portfolio

Portfolio analysis has also been introduced earlier, but to demonstrate how pricing strategy for one product may be affected by other products in the range, let us look at a fairly basic example. Assume that the retail selling price of a product could be '100', '110' or '120' (the units are immaterial) and that sales volume at these prices is estimated by market research to be 5000, 4800 and 4700 units. An *estimation chart*, devised by the producer, yields the following information:

Retail selling price	Price ex producer	Predicted sales volume	Revenue to producer	Total fixed and variable costs	Balance over cost	% return on sales
100	40	5000 units	200,000	160,000	40,000	20.0
110	44	4800 units	211,200	165,000	46,200	21.9
120	48	4700 units	225,600	169,000	56,600	25.1

Which of the three prices should the producer choose? If sales volume is being sought – perhaps to fill some spare production capacity or to launch a product in a market characterized by significant price elasticity of demand – the 100 price will be chosen. On the other hand, if senior management is signalling an increased need for high yield products to ensure that the profit performance of the company is in line with the planned longer-term growth of profits, then the 120 price would be chosen since this gives the best balance over cost. Or again, for very good reasons, the intermediate price of 110 might be chosen.

So the answer must be 'it all depends' and what this example seeks to demonstrate is that sometimes the aim could be to establish a price based not on the product itself but on the product portfolio and the projected performance of the organization as a whole. Thus, senior management should, at the least, have an overview of pricing decisions especially where the decision-making unit is the whole organization and where overall objectives are based upon a long-term target rate of return.

Pricing strategy and future trends

Enough has been said earlier in the text to substantiate the importance of planning for change. It is a vital part of management's responsibility to look ahead and assess the likelihood of changes in costs, demand, technology and competition over an appropriate period of time. The implications of such changes for prices and pricing strategies must be kept under review. Similarly, a current market situation which is dynamic may require dynamism in pricing strategy and policies instituted on how prices will be adapted to changed conditions. In the author's experience, for example, price reductions are usually more complex and difficult to manage than price increases, not least because of their effect on distributors, and adequate foresight will do much to smooth the changes.

One of the areas which can easily be overlooked is that of *production capacity* – 'will the organization be able *supply* the expected volume efficiently?' and 'at what break-points in volume will new patterns of cost emerge?' Needless to say, choice of raw materials and components suppliers, and the quality of strategic alliances, can have an immense effect on prices and profit performance. They should therefore be judiciously and continuously assessed.

Pricing decisions and marketing research

Implicit in the marketing approach is the value of the research function for decision-making purposes. No matter how experienced the executive, it is not possible for him to forecast with certainty how the market will react to a pricing decision. Therefore, any approach which will help to indicate the relationship between price and demand is undoubtedly useful. Surveys of user attitudes, modelling approaches and test marketing may all provide some indication of what will happen in the market place. With regard to modelling, according to the leading agency Research International (RI), recent advances in pricing research and the need to investigate more than one price for a product have led to a move away from pricing research as a *diagnostic* tool towards price modelling as a *predictive* tool. Research has been utilized to construct *brand switching models* employed to predict the probable gains or losses arising from different pricing strategies in competitive markets.

Below is a very brief description of some of the techniques used in pricing research.

Monadic approaches

The respondent is shown a single item (i.e. without competing products) and asked to respond to a single price or a number of different prices. The price(s) may be suggested by the manufacturer or the research objective may be for the respondent to generate an appropriate price.

This type of approach typically employs:

- *Scalar methods* – in which the respondent rates products at given prices on scales extending, for example, from 'definitely not buy' to 'definitely buy'. The ratings are interpreted by examining distributions of answers across the scale points and by comparing mean scores with the results from previous studies.

- *Simple Gabor Granger methods* – used to test new prices for an existing product or to resolve the optimum price for a new product, the pricing possibilities to be tested are prepared in advance and presented one at a time to the respondent; aggregation of responses over a large sample facilitates the construction of a demand curve showing the relationship between price and purchase intention or 'volume'.

- *Price Sensitivity Measurement* (PSM) – designed to overcome the limitations of presenting prices to respondents which are already fixed, and which may be well outside the range of prices acceptable to the consumer, PSM involves a number of questions designed to elucidate an acceptable price range; responses to points on a wide-ranging price scale indicating when the brand/product would be:
  – cheap or a 'bargain';
  – expensive or 'dear';
  – too expensive, so that a respondent would not buy it;
  – too cheap, so that quality would be doubted and purchase refused.

  This enables responses to be aggregated across the sample and plotted as four intersecting curves (Figure 9.3).

The 'core acceptable range' of prices, that is the price range within which most respondents feel the product is neither cheap/expensive nor too cheap/too expensive, is denoted as the area bounded by the intersecting curves. Price sensitivity measurement is in fairly common use for new product development, the repositioning of existing products and extension of the product range.

Competitive approaches

- *Extended Gabor Granger* – this is similar to the basic Gabor Granger method described earlier but priced competitive brands/products are introduced into the testing process. The respondent is asked to state his or her likely purchase behaviour (nature and/or volume) for the test product and other products in a display. A number of different prices are suggested for the test product and prices

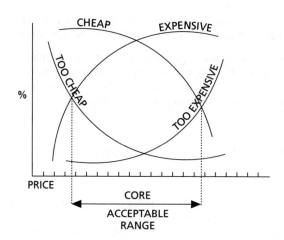

Figure 9.3. *Price Sensitivity Measurement (PSM)*

for competing products are held constant at their current market levels. The approach enables reactions to price to be made in a more realistic context.

- *Conjoint analysis* – this was described in some detail in the previous chapter. Research International have developed the conjoint approach, with their Brand/Price Trade-Off (BPTO) model. Here the brand entity is not decomposed into constituent attributes but traded-off as a fixed 'bundle of benefits' against the price being asked. BPTO is,therefore, in essence, a conjoint study with only two attributes – brand and price.

RI have also developed an *Options Model* which is designed for research into high-outlay durable type products.

The above outline gives some indication of the specialist support available for pricing decisions. Where problems of time and finance prevent adoption of more sophisticated approaches then canvassing the opinions of distributors and sales personnel will provide some help. Although managerial judgement is, in the end, central to the whole pricing process, any data which will inform that judgement, whether gathered formally or informally, should be carefully acquired and analysed.

The pointers we have reviewed in this section are intended to provide useful background considerations against which the pricing process can take place. Before leaving the section, however, a further factor should be examined and it is of overriding importance.

Pricing and organizational co-ordination

Robert Dolan (1995, p 175) makes the significant point that there are typically many participants in the pricing process and that problems will inevitably arise if a philosophy of wide participation operates without strong coordinating mechanisms.

Accountants provide cost estimates, marketers develop and communicate pricing strategy, sales staff provide input from specific customers, the production department sets the supply framework and finance establishes the monetary dimensions of the whole programme.

The system can rapidly become 'no system' if, the marketing department having set list prices, the salespeople negotiate discounts in the field, the legal department makes *post hoc* price adjustments in furtherance of legal and contractual compliance and the despatch department agrees price allowances because of delays in the shipment. Hence, while everyone is working with the best intentions, the results can often be less than the best. Some orders may be executed at a loss and some 'high-yield' products may achieve no more than break-even performance. Dolan suggests that: 'if there is no mechanism in place for creating a unified whole from all the pieces, the overall pricing performance is likely to be dismal' (1995, p 175).

If more support were needed for the principle expressed throughout this book that marketing must be a whole-organization activity, Dolan provides it with his practical illustrations of the 'dos and don'ts' of pricing. He believes that coordination of the pricing process is based on managers asking these questions:

- What is our pricing objective?
- Do all participants in the process understand the objective?
- Do they all have an incentive to work in pursuit of the objective?

The points we have just examined provide a useful background to the pricing process itself. We now turn to this process. Although relatively basic in its objectives and content the section which follows provides some useful insights into the part played by pricing strategy in the financial health of the organization.

The pricing process

The nature of product costs and the cost-plus approach

First, some thoughts about product costs, for sound pricing strategy must incorporate a thorough investigation and clarification of these.

If we were to scrutinize the cost accounting data produced by a manufacturing organization, let us say, we would discover that the *total cost* of its operations comprises various *types* of costs, for example:

- the cost of the human resources employed in the production processes;
- the cost of the raw materials 'consumed' in production;
- the cost of fuel used in heat treatment processes, etc.

These costs are classified as *variable costs* because, quite simply, they *vary* with the volume of output.

Then we would discover other costs clearly not directly related to the scale of output, for example:

- rent and rates;
- interest on loans;
- the purchase costs of buildings and equipment;
- maintenance and insurance costs;
- the costs of employing managerial staff.

These are classified as *fixed costs* – not fixed in amount from period to period but fixed in the sense that an organization has to provide for them regardless of the volume of its output. These costs are related to an accounting period, usually one year. This is an important point because, in the long run, as opposed to the short run, *all* costs will vary with changes in output. Nevertheless, the distinction between fixed and variable costs is significant for our purposes and we must keep it in mind.

Although markedly influenced by the price elasticity of the product, ultimately *forecasting sales* is obviously linked to the price at which the product is offered since sales cannot be obtained at *any* price. In the most rudimentary sense, the price structure for an individual product can be regarded as:

The variable costs of its production;

+ Its apportionment of the organization's fixed costs;

+ The organization's mark-up or desired balance over its costs.

Thus, if the variable cost per product = 60

and its apportionment of fixed costs = 20

and the desired mark-up per product = 20

then the total selling price *could be* 100, i.e. 60 + 20 + 20. 'Could be' are important words here because 100 is the *economic price*, based on the economics of production and arrived at by the cost-plus approach to pricing, as we have just seen.

Now the economic price *may* well be the price at which to market the product but on the other hand, the cost-plus approach is frequently criticized because it takes no account of the dynamic nature of markets and the prices prevailing there. Kotler and Armstrong (1990, p 296) make the point that, despite its popularity, using standard mark-ups to set prices is hardly logical but they suggest that the process remains popular for these reasons:

- sellers are more certain about costs than about demand;

- tying prices to cost simplifies pricing – sellers do not have to make frequent adjustments as demand changes;

- when all firms in an industry use the approach, prices tend to be similar and price competition is thus minimized;

- many feel that cost-plus pricing is fairer to both buyers and sellers – sellers earn a fair return on their investment but do not exploit buyers when demand increases significantly.

The break-even analysis approach

The break-even analysis approach is also cost-oriented and, being a useful tool in considerations of cost:volume:profit relationships and their effect on prices, it is also popular. Its use in setting prices can perhaps best be illustrated by a hypothetical example.

Bennett Engineering have developed a small electric motor which, despite its size, is capable of incorporation into a wide variety of products and processes. In spite of widespread competition, it should therefore enjoy substantial market potential. Just out of development, and unnamed as yet, it is known simply as Fhp 37/3.

It has all the standard hallmarks of good quality and durability. The range of possible prices, ex works, extends from £45 to £60 per unit, this being the final price to the industrial user. This means that the spread of £45–£60 represents the price 'confidence level' in the market.

Bennett Engineering intend to use distributors as the main marketing channel but will also supply larger users on a direct basis. Allowing for the usual distributors' discounts Bennett's price to the distributor, for a given minimum quantity of motors, is 40 per cent of the price to the user. The large distributive discounts allow key 'super' distributors, whom Bennett are keen to supply in bulk, to 'off load' supplies, in turn, to small local distributors.

Preliminary costs indicate that the Fhp 37/3 could be marketed at £50 each to the user, which would mean an ex-Bennett price to the distributor of £20 per unit.

Figure 9.4 is a break-even chart representing the pattern of costs, revenue, profits and losses at this £20 per unit price. We see, for example, that the total fixed costs, represented by line AA$_1$ are £80,000. Remember that whether, in this case, the output is nil or 1200 dozen units, these costs remain the same and so line AA$_1$ is horizontal.

Variable costs increase as production gathers momentum. The line AB illustrates this increase, the total variable costs being represented by the area ABA$_1$ and total costs by the whole area under the line AB. The trend in total sales revenue is represented by the line RR$_1$ and where this line intersects line AB is the break-even point (X).

The approximate values for X on the scales are:

- Quantity: 700 dozen motors;

- Equalization of total costs and total revenue at £168,000.

Below a sales turnover of £168,000, Bennett will be making losses (see area RAX) but will move into profit above this turnover (XR$_1$B).

It is easy to see how break-even analysis helps to structure thinking in respect of pricing strategy. The volume of sales required to break-even seems clear but, in most instances, the product is required to do more than break-even – hence the use of the chart for *target profit pricing*. Looking at Figure 9.4, total costs, total revenue and profits (XR$_1$B) have been determined. To obtain a target profit, that is a given rate of return on investment, it is necessary to relate any particular point in area XR$_1$B with the appropriate sales volume of electric motors at the price of £20 per unit. If the company wishes to make a higher return, then it may well consider charging a higher price or reducing its costs in some way.

To further illustrate the use of this type of approach – we did say earlier that the confidence level of prices established in the market for an electric motor of the Fhp 37/3 type and quality extended from £45 to £60 per unit, ex works. Imagine then that

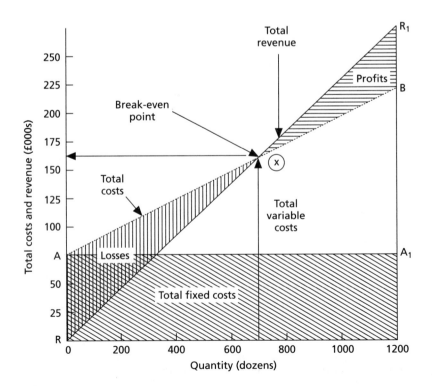

Figure 9.4. *Break-even analysis: Fhp 37/3 electric motors*

the four predominant prices within this range, and hence Bennett's price to distributors at 40 per cent of the final selling price were as follows:

Price to user, ex works £ per unit	Price from Bennett to distributors, ex works £ per unit
60	24
55	22
50	20
45	18

Figure 9.5 shows the break-even charts resulting from an analysis of the fixed and variable costs related to the production and marketing of the motor at each of the four prices from Bennett Engineering. The charts in Figure 9.5 depict how the most appropriate price may be determined from the revenue and quantity data appropriate to each of these break-even points and beyond.

Although break-even analysis is well-known and used in marketing circles, it does have limitations. The most fundamental is that it is essentially a 'laboratory' method, using the cost-plus approach and takes no account of the realities of the market place. It is one thing to say that 'we will break-even at sales of 700 dozen units', but what guarantee is there that they will be sold? In a dynamic market with a significant amount of competition it would be foolish to guarantee anything. So far we have looked at how the technique might be used in relation to a single price (Figure 9.4). Figure 9.5 indicates how it can be used for comparison purposes over a range of prices, Figure 9.6 is meant to convey how, supported by marketing research data, it can be used to take the realities of the market into account.

XY is the demand curve which shows *total* revenues obtainable at each of the four prices mentioned previously. It should be noted that the shape of the curve is different from the normal demand curve, which slopes downward and to the right as

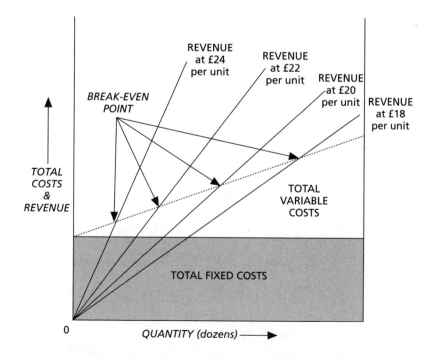

Figure 9.5. *A consideration of costs, revenue, volume and profit relationships at four ex Bennett prices for the Fhp 37/3 electric motor.*

in Figure 9.2 (i) and (ii). The reason for this is that the curve in Figure 9.6 depicts *total* revenues, whereas the more usual Figure 9.2 (i) and (ii) depicts *average* revenues.

It can be seen that the price of £22 per unit is the one at which the balance of revenue over cost is maximized since at point 2 the demand curve is at the greatest vertical distance above the total cost curve. Bennett Engineering would actually make a loss at the lowest price – £18 per unit, demonstrating that it is often as bad to be below confidence-level as to be above it.

To be effective, of course, the demand curve would need to be accurate. Well-conducted research, with users and distributors, would help to produce a realistic demand schedule. Even if the marketing budget is limited, ways have to be found to test the views in the market place to provide some basis for planning.

The perceived value approach

The last of the three approaches described in some detail in this Chapter takes the customer, not costs, for its focus. *Perceived value pricing* is based on the values of the product as these are perceived by its ultimate customer. User attitudes to the purchase of a product may be influenced as much by its psychological attributes as by its physical attributes which is why many organizations use the perceived value approach to pricing strategy. The price must 'fit' with the market segment being targeted and, in this regard, images of quality, durability, exclusivity, dignity, etc., may be evoked through packaging, presentation, distribution policies and the wording of advertisements.

Some of the fundamental factors underlying perceived value pricing are these:

● the concept of *confidence level*, i.e. the price or price band which buyers have come to recognize as synonymous with 'value for money' and the understanding that it may be just as unfortunate for the price to be below confidence level as to be above it, since customers may suspect the quality of what is being offered at the lower price;

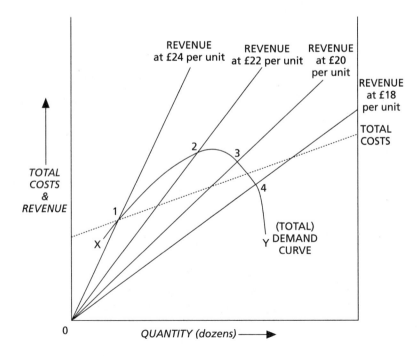

Figure 9.6. *Establishing profit performance through break-even analysis and the total demand curve.*

- the concept of the *total product* – in that what is being purchased is not simply a physical product or a basic service, but a bundle of benefits – a restaurant is providing more than a meal at a given price, for the standard of décor, nature of personal service and the provision of entertainment or otherwise will have a great bearing on the customer's view of what constitutes good value;

- the concepts of *marketing segmentation, product positioning, branding and brand management* and, not least, the belief that 'the sale takes place in the mind of the buyer'.

Obviously since significant subjectivity is employed, it is important that this approach is as informed as possible and therefore marketing research, employing such techniques as conjoint analysis, described earlier, is of great assistance.

Paths to pricing strategy

In this chapter we have so far considered many of the environmental and organizational factors that impinge on pricing and looked at some of the techniques and approaches used to assist price decisions. In this section we will look at modes of organizational thinking leading to decisions on strategy alternatives. In doing so, some additional pricing approaches will be mentioned, albeit briefly.

Students of marketing are always advised that the question to precede the development of strategy should be: 'What business are we in?' It is no bad idea to begin the pricing process in this way for the answer to the question will throw much light upon:

- the products or services involved;
- the market(s) involved;
- the industries and organizations which constitute the competition;
- possible strategies with which to counter competition.

The distinctiveness of the product (technological or otherwise) and the latitude this provides for price decisions, for example through product differentiation or 'monopolistic competition' on non-price factors, are among the principal variables in the equation, along with the proposed distribution and promotion strategies and the product's cost of production.

Cost data will provide a range of volume/price relationships and these can be measured against a detailed analysis of competitors' prices. Frequently, the costs of production will indicate the lower limit of possible prices while competitive prices may set the higher limit. Taking account of the competition does not necessarily mean adopting an identical price but maintaining perhaps a higher or lower price differential which, when other elements of the marketing mix are taken into account, renders what is being offered good value for money.

Three basic steps along the path to pricing strategy might be summarized as follows:

- *establish marketing objectives and decide upon the product's position in the target market* – objectives may range, for example, from short-term profit maximization to the pursuit of an image of product quality leading to longer-term profitability;

- *formulate the marketing mix to serve these objectives*, which will include examination of cost data and other internal and external influences on pricing strategy;

- *choose the pricing strategy and the tactics appropriate to that strategy*.

Pricing objectives will stem from marketing objectives which may be to aim for a given rate of return on investment, or to attain some particular market share, or may be designed to counter competition. Each of these objectives may give rise to different strategies. Such non-profit objectives as maintaining brand loyalty or providing full and continuous work for highly skilled employees may exercise entirely different influences on price decisions. Let us now look at some 'economic' pricing objectives in greater depth.

Percentage profit on sales/target rate of return on investment

The first of these is a *rate of profit* and is a function of a number of variables including price, product mix, production costs, marketing and administrative costs and, of course, sales volume.

The second (*return on investment*) is based on the *turnover of assets employed* or to put it more simply – the rate at which each invested £1 is generating sales pounds, a calculation based on assets employed in relation to sales volume during a particular time period. It is the *rate of utilization of assets* – plant and equipment, inventories, receivables and cash – and it provides a measure different from cost/profit calculations.

Return on investment is calculated as follows:

$$\frac{£ \text{ net profit}}{£ \text{ sales}} \times \frac{£ \text{ sales}}{£ \text{ investment}} = \frac{£ \text{ net profit}}{£ \text{ investment}} \text{ (i.e. assets employed)}$$

$$\therefore \text{ (rate of profit)} \times \text{ (turnover)} = \text{ (return on investment)}$$

To illustrate this with a simple numerical example and assuming a profit of 10 per cent:

$$\frac{£100,000}{£1,000,000} \times \frac{£1,000,000}{£ 666,666} = \frac{£100,000}{£666,666} = 15\%$$

$$\text{i.e. } 10\% \qquad \times 1.5 \qquad = \qquad 15\%$$

Thus, with a profit rate of 10 per cent and an asset turnover of 1.5, a return on investment of 15 per cent is produced. To improve the return on investment the organization could attempt to increase the profit rate, the turnover rate or both. Any of these moves might well have implications for pricing strategy.

Profit maximization

In this context we are discussing the maximization of *long-term profitability* rather than short-run profits. Currently there is, in any case, reducing opportunity to maximize short-term profits, even where it is ethically defensible to do so. The rapid diffusion of technological change, the presence of substitutes for many products, the role of governments and customs unions as watchdogs on pricing strategies and restrictive practices, all make 'short run maximization' less of a viable option. New suppliers are quickly attracted to markets in which good returns are in prospect and where demand temporarily exceeds supply. Even if the product is so startlingly novel it can command a very high introductory price, a number of factors combine to make short-run profit maximization socially undesirable. Increasingly articulate and well-organized consumer groups, consumer publications and television programmes are there to remind organizations of this fact.

The usual approach is to pursue profitability in the longer term and frequently an *investment-budget strategy* is the key to this. In launching a new product, for example, the organization may be prepared to budget for financial loss in say, the first year, to subsequently break-even, that is to equalize revenue and costs, perhaps in the second year, and to move into profitability at the next stage, for example year 3. In which case, ideally, the budgeted profit in year 3 should recoup the loss of year 1 and show some balance over the total costs for the three-stage period – which is termed the *payback period*. In highly competitive markets, this period can be quite lengthy. At the extreme, for instance, US manufacturers of soft-drinks have entered Asian markets on the basis of a 20 year payback period. If this indicates anything, it is the need to base pricing policies upon adequate and competent market research, with provision for this to continue where the payback period is lengthy.

Another point to be made under this heading is that organizations do not invariably seek profitability for every individual product or service. They may, and often do, regard profit targets as corporate goals in the sense that the range of products as a whole is looked to for the attainment of profit targets. This will allow some products to be offered as *loss-leaders* in order to generate goodwill and, hopefully, sales support for the more significantly profitable products. In this context, the line of reasoning evident in the section 'Price and the product portfolio', earlier in the Chapter, is pertinent. It is an approach often described as *price lining*. As Doyle (1994, pp 230–1) observes, by developing a graduated line of brands, a marketing-oriented company can adopt a differential pricing strategy. The price is an indicator of the quality differences between brands and, hopefully, users will feel motivated to 'trade up' to higher quality and, frequently, higher margin brands in due course.

Equalization of competition

In markets for highly standardized products there is often a *price leader* whom it is impossible to undersell because of the returns to scale the price leader enjoys. Since there is little opportunity for product differentiation the strategy may be to equalize the prices of the market leader, around which other supplying firms will also have based their prices. Operating at this confidence level of prices, the organization will then adjust its production and marketing operations so as to obtain the best possible return on its investment.

Known also as *parity pricing* or *going-rate pricing*, Kotler and Armstrong (1990, p 298) indicate that the approach is quite popular since the going-rate price represents the collective wisdom of the industry on the price which will yield a fair return. It also enables firms to avoid harmful price wars, which can occur when competitors are willing and able to meet any price cut.

Maintenance or increase of market share

Where the market is expanding and the organization is already earning a reasonable rate of return, the pricing objective might well be to maintain or to increase market share. Through continuous research services, market share can be monitored quite well in many instances, the important factor being the organization's sales trend line compared to the sales trend line of the total market.

In relation to considerations of market share it is important to mention the technique of *penetration pricing*, to contrast it with the technique of '*skimming*' and to outline some of the situational factors where use of one or the other might be appropriate.

As the term implies, the objective of penetration pricing is to obtain maximum penetration of the market. The price is kept as low as possible in order to reach a sizeable share of the market as quickly as possible. Where market demand is highly sensitive to price and it is relatively easy for competitors to enter the market, the penetration approach enables the organization to get away to a flying start and subsequently become that much more difficult to dislodge. Where lowering of costs becomes possible through economies of scale, the organization's considerable presence in the market might be enlarged through price reductions.

The *skimming technique*, by contrast, is a high price approach and is so called because the organization is 'skimming the cream' from the market. It is useful where a particular segment of the market is being cultivated because, for example, the product or service differs distinctively from what is currently being offered. Its quality and design features may foster an appeal to a more affluent segment of the market, which may be prepared to pay a premium price for a product different from those available to the mass market.

Where the market is being supplied by a large number of organizations, the skimming technique allows the newcomer a mode of entry and the restricted demand at the higher price, though attractive enough for the newcomer, is not so attractive that the main suppliers to the market are forced to take counter-measures.

The *skimming technique* is also appropriate where the product is a technological innovation, or is unique in some other sense and the high introductory price enables the supplier to recover his investment in research and development. The objective may then be to reduce the price progressively once market entry is well-established. Relating the approach to the product life-cycle in this way enables the innovator to deter other suppliers from entering the market if cost recovery is being reflected in a steady lowering of prices. The higher price at which the skimmer can operate, for one or more of the reasons outlined above, is sometimes termed the *opportunity price*.

Obviously, the technique adopted will be influenced by a number of factors, with the following being especially prominent:

- the nature of the product or service;
- the nature of the market;
- the nature of demand, e.g. price elasticity;
- the nature and extent of competitive activity.

Penetration pricing is appropriate where the objective is to generate maximum loyalty for the product from the early stages of its life and thus to obtain the benefit of long production runs so as to lower costs.

Once again, it is important to bear in mind that whatever approach is adopted, it must be related to the overall marketing strategy. Price is not an independent variable but an element in a strategic formula. It influences, and is influenced by, the strategies adopted for the product, its distribution and promotion and the human resources involved in supplier operations.

Pricing for industrial markets

Although so much of what has been said about pricing strategy is equally applicable to consumer and industrial products, a number of points concerning pricing for industrial markets are worth special emphasis. These are listed below.

Price is often related to providing a total product

The costs of provision may include substantial sums for user guarantees, maintenance throughout the life of the product, the training of operatives and trade-in allowances on obsolete equipment. A decision may have to be made on whether an 'all-in' price should be quoted or whether the offer should be 'unbundled' and separate prices quoted for each item, for example computing equipment and pre-loaded software.

Cross-elasticity of demand may be important

As noted earlier in the chapter, the demand for the product might be closely related to the prices for substitutes and complements. With regard to complements, capital equipment, for example a sophisticated photocopying system, may be installed at an especially attractive price, with the return on investment being generated via operating supplies – in this case photocopying paper.

Payment terms are usually more complex and of a wider variety

Payment by instalments, progress payments as the construction of a facility proceeds, credit facilities, and compensation by the supplier for any delays, are all features of industrial pricing. Since the extension of credit may be lengthy and for substantial sums, third parties, such as clearing banks and merchant banks, may be involved. Increasingly, suppliers are being asked to arrange for the *leasing* rather than the outright purchase of their products. Under a leasing contract, the supplier (lessor) grants the right to his customer to use the asset which is the subject matter of the contract (e.g. expensive capital equipment, a fleet of vehicles), for a given period of time in return for the periodic payment of fees or rent. Leasing can be regarded as a form of product differentiation. It is intended to broaden demand, bringing customers who would otherwise have found the product unaffordable within its scope. Even customers able to afford the product may find leasing more attractive if it enables them to make more productive use of financial resources.

Settling prices may be a matter of long negotiation

Frequently the distinctive and complex requirements of the customer necessitate long negotiations with a large number of influences/deciders. Prices are typically settled on a contract by contract basis, often as a result of *competitive bidding* in response to *invitations to tender* from customers. The contract concluded may be drawn from several options. Engineering contracts, for example, include firm price contracts, cost reimbursable contracts, target cost contracts, schedules of rates contracts, bills of quantities contracts, guaranteed maximum price contracts and compound contracts which combine two or more of these options.

Prices may be significantly affected by the business environment

While this may be true of all prices, in industrial markets it is fair to add 'only more so'. Often the supplier finds himself locked in a long contract and sudden political or economic change profoundly influences the risks and the returns involved. For this reason, the supplier may have to take a long view on prices and have some clear ideas on movements in inflation and currency exchange rates. The problem is particularly marked where the main supplier is dependent on foreign suppliers for materials, sub-systems, components, etc., or where the competition is such that an *escalation clause* in the contract is not a viable option.

The buying process may be particularly challenging

As a rule, industrial buyers are knowledgeable and technically proficient. Accordingly, they often know what constitutes a 'reasonable price'. Because they have to work so closely with suppliers they often know a great deal about suppliers' costs. Accordingly, they may press for contracts which will provide them with access to cost information and a share for their organization in any economies achieved by the supplier. Certainly, the 'buying atmosphere' is one in which price increases can only be justified by genuine cost increases or by product improvements, given that such increases are permissible under the contract terms.

Perhaps enough evidence has been provided in this chapter to support Williamson's (1979, p 81) view that pricing policy is 'the very nerve centre of the commercial process'. We can also see that industrial pricing adds to the complexity of the process. Speaking of the price variable, however, Morris (1992, p 365) is of the opinion that its potential is not fully realized in many industrial firms. He suggests this is because, in such firms, pricing decisions are often made by financial and production personnel who are invariably preoccupied with cost recovery and rates of return, when customer value and competitive activity should be significant factors. Because of this neglect 'cost considerations tend to play the predominant role in industrial pricing'.

Morris's comments underline the significance of an effective *marketing information system* for a creative pricing policy and another instance of its value can be found in the outline of a *competitive bidding model* provided by Jobber (1995, p 331). Many industrial and public works contracts are awarded on the basis of a *tendering* process. The buying organization draws up detailed specifications of its requirements and invites tenders from potential suppliers. The latter quote a price, in confidence, hence the process is frequently described as one of *sealed competitive bidding*.

Jobber described the use of a model based on the notion of *expected profit* to arrive at a recommended price for the bid, expected profit being equal to the profit at a particular bid price multiplied by the probability of winning. The most difficult aspect of the process is, of course, the assignment of probabilities of winning. Marketing information, however informal, can serve at least two clarifying purposes:

- since the buyer will, in most cases and all other things being equal, award the contract to the 'lowest price' supplier, identification of the likely level or range containing the lowest price;

- identification, as far as possible, of competitors' likely price intentions.

Provided their operations are in all respects ethical, sales engineers can provide a valuable research function in this context.

Pricing strategy: *an aide-mémoire*

From time to time in this chapter, the value of a creative pricing strategy oriented primarily to the user and the market has been highlighted. Clearly cost considerations cannot be ignored, for therein lies the road to ruin. It might therefore be prudent for marketing personnel to construct a checklist or aide-mémoire for use in developing pricing strategy. This will ensure that no important variables are overlooked. The details below might serve as a useful starting point for the construction of such a list.

User considerations

- Benefits of the product(s) to the user?
- Nature and strength of direct/indirect competition?
- User benefits provided by direct/indirect competition?
- Existence of substitutes?
- Typical buying motives?
- Actual/potential psychological appeals, hence possibilities of non-price competition?

Market considerations

- Actual/target market share for the product(s)?
- Competitive market share(s)?
- Market share trends?
- Price confidence level(s)? Elasticity/cross-elasticity of demand?
- Own tentative price(s)?
- Competitive price(s)?
- Competitive provision by way of 'total product' – warranties, after sales service, branding, packaging, etc.?
- Prevailing methods of physical distribution?
- Marketing channels typically used?
- Trade margins and discounts available at various stages in the marketing channels?
- Changes in the patterns of distribution? implications for pricing strategy?
- Competitive policies in relation to:
  - marketing communications?
  - trade and promotional support?
  - salesforce deployment and call frequencies?
  - granting of territorial selling rights?

Organizational considerations

- Implications of values statement, mission statement for pricing strategy?
- Product(s):
  - current/anticipated costs of production?
  - ratio of expected volume:plant capacity?
  - profit:cost:volume relationships?
  - break-even point(s) at alternative prices?
  - price–demand relationships?
  - desirable contribution to fixed costs?
  - profit target(s)?
  - life-cycle implications?
  - product portfolio implications?
  - marketing research implications? human resources issues (skills, training, etc.)?

Environmental considerations

- General economic prospects?
- Projected rates of inflation? stability of exchange rate?
- Legislation
  - effects on proposed price strategy?
  - monopolies and restrictive practices?
  - methods of quoting prices?
  - granting of credit and hire purchase facilities?
  - health and safety standards?
- Technology
  - stability of current technology?
  - any significant developments affecting prices?

The above list is meant to be illustrative rather than comprehensive but it is sufficiently detailed to show how, as a pricing aide-mémoire, it can help to clarify thinking on such strategic alternatives as:

- price leadership;
- differentiation;
- focus (i.e. identifying a niche in the market).

These approaches were outlined in Chapter 3. The issues relating to promotion and distribution incorporated in the aide-mémoire will become clearer as the book proceeds – the matter of *discounts*, for example, has important implications for pricing.

Pricing in practice

An example of how the pricing approach can be employed to serve broad strategic objectives is that of *dual pricing*, that is the policy of charging more or less for the same goods or services depending on *when* they are bought. This approach has been successfully adopted by airlines and telephone companies and in December 1997, Garner (1997) reported that retail analysts were researching the issue of whether and to what extent supermarkets and high street stores might charge more for purchases made in 'rush-hour' periods. 'Off-peak' shoppers and those who shop during the night would obviously benefit from such a policy.

Retailers charging more at the weekends and in the evenings would hope to encourage 'time rich, cash poor' customers, such as pensioners and single mothers, to shop in the quiet weekday periods. This would result in less congested stores at peak times, less traffic congestion and more car parking space for 'cash rich, time poor' shoppers who might well be prepared to pay more for shorter queues and better service. One of the clear benefits to the retailers is that of more even pressure on manning levels and a reduction of the need for staff to work too many unsocial hours.

The increasing use of loyalty cards means that the technology is available to support dual pricing strategies. Consumers could be awarded more points for shopping in off-peak periods. Since loyalty cards enable retailers to learn more about individual customers, the technology enables them to identify when people shop, why they don't shop at particular periods and when they need to be persuaded to shop.

In a fiercely competitive market, Garner (1997) added that one of Britain's largest retail consultancies was looking at 'fair and transparent' differential pricing strategies on behalf of several clients.

The strategic formula: Element 4:

Distribution – function and strategy

Utilities of place and time

Earlier, we have seen how the first element in the strategic formula, *marketing research* helps the organization to get its product or service 'right'. We then noted how the product was developed and priced, with both the interests of the customer and the organization in mind. This brings us to the 'place' element in the formula, the *distribution function*. Within the organization's overall mode of engagement with its market(s), the primary role of this function is to ensure that its output becomes available to the user:

- in the right place, and
- at the right time.

As the economist would say, these are the *utilities of place and time*. Defining them is simple enough:

- *utility of place* – ensures that the product or service is available at a location convenient to the user and not, for instance, at the manufacturer's distant premises or some similarly far away depot;
- *utility of time* – ensures that the product or service is available just when it is required.

Examples of these utilities are easily visualized. With regard to place utility, for instance:

- the consumer needing a disposable razor wants to get it from some convenient location – shop, hairdresser, etc. – and not at the factory in France where it is made;
- the truck manufacturer requires tyres at the place where he assembles his trucks, not in the tyre manufacturer's warehouse;
- the steel manufacturer, similarly, needs iron ore accessible to him at his blast furnace;
- the producer using a heat treatment process requires an appropriate source of energy – based on oil, gas, electricity, coal, etc. – readily 'on stream' and not at the refinery, rig, power station or the mine.

A first aspect of time utility is evident enough. The raw material, the component part, the finished product and the personal service simply must be available when they are needed. A business executive requiring a light-weight suit for his summer schedule of customer visits will not be prepared to wait until November for it. The manufacturer of calendars and diaries will have distributed these to appropriate retail outlets well before the Christmas shopping season begins. Perishable products such as milk, fruit and vegetables have a limited life. They must be distributed and consumed while they are fresh.

A further aspect of time utility is worth noting. It may well suit the economics of manufacturing production to make products in large quantities at infrequent intervals. On the other hand, the user may require the product in small quantities and often. To meet such demand, 'buffer' stocks may have to be created, either at the manufacturer's premises, his strategically located warehouses or, very often, at the premises of intermediaries such as wholesalers and retailers. So, as we shall see below, this *storage* function is one way in which distribution adds value to a product.

An additional word on storage which, to be strictly accurate, derives from the need to provide place as well as time utility, is that there are numerous reasons for storing goods other than arranging their accessibility to the market. For example, as Perlick and Lesikar (1975, p 283) have noted:

- the organization often has to anticipate demand, arrange output to meet it, and hold that output until demand becomes effective – the nature of marketing systems for most goods;

- output must often be stored because of seasonal variations in demand;

- storage often makes for economies in production – the manufacturer of nuts and bolts finds it less costly to arrange the continuous production of one size for a number of days, subsequently storing this production until other sizes are made, than producing small quantities of each size every day;

- the quality of some products is improved by storage – cheese, wine and timber must all be 'aged'.

Returning to place utility – we can also identify a *transportation* element here. More than 80 per cent of the products moved in the UK, whether to manufacturer's warehouses, intermediate producers, wholesalers, retailers or consumers proceed by road. Transportation may also be by rail transport, canal barge, container ship, freighter aircraft or by a combination of some or all of these methods depending on such factors as the nature of the goods, their destination, affordable costs and the required speed of transit. It is worth mentioning in passing that the present UK government is seeking, through its 'integrated transport policy', to reduce the amount of freight carried by road because of its adverse effects on the physical environment and the health and well-being of the population.

The distribution function

Basically, the distribution function involves the coordination and management of two elements:

- marketing channel activity;

- physical distribution.

The first of these involves assessing the costs and benefits of the routes or *channels* by which goods and services are made available to the target market. Zikmund and d'Amico (1993, p 450) point out that the word 'channel' derives from the French word for canal, which 'suggests a path that goods take as they flow from producers to consumers'.

In some instances, the channel is a direct one from the producer to the user. More frequently *channel management* involves the selection, use and support of *intermediaries* such as wholesalers, retailers, agents, brokers and others. Also, organizations do not invariably rely on a single mode of distribution and sometimes adopt a *multiple channel* approach.

The second element, physical distribution, encompasses such activities as transportation, warehousing, inventory control and, in some organizations, packaging, packing and order processing. In large organizations, particularly, physical distribution also encompasses the *inward* movement of products and materials, as well as the *outward* movement of finished products to customers. These two types of movement are often titled *inbound logistics* and *outbound logistics* as we saw in Chapter 3 (the value chain), logistics being an alternative term for physical distribution operations.

There are clear advantages in integrating the inward and outward movements of supplies and output, not least in ensuring the productive use of the organization's own transport. Sometimes a separate department, 'physical distribution' or 'logistics' is established, under the control of a physical distribution manager who may be, but is often not, responsible to the marketing manager. The process of physical distribution is, of course, of great significance for marketing effectiveness as we shall see presently.

There is abundant evidence for the distribution function's claim to importance. Obviously, the utilities of place and time are notable features of customer service. But customer service has significant costs. Doyle (1994, p 311), for example, points out that 'Marketing-channel costs and margins can easily account for up to 50 per cent of the price paid by the final customer'. In providing an example of one company's apportionment of product costs, Majaro (1993, p 141) relates 21 per cent of these to 'distribution and logistics'. We saw in Chapter 3, in the outline of value chain analysis, the benefits of clarifying a firm's cost position in relation to competitors. In Porter's schematic of the value chain, Inbound Logistics and Outbound Logistics feature as Primary Activities and are therefore of great salience for cost analysis and managerial effectiveness. In his description of the value system, Porter signifies that even if an organization's costs for its own activities are competitive, its *upstream value chain* – the operations, costs and profit margins of suppliers – and its *downstream value chain* – the operations, costs and profit margins of agents and distributors – may not be competitive, with adverse effects on the organization's own competitive position. So the organization can best protect its own position by perceiving itself as part of a larger system, as Figure 3.8 indicates.

Within a customer-led culture, no one would argue against the importance of customer service but the *level* of that service must come in for proper scrutiny. The relationship between level of service, defined as the percentage of occasions the product is available to the customer when and where he wants it, and the supplier's costs, hence his competitive position, is quite a dramatic one. As the level of service improves, costs increase not in a linear fashion, but exponentially, as Figure 10.1 indicates.

Christopher, Walters and Wills (1978, p 97) once expressed the view that it is beyond the 70–80 per cent level of service that the associated costs increase far more than proportionally. They suggest that management must therefore be very clear about:

- the level of service currently being provided;
- the manner in which the level of demand is influenced by the level of service;
- the incremental costs of improving the level of service;
- the extent to which increased costs, e.g. of stockholding, can be offset by the increased revenue derived from the increased demand.

Figure 10.1. *Costs increase exponentially as the level of service improves*

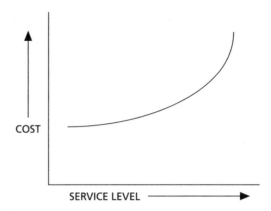

COST

SERVICE LEVEL ⟶

So *costs*, and therefore competitive advantage, together with *customer service* are the basic factors underlying the strategic importance of the distribution function. We can go well beyond this, however, as might be expected, given that *place* is a part of the strategic formula (marketing mix). Here are some reasons why.

- The more recent developments in transport methods, such as containerization and airfreight are not matters exclusive to the interest of the transport manager. They raise important questions of sales policy – e.g. sales representatives may be asked to increase order quantities so that the customer may take advantage of containerization and other 'unit loads'. They raise important questions of design policy – e.g. by some slight modification to shape how many more products would fit into the container module or the outer carton? So the distribution function is another operational facet underlying the need for departmental coordination.

- Because the cost savings of many of the developments in physical distribution are *indirect* rather than direct it is a first essential for marketing to recognize the nature and complexity of distribution issues and to coordinate their resolution. We shall see an illustration of this point later in the chapter.

- The increasing need for organizations to think and act globally increases the scale and complexity of distribution decision-making. Servicing world markets means that suppliers are continually faced with the need to extend product ranges, without increasing investment in inventories but at the same time providing an increasingly higher level of service in order to develop market share.

Among other developments, including the use of sophisticated management tools and techniques to support distribution decisions, this has led to the adoption of Just-in-time (JIT) programmes. The aims of JIT are to:

- minimize inventory and its costs throughout the supply chain;
- meet the requirements of each internal and external customer immediately on demand;
- achieve a continuous flow of production without delay or waste;
- ensure total reliability in the on-time delivery of required parts and material (Armstrong, 1993, p 150).

Usually JIT programmes area based on formal contractual arrangements between supplier and customer providing a *relationship marketing partnership* with all its advantages, but with an exceedingly high penalty for failure.

- Reverting to the issue of costs, some years ago research (Centre for Physical Distribution Management, 1981, p 11) indicated that total distribution costs seemed set to inflate at a rate which was 50 per cent greater than the projected rise in other industrial costs. It was anticipated that the freight transport element of distribution cost would increase from an average of 5.5 per cent to an average of 7.4 per cent of retail sales price.

Where sophisticated techniques and skilled management have not been applied to operations then, due to the labour intensity of some aspects of distribution, the dependence of transport systems on increasingly expensive fossil fuels and the ever increasing capital costs of maintaining adequate stock levels, experience has shown such projections to be sadly accurate.

Despite the importance of the distribution function which has hopefully now been demonstrated, it has often been described as the 'Cinderella' of too many organizations, a 'graveyard' where the bones of aspiring executives lie bleaching. Christopher and McDonald (1995, p 249), for example, point out that: 'More often than not the distribution channel will have taken its current form as a result of unplanned and haphazard development.'

This chapter will seek to demonstrate that organizations paying insufficient attention to the function are not only failing to manage resources effectively but are also excluding themselves from the opportunity to develop significant competitive advantage. As Brassington and Pettitt indicate:

> Place, or distribution, can become the element of the marketing mix which causes the biggest headache to the manufacturer. The other three mix elements remain under the manufacturer's control, but once the product is out of the factory gate, it is at the mercy of the middlemen within the distribution channel (1997, p 448).

That this is so means that management, particularly marketing management, should pay more, rather than less, skilled attention to it. When that happens the distribution function, once described as 'industry's dark continent', will begin to fulfil its vast potential. In a thoughtful article, Peter Martin (1997) has pointed out that, in the recent past, it was expected that, following the success of its companies in the fields of automobiles and consumer electronics, Japan would come to dominate the world markets for cosmetics, pharmaceuticals, household goods and other consumer products. This has not happened and Martin believes the reasons for this can be summed up in one word: *distribution*. The machinery of distribution in Japan's own internal market for such products has been compared most unfavourably with its world-class machinery of production. Zikmund and d'Amico (1993, p 456) describe Japanese distribution as 'a model of inefficiency' adding that when told Japan has one of the most cumbersome distribution systems in the world, many express astonishment. These authors point out that because of the length, expense and inefficiency of the distribution chain, by American standards, a Japanese camera costs more in Tokyo than in New York. Martin develops this point in a telling way:

> Outsiders never find it easy to break into established patterns of business, to acquire enough 'mental shelf space' in the heads of wholesalers, retailers and consumers to build sales to levels that offer economies of scale. Japanese companies have a special difficulty here: Japan's idiosyncratic methods of getting products from manufacturer to consumer offer little experience relevant to the rest of the world' (Martin, 1997).

If it were needed, this is powerful evidence for the importance of the distribution element in marketing strategy.

Channels of distribution

Types and functions

Zikmund and d'Amico's (1993) pointer that 'channel' derives from the French word for 'canal' is powerful, conveying as it does a route or method for the *flow* of goods from producer to user. As Hutt and Speh (1992, p 359) have written: 'The channel of distribution is the marketing manager's bridge to the market. Designing and managing the ... marketing channel is a challenging and ongoing task'.

In this section we shall examine the benefits and costs of marketing channels. In later sections we shall observe:

- how channels are assessed for their benefits pro rata to their costs and structured to reach and fit the needs of important market segments (*channel strategy*);

- how channel members, whose support and enthusiasm are crucial to the success of marketing strategy are selected, supported and motivated (*channel management*).

As we progress through these sections it should become clear why, in Doyle's (1994, p 311) words, channel efficiency is a key determinant of an organization's profitability and cost competitiveness. It should also become clear why Hutt and Speh (1992) regard this task as both 'challenging and on-going'.

Using consumer products as an example, Figure 10.2 indicates some of main channels producers use to distribute their products to users, for example the consumers, or 'ultimate customers'. The term 'ultimate' is used to differentiate product users from 'intermediate' customers who do not 'consume' the goods they buy, but purchase them for re-sale.

The first channel, on the far left of Figure 10.2 denotes the *direct marketing channel* in which products move from producers to users without the intervention of any intermediaries. Examples are given in Figure 10.3.

We shall be looking at direct marketing later in this chapter and return to it in Chapter 11. It is a very powerful channel, of increasing popularity in this information age, since it is very largely database driven. The emergence of the new electronic media, such as the Internet have increased its popularity and potential. Where the

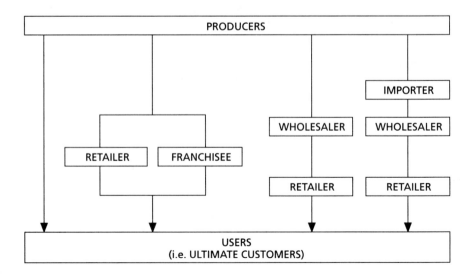

Figure 10.2. *Some types of distribution channel (consumer products)*

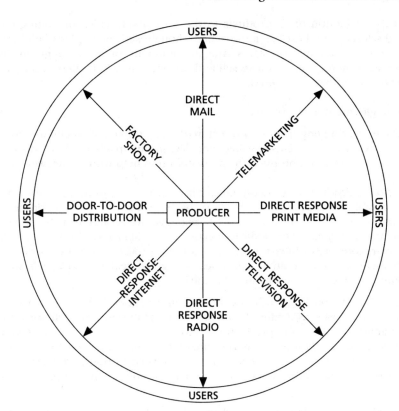

Figure 10.3. *Direct marketing channels*

supplier is distributing direct to the final customer, labelled here for brevity the 'user', the operation takes place through a *zero-level channel*.

The second route in Figure 10.2, a *one-level channel* makes use of a single intermediary – either a *retailer* or a *franchisee*. Next, a *two-level channel* appears in which the manufacturer distributes to the user via wholesale and retail intermediaries. Finally, a *three-level channel* is illustrated in which an importer appears as the first intermediary in the channel.

These channels are not mutually exclusive. Channel choice is determined by marketing strategy which is based on the needs of market segments and the type of products/services being distributed. Strange as it may seem, it might be perfectly feasible for a single producer to adopt a *multi-channel* approach utilising *all* the routes depicted in Figure 10.2. An example might help here.

A large, well-established manufacturer of an extensive range of glassware could justifiably adopt a multi-channel distribution strategy as follows:

- a range of advertising ware, i.e. ashtrays, jugs, etc. for use in pubs, hotels, restaurants, badged with logotypes or brand names of wine merchants, distillers, with whom sales and distribution are negotiated direct by the manufacturer's representatives (*zero-channel*);

- the manufacturer's high-quality lead crystal decanters and wine-glass products distributed via exclusive department stores and china and glass retailers (*one-level channel*);

- the major portion of the manufacturer's output, consisting of bulk-produced, medium-priced domestic glassware – water jugs, tumblers, inexpensive wine glasses, etc. to be distributed to its mass-market via wholesalers, distributing in turn to retailers (*two-level channel*);

- for the distribution of its products to the US market, which marketing research has disclosed can best be approached though six geographical regions each containing a number of states, the appointment of six strategically located importers (one per region) who sell and distribute to wholesalers and retailers in their regions (*three-level channel*).

Such strategies are not exceptional.

Given the increasing importance of direct marketing, the question emerges as to why intermediaries are so well-established and significant in channels of distribution. Some general facts about production and distribution help with the answer.

- *Location* – Production typically takes place in certain locations – sometimes at considerable distances from markets, or users. In the case of some products, e.g. cutlery, ceramics or footwear in the UK, manufacture is often heavily concentrated in some particular geographical location, e.g. Sheffield, North Staffordshire, Northamptonshire, whilst the markets for the products may be world-wide. As with the UK, so with other countries – a great deal of Germany's industrial production takes place in the Ruhr region.

- *Scale* – Production frequently takes place on a large-scale basis. The user of the product purchases, as a rule, the most minute proportion of what constitutes an economical volume of production. Moreover, in many cases, production processes are *continuous* whereas demand from the user, even for repeat-selling consumer products may be at irregular intervals or during particular seasons of the year. This means that stocks must be held, in both manufacturers' and distributors' warehouses.

- *Convenience* – In addition to purchasing his or her requirements in appropriate quantities, the user will wish to purchase them at some convenient location, usually near to the place of residence. Moreover, the user will wish to see quite a wide range of similar products from which to make a selection. This underlies the social appeal of shopping too.

- *Intermediaries* – Wholesale and retail organizations take part in the process of breaking down the scale of manufacturing quantities to appropriately sized user quantities, which are then made conveniently available. While some of the costs of distribution are initially borne by the manufacturer, e.g. those of moving goods from the point of production to distributors' premises, the wholesale distributor bears the costs of distribution to the retailer and the provision of retail premises is manifestly a cost of distribution. Of course, if we think about it, all the costs of distribution are ultimately borne by the user.

- *Production/demand priorities* – Except in a small number of cases, e.g. bespoke clothing or purpose-made furniture, *production must precede demand from the user*. The manufacturer must therefore invest in the production and accumulation of stocks of finished goods, in the hope that he or she will sell those products within a satisfactory period of time and at prices which will provide an adequate return on the committed resources. By manufacturing and investing in stocks prior to sale he or she is incurring *business risk*. Except in those rather infrequent cases where distributors buy on a sale or return basis, wholesalers and retailers share this risk with the manufacturer. Part of the financial return to distributors is a reward for sharing risk.

From these general facts, a number of the functions of the main intermediaries in distribution channels – wholesalers and retailers – can be discerned. Their functions are set out in more detail in Table 10.1, but before turning to this, a preliminary word about another important intermediary, the *franchisee* (see one-level channels, Figure 10.2).

Wholesaler	Retailer
Shares the financial risk by purchasing in advance of demand	Purchases and holds stock at the local level and shares the financial risk and commitment with manufacturers and wholesalers
Stocks products in locations convenient for the distribution process	Breaks down stock into smaller quantities appropriate for consumer buying (French verb *retailler* – to cut again)
Provides speedy and efficient delivery service to retailers to avoid 'stock-out' situations	
Frequently provides credit and other support services to the retailer	Where appropriate provides credit and after sales service
Breaks down bulk consignments from the manufacturer into appropriate retail consignments and arranges transport of these to retail premises	Through the provision of adequately trained staff advises the consumer on the quality, specifications, value and performance of products
Frequently maintains a team of representatives and/or electronic data interchange facilities to obtain orders and support retailing	Assists manufacturers and wholesalers to serve the market more effectively by providing up-to-date information on consumer reactions and choices
As an information exchange (manufacturer–retailer) assists the marketing of current products and the development of new products	Provides local display and promotional support in association with manufacturers and wholesalers
Provides assistance to both manufacturer and retailer in promotional campaigns	In some instances, and particularly for grocery products, pre-prepares the products for sale
Through purchasing and storage functions and financial support to retailers, evens out fluctuations in supply of, demand for, and price of the product	

In a *franchising* type of retail operation, the *franchiser* (usually a manufacturer of a product or service) provides the goodwill which attaches to his name or institutional image, e.g. Esso, Wimpy, Kentucky Fried Chicken, Dyno-Rod, as well as supplies of the product to be sold. Generally, the franchiser also provides financial facilities, usually by way of a proportion of the venture capital required, staff training and consultancy services covering such matters as the location of premises and the management and control of the business.

For his part, the *franchisee* provides most, if not all, of the venture capital and enters into an agreement to purchase his supplies exclusively from the franchiser. Following the lead of the USA, franchising is now big business in UK with sales of £5.9 billion per annum according to the 1996 survey of the British Franchising Association/ National Westminster Bank. Later in the chapter we shall take a further look at franchised outlets.

Channel strategy is based upon careful analysis of the costs and benefits of alternative methods of distribution. Taken together, Table 10.1 and Figure 10.4 are intended to provide a handy reference guide to the main benefits of using intermediaries. Obviously *costs* are incurred in providing time, place and other important customer utilities. We must now consider these and Figure 10.5 helps us to do this.

Costs and the ultimate selling price

Manufacturing any product entails using resources which must be paid for. Factory costs of production will include:

- the costs of raw materials used;
- the wages of production workers;
- factory overhead which typically comprises:

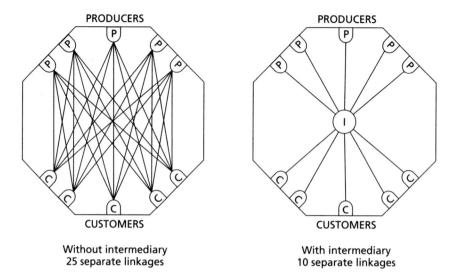

Figure 10.4. *Simplifying the distributive network through the use of an intermediary*

Without intermediary
25 separate linkages

With intermediary
10 separate linkages

- factory rent, rates, insurance,
- works salaries and 'non-production' wages,
- factory water, gas, electricity and repairs,
- allowances for the depreciation of plant and equipment.

A manufacturer will also incur costs for the marketing of his products, including their distribution. Among these costs, the following are examples:

● the costs of transporting goods to customers;

● the costs of advertising and promoting the products both to distributors and users;

● the costs of maintaining a group of representatives and/or a system of electronic media to sell the products.

It is also usual to provide sales representatives with financial incentives such as commissions and bonuses, etc. to induce them to achieve sales 'targets'.

Administration expenses will also be incurred, including the wages and salaries of the workers responsible for dealing with orders, enquiries, invoices, accounts and customers' letters, faxes and e-mail. Additionally, the manufacturer will add to the sum of all these costs a provision for directors' fees, bank interest, audit fees and bad debts.

The manufacturer must plan to recover all these costs by way of revenue from sales. Finally, he or she will add to his or her total costs a profit margin which will enable him to provide for:

● taxation of profits;

● dividends to shareholders;

● reserve funding to undertake research and development for new and improved products.

When an individual product has been allocated its due proportion of total costs plus its profit margin, the manufacturer knows its economic price to the distributor. Figure 10.5 attempts to illustrate this in simple form. This example assumes a distribution method which utilizes wholesaler and retailer stages *en route* to the consumer. The product price to the wholesaler is represented as '100'.

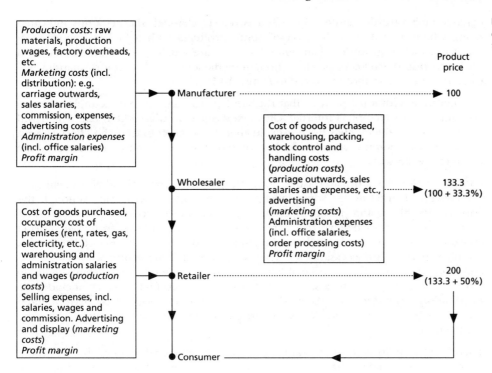

Figure 10.5. *Production and distribution costs and price to the consumer*

The wholesaler's costs include cost of goods purchased, warehousing and storage costs, outward carriage, selling costs, etc. So, as with the manufacturer, his or her costs can be classified under the broad headings of 'production', 'marketing' and 'administration'. Also, of course, he or she must include a margin to cover taxation and an adequate return on investment. Again, note that distribution, like production, generally precedes demand so the return earned by intermediaries is, in part, a reward for sharing risk with the manufacturer.

When the proper proportion of costs plus profit margin are allocated to the individual product Figure 10.5 indicates that the wholesaler must add to his '100' purchase price a gross margin or mark-up of $33\frac{1}{3}$ per cent. Consequently, the product's price to the retailer now becomes '133.3'. (Bear in mind that a 'mark-up' on the cost of goods may be alternatively termed a discount on the selling price.)

For his or her part, the retailer must provide attractive premises, often in expensive locations, receive and store the goods and then display them properly. Even in the smallest outlets, the retailer usually employs sales staff to advise and sell to customers. In the larger organizations, warehouse, office, transport and security staff will also be recruited. Local advertising is often undertaken in order to attract customers to the premises, advise them of the latest additions to the stock and of the special offers available. Figure 10.5 also provides a simple outline of the retailer's costs and it suggests that in order to cover them adequately and yield an increment of profit 50 per cent should be added to the price charged by the wholesaler. Thus, the price to the user – the retail selling price – becomes '200' (133.3 + 50 per cent).

Earlier in the chapter it was clear how distribution adds value to the product in the form of place and time utilities, the assortments available and the ability to buy in appropriate quantities. In turn, Figure 10.5 demonstrates how distribution adds to the product cost – in this illustration, a manufacturer's selling price of '100' becoming a consumer buying price of '200'.

This example is neither exaggerated nor unreal, being based on the author's own marketing experience. It would be fairly typical of a product such as medium-priced ceramic tableware distributed through a two-level channel, the mark-ups indicated being wholly realistic. In the case of some products with a higher frequency of purchase, such as groceries, distributors' margins are much lower. On the other hand for highly-priced, exclusive products bought by the affluent, distributors' margins will often be higher than those featured in Figure 10.5.

An important additional point is that the price progression in this example takes no account of such factors as internal sales taxes, such as value added tax, which will increase the product's final price even further. In some countries the effect is even more marked when the cascade effect of some turnover taxes burdens the cost of the product at every stage.

Our illustration has a broader aspect to it. Despite the current goodwill attaching to the concept, marketing, as some imagine it to be, attracts criticism. Although the costs of advertising and packaging come in for much of the odium, distribution has its detractors. Critics believe that across the range of products, from fast moving consumer goods to complex industrial plant and equipment, the costs of distribution are high, perhaps unnecessarily so. They suggest that if marketing is to act for the common good, as it claims to be able to do, it should attend to the seemingly indefensible fact that it often costs as much to 'sell' a product – which includes its distribution – as it does to make it. The fact that distribution costs have become indefensibly high is one of the factors contributing to under-consumption – so the argument runs.

Therefore, in addition to distribution's place in the value chain approach to competitiveness, there is a social dimension to its effectiveness and efficiency. Reverting to the individual firm, it is indeed the case that for many organizations the best prospect for outdistancing competitors may well be in distribution rather than production. In fact, where the latest production techniques are employed and human resources are fully trained in all the necessary skills, an organization might have its priorities wrong if it is pushing its managerial skills to the limit to make marginal improvements in product quality and production costs when it may have little idea of its total distribution costs.

The comments of R.J. Williamson, made 20 years ago, still hold good today, namely that:

> When Peter Drucker described distribution as 'industry's Dark Continent', he drew attention to the fact that distribution seldom seems to receive the attention in strategic and marketing planning that a function accounting for some 20 per cent of the country's gross domestic product would seem to deserve (1979, p 164).

It seems clear then that from both social and organizational standpoints the costs and benefits of alternative methods of distribution must be very carefully assessed. In fact, for the individual firm, distribution may offer the best opportunity to develop a distinctive competence and increase competitiveness. *Channel strategy*, which we shall come to presently, is the basis for doing this. Two further points are important before we leave the present section.

Other institutions and specialists

In addition to wholesale and retail intermediaries a number of other types of organization facilitate the flow of goods through channels. Some of the main ones are now described.

Sales agents and brokers

'Agent' is a term widely interpreted in marketing. Specialist organizations in marketing research and advertising are often referred to as agencies. Shipping and forwarding agents and air freight agents figure prominently in distribution, particularly for the physical movement of goods to global markets (see below). It is also the case that occasionally, intermediaries taking physical possession and title to goods are referred to, incorrectly, as agents.

Like *brokers*, however, *sales* or *commission agents* do not take title or physical possession of products, but negotiate their sale in return for a brokerage or commission on the value of transactions. Commission agents are frequently employed by organizations doing business with foreign markets, as we shall see in Chapter 13.

Merchants

These organizations, many of them substantial, take title to and, frequently, physical possession of, the goods in which they trade. Their stock-in-trade is very often unique knowledge of particular markets or of the products in which they specialize. Many of the UK's merchants are members of the British Export Houses Association and, to add to the confusion, some act as commission agents as well as merchants in the strict sense.

Merchants, sometimes labelled importers, see Figure 10.2, may be thought of as super-distributors and at the height of the Empire many of the UK's merchants had a network of branch organizations abroad. The rise of economic nationalism affected their power and influence, since newly independent countries favoured their own nationals in the granting of import licences, but they are still a significant force in distribution.

Other facilitating institutions

Other institutions facilitating distribution include transport organizations, credit information bureaux, chambers of commerce and forwarding agents. All of them play some part in the distribution of products, for example carriage, documentation and information on the creditworthiness of potential distributors. The 'groupage' services of forwarding agents often enable small exporters to enjoy the benefits of containerization and other distributive economies.

For all organizations offering credit to customers, the size and speed of their cash flow can be a significant problem. Small firms in particular, lacking the necessary working capital to finance their customers' debt, need to be paid promptly for goods already sold if they are to undertake further production.

One way to alleviate this problem is to engage the services of a *factor*. Although the methods and costs of factoring can vary, usually the factor will advance up to 80 per cent of the value of credit sales as they are made, with the remainder being paid when customers settle their account. The cost of factoring may extend from 1 per cent to 5 per cent of sales turnover depending on the volume of sales involved, the number and type of customers and the extent of the service required. At the extreme, particularly for trade with foreign markets, the factor may take over the whole of the financial and credit management involved.

Besides easing cash flow problems, the use of factors will save the costs of the administration and control of debt, for when the goods are despatched it is only necessary for the firm to transmit the invoice to the factor who then assumes responsibility for collecting the proceeds. The method is particularly useful when sales volume is growing rapidly.

The benefits of factoring must, as always, be weighed against its costs and also the non-financial advantages, such as the potential to build a relationship with the customer, of a firm administering its own credit sales. Yet more confusion – sometimes the word 'factor' is used to describe the 'super-distributor' type of organization purchasing in large enough quantities to re-sell profitably to wholesalers. Note the distinction.

The evolution of channels

Earlier in the text we saw some of the aspects making for marked and rapid change in the business environment, for example

- rising real incomes;

- the increasing pace of technological change;

- the rapid diffusion of world-wide communication systems.

Add to this the fact that many Western societies are becoming multicultural in their composition and outlook and the reasons for the dynamic nature of most markets become clear.

Organizations therefore learn to live with change as a constant companion if they are to survive. Nowhere is adaptation to change more pressing than within the marketing function and sensitivity to the need for change has to be as pressing an issue within distribution as in other parts of the framework.

Looking back once more at Figure 10.2 it is too easy to imagine that each channel member works in harmony with the others in a coordinated manner so as to deliver maximum possible value to the ultimate customer. But real life is not like that, for generally each channel member is an independent, autonomous business seeking to optimize its returns. Moreover, legitimately and understandably, the objectives of channel members may, to some extent, actually conflict. The manufacturer, for instance, may be aggressively pursuing market share on a high volume, low return basis, for a single product selling through numerous outlets. The retailer is concerned with a range of products, of differential rates of return no doubt, and seeks for competition to be limited as far as possible.

We also saw earlier how increasing competition was inducing the growth of *collaborative networks* and this is now also evident in distribution channels. *Vertical marketing systems* (VMS) is the term for an integrated approach in which all channel members pursue coordinated and mutually supportive objectives. Leadership in the channel structure may be provided by a manufacturer or a distributor. For example, and to take two of the best-known names in UK high streets, Boots the chemists is an example of a *forward integrated system* since it was originally instituted by the manufacturing division of that business. It is also a good example of a *corporate* VMS, a system in which one organization owns and operates all the levels in the channel. Marks and Spencer is a good example of a *backward integrated system* since leadership in the channel is provided at the retail end and extends backwards to a large number of manufacturers, all supplying to closely detailed price and quality specifications for the 'St. Michael' brand.

In addition to the corporate VMS operation, such systems may be *administered* or contractual. In an administered VMS, leadership is provided by one channel member, but with each channel member being legally and financially independent and autonomous. Technology has helped to speed the growth of such systems as evidenced by the EDI systems linking the large retail supermarket chains with their suppliers. As the title implies, a contractual VMS exists where channel members enter into legally binding agreements with each other on objectives and strategy. Perhaps the systems based on formal legal relationships between franchisers and franchisees, described earlier, provide some of the best examples of the contractual VMS concept.

In addition to the VMS trend, there is also a tendency for some distributors, which are in all other respects independent and autonomous, to collaborate in *horizontal marketing systems*. There are any number of examples of collaboration in distribution to exploit market opportunities. A number of ventures such as Supermarket Direct and Food Ferry have appeared in the London area specializing in direct to home deliveries from supermarkets. Increasing traffic congestion and the ability of the consumer to order groceries by 'phone, fax or computer and subsequently to have them delivered, is producing another battleground for the supermarket giants, despite their massive investment in superstores. The Sainsbury chain, as long ago as 1996 was negotiating with Supermarket Direct, to deliver its products direct to customers' homes and to co-brand the operation as a Sainsbury-endorsed service.

Perhaps, however, the term horizontal marketing system should strictly be reserved for collaboration between the same types of distributor – i.e. wholesaler–wholesaler and retailer–retailer links. Narus and Anderson (1996, pp 112–20), based on an extensive 1994/95 research study they conducted in the USA, provide a number of examples of how companies can increase customer service, while making major cost savings and productivity improvements, through the sharing of distribution channel resources and capabilities.

Narus and Anderson illustrate how strategic alliances and partnerships can make channels more flexible and responsive by outlining, among several others, the case of the Okuma America Corporation, a builder of machine tools and a subsidiary of Japan's Okuma Corporation.

Prohibitive costs attach to the stocking of a full range of machine tools, some of which cost more than $100,000 each, and a complete assortment of repair parts, which can be numbered in thousands. Because of this, distributors have historically been unable to provide a fully responsive service. To surmount this difficulty, Okuma has created an auxiliary support system labelled 'Okumalink'. The operation of the system is outlined below.

Okumalink

1. All Okuma distributors in North and South America, 46 in number, are required to carry a minimum specified inventory of machine tools and selected repair parts.

2. Okuma strives to ensure that either in its Charlotte, North Carolina warehouse, or somewhere in the distribution channel, virtually all its machine tools and parts are in stock at all times.

3. Through 'Okumalink', a shared IT system, distributors are kept informed of the location and availability of machine tools and parts in Okuma warehouses (Charlotte and Japan).

4. If a machine tool or part is ordered which an individual distributor does not have in stock, he can check its availability in Okuma warehouses through Okumalink. If in stock, it can be ordered electronically. If not, the distributor contacts other distributors through the Okumalink e-mail system to find the closest location. The 'in-stock' distributor then arranges for the item to be delivered direct to the customer's plant site.

5. Okuma also supports the availability of repair parts with a 'shipment within 24 hours' guarantee on all parts manufactured in Charlotte. If the parts are not shipped within 24 hours of receipt of order, *the customer will receive them free of charge*.

6. Okumalink will be upgraded to allow direct communication between all channel members. All distributors will log their inventories on Okumalink and be able to scan those of channel partners. Also, *they will be able to arrange intrachannel exchanges of machine tools and parts electronically*.

7. Investments and costs associated with stocking and handling inventory have been reduced for all members of the distribution network.

8. The possibility of lost sales because of distributors' 'out-of-stock' situations has 'plummeted'. Customer satisfaction has increased through Okuma's consistent delivery of a superior service.

Acknowledgements to Narus and Anderson (1996)

Two other aspects of channel evolution, *low-cost channels* and *multi-channel marketing* will be touched upon as the chapter proceeds.

Figure 10.6 aims to provide a simple illustration of the key factors which influence channel strategy. Below is an explanation of each of the headings, reading clockwise around the illustration.

The customer

If customer orientation and retention are to be more than slogans, channel strategy has to be based on a diligent and continuing study of user needs. Though the needs of intermediate customers must be assessed under this heading, the user, or ultimate customer, is the fulcrum on which the decision rests. User orientation implies the delivery of time and place utilities with optimum *convenience* and *availability* as key objectives.

- Where do users buy this type of product?
- In what quantities?
- Is this the most suitable method of making it available?

Finding the answers to such questions is the function of *distribution research*. This need not be sophisticated or expensive but it is quite vital and one of its concerns will be any evidence of a *changing pattern of distribution* (discussed later). With industrial products, supplies may be crucial to the user's day-to-day output and the seller often locates a warehouse, or even a factory, close to the user's industry so as to provide the intensively good service required. In the financial services field, a banking organization must ensure that any branch closures are not detrimental to customer needs and that they are replaced with an adequate spread of cash points and other electronic services. It is noteworthy that some of the newer entrants to the UK banking sector are providing extended branch opening hours to increase their competitive edge.

With the tendency for relational marketing, 'single-sourcing' and the just-in-time approach to develop further, it seems that 'the customer' is set to exercise even more influence over channel strategy.

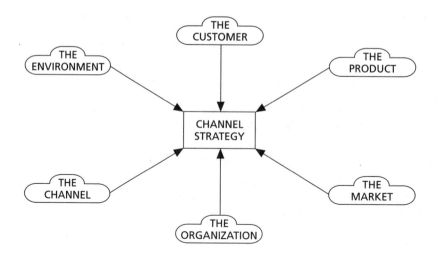

Figure 10.6. *Key influences on channel strategy*

The product

The nature of the product has a fundamental influence on channel choice. Some examples will make this clear. Let us begin with a rudimentary classification of product types. These can be categorized as follows:

- *fast moving consumer products* – food, drink, confectionery;

- *durable consumer products* – television sets, personal computers, motor vehicles;

- *industrial consumption products* – chemicals, lubricants, cement;

- *industrial durable products* – lathes, furnaces, machine tools.

Now let us think about how these various products can be provided with the necessary utilities to the user. Some ideas are summarized briefly below.

- *Fast moving consumer products* – bought regularly and requiring maximum availability, they are typically bought in a variety of retail outlets including supermarkets, department stores, specialist food shops, confectioners, newsagents, the local corner shop, garage forecourt shops, etc.

- *Durable consumer products* – tend to require specialist outlets such as car dealer showrooms, radio and electrical shops – e.g. Dixons, PC World – where specialized information and after sales service are available to the user.

- *Industrial consumption products* can be distributed in numerous ways since this heading includes several types of product. Where detailed specifications and close control of quality and performance are called for, as with many refined and processed raw materials, the manufacturer frequently markets his products direct to the user. Servicing supplies, such as lubricants for industrial processes and small machinery might be marketed in bulk quantities to distributors who, in turn, would distribute them to a multiplicity of industrial users along with the products of other manufacturers such as small tools, cleaning materials for tanks and drains and other maintenance supplies. Bolts, nuts, rivets, valves, pipe fittings, pulleys and belting, protective clothing, welding materials, etc. will similarly reach the user via engineers' merchants and suppliers.

- *Industrial durable products* are, for the most part, distributed direct to the user. Distribution typically follows a lengthy negotiation period in which details of the specification and performance of the required capital equipment or installation are exchanged between user and supplier. The result is often a purpose-built product or system installed by the maker on the user's premises with a high degree of after sales training, consultation and service being provided as part of the contract – as would be the case, for instance, with a new IT system.

Examples of the product's influence on channel strategy are legion. Here are just a few other examples:

- perishables must be marketed while they are fresh, so middlemen must be few – on the other hand, intermediaries may figure prominently in the distribution of canned groceries;

- products that have a high unit value, e.g. expensive furniture, are usually sold to specialist retailers or sometimes direct to the user;

- if the product has a high rate of retail turnover, where replacement stocks must be readily to hand, wholesale organizations and centralized buying and warehousing by retail multiples may figure prominently in the channel – which will obviate the need for the manufacturer to establish his own strategically located warehouse network;

- a high quality 'exclusive' product, such as an expensive perfume or high priced jewellery must be distributed to the type of outlet capable of attracting appropriate clientele and fostering the necessary level of appeal for the product e.g. a similarly exclusive department store or the type of jewellery store found in Bond Street or the Via Veneto.

Earlier in the chapter, Figure 10.2 illustrated some typical channels for the distribution of consumer products. Figure 10.7 gives some indication of the direct and indirect channels employed for industrial products.

The market

To some extent each of the key influences in Figure 10.6 overlap. In fact, it is on the analysis of their overlap and interaction that channel strategy is based. Obviously in considering the influence of the 'market' on strategy one must re-visit to some extent the earlier analysis of the 'customer'. There is an important difference however – in that under the heading of the market we move beyond factors of convenience and availability for the individual customer to questions of the *size of the market*, that is the number of actual and potential customers and its *geographical make-up*, that is how customers are dispersed throughout the country or region being scrutinized. The issue has even more significance if the product or service is being directed to particular *segments* of the market. Quantitative information under this heading is a vital input to decision-making and research agencies can offer much help either through 'quarrying' and presenting information from published sources or conducting specially commissioned surveys.

The *stage of development* of the market, including its language and literacy levels may be an important consideration, especially for products of some complexity. Information on the market's *promotional media availability* and its *facilities for physical distribution* may also influence strategy – and both of these are examined later in the book.

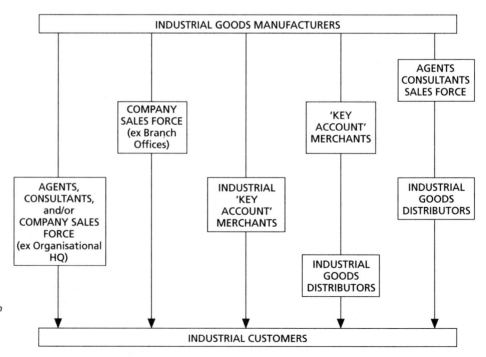

Figure 10.7. *Some distribution channels (and types of sales organization) for industrial products.*

Important decisions on factory and warehouse sites, the comparative costs and benefits of nearness to raw materials, port facilities and customers may well have to be taken as a result of careful assessment of quantitative and qualitative data relating to the market.

The organization

The size of the organization, the extent of its resources and its strategic objectives will have a great bearing on its channel policy. The organization might be so small that rather than set up a distribution network it might be more profitable to approach a large multiple-branch organization and offer some or all of its production capacity for the manufacture of the multiple's own brand products. At the other extreme, the organization may be so large that it is economically justified in setting up its own branch outlets throughout the market rather than rely on intermediaries to provide the intensively good service, and perhaps the after sales service, that is required.

Most organizations lie between these two extremes and therefore intermediaries figure prominently in their distribution strategy. The financial and administrative costs of alternative strategies have to be carefully assessed and kept under review. Stockholding costs, order processing and invoicing costs, transportation costs, the costs of advancing credit, selling costs, etc. are all influenced by channel strategy. Economies can be made by using intermediaries rather than direct methods but to use intermediaries is to some extent to lose total control of marketing operations.

On the other hand, the status of the intermediary can be of powerful support to marketing objectives – which is why an insurance company may seek to sell its services through a well-known bank or why a newcomer to a foreign market may seek to place his or her products with a prestigious retailer.

The channel

Typically, this heading requires careful deliberation. First, because the choice of channel is influenced by the nature of the product, as we have seen. Within a product group – books, toys, footwear, fashion – of a similar quality and price range, there is usually a standard channel practice or *prevailing method of distribution*. The supplier must, in the first instance, decide whether it is prudent to go along with, or to depart from, the prevailing method of distribution – *assuming there is sufficient room in the prevailing channel for another product or another service*.

This last point is very important, hence its emphasis. Many would-be exporters, for instance, including the author, have visited potential foreign markets armed with checklists of criteria for choosing distributors only to discover that the most notable were already taken-up by competitors. It is in the light of such discoveries that the marketing effort really begins.

The capabilities of the channel, its enthusiasm for the product, its likely measure of motivation to sell and service effectively, its facilities for promotion and display, the prestige or otherwise attaching to its name, the possibility of its developing as a competitor with its own brand of the product, are all significant.

The quality of distributors' operations can, of course, be improved by *effective channel management*, which we shall examine presently. Also, enough has already been said in this book on relational marketing and partnership approaches for it to be clear how these can improve channel effectiveness.

Yet, it is no rare occurrence for a marketing executive to discover that, having considered the number and type of intermediaries available, the competitive products they handle, the quality and strength of their selling efforts and the stock-holding policies they adopt to service the market, particularly for urgent orders, emergencies, peak selling periods, etc., there is little opportunity to enter the market by the prevailing method. Accordingly he or she might decide to break with tradition, adopt a bold policy of specialization and, within affordable resources, find an alternative route to the user. It should also be clear that the use of marketing research can assist in making appropriate decisions here. And we must bear in mind that although this outline is written in terms of establishing channel strategy from scratch, there is usually no 'blank-slate' situation and the marketing executive finds him- or herself working within an established strategy. Here his or her emphasis, again assisted by research, is to constantly review the costs and benefits of channel strategy and the extent to which a *changing pattern of distribution* means that the existing strategy is falling behind alternatives.

The environment

Obviously the context within which channel strategy operates will have some bearing on its nature. *Legal regulations* are clearly important and vary from trading bloc to trading bloc and country to country. Strategy will be influenced, for example, by the laws on product liability and contracts for the sale of goods. Where legal responsibility is placed on the retailer, the manufacturer will need to ensure that those chosen have the necessary resources and commitment to operate legally. Laws on import formalities, customs presentation, the regulation of customs free zones and freedom of non-resident carriers to provide services may, in the end, affect channel choice as may legislation in force designed to prevent the restriction or distortion of competition.

The distribution strategies of *competing firms* must also be carefully assessed. The channels used, the quality and motivation of channel members and the effect of the length of channels on final price must all be scrutinized – 'how do we differentiate ourselves from the competition?' and 'how can we improve on current distribution?' are obvious questions.

Formulating the strategy

Channel strategy is evolved by considering the factors just described, their interrelationships and impact on each other and relating these to more general strategic objectives, for example on sales revenue, return on investment, market share, etc.

In effect, the alternatives listed below apply in most cases.

- *Intensive distribution* offering a high *penetration* of the market will be sought where goods are low-priced, mass produced and possess a high 'convenience' or 'impulse' characteristic – the emphasis is on achieving high visibility through finding as many outlets as possible.

- *Exclusive distribution* will be the channel strategy for expensive, high quality products. Stockists will be sought who are capable of fostering the ideal 'brand image' for the product and catering for the more affluent. Stockists will be relatively few in number and may be given territorial exclusivity. The manufacturer hopes to gain increased control over the sale and servicing of the product with this strategy.

- *Selective distribution* is a compromise between the two preceding strategies. The manufacturer may require volume sales and therefore a large measure of product visibility but feel that for it to be seen in every outlet will be self-defeating. He may therefore restrict the number of dealers to less than the maximum, selecting them carefully and generating their motivation and support.

- *Dual distribution* may be employed, especially where a manufacturer produces two or more grades of the same product and his strategy is consequently based on the use of two or more channels. A manufacturer of ladies' fashions might distribute an exclusively modelled, expensive version of the range through high-class department stores and fashion shops. He or she might also manufacture a cheaper range designed for a mass-market, distributing this via the wholesale trade which decides where best it should be retailed. This strategy would be based on careful assessment of costs and profitability, so as to optimize the use of production facilities through a proper regard for user needs, tastes and purchasing power. The required number, locations, levels and types of intermediary in each channel are then established with these criteria in mind.

At least two other variables enter into this distribution equation:

● the *positioning strategy* being adopted, and

● the relationship of channel strategy to other elements in the *marketing mix*.

With regard to *positioning*, if a *differentiation* approach is being adopted, avoiding direct comparisons with competitors, this *avoidance* strategy may extend to the outlets chosen. A policy of selective distribution may be the governing philosophy, supported perhaps by territorial agreements with, as far as possible, intermediaries being employed different from those of competitors. An *engagement* positioning strategy, meeting the competition *head-to-head*, would probably call for an intensive distribution strategy in which competition is confronted in as many outlets as possible.

The relationship of channel strategy and elements of the marketing mix has been touched upon at several points in this chapter, for example the suitability of the channel for the product and the influence of the channel on the ultimate selling price. At least one other point is worth mentioning. Where a 'sales push' strategy is being adopted, the intermediaries have a great deal of influence on the outcome. They must therefore be chosen carefully for their commitment and enthusiasm and motivated to do well through adequate rewards for their sales efforts. For this reason, short channel strategies – zero or one-level – are more appropriate for a sales push approach since they enable a manufacturer to retain a great deal of control over the selling effort.

On the other hand, with a 'market-pull' approach, the manufacturer must do a great deal more than supply the product and wait for results. He or she must arrange for advertising and sales promotion to create a 'back-demand' on the intermediaries so as to 'pull' his or her product through the distributive network. Intermediaries must again be chosen carefully, but primarily for the support they provide for the advertising campaign by their arrangement for displays, demonstrations and sampling sessions, etc. Perhaps the dealers may also agree to bear a proportion of the costs of local advertising. Where long channels are employed (e.g. two or three level) the market-pull strategy enables the manufacturer to guard against the danger that his sales message will lose impact in transmission. So we can perceive how channel strategy influences and is influenced in turn by the promotional element of the mix.

In drawing attention to the importance of channel strategy, and more specifically, the evaluation of channel options, Doyle (1994, pp 319–20) has suggested that objectives, and the channel attributes that constitute the criteria for their employment or otherwise, should be carefully examined with the criteria being rated for their importance. Channel alternatives can then be scored in accordance with these weighted criteria. Certainly, sound channel strategy will repay the care and time taken in formulating it.

Channel management

In responding to his own question 'What's an intermediary worth?', Michael Morris (1992, p 490) makes two important comments:

- even if you eliminate the middleman, you can never eliminate his functions, listed incidentally in Table 10.1 of this Chapter, and

- an intermediary who specializes in certain functions may well provide those functions at lower costs than could the manufacturer bent on eliminating the middleman.

In short, far from the view expressed from time to time that intermediaries are virtually no more than parasites inflating the cost of products, a more studied look at their activities suggest they can often improve efficiency in the channel and reduce costs. The ideal is that the margin that the intermediary adds to the product should be commensurate with the value he or she adds, based on the utilities of time and place. Achieving this ideal is the objective of effective *channel management*. Some thoughts on this are now outlined, under the headings of *selection*, *motivation*, *assessment* and *conflict*.

The selection of intermediaries

Rightly, selecting intermediaries is often described as one of the most important in the whole gamut of marketing decision-making. It is easy to see why. However good the product, and other elements of the strategy, it is not likely to succeed if its distributors are inappropriate and half-hearted. Nevertheless it is important to take a balanced view. It is possible to extend the checklist of desirable attributes until the distributors being sought are expected to be paragons of all the virtues. This is not only unrealistic, since the most 'virtuous' distributors have long ago been taken up, it misses the important point that, as Jobber (1995, p 479) has said, the distribution problem is not so much 'selection' as 'acceptance'. A large retail multiple with countless branches generally 'selects' its suppliers. It is not the other way around and small/medium sized producers, in particular, quickly realize this.

Nevertheless, the choice of distributors does call for sound judgement and listed below are some common-sense observations designed to assist that process. The headings are general in nature so as to apply to both wholesalers and retailers. The criteria are as listed.

- The types of customer, market segments catered for and knowledge of market trends, competition, customer needs and expectations.

- Products presently handled – their reputation, market standing, extent to which they are complementary to or competitive with the supplier's own products and the level of product knowledge within the distributors' organization. Facilities for after sales service and implementing user guarantees where these are appropriate.

- Geographical area *effectively* covered and the location of premises in relation to the composition of the market.

- Estimation of present sales turnover and an assessment of the underlying trend of sales. Whether the size of the distributor is appropriate to the supplier's own anticipated sales development, though bearing in mind that a small energetic distributor may be more effective than a large organization already handling many products.

- Size and level of expertise of the distributor's staff, their attitude to customer service and enthusiasm for the supplier's own products.

- Financial standing, capital structure and past trading history of the distributor – information which can be readily obtained through credit information bureaux or the supplier's own bank. This type of information assumes less importance where the distributor is large and well-known but smaller suppliers may wish to satisfy themselves on the speed with which distributors make payment because of the implications for their own cash flow.

- The standards of showroom/retail display space – their appropriateness for the supplier's products and any planned promotional activity.

- Management factors. This is not easy to summarize briefly but it is important. Some assessment has to be made of the quality of the distributor's vision, ethics, forward planning, customer orientation and use of effective systems. All of these are the proper concern of its senior management. A fundamental question is: would we wish to develop a partnership strategy with this distributor?

The list could be extended no doubt but, if the above criteria were used, they would be sufficient to assist sound selection. Obviously the significance of each criterion will vary according to the size and nature of supplier and distributor. For example, a small supplier on a simple transactional (i.e. order to order) basis with a small distributor may not wish to scrutinize the latter's internal systems very closely. A large supplier seeking a partnership arrangement featuring EDI with a large distributor would be very interested in the 'systems' criterion.

Sources of recruitment for potential distributors, in addition to the supplier's own sales force include exhibitions, conferences, the trade and technical press, business magazines and trade associations. Where it is necessary, the use of marketing research might also be warranted.

The motivation of intermediaries

From a marketing standpoint, the ideal channel is comprised of customer-oriented, mutually supportive members. Intermediaries will not be enthusiastic, however, unless they want to be. They will want to be if they feel motivated to be.

In addition to products and services that are highly satisfactory to users, distributors are minimally entitled to:

- trade margins, discounts and credit policies which provide them with an adequate return for their role in sharing risk and arranging distribution;

- the reliability of the supplier on delivery promises and the maintenance of quality and value standards;

- reasonable policies with regard to the stipulated size of their orders and adequate marketing opportunity to liquidate their own investment in such order quantities – which raises the issue of the physical proximity of other distributors and the granting of territorial selling rights, where appropriate;

- where relevant, assistance with stock-turn through promotional campaigns, exhibitions, retail display materials, user manuals, etc.;

- where necessary, suitable support in arranging for an adequate level of after sales service, including the training of distributors' staff;

- effective and ethical systems for dealing with order processing, invoices, emergency situations, urgent orders and complaints.

Since financial return is a basic factor in this minimal entitlement, some words of explanation are appropriate here.

Distributor's margin
This is the amount added to the distributor's buying price in order to cover the distributor's costs and yield him a profit on his investment. For example, in the case of good quality ornamental glassware and a two-level channel, it might be usual for the wholesaler to add a gross margin, or 'mark-up' of $33\frac{1}{3}$ per cent on the manufacturer's price to him and for the retailer to add 50 per cent on the price from the wholesaler. Such a price structure then makes for a retail selling price which is

double the manufacturer's selling price to the wholesaler, in accordance with the following simple calculation:

	Product price
Ex manufacturer to wholesaler	100.0
Wholesale mark-up on cost	33.3
Price to retailers ex wholesaler	133.3
Retail mark-up on cost (50%)	66.6
Retail selling price	200.0

It should be noted that this simple outline takes no account of sales taxes, e.g. VAT which may or may not be applicable from time to time according to the product(s) and the market(s) in question.

The margin or mark-up on the cost price may alternatively be expressed as a *discount* from the selling price, for example $33\frac{1}{3}$ per cent on cost price = 25 per cent discount from the selling price. In the above example $\frac{33}{133} \times \frac{100}{1}$ = 25 per cent. Frequently, the distributor's margin is set out as a discount.

Also, it is customary for the distributor's discount or mark-up to be related to a minimum quantity consignment or minimum order value, for example 'the 25 per cent wholesale discount will be based on orders of not less than 10 standard packs. Each standard pack contains 36 items'.

Quantity discounts

As an inducement for distributors to carry stocks above the stipulated minimum quantities, particularly in advance of advertising campaigns, the manufacturer may offer additional discounts (e.g. $2\frac{1}{2}$ per cent; 5 per cent) for the purchase of stocks at fixed levels above the qualifying minimum for the normal discount to the distributor. Alternatively, the discounts may be set out on a scale relating to ascending order values, for example:

Minimum order (no. of packs)	Discount from selling price (%)
10	25
11–19	$26\frac{1}{4}$
20–29	$27\frac{1}{2}$
30–39	30
40–49	$32\frac{1}{2}$
50 or more	35

The manufacturer would be able to offer these increased discounts if his or her cost calculations indicated that economies in packing, transport, stockholding, administration and/or increasing returns to scale of production made them possible.

This sliding scale of discounts approach is also very useful where a manufacturer is pursuing a *dual distribution* strategy in respect of the whole product range and not just for two or more grades of the same product as mentioned earlier in the chapter. Figure 10.8 depicts this in relation to a manufacturer of glassware (medium-price and quality).

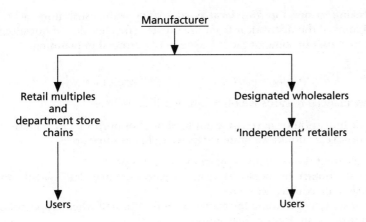

Figure 10.8. *Dual distribution: medium-price/quality glassware*

Use of the sliding scale enables the manufacturer to deal direct with those retail organizations which, by combining the orders of their multiple branches, are able to place substantial orders. At the same time the single-outlet china and glass shop would be supplied by carefully selected wholesalers perhaps given sole selling rights for such outlets in designated areas. Provided there was sufficient sales potential, and this the manufacturer must ensure, the wholesalers will feel motivated to distribute this range of glassware although significant quantities of it are being sold direct to large retailers. From the manufacturer's standpoint, of course, the nature of this bulk-produced product means that he must find as many outlets as possible taking care that each distributor has an adequate rate of return from sales.

Settlement discounts

Among many other things, marketing planning entails a careful assessment of the timing and amounts of sales revenues. These cash flow predictions may indicate that at some points in the timetable finance may have to be borrowed and the anticipated return on investment may have to be adjusted for the cost of this borrowing.

In order to minimize cash flow difficulties, and costs, an organization's normal payment terms frequently contain some inducement for traders to settle their accounts within a reasonable time, for example $2\frac{1}{2}$ per cent discount for settlement within 28 days of the date of invoice. According to its requirements to increase cash flow it may increase its inducements on the lines of a sliding scale, for example $3\frac{3}{4}$ per discount for settlement within 14 days of the date of invoice, 5 per cent for settlement within 7 days. The scale of the discounts would be carefully regulated in accordance with the alternative cost of bank borrowing.

Other distributors' allowances

Where these are offered, other incentives to distributors usually consist of discounts or allowances for retail displays, joint ventures at exhibitions, the shared costs of local advertising, etc. and may be in cash (as deductions from invoices) or kind (e.g. additional quantities of the product). Fees may be paid, if applicable, for product assembly and maintenance services and rentals for showroom or store space.

Before leaving this topic, it should be noted that students frequently refer to distributors' margins or discounts as 'profit'. This is obviously incorrect, since distributors' profit can only be calculated after the deduction of distributors' costs from the revenues produced by the distributors' margins.

At the beginning of this section, the key minimal expectations of distributors were outlined. The operative word is 'minimal' because, of course, achieving minimal standards will achieve no more, at best, than matching competition whereas strategic advantage stems from surpassing it. Going beyond an attractive financial return means seeking to develop *long-term partnerships* with distributors, acknowledging the standpoint of the distributor from the outset. The checklist of questions below is intended to mark out some of the key aspects of partnership planning.

Planning distributive partnerships: Questions for guidance

- Are the financial rewards we offer sufficiently attractive?

- Does each distributor have sufficient territorial opportunity to achieve satisfactory sales turnover? Should we grant exclusive rights in some areas?

- To what extent do we really *support* our distributors by:
  - regular contact by personal visits, correspondence, fax, e-mail, distributors' newsletters, conferences, etc.;
  - the provision of training for managers and sales staff where appropriate;
  - advertising and promotional support;
  - providing up-to-date information on the organization, its new products and processes, marketing policies;
  - sufficiently helpful credit policies and the provision of financial assistance where it is prudent to do so?

- Crucially, do we demonstrate our sincere commitment to partnerships by arranging for a frank interchange of ideas and views and, where it does not breach confidentiality, for the development of markets and the introduction of new products based on *joint planning*?

- Do we show enough timely and genuine appreciation of distributors' performance and achievements on our behalf?

Although the above questions do not exhaust the subject there are enough of them to indicate that developing partnerships will exert significant pressure on resources. As in all other things, management must therefore set out to achieve the best results from what is affordable. Most channel partnerships will be informal, though losing nothing in commitment for that. Increasingly, however, and especially with the adoption of single-sourcing and JIT, formal partnerships are appearing. In the UK, for example, one company adopts an open-book policy with its haulage contractors showing them its sales and profit forecasts and arranging an extra margin for the contractors if this is improved upon and if the contractors better the contracted proportion of complaint-free deliveries.

In summarizing their views on marketing channel strategy, Christopher and McDonald have this to say:

> Development relationships with channel intermediaries based on partnership can be a powerful means of developing competitive advantage. The aim should be to develop marketing programmes that are attractive to all members of the distribution channel and not just to end users (1995, p 259).

When competitive advantage *is* the objective we might add a gloss to this and say that sound channel partnerships mark the route to end-user satisfaction.

The assessment of intermediaries

Although it is legitimate to speak of '*control* of channel members' and the exercise of '*power* in the channel', such phrases seem to jar when related to the concept of a channel as a number of linked partnerships.

Nevertheless, if marketing objectives are to be achieved some assessment has to be made of the performance of intermediaries. There are some clear criteria which can be employed here, for example:

- sales volume by level and type (i.e. by target market segments);

- the intermediary's contribution to the producer's profitability;

- the level of stocks held;

- support to advertising and sales promotion campaigns;

- satisfaction levels of the intermediary's customers;

- sales and technical expertise, training undertaken, quality of management;

- the creation of new business;

- amount and quality of market 'feedback', etc.

All producers must seek to exert some control over the channel if the concept of pursuing objectives is not to become meaningless. Some distributors will fail and unless their performance can be improved, by training or other support for example, they may have to be replaced. The extent to which the producer can exercise control will depend upon the relative bargaining strengths of the parties. If the producer is a large organization, with popular, sought-after products, attractive trading policies and significant marketing resources, he will be able to exercise *channel leadership* based on his power. This power will be increased where there is a large number of distributors available from which he can select.

On the other hand, if the producer is a small organization supplying a large retail multiple, power and leadership in the channel may belong to the multiple, which may refuse even to produce the information on which its performance can be assessed.

So however informal or otherwise, some evaluation of intermediaries is inevitable but it should be a careful, thoughtful and balanced process. It can be made much more effective if intermediary selection is judiciously carried out and if the actual assessment is based on a framework of objectives which were mutually agreed at the outset. It is often the case, particularly in overseas marketing, that formal contacts are negotiated between channel members. These usually provide that the relationship be for an initial trial period, to be mutually reviewed in the light of the results achieved, with subsequent reviews at appropriate intervals – year by year, for example. Such an approach institutionalizes assessment, which should also be more palatable where the channel atmosphere is a positive one based on the trust which has been built up between members.

Given that marketing is to do with return on investment as well as customer satisfaction Michael Morris (1992, p 513), adapting the ideas of Bowersox *et al.* (1980), suggests that a *profitability index* has some merit for evaluating middlemen. First, from the sales revenue obtained via each distributor the cost of goods sold (i.e. variable manufacturing costs) is deducted. From the balance remaining, the marketing and physical distribution costs allocated to each distributor (e.g. trade margins, warehousing, transport, inventory costs) are then deducted to produce an 'annual middleman contribution'. From this figure, the fixed costs directly assignable to each distributor (e.g. the cost of staff salaries, trade advertising, bad debts, etc. incurred per distributor) are then deducted.

The balance remaining, termed the '*annual middleman-controllable contribution*', now available for each distributor, can then be expressed as a percentage of this contribution for the whole of the company. This *profitability index* ('middleman controllable margin-to-sales ratio') may not only demonstrate that Distributor A, though producing more sales revenue than Distributor B, may have a lower margin-to-sales ratio than Distributor B. It may also be useful in identifying how dealings with distributors low on the profitability index can be made more efficient.

A more subjective method of assessment, not requiring a mechanism for the strict apportionment of costs is also outlined by Morris (1992). This is the *weighted-factor approach* and depends on four basic steps:

- identification of the criteria judged to be decisive for the distributor's success e.g. selling ability, quality of management, stockholding, knowledge of the market, etc.;

- allocation of an importance weight to each of these criteria – e.g. by dividing weights across the criteria so they add to 1.0: selling ability 0.40, quality of management 0.20, stockholding 0.15, knowledge of market 0.15, advertising/ promotional support 0.10 (assuming 5 decisive criteria only);

- evaluation of each distributor's performance on each weighted factor – e.g. on a scale of 10: thus Distributor A: selling ability $6 \times 0.40 = 2.4$;

- the summing of each distributor's range of factor scores to produce an *overall performance rating* for comparison with other distributors and the average overall performance rating.

Though simplistic the weighted-factor approach does provide *some* rigour for the assessment process and has the advantage for the smaller manufacturer that it is relatively speedy and economical.

Channel conflict

If trading relations are being built on a genuine partnership approach and a mutually supportive atmosphere exists in the channel, this will do much to minimize conflict. It would be unrealistic to imagine, however, that commercial relationships between autonomous organizations will be conflict-free, for each of the partners perceive the 'reality' of a situation through the eyes of their own objectives. Since these can never be wholly identical, the opportunities for conflict are many and varied.

We have only to use the six elements of the strategic formula for guidance as to how conflict can arise through the differences in perception of manufacturer and distributor. Each is now briefly considered.

Preparation (marketing research)
The manufacturer may look to the distributor for timely feedback on market conditions, product acceptance, etc. The distributor may feel his sales force will be more productively employed in selling than in conducting research for a single supplier.

Product
The manufacturer may pride himself on his strategy of frequent product introductions and continuous product improvement. The distributor may view this as burdensome giving rise to more expenditure on maintaining inventory, lower rates of stock-turn per product, embarrassing out of stock situations and split deliveries.

Price
The manufacturer may be pursuing a strategy of low prices to the user in order to achieve sales growth. The distributor may feel there is an insufficient margin for his efforts in this low-price strategy.

Place
Believing it important that his output finds as many outlets as possible, the manufacturer may have adopted a multi-channel approach and a least-cost policy of physical distribution. The distributor may feel resentful that so many competitors are being supplied and that least-cost physical distribution is not always *timely* distribution.

Promotion

The manufacturer may wish to keep promotional expenditures as low as possible and expect the distributor to share in this outlay. The distributor may look to the manufacturer for an increased promotional 'spend', arguing that his own margins preclude any significant contribution, even on a local basis.

People

The manufacturer may look to the distributor to provide members for his training programmes on sales, servicing, new products, database systems, etc. The distributor may view the release of staff as costly and burdensome and prefer them to be 'in the field' or the department.

To this framework can be added a list of other opportunities for conflict based on day-to-day operations, for example complaints on product quality, down-time on equipment through poor service scheduling, late payments from distributors, poor sales performance, a returns policy viewed by the distributor as uncooperative.

Developing an atmosphere of trust and cooperation in the channel requires commitment and hard work. It is essentially a long-term process in which the establishment of commonly agreed objectives is a significant starting point. Diplomatic staff, compatible with their counterparts in other member organizations, and with adequate training and experience, can build on this beginning. The development of joint projects, perhaps based on the market-testing of new products or the sharing of marketing information is a further basis for integration. When things go seriously wrong, accessible and easy-to-comprehend disputes procedures can help to resolve the situation. These may be available through joint membership of a trade association which can also foster cooperation and mutual respect.

Power in the distribution function

This is a subject with marked implications for economic life in general and marketing strategy in particular. It is complex and extensive enough to justify a text of its own. In a book of this length we can only catch a glimpse of it and we draw on the field of consumer goods, in the main, to illustrate some of the issues.

Historically, manufacturers have been able to exercise significant control over their distribution channels, particularly where their products were popular, branded, heavily advertised and therefore well-known. Also, where a product is expensive and positioned to attract an affluent segment of the market, they would carefully control the number and type of their outlets so as to project an appropriate image for the product.

Another aspect of control emerges where a retail stockist is granted sole selling rights for a particular area in exchange for a guaranteed minimum sales turnover for the products. This is a strategy still in vogue with motor vehicles, cameras, optical equipment and other products requiring skilled after sales service.

Again, through his or her pricing structure to the trade, and the margin/discount policies, the manufacturer can exercise significant control over the prices of his or her products to the user so that frequently articles are marked with a 'manufacturer's recommended price'. Before 1964, however, in the UK the manufacturer could *legally fix* the retail selling price and distributors had to abide by this pricing policy or cease to be supplied. Today, while the manufacturer's recommended price *may* be the price generally prevailing in the market, it is often used in order to announce the distributor's bargain offer, thus:

Manufacturer's recommended price £299
Our price £250!

There are other features of reduction in the channel power of manufacturers. Let us see why.

The changing pattern of distribution

A population with a high average income, such as that of the UK which has mass-produced consumer goods readily available to it, will usually experience the phenomenon that has occurred in the UK, and other industrialized countries, with regard to the pattern of its retail trade.

In effect, the country's retail sales become concentrated through fewer and larger outlets and there is accompanying pressure on the small shopkeeper (i.e. the single outlet independent retailer) who will either go out of business or converge defensively with other independents and with wholesalers into *buying groups* in order to survive.

This process of concentration has been due to the ever-increasing proportion of total retail turnover taken by multiple retailers to the detriment of other types of retail organization, such as independents and department stores.

In the UK, historically, the 'multiple' has been defined as a retail organization with ten or more branches, but excluding retail cooperative societies. On this definition, the smaller multiples with two to nine outlets have traditionally been included with the 'independents'. In the past also, the 'specialist chain' has concentrated on a cohesive group of products, for example food (Tesco, Sainsbury), books and stationery (W.H. Smith), footwear (Dolcis, Clarks), clothing (Burton), but increasingly, as we shall see below, growth in a number of instances is now being achieved by diversification into other products, services and methods of trading.

In 1950, the multiples obtained 19 per cent of total UK retail sales and the independents 62 per cent. By 1986, the multiples' share had grown to 58.6 per cent and the share obtained by the single-outlet retailers had shrunk to 29 per cent, with a further fall of 1 per cent by 1990. According to UK government statistics the number of the country's retail businesses shrank from 368,222 to 244,285 in the relatively short period 1971–86.

The trend has continued to the present day, and, so it is forecast, will do so in the immediate future. Concentration has been particularly marked in the food sector where, by the early 1990s according to the A.C. Nielsen Company, the stores of over 10,000 square feet belonging to the top five multiple grocery retailers, Asda, Gateway, Safeway, Sainsbury and Tesco accounted for approximately 50 per cent of grocery sales. In the period from the mid 1980s to the present, competition between the grocery multiples has seen their diversification into fashion, pharmaceuticals, banking and travel services, insurance, gardening products and DIY equipment. They have emerged as political donors, patrons of the arts and sponsors of public education and charities. Their staggering strength, not only in the distribution channel but in the influence they wield over the economic and social life of the country, can be gauged from the data in Table 10.2.

The substantial transfer of control and power in the distribution of consumer goods has been due to a number of factors. The following are prominent:

- the abolition of resale price maintenance, i.e. the power of the producer to legally fix the price of his product to the consumer;

- the spread of branding and advertising of output by producers, guaranteeing consistency and quality and the subsequent emergence of 'private brands' owned by the large retail organizations;

	ASDA (Year to 29 April 1995)	ARGYLL (Safeway) (Year to 1 April 1995)	J. SAINSBURY (Year to 9 March 1996) Includes contribution from Homebase and US operations)	TESCO (Year to 24 February 1996)
Stores:	206	369	362	545
Employees:	75,000*	66,000*	110,000*	130,308*
Sales:	£5.285 billion	£6.217 billion	£13.5 billion	£13.03 billion
Profit before tax:	£257.2 million	£175.6 million	£712.0 million	£675.0 million

Table 10.2. *Size and financial performance – four UK multiple organizations*

Source: The Times, 9 May 1996.

* Full and part-time

- increasing consumer affluence and use of private cars underlining the importance of adequate, trouble-free parking facilities;

- high employment and its effects on labour costs, increasing the importance to distributors of labour saving techniques, e.g. self-service and 'check-out' systems;

- the increase in the number of working wives, inevitably with less time for shopping, and the conversational, personal approach of the 'corner shop';

- the general benefits to organizations of information technology, enabling greater control over day-to-day operations, the tracking of sales, inventory management and electronic data interchange with suppliers.

These and other factors which have influenced markedly the concentration of retail buying power outlined earlier and, in the past few decades, the 'new dynamics' of retailing, of which some examples are listed below, have become firmly established in the UK.

- *Supermarkets.* Self-service retail outlets with a minimum selling area of 2000 square feet, having three or more check-out points and offering a full range of foodstuffs and household requisites.

- *Hypermarkets.* Stores of at least 50,000 square feet of selling space – all on one single level, offering a very wide range of products, both food and non-food, with self-service retailing, 15 or more check-out points and free car parking at least three times the size of the selling space.

- *Superstores.* Stores of at least 25,000 square feet of selling space on a single level, with a wide range of food and non-food products, 10–20 check-out points and free car parking facilities of one to three times the area of the selling space.

- *Discount stores.* Stores based on the selling of branded goods at prices below manufacturer's recommended retail selling prices and with little or no provision in the way of customer services or facilities, 'self-service' being well to the fore – in the UK the Argos and Comet organizations have been prominent in this sector.

- *Voluntary groups and chains.* Organizations which aim to maintain the competitiveness of wholesalers and retailers through cooperation – particularly through bulk-buying, single-source purchasing and the adoption of operating efficiency techniques. Spar and V.G. are examples of these organizations which, by the 1980s were said to account for over 50 per cent of independent grocery trading. Nu-Mark and Unichem have been important examples of this type of development in the chemists' field and these voluntary associations are also active in the hardware and textile trades.

- *Retail parks.* On the fringes of towns and cities, these usually consist of a number of large single-storey buildings (termed 'sheds' by developers) operated by retailers of DIY products, electrical equipment, furniture, carpets, personal computers and office supplies. Each 'shed' is provided with ample parking facilities.

- *Out-of-town shopping centres.* Very large scale developments containing a wide variety of retail organizations from independents to branches of the 'high street' multiples and department stores. All types of consumer goods are available and many types of service, e.g. banking, travel and restaurant facilities. A vast amount of parking space is typically available. The Metro Centre at Gateshead and the Lakeside Centre in Essex are good examples of this type of development. At the time of writing, an extensive new development is under construction in Greater Manchester (the Trafford Centre). The centres have very large catchment areas. The Gateshead Centre draws customers from as far away as Scandinavia while the Essex centre is patronized by customers from the near Continent.

A number of these retailing ideas originated in the USA, although the Spar voluntary group organization, the forerunner of its type, originated in Holland. In Europe, the Western part of Germany as well as Switzerland, Holland and the Scandinavian countries quickly developed the concentrated and sophisticated distribution systems which have emerged in the UK. Belgium, France, Austria and Italy have also developed these types of system although at a somewhat slower pace, whilst it would be broadly true to say that Greece, Portugal, Spain and Turkey still have more traditional systems in which the independent trader is prominent.

In the UK there are signs that these tendencies to concentration and the growth of the large-scale retail enterprise may be reaching something of a watershed. Individuals and organizations are pointing out that such developments have been achieved at significant social cost, for example:

- the fact that many of the nation's high streets are now dominated by the branches of retail multiples, including fast-food outlets, so that the distinctive character of many towns and cities is being lost;

- the demise of the independents means that the more vulnerable sections of society, lacking transport facilities, have markedly reduced shopping provision;

- residents within the vicinity of shopping centres and supermarkets complain of reduced quality of life due to traffic congestion, noise and pollution;

- some suppliers to the grocery multiples, particularly small organizations, feel they are being driven to produce at little or no margin over costs;

- some consumers believe that the products being offered are bland in nature, based on 'common denominator' taste and they regret the reduction in the number of specialist outlets;

- there is fear that the oligopoly situation now emerging could result in higher rather than lower prices;

- there is concern that suppliers in Third World countries are being exploited and are, in consequence, paying their employees bare subsistence wages.

We are examining these aspects of the changing pattern of distribution because of their implications for marketing strategy. Certainly, the importance of scanning the social, as well as the economic, aspects of the business environment is amply illustrated by the distribution function. In the retailing of fast-moving consumer goods, for example, the situation is both fluid and highly competitive. Each day, the press, television and other media provide some examples of these trends, indicating at the same time that each trend, which must be considered for its strategic import, may be only a still in a fast-moving picture. Below are some practical illustrations of the various points made in this section. They constitute a small selection of the many newspaper articles gathered by the author on this subject while this book was in preparation:

Britain's food shoppers are getting harder to please. Price is no longer the sole determinant of a supermarket group's success – good service and convenience are playing increasingly critical roles. Customers are not prepared to travel as far to a store as they did five years ago, are doing more frequent, smaller shops and are often left dissatisfied with their chosen supermarket. This is the world of food shopping, according to Harris International Marketing (HIM), a firm of consultants (The Times, *26 February 1996*).

French boulangers and the country's corner-store culture scored a victory to savour over aggressive hypermarket rivals yesterday when the government announced tough regulations to counter 'predatory pricing'. The battle of the baguette has symbolised the growing conflict between large retailers and corner-store shopkeepers, who have complained that the bread sticks were sold as a loss-leader – sometimes at less than FFr.1 each – by hypermarkets (Financial Times, *27 February 1996*).

Rome: swift and intelligent support measures may yet save many of Italy's threatened small shopkeepers from extinction ... (Financial Times, *18 November 1996*).

The Burton Group, the U.K.'s second largest clothing retailer ... will launch Web sites containing 1,200 pages devoted to its stores and products, giving it what it believes will be the most extensive retail presence on the Net (Financial Times, *18 November 1996*).

Out-of-town superstores will account for most of the growth in UK retail sales in the next five years, in spite of ever tougher planning restrictions, according to a report published to-day by Verdict, the retail consultants (Financial Times, *30 April 1996*).

Petrol stations get retail top-up. Forecourt convenience stores prove profitable for oil companies (Financial Times, *22 December 1996*).

Asda is planning to introduce drive-through take-away diners at some of its stores later this year. It will be the first time the concept has been tried by a UK supermarket, though similar ideas exist in the U.S. (The Independent, *16 February 1998*).

Baked beans – and a mortgage. Supermarkets are leading the stampede to sell insurance and other investments (Financial Times, 16 February 1997).

You don't expect to see supermarket clothes in the fashion pages, let alone clothes from Asda. Yet in the past five years the once poor relation of super-markets has overtaken Safeway in terms of market value and sales – with its George range of clothing leading the re-emergence (The Independent, *31 December 1997*).

Asda yesterday announced a three-pronged attack on the home shopping market with plans to launch a grocery home delivery service, an on-line home entertainment offer and a digital television channel selling non-food lines like its George range of clothing (The Independent, *26 June 1998*).

In Japan, they call them 'roboshops'. They are 24-hour stores with such sophisti-cated computer technology that human staff are superfluous. Shoppers are invited to choose from single display items placed in long cabinets and marked with a number. They make their selection, punch the number into a computer and pay with plastic. The goods are promptly delivered down a chute (The Independent, *1 January 1998*).

Types of retail outlet

Hollinger (1997) draws our attention to the fact that:

Retailing around the world has become big business – and nowhere is this so evident as in the UK, where almost 10 per cent of the working population is involved in selling goods to consumers in Europe's fourth largest consumer market. The retail sector in Britain accounts for almost 40 per cent of all consumer expenditure, and is worth an estimated £143 billion a year.

She adds that the UK employs in retailing a greater proportion of its working population than any other European country except Italy. It is one of the most mature retail markets in the world, and is becoming ever more competitive.

Early in this chapter we reviewed the role of the retailer in general. This section provides a short summary of the various types of outlet and methods of retail trading.

Independents

The recent history of independent trading has been outlined. Contraction in the sector has not been confined to fast moving consumer goods (fmcg). In 1994 there were 7000 motor car dealerships in the UK. It is expected that this will reduce to about 5000 dealerships, the rationalization taking place at the expense of small, private dealers.

Even so, it must be borne in mind that in some product groups, the independents are still prominent, for example:

- in books, newspapers and magazines (despite the presence of such significant multiples as W.H. Smith, Waterstones and Dillons);
- in florist, plant and garden products,
- in dress fabrics, knitting yarns and soft furnishings;
- in antiques, works of art, stamps and coins (where independents still hold about four-fifths of the retail market).

Independents also hold an above average market share in the following fields: novelties, souvenirs and gifts; carpets; pharmaceutical products (in spite of the significant presence of multiples such as Boots); sports goods, toys, cycles and camping equipment.

Reduced numbers of outlets has also meant that many skilled and intelligent people must find ways of earning their livelihoods and that there are many empty premises available often on reasonable terms. The wise marketer will therefore:

- continue to monitor the trends described;
- recognize that, particularly for certain products, independents will continue to be important channel members;
- adopt perhaps a strategy of bold specialization in favour of the independents where larger competitors are devoting most of their attention to the multiples.

Multiple organizations

Little more needs to be said on the ever-increasing power of the multiples. It should be noted, also, that in addition to the type of multiple which has concentrated on a cohesive group of products – food, electrical goods, footwear, chemist goods, etc., there are the *variety chain stores* which also figure prominently in the sector. These sell a wide range of products, as implied by their title, examples in the UK being Littlewoods, Woolworth, British Home Stores and Marks and Spencer. The last of these was ranked third in a list of the top 12 retailers in the UK with annual sales of over £7 billion (as at 31.3.1996).

To distinguish them from this group, multiples concentrating on a narrower range are sometimes referred to as *speciality chain stores*.

Department stores

These are defined as establishments employing 24 or more persons and selling a wide range of goods including clothing, textiles and at least four other major product groups, e.g. furniture, electrical goods, leather goods, footwear, etc.

Although every capital city in the world boasts its 'high visibility' department stores, such as Harrods and Selfridges in London, it is a method of retailing which has suffered severe competition since the 1950s due to social and economic trends, not least the growth of the multiples. Consequently its share of total UK retail sales has been under constant threat and by 1996 this had been reduced to 4 per cent. In the period 1980–96 the number of stores contracted from 700 to 570.

However they cannot be dismissed as the dinosaurs of retailing for there have been welcome signs of their change and adaptation for trading in the twenty-first century. In 1996, for instance, it was announced that:

- Harrods planned to open a large number of international satellite stores;

- Harvey Nichols was expanding into the UK regions and hoped to open four stores and up to ten restaurants;

- Debenhams planned to expand its British network by '12 to 100 stores' (Bernoth and Olins, 1996, p 3) and was also moving onto the European continent;

- John Lewis opened its new store in Cheadle (1995–96) and planned four more stores – in Bluewater Park, Kent; Bristol; Glasgow and Leeds;

- Selfridges had spent more than £200 million refurbishing its Oxford Street store, intended to expand it by 200,000 square feet and would be opening at least four other outlets in the UK including a 160,000 square feet operation in Greater Manchester's new Trafford Centre;

- Internationally famous French store, Galeries Lafayette, opened a glittering, glass-plated new store in Berlins's Friedrichstrasse.

A spur to this sector's reinvention of itself may have been supplied by the Verdict retail research group which also announced in 1996 that the number of core consumers for the UK department stores would increase in the next five years. The 50–64 age group was set to increase by 11 per cent and the segment more recently converted to department stores, the 15–19 year olds, would grow by 7 per cent in the same period (Bernoth and Olins, 1996, p 3).

When the world's first department store, Bon Marché, opened in Paris in the 1850s, Emile Zola said it represented 'democratised luxury', with the first stores becoming shop windows for the new industrial age. The development of this method of trading, that is of several shops within a shop, was based on the provision of good quality, reasonably expensive merchandise to the growing middle classes. Historically this clearly differentiated them from the variety chain stores, a distinction which has far less meaning today.

Since very many of Britain's department stores belong to large groups, for example John Lewis Partnership, Debenhams, House of Fraser, etc. they could, strictly, also be classified as multiples, though not in their method of trading. Typically, they occupy large central sites in urban areas, devote a great deal of their advertising to 'events', 'sales', etc., in order to bring customers to their premises from the large geographical areas they serve. Also, unlike the 'real' multiples they offer a range of ancillary services including budget accounts and other credit facilities; hairdressing facilities; delivery services, restaurants and theatre booking facilities. However, in some respects, these distinctions are not as clear as they once were. Many manufacturers retail their own merchandise by way of 'leased departments' in these stores.

Co-operative retail societies

These belong to what is more accurately described as the 'consumer co-operative movement', to distinguish it from those groups which are wholesaler and/or retailer inspired.

The ideas of the Rochdale Pioneers who founded the movement have a place in Britain's history. In 1844, they founded a retail organization or 'society', based on open membership, democratic control ('one man one vote') and profit sharing for members linked to their purchases with the retail society. Although since the Second World War price cutting and dividend stamps redeemable for cash took the place of the old-style dividend distribution, the guiding principles are still much the same as they were in 1844. In the recent past some area testing has taken place for the re-introduction of the dividend concept (through The Co-op Dividend Card Scheme) and it will be interesting to see if this re-emerges broadscale.

Since the movement's inception, co-operative retail societies have become the owners of thousands of outlets in a number of countries and, in the UK they are joint owners of one of the largest distributive organizations in Europe – the Co-operative Wholesale Society (CWS). The CWS also operates highly successfully in the banking and insurance fields and is the largest UK owned provider of funeral services.

The movement is particularly strong in some countries, for example Switzerland, Denmark, Finland, Sweden and Norway. In the UK its share of total retail trade has declined in the last few decades and was down to 5 per cent by the late 1980s. Detailed research by Eliot (see McGoldrick, 1990, p 37) has indicated that this is due to:

- failure to keep pace with retail developments – despite having pioneered self-service techniques in the UK; and
- lack of a unified trading image due to a fragmented organizational structure in which individual societies have been bent on pursuing their own trading policies and trading names and have been reluctant to merge so as to match the power of the other types of multiples.

Even so, the CWS and its retail societies are a major feature of UK distribution and consumer services. In food retailing, the organization operates 300 convenience stores, 300 supermarkets and 30 superstores. Many of its 36 non-food stores are undergoing substantial refurbishment and Co-op Travelcare, the largest UK travel agent chain independent of tour operator control, now offers a sophisticated telephone sales facility to complement its network of over 250 branches.

The CWS Group as a whole employs over 50,000 employees and in 1997 achieved sales of £3.13 billion. Not least, it is an organization which places strong emphasis on ethical trading and community involvement. It has been highly visible, for instance, in informative and responsible food labelling, while the ethical policy of the Co-operative Bank, devised in 1992, has been cited as a standard for others to follow.

Mail order and direct response selling

It is not easy to describe this sector of retailing in a brief outline. To take the sector step-by-step a number of organizations can be distinguished which are collectively described as 'mail order'. These are:

- The small-scale operator offering one or a few products (e.g. gardening requisites, DIY items) through the postal shopping sections in newspapers and magazines. In some hobby and special interest magazines these advertisements are read as avidly as the editorial features.

- The large-scale wholesaler – retailer organization offering goods to the public by way of an illustrated catalogue, orders being obtained by postal response or through agents remunerated by a commission on the value of sales (but see below). This type of organization dominates the mail order trade and includes such traditional specialists as Littlewoods, Grattan and Great Universal Stores (GUS). Recently they have been joined by smaller, innovative operators including Next Directory, Land's End, Racing Green and Cotton Traders.

- The 'postal service' section of department stores and here it is noteworthy that these may be augmented by a similar service from the multiples – Marks and Spencer, for instance, is currently (1998) carrying out area tests in this connection.

- The type of operation, really an extension of the first in the list (see above), which is conducted by direct response advertising in the colour supplements of the national Sunday newspapers. Designed to reach the more affluent customer, both manufacturers and wholesale organizations use this direct marketing approach. Front runners in this field have been Scotcade and Innovations (Mail Order) Ltd.

Direct marketing, or *direct response* evolved from the use of direct mail as an advertising medium, but now there are many media which are used to promote direct response sales including advertisements in newspaper and magazines, on television, radio and the Internet (see Figure 10.3). Selling by telephone is another way of evoking direct response. In addition, direct response *advertising*, as opposed to selling, is frequently used to attract buyers to the seller's location (stores, market, etc.) or to obtain an interview for the seller at the buyer's location (home, office, etc.).

Clothing, footwear, furniture, books, video and audio cassettes, insurance, investments, credit facilities, sports and leisure goods, beauty products, jewellery and any number of household products are just some of the goods sold successfully by direct response methods.

Home shopping, traditionally by mail order catalogues, grew significantly in the immediate post-Second World War period (1950 – 1 per cent of total UK retail sales; 1970 – 4.2 per cent). By 1996 it still accounted for only 5 per cent of retail sales, but according to Cunningham (1996, p 25) 'is growing very fast and is very competitive'. She adds that it has enough potential to attract the attention of 'high street heavyweights such as Burton and Marks and Spencer'. The head of Burton's catalogue operations adds: 'We think mail order is going to grow faster than the high street and we also see huge possibilities to augment sales in our shops through catalogues.'

It may well be a method of trading 'whose time has come' in that an increasing proportion of women in the UK and Europe now go out to work and increasing traffic congestion in city centres deters people from shopping. In fact, as these lines are being written, the UK government has announced measures to reduce the number of cars in the centres of towns and cities. These trends are beneficial to direct response and social change means that the role of the agent who shows the 1000 plus page catalogues to friends, families and neighbours, ordering goods on their behalf and being rewarded by a commission, is now in decline. Catalogue trading is therefore becoming more 'direct'.

The sector provides a very good example of *niche marketing* too. N. Brown, a Manchester-based organization, decided to differentiate its approach from the large catalogue sellers and concentrate on selling clothes to middle-aged and elderly women in a wide range of sizes. By 1996 it had cornered 25 per cent of the direct mail order (i.e. non-agency) business in the UK and had become well-known and respected in the industry.

Franchising

In this type of operation, the franchiser provides:

- the goodwill attaching to his brand or organizational 'image';
- the product to be sold;
- consultancy services on location, management, financial control, etc.,
- in some cases, financial facilities – usually by way of a proportion of the venture capital required.

In the UK, the banking sector is prominent in providing start-up funding, the five leading franchise lending banks being NatWest, Lloyds, Barclays, Midland and the Royal Bank of Scotland. The last named, for example, will provide up to 70 per cent of a franchise investment, whereas its limit for a stand-alone business is likely to be in the region of 50 per cent of a start-up project's costs (Gourlay, 1996, p 13).

From the standpoint of the franchiser's marketing strategy, particularly where a bank is providing some franchise finance, the method provides an attractive way of expanding the business while reducing the need for capital but speedily distributing the product to a wide market. In the USA, for example, according to Gourlay (1996, p 13) franchising accounts for 12 per cent of retail sales. No doubt this is due to the fact that because of its vast collection of diverse markets, utilizing the local market knowledge of enthusiastic entrepreneurial individuals has proved very fruitful.

In the UK, according to the 1996 study by NatWest Bank on behalf of the British Franchise Association (BFA), business format franchises accounted for 3.7 per cent of total retail sales. Other points from this survey were:

- There were 474 business format franchises at the end of 1995, against 414 in the previous year.
- These supported 25,700 franchisees employing 222,700 people, up from 192,300 in the previous year.
- Sales for 1995 were £5.9 billion against £5.5 billion in 1994.

Gourlay adds that while franchising in the UK lags markedly behind the USA, in Europe's large economies, such as Germany and France, it has achieved similar penetration. Moir (1996, p 15) suggests that franchisees who can offer local expertise to groups with pan-European ambitions 'should find themselves at a premium'.

For his part, the franchisee arranges for the provision of most, if not all, of the venture capital and enters into agreement to purchase his supplies exclusively from the franchiser. The system has been used successfully in the catering field (Wimpy, Domino's Pizza), business services (Prontaprint, Kall Kwik), homecare services (Dyno-Rod), wedding attire and soft drinks. Its influence continues to widen with management and consultancy services, recruitment services industrial signs, damp proofing, drive laying and numerous other ventures now being franchised.

Traditionally it was thought franchising was particularly attractive to the redundant worker but according to the NatWest bank, only 20 per cent of franchisees are the newly redundant, 40 per cent are already self-employed and the remainder are in paid employment. Moreover, since franchises cost, on average, £45,000 each plus the cost of income support until a salary can be taken out of the business, not many franchises can be bought with average redundancy payments (Moir, 1996, p 15).

For these and other reasons sound advice is important before a franchise contract is concluded. In the UK the British Franchise Association is an important organization in this respect since before they can become accredited members, franchisers must satisfy the Association that they can meet the standards for contracts and support systems set out in the BFA manual. Lawyers, banks and accountants can also offer objective views on the costs and benefits of franchising and on the integrity of franchisers and their contracts.

Automatic vending

Vending machines are all around us – in the college, university and office block; at the shopping precinct, railway station, seaport and airport; in the library, community centre and sports stadium.

The spread of products sold in this way continues to expand – food and confectionery, books and newspapers, insurance and banking services, document copying, clothing, hosiery and cosmetics. These are just some of the items retailed and since the 'roboshop' development in Japan, mentioned earlier in the chapter, is really automatic vending in a more sophisticated form, the range of items will continue to widen.

The attraction to the consumer is accessibility of products and services around the clock – but machines that are out-of-service or out-of-stock generate frustration and ill-will. From the marketer's standpoint, therefore, maintenance and stocking procedures are key factors. For this reason, vending is not the cheapest method of retailing but the consumer is generally willing to bear some extra cost for the convenience of the method.

Though we are inclined to regard vending as a twentieth-century development, particularly as the vending machine becomes even more streamlined and automated, it is Kotler and Armstrong (1990, p 365) who point out that in 215 BC Egyptians could purchase sacrificial water from coin operated devices. *Plus ça change.*

Other methods of retail distribution

Electronic shopping or *teleshopping* was hailed as a development which would revolutionize retailing but, in the UK at least, it had not made a noticeable impact up to the mid 1990s. Early systems linked the consumer to the seller's databank, either by means of a television set with a keyboard device connected to the system by two-way cable, or by means of a telephone and a home computer. 'Videotex' is a service providing a 'catalogue' of products and services from retailers, banks, travel agents, etc. After comparison of items and prices, the purchase is made using a charge card.

Further development of the approach would entail attracting more distributors and their customers and the introduction of more attractive, user-friendly technology. Even then, it may not be able to surmount the difficulty that for many, 'going shopping' is a pleasant, social experience. None the less, the marketing fraternity will watch the development of electronic shopping very carefully. In November 1996, Tesco became the first UK supermarket to provide an online service via the Internet. It allowed customers to order from the complete 20,000 item range of a conventional superstore and was available to customers living within five miles of Osterley, West London. The scheme was launched using a CD-Rom so that customers could select their purchases before ordering online through CompuServe. In December 1996 Sainsbury announced that it would launch its Internet supermarket, developed in conjunction with computer group Hewlett-Packard, in March 1997. Restricted initially to 200 shoppers in Watford and Bracknell, by the second half of the year the company planned to test the programme on between 500,000 and 1 million customers in the catchment areas of five to ten stores.

Door-to-door retailing is a well-established method of direct-marketing particularly for cosmetics, in which the Avon company is prominent, and household products – Kleen-E-Ze and Betterwear being significant names here. *Party selling* (e.g. Tupperware plastic products) has been a notable later development in this method of distribution. The personal integrity and quality of the service and advice offered by the agent or salesperson is a crucial factor for success.

The term 'market' covers a number of methods of trading and types of products and services, for example:

- *the covered or open-air markets* in which a wide range of products are retailed to customers – fish, fruit, vegetables, confectionery, clothing, antiques, etc.;

- *the product or commodity markets and exchanges* through which buyers and sellers can make contact and which specialize in fixing prices and grading commodities. Foreign exchange, insurance, stocks and shares, shipping, rubber, tea, coffee, etc., are some of the products and services dealt with in these specialized exchanges.

Both types of market are an important feature of the commercial scene and many are of world-wide reputation, from the street markets of London to the financial markets in the major centres of the globe.

Physical distribution management

Early in this chapter, we noted that:

- physical distribution is the second major element in the 'place' element of the strategic formula;

- that though the level of service to the customer is undoubtedly important, improvement in this level entails an exponential increase in costs (see Figure 10.1);

- that the process of physical distribution or 'logistics' is of great strategic significance, a fact infrequently recognized by senior managers, including those responsible for marketing.

We also noted that, particularly for large organizations, there are clear advantages in integrating the inward and outward movements of supplies and output so that a *logistics management* approach can make the most productive use of resources, including transport. This section provides some further thoughts on the physical distribution function, concentrating on the decisions relating to supplying the customer.

It is impossible, of course, to maximize the level of customer service and, at the same time, minimize physical distribution costs. Here, decision-making has to do with finding the best balance between frequently opposing variables. The 'best balance' is the one providing an effective level of service and also helping to meet organizational objectives, e.g. return on investment. How are the variables opposed to each other? Let us look at some examples.

Choice of transport

The supplier usually has the following options: road haulage; rail transport; canal transport; coastal transport; air freight; postal delivery; parcels and small freight delivery services.

With regard to road haulage (the most favoured method in the UK, to the detriment of its environment) the choice has to be made between owning and operating a fleet of vehicles, contract hire or payment for haulage company services.

Each of the transport modes listed above has its advantages: the flexibility of road transport; the accessibility to dock systems when the loading ports handle barge traffic and the country has a well-developed canal system; the speed of air freight. But all these modes produce a different pattern of costs and, in general, the greater the advantage, the more the costs. Choice of a transport mode means considering a number of factors, including:

- any special requests of the customer;
- the required speed of transit or delivery lead-time;
- the nature of the journey;
- the volume/weight/value of the consignment;
- the physical nature of the goods – perishable, fragile, etc.;
- the freight, packing and insurance costs entailed with each option.

Another crucial factor, rarely found in such checklists is the quality of service offered by the carrier. More and more organizations are now realizing that the understanding, cooperation and flexibility of the carrier is so important that, as noted earlier, they are concluding long-term contracts with carriers to which penalties and bonuses are attached.

A combination of two or more modes may also be an option. In export movements, for example, the rail trunking of road vehicles, using 'kangaroo' trailers, offers both the high speed of rail and the flexibility of road transport for the 'through' carriage of consignments. So the choice of transport mode, even for a single consignment, can be quite a complex issue.

Where the whole volume of required movements with a given time period, say a financial year, is under review, the examination of all the variables can be extremely complex, with a great deal depending on the accuracy of a firm's demand analysis for its output.

Inventory policy

The *level of service* issue has already been outlined. The question of an integrated policy is also important. The production manager may veer towards high stock levels because of the increased discounts available on bulk purchases of raw materials, the benefits of long production runs and the reduction in setting up time. The sales manager may also favour high stock levels so as to shorten delivery lead times and ensure no sales opportunity is lost. On the other hand, the finance manager may be canvassing reduced inventory because of the costs of interest entailed by high levels and because 'tied up' capital may mean losing lucrative possibilities for alternative uses.

The marketing manager must be able to determine which policy will best serve overall strategy and then share his perception with senior management colleagues.

The role of the marketing manager

Looking at these two aspects of physical distribution, choice of transport mode and inventory control we can see that logistics is an important and complex function where optimal solutions are unlikely to be achieved by guesswork and 'experience' ('we've always done it this way'). What then are the implications for the marketing manager?

First, it is essential that he or she recognizes the nature and complexity of physical distribution issues. It would be an abrogation of responsibility for him (or her) to say 'I leave such matters to the transport manager, he's very shrewd'. The techniques of transport raise questions beyond the responsibilities of the transport manager. For example, how far can representatives and agents be encouraged to increase order quantities so as to take advantage of containerization or some other type of 'unit load' carriage? This is an aspect of sales policy. The marketing team might ask itself 'how many more products can we fit into a container module by some modification to the product's shape and if we modified the shape, would this affect demand?' This is an aspect of design policy. The transport manager's remit does not run to sales and design policy.

Also, it is conceivable that, in making judgements on transport methods, busy transport managers are preoccupied with freight rates. Yet the freight cost element is merely one cost among many for any method of transportation. Accurate comparison between methods entails taking into account items additional to the freight rate, including warehousing costs, interest on capital, insurance premiums and packing costs. Not all of these are within the scope of the transport manager. For example, the use of air freight will probably entail higher freight charges than sea transport for the average consignment. On the other hand, air freight movements usually entail lower packing costs and lower insurance charges, because of reduced transit time. The lower lead time also means less interest on the supplier's capital – an item which would be taken into account by a comprehensive total distribution cost analysis, again something which is hardly the province of the transport manager, important though he or she may be.

So, although a mode of transport may be more costly from the freight charges standpoint its use may still be justified on the basis of overall economy. That may be the situation for a single consignment but to refine our decision-making still further, what would be the situation concerning the *total sales volume* predicted to be sold in a given market over a given time period and how does the costs situation alter over and above that volume? Let us look at an example.

Imagine that a UK manufacturer of engineering components has established a warehouse in Brussels to provide an intensively good service to customers with mass-assembly plants on the near Continent. He is now considering alternative methods of physical distribution as indicated in the *total distribution costs* (TDC) analysis approach outlined below.

- *Method A*   By sea ex UK → Brussels warehouse → customers' assembly plants by road.

- *Method B*   By air freight ex UK → by local delivery ex airports → direct to customers' assembly plants.

The approach begins by classifying all the distributive costs of each method as either fixed or variable. Fixed costs are those which would still have to be allocated even if there were no engineering components in the pipeline, i.e. at 'zero throughput'. The analysis might be structured as shown.

Method A (sea/Brussels warehouse/road)

- *Freight costs of transportation* – classified as variable costs.

- *Warehousing costs* – classified as partially fixed/partially variable, e.g. the fixed costs in this instance are the costs of occupation, local rent, rates, etc.; depreciation of fixtures, fittings, stock handling equipment and delivery vehicles.

- *Interest on stocks held* – classified also as partially fixed/partially variable e.g. the interest on the minimum allowable stock level may be used for calculation purposes as the *fixed* element.

Method B (air freight and local delivery to customers)

There is clearly a much lower element of fixed costs by this method. There are now no warehouse occupancy costs and the minimum allowable stock levels held in the UK can be lower because the lower lead time of air freight requires a lower level of 'buffer' stock.

Let us assume that when the classification of cost data is completed, the analysis appears thus:

		Fixed costs (%)	Variable costs (%)
(A)	Sea/Brussels warehouse/road	35	65
(B)	Air freight and local delivery	20	80

A cross-over chart can then be constructed (see Figure 10.9). From this figure it can be seen that until a break-point in sales volume of 25,000 units is reached, it is uneconomical for the supplier to have a warehouse in Brussels. Obviously, if a volume break-point can be established for each transport method to each market it serves, the firm can alter its method of moving goods to a market according to how and when the volume of business transacted with a market or group of markets, expands.

TDC analysis can be criticized on the grounds that it is an 'ideal' method, entailing a great deal of work. Certainly it calls for more information on distribution costs than many firms possess but if marketing *is* to do with measurement, since many physical distribution decisions are too far reaching to be delegated to managers with a narrower functional perspective, then marketing managers must be involved at least to the extent of knowing the complexities of logistics and their ultimate effect on selling prices and being acquainted with the numerous techniques which can be employed in decision-making.

It was reported in July 1998 (Trapp, 1998b, p 6) that management consultants AT Kearney, currently carrying out research in association with the European Logistics Association, had this to say regarding their study, which is a follow-up to similar

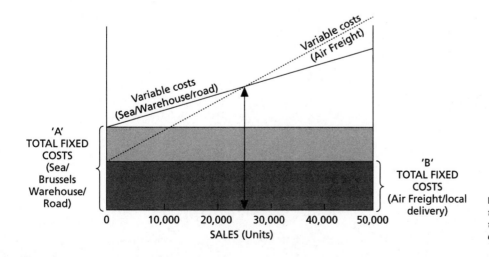

Figure 10.9. Comparison of two methods of physical distribution – a total distribution cost (TDC) analysis approach.

surveys in 1982, 1987 and 1992: 'Companies are recognizing the importance of approaching logistics in a strategic and high level manner ... we expect to find that attitudes have radically altered'.

The strategic formula: Element 5:

C·H·A·P·T·E·R

ELEVEN

11

Promotion – function and strategy

'Promotion' or 'marketing communications', has a number of elements:

- advertising;
- sales promotion;
- public relations;
- personal selling.

Let us begin by broadly defining these.

- *Advertising* consists of purchase and use of space in newspapers, magazines or outdoor locations or the purchase and use of time on radio and television by an identified sponsor (i.e. the advertiser) for the promotion of goods, services or ideas. Expenditure on direct mail is also classified under this heading.

- *Sales promotion* often complements the other communications elements, especially in the field of fast moving consumer goods (fmcg). It includes those activities designed to encourage user-purchase at point of sale, to increase dealer effectiveness and to reward customer loyalty. Examples include in-store displays, demonstrations and exhibitions. Sales promotion also covers expenditure on 'special offers', competitions, etc.

- *Public relations*, in its broadest terms, can be taken to mean the deliberate and sustained effort to maintain mutually beneficial relationships between an organization and its stakeholding 'publics' – customers, suppliers, employees, shareholders, the community, etc. In relation to marketing operations it entails the creation of a favourable atmosphere within which marketing can take place. This is usually achieved through 'free' publicity in newspapers, magazines, and on television, radio, etc. in which the organization and/or its personalities, products, processes, technical achievements and commercial successes receive favourable mention.

- *Personal selling* consists of oral or written presentation and/or presentation by sound and vision for the purposes of making sales. It is essentially a negotiation process carried out by members of the organization's salesforce. The process may be with actual or potential customer firms, as in industrial marketing, with distributors or, in the case of direct-to-user methods of distribution, with consumers.

Marketing, or more accurately, what passes for it in the public mind, has always had its critics and their worst attacks have generally been reserved for the promotion function on the grounds of its economics and its ethics. We shall now consider briefly the economics and ethics of promotion and although all four of its elements in their turn have come in for criticism, we shall focus on advertising in responding to these criticisms.

The economics of advertising

In 1997, total advertising expenditure in the UK reached an all-time record figure of £13.1 billion. At current prices, this was an increase of 9.3 per cent over 1996 – 6 per cent in real terms. In the early 1990s, a period of economic downturn in Britain, advertising expenditure declined from the previous all-time high figure recorded in 1989. The 1997 total was the sixth consecutive year of increase at constant prices since that period of decline. The expenditure represented 1.94 per cent of gross domestic product, very slightly below the 1989 record share of GDP – 1.96 per cent (see Figure 11.1).

The curve in Figure 11.1 has another interesting feature, for it demonstrates the stability of advertising expenditure which, over a period of more than 40 years has never exceeded 2 per cent of GDP. McCann (1998, p 15), commenting on the 1997 figure makes the following interesting observation: 'The reason the Government should be paying close attention to this figure is that advertising has proved itself repeatedly to be a very responsive indicator of economic health.'

In reasoning that advertising's consistent ability to be an early indicator of economic slowdowns and upturns should make the Government study the expenditure figure more closely, he points out:

- that the trading system of commercial television in Britain is geared 'to allow advertisers to come on air at the last moment if they so wish, and so media spend is again something which companies do not have to plan years in advance';

- that in the strong daily newspaper market the lead times for advertisements can be as short as a few hours, meaning that a large proportion of advertising expenditure can be flexible;

- that together, television and the press display advertising account for £10.6 billion of the £13 billion total.

So we note the way in which advertising expenditure links closely with the state of the economy and how advertisers seek to relate their spending to economic opportunity. This point and the relative stability of the curve in Figure 11.1. run counter to

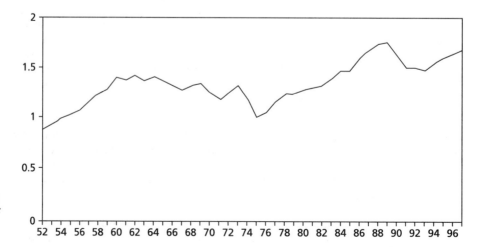

Figure 11.1. *Advertising as % of GDP at factor cost. Source: The Advertising Association, news release 15 June 1998.*

the allegations that spending advertising money is a reckless business, which is wasteful, unnecessary and a strong force behind rising prices. On this last point, Britain's highest years for advertising expenditure have been among its best years for price stability.

Perhaps the best general economic justification for advertising came from the experienced practitioner, John Hobson (1988) who drew attention to its vital role in a free society. He described it as one of the key tools of competition and innovation which maintain the dynamics and initiative of industry while providing an outlet for the results of research and development, without which any industrial nation must go into decline. Hobson continued:

> Advertising helps to maintain employment and the uses of all resources, at a steady pace, without undue swings in supply and demand. It increases the aspirations of the public so that the desire to work harder and earn more money are increased. It improves the quality of material life for the mass of the public. It may be objected that it puts too much emphasis on material aspiration and well being, but advertising is only responding to social trends, encouraged by the redistribution of wealth over the last century (Hobson, 1988, pp 253–4).

At least three other relevant observations can be made:

- an economy's advertising expenditure typically contains a highly significant proportion about which few, if any, would argue, e.g. for government services to the public; health care; crime prevention; famine relief and many other charitable appeals;

- the alternative to a free society in which demand is influenced by advertising is one in which all economic activity is planned 'from the centre' – the breakdown of communism in the USSR and Eastern Europe attests to the failure of this approach and to its dire consequences;

- throughout this book, the point has been made that, for most products and markets, competition becomes ever more intense – the customer therefore has wide freedom of choice and if the advertiser's products and services do not live up to the claims made for them, the customer's affection will soon be transferred to the competition.

John Kay affirms this last point when commenting on the spending of advertising money:

> It tells you that the advertiser is committed to the product and the market. If he were not it would be absurd for him to spend so much. And if he is committed to the product and the market, it also makes sense for him to devote resources to ensuring the quality of his product (Kay, 1997, p 16).

As with the other elements of the strategic formula, the case made for the *promotion* element in this book is that organizations adopting the marketing approach must plan their promotional expenditure very carefully and in relation to clear objectives, for organizations lacking cost-consciousness will succumb to competition and cease to exist.

No one would claim that advertising is an exact science, but in outlining how it has become more scientific, Winston Fletcher (1996) suggests that the recent boom in retail advertising is 'attributable to the simple fact that retailers now measure advertising's sales effects with considerable precision, aided by bar coding and sophisticated inventory control techniques which have increased the speed and sophistication of their calculations.' He goes on:

For manufacturers of consumer branded goods such quantification is still, as it always has been, a tad trickier. But with a little planning it can usually be done. With faster and more accurate sales audits, continuous consumer purchase panels, awareness tracking studies and the panoply of modern information technology, advertisers can stop guessing and start assessing (Fletcher, 1996, p 15).

Later in the chapter we shall see some ways in which marketing research can assist in the planning of promotion.

The ethics of advertising

It is important to note that the views expressed under this heading are exclusively those of the author, so they might not find universal acceptance. Nevertheless, they are set out in good faith to record for the reader some thoughts on a key facet of marketing communications.

An economic justification for the promotion function comes easily to this author. He is less at ease with some examples of promotional activity viewed from an ethical standpoint. Here are a few samples.

A current television advertisement for a car is almost entirely taken up with a lady taking off her clothes. After entering the car she drops her last item of clothing through her open window and drives off – leaving the viewer with the clear impression she is driving the car totally naked. Apart from a few words at the end of the commercial, nothing is said about the car itself. It might be claimed that the purpose of the advertisement is to generate interest in obtaining further information about the car. If so, this seems an economically doubtful strategy leaving this author with the impression that the advertiser's money has not so much generated interest in the car as provided sexual titilation for the viewer. Whether or not it has been effective in commercial terms, there is the question of whether it is unethical because it has caused offence. The author found it offensive and feels he was not alone in this. It might be worth adding that the author, in the market for a new car at the time declined to consider this manufacturer's products and bought from the competition.

In February 1998, Blackstock (1998) reported that a jeans company intended to promote its products by 'depicting scenes of human mutilation, a denim-clad Virgin Mary, groping OAPs and a spoof of a soft-porn movie ...'. He believed that the advertisements were 'likely to draw gasps from even the most liberal-minded'. They were intended to appear on buses, poster sites and the London Underground although the more controversial ones would be confined to magazines.

Donegan (1997), in August 1997, noted that advertisers had been warned against using 'speed and acceleration' claims to sell cars after two television commercials were taken off the screen because they broke road safety guidelines. The Independent Television Commission (see Chapter 5) had given notice in its latest advertising complaints report that it would take action against 'a wholesale drift in standards' from guidelines which ban advertisers from using aggressive or illegally fast driving.

Reporting in February 1998, Watson-Smyth (1998) drew attention to the fact that two of the world's largest car makers had to withdraw advertisements following complaints that they were insulting and racist. On the point of racism, a study carried out on behalf of Race for Opportunity, the Business in the Community campaign promoting economic activity among minorities, found that ethnic minorities are often alienated by big companies' marketing and advertising campaigns, many of which reinforce their sense of exclusion from mainstream society.

The vast majority of UK advertisements are completely in line with the stipulation of the Advertising Code (Chapter 5 q.v.) that they should be 'legal, decent, honest and truthful'. Yet it has to be said that a minority are not prepared with a due sense of responsibility to consumers and to society. Of course, organizations challenged on the ethics of their advertisements often lament the general decline in moral standards but point out that they are merely reflecting society as it is and not as they would wish it to be. Their argument is grounded in *normative moral relativism* which holds that it is wrong to pass judgement on others who have substantially different values, or to try to make them conform to one's values, for the reason that their values are as valid as one's own. Here a reasonable man would ask the question 'but where do you stop?' and may well believe that what politicians describe as our 'fractured society' and what those in other cultures refer to as the 'decadence of the West' can be laid at the door of moral relativism. The author would add that to allow advertisers to say 'we merely reflect the decline in ethical standards' is to let them escape their part in creating that decline.

There is abundant evidence that *consumerism* is well-established in the West, as noted in Chapter 5. Its already influential voice becomes steadily stronger. There is also evidence that, in choosing between brands, the consumer is becoming more and more concerned with the reputation and integrity of the supplier. As Roger Trapp (1998c) indicates, integrity is not just an image – companies must live up to their brand identities in all phases of their operations and management. This is, after all, what is meant by *integrated marketing* – which 'is based on the fact that everything a company does, and sometimes what it doesn't do, sends a message' (Duncan and Moriarty, 1998).

The view taken in this book is that an organization driven by ethical values, practising integrated marketing, is more certain of securing its objectives, profit and non-profit, than it would be by any alternative approach. Its promotional strategy should be the outward sign of such a strategy. In this way it will be contributing to the *long-run welfare of society*, as well as selling its goods and services – another tenet of the marketing philosophy.

Marketing communications: *process and function*

Communication: meaning and process

Communication is frequently taken to consist solely of sending messages. This is incorrect. A dictionary definition of communication is: 'to succeed in conveying one's meaning to others' (*Chambers Twentieth Century Dictionary*, 1972, p 263). Phrases such as: 'to give a share of', 'to have something in common with another' are also used in defining the word. Therefore, there are at least *two* parties to the process – a *sender* and a *receiver* and unless the receiver understands the sender's message they are not communicating. This fact is simple enough but it is highly important for marketers, as we shall see.

Figure 11.2 depicts an outline of the elements in the communication process, as classically defined by Shannon and reported in Ritchie (1991). In a marketing context, an interpretation of Shannon's visualization of the process is set out below.

- A marketing organization, as *source* or sender, *encodes* a message – that is forms the message into words, pictures, etc. using terms, symbols judged to be readily understandable by the *receiver*.

- The message is then transmitted via a *channel*, i.e. a medium of communication such as television, the press, radio, etc. In practice a number of media are frequently used to complement each other and reinforce the message.

- The message is then *decoded* by the receiver, which means, hopefully, it is interpreted in a way the marketer intended. This is a prelude to action by the buyer

Figure 11.2. *Elements in the communication process*

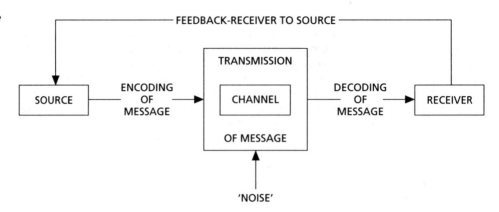

who then responds positively, e.g. by buying the product, subscribing to the charitable cause, noting the price change or, in the case of corporate advertising, adopting a favourable attitude to the organization itself.

● The *receiver* may provide the source with some *feedback*, e.g. expressions of opinion, complaints, submissions of requested information, responses to advertising research, etc.

● The process is subject to a greater or lesser degree of what is known technically as 'noise'. This may interfere with or distort the transmission and decoding of the message. In marketing operations 'noise' may result from competitors' advertising, some dramatic change in the business environment and so on.

As Scott Poole (1998, pp 85–7) indicates, distortions may emerge during encoding and decoding, through the introduction of error or if the source and the receiver have different codes.

Several points of practical significance for marketing can be discerned from these outlines of the communications process:

● the message must emanate from clear objectives – in the sequence:
corporate–marketing–promotional objectives;

● the organization must *know its market* for, as indicated in Chapter 7 (see Figure 7.2 et seq.) the characteristics of the buyer will affect the outcome, positively or negatively, of the stimuli received – his or her level of understanding and predisposition to receive the message affect its decoding;

● it follows from this that, generally, the message must be expressed in simple terms, in the language of the receiver and via an appropriate channel as free as possible of distortion;

● the marketing organization should try to obtain feedback on how the message has been received and whether it has been fully understood.

The function of communication

An example of this was given in Chapter 7 when the distribution of a consumer product was outlined and push and pull strategies were explained (see Figure 7.1). It may be useful to say a little more here.

We can safely assume that when an organization invests in the production of a product or service it genuinely believes that what it offers will provide the user with good value for money. If it proceeded otherwise it would be acting unethically, perhaps illegally and certainly with economic lunacy. Moreover, if marketing research had been undertaken prior to production, it should have enough evidence that its confidence in a return on its investment is not misplaced.

At this point, if it could inform the user of all the benefits of the product or service, it might have a reasonable chance of securing sales. We know, however, that frequently the producer is physically separated from the user by intermediaries – particularly so in consumer markets, as indicated in the simple illustration in Figure 11.3.

For the intermediaries, an individual manufacturer's product is invariably one among very many. Consequently, the intermediary will not have a detailed mastery of its 'reasoned selling argument'. The manufacturer must guard against any loss in transmission of the power of that argument. He must also guard against its distortion. The potential user must have the fullest, clearest information on the product's attributes, performance, economy or whatever – there must be no garbled version.

Typically, and as indicated in Figure 11.3, the manufacturer therefore decides to inform the potential user in a direct manner about the benefits of his offer and this is the function of his promotion. As noted earlier (Chapter 7) in this instance he is selling *through* the intermediaries rather than *to* them – attempting to *pull* his products through the channel by creating demand through consumer promotion.

Obviously the products must be in the channel before consumer promotion commences for, as the old saying goes: 'to send consumers to the shops for goods which aren't there is to fling them into the arms of competitors'. Also, especially where new products are concerned, intermediaries are loath to handle these unless demand is being created through direct-to-user promotion. For these reasons, most promotional campaigns are a combination of trade 'push' and consumer 'pull'.

For mass-produced consumer products, advertising on television and the national press is used to create consumer demand. This prompts the question of whether advertising is the most cost-effective method of generating that demand. The answer, in large part, depends on the product and the market. Often advertising is one element in a total promotional plan which might also employ point-of-sale display, exhibitions, editorial articles and personal selling. The task then is to strike the correct balance between all these elements in a cost-effective manner. In most cases, the case for the inclusion of advertising is beyond dispute, certainly for fast moving consumer goods (fmcg).

Consider a new breakfast food or bedtime drink. How can its benefits be introduced to potential users? Effectively, this means telling the product's story to 20 million households. To attempt to do so with a team of sales representatives calling at every household would cost so much as to raise the price of the product to astronomical proportions. A full-page advertisement in a mass-circulation newspaper or a 30 second advertisement on television at peak viewing time may each cost several thousand pounds but only a fraction of a penny for each household seeing these advertisements. The creative challenge for the advertiser is to achieve the impact of the sales representative's direct approach through the indirect method of advertising.

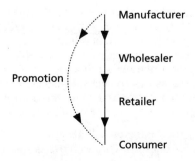

Figure 11.3. *The function of promotion in a two-level channel (consumer products).*

The objective of the communications campaign may be to:

- launch a new product;
- maintain sales of an existing product;
- increase sales of the product by attracting new users;
- announce a price change;
- support the efforts of the salesforce;
- improve the reputation of the company and its service;
- improve customer retention;
- increase recognition of the brand;
- increase the number and quality of channel members;
- generate enquiries for the firm's home shopping catalogue, financial consultancy, insurance services.

  etc.

These are ten examples from a much longer list of possibilities and they are not mutually exclusive, as will be perceived. The key point here is that the strategy to be adopted and the financial budget required must emanate from the overall marketing strategy and must be based on clear and realistic promotional objectives. Any form of marketing communication is not some creative activity unrelated to profit or non-profit objectives – it is organized creativity in the service of objectives.

Devising the strategy

From what has been said so far it is clear that, as with all marketing activity, promotion must be based on sound knowledge of the customer. The market segment will have been carefully chosen and the product or service developed or 'positioned' for maximum appeal to the segment. The role of promotion is to develop a message based on clear objectives and to communicate with the customer via that message, which may be to do with quality and value of a product, the reputation of the supplier, etc., as we have seen above.

There are a number of models used in marketing to depict the progression of the potential customer from a state of unawareness of the advertiser's message to taking action as implied by its objective. One of these is the AIDA model, an acronym which means that the message should be so structured so that it

- obtains Attention   –   the receiver's *cognitive* stage
- develops Interest   –   ⎫
- arouses Desire   –   ⎬   the *affective* stage
                           ⎭
- impels Action   –   the *conative* stage (e.g. the product purchase).

The AIDA model of the targeted stages of promotion's effect on the receiver is rather simplistic and as Yorke (1998) points out logical progression through each of the stages is not always possible with much depending on the product or service offered and the target group of receivers. Nevertheless it is well-established and is a useful tool to structure the promotion planner's thinking. Ideally, research should be used to provide before and after measures so that the success of the promotional strategy can be analysed. Later in the chapter when some research procedures are described reference will be made to DAGMAR – another significant model.

In developing the message the marketer will always seek to discover the significant benefit which is unique to his offering. The objective is not to expand the market for the whole product group, including competitors' products, but for the marketer's own specific product. And just as the product has been 'positioned' so too must the message be positioned upon the unique benefit. Hence the importance of another acronym in marketing language – the USP (*unique selling proposition*).

Here is the underlying reason why a popular objective in promotional campaigns is the establishment of *brand identity* – a process to which organizations are prepared to devote much time, money and effort. An excellent illustration of this was provided in 1996 by the Pepsi-Cola Corporation. According to Alexander (1996) the organization embarked on 'the most extravagant promotion in its 98 year history'. It persuaded the UK's Daily Mirror to turn 'blue for a day' and Air France was persuaded to paint a Concorde blue. Cosmonauts aboard the Mir space station were paid to hold up a Pepsi advertisement before television cameras – the first commercial message from space.

Globally, US $500 million (£327 million)was spent to draw attention to Pepsi's decision to change its colours from red, white and blue to predominantly blue. Pursuing the decision to make a major marketing effort internationally Pepsi decided to differentiate itself as much as possible from its main rival Coca-Cola which, with its red cans, was dominating displays and promotion. Both companies have also faced competition from new entrants to the market – in the UK from Virgin and from the own-label brands of Sainsbury and others. Pepsi, therefore, decided to dispense with a policy of heavy discounting to retailers in order to protect its market and moved to strong manipulation of its brand image via expensive promotional campaigns in global markets where it already had distinct advantages over smaller competitors.

Basically, the development of a promotional strategy hinges on the issues of:

- *what* should be said;
- *where* it should be said; and
- *how* it should be said.

The *what* question involves consideration of benefits to the user, the nature of the target market and what is unique or distinctive about the offer (i.e. the USP). When a company is operating in many markets throughout the world, typical issues are:

- should there be a standardized approach for all markets? or
- should there be a separate approach for each market or group of markets? or
- should there be a standardized approach but with local variations to take account of differing cultures, literacy levels, etc?

The *where* question relates to the use of the various *elements* of the communications mix (e.g. advertising, public relations, etc.) and of the *media* within these elements (e.g. television, newspapers, etc.) – more on this later in the chapter.

The *how* question, as its name suggests, relates to the way in which the message will be transmitted and involves a consideration of:

- the creative approach to be adopted (e.g. functional, humorous, frivolous, emotional or with an emphasis on the ethical dimension);
- the relationship between the creative options and the financial resources available (the development of a cartoon for a TV commercial will be more expensive than a 'live action' presentation from a simple studio set);
- the market segment to which the message will be directed (e.g. it is unlikely, though not impossible, that a frivolous approach would be effective in promoting a high quality, expensive product to rich and discriminating consumers).

The communications mix

The need for integration

The four main elements of the communications mix were listed at the beginning of the chapter and described in some detail. The word 'main' is used advisedly, for in promoting an organization and its products there are many elements including the firm's stationery (letterheads, invoices, catalogues), its transport, its packaging and often the working dress of its employees, which should all be integrated to powerfully project the institutional image the organization wishes to convey, in accordance with the concepts expressed in its values and mission statements.

Here it is interesting to note the report by Roger Trapp (1998a) which alludes to a publication from the Centre for Tomorrow's Company on the subject of *company* annual reports. The Centre advises that the purpose and value of these reports would be increased if the watchwords for their publication were 'Sooner, Sharper and Simpler'. The Centre's document points out that while the primary audience for the reports is the companies' shareholders, an important secondary audience consists of the companies' stakeholders – customers, employees, suppliers and communities, including financial analysts, the media, policy makers and commentators. 'Companies now need to review their annual reports, in terms of their concept, their content, their delivery and their timing, and ask how effective a part they play in the total process of communication with their audiences', suggests the document (see Trapp, 1998b).

Packaging is another key feature of many a well-integrated communications campaign. It can also reveal a great deal about how ethical, or otherwise, an organization really is. As Cowe (1998) points out, concerning the labelling of packages:

- flavourings don't have to be listed by name and additives such as solvents and enzymes, used in processing and which may remain in the food, also escape listing;

- fruit and vegetables are not labelled but they may contain pesticide and insecticide residues and it is also possible that other chemical contaminants come from plastic packaging;

- processed food contains unhealthy fat, sugar and salt but the quantities may not be listed, while nutrition labelling is also voluntary;

- some labelling is based on half truths – '90 per cent fat free' really means with 10 per cent fat – over the accepted guidelines for a low-fat claim.

The public concern underlying such facts was demonstrated in March 1998 when a petition on the subject, signed by 1.3 million people, was delivered to the UK Prime Minister at 10 Downing Street.

The way in which communications are integrated is often demonstrated by the use of an organization's logotype. The *logotype* (or 'logo') is the term for its corporate symbol. This may be a badge (as on the bonnet of a motor vehicle), a stylized form of lettering, a coat of arms or some device which in the mind of the public becomes precisely and unmistakably identified with a particular organization. Often too, the logotype is produced in a distinctive colour or colour combination – the organization's livery colour(s). Examples are easily found – turquoise (Barclays Bank); red, white and blue (Esso Petroleum); green and yellow (B.P.); blue and white (Fiat); yellow and blue (Walls Ice Cream); red (Typhoo tea, Coca-Cola); green and gold (Marks and Spencer).

Vauxhall, Rover, Renault, Porsche, Kelloggs, Sainsburys, Hotpoint, Zanussi, BMW, Boots, Heinz – we live our lives against a background of corporate symbols, livery colours and general corporate communication. The subject of corporate marketing we shall return to, but at this point it is the need for *integration* which is being emphasised.

Every product, every service, every package, every advertisement and every promotional campaign must be so closely linked with each other and with every other possible aspect of an organization's operations that each new happening – a product, a merger, a technical achievement – benefits from the cumulative, repetitive force of what has gone before.

Promotion 'above and below the line'

Marketing practitioners often refer to some of the elements in the promotional mix as being *above the line* and to others as being *below the line*. The difference here is that the specialist firm handling a client organization's communications campaign (the advertising agency) will receive a commission from the media owners – newspaper publishers, commercial TV companies, etc. – on the client's communication expenditure which is 'above the line'. On 'below the line' expenditure, for example on such sales promotion expenditure as consumer competitions, reduced price offers and in-store displays, it will not.

Some say that the origin of these expressions derives from the line drawn by the advertising agent in his accounts which showed the items above the line on which commission was owing to him. Others say its origins lie in the UK tax regulations of former days.

Whatever the origin, the agency will receive up to 15 per cent of the value of press and TV advertising from the appropriate media owners, whereas for the below the line expenditure of his client in which he is involved, and for integration purposes he is invariably involved, he will negotiate a fee payable *from the client*. We shall come to the work of the agency and the related process of 'rounding up' the charges for its services before the end of the chapter.

Interrelationships between elements of the promotional mix

It may be the case that a promotional campaign on behalf of a 'major brand', that is an acknowledged leader in its field, will make extensive use of above the line advertising, for example large and often repeated newspaper advertisements and lengthy and frequent TV commercials. The sales volume achieved by the brand will probably generate the required promotional expenditure, which may amount to millions of pounds or dollars, without much difficulty.

On the other hand, it *could* be the case that a campaign is conducted solely through below the line media, for example a small organization lacking the funding for advertising may introduce a cheap kitchen tool by demonstrations in the housewares departments of large stores. Campaigns conducted exclusively below the line happen much less frequently, for it is usually the case that the 'above' and below the line elements are used in combination. An illustration of how this strategy operates and the underlying reasons for its adoption are provided by the 'case study' of an imaginary firm, which now follows.

Beautilux plc
Beautilux is renowned for its good quality bone china tableware (teasets and dinner sets). Its range has appealed hitherto to a number of income groups, hence the company's advertising slogan 'Real bone china – at prices to suit every pocket'. It has decided to introduce a new collection:

- of superb quality;
- with the most expensive types of patterned decoration;
- which it proposes to call its 'Flawless' range of 'heirloom tableware'.

Since the Flawless range will be at the very top of the price levels linked with this quality of product, the company is clear from its research that the market segment to be aimed for can be broadly described as the 'AB social grades, with some upwardly mobile C_1s'. This point is a key aspect of what can be described as the *positioning identification stage*.

The second stage entails deciding how best to secure that position in the market. Consequently, Flawless ware is expensively packaged in restrained and dignified colours and the Flawless brand symbol is rendered on the package in a rich, traditional form of lettering (i.e. 'typeface'). Distribution is confined to a limited number of high-class department stores and china shops which cater for a discriminating clientele.

These stores are listed in the advertisements for the Flawless range. The message (i.e. copy) in the advertising is somewhat subdued – it does not exhort consumers to dash out and buy the product, rather it advances the respectful suggestion that anyone seriously interested in seeing heirlooms of the finest craftsmanship and quality would do well to inspect the Flawless display cabinets in the listed stores. The advertisements are restricted to the expensive homemaker magazines and the colour supplements of the quality Sunday newspapers. So from this we can see how elements of the marketing mix – preparation, product, price, place and promotion are brought together to secure the envisaged market position. As to the 'people' element – employees are specially trained and selected for the production of Flawless; they are what Beautilux would objectively describe as its master craftsmen.

It transpires that the introduction of the Flawless range is a marked success and for the next few years the marketing strategy of Beautilux is to maintain its market position. It is able to do this with a promotional budget somewhat reduced from the level employed at the introductory stage, but it skilfully employs public relations techniques to sustain its image, for example business magazines feature articles on the total quality management techniques employed at the factory and the more general magazines report the visits of national and international celebrities to the Flawless production unit.

One or two competitors then introduce their own range of top quality bone china tableware using the Flawless approach, but Beautilux counter this subtly by advertising copy which emphasizes 'the originality and timelessness of a genuine heirloom'. Moreover, the company resists any appeal to widen its distribution beyond the original list of stores.

Several years pass, during which Beautilux has so developed its production techniques and employee skills that it can manufacture and market Flawless at lower costs and prices without the slightest reduction in quality. After continuous annual growth, however, sales are now beginning to level off. The marketing manager tells the board of directors:

> 'Flawless' is at the maturity stage of its life-cycle. To avoid decline we need to change its positioning. In my judgement, without breaking faith with existing customers, we can reduce it slightly in price and extend our distribution network a little. In this way, we shall widen our appeal among the C_1s and, if we offer the range through a number of 'starter packs', the young marrieds.

The changed strategy is agreed. It is based on a new advertising slogan – 'rarity with value' and potential customers are told that Flawless is available 'in many well-known stores and china shops'. Advertisements appear in 'middle-brow' magazines and, to a limited extent, on television. The new strategy is carefully explained to the limited number of original distributors. With few exceptions, they are persuaded that the increased sales potentially available through the change can usefully be traded off against their loss of local exclusivity.

Comment

The case study provides an example of how *positioning* provided the basis for a marketing strategy. We also saw how the promotional strategy served the marketing objectives as the positioning was:

- identified;
- secured;
- maintained;
- changed.

The promotional campaign consisted of restrained and dignified advertising in expensive homemaker magazines and quality Sunday colour supplements. This was the above the line promotion. It would be read at leisure and might lead to a family discussion, not least because the purchase of Flawless would be costly.

It was unlikely that the family would immediately dash out to inspect the tableware – few, if any, stores would be open when the Sunday supplements appeared in any event. Yet Beautilux knew that the well-to-do (its target market) are surrounded by the competing clamour of many advertisements. In order not to dissipate the force of its message it listed the stores where Flawless could be found and where, it suggested, the display cabinets could be inspected. The cabinets were part of its sales promotion, that is below the line expenditure and were an important link through which Beautilux hoped to lead prospective buyers through the sequence of:

- Attention;
- Interest;
- Desire;
- Action.

To obtain space for the cabinets in the leading stores targeted for distribution, Beautilux sales representatives visited their buyers well before the start of the consumer advertising in order to:

- acquaint them with the virtues of Flawless as a product;
- explain how its distribution was being arranged – i.e. on a restricted basis, through leading stores, each of which would be given sole selling rights for a precise geographical area;
- show the copy (words) and artwork (illustrations) for the proposed advertisements, together with a media schedule which listed the titles of the publications to be used, with the amount to be spent in each and in total;
- show details of the display cabinet, its specifications, quality, space and power requirements and negotiate its location;
- finalize a dealership contract and book the order for the introductory consignment of the tableware.

This process of achieving distribution had to be completed before the consumer advertising campaign otherwise an enterprising dealer would simply direct any enquiry for Flawless towards competitive high-quality tableware.

The role of public relations was also outlined in this brief case study. The articles concerning quality control and celebrity visits were intended to create a favourable atmosphere in which the effective selling of Flawless could continue.

So it becomes apparent how the elements of the communications mix – advertising, sales promotion, public relations, personal selling – were brought together in a co-ordinated campaign. The interrelationships between the elements can also be perceived – many dealers, for instance, though impressed with the product, would also seek reassurance about the measure of communications support being made available to pull the product through distribution, enabling them to make a speedy and satisfactory return on their own investment.

It is useful to note that it is not only above and below the line media which can be combined in communications campaigns. Where the consumer has to be 'educated' as well as 'informed' – as in the case of a technical product or one based on a revolutionary concept – television may be used as the primary medium to show how the product operates, with the press used as a secondary medium in which the technicalities involved are explained at greater length.

Or again, since television is an expensive medium, thus featuring short, sequential advertising ('it's there, it's gone') it is often used as the primary medium in a campaign with outdoor advertising (e.g. posters, transport advertising) acting in the secondary role of reminding the public of the product and the advertising theme when next they are in the vicinity of the shops.

Planning the promotional campaign

The *medium* (plural: media) is the channel of communication through which promotional effort is directed. Campaign planning involves the use of media in a combination balanced in a manner appropriate for the product/service and its target market.

Choosing a medium entails an examination of:

- its characteristics;
- 'atmosphere';
- quantitative coverage;
- cost.

The *characteristics* of the medium are the attributes it will make available to the communicator – its facility of sound, colour, movement, the printed word. The medium may offer the possibility of lengthy advertising content, or constant repetition of a brand image through the use of a catchy tune (a 'jingle') or the ability to remind the user of the message that has gone before in some other medium.

Other important characteristics are geographical coverage, composition of the audience it reaches (e.g. by age, sex, social grade, product usage, life-style, etc.), the frequency of its appearance (daily, weekly, monthly) and its power to reach special groups. In this last respect, some media may be so influential with special groups that their standing will extend to the advertisers' product. In fact, we might say of them that 'the medium is the message'.

Swindells says this of *atmosphere*:

> If we cannot measure atmosphere, at least we can try to define it. The atmosphere of an advertising medium derives from the state of mind of the readers, viewers or listeners at the time of exposure to the advertisement. It is generated partly by the medium and partly by the people themselves and what they are doing at that moment (Swindells, 1966, p 40).

Swindells goes on to say that the 'atmosphere' in any medium relates to nine factors. If we consider just two of these it will perhaps clarify the term:

- *The type of people using the medium.* The cinema is patronized mainly by 'young adults' (i.e. 15–24 age group); the 'atmosphere' of the medium is therefore youthful, light-hearted, escapist. *The Times* newspaper is read by affluent and influential people in business, politics, the arts, etc. They might be thought of as the leaders of opinion. Reflecting their needs and tastes, the atmosphere of *The Times* is therefore somewhat dignified and authoritative.

- *The conditions under which the medium is used.* Many of the morning and evening newspapers are read by people on their way to work – they are rushed and preoccupied but, even so, are looking for *news*, which must be presented as briefly as possible and with an adequate note of urgency. The atmosphere of the colour supplement to a national Sunday newspaper, because it is read in a more relaxed situation, will provide a different atmosphere for the advertiser. Because the atmosphere provided by the cinema is one of entertainment, the advertiser must bear this in mind in his or her creative approach. The advertiser on television must similarly bear in mind that the viewing population consists largely of family groups.

Quantitative coverage. Some of the ways in which the audiences for various media are analysed and described have been set out in the section on promotional research in Chapter 7. Coverage must be so planned that it overlays the target market as precisely as possible with minimal costly overlapping of other segments of little or no use to the advertiser.

Cost is self-explanatory. Frequently the expense of reaching the target market is measured in 'cost per thousand' terms. Obviously the *value* that a medium offers can only be assessed in relation to the other factors – characteristics, atmosphere and coverage. For example, a newspaper which predominantly caters for the lower social grade reader may nevertheless offer a better 'cost per thousand' coverage of the well-to-do than a more 'upmarket' newspaper. The editorial 'atmosphere' of the large circulation newspaper may be so unsuitable to a high quality product, however, that its producer would not think of advertising in it.

The ways in which decisions on the choice of media (television, newspapers, etc.) are made within the general planning framework are described in the section which follows.

The campaign plan

Among the major steps involved in the planning process, those set out below will be prominent.

Consideration of the objective(s)
This may be to introduce a new product or service; to remind users about an existing product; to develop some desired company 'image'; to give information about changes in price, specification, etc.; or one of a host of other objectives.

Consideration of the target market for the product or service
The 'market' here is taken to mean the ultimate users of the product or service and these must be described as precisely as possible in terms of age, sex, social grade, special interests, type of manufacturer, size of organization, geographical location, size of household, ownership of consumer durables, or whatever the appropriate classification may be.

The nature of the distribution channels
Examples include direct to manufacturers; direct to consumers (by mail order, advertiser's own showrooms or retail outlets); to consumers via retailers; to consumers via

wholesalers and retailers. This will be of particular importance where part of the advertising budget will be deployed to trade advertising.

Considerations of how the nature of the product or service will influence the nature of the message

Can it be treated humorously or seriously? Should the emphasis be on lengthy, technical explanation of the product in operation? Is visual treatment important? Is the product or service best portrayed in an atmosphere of escapism or romance? What is known about why users buy this category of product or service and how will this influence the nature of the message?

The budget available and the time period of the campaign

This really needs no explanation and although the most expensive campaigns are not necessarily the best ones, the advertiser has to be realistic about what media to use, what size of spaces to be purchased, the frequency with which advertisements are repeated during the campaign and whether certain facilities, such as colour, can be employed, for all of these are influenced by the size of the budget available, in absolute terms and in comparison to competitors' budgets, and the time period during which the budget will be employed (three months, six months, one year).

The characteristics, 'atmosphere', quantitative average and cost of advertising media

Examination of the media will ultimately lead to decisions on which media will be used as primary media and which (if appropriate) as support media; the balance of expenditure between media; the size of spaces and/or time segments for (a) impact and (b) repetition. Both above the line and below the line media are considered, if they are relevant to the product or service in question. The characteristics and 'atmosphere' of the various media have been outlined earlier. Details of the media readership and composition of television audiences are available from such sources as the National Readership Surveys (NRS Ltd) and the BARB TV audience surveys conducted by Taylor Nelson Sofres. Such syndicated services as the Target Group Index (TGI) are also very helpful and a number of independent surveys are carried out by media owners and are available for the scrutiny of the media department of the advertising agency. Media analysis and media 'schedule building' are often complex tasks requiring a great deal of knowledge and experience of the media and of their suitability for various products, services and objectives. The computer is used as an aid to planning the larger and more complex media schedules. All other things being equal, the buyer is seeking on behalf of the advertiser the largest coverage of the 'target' market at the lowest cost per thousand. (UK students who wish to acquaint themselves with the current costs of the various media should ask at their local Reference Library to see an up-to-date copy of *British Rate and Data* (BRAD) – an important guide to media buyers.)

The phasing of advertising through the campaign period

This is closely allied to the previous heading and involves a consideration of how the 'weight' of advertising should be spread through the period of the campaign. In a one-year schedule to launch a new product, for example, a disproportionately high amount of advertising may be undertaken in the first three months. The timing of the campaign will be of significance particularly if the demand for the product is seasonal. Also of importance will be the timing of the campaign to distributors preceding the main campaign to users. A 'contingency reserve' of funds is usually held back from the budget in order to meet situations arising during the campaign.

Integration of the campaign with other marketing activities

Included here will be considerations of personal selling programmes, point-of-sale display schemes and such other marketing activities as competitions, premium offers, 'celebrity' participations, sponsorship activities – all of which must be coordinated with the advertising in the service of the overall marketing objectives.

The budget and its control

If what has been said so far in this book about the marketing approach and the prudent use of resources is genuine, you would expect it implies, therefore, a rigorous analytical approach to fixing the communications budget.

Your thinking would be correct but there is a significant problem in that no model exists which demonstrates a clear relationship between communications expenditure and sales volume. Because we cannot absolutely predict how sales volume will vary relative to variations in promotional spending all that the marketing approach can ensure is that the element of managerial judgement necessary in fixing the budget is based on the best information available.

This at least enables us to dispense with the *arbitrary figure approach* (i.e. 'We spend £250,000 every year on advertising, come what may'). This bears no relation to sales volume or profit and gives no indication whether the figure arrived at is too much or too little. In either case, barring some miracle, it is bound to be wasteful.

The *percentage of sales method* has a more comforting ring to it and it has been popular. The appropriate percentage of expenditure required to achieve sales for the product group is applied to the forecast of sales revenue. The percentage varies according to the nature of the product (some products, e.g. fashion goods, will require a higher percentage of advertising support than staple commodities in consistent demand, such as nuts and bolts). It is obviously much more realistic to calculate the budget on the basis of *expected future sales* rather than past sales, for 'historic' data take no account of the changing nature of markets and, where the budget transpires to have been fixed at an artificially low level, it will have deprived the organization of taking advantage of favourable market opportunities.

The *level of competitors' expenditure* is another factor to be borne in mind, but merely to equalize it would again be basically wrong. It is a fact that, through syndicated research services (e.g. Nielsen) it is possible for advertisers of some products to learn what brand share of the market is being obtained by competitors for their weight of advertising expenditure. But each organization and each product is unique and to copy competitors may prove a poor strategy on several counts: it suggests, for example, that competitors have a closely controlled, analytical approach to calculating the budget, an assumption which may be without foundation. It also presupposes that the organization's promotional mix has the same proportionate make-up as that of competitors – but a competitor may be spending more on advertising because it has fewer salespeople.

Another approach can be described as the *margin remaining method*. Here the budget available is taken as the amount remaining when production costs plus marketing costs plus the desired return on capital are subtracted from anticipated sales revenue. Unhappily, this has its drawbacks too, for as volume and, hence, revenue expands, more funds are automatically available for advertising and other promotional activity but, since a certain 'momentum' has been developed, it may not in fact be needed. Conversely, if volume is static or contracting the supply of promotional funds is constricted at a time when heavier investment in promotion may be necessary to sustain the product's life.

Other approaches have included the use of *marketing models* to determine whether budgets were too large or too small and *media-weight tests* whereby different ITV regions have been subjected to different levels of advertising exposure for a given period, in order to assess the resulting changes in brand sales and market share. Experiments will also continue using *sensitivity analysis* via spreadsheets supported by the computer. These and more sophisticated techniques are being used in the search for rigour.

Given our incomplete knowledge of how advertising works, a more realistic approach to fixing the budget is provided by the *task method*. Here the objectives of the communications campaign are carefully defined and a scheme to accomplish these is designed. This scheme is then accurately costed and compared with the finance which appears to be available. If the plan is beyond the affordable resources, then consequential adjustments are made to it. If it still appears to be worthwhile, given that some revision of objectives will have been necessary, then it is adopted. Baker (1991, p 415) has described the task method as at least 'a realistic statement of what the firm can hope to accomplish related to current resources'. He has quoted data available from a survey of the British Institute of Management which showed that approximately one in five of the respondent firms adopted this method. Virtually the same percentage is reported by Crosier (1987, p 311) based on analysis of a number of surveys in the UK and USA during the period 1970–85.

In one sense, the organization should regard the promotional budget as a *cost*, but it is also true that it can be properly regarded as an *investment* and this is particularly so for the launch of a new product. Regard should also be paid to the various stages in the product life-cycle since this may have clear implications for budgetary strategy (e.g. a disproportionately high level of funding at the introduction stage and possible withdrawal at the decline stage).

This is a necessarily brief glance at the budgetary factors in marketing communications, a field for decision-making where there are no absolutes and in which there is room for intuitive judgement but where decisions must be better for having been made against a background of relevant information. In this respect, the organization's own past history of the influence that promotional expenditure has had on sales volume is an important input.

Dr Simon Broadbent (1984, p 203), a well-known British writer in this area of decision-making, once recommended that the organization ask itself four questions about the budget:

● What can the product afford?

● What is the advertising task?

● What are competitors spending?

● What have we learned from previous years?

Broadbent suggested that the questions approach the problem from different directions and rarely lead to the same answer, but they enable the organization 'to bracket the area in which a sensible answer lies'.

With regard to *control* of the budget, the principles of budgetary control apply to the promotion function just as assuredly as they do to the other functions (production, personnel, etc.). The schedule produced from the campaign plan will show the various periods and times to which expenditure has been allocated. Sales volume and cash flow projections must be monitored carefully in relation to this expenditure so that it can be increased, reduced or, at worst, curtailed, if actual results differ from the plan.

In this connection, the usual practice is to hold back a proportion of the budget, perhaps $7\frac{1}{2}$ per cent or so, as a *contingency reserve*. It may be left unspent if the main budget seems to be generating sufficient sales, it may be used to exploit a favourable situation, or it may be spent to meet any increase in the costs during the campaign (which would otherwise affect the planned frequency of advertisements, for example).

Information technology, providing speedy retrieval of data on sales pro rata to expenditure, makes possible quick control decisions and timely corrective action where necessary.

Before leaving the budget issue, it might be useful to mention the results of a research survey conducted by the London Business School on behalf of the Chartered Institute of Marketing and reported on briefly by the *Financial Times* in April 1996. The research was an attempt to discover some marketing performance norms for financial services companies, including the productivity of the marketing budget. At a conference, the leader of the research team reported: 'Our results suggest that it is difficult – if not impossible – to develop general industry-wide rules for spending on particular marketing activities. In fact, our results suggests there are no rules' (Swartz, 1996). In spite of this, the conference was told that:

- on average, companies in the sample saw twice the sales response for each £1 spent on below the line activities, than when spending above the line;
- that while *how* the budget is spent is undoubtedly important, *why* is it spent may be even more so, for example :
  - marketers focusing their expenditure on brand strength could expect to see increased customer retention,
  - a focus on customer satisfaction was associated with increased product profitability with satisfied customers being willing to pay a price premium while their satisfaction continued,
  - that the companies focusing on the development of new products and services are more effective in acquiring new customers.

This was one study of one industry but it does give food for thought not least because the researchers felt the findings did 'validate the importance of basing marketing decisions and marketing budgets on key marketing concepts'. Importantly too, the study suggested that individual companies must allocate funds for the development of cause-and-effect marketing models. Researchers felt that many organizations in the sample were failing in this regard (see Swartz, 1996).

We have now looked at the various elements of the communications mix and considered some aspects of their role. In the section which follows further thoughts are set out. The section begins by looking at the various advertising media.

Advertising

In the UK advertising attracts about a quarter of the total expenditure on marketing communications, the other main components of which are sales promotion and personal selling. It seems reasonable to suggest that advertising's proportion will be similar, at the least, in other advanced economics.

As we saw in the AIDA model, it can be used to inform the market about the product and arouse interest in it. Where the product is new advertising has an educational function to perform. In order to develop desire the advertising campaign must persuade the market that the product delivers substantial user benefits compared with its costs. It must also stimulate purchasing and as we have seen, this often means a two-stage process of primary advertising to convey the reasoned selling argument for the product, based on the 'unique selling proposition' (USP) and reminder advertising at or near the point-of-sale.

Because of the doubt and uncertainty which often arises after purchases (and particularly major ones), *reassurance advertising* has an important part to play in countering this *cognitive dissonance* (see Chapter 7). When supported by an adequate after–market service, reassurance advertising helps to establish the conviction that the purchase was indeed a wise one.

Sir William Crawford, one of the great early practitioners of advertising, expressed the view that sound advertising tactics can be summarized in the three word precept:

Concentration – Domination – Repetition

- *Concentration* implies careful selection of the appeal best calculated to gain favourable response from the target market (i.e. the USP).

- *Domination* means amassing the financial and presentational power to create a dominant impact on the potential user. This usually means using large advertisements in the early stages of a campaign to outweigh the competition. Where the budget is insufficient to cover all possible prospective users, a choice may have to be made to dominate a smaller geographical area or some other medium.

- *Repetition* implies that the campaign must be continued over an adequate period of time. Products drop too easily out of mind, the first stages of the campaign will not reach everyone targeted and, with most consumer products, it is the repeat purchases which bring a return on the investment.

Of Crawford's precept, Hobson says: 'It is still, and must always be, the clearest reflection of the processes which go to make up mass selling' (1988, p 261).

The various advertising media available in the UK are described below. Their attributes hold good for advertisers in all countries except that the relative importance of some media will change somewhat from country to country – for example, radio is a minor medium in the UK (3 per cent of national advertising expenditure) but in some countries with low levels of literacy it is a very significant medium.

Before saying more about the various advertising media, based on UK experience, the data in Table 11.1 are set out to fix each of media within the overall framework.

The press

The term 'the press' covers an extensive range of publications including national newspapers, regional newspapers and magazines. Uniquely, Britain has both daily

Media category	Expenditure (£ million)	Percentage of total
National newspapers	1,650	12.6
Regional newspapers	2,237	17.0
Consumer magazines	660	5.0
Business and professional	1,106	8.4
Directories	737	5.6
Press production costs	577	4.4
Total press	6,967	53.0
Television	3,651	27.8
Direct mail	1,540	11.7
Outdoor and transport	500	3.8
Radio	393	3.0
Cinema	88	0.7
Total	13,139	100.0

Table 11.1. *Total UK advertising expenditure by media category, 1997*

Source: The Advertising Association, 15 June 1998.

and Sunday newspapers that are truly *national* – they have large circulations and are useful, therefore, for mass marketing.

Although the distinctions are a little less clear of late, their writing style, feature material, layout and political/economic content enables them to be divided into 'qualities' and 'populars'. In turn, this enables advertisers to direct their message to particular segments of the population in accordance with marketing objectives. The national newspaper circulation, that is the sales figure ratified by the Audit Bureau of Circulations (ABC), is given for September 1997 in Table 11.2. It has been divided into quality and popular classifications.

The flexibility of the national newspapers – in addition to their ability to reach all types of target markets – extends to the size of the advertisement it is possible to feature (from a large 'display' advertisement to a 'classified' one of a few words of copy). Colour facilities are also generally available either in the newspaper itself or in the colour supplements.

The *regional press* is an even bigger medium than the nationals (in 1997 it attracted 17 per cent of total expenditure, 4.4 per cent more than national newspapers). It is rooted in the affairs of the local community and some observers believe it is read more closely than the national press. A great deal of the advertising is of the classified type and in the last three decades the regional press has been supplemented by the *freesheet press* which is distributed without charge to households, being paid for by advertising revenue and which has succeeded in attracting national as well as local advertising.

Magazines can be divided into the following groups:

- *general interest* (e.g. *Ideal Home, Readers Digest, TV Times*) which are similar to the national press, being frequently used for national advertising campaigns;

- *specialist interest* (e.g. *Amateur Gardening, Amateur Photographer, Motor*, etc.) which cover highly particularized markets and whose advertisements are often read as closely as the articles they contain;

- *trade, technical and professional magazines*, which are excellent channels of communication to retailers (to induce them to stock up in advance of advertising) and to announce news of new products, processes, developments, etc., to engineers, accountants, medical practitioners, etc.

The magazine field is one of continuous and interesting developments. The latest of these are as follows:

- the ever-increasing number of specialist magazines which are targeting readers in need of advice on personal finance, and

- the steadily increasing number of *contract magazines* which, because they are produced for a select mailing list, offer advertisers a more tightly targeted readership than many conventional magazines – the country's largest title in this sector, *AA Magazine*, is despatched to nearly 4 million of the Association's members.

Qualities				Populars			
Daily		**Sunday**		**Daily**		**Sunday**	
Telegraph	1,129,777	The Times	1,449,113	Sun	3,877,097	News of	
Guardian	428,010	Telegraph	938,253	Mirror	2,442,078	the World	4,620,415
The Times	821,000	Observer	498,086	Record	703,090	Mirror	2,424,000
Independent	288,182	Independent	311,321	Star	729,991	People	2,001,978
Financial Times	326,516			Mail	2,344,183	Mail	2,322,423
				Express	1,241,336	Express	1,261,690

Table 11.2. *UK National newspaper circulation – September 1997*

Source: Audit Bureau of Circulations (ABC).

Television

This is a mass medium (nearly all UK households own a television set) but a flexible one in that campaigns can be built up into national proportions through extending them region by region.

Large families with young children are an important segment and the medium has revolutionized advertising in the latter half of this century offering as it does the facility to demonstrate products, supported by colour and sound facilities.

The presence of a relaxed, family atmosphere also offers its special advantages to the advertiser and the musical jingle often used to develop 'brand identity' for a product or service has proved a powerful phenomenon. Because television is sequential ('it's there – it's gone') the advertiser must tell his story in fairly stark and simple terms. Press advertising is therefore often used in conjunction with TV, so that the potential user can seek more detailed information on colour, size, price, etc.

As will be noted from Table 11.1, in the UK, television recently accounted for virtually 28 per cent of total advertising expenditure. Another striking development in this medium is the radical alteration in the number of commercial channels available. In addition to ITV (Independent Television), Channel 4 and the recently opened Channel 5 have provided advertisers with national terrestrial commercial stations. Additionally, up to the end of 1996 there were between 40 and 50 satellite and cable channels available to the advertiser. Moreover, although the Internet is still in its infancy it is being steadily recognised as a valuable channel with which to reach lucrative markets.

Archer (1996) points out, however, that this 'embarrassment of riches' will enable organizations to better target their commercial messages, for example to 18–34 year old ABC men or C_2DE housewives with children rather than just all adults. She points out, however, that to late 1996 this proliferation of choice had not increased either the number of TV viewers or the average hours per week spent viewing.

Because the audience share of ITV has been reduced by this fragmentation, advertisers seeking to reach large markets can no longer do this through the uncomplicated use of a single channel (ITV). As Archer explains, the process of constructing a TV schedule that delivers the right amount of *cover* (numbers of people reached) with the required *frequency* (number of times those people are reached) is now far more complex.

It will be interesting to see how further developments affect the use of this powerful advertising medium particularly when the methodology becomes available to measure the value of the Internet for promotion purposes and digital TV becomes widely available.

Direct mail

One of the most important attributes of this medium is that a particular target market can be approached with minimal wastage. For this reason it is particularly suitable where the total market is carefully defined and documented, as is the case with manufacturers of specialized industrial products and members of particular trades and professions. In the case of the industrial buyer, for example, the catalogues and price lists of supplying firms, with all the accompanying technical data, become part of his 'stock in trade' and much of it is filed away carefully.

Although it is a highly selective medium, it is also used in conjunction with mass-produced consumer products, usually accompanying the launching of new products with offers of samples, gift coupons, bonus offers and price reductions (although in this case the distribution is often carried out on a door-to-door basis rather than through the mail). Although the medium is relatively inexpensive, in fields where it is widely used the advertiser would do well to make the literature and the accompanying letters as attractive as possible, so that the material is handled and studied rather than despatched to the waste bin. It is particularly suitable for products and services for which a 'private' approach is important and it is of powerful assistance to other types of marketing communication, particularly personal selling.

It is interesting to note that while the respective shares of UK national expenditure for each of the media have largely held good for the last ten years, direct mail has increased its share from 7 per cent (1987) to approaching 12 per cent (1997). Its popularity widens as direct marketing, noted earlier in the text, continues to develop. In this respect the heading 'direct mail' should perhaps be more accurately subsumed under the 'direct marketing' label for in addition to the post, it is possible to conduct one-to-one communication with customers via the fax machine, e-mail, the Internet, a network of personal computers, not to mention the telephone and the personal sales visit.

Reverting to direct mail itself, it is a medium which attracts a fair amount of the criticism levelled at what is mistakenly called 'marketing'. Its critics point to the costs and irritation generated by 'junk mail'. The Direct Marketing Association has countered that one-to-one direct mail is only junk mail when it is inappropriate, poorly targeted and badly written. Quoting statistics from the Direct Mail Information Service, Craig Seton (1998) draws attention to the following:

- consumers spend on average about £83 for each item of direct mail to which they respond and they make, on average, three responses per year;
- direct mailings in Britain rose by 126 per cent to 3173 million items in 1996 – two-thirds to consumer households, one-third to business;
- 84 per cent of business direct mail is opened, 17 per cent redirected to a colleague and 13 per cent is filed or answered;
- 77 per cent of consumer direct mail is opened, 63 per cent is opened and read and 33 per cent is kept or passed on to someone else;
- almost one in 10 items of direct mail is requested by consumers.

The medium has pronounced value for *customer retention* which, as previously noted, is a more profitable process than seeking to establish new customers. Keeping in touch with customers by way of thank-you letters and seasonal greetings augment the effectiveness of the sales letter. According to Rodney Hobson (1997) research supports the view that companies need to do more to keep in touch with their customers as an essential ingredient of keeping their trade. He cites the experience of publishers McGraw-Hill who found that two-thirds of customers who switch suppliers do so because they are treated with indifference. Only one in six drifted away through dissatisfaction with the product or service.

Direct mail is a medium likely to increase its share of the national advertising spend. The UK's Royal Mail service obtains about £800 million per year from postage revenue through direct mail and, as its national business marketing director points out, the rapidly falling costs of building high quality databases and acquiring the IT tools to manage them means a cost-effective direct mail system is now possible for even very small firms.

Although the smaller media – poster and transport, radio and cinema – collectively accounted for only 7.5 per cent of total advertising expenditure in 1997, as the Advertising Association indicates (1998) that amounted to £981 million, which is hardly insignificant. It is also important to say something about the characteristics of these media and their potential value for advertising campaigns, hence the short descriptions which follow.

Outdoor and transport media

Although occasionally the theme of a campaign can be condensed within the limitations of outdoor media so that they can be used as main media, the primary function of most outdoor advertising is to *remind* the potential users of the product or service whilst they are at or near the point-of-sale. Mostly the message confines itself to a simple statement, a short slogan, an illustration or a brand name. It has to communicate its message quickly – because a quick glance may be all it will receive. Often the reminder function is to help the user to recollect the other advertising (e.g. on television, in newspapers) where the benefits of the product of service were set out at greater length. Thus the term 'support medium' is frequently used to describe this type of advertising. Products whose sales message can be briefly conveyed, for example petrol, food, drink and travel, figure prominently in the medium. In addition to the sites available on highways and in streets and shopping precincts for posters, painted signs and illuminated displays, etc., 2000 railway stations and 21,000 buses offer sites for the UK advertiser.

A most important characteristic of the medium is the opportunity it provides for using a wide range of colours to the best and most imaginative effect.

It is interesting to note that in early 1998 a firm of accountants undertook a £500,000 poster campaign to get its brand name noted and as a prelude to a follow-up call to companies. It seems odd that accountants should use a medium of mass-marketing when they have precise information on their target markets. As Lee (1998, p 13) suggests, however, in a field characterized by acquisitions and mergers there is a trend for firms to re-evaluate the way they market themselves. Perhaps it is also an indication that, in seeking differentiation from competitors, there are no absolutes.

Radio

Like outdoor advertising, radio is used in the UK mainly as a support medium. However, in the last 25 years a network of local commercial radio stations has become established, its weekly coverage extending to very many urban areas and reaching approximately half the total population. Through this network it is therefore possible to construct what would amount to a national campaign.

The audience consists mainly of housewives during the hours of daytime broadcasting, while young adults predominate in the evenings. The morning and evening commuter rush hours are important segments within which to reach motorists. It has the important characteristic of sound with which to build the appropriate advertising atmosphere, but it is not likely to develop its appeal to advertisers in general beyond the support function.

Even so, radio has increased its share of total expenditure from 1.8 per cent in 1990 to 3.0 per cent in 1997. In this context, the figures for 1995 indicate significant increases in the expenditure of the medium's leading advertisers (see Table 11.3). Although the medium has benefited from the large increases of two relative newcomers, Coca-Cola and lottery organizer, Camelot, other advertisers including Ford have registered notable increases.

Cinema

This medium attracts less than 1 per cent of total advertising expenditure. It suffered greatly from the advent of television so that its vast audiences of the 1940s and 1950s have vanished. Today it is primarily a medium to reach young adults (15–24 age group) and therefore such products as soft drinks, confectionery, cosmetics and health and beauty services are best suited to it.

Building societies also use the medium because the audience contains a significant proportion of young marrieds as well as prospective marrieds. Cinema advertising is

Advertiser	Expenditure 1994	Expenditure 1995	% Increase
McDonalds	3,634	3,952	8.0
Dixons Stores Group	1,383	3,603	160.5
Kimberley Clark	2,033	3,159	55.4
Coca-Cola	486	3,013	520.0
Camelot Group	531	2,620	393.4
Carphone Warehouse	1,486	2,397	61.3
Renault	1,378	2,094	52.0
Ford Motor Co. Ltd.	350	2,014	475.4
British Telecom	1,936	2,014	4.0
Mirror Group Newspapers	769	2,010	161.4

Table 11.3. *Leading advertisers – UK radio (expenditure in £000s)*

Source: MEAL/Radio Advertising Bureau and the Observer, 10 March 1996 issue

also an important vehicle for local organizations, particularly retailers. It offers colour, sound and its own particular 'atmosphere' for advertising, as described earlier. Apart from the slide advertising used mainly by local organizations, 30-second and 60-second films are available.

Sales promotion

It seems likely that UK organizations spend marginally more in total on sales promotion than they do on advertising. It is therefore an important industry, engaging significant creative thinking and with its own rewards for excellence via judges acting on behalf of the Institute of Sales Promotion (ISP). In this section we shall be looking at the key elements in sales promotion expenditure.

Incentive and loyalty schemes

Marketing organizations wishing to expand sales, reward the loyalty of existing customers, or find new customers, often use sales promotion schemes as part of their promotional mix. Perhaps the best way to describe types and functions is to provide one or two examples from the vast number employed each year.

In the highly competitive civil aviation markets, airlines work hard to attract customers' business and reward loyalty generously. A popular method of sales promotion is the use of *air miles*, originally used by British Airways and now employed by many of its competitors. In outline, air miles work as follows:

- they are reward points given free to customers by an airline;
- they can be exchanged in many ways, e.g. for more air travel or for car hire, hotel accommodation, holidays, etc.;
- these reward points are increased as the customer increases travel with one airline;
- advance booking or travel at unpopular times is often rewarded by an increased ratio of air miles awarded:miles travelled;
- air miles are awarded to the individual business traveller even if the employer pays the air fare;
- incentives extra to the airmiles may also be offered to 'club members' who qualify for membership by their frequent travel.

Lufthansa provides a glimpse of air travel in an earlier age through one of its 'fantasy awards' in which air miles can earn a 30 minute flight on its refurbished JU 52 which first entered service in 1936. Passengers of KLM can exchange their loyalty points for a cookery course in Paris. United Airlines invited customers to bid their travel points in an auction, with an aircraft being named after the winner.

Sales promotion schemes are also highly visible in the consumer banking section. A bank may, for example, devise a promotional package for the student segment offering interest free banking, free overdrafts, a gift of cash and a scratchcard offering free rent to the lucky card holders. TSB, focusing specifically on 16–20 year olds, built on its association with the cinema medium and offered vouchers redeemable at 300 UK cinemas.

Point-of-sale display

Sales promotion also includes the use of showcards, window-stickers, 'mobiles', illuminated displays, electrical signs, 'crowners' (to fit over cans, jars and other containers) and leaflets, booklets, folders, etc. This is alternatively termed 'merchandising material' – a reasonable definition of 'merchandising' being 'anything at or near the point-of-sale which is designed to assist purchase'. Where illuminated displays and external signs are used which show the distributor as an 'approved stockist', it is frequently the case that the distributor provides an after sales service for the product, including the supply of spare parts and/or has exclusive selling rights in that geographical area.

Point-of-sale display material is often linked to sales promotion schemes including coupon, special pack, premium offers and other methods of inducing users to try a new product or remain loyal to an existing product or brand. Marketing organizations occasionally use consumer competitions as part of their communications strategy – this is also helpful in indicating the preference points of the consumer and can be an aid to further product development. Point-of-sale material often has an important role in promoting such competitions.

As a medium, it offers the advertiser the facilities of motion, colour and even sound. The message it carries, which may be no more than a representation of the brand and a simple slogan, must be integrated with the rest of the campaign and should instantly remind the viewer of what is being communicated in that campaign. In this way it will increase the productivity of expenditure in other media. It must be attractive and eye-catching. Not only is this important for its promotional task but also to secure retailer cooperation – for it can undoubtedly help to increase the rate of sales at retail level and thus also help to extend the number of retailers willing to stock the product.

The merchandising function (which consists of assembling the display material, placing it in a visible and busy position in retail premises and, if appropriate, keeping it adequately stocked) is sometimes carried out by the retailer's staff, sometimes by the advertiser's own salespeople and sometimes by both. Where distribution channels include wholesalers, the point-of-sale material is often included with the products and offered 'free' to retailers as an inducement to purchase standard packs which obviate the need for breaking bulk into very small quantities. Merchandising material is particularly effective in increasing the rate of retail sales ('stock-turn') of products bought on impulse.

Packaging

In Chapter 8, the functional and symbolic role of packaging was described enabling us to understand it as a vital link in the promotional mix. Unless the design and other features of the package are tightly integrated with the message being conveyed by the other media then the campaign can only lead to confusion and may indeed fail.

Another reason for the significance of packaging arises from the dominance of the multiple chains in retail distribution. Since their method of selling excludes the use of point-of-sale material in the store, the package must take on this role and become the 'silent salesperson' on the supermarket shelf.

Earlier mention has also been made of the legal and ethical aspects of packaging, particularly with regard to food labelling. In its February 1997 report 'Messages on Food', the National Consumer Council urged the UK government to consider banning such claims as 'nature's way to reduce cholesterol' and 'essential for healthy living'. The Council considered that the proliferation of health messages on foods 'is confusing consumers and may be obscuring advice about a healthy, balanced diet' (Maitland, 1997).

Packaging is an important marketing tool and its design and development must be given careful attention if it is to work in the manifold interests of the customer.

Exhibitions

Exhibitions encompass a broad media heading and it includes:

- the giant international fairs – e.g. the world's largest industrial fair at Hanover;
- national exhibitions for the general public – e.g. the UK's Motor Show, DIY and Home Improvement Show, the Good Food Show;
- national trade exhibitions for wholesale and retail distributors – e.g. the Gifts and Fancy Goods Fair, Toy Fair;
- national technical exhibitions for manufacturing users – e.g. The UK Machine Tools Exhibition;
- local exhibitions – e.g. the UK's County Shows and exhibitions organized by local chambers of trade.

Fairs and exhibitions have a hallowed tradition of importance to economic activity and a great deal of our commercial law sprang from the need to regulate trading at these fairs. The keynote throughout this book has been that all marketing activity should be closely integrated. Alles clarifies this when he says of exhibitions: 'If marketing started in the market place and exhibitions claim to be directly descended from the great markets which became great trade fairs, then it is only appropriate that exhibitions should be studied for what they are – marketing tools' (Alles, 1973, p 11).

Exhibitions enable the seller not only to display his or her products, to obtain orders and to negotiate selling agreements for them, but also to obtain, at first hand, important reaction to the product and its distribution and promotional policies. Because the actual product can be shown, operated, dismantled, heard, tested, lifted, adjusted, etc., exhibitions are particularly important to industrial advertisers. Consequently, they often attract a substantial part of the communications budget for the marketing of industrial goods.

From the buyer's viewpoint, exhibitions provide an important shop window in which the comprehensive range of products available can be carefully assessed, prices and delivery terms can be negotiated and purchasing contracts can be finalized. At large general exhibitions within a particular field, for example engineering, the seller can also place orders with other exhibitors (e.g. for components, sub-assemblies). Participation at important international exhibitions often enables marketing organizations to enter overseas markets and to assess potential competitors.

The design of the exhibition stand, the efficiency and knowledge of the selling staff and the speed with which enquiries and orders are dealt with, all enable the organization to project itself powerfully to its markets. What is more, where the exhibition is specialized, the exhibitor knows he has the increased opportunity of making productive use of the time and expenditure involved.

Recently there have been a number of dramatic developments in the use of graphics on exhibition stands which have markedly increased their impact and pulling power. Digital imaging and large format high-resolution printing are important factors here. The National Exhibition Centre in Birmingham launched its own television station in March 1998 broadcasting through 250 screens across the entire complex. This means, among other things, that all exhibitors at the NEC can operate interactive display systems, increasing the attractiveness of their stands for potential clients.

According to a survey of members by the Incorporated Society of British Advertisers (ISBA) reported in March 1996, UK companies spend more on exhibitions than they do on radio, posters and cinema combined – approximately 8.7 per cent of *all* UK media expenditure. According to Ellings commenting in April 1998, the exhibition industry was then growing in the UK by at least 10 per cent per year, both in terms of metres (i.e. the amount of space on show) and money. He added: 'Business is booming in part because exhibitions are now seen as a valuable opportunity to target exactly those hard-to-reach groups that other media struggle to target' (see Cook, 1998).

Public relations

At the beginning of this chapter, we noted that *public relations* (PR) entailed a deliberate and sustained effort to create mutually beneficial relationships between an organization and its stakeholding publics. We also recognize that an organization has many such 'publics' – its employees, suppliers, shareholders, the citizens of the community where it is located, departments of central and local government, etc., and, by no means least, its customers – both users and distributors. The role of public relations is to establish and maintain understanding and goodwill for the organization's products and services, activities and operating policies. The organization may have a new product, a new process, it may intend to build a new factory, to merge with or acquire other organizations, or it may have secured a large contract. It thus has a story to tell, or a policy to explain; or it may be called upon to defend its manufacturing processes by some anti-pollution lobby (assuming the processes *are* defensible). It will approach the national and local press, the specialist magazine, radio or television, in order to obtain editorial coverage or air time so that its story can be told. In these instances, the business organization has no control over the content of the communication, the editorial decisions being taken by the media owners. For this reason, it is important that the items being put forward are newsworthy and attractively presented – for there is no shortage of other organizations believing that they are 'doing good and hoping to get the credit for it'.

So it can be seen that public relations is not only concerned with communicating for marketing purposes, but also for the broader purpose of creating a favourable atmosphere within which the organization may operate successfully. Where it is used to support the marketing of new products, it is usually the case that the product is novel, of some technical complexity, or likely to meet with prejudice or doubt. In this case the organization will attempt to obtain an editorial feature or a segment in a television programme (of the 'Tomorrow's World' type – 'popular' science aimed at the family audience) so that its operating principles and benefits can be explained.

The field of public relations includes *press relations*, which attempts to serve the same range of organizational objectives, but exclusively through the medium of the press. To illustrate how press relations operate, let us consider an imaginary, but none the less realistic, example.

The Chopit (Wundacut Machine Company)

Wundacut is a leading manufacturer of lawn mowers. It manufactures and markets an extensive range of these in various cutting widths – 12 in., 18 in., 20 in. and 24 in. Petrol and electrically driven models are available in each of these widths. The company also produces a cultivator for mixing and aerating topsoil and a range of electronically driven chain-saws.

From its marketing research it has recently learned that, despite the established competition, a substantial demand exists for a hand-held, portable, lightweight garden tool capable of trimming lawn edges and cutting down weeds, particularly in such relatively inaccessible places as the bases of walls and trees and the spaces beneath garden fences.

After careful research and development Wundacut produces the Chopit, a battery operated cordless trimmer/weeder which utilizes an automatically fed nylon line as its cutting mechanism. A prototype Chopit is then extensively tested by a consumer panel of 24 amateur gardeners, so that its engineering, design and safety-in-use come in for careful scrutiny. These gardeners are told that while the trimmer/weeder is designed for the amateur market it is, in fact, capable of heavier-duty work than competitive products. Because of this and a number of other quality features the Chopit will retail at a top-of-the-market price of £100 inclusive of a full one-year warranty.

Tests within the panel are successful and there is no aversion to the proposed price. In fact, the tests demonstrate that Wundacut has succeeded in devising a garden tool which, speedily and effectively, trims areas around trees, shrubs, walls, paths and patios with minimum breakage of the cutting line. When breakage does occur, the automatic feed device enables the trimmer to become fully operational within seconds.

Having evidence of such positive user-response, Wundacut decides to market the product from 1 January in order to have the product accessible to users in time for the 'gardening season' beginning at Easter, when it is planned that television advertising and full-page advertising in such specialist magazines as *Amateur Gardening* and *Popular Gardening* will begin to appear.

During the tests, a member of the consumer panel, agreeing that the Chopit would do somewhat heavier work than other trimmer/weeders designed for the amateur added 'It's certainly no toy – but using it is child's play'. Following agreement of the panel member and an unsolicited gift from Wundacut, the advertising agency planning the promotional campaign introduces the Chopit to the market with the slogan 'No toy – but child's play' as a constantly recurring theme in all the advertising and the sales promotional material sited in gardening centres and DIY stores.

Before the main advertising campaign commences, Wundacut releases to the national and the specialist press a detailed description of the special attributes of the Chopit and why the company has decided to add a trimmer/weeder to its range of products. The *press release* incorporates the results of the user trials and is accompanied by a video of the Chopit in action, presented by a nationally known figure in the gardening world, who also appears in life-size, cut-out point-of-sale material holding the Chopit. The PR activity of Wundacut also includes efforts to have the Chopit used and discussed in TV gardening programmes.

This is an example of how PR activities can be used in an integrated campaign and how it can cross-brace the use of other promotional media. We have to remember, however, in the context of PR, that the media approached are not working for Wundacut but for their own readers, viewers, listeners and shareholders. So the 'news' in the press release has to be really newsworthy to gain attention and space. The Chopit, after all, is hardly revolutionary – a number of competitive versions are already on the market. The production of a good quality video is a skilled business, probably requiring the services of a specialist production unit. A good visual, however, may convey more than a thousand words particularly with a product crying out for demonstration.

Public relations can also be organized through articles in house journals, by the production of films for showing to relevant 'publics' and by provision of facilities for factory visits. In such cases, the organization *does* have control of communications content and communication is again an exchange process, in that ideal opportunities exist for canvassing the opinions of actual and potential users, essentially for conducting consumer research. As a leading writer, Norman Hart, has pointed out, in developing its public relations activities to support its marketing strategy, a firm's procedure will follow the same principles of planning as for other activities, but with written objectives broken down under 'publics' instead of 'products'. The same media may be used for achieving these objectives as are used in the marketing communications campaign (e.g. press advertising, television, etc.). Sponsorship is another important medium through which the organization can develop the necessary corporate image in its external environment to support its marketing operations. Sponsorship is outlined later in this chapter.

It must be remembered that the external environment comprises more than consumers and society in general, important though these are. Success in a marketing campaign clearly requires the enthusiastic support of dealers. A flow of regular communication to them by way of newsletters, conferences, exhibitions, etc., is an important public relations activity. Similarly, suppliers must be made to feel an important 'part of the team' if quality and reliability are to be among the hallmarks of the firm's market image. And we must not forget that the 'internal' environment is one that must be carefully nurtured and cultivated too – many companies today have some form of employee communication designed to develop the customer orientation of production, sales and other members of the organization. Video presentations are also being increasingly widely used for training and communication.

As we shall see in Chapter 13, where *corporate marketing* is outlined, public relations can do much to create a favourable climate in which effective marketing can be carried out. But it is not for the unskilled and it requires as much planning and organizing as every other part of marketing activity. Writing in 1998, Pritchard made the point that though its practitioners are image-builders, public relations 'is a business with a less than positive image' so that 'Super salaried spin doctors and pushy publicists grab the headlines, seemingly as often as their clients' (Pritchard, 1998, p 13).

Pritchard added, however, that away from politicians and stars, public relations is a serious and fast-growing business. The Institute of Public Relations (IPR) in the UK reports annual membership rises of 7 per cent. It is also a business which is becoming more professional, one where qualifications play an increasingly important role. Pritchard notes that Stirling University's M.Sc. course in public relations, now in its tenth year, includes units on research methods, international media and ethics. Among institutions developing new programmes is UMIST's Manchester Business School (MA in corporate communications) supported by ten companies including British Gas, British Aerospace, Tesco and United Utilities. As this chapter was being written, the IPR intended to launch its own diploma programme in September 1998, a 24 week course for people already working in PR, but who have no relevant qualification.

Pritchard also indicates that companies are putting more emphasis on public relations and shifting resources away from advertising and adds that at Stirling, most of the UK students have job offers before they complete the M.Sc. programme. We will return to the subject of PR in Chapter 13.

Personal selling

Personal selling is the form of sales communications in which negotiations are conducted *directly* with potential customers, usually at the customer's premises or at exhibitions. As Doyle (1994, p 239) indicates, personal selling accounts for the largest proportion of the UK's communications mix expenditure by far. Sales personnel play a vital role in the achievement of sales and marketing objectives – as someone once wisely remarked 'Nothing happens until somebody sells something'. Yet the function of sales personnel extends well beyond their key task of generating sales revenue, as Figure 11.4 illustrates.

The illustration aims to convey how, in their boundary role between supplier and customer, sales personnel are prominent in the two-way exchange of information. This is one of the many ways in which adequately trained and informed sales personnel are significant contributors to the concept of 'market-induced flow'. Let us now look at some aspects of personal selling operations.

Face-to-face selling is particularly appropriate where the product or service is relatively complex and requires detailed explanation and perhaps a demonstration in use. It is thus an important element of communication in the marketing of industrial products and allows also for clarification of the terms and conditions of after sales service, which is frequently an important aspect of negotiations in this field. It is also widely used in the marketing of consumer products although, where these are mass-produced and widely advertised, the salesperson's role in the interview is more concerned with explanations of suppliers' discounts and advertising support than with the features of the product.

Where the organization is new, where the product is new, or where the organization is entering new markets, the face-to-face interview is an important and powerful

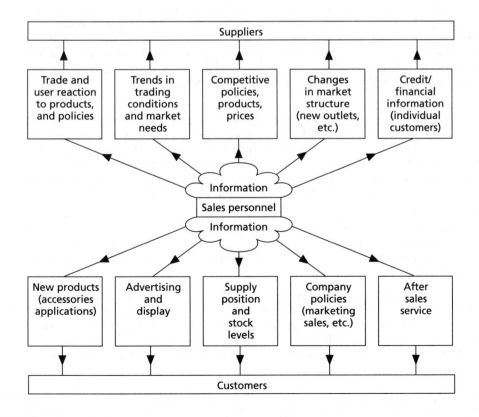

Figure 11.4. *Sales personnel as the information link between suppliers and their customers*

method of sales communication, if properly conducted by an adequately prepared and knowledgeable salesperson. Where it is important for the salesperson to observe at first hand the needs of the customer and adjust his or her proposals accordingly, there is, of course, no substitute for the face-to-face interview. It is also of value where the organization relies on its salesforce for feedback of marketing research information. Where negotiations are likely to be detailed and protracted, the face-to-face interview allows the prospective buyer ample opportunity to raise queries concerning the specifications, price, colour, output rate, etc., of whatever is being offered and, in most cases, the salesperson has an equal opportunity to deal with these and to underline the reasons why, in the marketing organization's view, the product or service on offer is preferable to competitors' products or services.

Face-to-face selling in the consumer goods field is often an important adjunct to other means of marketing communication: in order to ensure that advertising to the consumer is suitably productive, distributive outlets have to carry sufficient stocks of the product and display reminder advertising where this is appropriate. (The face-to-face interview is sometimes the most effective method of attending to other important aspects of the supplier's business, such as the collection of outstanding accounts! Cash flow considerations become extremely important when the supplier also has to finance an extensive advertising campaign.)

Where a number of personnel, either in the supplying organization or the customer organization or in both, are involved in sales negotiations face-to-face communication is of great consequence.

Telephone selling is a relatively cheap method of making contact with potential customers and attempting to sell to them – it is certainly much more economical than the salesperson's call. Against this, it does impose constraints on the communicator who must secure favourable attention very quickly and convey, briefly but effectively, the details of the sales proposal. For this reason, the argument in favour of what is being offered must be capable of being condensed into headlines, leaving little in the way of requisite explanation. The method has been successfully used in the UK for the selling of advertising space in newspapers and of time segments for television advertising. The prospect knows the medium well enough and interest will therefore centre on the cost, together with details of any special discounts available, or special prices being quoted as a result of cancellations, etc. The media very often use the telephone to secure flanking advertising support for editorial special features (although in the author's opinion these are often overdone).

Where the organization is known to the potential customer and its products or services equally known and accepted, the telephone can be a low-cost, effective method of sales communication. It is obviously well-suited to obtaining repeat business, therefore. In practice, where the product is branded and/or standardized in quality, leaving only one or two variables in the sales proposal (e.g. price, discounts, special offers), it is particularly suitable. Frozen foods and other grocery products are frequently sold to retailers on this basis – the telephone call establishing whether stock levels are adequate.

When the telephone becomes widely linked with visual display units ('videophones') enabling the sales negotiator to contact the potential customer and conduct, if need be, quite lengthy interviews, then it may well become a more extensively used means of communication.

Direct selling by correspondence is frequently a vital aspect of the promotional mix. As Wilmshurst (1978, p 159) indicates, it is perhaps too easy to emphasize the importance of the salesforce 'in the field', whereas of course many people *inside* the organization have an important selling contribution to make. Much of their contact with customers is by means of correspondence, which again is especially significant for obtaining repeat business.

Correspondence is of great consequence where business is obtained by the submission of tenders. These are usually vetted by committees in public sector organizations and the role of the salesperson is to obtain all the relevant information on customer needs on which the tender can be based. The correspondence accompanying the tender documents often contains valuable supplementary information and should also project a powerful image of the prospective supplier as an efficient organization. Correspondence is similarly of great consequence in dealing with distant customers and enquirers, particularly those in overseas markets. The function of this type of sales communication is to keep overseas customers' requirements adequately serviced in the periods (which may be necessarily protracted) between salespeople's calls.

Finally, we come to the last link in the communications chain – the *dealer's sales staff*. All the marketer's expenditure on marketing research, product development, distribution, advertising and promotion can come to nothing if the potential user is faced with indifference or a lack of knowledge on the part of the dealer's sales staff.

For this reason, the marketing organization will do much to ensure that these staff are trained and motivated to sell its products and services. Explanatory manuals, videotapes and presentations by the organization and its salespeople, enabling dealers' staff to be knowledgeable and enthusiastic with users, are frequently a key feature of the communications campaign.

This type of training can be arranged at the dealer's store or premises, at a specially arranged dealer conference or at the premises of the marketing organization – which is often the case where the product is an item of complex and costly equipment (such as a motor vehicle).

Conferences for dealers often include a pleasant social component designed to make sales assistants feel a part of the supplier's organization. Motivation to sell its products is stimulated by competitions, bonuses and other rewards designed to recognize selling effort.

The 'last link' in the promotional chain is often the vital one and it can be ignored only at the supplier's peril.

One of the key tasks for which the marketing manager is ultimately responsible is the deployment and motivation of 'field' sales personnel. Comments on this task are included in the next chapter on 'the people element'.

Sponsorship

No review of the promotional mix would be complete without a mention of *sponsorship*. It is an activity which is usually classified as a method of sales promotion, albeit an indirect one. From the sponsor's strategic viewpoint, sponsorship may be undertaken for one or more of many motives, for example:

- direct return on investment – where sales will result from the sponsorship;
- to enhance the organization's reputation – for generosity, civic-mindedness, etc.;
- to obtain prestige from the type of event being sponsored.

A good illustration of the link between sponsorship and *place marketing* was provided by the *The Times* newspaper advertisement of February 1996 in which the Manchester City Council and the Games Organizing Committee were seeking to appoint a 'Television Marketing Rights and Sponsorship Consultant' for the Manchester 2002 Commonwealth Games.

The last two decades have seen a marked growth in sponsorship in the UK, despite some setbacks during the world-wide recession of the late 1980s to early 1990s. In that period many sponsorship budgets were either axed or severely cut back and the search for sponsors became more arduous. What then emerged was a discernible trend towards sponsorship of the more modest community project rather than sponsorship of the prestigious event with national appeal in the nation's capital. Obviously, the external environment influences sponsorship as it does any other type of marketing activity and sponsors have to be socially as well as economically sensitive to the spending of large sums of money at a time of rising unemployment.

The subsequent up-turn in economic activity brought a resurgence in sponsorship, helped by such landmark events as the 1996 Summer Olympics in Atlanta, Georgia, the Euro '96 soccer tournament and France's 1998 soccer World Cup. The special events planned in many fields for the year 2000, including the construction of London's Millennium Dome, will doubtless provide a backdrop for sponsorship funding to reach new, high levels.

With the growth in sponsorship has come an increasing professionalism among both sponsors and sponsored, with fully-fledged sponsorship departments being established on both sides. As competition for funding sources has intensified so has the need for appropriate research and, in the UK, organizations such as ABSA (Association for Business Sponsorship of the Arts) have played an important role in finding new sponsors. ABSA was prominent in coordinating the recent three year sponsorship of the London Jazz Festival by Oris Swiss Watches through funding from UK distributor Duval. This particular move was a demonstration too that arts sponsorship is no longer the exclusive preserve of corporate giants such as British Telecom and NatWest bank.

There are many fields and activities in which sponsorship is now an important feature. In *sport*, for example, cricket, motor racing, athletics and soccer and a host of other sports benefit from sponsorship. In soccer this extends from the team's kit, to the league or cup competition and even to stadia. Sponsors are prominent in *education* endowing, among other things, university buildings, specialist departments, including management schools and professorships. Music, ballet, art and drama are among the *arts* which have been supported and, in the *health care* field, some research institutes and hospital wards owe their existence to sponsorship. Sponsors are now prominent in television drama and light entertainment, their funding extending from 'Inspector Morse' and 'Rumpole of the Bailey' to the weather forecast.

The marketing approach to sponsorship requires the amount of funding made available and the events sponsored to be as carefully regulated by organizational objectives as any other aspect of promotion. An interesting comment here is that ABSA, mentioned above, was 'set up to encourage business to support the arts for commercial rather than philanthropic reasons' (Tweedy in Oldfield, 1996).

The signs are that the UK and other advanced economies will follow the lead of the USA where it was estimated that companies would spend (1996) $3.5 billion on sports sponsorship alone. It was also notable that while IT organizations had lagged behind makers of cars, cigarettes, soft drinks and household products in expenditure it was now one of the fastest growing sectors in sports sponsorship, as witness IBM's sponsorship of the Atlanta Olympics and Hewlett-Packard's backing of World Cup soccer.

From a strategic standpoint some other facts are worth noting.

● *Sponsorship can sometimes be undertaken as a joint venture* – an intriguing example was the Autumn 1992 exhibition of Tibetan Art at the Royal Academy which was sponsored by Silhouette Eyewear (which had just launched a 'Tibet' range of spectacles) and two Swedish property developers (Vistech

International/Redab UK) which were concerned about the ecological damage which has been done in Tibet.

- *Multinational corporations have been particularly visible in the field* (e.g. the 'Coca-Cola Cup') since it assists their localization strategies. The corporation does not wish to be regarded as 'foreign' but rather as part of the host nation's culture so it 'takes on' some aspects of that culture through sponsorship. Japanese companies have found this approach appealing.

- *Some industries are moving beyond the traditional use of corporate sponsorship as a form of 'brand marketing'.* This applies particularly to the IT industry for in many instances computer and software companies also provide the equipment and IT services required by big events. For Euro '96, Sema Group, the Anglo-French computer services organization, Microsoft, the US software developer, Digital Equipment and British Telecom combined to form the technology team for the matches which took place in eight football grounds from Anfield in Liverpool to Wembley in London.

Promotional research

The tenets of the marketing philosophy influence the marketing communications process in these ways:

- expenditure on marketing communications must be calculated as carefully as expenditure on human resources, raw materials, distribution, administration and every other aspect of operations;

- such expenditure must be undertaken in relation to clear objectives – communications objectives stemming from marketing objectives with the communications plan as an integral part of the marketing plan;

- before, during and after the communications campaign the costs and benefits of the strategy adopted must be measured and weighed against alternatives to determine whether there is a more cost-effective way of achieving objectives.

The measuring and weighing activities referred to above is the function of the *promotional research*. This is a vast field and one which we can look at only in outline here, with a few examples of research methodology. Even so, it should be sufficient to dispel the idea that marketing promotion is the haphazard spending spree its critics would claim.

Taking *advertising* as our first example, if this is properly to be considered as an investment and not simply as a cost there has to be some adequate measurement of what advertising money will buy. At a rudimentary level, for instance, press advertisers will seek some ratification of the *circulation*, that is the number of copies of each issue distributed, for the publication(s) concerned. If this figure is certified as correct by the Audit Bureau of Circulations (ABC), or is otherwise independently attested, this is to be preferred to the publisher's own statement, valid though this may be. For certain technical publications, the national postal service may issue certificates of posting, as does the Royal Mail in the UK, and these again serve to assure the advertiser.

Circulation is only a starting point because it is next necessary to know:

- how many people *read* each issue, and

- whether these are likely to constitute a target market for the advertiser.

In the UK, The National Readership Survey (NRS) which represents the interests of media owners, advertising agencies and advertisers, describes the readership of more than 200 major consumer press publications in great detail. A broad description of the readership of local newspapers is also provided and the Survey's reports are issued twice each year covering January to December each year and July (one year) to June (following year). A sample of 27,500 adults is interviewed each year to provide the raw data which have become, historically, an essential part of every media planning model. Readership information provided by the Survey is classified according to age, sex, social class, Registrar-General's regions, ITV regions, special categories, for example petrol buyers and exposure to other media such as commercial television, radio, cinema. The purpose of such classifications is to provide data of more value to advertisers, enabling them to discriminate between media in the light of their own segmentation variables.

Despite the obvious value of such data, common sense suggests that a product/market might best be defined in terms of *usage of the product itself*. Readership figures that discriminate in terms of light users and heavy users might be even more valuable. Indeed, research does indicate that a skewed purchasing pattern often does apply – even to products intended for a mass-market. Fifty to 80 per cent of the purchases of some commonly bought products are made by 20–30 per cent of all UK housewives. So, some type of *product–media survey* might possess more value for the advertisers than demographics alone.

Based on this premise, the British Market Research Bureau (BMRB International) established in 1969 the *Target Group Index* (TGI), a product and media continuous survey which has become a key source of consumer research data for the UK and Ireland. It is based on samples of 25,000 interviews each year in the UK mainland, a further 1500 in Northern Ireland and 3000 in the Irish Republic. According to BMRB it produces 'the largest single-source marketing database in Europe'.

Each interview questionnaire yields essential data on an individual's product and brand use, his or her media usage patterns and his or her demographic details. The survey includes some 4000 brands in over 500 product fields covering all major fast-moving consumer goods sectors. TGI also collects a wide range of attitudinal data known as 'Lifestyle' which is particularly useful to TGI subscribers as a source of new perspectives on familiar markets.

The data are available by subscription to advertisers, advertising agencies and media owners. Results are available on an annual basis in the form of printed volumes of data with each product field and major brand cross-referenced against a standard list of demographics and media. All data can also be accessed by computer. To provide an even sharper focus to appropriate advertisers on product–media usage BMRB have also established Premier: The Upmarket TGI, which provides data 'on the country's most conspicuous consumers', and the Youth TGI and TGI Ad Hoc for clients requiring a tailor-made approach to their research problems.

Many years ago, Simon Broadbent (1979, p 110) concluded that: 'For the national press, research means above all two sources: The National Readership Survey and the Target Group Index'. Certainly these two forms of continuous research provide evidence that the criticism about waste in advertising is often misplaced. 'Cost per thousand' of the target audience supplied by the printed media and the number of 'opportunities to see' (OTS) for television, posters and the cinema have become standard inputs to media expenditure models.

For *posters*, OTS are measured by the traffic past sites including pedestrians. In the UK 130,000 sites are surveyed by the OSCAR (Outdoor Site Classification and Audience Research) service. This enables expenditure to be undertaken based on such factors as visibility of the site, competition (number of posters per site), its angle of vision, height above ground, illumination and measured weekly traffic past the site. The CAVIAR (Cinema and Video Industry Audience Research) and RAJAR (Radio Joint Audience Research) surveys provide similar measures of coverage for their media.

Television audience research in the UK is supervised by the Broadcasters' Audience Research Board Ltd. (BARB), a joint company of the British Broadcasting Corporation (BBC) and the Independent Television Companies Association (ITCA). To measure audiences the research system is based on electronic meters which are attached to a UK representative sample of television sets. The meter records whether the set is switched on and, if so, to which channel. The data obtained are supported by diaries recording the personal viewing of members of the household. The contractor(s) appointed by BARB are responsible for establishing the sample of homes in the panel, metering all TVs, videos, satellite or cable decoders in the panel households and for the processing and distribution of the audience data.

The meter allows household members to register their presence when viewing and the overall system enables viewing to be described by such classifications as family size, age of housewife, socio-economic status, presence of children and actual weight of television viewing. More recently, BARB has also started collecting data on Additional Panel Classifications (APCs) covering a limited number of product or service oriented market definitions.

However, since the historical focus of BARB's data has been demographic classifications, advertising planners have been able to pinpoint, for example, ABC_1 adults aged 45 plus linked with TV viewing but have not been able to identify, for example, unit trust holders within that group. Accordingly, in 1990 BMRB International embarked on the valuable task of fusing its Target Group Index data onto BARB's 9000 adults. The specific objective of this significant venture was to create a database of TV viewing which enables planners and advertisers to assess audience delivery by brand and product usage – as with the print media – rather than just the usual demographics. Target Group Ratings (TGRs) have thus emerged as a significant extension of the BARB system's capabilities.

All of these types of data from NRS, TGI, BARB, etc. are valuable when undertaking expenditure in large, general markets. Where the market can be defined precisely, the choice of media is less of a problem. If publications such as *Accountancy Age*, *Architectural Review* and *Building Equipment News* are appropriate for their purposes, advertisers have little need for further research beyond the coverage and costs of alternative titles in the specialist field in question.

So much for a glimpse into the 'measuring and weighting' process but what of the advertising itself? How can the advertiser know whether the proposed creative approach is along the right lines? Where the *pre-testing of advertisements* is undertaken, copy research for press advertising is carried out by showing mock-up advertisements to consumer panels of appropriate composition, who are asked to state their preferences and/or to rank advertisements in order of appeal. One method of pre-testing television 'commercials' is to show them to invited audiences, again of appropriate composition. Usually, the advertisements are interspersed with a feature film and cartoons. The audience is asked to rank-order a number of brands before and after the film programme – any changes in preference being assumed to be as a result of the advertisements.

The *post-testing of press advertisements*, i.e. the evaluation of their effectiveness after actual use in a campaign is usually done by a process of *aided-recall*. The interviewees are taken through the press publications used for the campaign, page by page, and asked which advertisements they recall. Post-testing can also be done by the use of *coupon returns*, the coupons being 'keyed' so that the advertiser is aware of the publications in which they appeared. Simple cost-per-enquiry or cost-per-order calculations can then be made for each publication used. In direct marketing campaigns, the *volume of sales generated* per medium is, of course, readily to hand and this is the best of all criteria. Through *test-marketing*, promotional methods can also be tested in simulated campaign conditions.

The scope of promotional research and the range of research services available in developed economies such as the UK would again merit a textbook in itself. Though we can take no more than a glimpse into it, mention must be made of the *advertising expenditure measurement* services available from AC Nielsen •MEAL, whose primary purpose is to monitor continuously advertising activity as an aid to client/agency review procedures. Its monitoring activities extend to television, radio, national daily and Sunday newspapers and colour supplements, regional daily and Sunday newspapers, all major consumer magazines, selected leisure interest magazines, trade and professional magazines, cinema and outdoor advertising. Its Product Group reports are classified by over twenty product categories, for example finance, food, holidays, household appliances, pharmaceutical, publishing, etc. and relate to several hundred product groups.

Nielsen •MEAL's regular services relating to these categories and groups include brand expenditure by media groups and television regions. A digest is also available which shows the total advertising expenditure for the latest quarter, each month of the quarter and during the preceding twelve months. The proportion of expenditure on television, radio and the press for each brand and product group is also shown.

Obviously AC Nielsen •MEAL information is most helpful to advertisers in tracking new product launches and comparing competitive expenditure. With the rise of global marketing the service is rapidly expanding and, through sister companies, covers Western Europe and the major markets of Eastern Europe, Asia, North America and Latin America. The information can be delivered in a variety of formats, for example in addition to hard copy reports such as the Quarterly Summaries, *AdQuest* is a powerful and detailed PC-based system and *Dataview* is a PC-based interrogation tool. Data management services, analysis software and customer support are also available to clients.

Reinforcement for the claim that organizations, by and large, seek to safeguard the productivity of their promotional expenditure is apparent from a review of the services available from marketing research agencies – brand image analysis, usage and attitude studies, advertising pre-testing, promotions research, advertising tracking, evaluation research and so on. The underlying difficulty, as indicated by Jobber (1995, pp 362–3) is that the debate on how advertising works still continues and there can be 'no single all-embracing theory that explains how all advertising works because it has varied tasks'. He mentions the criticisms the AIDA model has attracted, despite its popularity in the USA and outlines the ATR model (awareness, trial, reinforcement) which has received support in Europe. ATR is a 'weak' theory of how advertising works, as opposed to the 'strong' AIDA theory and suggests a process whereby the awareness and interest of the customer is aroused, followed by a move towards an uncertain first-trial purchase, then reinforcement and reassurance after first purchase is provided by the advertising.

A model of advertising effectiveness, hailed as a landmark at its introduction in 1961, is DAGMAR (Defining Advertising Goals for Measured Advertising Results). Employing the model entails establishing a benchmark measure of the position along the spectrum – unawareness, awareness, comprehension, conviction, action – to which members of target group(s) have progressed. Objectives are then fixed, advertising undertaken and a further measure taken to discover whether or not any effective shift has occurred, that is whether objectives have been met. Leo Bogart (1990, pp 48–9) doyen of American advertising, reports that 20 years after its introduction a study by the Advertising Research Foundation found the DAGMAR model still being widely applied to define strategy and copy research objectives. Yet as Yorke (1998, p 147) has commented on the DAGMAR model: 'Precise measurement is impossible as so many other variables are present. Furthermore, such variables become more numerous the further one moves towards action.'

As the marketing manager fixes communications objectives, establishes the campaign budget, agrees its allocation to media, endorses the specialists' strategy and evaluates campaign results he or she is constantly aware, if he or she is responsible and effective, of the dangers of waste and the forces of competition. Only the cynic would disagree with this.

Perhaps the last word on how 'scientific' marketing communications can be should be left to Winston Fletcher (1996, p 15). Fletcher believes that the search for universal rules is over for, echoing Jobber, he points out that retailers' advertisements work differently to manufacturers' advertisements; direct response advertisements differ from image advertisements; recruitment advertisements work differently from corporate advertisements, etc.

The UK's Institute of Practitioners in Advertising (IPA) effectiveness awards have conclusively demonstrated that advertising operates in a plethora of ways, according to Fletcher. He believes that the case histories on which the awards are based (approximately 600 by 1996) are now established as 'the most authoritative collection of advertising case histories in the world'. He believes that these should be classified to group 'certain types of campaign which resemble each other, like species'. Some viable pointers for advertising effectiveness, related to the species of campaign, might then emerge.

Were the efforts typically made to minimize waste in the promotion function to become more widely known, the cynic might be moved from cocksure ignorance to, at the least, thoughtful uncertainty.

The strategic formula: Element 6:

People

Early in this book, the importance of the people element in strategic marketing was emphasized. Among the points made were these:

- since marketing has been elevated to a 'whole organization' concept – everyone acquires some responsibility for the quality of marketing effort (Chapter 2)

- people responsible for achieving objectives must be made to feel they own the strategy and feel motivated to implement it (Chapter 2);

- the whole organization can best learn how to learn ('double-loop-learning') through a 'bottom-up' participative approach to planning (Chapter 2);

- employees are important stakeholders and many of the most effective organizations are founded and run on stakeholder lines (Chapter 2);

- 'shared values', 'skills' and 'staff' are important components in the framework for effective strategic change (Chapter 2);

- the development of an appropriate 'management style' is a key component of effective strategies (Chapter 3);

- managers must constantly be looking for ways in which to achieve synergy through coordinated action (Chapter 3);

- given the salience of the 'people' element there is a case for establishing it as one of the ingredients of an enlarged marketing mix, consisting of *preparation* (marketing research), *product, price, place, promotion* and *people* (Chapter 3);

- people figure prominently in the *value chain* and the *value system* and employee satisfaction and turnover are significant factors in the *balanced scorecard* approach to the measurement of results (Chapter 3);

- the quality of *communication within and between units* is an important aspect of the design and management of organization structures (Chapter 4);

- core capabilities have to be shared not only within the individual organization but often across quite separate organizations because of the increasing importance of *strategic alliances* (Chapter 4);

- the pattern of shared values and beliefs, which are the basis of an organization's culture, is a key determinant of how an organization functions (Chapter 4);

- in highly competitive, rapidly changing markets the hierarchical structure often impedes timely and flexible response (Chapter 4);

- the characteristics of an effective system include:

  - its acceptability to organization members, and
  - its appropriateness to the skills and aptitudes of the organization's members (Chapter 4);

- information technology and electronic data interchange now increase effectiveness through the development of *networks* (Chapter 4);

- some research has demonstrated that:

  - most employees do not see how their jobs have anything to do with customers or customer needs,
  - most functional areas do not really understand the roles of the other functions in the company, so they have no basis for cooperation,
  - most functional areas have little or no meaningful input to the marketing direction of the company (Chapter 5)

- the tendencies to *departmental conflict* are numerous and varied, as depicted in Figure 5.1 (Chapter 5).

This is a relatively short chapter on the 'people' element in strategic marketing. It does not deal with *human resource management* (HRM) in depth, for that would be beyond the scope of this text. Its purpose is to offer some views on how best the points just listed might be acknowledged and addressed in the development and implementation of strategy.

As noted earlier too, in the 1990s the desirability of building *competence* in one or more *core activities* to achieve strategic advantage has gained substantial credibility and in this regard, some writers have drawn attention to the commitment of Japanese management to:

- cradle, and progress towards, a vision of a desired future;

- use this vision to integrate the efforts of the whole organization for a common purpose;

- through this common purpose, identify and develop the core competences to achieve the vision.

The specific objective of this chapter is to review some of the thinking on such aspects of managerial work particularly from the standpoint of the marketing executive.

Jeffrey Pfeffer, Professor of Organizational Behaviour at the Stanford Graduate School of Business believes that the 'conventional wisdom' that organizational returns are related to factors such as access to economies of scale, associated cost efficiencies, dominant market share, technological leadership, being in the right industry, etc., is wrong (Pfeffer, 1998, p 5).

Based on various research studies, related literature and his own personal observation and experience Pfeffer sets out the following seven practices which characterize successful organizations (1998, pp 64–5):

- employment security;

- 'selective' (i.e. with care and sophistication) hiring of new personnel;

- self-managed teams and decentralization of decision-making as the basic principles of organizational design;

- comparatively high compensation contingent on organizational performance;

- extensive training;

- reduced status distinctions and barriers, including dress, language, office arrangements, and wage differences across levels;

- extensive sharing of financial and performance information throughout the organization.

Pfeffer's case for 'building profits by putting *people* first' is detailed and well-organized but he believes that while numerous rigorous studies, within and across industries have demonstrated the 'enormous economic returns' from participative management and employee involvement practices, many managers are moving in the exact *opposite* direction to what this growing body of evidence prescribes. This chapter will illustrate why Pfeffer's seven practices deserve careful consideration and implementation to the degree that is appropriate and feasible.

Echoing Pfeffer, Wheeler and Sillanpää (1997) argue that British businesses have hindered themselves by undervaluing their workers. Further, they point out that effective two-way dialogue with stakeholders is considered essential in numerous high-performing companies in Europe, the Far East and North America. On an ethical note, Cole observes that employees could be considered as a dependent category of stakeholder, adding:

> Employees are individuals who, over a given time, invest a large proportion of their lives in their organization. Thus, much of their personal lives (e.g. as bread-winners), as well as their role as employees, depends on the success or otherwise of the corporate strategy adopted by their employer (Cole, 1994, p 172).

Cole's comments set the tone for much of what follows in this chapter and it is appropriate that in the next section we look further into the ethics of the people element.

The ethical framework

Marketing strategies and operations are clearly the most public aspects of organizational behaviour so that the majority of ethical issues appear to be linked to the marketing function. If we think about the *marketing philosophy* as it has been described in this book it will appear, essentially, as being about exchange relationships that are both voluntary and active and in which the role of trust in consumer and industrial transactions is paramount. In discussing law and ethics (Chapter 5) we glimpsed what organizations *must* do (the legal framework) and what they *ought* to do (the ethical framework). In this section we will take a further look at marketing within the ethical framework.

It takes little imagination to perceive what can occur when an organization acts unethically – sadly we see too many instances of it. At the strategic level, the dangers of concentrated power may lead to restrictions on innovation, reduction of the pressure for quality improvement, the erosion of competition and the opportunity for increasing prices. At the operational level, let us take one or two examples of unethical practices from the elements of the marketing mix:

- *preparation* (marketing research) – misrepresentation of other activities as 'research', lack of objectivity, lack of data validation;

- *product* – 'passing off' products as those of competitors, inadequate information on changes in product quality, inadequacy of after sales service;

- *price* – false price comparisons, misleading meanings of 'sale', 'clearance' and 'discount', unethical issues in tendering procedures;

- *place* – faults in the accessibility of goods and services to the poor and vulnerable sections of society, distribution of power among channel members – its influence on minimum order sizes, product mix selections, etc.;

- *promotion* – manipulative/deceptive sales promotion, the advertising of promises that cannot be kept – health, beauty, etc., ethical issues with respect to demonstrations, endorsements, testimonials.

- *people* – discrimination in the workplace, ethical issues in working conditions and rewards, the special problems of restructuring, re-engineering.

In some areas of potential misconduct, there will be a legal prescription and a penalty, other areas will pose an *ethical dilemma* in that matters of right and wrong have not been so clearly identified and disagreements may occur about the 'proper behaviour' to be adopted. So top management has an obligation to its people to clarify matters. Ensuring the *values statement* is acted upon, conducting an *ethical audit*, and developing a *code of ethics* are important steps along the way. Some organizations have gone beyond this and established an *ethics committee* to rule on questionable issues and discipline violations. Again, some have appointed an *ethical ombudsman*, to act as the corporate conscience, to hear and investigate ethical complaints and to forewarn top management of potential failures in the organization's ethics.

Management has a responsibility to employees to clarify what decisions and actions are within the domains of law and ethics and what are in the domain of free choice. As has been said (Daft, 1991, p 93) the ethical domain has no specific laws but it does have standards of conduct based on shared principles and values about moral conduct which guide the individual and the organization. Above all, top management must create an *ethical climate* of openness within the organization on ethical issues so that an individual can raise ethical questions without fear of direct or indirect consequences. And as Kreitner (1998, p 149) says the challenge for today's management is to create an organizational climate in which the need for 'whistle-blowing', that is reporting perceived unethical organizational practices to outside authorities such as government agencies or public interest groups, is reduced. Better yet to say 'nonexistent' than 'reduced' and though this may be an ideal, why should management not strive for the ideal?

As with the organization in general, so with the marketing function in particular, for the chief marketing executive is responsible for creating an ethical climate within it. He should recognize, however, that developing a *marketing code of ethics* is only a step along the way and that it will fail to encourage ethical conduct unless it satisfies two criteria, as Kreitner (1998) also indicates:

- *it refers to specific practices*, e.g. the acceptance of bribes, the receiving of gifts, falsification of records and misleading claims about products or in advertising;

- *it should be supported by top management and equitably enforced through rewards and punishments* – for 'selective and uneven enforcement is the quickest way to kill the effectiveness of an ethics code' (Kreitner, 1998, p 149).

It is true, of course, that largely because of intense global competition, a new social contract between employer and employee has now emerged based not on the concept of a 'job for life' but on a shorter-term relationship of convenience and mutual benefit. In the new situation the employee must work at increasing his own long-term value, and the employer and the employee must invest in each other as together they face the market. Stability of employment then depends on the degree of their success.

This is not to say, however, that the employer should not strive for the ethical goal of providing, as far as possible, employment security. We note here Pfeffer's point that this also makes good economic sense. Moreover, it should be employment which recognizes and acts upon the continuing legal and ethical pressure for equal opportunity. There should be no 'glass ceiling', that is to say no transparent but strong barrier which keeps women and members of minority groups from moving up organizational ladders.

Corporate social responsibility is based on the belief that an organization has social obligations above and beyond making a profit. Implicit in this belief is an attitude which sees workers as an asset rather than an expense. The social consequences of decisions about workers should be analysed before they are made and their social costs should be minimized where appropriate.

If ethical conduct by employees is to be encouraged perhaps it would be prudent to provide a place for discussion of ethics cases and of ethical issues specific to the organization in its training programmes The case for it seems substantiated by the comments of noted ethicist Archie B. Carroll (1987). Carroll has labelled managers lacking ethical awareness as *amoral*, that is neither moral nor immoral but *indifferent* to the ethical implications of their decisions and actions. Carroll considers that the amoral managers greatly exceed in number the moral or immoral managers. This seems to identify a 'training gap'.

In discussing organizational effectiveness, Kreitner (1998, p 269) restates the view that no single approach to evaluating effectiveness is appropriate in all circumstances and for all organizational types. He then points out that: 'More and more the effectiveness criteria for modern organizations are being prescribed by society in the form of explicit expectations, regulations and laws. In the private sector, profitability is no longer the sole criterion of effectiveness.'

In this context, the *balanced scorecard* approach described earlier in this book, and which among other things assesses an organization's performance in relation to its *people*, seems an idea with much to commend it. As Cannon has said (1997) business success will demand that organizations are capable of absorbing, responding to and initiating change. This capacity is highly dependent on the degree to which people trust those initiating change. We might add that an atmosphere of trust is best built by the organization which acts ethically towards its employees and other stakeholders.

Human resource management

An excellent definition of human resource management has been provided by Armstrong, namely that:

> Human resource management (HRM) is a strategic and coherent approach to the management of an organization's most valued assets – the people working there who individually and collectively contribute to the achievement of its objectives for sustainable competitive advantage (Armstrong, 1993, p 371).

The fundamental philosophy of HRM is grounded in the following beliefs:

- sustainable competitive advantage is achieved through people;

- close attention should be paid to integrating corporate and human resource strategies and to the development and sustenance of an appropriate culture;

- human resources can best be utilized through policies which generate organizational commitment and make the best use of the skills, creativity and energy of people;

- HRM is owned by line management – where a personnel function exists separately it has an enabling role in the effective management of people by line management.

Figure 12.1 is an attempt to depict, in brief notation, Armstrong's summary of the aims of HRM which he perceives as deriving directly from its philosophy. In an operational sense, HRM combines several activities and approaches including planning, job design, selection, recruitment, training, the design of working conditions and rewards, manpower budgeting, management development and so on. The purpose of this section is not to provide detail on the several aspects of HRM but to provide some thoughts on its application. The relevance of these to the chief marketing executive and other line managers within the marketing function should be apparent.

In Chapter 14 we shall be looking at the marketing planning process in some detail. For now, let us recognize that planning will get underway with the demand analysis and sales forecasting which accompanies the evolution of strategy. This will prepare the way for confirming the adequacy of the current organizational structure or indicate the need for it to be reshaped. Settling the structure will enable *human resource planning* to take place at the next stage. Simply put, the desired result is for the organization to possess the right number of appropriately skilled people in the right jobs at the right time. The patterns and criteria for effective recruitment, selection, training and performance appraisal should then become clear. Subsequently, as performance and strategy are reviewed, so the planning of human resources will be reviewed. The 'staffing strategy' will be evaluated and updated as part of an iterative process.

Where a marketing manager does not have the support of a personnel department in developing his or her human resources, he or she may find it valuable to call on the services of *external agencies*. With regard to recruitment, for instance, in Chapter 6, an outline was provided of the services of marketing research specialists BMRB International in respect of both the *recruitment* and *retention* of staff. With respect to training, Furnham (1997) professor of psychology at University College, London draws attention to the fact that many large organizations 'have discovered the attitude to, enthusiasm for, benefit of and cost incurred by training is improved if the whole department is outsourced'. He believes the ideal is to have a portfolio of external trainers whose individual expertise enriches a company. Cryptically, he comments that the optimal solution is for trainers to be 'hired when required and fired when tired'. Given the undoubted importance of training, not least for implementing necessary and often overdue change, it was sad to note Donkin's (1997) report of a study released at the March 1997 London Conference of the Institute of Personnel and Development. The study, based on a survey of 205 UK companies indicated that many companies 'would still rather poach trained staff from competitors than train their own employees' and that 'some companies still find it hard to accept that training pays business dividends'.

Building an atmosphere of trust to which all employees can relate is undoubtedly a long, hard battle. Cole (1994, p 178) draws attention to the importance of adequate policy guidelines and some examples of such policies, which can be briefly summarized as follows:

- no organizational changes without thorough consultation and discussion;
- all job vacancies to be advertised internally before recruits are sought from outside;
- every new staff member and internal appointee to a new post to be entitled to a period of induction training;
- all employees to be encouraged to avail themselves of the company's training opportunities regardless of length of service, race, sex, etc.;
- management succession plans to be influenced primarily by performance appraisal reports.

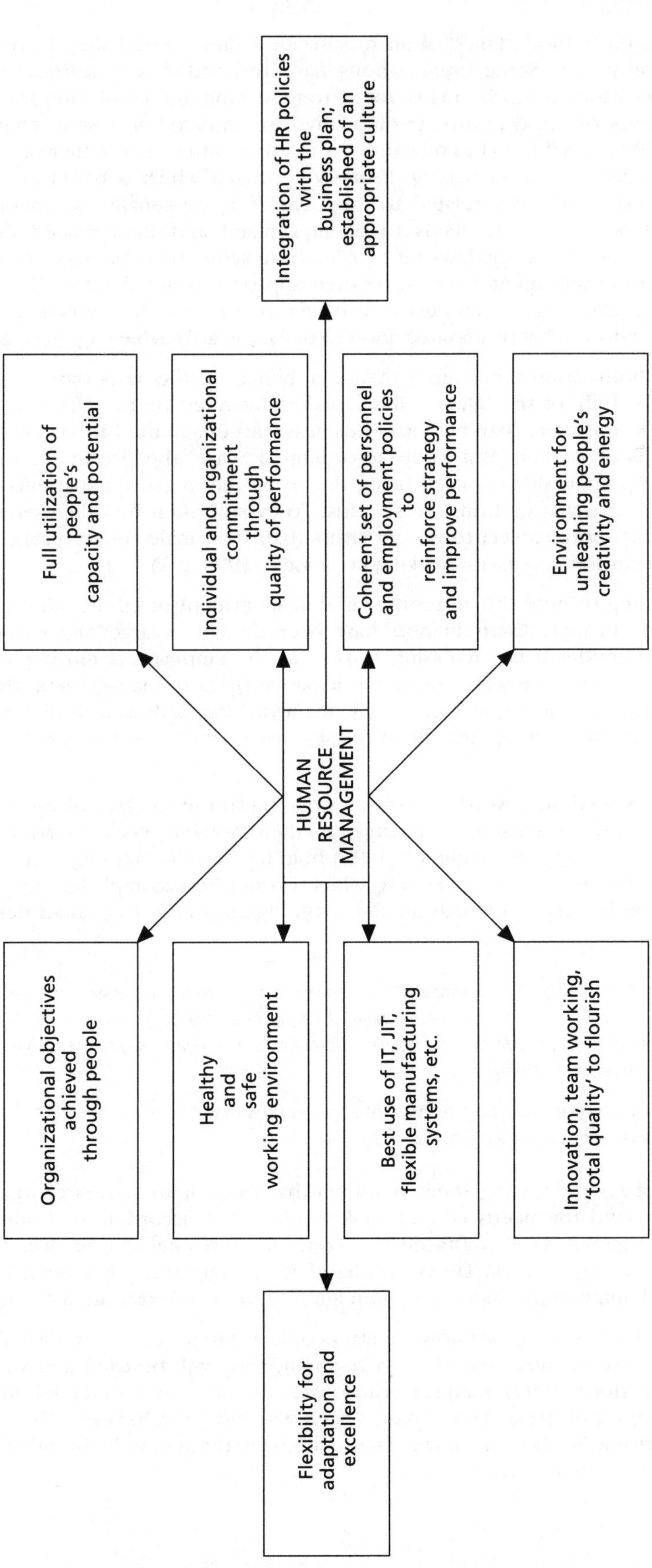

Figure 12.1. *The aims of human resource management (HRM) – Adapted from Armstrong, M. A Handbook of Management Techniques, 1993, see reference*

Nowhere is the ethical stance of an organization more tested than in the field of equal opportunities. Some organizations have responded with *affirmative action programmes* which comprise plans 'for actively seeking out, employing and developing the talents of those groups traditionally discriminated against in employment' (Kreitner, 1998, p 325), including women and ethnic minorities. Other organizations have responded with a *managing diversity* approach which is based on the belief that *difference* – whether related to race, age, sex, personality or whatever, is a commercial benefit which needs to be maximized and then related directly to business. It is good that the laws on equality have achieved some major changes, say the adherents of managing diversity, yet their approach is not about legal compliance but business goals, which can best be achieved by treating each person as a unique and valued individual with a contribution to make towards achieving those goals.

Ultimately both approaches encapsulate a belief in the importance of *people*. Certainly the folly of the 'glass ceiling' is demonstrated by the fact that, as Scase (1998) points out more than half of all business start-ups in the UK economy are now in the hands of women. But sadly, according to Scase, the rise in the number of female entrepreneurships is itself being driven by the negative experiences women encounter in many large firms. Scase adds: 'They still often find themselves passed over for promotion, subject to greater stress than their male counterparts, and marginalised in corporate decision-making processes' (1998, p 1).

It is interesting to note the entrepreneurial skills evident in ethnic minority groups which, often through discrimination, have been denied to larger organizations too. Reverting to gender bias, increasingly today, as the emphasis is moving away from hierarchical structures towards more participative styles of management, the 'softer' interpersonal and communications skills, teamworking skills and flexibility are very much in demand. These are all attributes with which women are particularly identified.

Finally in this section, a word on how an organization in the face of ever-increasing competition, prepares itself for *change*. In their notable work *Reengineering the Corporation*, Champy and Hammer (1993) hold to the view that long-term success is about *business process re-engineering* which cannot be accomplished by small and cautious steps but tends towards an all-or-nothing approach. As Crainer describes it, this means:

> *stripping away what a company does, analyzing the core processes which make up its business and then reassembling them more efficiently in a way which is free of functional divides and needless bottlenecks. Re-engineering returns organizations to first principles.*
>
> *A common image associated with re-engineering is that it takes a blank piece of paper and starts again* (Crainer, 1996, p 152).

The aims of re-engineering seem praiseworthy: to seek to re-create organizations designed around the needs of their stakeholders, but according to Crainer, while many corporations have embraced the concept of re-engineering, few have succeeded in making it work. He concludes that re-engineering has been held back because its human implications 'are often ignored, overlooked or under-estimated'.

Until organizations recognize how central people are to success, it is likely that more and more powerful nostrums such as re-engineering will be tried and will fail. Dr Thomas Stuttaford (1997), medical writer, states that insecurity in the job market has produced a level of stress such as hasn't been witnessed for 70 years. This cannot be ethical, particularly when the new technologies were thought to be bringing enriched and happier lives to everyone.

The communication process

In Chapter 1 it was emphasized that *effective communication* was the starting point in creating a customer-led culture. The four purposes of communication, as perceived by Francis (1987) were then listed, namely:

● for sharing the compelling vision;

● for integrating the effort;

● for sustaining a healthy community;

● for making intelligent decisions.

Based on an analysis of Francis's work, Figure 12.2 illustrates the twelve components underlying these purposes. Starting from the top left quadrant and reading clockwise, some words of explanation are listed below for each of the twelve components.

Sharing the compelling vision
If the vision is to be communicated in ways that are clear, exciting and inspiring, the organization must be:

● sensitive to environmental change, its opportunities and threats;

● have a vision which 'specifies the strategic driving force of the organization and contains the basic values which determine policies' (Francis, 1987, p 12);

● have managers with the persuasive strategies and skills to inspire people to work together towards common goals.

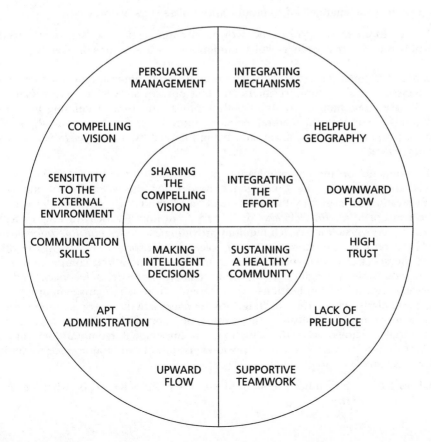

Figure 12.2. *The twelve components of organizational communication. From Francis (1987) Unblocking Organizational Communication*

Integrating the effort

Integration is best achieved by having:

- systems and procedures which bring together the efforts of specialists, departments and groups;
- workplaces so designed that they foster communication within and between teams;
- an effective downward flow of communication so that everyone knows what to do and how to do it.

Sustaining a healthy community

Commitment to an organization's goals and policies depends upon:

- an atmosphere of trust,
- which is free from destructive prejudice, and which is
- based on a respect for differences and the value of everyone's contribution so that people cooperate effectively.

Making intelligent decisions

If the decision-making team is to make intelligent decisions the whole process should be fostered by:

- openness in management which values the ideas, creativity, knowledge and experience of all employees;
- streamlines the channels of communication to assist its two-way flow;
- the development of spoken and written communication skills and other skills (e.g. being an active listener) which minimize communications blockages.

We noted in Chapter 11 that a dictionary definition of communication is to succeed in conveying one's meaning to others and that phrases such as 'to give a share of' and 'to have something in common with another' are used in defining the word. Such phrases support the central concept underlying the Francis analysis of a common purpose emanating from, and being fostered by, a truly *participative style of management*.

In his comments on the communication process, Kreitner (1998, pp 354–5) incorporates an outline of the contingency model for the selection of media of communication proposed by Richard Lengel and Robert Daft. Their model is based on the concept of *media richness*. Media vary from high (or rich) to low (or lean). Face-to-face conversation is a rich medium providing as it does *multiple information cues* based on message content, tone of voice, facial expressions, etc. At the other end of the spectrum, *lean media* such as bulletins, generalized computer reports, etc. provide only a single cue, do not facilitate immediate feedback and are impersonal. Again, the implications for an 'open', 'in touch', management style are clear, particularly where the challenge for management is to stir commitment or create a more positive culture. The contingency approach indicates the need to match media richness with the situation. An impersonal memorandum may be sufficient to deal with a routine, administrative issue but not to announce redundancies or short-time working.

A final note from this author – communication is often achieved by what we *do* as well as by what we *say*.

Motivation

Pfeffer (1998, pp 31–3) indicates that there is a 'substantial and rapidly expanding body of evidence, some of it quite methodologically sophisticated' establishing a strong connection between how firms manage their people and the economic results they achieve.

Pfeffer believes the evidence demonstrates that management approaches which foster high commitment produce tremendous gains because:

- people work harder, as a result of their increased involvement and commitment, which stem from 'having more control and say in their work';

- people work 'smarter' if management helps people to build skills and competence and, as importantly, helps them to apply their wisdom and energy;

- giving people more responsibility saves on administrative overheads and minimizes the other costs 'associated with having an alienated work force in an adversarial relationship with management'.

What underlies 'high commitment management practices'? In other words, how can people be motivated to work enthusiastically to attain an organization's objectives? The question of motivation has long occupied the attention of managers and social scientists. Early work was associated with the Maslow hierarchy (see Chapter 7) and Herzberg's two factor theory both of which have been criticized for their lack of a substantial empirical basis. Nevertheless, as Kreitner (1998, p 388) points out Maslow does teach one important lesson, namely that a *fulfilled* need does not motivate an individual – economic security may fulfil a *safety* need but added security will probably *not* provide the motivation to work harder. On the other hand 'because challenging and worthwhile jobs and meaningful recognition tend to enhance self-esteem, the esteem level presents managers with the greatest opportunity to motivate better performance' (Kreitner, 1998).

Similarly, despite its alleged weak empirical basis, Herzberg's two factor or 'motivation-hygiene' theory has secured its place in the canon of managerial concepts emphasizing as it does that it is not possible to motivate people solely by improving the 'hygiene' factors (e.g. the betterment of working conditions and monetary rewards). Herzberg held that this would probably decrease dissatisfaction but that true *motivation* emanates from factors associated with the job itself and relies on opportunities for achievement, recognition and responsibility. It will be seen that both Maslow and Herzberg reinforce what Pfeffer is saying about the beneficial effects of enlarging the discretionary component of people's work.

As reported by this author in another text (Frain, 1993, p 51), more recent work on motivation has involved an examination of the cognitive processes entailed. One significant 'process' approach utilized ideas about the *expectations* people have about the consequences of their behaviour (Lawler, 1973). In essence, this theory suggests that the amount of effort people are prepared to invest in a task depends on three factors:

- *expectancy* – whether the effort involved will result in better performance;

- *instrumentality* – whether the performance will result in beneficial outcomes, such as rewards;

- *valence* – whether the possible outcomes are attractive for the individual concerned.

According to Robertson and Cooper (1983, p 83) theories involving the concepts of expectancy, instrumentality and valence (called either expectancy theory or expectancy/

valence theory) form the basis of much current research on motivation and work behaviour (vide Steers and Porter (1979)). The theory emphasizes that the attractiveness of specific outcomes or rewards is a very individualistic issue. What is attractive to one person may be irrelevant for another. So that although expectancy theory seeks to provide a general model of the factors involved in determining effort and performance for all employees, the individual differences between people is an integral part of the theory.

Nadler and Lawler (1979) have summarized some of the main implications for organizations.

- Design pay and reward systems so that desirable performance is rewarded (do not reward mere membership by linking pay with years of service). The relationship between performance and reward is clear. Rewards such as upgradings resulting from good performance should be clear and explicit, rather than ambiguous and secret.

- Design tasks, jobs and roles so that people have an opportunity to satisfy their own needs through their work, but do not assume everyone will want the same things. Some will look for enriched jobs with greater autonomy, feedback, etc. Others will not.

- Individualize the organization. Expectancy theory proposes that people have different needs, valences, etc. Because of these individual differences it is important to allow people some opportunity to influence not only the type of work they do but many other aspects of organizational life.

Another latter-day approach to motivation is based on *goal-setting theory*, which has been researched more rigorously than a number of alternative approaches. In an organizational context, *goal setting* is employed to improve individual or group performance by way of formally stated objectives, deadlines or quality standards. The theory's model is a generic one in that the motivating power of goal-setting is the same whether in the fields of business, sport, academe or whatever. The life stories of the successful often demonstrate that they set themselves clear goals and were stimulated through the challenge to achieve them. Research, according to Kreitner (1998, p 392) indicates that the motivational function of goal setting emanates from four factors:

- the goal, an exercise in selective perception, directs *attention* to a specific target;

- it then encourages one to exert *effort* to achieve something specific;

- because a challenging goal requires sustained or repeated effort, it encourages *persistence*; and

- fourth, because it creates the task of moving from an actual to a desired state, it fosters the creation of *strategies* and *action plans*.

Goal setting is usually employed in approaches such as *management by objectives* (MBO) where goals are set by negotiated consensus between the manager and the individual and performance is then appraised in relation to these goals.

Of all the people to be motivated to work enthusiastically to achieve an organization's objectives, none are more important than the field sales representatives – the people who deal with actual and potential customers on a face-to-face basis. All the marketing research, planning, strategizing and re-structuring will come to nothing if the salespeople are ineffective and inefficient. To add another military analogy, an army's infantry is often referred to as being 'at the sharp end'. We can safely regard an organization's salesforce as its infantry. The conclusion of this section might be a suitable point to provide some thoughts on how salespeople might be managed and motivated.

The management and motivation of the field salesforce

Doyle (1994, p 277) has rightly pointed out that employing sales people is expensive, indicating that as the largest element in the communications mix, the average cost of maintaining a salesperson in the field, including relevant overheads, was £40,000 in 1992. By the time this section is being read it might be necessary to add 5–10 per cent to this figure. It is therefore clearly evident, both in terms of the importance of its work and the nature of its costs, that much skill and insight must be brought to the management and motivation of the field salesforce. The outline below provides some pointers in this respect.

Attaining general objectives is linked to the attainment of marketing objectives which is directly related to the attainment of sales objectives. Suppose that a general objective is to increase the rate of return on investment by 2 per cent. A firm can attempt to do this by increasing sales, hence revenue; by decreasing costs; or by a combination of both. How can personal selling objectives be linked to one or more of these measures? Quite simply, the field salesforce must be so organized and motivated that it strives to obtain a 'target' volume of revenue from sales at a 'target' level of cost. Planning to do this means addressing a number of key questions, including those listed below – (note that in order to provide a clear illustration of what is involved we assume here that the organization can start with a 'blank slate' – in practice, however, re-adjustment or re-ordering of an existing salesforce and an incremental approach may be the only viable process).

- What is a suitable balance between the personal selling function and the other components of marketing communications?

- Closely related to the above point, what number of sales representatives should be employed and how should their efforts be organized? This will entail consideration of the following:

  - the nature of the salesperson's task; e.g. how much 'selling', technical, advisory or merchandising work is involved;
  - the number and location of existing customers (e.g. consumers, trade outlets, manufacturers);
  - the purchasing policies, comparative size, informational needs and other characteristics of potential customers;
  - the financial resources available to the company;
  - the maximum affordable cost of the salesperson's call on customers, and related to this, the minimum sales volume required from customers supplied 'direct' by the company;
  - the range of products marketed by the company and the extent to which these should be sold by the same team of salespeople;
  - the distribution policy (e.g. mass distribution or selective distribution);
  - the nature of the competitive selling policies.

- The type of personnel required for the selling task, with regard to age, experience, technical and other qualifications; the level of remuneration appropriate to this personnel and task 'profile'; the component parts of remuneration, i.e. the balance between salary, commissions, bonuses; the type of initial and continuous training required, etc.

- The level of salespeople's travelling, hotel, subsistence and other expenses.

Consideration of these factors will lead to decisions as to whether the salesforce should be deployed on an area, industry or other basis, and on the establishment of objectives for individual salespeople in terms of sales turnover to be achieved per time period (e.g. one month, one year), the required average number of calls per day, the target ratio of orders:calls, the target ratio of sales revenue:selling costs, the mix of products to be sold; the type of markets/customers to be approached.

Some elaboration on the *selection and training of salespeople* needs to be made here. First, the concentration of buying power, outlined earlier in the book, the development of relationship marketing and the application of the marketing concept have all changed the nature of the selling role. Fewer salespeople are now needed, capable of taking a broader strategic view in their negotiations: see Figure 11.4 in this regard. This has implications for training, as well as selection, with 'sales training' programmes, now necessarily covering issues relating to:

- company values, missions, ethics;

- marketing as a whole organization activity;

- the contribution of salespeople;

- the selling process (e.g. finding prospects, pre-approach investigation, the approach, presentation/demonstration, handling objections, pre-closing and closing the sale, maintaining customer relationships);

- administration – e.g. company systems, reports, records, accounts settlement (where appropriate), customer credit issues;

- productivity – time management, organizing territorial coverage, optimum levels of customer service.

It is quite vital to provide continuous as well as induction training and much of this is provided in the field by sales supervisors. Needless to say these staff members should be selected for their experience and ability to provide understanding, supportive and inspirational leadership.

Setting objectives for sales personnel will obviously depend to a significant extent on the nature of the product/service and its market. A target ratio of orders gained to calls made would be inappropriate for the sales representative of a pharmaceutical company whose role is to call on medical practitioners solely with an educative/advisory function. In this case, some other measure of productivity must be devised.

Establishing clear, attainable objectives applies both where the selling function is being initially established and organized and where an existing organization is being reappraised. In the latter case, continuous monitoring of sales revenue in relation to costs may have suggested a need for re-examination. One of the factors which may induce this is a change in the market for the product, for example changes in the pattern of distribution (see Chapter 10) or, in the case of industrial marketing, diversifications or developments in user industries affecting the use of the product.

The objectives set for individual sales personnel in terms of sales turnover, costs, calling rates, etc., will become their *performance indicators*. Managing a salesforce means motivating and controlling it so that it operates in accordance with these indicators. Adequate performance will depend upon the quality of its leadership, the quality of its training and the design of a system of working conditions and rewards that encourage sales personnel to be constantly 'up and doing'. 'Working conditions' include allowances for expenditure that are at least reasonable and the provision of an adequate means of transport or a suitable allowance for this. 'Rewards' means a method of payment (usually some combination of salary, commission, bonus on turnover, bonus on cash received, etc.) that is a fair reward for effort.

It is said that salespeople 'must be happy in order to produce'. This is a wise statement for the organization must value its sales personnel not only for their sales-generating capability but also for their role as the information link between customers and suppliers.

Probably enough has been said in this and earlier chapters concerning the role of sales personnel for the reader to deduce how they operate as an information link between customers and suppliers. Perhaps the best way to summarize this is to represent it diagrammatically and Figure 11.4 (see previous Chapter) attempts to do this.

It could be said that the salesperson occupies a *boundary role*, being at the boundary of the supplying organization and in close contact with other organizations, that is actual and potential customers. The role is one, not only of selling, but of interpreting the policies and activities of each organization to the other. Boundary roles are said to be stressful, for customer and supplying organizations do not necessarily share the same objectives and the salesperson must bring the two organizations into mutually beneficial contact and cooperation with each other without compromising his or her integrity and loyalty. In this respect one sales manager sums up his thoughts with the comment that: 'I don't mind the sales force being representatives of their customers to the company, provided I know they are equally good representatives of the company to the customers'.

Team management

We have noted that all organizations now operate in conditions of rapid change. It is also clear that organizations are developing 'flatter' structures, are becoming less hierarchical and have shorter lines of communication – principally because of their changing environments. Recently, in some instances, flow line methods of production have been replaced by the cellular approach. Again, as we saw earlier, strategy is frequently becoming a matter of *collaboration* rather than simple competition.

All of these trends have given rise to the current emphasis on 'teamwork', 'team building' and 'team management'. In fact, in some instances it is easy to visualize an organization as an interlocking network of teams rather than as a hierarchical structure in which functions predominate.

Enterprising managers have long since recognized the importance of the *informal groups* which develop purely by people coming together and interacting regularly in the work situation. These are groups which are additional to, and exist outside of, the formal organization structure. Primarily they fulfil the 'belongingness' needs identified by Maslow. People affiliate to them for friendship, support and in some cases protection from the more exploitative employer. They develop their own norms of behaviour, that is socially sanctioned rules of conduct which, from the organization's standpoint can be positive ('shape up with your output') or negative ('don't be a rate buster'). Informal groups provide, for the individual, status, security and social satisfaction particularly in large organizations where the employee can feel unknown and faceless. Solidarity emerges as members face a common situation and share common experience.

The informal group will oppose organizational objectives if these are judged harmful to group interests, for example too high output standards, too low pay rates. On the other hand groups can operate decidedly in organizational interests. At one level, their social activities can strengthen people's ties to the organization. At another because they can be highly adaptive they are often of great benefit to organizations in times of change and crisis. Knowing that these grassroots social networks can either impede or advance the organization's performance, the effective manager learns to work with them, use them as a means of communication and makes a clear effort to infuse them with the organization's values and goals.

Beyond this, however, and because of rapid change in markets, technologies, etc., there is now a strong focus on the formation of formal groups and the development of *team management*, 'the process of improving the quality of teamworking throughout the organization' (Armstrong, 1993, p 39). Armstrong lists a considerable number of techniques for improving teamwork. Some of these are listed below to convey the essence of his advice.

- Pick people who will fit the culture and work well with others but who are still capable of taking their own line when necessary.

- Keep on emphasizing that constructive teamwork is a key core value in the organization.

- Set up overlapping or interlocking objectives for people who have to work together. These will take the form of targets to be achieved or projects to be completed by joint action.

- Set up interdepartmental project teams with a brief to get on with it.

- Clamp down on unproductive politics.

- Recognize and reward people who have worked well in teams. (See Armstrong, 1993, p 39.)

Obviously, managers responsible for building teams will require training to develop the necessary skills, for example T-group and interactive skills training. This type of training is designed to increase the team-builder's perception of the team's reactions, the state of its relationships and to increase the effectiveness of interaction with and among the team. This is known as *group dynamics* training, which Armstrong (1993, p 432) describes as 'a form of training designed to help groups to analyse and improve the processes they use to make decisions, solve problems, resolve conflict and generally work effectively together'. Ideally then, it should be available to all members of the work groups if the organization is committed to team working.

The effectiveness of a team is very much influenced by the degree of mutual trust between the team's members and the organization's members. Kreitner puts this well:

> *Trust is a fragile thing. As most of us know from personal experience, trust grows at a painfully slow pace, yet can be destroyed in an instance with a thoughtless remark. Mistrust can erode the long-term effectiveness of work teams and organizations* (Kreitner, 1998, p 438).

Kreitner reports the view of management professor and consultant Fernando Bartolomé that to build trust, managers need to concentrate on six areas. These are summarized briefly below and serve to affirm yet again the importance of an ethical climate for the well-being of the organization and its members.

- *Communication* – e.g. supply information, provide feedback, explain decisions and policies, be open about problems;

- *Support* – e.g. show concern for subordinates; be available and approachable; help, coach, and encourage people; defend them when necessary;

- *Respect* – e.g. delegate to subordinates; listen to them; act on their opinions;

- *Fairness* – e.g. give credit where it is due; be objective and impartial in appraising performance; praise liberally;

- *Predictability* – e.g. behave consistently and dependably; keep explicit and implicit promises;

- *Competence* – e.g. show technical and professional ability and good business sense.

Leadership ⋮

Whatever the individual historian's field of interest and enquiry – politics, war, economics, society, etc. – sooner or later he or she will say something about *leadership* – its presence, absence or quality in the period under review. Since it is also held to be a decisive factor in the health and well-being of organizations, management literature provides an abundance of material on leadership. In a few short paragraphs we can do no more than consider this material in inevitably selective outline, then take a closer look at an example of some thinking appropriate to the conditions currently confronting organizations.

A number of analytical approaches to the study of leadership can be identified. The earliest of these, the *qualities or traits approach* attempted to identify the common, and therefore hopefully generalizable, characteristics of successful leaders – for example intelligence, charisma, initiative, self-confidence, etc. It shed little light on how to differentiate between leaders and non-leaders.

Next, the *situational approach* emphasized the importance of the professional/ technical skills of the leader, rather than personality traits, and related these to the *situation* in which the leadership is exercised. In other words, leaders are not the only critical component of leadership. The followers, and conditions in which operations take place, are also highly relevant. This approach provided a better basis for the training of leaders.

The *functional* approach, as its name suggests, concentrated on the functions of leadership rather than on the characteristics of the leader or the particular situation. As Mullins explains:

> The functional approach views leadership in terms of how the leader's behaviour affects, and is affected by, the group of followers. This approach concentrates on the nature of the group, the followers or subordinates. It focuses on the content of leadership (1989, p 426).

As an illustration of the approach Mullins points to John Adair and his concept of *action-centred leadership*. Adair's ideas are that to be effective, a leader must meet three areas of need within the work group, namely:

- the need to achieve the common *task*;
- the need for *team maintenance;*
- the *individual needs* of group members.

The common task would centrally involve the *objectives* of the group. Team maintenance needs would very much include such matters as maintaining morale and building team spirit. Individual needs would encompass giving praise and status to the individual, reconciling conflict and provision of the individual's training. Adair adds that any action by the leader in one area of need will affect one or both of the other areas of need and he denotes these various areas of needs as three overlapping circles. It can be perceived from what has been said on team management in this chapter that Adair's views are still relevant and valuable.

Consideration of *leadership style* and leadership as a *category of behaviour* are further approaches in the study of leadership. In the first of these, the *authoritarian style*, in which the leader alone exercises great authority and is responsible for all decisions relating to policies and procedures, is contrasted with the *democratic style*, at the other end of the continuum, in which leadership is shared with group members who have a great say in decision-making. In the *laissez-faire style*, if it is genuine and not just an abdication of responsibility, the leader carefully observes the performance of the group, allows it freedom of action if its progress is satisfactory, but is available at all times if needed. The assumption underlying the 'style' approach is that group members will work more effectively if their leader employs a particular style of leadership rather than some alternative style. The *behavioural category* approach is closely identified with the research conducted at Ohio State University into:

- the types of behaviour employed by leaders, and
- the effects of leadership on group performance.

Two major dimensions of leadership behaviour emerged from the research:

- *consideration* – indicating a leader's concern, warmth, support and consideration – as a means of establishing trust and respect, and
- *structure* – indicating the extent to which the leader defines goals and organizes group efforts for their attainment.

From these two dimensions it is possible to identify four categories of leadership behaviour namely, leadership which is:

- low on consideration and low on structure;
- low on consideration and high on structure;
- high on consideration and high on structure;
- high on consideration and low on structure.

It appears that, while the evidence is not conclusive and 'much seems to depend on situational factors' (Mullins, 1989, p 432), a leadership style which is high on consideration and high on structure is generally more effective both in terms of group performance and the satisfaction of group members.

In fact, the importance of situational factors emerges from several studies of leadership. The *contingency theory* of leadership attempts to identify situational variables and relate these to the most appropriate leadership style to suit the circumstances. A well researched contingency approach and one with which this author is well acquainted centres on the work of F.E. Fiedler, Professor of Psychology and Director of the Organizational Research Group at the University of Washington.

Fiedler's research programme into the nature of effective leadership was carried out in a large range of organizations including businesses, civil and military governmental agencies and voluntary organizations. The studies concentrated on work groups rather than on organizations in the round.

'Effectiveness' was defined in a robust way: how well the group performs the primary task for which it exists, for example output levels for production managers, students' standardized achievement-test grades for school principals.

Fiedler identified two main leadership styles. *Relationship-motivated* leaders obtain their main satisfaction from good personal relationships. They are very concerned with what group members feel. They encourage subordinates to participate and to offer ideas. *Task-motivated* leaders are pre-eminently concerned with the successful completion of any task assigned to them. Their style is based upon clear orders and standardized procedures for subordinates.

The *Fiedler contingency model* is one of some elaboration and its precise description here would be out of place. What can be said, quite simply, is that either of the above styles can be effective in appropriate contexts. He takes a *contingency* approach to leadership and rejects the belief that there is a best style which is appropriate for all situations. Fiedler's tenet is that what is effective leadership will be contingent on the nature of the task which the leader faces and the situation in which he operates. As an aside, when he was Principal of a large, diversified college, this author found the Fiedler approach provided a useful framework for the functions of leadership in inducing organizational change.

As Crainer (1996, pp 182–3) indicates, latter-day approaches to leadership have drawn on:

- *Transactional theory* – which emphasizes the mutual benefit from an exchange-based relationship with the leader offering resources or rewards in exchange for the follower's commitment or acceptance of the leader's authority.

- *Transformational theory* – which, unlike transactional models (which are based on the extrinsic motivation of an exchange relationship) are based on intrinsic motivation. The emphasis is on commitment from followers rather than compliance. In Crainer's words: 'The transformational leader is, therefore, a proactive, innovative visionary.'

What then, is to be learned from this outline of approaches to leadership? Currently, organizations are seeking highly skilled, well-qualified employees to cope with the opportunities and threats of complex and continuously developing technologies and markets. In this situation, the autocratic, 'macho' style of leadership looks increasingly out of place. The subtle management of relationships, recognizing human worth and fostering commitment looks more and more appropriate. MacFie seems to sum up the requisite qualities for leadership today when he says:

> These qualities are: the capacity to develop and communicate a vision and future direction; an ability to manage and inspire other individuals and teams; a capacity to handle ambiguity and complexity; an ability to articulate and embody a clear and relevant set of values, and an attitude of openness to innovation. In addition, the world literature suggests that certain personal qualities are advantageous: these include energy, flexibility, sense of humour and balance, determination, self-confidence and the ability to relinquish control when necessary (MacFie, 1998, p 3).

Marketing managers please note.

Managing change

Often, if marketing is to be adopted as a whole-organization concept, there will be need to bring about *change* in the organization's policies and operations. *Change management* is the process of bringing about organizational change successfully. While we often speak of change in general terms it is necessary to identify various *types of change*. The types below are drawn from the Nadler-Tushman model (n.d.) and the examples of each type are related to the marketing function.

Types of organizational change (Nadler–Tushman)

- *Anticipatory change* – this is planned change based on expected situations, e.g. the launch of a new range of product(s) or entry into new markets.

- *Reactive change* – which is change made in response to unexpected situations, e.g. the sudden appearance of a large, well-resourced competitor in the organization's market(s), calling for significant change in production, personnel, marketing, etc.

- *Incremental change* – subsystem adjustments required to keep the organization on course, e.g. review of salesforce incentives and marketing research expenditure to increase sales volume.

- *Strategic change* – altering the overall shape or direction of the organization, e.g. following the decision to change a *production-oriented* organization to one which is *customer-led* in all phases of its operations.

The literature tells us that managing change is never easy – at worst, that it can be a hard, unremitting struggle because people resist change. Kreitner (1998, pp 484–6) lists many reasons for this resistance, some of which are:

- change can come as an unpleasant surprise if introduced without warning;

- we all wish the context in which we operate, emotionally and technologically, to be as safe, secure and predictable as possible;

- without adequate preparation and training, change may be perceived in a negative light;

- there may be a clear sense of loss, particularly if change results in the break-up of well-established work groups;

- where management is disliked or distrusted, it is a poor conduit for change;

- lack of tact, poor timing and perceived threats to job status all act as blocks to change.

Of course, sometimes change means reductions in hours, pay, worsening of working conditions and curtailment of other benefits, in which cases change can be *very* actively resisted.

Management can do a great deal to mitigate the negative aspects of change. Where, for instance, it provides committed and strong leadership, is perceived as understanding people's fear of change and is clearly supportive in helping employees to face change, the transition will be brought about more smoothly. Such commitment must also be perceived as emanating from the very top.

It is important that the managers and others who are acting as the *change-agents* have the personal qualities and skills to lead change. It is interesting to note Eadie's comments (1998) on the role of consultants in this regard, particularly in the current frenetic merger and acquisition activity in pharmaceuticals, banking and other financial services. Consultant Frances Cook, managing director of the UK's largest outplacement and career management organization, makes the important point that the way change is managed, particularly where job losses are inevitable, can have a significant influence on an organization's image:

> If the organisation has been seen to throw employees out on the street, it will find it hard to attract good people. Customers and suppliers are also affected. The way employees are treated influences the future prosperity of the organisation (Cook, 1998).

Cook explains that if departing staff are treated decently, those remaining feel better about continuing to work for their employer. Tangible evidence of the employer's concern is provided when they are happy to pay for outplacement counselling so that their former workers can be resettled.

Earlier in the text, mention was made of the development of the *learning organization* (see Chapter 2). Where this has been achieved a working environment results which is conducive to change and if a reward system can be devised which recognizes innovations and contributions in achieving change, so much the better. As Armstrong counsels (1993, p 42) except in crisis conditions, change is best tackled incrementally with the overall programme 'broken down into actionable elements for which people can be held accountable'.

While establishing the need for change is much easier than actually bringing it about, concrete evidence and data on the need for change are vital if those affected by the projected change are to be adequately informed and persuaded about its inevitability. This points out the need for a *management information system* (MIS) of acknowledged adequacy. Needless to say a vital feature of the overall system will be a *marketing information system* (MKIS) which makes an important contribution to the organization's environmental scanning.

Bernard Burnes (1996, pp 332–3) who has written authoritatively on managing change suggests that the planning of change involves six interrelated activities. Figure 12.3 attempts to sketch in the outline of these six activities. Clear and comprehensive detail on these can be found in Burnes (1996).

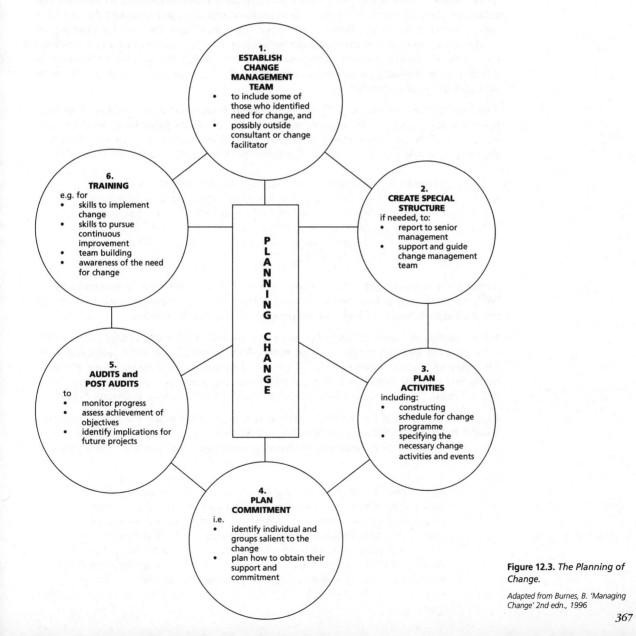

Figure 12.3. *The Planning of Change.*

Adapted from Burnes, B. 'Managing Change' 2nd edn., 1996

In all forms of organizational life, change is now a constant. Perhaps, in summary, the last word can be left to Armstrong, who says:

> In an age of global competition, technological innovation, turbulence, disconti-
> nuity, even chaos, change is inevitable and necessary. The organization must do
> all it can to explain why change is essential and how it will affect everyone.
> Moreover, every effort must be made to protect the interests of those affected
> by change (1993, p 42).

Creating a customer-led culture

We have noted earlier in the text how an organization's culture, which has been described as the 'chemistry' and 'vibrations' that permeate the work environment, is an amalgam of values and principles communicated by management, its policies and ethics, its stakeholder relationships, its traditions, management style and the attitudes and behaviour of its employees. We have also seen how the implementation of marketing in its fullest sense can only be achieved by the creation of a customer-led culture permeating the whole organization. Kotler (1997, p 54) is relevant here for he advocates the building of customer satisfaction through quality, service and value by way of *total quality marketing*.

Total quality management (TQM), outlined in Chapter 8 is an organization-wide approach to continuously improving the quality of all its processes, products and services and it provides the foundation for *total quality marketing*. Beckham expresses the responsibilities of the marketer, in this regard, clearly and forcefully:

> Marketers who don't learn the language of quality improvement, manufacturing
> and operations will become as obsolete as buggy whips. The days of functional
> marketing are gone. We can no longer afford to think of ourselves as market
> researchers, advertising people, direct marketers, strategists – we have to think
> of ourselves as customer satisfiers – customer advocates focused on whole
> processes (in Kotler, 1997, p 55).

'Getting the culture right' is one thing, however, but achieving it is something else. We have noted earlier how organizational politics and the various reasons that people resist change constitute blocks to the process of shaping the culture.

While, in theory, strategy and objectives are rooted in the *marketing plan*, Piercy (1992, p 233) for one, points out that what often occurs in practice is quite different, for many executives have no idea what the organization's strategy is, let alone its marketing plan. Moreover, planning is frequently regarded as unnecessary, time wasting, inflexible, inaccurate, a killer of initiative and a 'meaningless, pointless ritual'.

Piercy believes that if the strategic plan is not to be left on the shelf, less attention should be paid to planning techniques and sophisticated models and more to culture, management style, information flows, participation and the like. His conviction is clear:

> My firm belief is that the most important and productive thing to focus on in
> marketing planning is not the techniques and formal methods, it is quite simply
> commitment and 'ownership'. It is a hard life. There are no real rewards for
> beautifully designed planning systems incorporating the latest computerized
> models. The rewards come from getting our marketing act together and getting
> people excited and motivated to do the things that matter to customers in the
> marketplace. That is, after all, the only source of real rewards (Piercy, 1992, p 233).

We can see the importance of *communication*, from top management downwards, as an important factor in stirring commitment and the application of a *planned approach to achieving change* (Figure 12.3) as also of relevance and value. And if marketing is to become everyone's job then, as Kotler says, marketing people must spend time and effort not only to improve external marketing but also to improve internal marketing and the marketer must complain like the customer complains when the product or the service is not right.

The organization's *corporate marketing* efforts (see Chapter 13) also have a significant influence on employee commitment. If these efforts succeed in projecting the organization as effective or superior along critical dimensions and *provided the reality matches the projection*, employees will want to identify with it and become proud of its objectives and ideals.

Also, when employees can acquire *ownership* of strategies and plans, through having been consulted and asked for their opinions and suggestions, they are more likely to play their part in making strategies work. Lupton (1986, p 57) points out that the notion of hierarchy dies hard, as does the associated idea of managerial prerogative, 'ill those these notions seem to have served'. He believes that becoming a manager does not automatically confer wisdom greater than that found among people who are not, and are never likely to become, managers. A manager might be wise about some specialized matters but cannot be wise about all things all the time; he or she is bound to be less knowledgeable and less wise about the jobs of some of his or her subordinates than they are. Lupton's belief in the 'competences of the underdog' is well stated, for example:

> Increasingly the packaged general solution to these problems will have to be abandoned for a method of diagnosing just how flexible, how adaptable, a particular organization (or different parts of it) needs to be, to cope with its environment and its technology of manufacture or service. Which, once again, calls for detailed knowledge and the collaboration of everybody who knows anything that is necessary (Lupton, 1986, p 57).

If a marketing plan is realistic and achievable, based on a thoroughly objective assessment of what the organization can do, people are more likely to commit to it. The likelihood is increased if the gentle art of persuasion, and the subtle management of relationships are clearly part of the management style. What must also be clear is the conviction of all managers that marketing is everyone's job. This is not easy to achieve. Suspicion and mistrust about the motives of the marketing department can be allayed, for example:

- by cross attendance at departmental meetings – production to marketing, marketing to production;

- by a strategy which requires each departmental head to spend time in the field meeting customers;

- by arranging a programme of factory visits and discussions for sales distributors and agents;

- by the development, wherever appropriate, of *cross-functional teams* and *task force structures* (see Chapter 4).

But it is a long haul and impatience for results has its dangers. Here, Doyle (1997) is helpful, for in commenting that while rationalization and cost-cutting can provide an immediate jump in profit but only revenue growth gives long-term increases in earnings, Doyle concludes: 'Sudden rapid growth is rarely a formula for long-run performance. Sustainable growth depends upon building an enduring reputation for superior quality and value and this is a long and unglamorous road' (1997, p 19).

In the end, only informed, committed and well-led people can deliver sustainable growth.

The broader base of marketing

C·H·A·P·T·E·R

THIRTEEN

Introduction

We have looked at many facets of marketing in this book. Inevitably perhaps most of our concepts and examples have been related to consumer products and services. So, although we have suggested that the differences between industrial and consumer marketing may be more of degree than of kind, and although attention has been drawn to some of the special features of industrial marketing, it might be prudent to say more about it.

Similarly, much of our review has concerned itself with operations in the home, or domestic market. But markets can no longer be looked at in isolation. The pace of their integration is such that an organization failing to think globally will find it increasingly difficult to hold on even to its domestic market. Therefore, we need to look at marketing activity as it is impelled to move more and more across frontiers.

Finally, although much has been said about corporate objectives and how these influence marketing objectives, only a comment or two has been made on how the organization itself should be marketed. Further observations may be helpful.

So, though it could be said that 'it's all marketing anyway', the purpose of this chapter is to look at marketing in a broader perspective, that is with reference to industrial, global and corporate marketing.

Industrial marketing

'Loving the product more than the customer'

In earlier parts of this text, some observations have been made on:

- the nature of industrial products and services;
- the nature of the (derived) demand for those products and services;
- the nature of industrial customers.

Beyond these observations, a number of substantial differences between industrial and consumer marketing must be recognized. Webster (1991), for example, echoes Baker's view that these differences are often of degree rather than of kind, but adds that the degrees of difference are themselves quite marked. Webster points out that management consultant B. Charles Ames has suggested that there were four key aspects of applying the marketing concept to industrial organizations. These were:

- concentration on improved profit performance;
- the (detailed) identification of customer needs;
- the increased significance of market segmentation;
- the design of the (particular) product/service 'package'.

For Ames, sales volume and market share were not, of themselves, as important as in consumer marketing. Identifying customer needs entailed examining the economics of the customer's operations and looking carefully at the customer's industry and the nature of its competition. The selection of particular customer groups (segmentation) on which to focus marketing operations is, if anything, even more important in the industrial field. Finally, the product is frequently non standard – it must be 'invented' and packaged with services which are often as important as the product itself.

Ames therefore concluded that:

> From all this, one conclusion is clear: marketing in the industrial world is much more a general management responsibility than it is in the consumer products field. For in a consumer goods company major changes in marketing strategy can be made and carried out within the marketing department, through changes in advertising emphasis or weight, promotion emphasis or type, package design, and the like.
>
> In an industrial company on the other hand, changes in marketing strategy are more likely to involve capital commitments for new equipment, shifts in development activities, or departures from traditional engineering and manufacturing approaches, any one of which would have company wide implications. And, while marketing may identify the need for such departures, general management must take the decision on the course the company will take to respond to the market – it must provide the follow-through to ensure that this course is pursued in every functional area (see Webster, 1991, pp 11–13).

Of course, Ames' views date from 1970 and they can be challenged on at least two counts:

- they pay insufficient regard to the expense and effort put into the innovation and development of consumer products, which increase as technology develops and becomes more complex;
- they convey the idea of marketing in the industrial goods field as a sort of 'bolt on' activity whereas, as we have seen in this text, when the concept is truly implemented it is a *whole organization activity* emanating from the top with *all* directors and senior managers responsible for developing a marketing culture and commitment.

However, there is much in what Ames says, which is why it is included here and in developing his views, Webster (1991) makes these additional points:

- The effectiveness of industrial marketing depends to a greater degree on other business functions, especially manufacturing, research and development (R&D), inventory control and engineering. This high degree of *functional interdependence* is a major characteristic of industrial marketing.
- Industrial marketing is also unique because of the typical product's *technical complexity*. The major barrier to a true marketing orientation in the industrial firm remains excessive product, engineering, manufacturing and technical orientation.

Frequently the business strategies of industrial companies call for a high degree of technical innovativeness and risk taking with related high expenditures for research and development. 'In such companies, top management is likely to have been grown in the engineering and research garden and technical values may be predominant in management decision-making', says Webster. The real risk in these cases is 'loving the product more than the customer', that is becoming so enamoured with a technical accomplishment or particular product parameters that the necessary flexibility for responding to customer needs in a competitive market place disappears. As a result, one of the most common business faults can be the outcome: trying to change the customer to fit the product.

This author has had considerable experience in the field and can support Webster's comments in that, while implementing the marketing approach is never easy, in industrial marketing it is, if anything, even more difficult because of addressing the serious problem of product, and production, orientation. The industrial marketing executive is worthy of his or her hire if he or she succeeds in inculcating Corey's (1976, pp 40–1) beliefs that:

- in marketing strategy, the form of the product is a variable, not a given – products are planned and designed to serve customers;

- the product is what it does; it is the total package of benefits the customer receives – extending beyond the functional utility of the product to technical assistance, assurance of dependable supply, product service, supplier's reputation as an advantage in marketing to users and the range of personal and technical relationships between supplier and customer organizations.

Supplier–customer interdependence

From what has been said, it can be deduced that effectiveness in industrial marketing depends very much on a healthy mutual reliance between buyer and seller. If we imagine a long continuum, the actual sales transaction is only one point on it. Before that point there is often an extended, complex negotiation process. After that point there is often an equally long and continuing 'support' phase. Adequate product performance is a *sine qua non* but beyond that, the buyer frequently expects, and obtains:

- technical assistance;

- guaranteed dependability of supply;

- satisfactory service after sale (e.g. trouble free maintenance, an assured supply of repair parts, components, raw materials, etc.);

- the extension of financial and credit services.

The customer's own marketing effectiveness is very often bound up with the possibility of:

- achieving cost reductions;

- raising quality standards;

- exploiting new technologies.

Increasingly, customers look to their suppliers for insights and practical cooperation on these and other issues. Where the supplier's technical and sales personnel are 'assistant buyers', dedicated to customer service, such support will be readily given.

Moreover, buyer–seller interdependence is increasing. Throughout the last 15 years, a key trend in buying policies has been that of 'single-sourcing' for the acquisition of major parts and materials. This has resulted from the widespread adoption of just-in-time (JIT) methods in:

● production planning and control, and

● stock planning and control.

Products delivered have to meet conformance standards without goods inwards inspection by the customer, which means that the supplier has to compete with stringent requirements for *quality assurance*. Products have to be delivered on time, which in terms of JIT requirements can be very specific (e.g. '12 noon on Tuesday, 3 November', rather than during the first week of November).

Suppliers have to plan ahead very thoroughly to comply with such requirements, which means that they also need to have a detailed, accurate and thorough grasp of the *customer's forward planning*. Inevitably, suppliers who are ill-prepared for JIT are invariably dropped because more and more, suppliers of major purchases are seen as extensions to the customer's own organization. They are taken into the purchasing organization's confidence about its future plans and problems, to be resolved jointly for mutual benefit.

Obviously, this means that former patterns of purchasing, in which two or more suppliers are in competition with each other, are being significantly altered. It follows that the supplier with a total *marketing corporate environment* is the one likely to benefit from the continued increase in single sourcing.

Complexity in the buying process

In Chapter 7 we noted the complexity in many industrial buying decisions resulting from several variables, including the large numbers of persons frequently involved, the complex technical and economic factors to be considered and the large sums of money which may be involved in the transaction. Of course, the question of *degree of difference* must also be borne in mind – in that for a straight rebuy of a standardized component or raw material the buying process will be very similar to that for a consumer product.

On the other hand, the process for buying a complex item of capital equipment or a completely new, state of the art, system of information technology will usually be lengthy and immensely detailed. Often too, the buying organization will utilize quite complex decision-making tools including mathematical models, life-cycle costing, value analysis and time-based buying strategies. We must also recognize the current development of *collaborative effort among suppliers* as another variable adding complexity to industrial marketing. Looking back the Chapter 2, Figure 2.6, the European Airbus project, we have a graphic illustration of this – especially when we remember that Figure 2.6 is a much simplified outline of the real-life situation since it takes no account of the work of the contracted suppliers involved.

Special trading practices

Generically where skills are shared across quite separate supplying organizations the strategy is termed a *joint venture* – for example, two (usually large) organizations might combine their resources in order to obtain a particular construction contract. When a number of organizations is involved, as in the Airbus project, the strategy is described as a *consortium* arrangement.

Joint ventures and consortia approaches are two of the *special trading practices* which often contribute to successful industrial marketing. As Chisnall (1987, pp 352–3) points out, such practices also include:

- *Reciprocal trading* – in which buying and selling firms agree to trade with each other for certain products, wherever possible.

- *Project management* – frequently called 'turnkey operations' and applying to large capital projects: the approach here is for one 'turnkey' contractor to co-ordinate all aspects of the project on behalf of the client.

- *Leasing* – in the drive to become 'leaner and meaner' many organizations now lease rather than purchase industrial products, particularly those in which they incur large capital expenditure; the supplier must arrange marketing and financial strategies accordingly.

- *Licensing* – organizations can generate substantial income by licensing their technical know-how and access to their patents and trade marks.

For Webster (1991, p 17), four sources of uniqueness in industrial marketing arise from:

- marketing's greater dependence upon other business functions for its effectiveness;

- product complexity extending to virtually all economic, technical and personal relationships between industrial buyer and seller;

- a high degree of buyer–seller interdependence extending well beyond the transaction itself, and

- the complexity of the organizational buying process.

Webster adds that *complexity* is a word often used appropriately, to summarize the unique features of industrial marketing. To his list we can add further complexity variables, arising from:

- *derived demand* – which makes the marketing research process more complex since it often entails examination of the customer's patterns of demand as well as those of the organization itself;

- *collaborative effort* – the need for which arises from pressures to innovate, accelerating rates of change in technologies and markets, and the high costs of new product development and market entry;

- *special trading practices* – some of which have been listed above.

On this subject of complexity Webster adds that, almost as often, it is used as an excuse for not developing and adopting more rigorous analytical approaches to problem solving in industrial marketing. It might therefore be useful, in concluding this section, to review some of the ways in which industrial marketing might be made more effective.

Effective industrial marketing

The development of an appropriate and attractive strategic formula within a customer-led culture is a giant stride in the right direction. Beyond that, a number of concepts and approaches, already outlined in this text, have a special value. These include:

- emphasis on the potential benefits of fostering *long-term customer relationships* – see, for instance, Figure 1.6, Chapter 1;

- recognition of how *processes*, as well as products, can provide marked competitive advantage for alert and adaptable organizations – as exemplified by the application of *rapid prototyping technology* and *optimized production technology*, outlined in Chapter 2;

- the development of sustainable competitive advantage through *synergy* across departments and SBUs – instances of which are provided by the Bursley Group case study in Chapter 3;

- the advantages to be gained from the *application of particular techniques*, e.g. value management, TQM, and 'openness' to the *potential of new techniques*, e.g. the six sigma programme (Chapter 8);

- the advantages, where appropriate, of adopting particular organizational forms for speed and flexibility – see 'Task force structures' (Chapter 4).

Locating the strategic effort

Among the many variables management has to consider in devising strategy is the key one of *where* organizational, hence marketing, resources and effort should be applied. To what areas, regions and nation states? is a fundamentally important question. The emergence of global competition has been mentioned a number of times in this text. It has occurred as the layers of protection for home market operations have been reduced or have disappeared. Falling transport costs have counterbalanced the drawbacks of geographical distance. The liberating influences of deregulation of markets and tariff reductions have intensified with the creation of trading blocs such as the EU and free trade areas such as NAFTA (North American Free Trade Agreement). Significant political change has germinated both opportunities and threats, from Eastern Europe and China for example.

Such sweeping changes have forced organizations to recognize:

- the opportunities that now exist beyond the home market, and

- that even where home market dominance has been achieved it is now threatened by intense international competition.

Even if the organization is small or medium-sized, its strategists must increasingly confront the issue of whether and to what extent it should deploy its resources to developing internationally. For such companies it means being realistic about the resource levels available – creating a global presence and establishing a global brand is inherently risky and certainly highly expensive. Organizations committed to operating abroad tend therefore to 'work their passage' along the exporting–international marketing–global marketing continuum, coming to rest where the coordinate of skills and resources meets the one of risk and complexity. In the sections which follow we shall look at some of the issues involved as an organization seeks to operate at each of these three levels of sophistication.

Export marketing

'Exporting', one aspect of the broader activity we term 'international marketing', can generally be taken to mean the supply of finished, semi-finished and 'knocked-down' products from one country to one or more foreign countries. (The term 'knocked-down' will be explained later.)

Exporting can be undertaken *indirectly* (e.g. through merchants and buying agents in the UK or through the UK buying offices of foreign firms) or *directly* (e.g. through sales agents in the markets concerned or UK-based travelling representatives, or via a sales office established abroad by the exporter to serve a market or group of markets

– if the products require substantial after sales service, a service depot may be established there too).

Often an organization comes into exporting quite by chance (through the visit of a buyer or agent to the factory or showroom) and if the products are appealing, trade develops from there.

While no prospects for business should be neglected, the marketing concept calls for a planned approach, related to the overall mission and objectives of the organization and based upon sales volume:cost:profit considerations. This is of increasing importance as competition in world markets intensifies.

Successful exporting calls for investment on three counts:

● *Investment in time* – patience and sustained effort are usually necessary before the correct combination of product and marketing strategy is found.

● *Investment in finance* – breaking into highly competitive markets may require a type of investment budget procedure, with a subsequent payback period of two, three or more years.

● *Investment in personnel* – exporting, even on a limited scale, means developing appropriate marketing mixes and calls for the study of shipping procedures, modes of transport, insurance cover, export contracts of sale, tariffs, quotas, import licensing restrictions, credit and 'political' risks, etc. It cannot be left to personnel already heavily committed in domestic marketing activity.

Because of the implications for cost and profit objectives, marketing research must be well to the fore, however basic this may be.

A strategy for approaching export markets must be based on an assessment of at least these factors:

● present and potential size of the market(s);

● degree and type of competitive activity;

● prevailing price levels, trade margins, discounts;

● required advertising, promotional and servicing support;

● quality/performance comparisons with competing products and services, plus suggestions for modifications;

● assessment of tariff and non-tariff barriers to trade;

● assessment of cost/effectiveness of various methods of transportation and distribution;

● assessment of short- and long-term return on investment targets;

● related financial implications of all the above, including an assessment of the credit and political risks involved.

Since some of the terms in the above checklist may be new to readers, here is a word or two of explanation:

● *Tariffs*. These are duties imposed on products by the governments of importing countries and, of course, they increase the price of the goods in the market. They may be imposed on the value of the goods (*ad valorem* tariffs), be imposed by weight or may be specific to the classification of the goods concerned. The objectives of tariffs are to raise revenue, or more usually, to protect the industries of the importing country. Trading blocs (e.g. the European Union) and frameworks such as WTO (The World Trade Organisation, formerly GATT – General

Agreement on Tariffs and Trade) aim to liberalize international trade through the reduction and subsequent abolition of tariffs. Nevertheless they still widely exist and understanding the tariffs of some countries can be quite complex.

● *Non-tariff barriers to trade*. An exporter may discover that in order to sell his products in a foreign market they may have to comply with strict regulations (e.g. health and safety) that go beyond the requirements in his own country. Or, goods may be barred from importation unless they utilize a proportion of local labour or contain local raw materials. Again, sometimes the objective is to protect the industries of the importing countries.

● *Credit risk*. The risk that a supplier may part with his goods and not get paid for them is increased in exporting because the buyer may be relatively unknown to the supplier, may be geographically distant and will be operating under a different legal system. The supplier could ask for cash with order but is hardly likely to do any business. The buyer would prefer lengthy credit (e.g. 90 days or more) so that he or she can import the goods and sell them before the exporter's bill has to be met. Some compromise has to be reached (this will be explained later). The exporter could insure against this risk and invariably does, but costs are incurred, which must be 'absorbed' or added to the export price.

● *Political risk*. Due to wars, or civil commotions, the exporter's consignment may be delayed or lost, it may not be possible to recoup payment for his or her sales and, at worst, his or her assets may be seized. In these respects, some countries are more problematical politically than others. The political risk is a peril that can be insured against, but at a price.

The export marketing mix

Perhaps the best way to complete this short description of export marketing is to outline some of the typical issues that arise in developing various elements of the mix so that there is an 'in-built acceptability' about the exporter's offer.

Product

It is often the case that the product has to be adapted or reformulated to be acceptable to markets abroad. Differences arising from geographical and climatic conditions, the technical skills of operatives in the importing country, the voltage rates of electricity supply, health and safety regulations, taxation and political requirements (e.g. necessitating the use of locally made components) may give rise to the need for products with different design features, colours, sizes, materials used, etc.

Cultural considerations (e.g. tribal, social and religious factors) may have significant implications for food products, additives, ingredients and for brand names and symbols.

Tariff and non-tariff barriers can sometimes be overcome by exporting products in a semi-finished state or 'knocked-down' state (partially or completely, and known as p.k.d. or c.k.d.). For example, a car manufacturer separately crating six engines, six body shells and six chassis for export would provide employment in the importing country in building up six complete vehicles.

> An excellent illustration of fitting a product to a market is provided by Walkers Shortbread Ltd., which exports 40 per cent of its output. The firm's managing director, visiting Australia in 1994, was worried about the effect on sales of the then current 'Buy Australian' campaign. A customer suggested that the competition might be countered if Walkers made more use of Australian ingredients. As a result, a completely new shortbread was developed made with Australian Macadamia nuts. The Australian content of the product was emphasised on its packaging as was the use of Australian stem ginger on

another product 'Ginger Royals'. These moves enabled the company to stabilise its leading position in Australia and led to the successful introduction of Macadamia Shortbread in the Far East, the UK and other markets ('Export Winners', Department of Trade and Industry, January 1997).

Price

Fixing the price is frequently a lengthy and complex process and we can only look at it in outline here. Tariff classifications, freight and insurance costs, handling and storage costs, agents' commissions, trade margins and discounts and local taxes (e.g. value added tax) are some of the factors that must be discovered by marketing research. To these must be added any extra production or development costs to be incurred in fitting the product to the export market.

The product must be compared to competing products in terms of its specification, performance, design, durability, accessories and after sales service to assess the *value* it offers and whether the best marketing strategy would be through *non-price competition*.

Finally the price should be quoted in a manner that 'makes it easy for the buyer to buy'. An *ex-works* or *free-on-board* (f.o.b.) UK export quotation in sterling, for example, would be a definite impediment to sales. A *delivered* price to the buyer's premises in the buyer's currency, or at least a *cost, insurance and freight* (c.i.f.) quotation in the buyer's currency, to his nearest port or airport, would be very much better.

The extension of credit to the buyer, or otherwise, is a related and important aspect of fixing the price. Figure 13.1 attempts to summarize the issue. It is meant to convey that whatever is best suited to the exporter (+) involves the importer in the most expense and trouble (−) and vice versa. The quotations between the extremities ('Open account' and 'Cash with order') denote the other points on the continuum.

The price quoted to a buyer may or may not take account of the costs and services associated with supply. For example there is a world of difference between the two following types of price:

● *ex works* – which is a quotation for goods at the factory gate, with or without the cost of packaging and packing, leaving the associated costs of transport and insurance as the responsibility of the buyer;

● *delivered duty paid* (DDP) – which covers *all* the costs of delivery to the buyer's premises, including any duty payable, and which provides the buyer with an accurate and speedy means of fixing his own (re-sale) price for the goods.

It is important, so as to avoid misunderstandings, friction and, at worst, repudiation of contract, to be precise and absolutely unmistakable about what the price covers. The International Chamber of Commerce has done significant work in eradicating the dangers of misunderstandings. In its *Incoterms* guide it has published standard

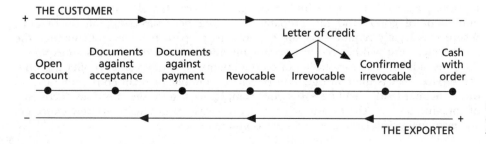

Figure 13.1. *Methods of export payment: risk and security*

interpretations of the most commonly used quotations – f.o.b., c.i.f., etc. – setting out clearly the respective obligations of buyer and seller. This has been widely adopted for application to international sale contracts. The exporter can therefore make the proposed extent of his own responsibility transparently clear merely by adding the suffix 'Incoterms' to his quotation together with the applicable publication date of the guide being used (1990 being the latest edition at the time of writing). If he refers the buyer to the appropriate edition and the buyer agrees to be bound by these terms there should be no problems.

As indicated earlier, exporters can obtain insurance protection against non-payment by overseas buyers for either commercial or political reasons. Various types of insurance policy, general or specific, are available. In the UK, for example, NCM Credit Insurance Ltd. is the largest provider of short-term (up to 180 days) credit insurance for exporters. A number of other institutions also provide cover. In the first instance the exporter will invariably seek the advice of his or her own bank on this.

Place

In terms of considerations of place there are two basic aspects:

- methods of physical distribution, and

- marketing channel policy.

Physical distribution

Balancing costs and benefits means considering:

- any special requests of the customer;

- required speed of transit;

- climate and geography of the journey;

- volume/weight/value of consignment(s);

- nature and chemical composition of the products;

- freight, packing and insurance charges of various methods of physical distribution.

Reviewing these factors will, in turn, mean considering:

- the whole broad field of containerization;

- the economics of palletization and other 'unit-loads';

- the pros and cons of 'roll-on/roll-off' road vehicle services, air freight services, train ferry services;

- use of company transport or contract haulage;

- availability of forwarding agents groupage services.

A word here on *forwarding agents* – organizations which can advise on methods of transport, appropriate routes and packing. They are also able to arrange for the movement of goods and the preparation of the necessary shipping documents. Where it is legally required for the exporter to prepare particular documents, the forwarding agent will be able to give suitable advice. Since the agent is an expert in the consolidation and forwarding of consignments he is often able to offer a group-age service, that is the consolidation of a large number of small consignments into one container load, enabling SMEs, for example, to acquire the speed and economy of containerization. The forwarding agent's services are invaluable to new exporters and even many very large exporters rely on them exclusively.

The cost savings of the newer techniques of physical distribution are *indirect* (through reduced packing, insurance and interest on capital due to reduced journey time) rather than *direct* (through freight rates). An exporter preoccupied with freight rates might therefore miss an excellent opportunity of obtaining a competitive edge. This is a reason why marketing should involve itself in the transport function, as indicated earlier in the text.

Channel policy

At the first stage channel policy involves an examination of the *prevailing method of distribution*. Is it better to 'go with' this or seek to establish an alternative method? For a new exporter it may be unrealistic to attempt to divert business from the customary channels. On the other hand, if the members of those channels cannot effectively handle any additional products, the exporter has to weigh the alternatives carefully.

What is the 'structure of the market'? For industrial products, is there a concentration of buying power? For consumer products, what is the relative importance of 'independent' retailers, multiples, department stores, consumer cooperatives and mail order organizations? How significant are the wholesale trade, franchising and direct response marketing?

Distributors' profit margins and discounts, quantity discounts, sales taxes, the credit-worthiness of distributors, the necessity of holding stocks in the market and the possibility of negotiating contracts for the supply of own-brand merchandise must all be weighed carefully in fixing the channel policy.

Some exporters have discovered that introducing products through local manufacturers of allied, or even similar, lines can be effective.

Promotion

In terms of promotion, there are three points to consider:

- *what* should be said;
- *where* it should be said;
- *how* it should be said.

The responses will depend on the availability of media, the degree of sophistication required in media choice and creativity, the buyers' motives and informational needs (which will vary from market to market), the budget available and the presence or absence of the firm's own sales organization in the market.

The legal regulations affecting the *content* of advertising (especially concerning claims for the product); the social and religious conventions of the market (e.g. relating to the role of women), the influence of particular colours in certain markets and cultures and the absolute necessity of obtaining correct idiomatic translations of advertising 'copy' and public relations material are some of the important factors to be reviewed in planning campaigns in export markets.

Exhibitions in foreign markets are popular with exporters, as a way of introducing products and also of conducting basic marketing research. As in the UK, participation is very often supported by government funding for new exporters. Government services are also usually available to support publicity and public relations activity in foreign markets.

An increasingly common issue for debate is the extent to which communications campaigns can be standardized, that is whether one campaign and one message may be utilized throughout many markets. This will be discussed further when we consider *global marketing* later in the chapter.

People

Several references have been made in this text to the importance of the people factor. Chapter 12 provided an outline of ways in which the organization might develop a customer-led culture. If implementing marketing as a whole organization activity is important for success in the domestic market it is even more important for foreign markets. The example below, based on an actual firm, provides a splendid illustration of how it might be done.

Nectar Manufacturing Ltd: Total customer satisfaction

Nectar Manufacturing Ltd. based in Carrickfergus, Northern Ireland, employs 120 people in the manufacture of natural hair and skin products and cosmetics. The Company is strongly focused on understanding its customers and on providing them with the highest standards of service. The Company's Total Customer Satisfaction programme includes problem solving committees and an employee award scheme under which, every six months, two or three high achieving employees spend a week working with customers overseas. Upon their return, a report is written and circulated within the company:

- *employees experience the customers' problems first-hand and are encouraged to respond: e.g. an employee from the packaging department saw the state orders arrived in and was able to suggest improvements to the packaging process;*

- *responsibility for effecting changes that will improve customer service is devolved to all levels within the company.*

('Export Winners', *Department of Trade and Industry*, January 1997).

Perhaps enough has been said in this outline to clarify why exporting calls for:

- investment in time;

- investment in finance;

- investment in personnel.

The one element of the enlarged marketing mix not yet mentioned in this section is, of course, the *preparation element*, marketing research. Research for exporting typically comprises:

- *desk or 'armchair' research* – usually based in the exporter's country, e.g. the UK and

- *field research* – in the market(s) abroad.

Desk research involves the gathering and analysis of *secondary data*, for example published statistics from government and other sources, such as the Country Forecasts (58 in number) from the Economist Intelligence Unit. *Field research* involves the gathering and analysis of *primary data*, that is marketing information tailored specifically to the needs of the organization and obtainable from surveys and other research work in the market.

Chapter 6 contains a significant amount of information on both types of research and their methodologies and sources (it is important for examination students to remember which are primary data and which are secondary data, for they are often described incorrectly in answers).

'Export Winners', published by the DTI in January 1997 and referred to earlier in this section was a report containing the views and experiences of 75 successful UK exporting companies. Over two-thirds of these were SMEs and approximately one-quarter were in the service sector. Regardless of the size of the company or the nature of its business, a number of 'core ingredients for success' emerged from the interviews involved. These were:

- vision;
- commitment;
- planning;
- market visits;
- relationships;
- culture and languages;
- documentation and procedures;
- quality.

International marketing

International marketing is the broader activity of doing business with foreign markets, of which exporting is one aspect. The purpose of this section is to describe some of the other aspects.

Licensing and royalty agreements

As a result of researching markets for opportunities to sell finished products abroad, it is often discovered that the best method of market entry is to arrange a *licensing* contract with a local manufacturer.

It may be difficult to export finished products because of import controls or freight and distribution costs. Again, the design and specification for acceptance abroad might be impractical or uneconomic for the exporter. Or again, plant capacity or lack of capital funding may prevent the organization from reaping the rewards of its natural inventiveness.

In addition to any registered patents the firm may possess (and it should seek specialist advice on how these should be protected in foreign markets), it may be possible to license the use of the following 'know-how' (termed *intellectual property*):

- the results of technical research;
- a novel, important feature of product design;
- use of the firm's name or trade mark where this has clear market value;
- special features in capital equipment which increase output, enhance safety, etc.

Income may be by:

- disclosure fee;
- royalties on sales achieved by the licensee;
- usually, a combination of the previous two items and perhaps
- payments for continuing technical assistance.

Too often in the past licensing has been regarded as a last resort. Yet accurate assessments and costings may reveal that a firm's blueprints, drawings, prototypes and technical knowledge would yield it a better return on investment than its finished products. So it should always be regarded as a fundamental aspect of the marketing approach.

Franchising, which has been described in Chapter 10, is a very similar method of market entry.

Contract manufacturing

Under contract manufacturing the organization will seek a suitable manufacturer in the foreign market and arrange for its products to be manufactured there. Usually, the agreement covers manufacture and/or assembly so that the firm entering the market will retain control over marketing, including distribution.

Contract manufacturing is often an important first step in setting up the organization's own manufacturing plant abroad, and it allows speedy entry, skirting tariff and non-tariff barriers to trade, with limited investment being required. Since the organization could to some extent lose control over its production the agreement may provide for the local firm to maintain stipulated quality and cost standards and give the organization the right of inspection in this regard.

Management contracting

Management contracting is really the export of management and consultancy services. A local organization may provide the funding for a capital project (e.g. the construction of a tourism complex, including accommodation, entertainment and shopping facilities). Though the local firm has the funds it may lack the expertise to operate and manage such facilities and so concludes arrangements with a well-established consultancy company, with considerable experience in the field.

The consultant organization, having satisfied itself through prior research that this is the most realistic and profitable way of dealing with the market concerned, will find the method appealing – it is a low-risk strategy and the agreement usually provides for consultancy and management fees, etc. to be paid from the outset of the project.

Joint ventures

Apart from exporting, all the methods of international marketing so far reviewed can also be described as *joint ventures*.

A local organization is identified as a suitable partner and the market is developed jointly under the terms of a contract. The partners often retain their own identities and corporate structures in the venture but cooperation may go beyond this, for example:

- a UK firm may purchase an interest in an existing foreign company, or
- a foreign firm may acquire a share in a company already established in the market by a UK 'parent' firm, or
- the UK company may jointly set up and operate a completely new business enterprise with a local company.

It is very important for the UK firm, for example, to recognize that if local company law prevents majority shareholding by foreign nationals it may not have the power to improve matters which are not to its liking. Therefore, a great deal of thought must be given, at the outset, to such matters as:

- *allocation of dividends* (e.g. for distribution or re-investment?);
- *commercial policy* (e.g. does the local firm subscribe to the 'marketing' approach?);

- *business ethics*;
- *product policy* (e.g. affecting matters of health and safety).

There must be complete *unity of purpose* for the venture to succeed and all potentially contentious matters must be fully anticipated and provided for in the contract of agreement.

Wholly owned subsidiaries

A clear trend throughout the world in the last two or three decades, hastened by the formation of trading blocs and free trade areas has been that of direct investment in foreign markets through setting up or acquiring *wholly owned subsidiaries*.

The development has encompassed services as well as products with retail organizations, consultants, advertising and marketing research organizations well to the fore – as indicated in earlier chapters of this book, in fact.

Whatever the class of subsidiary – manufacturing, retailing, after sales servicing, sales/ marketing, etc. – to own and operate one abroad requires extensive marketing research and expert legal advice on company formation and operation and on taxation matters. An accurate assessment of the capital and operating costs involved will clearly be a decisive factor too.

Despite the need for caution and care, it is clear to an increasing number of organizations throughout the world that a full local presence may so reduce costs and increase speed of service that the firm's competitiveness is markedly improved. A high level of involvement means a high level of risk, of course – particularly where a changed political situation could amount, at worst, to the freezing or seizure of foreign assets. This only underlines the importance of extensive, high-quality prior screening of market opportunities.

Multinational corporations

Until recently, multinational corporations, giant international companies operating across the world, represented the highest level of sophistication so far as international marketing is concerned. With headquarters in either America, Europe or the Far East, they have assumed tremendous importance and, outside of the former Eastern bloc countries, the ownership and control of the means of production and distribution by giant corporations had reached such remarkable significance by 1967 that J.J. Servan-Schreiber, in his best-selling (see Keegan, 1989) book *The American Challenge*, predicted that in 15 years the multinational corporation would become the world's greatest industrial power after the USA and the USSR. (By the early 1970s multinationals accounted for almost one eighth of Britain's output and one fifth of her exports).

Though relatively few firms enter the lists as multinationals, the economic power and influence wielded by such firms as General Motors, General Electric, Ford, Fiat, Nissan, Mitsubishi, Siemens, ITT, IBM, ICI, British Petroleum and Royal Dutch/Shell has been evident for all to see, particularly in the last four decades.

Paliwoda offers the following 'working definition' of a multinational:

> *A multinational enterprise is a corporation which owns (in whole or part) , controls and manages income-generating assets in more than one country. In so doing, it engages in international production, sales and distribution of goods and services across national boundaries financed by foreign investment (1993, p 25).*

Paliwoda believes the multinational meets the following two important criteria, with particular emphasis on the second of these:

- foreign direct investments either in manufacturing or service industries in more than two countries, and

- corporate planning which employs a world-wide perspective, and impartially allocates resources and funding on a global basis.

Governments have been keen to attract multinationals since they provide for their host countries employment opportunities, capital investment, advanced and even high technology and marketing skills. Against this, of course, their size and the fact that their strategies are planned internationally means that rationalization of their production, movements of capital and pricing strategies may have marked effects on a nation and its balance of payments.

All in all they bring to a nation far more advantages than drawbacks, though noted author Warren Keegan (1989, p 7) believes that as a method of operation the multinational is yielding primacy of place to the *global corporation* which we shall be looking at later in this chapter.

Concluding comments

This is an outline of various methods of market entry which are collectively labelled international marketing. However, these methods are not mutually exclusive. A company operating successfully in international markets may employ a variety of methods – indirect exporting, direct exporting, licensing, franchising, contract manufacturing, etc.

The methods it will employ will depend upon:

- the organization's size, resources, mission and objectives;

- the nature of the markets in which it chooses to operate.

An additional method worthy of mention, because it has proved useful from time to time, is that of *countertrading* in which an importer can pay for goods and services by barter. This has been particularly useful in trade with former Communist countries which lacked acceptable hard currencies with which to meet their bills. Hibbert (1989, p 137), for example, reports that Schweppes in Britain accepted Bulgarian tomatoes as part of a deal to sell its beverages into Bulgaria.

Obviously, from the exporter's point of view, *barter trading* is not without its difficulties but it has enabled organizations to develop markets well beyond anything that could have been attained on the more usual exporting lines.

Global marketing

This is a large and complex subject. Reducing even its main features into a necessarily brief outline presents quite a challenge. One way to begin is to trace the development of the global corporation as it was perceived by Keegan (1989, pp 7–9). Keegan suggested that, at the first stage, companies are domestic in their 'focus, vision and orientation' and that their environmental scanning is limited to the geographic scope of their domestic market.

At stage two, the evolution of the global corporation begins. The company is still oriented towards home market operations but it decides to pursue international opportunities. The product strategy of the 'stage two' company is one of *extension* – products designed for the home country market are 'extended', wherever possible, into international markets.

At stage three, the company discovers that the differences in markets around the world demand adaptation of the marketing mix. So it responds to differences in markets and evolves into an organization pursuing a *multidomestic strategy* which responds to the needs of each specific national market, its dynamics and its competitive structure. Keegan suggests that it is now 'multinational' in focus, as opposed to 'home country'.

Stage four sees the company still extending products wherever possible (the stage two approach) and adapting products (the stage three approach) whenever necessary. In addition to this, however, a company at stage four also focuses on emerging global markets, that is markets that can be reached with the same basic appeal and message and with the same basic product. Keegan adds: 'The essential difference between the global corporation and the multinational corporation is that the global corporation seeks to serve a basically identical market appearing in many countries throughout the world.'

The word 'basic' is important, for the product and the message may require *some* adaptation to local customs and practices, for example a right-hand drive 'world car', such as the Ford Mondeo must be adapted for those countries requiring left-hand drive. The global corporation consequently has a mixed structure to allow for these operational alternatives.

Hibbert (1989, pp 104–5) suggests there are strong forces in the business environment of today leading towards global marketing strategies, for example:

- demographic, cultural and economic convergence in consumer markets;
- increasingly identical requirements in world-wide industrial markets (e.g. machine tools, plant construction);
- increasingly significant economies to be achieved through standardization in purchasing, manufacturing, distribution, etc.;
- the impact of technology on manufacturing (requiring large-scale production of standardized products to recoup investment);
- changes in regional economic cooperation (e.g. European Union) leading to freer movement of goods, labour and capital;
- the impact of technology on transportation and distribution;
- the deregulation of national markets in airline, banking and financial services and the denationalizing of telecommunications, power generation, etc.

These influences for change are readily apparent to all of us and there can be no argument about them. However, as Richard Koch, writing in 1995 points out we must now extend our definition of *globalization* beyond a process 'whereby global tastes and product offerings converge and are increasingly satisfied by global products rather than local ones'. This is one aspect of globalization but the term is:

> Also used to indicate something much more significant and far reaching. Few real global products exist, but globalisation is a reality for most of the world's largest companies, in the sense that they think and operate with a global perspective on customers, technology, costs, sourcing, strategic alliances and competitors (Koch, 1995, p 226).

Koch describes the trends identified by Hibbert, adding that they do not require 'product universalism': *product localization* is necessary for global success in most businesses. Such trends and circumstances have given rise to the cry for organizations to 'think global and act local'. The Sony Corporation coined the phrase 'global localization' to describe the process of adapting a global product to local tastes by low cost customization. The process provides the supplier with the low-cost advantages of volume output but provides a measure of product differentiation tailored to specific customers and markets. The Sony phrase has subsequently been contracted to 'glocalization', which has implications for organization structures as well as product policies. The neat summary of Bartlett and Ghoshal (reported in Kotler, 1997, p 424), provides us with a useful way of concluding this outline. They distinguish three organizational strategies:

- a *global strategy*, which treats the world as one market;
- a *multinational strategy*, in which the world is regarded as a portfolio of *national* opportunities;
- a *'glocal' strategy* in which certain core elements are standardized and other elements are localized. (They instance the example of telecommunications here, in that the supplier can obviously standardize some core components but each nation requires some adaptation of its equipment).

Corporate marketing

Let us begin our review of this topic with an imaginary case study.

Fortuna Fine Chemicals

Fortuna Fine Chemicals, which recruits a large number of graduates each year, is concerned about the quality of candidates coming forward in response to its recruitment drives. Despite economic recession and rising unemployment, the company feels that many of the candidates appear to lack the motivation and the level of knowledge to become the type of skilled manager needed in the next decade, particularly in relation to global markets.

When a marketing research agency is briefed on the problem it suggests there may be a significant gap between the company's perception of itself and how it is regarded by other groups, including potential employees. The company sanctions a survey of its corporate image. The agency begins this by conducting discussion groups among third-year university undergraduates. The preliminary findings are that in comparison with its competitors the company is seen as 'colourless and ordinary'.

Learning of these findings, Fortuna sanctions a full-scale survey among all third-year undergraduates based on a detailed and quite lengthy questionnaire which, gratifyingly, obtains a high, representative level of response. The survey results confirm the hypotheses generated by the discussion groups. The company is indeed perceived as 'colourless and ordinary'. Moreover, as a result of a discharge of effluent from one of its main manufacturing processes some years before, which received adverse publicity at that time, the company is perceived to be uncaring about the environment despite the fact that the process had been replaced by one which is far safer and cleaner environmentally.

As a result of these findings the company undertakes a promotional campaign in order to build a strongly favourable company reputation attractive to both current and potential employees and a number of other sectors including customers, investors and the general public. This communications campaign involves an analysis of the design of company packaging, publicity materials, stationery and company reports as well as that of its advertising and public relations at all levels.

This 'case study' should clarify for you something of the process and objectives of *corporate marketing*. This book has outlined the process of marketing goods, services and ideas, but has said little about the marketing of the organization itself.

And what would be the point of an organization advertising its brands extensively and being resolute in providing its consumers with superb value for money if the organization itself remains unknown or 'colourless and ordinary' – or worse, is seen as aloof and uncaring?

An extensive study conducted for *Time* magazine by Yankelovitch, Skelly and White (1985, p 39) suggests that corporate communications can play an important role for those corporations that use it regularly. This is self-evident if we think about it, but two points do need to be stressed here:

● Corporate marketing is no substitute for 'doing good'. Having 'done good', there is no harm in the company getting the credit for this through corporate marketing. What corporate marketing must never be is unethical and manipulative – designed to convey the idea that the organization is better than it really is. Such an approach is, in any event, bad business in the long run. As someone once said of advertising, it might well sell anything – once.

● As with all marketing activity, every aspect of it should be integrated and project a *consistent* message. It is pointless for a company fearing a hostile takeover bid to conduct a direct mail campaign to its shareholders which asserts its sense of responsibility to them if, at the same time, it is undertaking the sponsorship of particular events which give it a frivolous image.

Perhaps the best way it can ensure it is 'doing good' and project an image which supports this is to 'begin at the beginning' with a formulation of its objectives.

In Chapter 2 we noted that the *stakeholder concept* suggests objectives should not stem from the organization exclusively but from the claims upon it by its various stakeholders – its customers, employees, distributors, shareholders, suppliers, central and local government, the general public, that is all parties who have a stake in its well-being and are affected by its operations. The proposed objectives should constitute a reasonable balance of all their claims upon the organization. Figure 13.2 is intended to convey this concept.

Corporate marketing in action

The evidence of corporate marketing has been all around us, particularly in the last two decades. As a result of the oil crises of the 1970s, for instance, when supplies were reduced and prices rose dramatically, the oil companies had to reduce their heavy advertising expenditures. They no longer needed so much to persuade the public to buy petrol as they needed to keep their name before the public in a favourable light – not least because, like most other profitable multinationals, they were increasingly being regarded with some suspicion, hostility even.

Consequently most oil companies, in emphasizing their corporate as opposed to their brand image, based their promotional campaigns on their exploration activities in the North Sea, Alaska and other treacherous locations – drawing attention to the costs and the risks being undertaken in order to discover new sources of oil.

One might say that this was undertaken as an aspect of *crisis management* due to a change in the business environment. This is also visible in the corporate advertising and public relations campaigns undertaken *defensively* in the wake, for example, of a public outcry about the location of a factory or a process, or in the wake of an environmental disaster.

While such activity is understandable from the organization's standpoint, what is being said in this section is that corporate marketing, in the fullest and best sense of the marketing concept, should be based upon prior objectives derived from the claims of stakeholders.

Figure 13.2. *Organizational objectives and the stakeholder concept*

Two other influences are currently at work in the development of corporate marketing. The first of these is that it may transpire that it is be more logical, and more productive, to promote the organization rather than its brands. This is particularly the case with large retail multiple organizations (e.g. Sainsbury, Tesco, Marks & Spencer) which, in any event, sell a very significant proportion of own-brand merchandise.

The second influence relates to the global integration of many firms and their need to project a world-wide image. A good example of this was the award winning approach of ICI (Imperial Chemical Industries) at the end of the 1980s. The objective was to transform the perception of ICI from a massive British industrial conglomerate with world-wide links to a massive world-wide industrial conglomerate which happens to have a British headquarters.

The organization's symbol – the ICI roundel – had been used in a piecemeal fashion (it was black and white in Britain, orange and white in other parts of the world) was changed to a uniform blue throughout the world and was accompanied by the slogan:

World Problems,

World Solutions,

ICI World Class.

The notion of corporate marketing as being no more than a public relations activity orchestrated by manipulative 'spin doctors' dies hard. The 1998 Workshop Programme of the UK's Institute of Public Relations contained a number of workshops related to traditional PR functions, for example:

- Writing for the Press;
- Introduction to Media Relations;
- Improving your Creativity;
- Professional Presentation Skills.

But it also contained workshops of a more strategic import, for example:

- Research and Evaluation Methods in Public Relations;
- Financial Aspects of Public Relations;
- Corporate Strategy and Public Relations;
- Management of Public Relations Programmes.

It was also notable that in early 1996 leading public relations firm Burson Marseller announced that it was no longer merely providing PR services. *Perception management*, a mixture of PR and management consultancy, had now emerged so that organizations needed to be thinking about communication as part of their wider corporate strategy – a development that now required more than engaging the services of media relations specialists.

In this context, Walker (1996) reported on how some local councils in Britain were upgrading their PR sections to centres of total communication. These councils had realized the necessity of thinking about communications as part of their overall management strategy. This meant moving on from the concept of a former journalist sitting in a press office 'fighting fires', to such matters as listening to what stakeholders were saying, thinking about the way their services were organized and informing the public of their entitlements and how to obtain them.

Here we can discern the marketing concept at work and thus what is meant by *corporate marketing* – a process in which all managers, all organization members for that matter, are accountable and ethical communicators.

Thoughts on forecasting and marketing planning

C·H·A·P·T·E·R

FOURTEEN

Preliminary thoughts

In an introductory work of this nature, it is not usual to devote a great deal of space to the planning process. Marketing planning is generally featured in the later stages of marketing courses and there are a number of texts available which deal with this rather complex process in detail.

However, much has been said in this text about the *strategic* importance of marketing and about the approach to developing strategy. The development and reinforcement of sustainable competitive advantage in the market place as the primary objective of strategy for the SME, the SBU and the product division has been emphasized. 'Sustainable competitive advantage', 'synergy', 'the value of core competences', and 'asset-based marketing', etc. are all useful concepts, but they do not occur by happenstance. Conscious action must bring them about and a planning process is necessary to do this. It therefore seemed important to offer some thoughts at least on marketing planning towards the end of this text so as to round off the earlier attention paid to strategy and its development.

As we saw in Chapter 2, managers bring together *scarce resources* to achieve *pre-set objectives*, their actions taking place within an *environment* in which forces are at work influencing what goes on.

The processes involved in managing an organization to further its mission and achieve its objectives are ones of:

● analysis;

● planning;

● implementation;

● control.

Much was said about the analysis process in early chapters, particularly those dealing with marketing research. The planning process is one of matching the resources of the organization with marketing opportunities so that the objectives laid down can be achieved.

Implementation means, simply, 'getting the job done' – the targets have been set, the timing has been established and the personnel involved have been allocated their allotted tasks. It now remains to put the plan into operation, that is to *implement* it, and, importantly, to scrutinize continuously the organization's performance, which is the process of *control*.

An activity which bridges the processes of *analysis* and *planning* is that of *sales forecasting*. Since it is concerned with the analysis of demand, and relying as it does on the systematic analysis of both internal and external data, sales forecasting is often regarded as part of the marketing research function. In this book, the author has separated sales forecasting from marketing research in order to relate it more closely to marketing planning. The next section deals with sales forecasting and serves also as an introduction to the overall planning process.

Sales forecasting

Status and purpose

A *sales forecast* may be defined as an estimate of sales which will hopefully be obtained during some specified future period of time (usually one year) based upon specified resource inputs.

Mention of resource inputs having been specified suggests that the plan has already been formulated and this might raise the query 'which comes first: the plan or the forecast?' In practice, forecasting takes place in a context of broad goals – the objectives of the organization – which may be taken as given. Linked to these goals, the forecaster must make certain assumptions about the resources (plant and equipment, raw materials, manpower and finance) which will be available in the period under review. In fact, the forecaster may be asked to introduce a range of levels of resources into his calculations so that the range of forecasts then emerging can be compared with the overall goals, and the forecast best suited to these goals can be adopted. This approach is particularly suited, for example, to forecasting the sales of new products. Therefore, it is this chicken and egg situation of planning and forecasting which Willsmer (1976, p 166) doubtless has in mind when he says: 'Forecasts shape plans and plans shape forecasts'. Once a particular forecast has been agreed it then becomes the key factor in the monitoring and control of all the organization's operations – cash flows, purchasing, production, marketing and sales activities and the budgeted expenditure allocated to these activities. All business organizations must therefore forecast, since forecasting is a major function in planning and budgeting. Even the executive who claims he or she has never formally undertaken any forecasting activity cannot possibly operate a business unless he makes some estimate about the future even if this estimate is one of 'no change' (a barely realistic conclusion in the present climate). Similarly, the non-profit organization lays claim to its resources based on its forecast of level of activity for the next period.

Marketing, as we know, has to do with an adequate return on investment for the business organization. That return will be derived from realistic company planning accompanied by adequate management controls and business budgets. A sales forecast which can be employed with reasonable confidence provides the basis for the planning and the controls. To understand why Schwartz (Schwartz, 1981, p 68) believes that the sales forecast is the most important operational procedure undertaken by a business, Figure 14.1 shows some of the operations within the major functions of the business that are governed by the sales forecast.

Steps in the forecasting process

Obviously, the degree of elaboration employed and the level of accuracy being sought will be related to the size of enterprise involved. The objective should be to develop a forecasting method which will be accurate enough for practical purposes within an affordable cost. So, although the forecasting process is described in some detail in the pages which follow, in practice, the 'adequate' necessarily has to be substituted for the 'ideal'.

Sales forecast

Production	Finance	Marketing	Personnel
Stock levels	Cash flows	Advertising appropriation	Company manpower plan
Plant and equipment	Operating costs		incl. selection and recruitment of direct and indirect labour; provision for training and retraining; provision for redundancies, etc.
Materials purchases	Operating margins	Sales promotion and publicity expenditures	
Packaging and transport	Capital requirements	Sales quotas and budgets	
Heat, light, power supplies	Profits	Marketing research incl. product research and development	
Plant maintenance and repairs	Interest and taxation		
Planning and inspection, etc.	Dividends, etc.	After sales service, etc.	

A comprehensive and logical procedure for the development of a forecast, for a business organization by way of illustration, is set out below. The key steps are as follows:

     1   Forecast general economic conditions

     2   Forecast market potential and industry sales

     3   Forecast company sales

     4   Forecast sales by products, operating units

The arrows indicate the forecasting sequence and are meant to convey that Steps 3 and 4 are part of the same stage in the total process.

With regard to Step 1, in Chapter 2 some of the economic influences in the firm's environment were outlined and ways in which these might affect its future performance were indicated. *Environmental analysis* is, therefore, a key feature of Step 1.

The next stage in the process (Step 2) is to forecast the size of the *potential market* in which the firm is engaged and the *anticipated sales volume* of the industry of which the firm is a member. The first figure (market potential) is a measure of the maximum amount that could be sold with maximum possible marketing effort and expenditure within a given external environment. The anticipated industry sales will be an estimate of lesser magnitude than market potential since not all firms involved will be deploying maximum possible resources and effort to their marketing activity. Forecasting at this stage must be based on comprehensive knowledge of the industry's markets and the manner in which economic variables affect its sales.

The third step in the process is to forecast the total volume of sales that can be attained by the firm itself within the expected environmental conditions for the period under review. We have seen that *market potential* is the theoretical upper limit of industry sales with the forecast of actual industry sales as a somewhat lesser figure. Think of this last figure as *actual market size* – the total sales that will be achieved as a result of the anticipated efforts of all firms in the industry. The individual firm must now forecast its *market share* – or *company sales volume* – which it expects will result from a given level of resources, including marketing effort.

Remember that the firm will know from past experience whether there is any clear relationship between industry sales and its own sales. If the firm belongs to an active and effective industry or trade association, reliable data on industry sales may enable forecasts to be made with some confidence. Also, if the firm operates in more than one industry then its anticipated proportion of sales must be calculated for each industry and then brought together to form the total of the firm's estimated sales.

As indicated earlier, the arrows between Steps 3 and 4 move in both directions to indicate that these cannot be separated in practice, but they are also there for another important reason. It is good management practice to develop a forecast from the 'bottom-up', that is through the contribution of the people whose job it is to attain the targets implied by the forecast as well as from the 'top down' through management.

Not only does this make good business sense, since the employees (e.g. salespeople in industrial markets) often have important knowledge of trends in markets, it also makes good psychological sense. Involving employees gives them a sense of 'planning ownership' in both the forecast and the budget. This fosters commitment and energizes and inspires people to achieve the targets laid down in the marketing plan. Creating the notion of 'shared futures' in this way also helps to dispel any negative attitudes to control systems. When results are constantly being monitored, everyone is keen to have news of how the plan they helped to create is progressing.

In Chapter 12, when some thoughts on the development of a customer-led culture were being outlined, Piercy's (1992, p 233) belief was noted that 'the most important and productive thing ... in marketing planning is not the techniques and formal methods' but 'quite simply commitment and ownership'. It is a dictum fit to inform the actions of every planner.

Steps 3 and 4 usually entail consideration of the following factors:

- current sales (products);
- current sales (territories/markets);
- current sales (calendar – monthly/yearly).

These data help to provide an answer to the question 'Where are we now?' – which we will further examine later in the chapter. The data then have to be adjusted for:

- anticipated sales of new products;
- the trend of sales over previous time periods;
- the current sales in relation to the size of the market;
- the review of general trading and economic conditions;
- the ration of promotional support and other marketing effort to be made available in the period ahead.

We will then be at the stage of the *initial forecast* – perhaps the first of several, linked with various levels of resource inputs. To move towards the formation of the *sales budget* and other budgets means that the forecasts initially produced have to be modified for such factors as:

- the profit earning capacity of the various products;
- the production capacity of the business;
- the marketing, administrative and other costs involved;
- the total financial requirements of the proposed programme.

The forecaster will then say: 'all other things being equal, this is what is likely to happen'.

The next stage in the process is to decide upon the *budgets*. A budget can be defined as the statement, usually in detailed statistical and financial terms, of what the organization will actually set out to achieve in its marketing plan. The budget becomes, in effect, the target for attainment and every part of the organization will have its own budget (or target) for attainment stemming initially from the sales forecast and all-important *sales budget*.

So far then, we can see that in setting out to achieve its objectives, that the sales forecast is linked to the *planning* operation and the sales budget, while linked to the planning operation, is also the basis for *implementation* of the plan and also provides for the basic information for *control* (i.e. the continuous assessment of progress to target). Fixing the sales budget will enable the organization to settle its *production budget* so that which products are to be made, when they are to be made and the approved expenditures on stock levels, labour, materials, packing, plant maintenance, etc., can all be established. The *marketing budget* can be finalized and will establish (from the sales budget) details of the sales to be achieved per product and per territory and time period (e.g. per month). This budget will also include details of the approved expenditures on promotion (advertising, public relations, etc.), marketing research and the salesforce (setting out the allowable salaries, commissions, expenses, etc., to be paid for the achievement of targets set out in the sales budget). The *personnel budget* will contain details of the numbers and related expenditure for employees in all departments and will make provision for the necessary outlay on the selection, recruitment and training of new employees.

The *finance budget* will contain a breakdown of the income and expenditure per time period and the target balance over cost for the whole plan. It will also clarify the cash flow requirements and the working capital that may have to be borrowed pending the receipt of income from sales.

So, we can see that first the sales forecast and then the sales budget are at the root of all planned output and expenditure – a clear illustration of the old saying that 'nothing happens until somebody sells something'. Ultimately, when a forecast is adopted it not only sets the framework for much marketing activity, including the marketing communications policy and the setting of targets for salespeople, it also influences all the organization's operations as indicated in Figure 14.1.

Types of forecast

The form of a forecast, the period it covers, the degree of detail and accuracy required, the frequency of its revision all depend on the needs of the organization and the size and nature of the organization itself. The main types of forecast are now described.

Broadly speaking, the short-term forecast covers a period of one to three or six months ahead and relates very much to tactical decision-making – on stock levels, production schedules, transport planning, buying schedules and short-term borrowing. Such forecasts are typically prepared in great detail by products, markets, sales regions, etc. and are reviewed on a monthly basis with adjustments being made as actual sales pro rata to forecast are monitored. This would certainly be the case with several consumer markets, but as Wilson (1973, p 289) points out, the short-term forecast in industrial markets might extend to three years. Hence, 'it all depends'. The short-term forecast might be considered by many organizations to include the one year forecast, although it might be seen as a medium-term forecast (a description covering the period from one to five years) in other organizations. All organizations then prepare one year forecasts. Where sales are seasonal, both the peak-selling and slack periods are therefore covered by the forecast. The forecast thus aligns itself with the yearly financial profit plan and is of primary importance in budgeting for expenditure and revenues, the planning of marketing expenditures, manpower levels, the mobilization of working capital and provisions for taxation. The forecast will be reviewed at monthly or quarterly intervals and as with the shorter term forecast (one to three months or one to six months) it must be as accurate as is realistically possible since the ultimate financial results will be markedly influenced by the short-term forecast.

Medium-term forecasting (e.g. usually from two to five years) enables the organization to plan its capital expenditure, its longer-term marketing strategy, its research and development programmes, its management development and its policies of mergers and acquisitions through the length of the typical business cycle. This period is the one usually required to bring new plant, equipment and production processes into commission and to bring new products through the various technical feasibility and market testing stages to commercialization. Long-range forecasts extend beyond five years and relate even more closely to programmes of replacement for production processes, plant, equipment and products (many of which will have completed their life-cycle). This is the stage at which company objectives, including its visionary objectives, come under review. Obviously less detail is required for both medium-term and long-term forecasts and a high level of accuracy is not so important and is, in fact, difficult to attain (but this is not to say that the forecasting process is any less skilled).

With regard to longer-term forecasting, mention should be made of *technological forecasting*. This is a branch of forecasting which attempts to predict the impact of technological change on both products and services, and upon processes and methods in customer industries. The wider social and economic implications of changing technology also come within its purview.

Forecasting: roles and responsibilities

The question of who does the forecasting must be related to the size of the firm. In a small organization, the marketing executive will probably make the forecasts. In a larger firm it may be delegated to one or more marketing assistants. In very large firms the role may be allotted to an economist/market researcher. In a survey, conducted some years ago, and reported by Wilson (1973, p 282), 60 per cent of the responding firms stated that an economist/researcher figured in the forecasting process. This is not to say that the forecaster must invariably be a trained economist but what is important is that he or she should have a broad understanding of the economic environment and the working of the economy and be conversant with the many sources of published economic forecasts and other data. Where the organization retains the services of economic or marketing consultants or marketing research agencies it is important that the forecaster is able to work with them at an appropriate level of complexity and understanding.

It goes without saying that the forecaster must be competent in the standard forecasting techniques with an adequate appreciation of the more complex computer-based forecasting routines. What is salient is that the forecaster has a good knowledge of the organization, its products or services, its objectives and policies, its consumer markets or user industries, channels of distribution, etc. Ideally, the forecaster will be closely involved with the development and operation of the marketing information system which informs and guides operations.

Methods of forecasting

The selection of a method best suited to an individual organization will depend on a number of factors. Some of the prominent ones are listed below.

- the type of business/field of activity involved;
- the size of the organization, the experience of the personnel at its disposal;

- the type of historical data available and their relevance to the forecasting problem;

- the organization's experience of forecasting;

- the status of the forecast within the organization, i.e. its importance as an integrated planning tool;

- the time period to be covered by the forecast and the time available to make the forecast;

- the degree of accuracy required, i.e. the margin of error that would be acceptable for planning purposes.

It will be useful to explain briefly the significance of each of these factors in turn.

- In the consumer goods field, marketing activity is much more widely documented, with retail stock audits and numerous continuous research services and *ad hoc* surveys providing information on market trends, brand shares, etc. This is not the case in industrial marketing. Moreover, the action taken by the consumer goods company on such matters as price, discount policies, consumer and trade 'deals' usually has a much more direct influence on marketing results than in the industrial goods field where demand is derived.

- The size of the organization will determine the number of forecasting personnel at its disposal (the very small firm may have none), and the extent of their qualifications and training. The small firm will not, as a rule, be adept at the origination and use of complex, sophisticated techniques using econometric models. The experience of personnel is equally important. Most methods are a combination of objective (i.e. statistical) and subjective (i.e. judgemental) techniques. Executive judgement, based on up-to-date and valuable experience of the products, the market, competition, user and distributor attitudes, etc., is a vital element in realistic forecasting.

- The amount and quality of internal data (sales by products, markets, calendar sales, sales expenses and expense ratios, promotional appropriations, unit costs of production, etc.) and the time period through which this has been accumulated will clearly be of great significance as will the availability of market data and their relevance to the forecasting problem.

- The more experience of forecasting the organization has, the more likely it is to get better at it, the more chance it has of determining which particular factors most influence its marketing results and the more prepared it should be to use the more sophisticated forecasting techniques.

- The value put upon the forecast as an aid to planning will determine the resources made available for forecasting, hence the time and care devoted to it and the extent to which sales, production and finance personnel can be mobilized as part of the forecasting team.

- Some factors significantly influence short-term forecasts but have little significance for other time periods. It may be that changes in customer/distributor stock levels markedly affect short-run demand, but this factor may safely be discounted for a five year forecast. The time available for forecasting may necessarily be short , e.g. prior to introducing a contingency or emergency plan, and an outline forecast may be quite adequate.

- Accuracy must be approached on a cost:benefit basis – a point that has been made earlier. Moreover, the purpose of the forecast is relevant here. Greater accuracy is required for a forecast related to incremental improvement in net profit performance than one which relates to the decision to enter a new market, where perhaps only a 'broad brush' estimate of size may be all that is required for a 'go/no go' decision.

In addition to the above factors, the extent to which the organization plans to do something different in the ensuing period (introduce new products; enter new markets; change marketing, promotional or distribution policies, etc.) may well affect the choice of forecasting methods.

The process or forecasting will be better understood, perhaps, if we take a quick look at some of the main forecasting techniques. A range of quantitative and qualitative techniques is available to the forecaster. At this point in time there is some emphasis on the use of qualitative techniques for it is suggested that quantitative techniques, many of which process past data in order to forecast the future, are less useful in times of rapid change. Nevertheless, quantitative techniques, in the broad scheme of things, play a valuable part and any competent forecaster must understand their use and application.

The techniques of forecasting

Quantitative techniques

One of the most common statistical techniques used in sales forecasting is that of *time series analysis*. Statistics relating to changes in the values of a variable over time (in this case, sales) are known as a time series. Examinations of such series of data commonly reveal four different effects of changes over time. Figures 14.2 to 14.5 below illustrate these effects.

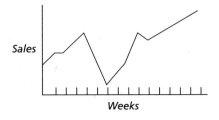

Figure 14.2. *Acme Foods – random fluctuation*

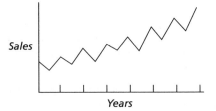

Figure 14.3. *Acme Foods – secular trend*

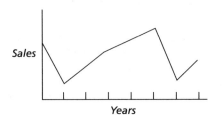

Figure 14.4. *Bennett Engineering – cyclical variation*

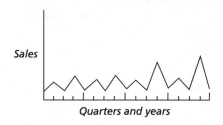

Figure 14.5. *Gladrags – seasonality*

Figure 14.2 illustrates the sales of Acme Foods during what normally would have been a busy quarter of the year. Unfortunately, a transport strike one third of the way through the period resulted in curtailment of deliveries of products and a break in supplies of raw materials. Sales were adversely affected by this unforeseen event (*random fluctuation*) and only began to recover towards the end of the quarter.

Figure 14.3 depicts the long-term movement of Acme Foods sales volume. It can be seen to have been increasing for several years. Such long-term movement is called the *secular trend*. It can be positive (upwards) or negative (downwards). Fortunately for Acme Foods their secular trend is positive.

Bennett Engineering have plotted their sales over a long period of time (Figure 14.4 is merely a section of a much more extended graph) and discover that in their section of the industry there is a cycle of growth and contraction over each five year period. This series of peaks and depressions, when occurring regularly over an extended period of time is a *cyclical variation*.

Gladrags have also chronologically classified their sales data (Figure 14.5). The type of fashion goods they produce have peak sales in the stores in the summer season and in the months before Christmas. Their own sales to the trade have peaks in the Spring and September. The sales curve shows this *seasonality* and it is notable that despite the sales growth of recent years, the level of sales in the off-peak periods is quite static. Gladrags intend to revise their product policy in order to improve this situation.

Recording these data graphically helps the firms in question to assess their future prospects to some extent (and, of course, it is perfectly possible for the sales curve of a single firm to exhibit all of these effects over time. And certainly in the case of secular trends, cyclical variations and seasonality, knowledge of the direction and magnitude of such changes will prove of some value in forecasting). In order to be more directly valuable, the trends in sales data require smoothing so that the overall trend lying behind the fluctuations becomes more apparent. One method of smoothing the trend is by the use of *moving averages*. An example may help to illustrate the process.

Premier Preserves

The company, relatively small but dynamic, manufactures jams and marmalades and markets these almost exclusively in the UK, at this stage. Growth has been good but laboured at some stages due to the contraction in the number of independent retailers (their main outlet), keen price competition from larger manufacturers and the appearance on more and more tables of substitute 'spreads' (e.g. peanut butter, chocolate). Sales data since 1984 are shown in Table 14.1.

In addition to the calendar sales, the forecaster has calculated the three year moving totals and the three year moving averages applicable to these sales figures (the supplementary note below the table outlines the method of calculation). The calendar sales are illustrated graphically in Figure 14.6.

Table 14.1. *Premier Preserves: yearly sales (standard packs)*

Year	Sales (calendar year)	Moving 3 year total	Moving 3 year average
1984	500	—	—
1985	622	1602	534
1986	480	2010	670
1987	908	2400	800
1988	1052	2775	925
1989	815	3270	1090
1990	1403	3630	1210
1991	1402	4080	1360
1992	1275	4500	1500
1993	1823	4848	1616
1994	1750	5364	1788
1995	1791	5706	1902
1996	2165	6210	2070
1997	2254	6588	2196
1998	2169	—	—

Note: 3 year total   1985 = 1984 (500) + 1985 (622) + 1986 (480) = 1602
1986 = 1985 (622) + 1986 (480) + 1987 (908) = 2010, etc.

3 year average 1985 = $\frac{1602}{3}$ = 534 (recorded against the mid year, here 1985, in each 3 year cycle).

Also illustrated in Figure 14.6 is the smoothed trend produced by plotting the values of each of the three year moving averages. Projecting the straight line (a process known as *trend extrapolation*), it is possible to deduce that on a continuance of the trend Premier Preserves could sell 2460 standard packs in 1999, a figure which it would be difficult to project from the episodic twists and turns of the curve of calendar sales (and despite the fact that the secular trend it portrays is so markedly positive).

The reader will doubtless have realized that trend projection from a time series has the major drawback that it assumes that conditions in the past will be largely the same in the future. The technique clearly takes no account of changes in the economic environment, in competitive activity, or changes in the firm's own product, promotional or other policies. For this reason, its results must be cautiously inter-preted and, in practice, it is seen as one input to the total forecasting process. A forecaster relying substantially on other techniques will invariably carry out a trend projection merely to serve as a starting point for subsequent ideas – to orient oneself to the task as it were.

For trend projection using moving averages it can be said that the technique is objective at least (i.e. not reliant on impressions and judgement) and simple to carry out. A refinement of the approach is provided by *exponential smoothing*.

In the example we have just examined, data from all parts of the time series were given an equal weighting in the process of calculation. Exponential smoothing is one of the techniques by which, because more recent data are judged to have greater typicality for the future than older data, the more recent data are given greater arithmetic weight. The weighting given in the data increases exponentially as the calculation progresses from older to the more recent data. Of great importance in the technique is the determination of an appropriate value for the *smoothing constant* or weighting factor which is applied. An approach would be to compare past forecasts

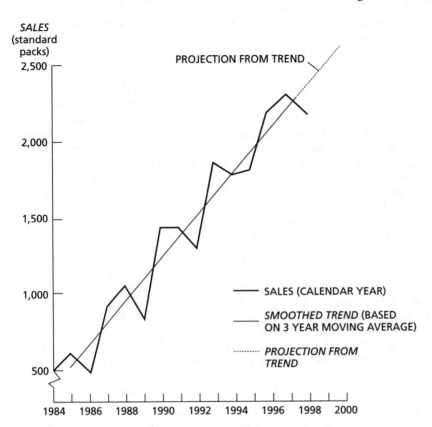

Figure 14.6. *Premier Preserves: calendar sales and smoothed trend (using 3 year moving average)*

PROJECTION FROM TREND

SALES (standard packs)

2,500

2,000

1,500

1,000

500

—— SALES (CALENDAR YEAR)

—— *SMOOTHED TREND* (BASED ON 3 YEAR MOVING AVERAGE)

.... *PROJECTION FROM TREND*

1984   1986   1988   1990   1992   1994   1996   1998   2000

with actual sales and to adopt the smoothing constant which would have produced the smallest forecasting error. The computer can be used for the most sophisticated forms of the technique. It is useful input, particularly to short-term forecasting.

Correlation and regression

As we noted earlier, the first stage in the forecasting process entails some appraisal of likely trading conditions and the economic outlook for the period under review. A key economic indicator will be *gross domestic product* (GDP), that is the total of goods and services which, it is predicted, will be produced in the country during the given period. If, from an analysis of past data, the forecaster can establish that some statistical relationship exists between GDP and the firm's own sales, or the sales of its industry, so much the better. Obviously the projected size of GDP will affect business confidence and hence the economic atmosphere in which the firm will be operating, but if GDP can be used as a *tied indicator*, in that GDP and the firm's sales move together, whether upwards or downwards, this is decidedly valuable to the forecaster. When a forecaster is considering the relationships between two variables (e.g. sales and advertising; sales and GDP; sales and rises in real income) then he or she will compare the relative values of the two variables by *regression/correlation analysis*. The strength of the relationship between the data is known as the *degree of correlation* and this is indicated (on a numerical scale between 0 and 1) by the *correlation coefficient*. Correlation coefficients of 0.8–1 indicate strong relationships whereas coefficients of 0–0.2 indicate little or no linear correlation. Thus a correlation coefficient of 0.8 for the relationship of new housing starts:sales of Arnolds ceramic kitchen and bathroom tiles, would indicate to Arnolds that statistics on new housing starts were an important input to their forecasting process (it is, of course, the lagged relationship – housing starts must logically precede the ordering of tiles). On the other hand, the firm would treat a coefficient of 0.5 for number of

UK marriages:sales of tableware with more circumspection. In both these cases, of course, the correlation is positive – variables can be shown to be negatively correlated (e.g. a negative correlation between hours of sunshine and sales of heavy, durable clothing would hardly be surprising).

In order to study the relationship between the two variables, the forecaster will probably construct a *scattergraph* (Figure 14.7). In the example below, the relationship between the sales of a basic raw material (e.g. china clay) and the output of some key customer industries (ceramics, paper, paint and cosmetics industries) is being examined. The values of the dependent variable (sales) are plotted along the vertical (*y*) axis and the values of the independent variable (industries' output) along the horizontal (*x*) axis. The scattergraph is measuring *annual percentage changes in output* (in order to overcome the difficulty of plotting values of vastly differing orders of magnitude). Sales and industrial output could be measured on a quantities basis, if this were feasible, or on a money values basis in which case, in order to compare like with like, the values would be computed at constant and not current prices.

The reader will note that each single point on the graph is the plot of the pair of figures (industries' output:raw material sales), the values having been obtained from a time series (1984–98). It will also be seen that a line has been added which passes approximately through the centre of the graph of the points. This is the *line of best fit*. It has been drawn by eye and in such a way as to minimize the total divergence of the points from the line. The value of incorporating the line of best fit is that for any value of the independent variable (in this case, industries' output) an appropriate value for the dependent variable (sales) can be read off from the graph. Thus, if for the forthcoming year a 3 per cent growth in output is being forecast an estimate of 2.8 per cent growth in sales of the raw material seems reasonable.

Now for a warning note – the figures produced for the scattergraph are *purely hypothetical*, in order to illustrate a principle. (For one thing, the reader will recognize

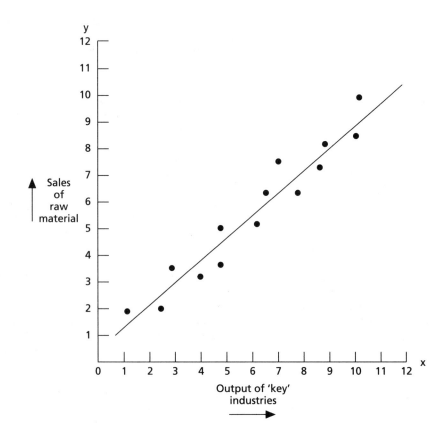

Figure 14.7. *The relationship between sales (raw material) and output of key industries*

that annual percentage growth rates of 9 and 10 per cent are totally unrealistic.) Moreover, the two variables are so closely related that the pattern of scatter of the points is such that it enables the line of best fit to be drawn with comparative ease. If in practice, the two variables were not very closely related, a line of best fit, certainly if drawn by eye, would not be a very reliable guide for making estimates.

We can see that the line of best fit in Figure 14.7 is, in effect, a straight line and therefore there is a *linear* relationship between the two variables (had the line of best fit been a curve, the relationship would have been *curvilinear*). To determine the correct position of the line of best fit when the pattern of plots on the scattergraph is not so clearly discernible as it is in Figure 14.7, a mathematical method is vastly preferable to human judgement.

The method is known as the *method of least squares*. The logic of the mathematical computation is that the line of best fit is the one that minimizes the total of the squared deviations and the line so drawn is called a *regression line*. In order to clarify what is meant by 'minimizing the total of the squared deviations' we must first look at Figure 14.8. The deviations of the points from the line are calculated by measuring either the *vertical* distance between a point and the line or the *horizontal* distance between a point and the line.

The general equation for a straight line on a graph is: $y = a + bx$ (where a and b are constants).

The two different methods of measuring the deviations, one minimizing the total of the squared deviations measured vertically, the other minimizing the total of the squared deviations measured horizontally would produce two different regression lines:

- the regression of y on x (vertical deviations);
- the regression of x on y (horizontal deviations).

The first of these (regression of y on x, to predict y from x), is the one most commonly employed. Determination of the line of best fit means finding the appropriate value of the constants a and b in the equation:

$$y = a + bx$$

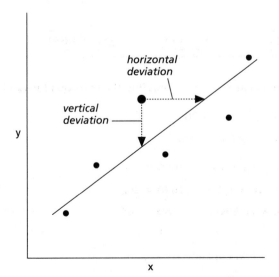

Figure 14.8. *Horizontal and vertical deviations and the line of best fit*

and for the regression of y on x, these can be discovered by the solution of the following two simultaneous equations:

$$\Sigma y = an + b\Sigma x$$

$$\Sigma xy = a\Sigma x + b\Sigma x^2$$

where n = the number of pairs of figures.

To the uninitiated, these notes may seem a little daunting but the essential simplicity of the technique can be illustrated by a straightforward practical example. Here is a 'database' for our hypothetical firm, Bennett Engineering.

	Bennett Engineering plc: Sales and Advertising Expenditure, 1994–1998	
Year	**Advertising (£100,000)**	**Sales (£100,000)**
	x	y
1994	2	60
1995	5	100
1996	4	70
1997	6	90
1998	3	80

Examination of the two equations shows that the only figures required are Σy, Σx, Σxy, Σx^2 and n; n in this case being 5 as there are five pairs of figures.

The other four figures can be quickly obtained by laying out the data in tabular form:

x	y	xy	x^2
2	60	120	4
5	100	500	25
4	70	280	16
6	90	540	36
3	80	240	9
$\Sigma x = 20$	$\Sigma y = 400$	$\Sigma xy = 1,680$	$\Sigma x^2 = 90$

It only now remains to insert these values into the two equations and solve for a and b:

(i) $400 = a \times 5 + b \times 20$

(ii) $1680 = a \times 20 + b \times 90$

Multiply equation (i) by 4, i.e. $1600 = 20a + 80b$

Multiply equation (ii) by 1, i.e. $1680 = 20a + 90b$

Subtracting upper from lower $80 = 10b$

$$\therefore \quad b = 8.$$

Now substitute 8 for b in equation (i), i.e.

$$400 = 5a + 8 \times 20$$

$$\therefore \quad 5a = 400 - 160 = 240$$

$$\therefore \quad a = 48.$$

The regression line, therefore is $\quad y = a + bx$

$$= 48 + 8x$$

This line is known as the *regression line of y on x* and is the line of best fit when the deviations are measured vertically, as indicated earlier.

To use this regression line is quite simple – it is only necessary to replace x in the equation by a value for advertising to obtain an estimate of sales, y.

If Bennett Engineering decide to commit £450,000 to advertising the estimated sales will be:

$$y = 48 + 8 \times 4\tfrac{1}{2} \text{ (n.b. £450,000} = 4\tfrac{1}{2} \times 100,000)$$

$$= 48 + 36 = 84, \text{ i.e. sales of } \underline{£8,400,000}$$

$$(84 \times £100,000)$$

So, in outline, this is how linear regression analysis can be used as a *contributor* to the forecasting process but remember that, in this instance, the line of best fit is a straight line and therefore there is a linear relationship between the two variables.

Remember too the other warning notes to be sounded:

- the technique assumes the future will be a projection of the past – dynamic markets may alter the reliance to be placed on this;
- it assumes the same relationship has existed between the two variables during the period from which the data are drawn – a matter for executive judgement;
- it assumes that one independent variable explains the variations in the dependent variable, whereas we know that the causes of most marketing outcomes are multi-variate;
- to be useful, the technique needs data extending over a lengthy period to be available – so much depends on the size and quality of the database;
- finally and importantly, do bear in mind that an organization would be extremely unwise to rely on the projections from a single technique.

On this last point, in attempting to forecast in a highly dynamic, perhaps unstable, situation clearly too much importance cannot be allotted to a single approach. Here it is important to mention that *multiple regression techniques* do take account of the various independent variables whose influence is judged to be significant, for example employment, income, population, output, level of advertising support, level of competitors' advertising, etc. Obviously these techniques are more complex because separate forecasts must be made for each of the independent variables and due weight given to the importance of each of these. The technique of *discriminant analysis* has been found valuable in this context.

Qualitative techniques

Having just taken a brief glimpse at the use of statistics in forecasting, we must now consider that side of the forecasting approach which depends upon the application of experience and the gathering and analysis of what are frequently termed 'soft data'.

Surveys of buyer intentions

This method consists of asking a representative sample of users about their buying intentions (how much of a given product they will buy at a given price). The approach has been used in both the consumer and the industrial goods fields and is said, if anything, to be more reliable in the latter field (especially when the market consists of a limited number of firms) since industrial users are very much more clear about the materials and equipment they will purchase in the year ahead, than is the average housewife. The sample must be large enough for prediction purposes and some organizations (e.g. the BBC) maintain continuous *consumer panels* to assist their forward planning. The purchase of 'question units' in omnibus surveys as described in Chapter 6 would be another way of gaining this information and related to it are the techniques of *attitude measurement*, a subject mentioned in Chapter 7.

The limitations of the approach include the doubt which attaches to the relationship between attitudes and behaviour and various forms of multivariate and taxonomic analysis are usually applied to attitudinal data in order to illumine this area.

Published information, such as the CBI forecasts, the *Financial Times* surveys, and the economic forecasts mentioned in the early parts of this chapter, may well contain suitable contextual data for this method.

Surveys of expert opinion (internal and external)

Such surveys are usually a significant element in most approaches to forecasting. The chief marketing executive and his senior marketing colleagues are judged to be the internal experts and their knowledge of the firm's products, its markets, its competition, etc. constitute their expertise. In forming their judgements they will typically have access to any statistical projections derived from the objective techniques (described in the last section) and these will serve as a starting point for their own ideas.

The external experts usually comprise any marketing consultants or advisers retained by the firm, advertising agency executives, and senior personnel in customer organizations. In addition to their knowledge of the firm, these experts may be able to make comparative assessments based on their knowledge of the market performance of competitive products or of similar products in other markets.

The procedures employed might be either formal or informal. For example, the external and internal experts may be gathered together formally, having already prepared their own personal analysis of the situation and within the meeting may have to defend their viewpoints against alternative predictions. The objective of the 'jury' or 'conclave' of experts would be ultimately to arrive at some mutually agreed forecast. This is undoubtedly a valuable element in the forecasting process although the external experts are less likely to be able to make forecasts for individual products of the firm than to be able to provide some reasonable estimate of its general prospects.

Surveys of salesforce opinion

The concept of building the forecast from the top down and the bottom-up has two aspects. There is first the idea of proceeding through stages of the forecast – as outlined earlier in the chapter. There is also the idea of including all relevant personnel in the process, from whatever level in the hierarchy. Thus the contribution of the senior marketing executive and his team, and the opinions of external experts, may be thought of as the top down element, whilst including a survey of salesforce opinion would be the bottom-up part of the process. Involving the salesforce has at least three points in its favour:

● The salesforce is closer to the market and user and distributor opinion: therefore it would be completely imprudent to overlook this source of opinion.

- Since the targets and quotas of the salesforce will be derived from the forecast it makes good sense to involve the salesforce in the calculations for this increases their sense of responsibility in achieving targets.

- When the management canvasses the salesman's views, it increases his sense of importance to the organization and acts as a motivator to his performance (shades of Herzberg).

The process is one in which the forecast of each salesman for his own territory becomes a *composite forecast* for the organization when individual territory forecasts are aggregated. There is always the possibility that, since the sales quota is derived from his forecast, the salesman might be tempted to produce an artificially low forecast. Two points can be made here:

- The process is one that can, and should, be approached in stages, each individual forecast being reconciled with that of the salesman's immediate supervisor before being passed on to the next stage where reconciliation again takes place. Thus territory → area → regional → company stages each provide a device for filtering out artificially low forecasts.

- Another check against the low forecast is by relating the level of approved sales expenses to the forecast.

The *salesforce composite* is such an important aspect of the forecasting process that it would be an irresponsible management which excluded such opinion from the process. It could, of course, be argued that salesmen are not sufficiently *au fait* with general economic considerations to take sufficient account of them in their individual estimates. Management must make allowance, where this is deemed to be so, in its own assessment of the salesforce composite forecast. Alternatively, as it develops experience with its forecasting and is able to isolate those environmental variables exercising the greatest influence on sales performance it can show the salesman how to adjust his own estimate accordingly. In one organization where the salesmen were trained in this way, the salesforce composite came to within 3 per cent of the firm's own top down forecast.

The Delphi technique

This is a technique which canvasses opinion from experienced executive members of the organization by a structured research method making use of a questionnaire. The executives do not meet in committee and therefore the respondent is not inhibited by the group dynamics of the committee situation. The responses from the first round of questionnaire distribution are collated and fed back to each respondent, so that if one executive's views are challenged by what appears to be the majority opinion that executive may be asked whether he or she would wish to modify his or her views or submit extra supporting evidence for them. In this way it is hoped that some consensus view will emerge which can be used as a basis for forecasting. The approach can be varied in that personal interviews may be conducted with each respondent at the feedback stage rather than the impersonal distribution of feedback notes and further questionnaires. Also, rather than deeper probing of a single issue, further questionnaires may proceed from the macro to the micro stages of forecasting.

The method has been frequently used and while some observers feel that Delphi is better suited to estimates of general trends in markets and technologies rather than to detailed estimates of individual product sales, some success has been reported with forecasting of the latter type.

Forecasting and the computer

The computer is enormously valuable for decision-making in marketing. First, there are the routine administrative tasks relating to sales, invoicing, order processing, stock levels and so on. The volume of data thus assembled can then be aggregated, analysed and displayed to the decision maker. Qualitative judgements on the performance of products, salespeople and market segments from the fine divisions of quantitative data so speedily made available, can then be made by the marketing executive.

At the next level, models of markets can be developed so that the sensitivity of a particular market can be reviewed when related to changes in specific inputs – price levels, advertising expenditure, etc. At the highest level of complexity, such models can encompass a large number of variables.

For the purposes of forecasting, the part of the computer system which stipulates how data are to be manipulated, the *software*, can range from simple *spreadsheets* to *advanced statistical packages*.

A *spreadsheet* is a form used for organizing and calculating numerical information. The use of computer-based spreadsheets has eliminated errors in calculating relationships between data and has also made it possible to rapidly change data. An electronic spreadsheet 'remembers' the relationship between data and thus provides a 'what if?' facility. What if the cost of a basic raw material increases by 10 per cent? How would this affect the price of the finished product? What would be the consequent effect on sales and profits? The value to the forecasting process is clear and whereas manual techniques would take a considerable length of time to produce answers, the computer makes the information available in seconds.

At a more sophisticated level, the *statistical package* is especially useful for exploring data in the early phases of analysis, for plotting and for regression analysis. As well as simple arithmetic operations on data, it enables correlation coefficients, regression, binomial probability and other routines to be easily performed.

At an even higher level of sophistication software packages become comprehensive tools for managing, analysing and displaying data. The facilities available can provide scattergrams, factor analyses, cross-tabulations, hypothesis testing, time series analyses, etc. If, for example, we are exploring the relationship between sales and some variable as we have seen earlier (Figure 14.7) a scattergraph enables two variables to be studied together. Sophisticated packages enable scatterplotting to be used in this context. Beyond the primary step of studying the relationship between two variables it is often useful to quantify the strength of their association by calculating a *summary index* and here, a commonly used measure is the Pearson correlation coefficient, r. The absolute value of r, which indicates the strength of the linear relationship, better enables the estimation of, for example, the amount of sales generated from a certain level of promotional expenditure.

Another process available via the use of software packages, the *Box-Jenkins procedure*, can be used to fit and forecast time series data. This procedure is designed to provide for easy and flexible model identification, estimation and forecasting. Several models can be examined in a single invocation of the procedure. Parameter estimates, forecasts and plots of the auto correlation function, partial auto correlation function, and forecasts at different levels can be included in the output.

Analyses that would otherwise take weeks of work can be conducted economically and at great speed. The nature and impact of the computer has enabled better decisions to be made within the forecasting function, as in many other areas of marketing management.

Concluding comments

It has been said that the only certain thing that can be said of a sales forecast is that it will be wrong. This does not detract from the value of forecasting as a planning tool nor is it meant to deter the forecaster in his quest for accuracy. What it does highlight is the need for constant review of actuals:forecast, particularly where many factors influence sales. It should also again be added in this context that the more forecasting the organization does, the more likely it is to develop its accuracy.

Our view of the forecasting process has been a necessarily restricted one. The subject is treated comprehensively in a number of textbooks, including the one by Gordon Bolt (1994).

Marketing planning

One of the fundamental beliefs of the marketing approach is that an organization must *plan* in advance of its operations. Planning:

- makes clear the threats and opportunities open to the organization;
- provides a framework by way of which
  - objectives can be pursued,
  - performance standards can be established and monitored,
  - effort can be assessed and rewarded;
- clarifies the costs and benefits of alternative courses of action, so assisting the effective allocation and use of resources;
- helps in the development of effective communication within the organization;
- through its call for continuing and reliable information helps the organization to monitor change and prepare for it;
- helps to increase employee participation and commitment when properly carried out.

Twenty years ago, when the first edition of this text was being prepared, the author suggested that a framework for planning could be developed if the organization asked itself a number of questions. It was gratifying to note that this idea commended itself to other writers in the field. The importance of this question sequence still stands and it is set out in Figure 14.9. To the right of these questions the formal procedures relating to the questions are also set out, and a short description of what each of the procedures entails then follows.

1. Where are we now?	Organizational framework; Situation analysis; External and internal audits.
2. Where are we going?	Opportunities and issues analysis; Assumptions and objectives; SWOT Analysis.
3. How will we get there	Strategies and tactics.
4. When will we get there?	Time schedules and priorities.
5. What are the costs and benefits?	Operating resources and budgets; Revenue predictions; Projected profit and loss statement(s).
6. How will we know we've arrived?	Control and evaluation procedures.
7. Who will be responsible for getting us there?	Personnel and organizational details.

Figure 14.9. *A suggested framework for marketing planning*

1 Where are we now?

The plan may relate to a whole organization, as in the case of a small or medium-sized enterprise (SME), an SBU within a large organization, a product group, or in some cases an individual product. The place of the SBU, product group, etc., in the *organizational framework* should be clearly detailed as should its own *mission statement* with, where appropriate, an explanation of how this relates to the *corporate mission statement*.

The *situation analysis* comprises an outline of the organization, department or unit, etc. – its size, location, ownership, market share, market strengths, competitive position. An analysis of the industry in which the unit operates should be provided along the same lines with an indication of its key trends and other factors likely to influence marketing operations, e.g. proposed mergers, acquisitions, strategic alliances, trends in types, volumes and values of output and sales.

The *external audit* will be based on an up-to-date environmental analysis, highlighting any economic, political, technological, social, or legal influences significant for future operations – as outlined in Chapter 2. Obviously, governmental forecasts of GDP and likely movements in interest rates are examples here. This audit should also include an analysis of the *competition* – its major sources, any threat of new entrants to the market(s), strength of buyers and suppliers, potential substitutes, etc. The current strategy of main competitors should be detailed, as well as their current strengths, weaknesses, size and market share. Some assumptions should be made on the satisfaction of competitors with their current strategies and whether there are likely to be any future strategic 'shifts'.

A most important component of the external audit relates to *customers* – their numbers, types, segments, geographical dispersion, analyses by size and value, patterns of demand, buying criteria, retention rates, satisfaction levels and, not least, profitability (where applicable). These data should be closely examined for any trends likely to influence planning and should be used to set the tone of the plan, that is to say that that marketing is about satisfying customers.

The *internal audit*, or *marketing audit* is the planned, systematic and regular evaluations of the total marketing function and encompasses an assessment of:

- the formulation of marketing objectives;
- the processes employed to devise strategies and tactics to meet those objectives;
- organizational performance, i.e. the extent to which the strategies and tactics achieve the stated objectives;
- the processes by which the activities necessary to achieve the objectives are organized;
- the selection, recruitment, training, motivation and performance of the people carrying out marketing operations and the manner in which they are structured;
- the various procedures involved in the total marketing function including forecasting, planning, administration and control.

The enlarged marketing mix, described earlier in the text and comprising *preparation* (marketing information), *product, price, place, promotional* and *people* would provide a useful core for the framework adopted to conduct the audit. The marketing audit has been described as an 'organizational spring cleaning' process and should compare performance with any external measures or information available, for example market growth, competitors' sales and profitability, etc. Importantly, performance should also be weighed against measures of customer satisfaction and retention.

A number of concepts and techniques are valuable in the context of the audit – see for instance Pareto analysis and PIMS (Chapter 3) and, in respect of the people factor, the McKinsey 7-S Framework (Chapter 2).

2 Where are we going?

Information on new markets, changes in existing markets, environmental changes, the operations of competitors, etc. provides the basis for *opportunities analysis*. Marketing opportunities may consist of:

- *market penetration*: selling more of existing products to existing markets by increased promotion or salesforce activity;

- *market development*: increasing sales volume and profits by finding new markets, overseas perhaps;

- *product development*: introducing new or improved products to present markets;

- *forward integration*: by diversifying activities – Arnolds, for example, may diversify from tableware into wall and floor tiles, into industrial ceramics, laboratory ceramics, refractories, etc. Diversification may take place through mergers with other companies, the acquisition of other companies and may be *horizontal* (e.g. the acquisition of competitors), or *vertical*, and if the latter, may consist of acquiring raw materials producers.

Again, the organization may see opportunity for growth by acquiring its own retail outlets.

Accompanying the identification of opportunity should be an *issues analysis*. For example, the cultivation of new markets or market segments may necessitate increased production and R&D facilities, increased advertising and sales promotion expenditures, a decision for the organization to divest itself of certain products or services, or of altering distribution policies in order to take advantage of changes in patterns of retailing.

In this section, planners also need to detail any *assumptions* being made, for example:

- that the rate of market growth or contraction will continue;

- that changes in the distribution system will accelerate;

- that 'brand switching' will intensify;

- that competitors will maintain their present course.

Markets and segments will be carefully described and quantified and related to competitive advantage, customer benefits and the organization's overall mission. Demand analysis and sales forecasts will be reviewed and a rationale incorporated for any review of forecasts.

Concurrent with this review of *opportunities* and *issues* and taking note of any *assumptions* being made, the planners will relate organizational *strengths and weaknesses* to the *opportunities and threats* becoming evident. Much of the data for this *SWOT analysis* approach will have become available through the *marketing audit* and the *opportunities/environmental analyses*. An effectively conducted SWOT analysis should clarify:

- ways in which the organization can achieve *sustainable competitive advantage*, and

- what *critical success factors* are necessary to achieve this.

It should now be possible to determine marketing objectives which should be clear, realistic and internally consistent with corporate objectives. In this way, a single marketing plan becomes an important, but none the less individual feature in a larger planning landscape. Senior management will have defined what the overall objectives of the organization must be. This is one planning parameter. Another parameter will be a description of the alternatives available and clarified as a result of the processes just described. The marketing executives now set out their belief as to what marketing objectives will best support corporate objectives. The two points listed below are worth noting in this regard.

- Overall corporate goals may be a mixture of economic and non-economic objectives, e.g. 'a superior, sustained rate of return on investment' and 'safety'.

  So that, in addition to effectiveness in economic terms, an organization may pursue within its overall goals non-economic objectives such as leadership in its field for innovation, or quality, or financial security (as with a bank) or environmental concern (of great significance for a chemical company, for example).

  The planners must see to it that what they propose meets both types of objective and resolve, satisfactorily, any *conflict of objectives*.

- Whilst objectives can be, and are, couched in both quantitative and qualitative terms, it is important that marketing objectives are translated into quantitative terms wherever possible – so that the actions necessary are clearly apparent and performance can be measured. Thus a corporate objective concerned with a 'sustained, superior rate of return on investment' may become, for a one-year marketing plan 'an increase of 2 per cent in profits before interest and taxation'.

In this way, objectives provide direction for the various managerial levels, serve as motivators to achievement, provide a basis for monitoring and control, make corporate philosophy abundantly clear and help to create a unity of purpose throughout the organization.

3 How will we get there?

Answering this question entails making proposals on the *strategies* and *tactics* to be adopted. Strategies were considered at some length in Chapters 2 and 3. One or two other points can be added here.

Defining the organization's mission entails making broad policy statements which are long-term (valid perhaps for five years or more). Statements on *strategy* are similarly broad in scope, indicating the directions in which the organization will move to achieve its objectives and are, as often as not, quite long in term, for example two to three years. *Tactics* are the actions deemed necessary if particular strategies are to be adopted and are usually short-term (usually reviewed yearly).

An example may help here. Corporate objectives may hinge on the growth of sales revenue and profits. In this context, alternative strategies are typically reviewed before a strategic recommendation is made. The strategies being evaluated may consist of:

- retention of existing markets;
- entry into new, but similar markets, with existing products;
- entry into new, but similar markets, with new products;
- diversification into radically different markets.

The strategies are not mutually exclusive and some combination of them may be adopted.

A sequence of questions of the following types will be used to determine the tactics:

- *retention of existing markets*: what tactics best serve this strategy? – product modifications? increased advertising? extension of the distributive network?

- *entry into new markets with existing products*: how best do we enter overseas markets? – through export houses? agents and distributors abroad? UK based representatives?

- *entry into new markets with new products*: how should these be priced, promoted, distributed? shall we adopt the tactics prevailing for the marketing of similar products or devise new tactics?

- *diversification into radically different markets*: e.g. the manufacturer of standardized engineering products may decide to seek contract work for construction programmes; but a warning note here; where such diversification can be undertaken with minimal modification to production techniques, manpower planning and organizational structures it is essentially tactical, otherwise strategic decisions are entailed.

Of course, like the other steps in the planning process, tactical decisions call for an accurate appreciation of competition and realistic assessment of the resources which will be available. Thus, although we shall be considering resources below ('what are the costs and benefits') these steps do not necessarily follow each other. In practice, resource considerations are weighed in the balance when alternative strategies and tactics are being studied for their feasibility.

Strategy formulation will often include some consideration of the positioning strategy to be adopted (e.g. 'head to head' or 'avoidance'?) as planners recommend how best the organization should be perceived by its customers in relation to competition.

Tactics will usually describe in detail:

- product plans, modifications to products and the product range and proposals for the introduction of new products;

- pricing tactics, including any plans for changes in trade margins, discounts, any introductory offers, etc.;

- proposals on physical distribution, channel(s) policy, stock levels, key account policy, etc.;

- promotional tactics including types and levels of sales force operations, the advertising appropriation and media plan, creative approach, consumer and trade sales promotions, public relations and publicity campaigns.

4 When will we get there?

Planning takes place within a time framework:

- a planned growth of profits over a five year period;
- the annual marketing plan;
- the *time* required to develop and re-launch the modified product, etc.

Time scheduling specifies what must be done and when it must be done, which actions must precede others and what aspects of the plan must be given priority. Moreover, setting the marketing plan within a time frame provides a time frame for the other departments of the organization, setting off a form of chain reaction.

For example, assume that in the ensuing financial year (1 January–31 December) the *marketing objective* of a firm is to generate £3 million in sales revenue by selling 3 million units at £1 per unit. Consequently, according to the following calculation, this means a *production objective* of 3,250,000 units, thus:

January 1 Opening stocks and work in progress	100,000 units (A)
January 1–December 31 Projected sales	3,000,000 units (B)
December 31 Desired closing stock	350,000 units (C)
∴ Production objective	3,250,000 units (B−A+C)

When a range of forecasts is being reviewed, the production department will be consulted on whether the projected sales volume constitutes a balanced programme from its standpoint.

The overall *financial objective* will comprise a series of sub-objectives based on time scheduled purchases of raw materials and components, direct and indirect labour costs, factory overheads, marketing and administrative costs, packing and transport costs, projected borrowing (and its costs) for peak periods in business activity and projected cash flow.

The *personnel objective* will be based upon a time scheduled plan of the number and types of people to be employed and trained or retrained and provision for recruitment, redeployment, etc.

This outline can be thought of as a *means–end chain*. The attainment of the time scheduled objective for each organizational function constitutes the way in which each *ensuing* department or function attains *its* objective which in turn enables the organization itself to attain its objective.

The plan of schedules and priorities can be as simple or as complex as circumstances dictate. The small firm with a limited range of products or services may find a simple sheet completely adequate. A complex organization with several operating divisions may plan its sequential interrelated activities utilizing such techniques as *network analysis* (e.g. either the critical path method or the programme evaluation review technique). Planning the development of a new, complex product which will affect production methods, manpower planning and marketing programmes over an extended period of time and require successive increments of capital investment will require quite sophisticated scheduling. A modification to an existing product entailing minimal 'adjustment' to the way in which departments operate will require clear but relatively simple scheduling methods.

5 What are the costs and benefits of getting there?

This question is posed in order to project revenues, budgets and profits and, as one writer has put it (Green, 1970), enables the marketing department, and hence the organization, to develop 'a programme of action with price tags'.

Here the organization is evaluating alternative courses of action and assessing their costs and benefits so that ultimately a plan is agreed with an accompanying logistical appreciation which will enable the managers concerned to obtain the right resources, of the right quality and quantity, in the right place, at the right time and at the right (i.e. acceptable) level of cost.

The process entails making forecasts of sales revenue, capital, manufacturing and marketing expenses, labour costs, plant capacity and projected return on investment, among the many other factors involved. The plan for the immediate period ahead (usually one year) will have detailed forecasts and budgets; the plans for succeeding periods (so as to complete a three or five year period, for example) will be less detailed. Planning procedures for this latter stage may not always call for strict mathematical accuracy so much as sound indications of the 'gap', if any, remaining in the desired quantum of sales volume, revenue, profits or whatever.

One other important point: the 'how much will it cost us?' question is only a convenient shorthand to describe this stage in the planning process. Financial considerations are important here, but a review of resources means screening *all* the wealth producing assets that are available to the firm – its plant capacity, its equipment, the skills of its labour force, its technical know-how, its 'institutional image' in the market, the opportunities for selling its by-products, etc. In short, 'positive thinking' is important here and the review of resources must be undertaken not in the spirit of what constraints it will impose but with an eye to the opportunities it will offer.

A projected *profit-and-loss statement* should constitute the final answer to this question. Senior management will then review it and either approve it or request it be modified. When finally approved, its detail will constitute the basis for the approved budgets relating to all operations. To arrive at an overall *profit-and-loss* statement and where a multi-product marketing plan is being developed, individual financial forecasts may be needed for each product. The example below relates to a new product, for which the brand name has not been finalized and is therefore referred to by its type number and which, unusually, is expected to make profits from its first year.

Product R.37/2: Target Profit Plan, 1999

1	Forecast of 1999 ex-factory sales	10,000 standard packs.
2	Proposed price to distributor per standard pack	£200.
3	Estimated sales revenue (1 × 2)	£2,000,000
4	Estimated variable costs (manufacturing cost + packaging + physical distribution)	£1,100,000
		(£110 per standard pack).
5	Estimated contribution margin for fixed costs, marketing costs + profit (3 − 4)	£900,000
6	Estimated fixed costs: £15 per standard pack × 10,000	£150,000
7	Estimate of marketing costs	
	Advertising £250,000,	
	Direct sales expenses £100,000,	
	Other costs £100,000	£450,000
8	Estimate of target profit [5 − (6 + 7)]	£300,000
		(= 15% on sales).

---

6 How will we know when we've arrived?

To answer this question, it is necessary to provide processes for the *control and evaluation* of the plan. Control means to check while evaluation means to determine the value of the plan itself. Together, these processes entail:

- continually monitoring the results actually achieved against forecasts and budgets, so as to affirm progress to objectives or determine any differences between projections and performance;

- where differences do exist, probing into the causes for those differences;

- taking corrective action, either within the current programme or by making necessary adjustments to the programme for the immediate next period(s).

The first two steps relate to the control of the plan and step three, making adjustments, to its evaluation. Figure 14.10 attempts to illustrate these processes as an iterative, that is repetitive, exercise.

The plan may have been devised and approved but it does not become a plan for action regardless of the consequences. In a profit organization, for example, when it is put into operation, the company's progress with regard to the plan is carefully monitored, particularly the sales being achieved, the pattern of costs involved and the stock levels being built up. The plan will also indicate how and when (e.g. weekly, monthly, quarterly) the plan is to be reviewed by senior management. In these reviews, the chief marketing officer will relate results to surveys of the current scene and, where divergences are significant, make recommendations for changes in strategy, if need be (see Figure 14.10). Less significant divergences may entail reduction of projected expenditure if sales are not meeting forecasts or increased expenditures and other marketing activity to exploit a favourable situation.

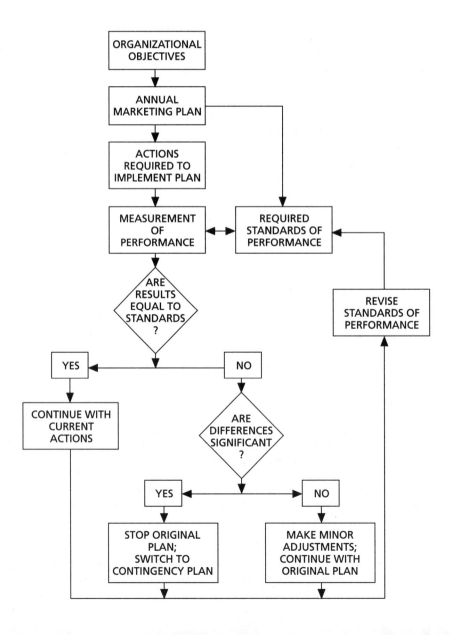

Figure 14.10. *Controlling and evaluating the marketing plan*

Importantly, if only in 'broad brush' terms, the marketing planners are usually expected to devise a *contingency plan*, so that if new challenges or opportunities emerge the organization will already have given some thought to response strategies. A change of direction can then be taken but any negative effects of it can be reduced.

On the subject of *measuring performance*, as Mullins (1989, pp 458–9) points out, 'control' is a term which can be misunderstood. Mullins believes that people may be 'suspicious of control systems and see them as emphasizing punishment, an indication of authoritarian management and a means of exerting pressure and maintaining discipline'. He goes on to explain that in an effective organization control is not like that and can stand for order and reliability. Beyond this, of course, as occupational psychologists affirm, *knowledge of results* can be a powerful motivating force. As a rule, and when all other influences on achievement are in place, people will strive to attain the targets set for them, particularly when they have been part of the target-setting process.

In a profit organization a marketing executive has two primary standards by which to measure performance:

- *Sales volume* analysed by products, territories, customer groups, industries, etc. as well as by time periods (daily, weekly, monthly, quarterly and cumulative).

- *Marketing costs* analysed under the headings in which they appear in the company accounts (e.g. salaries, commissions, travel expenses, advertising expenditure, etc.) or better still by functions (e.g. advertising, salesforce, distribution, etc.), or even better still by market segments (e.g. by customers, territories, industries, etc.) – the degree of refinement of the marketing information system being a function of the size of the firm and its affordable budgets for the administration of its controls systems. Certainly the higher the degree of refinement the better management can determine where the trouble spots lie.

The marketing executive has a number of techniques at his disposal when measuring performance. One of these is *ratio analysis* and among the key ratios valuable for this purpose are these:

- gross margin percentage $= \dfrac{\text{gross margin}}{\text{net sales}}$

- net profit percentage $= \dfrac{\text{net profit}}{\text{net sales}}$

- operating expense percentage $= \dfrac{\text{total expenses}}{\text{net sales}}$

- returns and allowances percentage $= \dfrac{\text{returns and allowances}}{\text{net sales}}$

- stock-turn rate $= \dfrac{\text{cost of goods sold}}{\text{average inventory at cost}}$ (one of a number of approaches)

Last, but not least,

- return on investment (ROI) $= \dfrac{\text{net profit}}{\text{sales}} \times \dfrac{\text{sales*}}{\text{investment}}.$

* These two elements in the formula enable planning to take place by a 'what-if?' approach, altering the values of all the variables then considering what is the most pragmatic of the options, for example increasing the ROI by decreasing 'investment', such as the size of the inventory, while obtaining the same levels of sales and profits.

A number of textbooks provide a comprehensive treatment of the financial aspects of marketing including the one by Schmidt and Wright (1996).

7 Who will be responsible for getting us there?

At the beginning of this section it was stated that when properly carried out, planning helps to increase employee participation and commitment. Plans can only be achieved through *people* who need to be informed and motivated, for a plan is no better and no worse than the way it is communicated and accepted by the people designated to carry it through.

Like forecasting, planning should be a bottom-up as well as a top down process. There is no problem for the owner of a small business to generate 'ownership' of, and commitment to, the plan. In larger organizations senior management must ensure that the communications networks, both vertical and horizontal, are effective or the concept of marketing as a 'whole organization' activity will be an illusion.

Responsibility for obtaining results must be defined, fixed and published. A detailed description of the actions necessary, their timing and the people who will carry them out will be set out in the *action plan*, which often accompanies the main plan in the form of an appendix. For its *corporate plan*, the organization obviously needs to be clear on the number of people who will be involved in its execution, their grades, skills, levels of training and how their activities are to be organized and coordinated.

This applies with equal force to the *marketing plan*, where such issues as the size of the salesforce and their required level of technical and sales training for the introduction of a new product often emerge at the tactical level. At the strategic level answering this seventh question may entail applying the existing organizational structure to projected operations and assessing its 'fit'. The marketing plan may, in fact, necessitate some radical alteration in organizational structure, for example moving the salesforce from a structure based on products to one based on industries or markets (see Chapter 4).

The author makes no apology for repeating that results are obtained only through *people*. Accordingly, they must be clear about:

- what they are expected to do;
- what authority they have to do it;
- how their performance is to be measured.

A factor implicit in the planning process is some form of *performance appraisal* for the people involved. This may be carried out at different levels of sophistication. Performance appraisal for a salesman in a small firm may largely comprise scrutiny of sales, expenses, new accounts opened and feedback from customers. In a larger organization it may mean a formal appraisal interview, the agreement and documentation of personal objectives and subsequent review of progress at fixed intervals.

The skills and commitment of the people involved, their numbers, the methods of organization and empowerment employed and the way in which their activities are reviewed and rewarded obviously have a critical influence on the success, or otherwise, of the plan. Perhaps enough was said in Chapter 12 to substantiate this statement.

Final comment

This section has offered some thoughts on marketing planning. Hopefully, it will have provided a suitable basic introduction to the subject. Again, a fuller treatment can be found in a number of textbooks including the most recent edition of that by McDonald (1999).

Marketing in the new millennium

Looking to the future

Charles Franklin Kettering (1989) once observed that: 'We should all be concerned about the future because we will have to spend the rest of their lives there' (1989, p 703). Marketing practitioners must be concerned more than most, because forecasting the future, and suggesting how resources may best be allocated to meet it, is at the heart of all their activities.

Yet predicting how the business environment might develop over the first decade of the new millennium would daunt even the most self-assured forecaster. When the third edition of this book was published in 1994 it was noted that, whereas there was once a fear that the USA would dominate the world economy, this had by then been replaced by the fear that Japan would do so, but, by the early 1990s, it was the giant corporations emerging in the Pacific Basin which were now moving to centre stage. Coupled with that, the collapse of communism in Eastern Europe would un-doubtedly have its effects on the business environment as the countries there moved rapidly to the development of market economies.

A few years on and by August 1998 world markets were in turmoil with the collapse of Russia's currency and the fear that global recession was imminent was reflected by the world's plummeting stock markets. Russia's economy and government were in gridlock and before the end of August, according to Jamieson (1998), the total value of its stock market was less than the value of the British retailer, J. Sainsbury.

As for the new dawn emanating from the Pacific Basin, 15 months earlier Thailand's currency collapsed, its stock market fell by more than 80 per cent and its bad debts were approaching 40 per cent of total loans. Soon this pattern extended through South East Asia, with Indonesia's stock market down 88 per cent in value, its currency values diminishing rapidly and its debt mountain standing at $140 billion. Japan was in deep crisis too, with estimated bad debts of $1 trillion, one fifth of its GDP and, according to some assessments, with 19 of its top 20 banks technically insolvent. As this economic free-fall extended to South America, notably Brazil, the International Monetary Fund (IMF) poured in funding to rally confidence, halt the slide in markets and stave off world recession. If those responsible for scanning the business environment on behalf of organizations have learned anything, then, from the closing years of the old millennium, it is the meaning of the word 'turbulence'.

These developments increase rather than diminish the importance of environmental scanning and forecasting and necessitate their becoming continuous rather than episodic processes. For its part, this text in its final paragraphs will try to provide some indications of the future as it might affect marketing activity though, under-standably, with the emphasis more on aspiration than prediction.

So far as the physical environment is concerned, the chief worry is global warming whose best known man-made cause is the burning of fossil fuels by the world's industries and its populations. Detrimental climate change, and a rise in sea levels as well as temperatures, have been linked to this and it is to be hoped no more disasters on the scale of those in Bangladesh and Nicaragua have to occur before the international community acts on, rather than talks about, this dire situation.

Ironically, according to Boulton (1996) the business of energy efficiency has received considerably less attention in recent years as oil and gas prices have fallen and large new reserves have been found around the world. According to the UK's Energy Saving Trust, households, which account for 30 per cent of the nation's energy consumption, could save £3 billion per year on energy bills for a one-off investment of £8 billion – which is an attractive return. According to the chief executive of the Trust, the main reason why this investment is not taking place is a lack of knowledge of the abundance of free advice on how to make such savings and the cash incentives available to instal energy efficient appliances such as gas-condensed boilers. This is surely an area in which marketing techniques should be well to the fore, working for non-profit as well as profit objectives. The wider acceptance and use of reformulated petrol which recently produced for Los Angeles its best result in more than 40 years of air-quality measurement (Parkes, 1997) provides a similar opportunity for skilled marketing activity, as does the use of compressed natural gas (CNG), particularly for larger vehicles, such as buses, operating in polluted cities.

Technology and its ever-increasing development will continue to provide marketing opportunities not only in the shape of new and better products and services but in the technique of marketing itself. Nothing provides a better example of this last point than the Internet. What the Net offers to marketers has been handily summarized by Bickerton as follows:

- a changeable brochure or magazine issued to tens of thousands of potential customers for no distribution or print costs;
- a remote camera telling you what your customers find interesting about your material;
- a live advert that your customers choose to watch;
- an eternal exhibition stand;
- a 24-hour telesales person covering the world;
- a mechanism to reach millions of new customers;
- a return coupon that automatically fills your customer database;
- a new trading medium which gives customers the opportunity to order what they want, when they want, wherever they are. (Bickerton, 1996.)

Bickerton emphasizes, however, that its benefits will best be realized if organizations remember their Web site must give customers what they want, be interactive, and provide a visit which is interesting, enjoyable and dynamic, in the sense that it offers new information when customers return to it. She also points out that the site must be of high quality and made to pay for itself, for example by online ordering. The site should be well integrated with the rest of the marketing mix, well promoted and used for test marketing purposes. A final point to bear in mind is that: 'The issue is not just about having a presence, but using it to deliver business benefits'.

Digital television is another technological arrival which will doubtless have its effects on both markets and marketing practice.

The forces which make for the globalization of markets including the globalization of media, the growing importance of global brands, and the growing size of commercial risks, will all still be in place. As McRae (1998) points out, however, there are countervailing tendencies which indicate that small organizations as well as large ones can thrive on the global scene. Such tendencies include:

- increasing use of the Internet, which cuts the costs of global market entry for small businesses and enables purchasers to find them;
- the continued growth of personal and professional services which provides a place for small operators;
- the growing consumer search for 'exclusive' goods and services which enable specialist producers to sustain higher margins than mass producers.

The marketing approach, which as we have seen, is not the prerogative of big spenders, will undoubtedly help the small provider to counter the concentration of power in world markets.

It is firmly to be hoped that the sensitivity to the ethical dimension of management now becoming apparent will increase and that organizations will take on board, to a greater extent, the social as well as the economic effects of their activities. Certainly there is growing recognition that ethical behaviour and increase in shareholder value are not mutually exclusive objectives. Here it is heartening to note the following two points:

- In April 1998 Royal Dutch Shell terminated its membership of a powerful industry group which lobbies against tougher environmental controls and 'launched a major initiative to raise its profile on social and environmental issues, giving them as much importance as financial issues' (Harrison, 1998).
- Supermarket giant J. Sainsbury launched an experiment in August 1998 to assist village shops by acting as a wholesaler and allowing village shopowners to sell its products to their customers – here it should be noted that by 1998 over 70 per cent of the parishes of England and Wales of up to 10,000 residents had no general store and nearly 60 per cent had no garage.

In an improving ethical atmosphere it is good to see the widening development of *cause-related marketing* and it is to be hoped that as more socially-related marketing activity becomes visible those too ready to link 'marketing' with the materialism of the West will be moved, at the least, from cocksure ignorance to thoughtful uncertainty about its value. Though few of the cynics would understand why marketing has as much to offer to the poor and the vulnerable as it does to the prosperous, it can be a powerful weapon against the widening inequality now posing a growing threat to the USA, the UK and other societies.

Marketing as a career

It should be clear that marketing offers immense prospects to young women and men possessing the necessary personal qualities and professional skills. A notable observer of the business scene, Professor Cary L. Cooper of the Manchester School of Management believes (see Altman, 1997) that the two major disciplines which have been the driving force in recent years have been and still are finance and marketing. In 1997, a report of a survey (see Ashworth, 1997) published by the Economist Intelligence Unit (EIU) indicated that marketing had become 'the fastest route up the corporate ladder'. Professor Peter Doyle (1997), in a thoughtful article outlining his view that manufacturing is now rarely a source of competitive advantage for large Western companies, suggested that: 'Investors should avoid companies run by managements which do not understand that the key value-adding skill is marketing.'

In addition to such personal qualities as enthusiasm, creativity, adaptability, good health, self-sufficiency and common sense, success in marketing calls for customer orientation, planning ability and an expertise broad enough to be tested, increasingly, in the global sphere. Also, although 'being a team player' is perhaps the most boring cliché of our times, it contains significant truth. As the EIU report just mentioned indicates, growing competition and wider global presence will make the present style of leadership, still often centred on one person at the top of a hierarchical pyramid, increasingly counter-productive. Respondents to the EIU survey 'expect the scales to tilt in favour of teams' (note the appropriate section of Chapter 12 in this regard).

The list of necessary attributes appears formidable but will not deter the committed entrant to the marketing profession. Also, it should be noted that, at the outset, in addition to intelligence and the commitment to succeed, what is needed above all is the belief in the value of marketing to economic and social well-being and an enthusiasm to serve others.

A career in marketing is full of challenge and intellectual stimulation. It will particularly appeal to a young person with a spirit of adventure. It will also bring its share of disappointments and call on a capacity for endurance. Here it is useful to remember the view of Samuel Smiles who said that many people of possible distinction and brilliance had been lost to the world simply because nothing interrupted the course of their prosperity. It is important to bear in mind that, for its high risks, marketing offers high rewards as well as special psychological satisfactions which only those engaged in marketing can ever appreciate.

A personal quality omitted from the earlier list is *integrity* – the most important attribute that can be brought to any role. Our final thought should be about this, for without it, all else fails ultimately. In recent times the world has been dismayed at the behaviour of some members of the business community. What it now needs are virtuous and dedicated people who will be rallying points for integrity. Marketing needs them especially, for unless it is ethical, marketing will never deliver what it truly can deliver.

Aaker, D.A. (1995) *Strategic Market Management* 4th edn, New York: John Wiley & Sons.

Advertising Association (1998) Press release, 15 June.

Aldersey-Williams, H. (1994) 'Brand new Birmingham', *Financial Times* 24 February.

Alexander, G. (1996) 'Pepsi Challenge', *Sunday Times* 7 April, Business Focus, p 3.

Alles, A. (1973) *Exhibitions: Universal Marketing Tools*, London: Cassell/Associated Business Programmes.

Altman, W. (1997) 'So you want to be top of the heap?' *The Times* 9 January, Premier Appointments, p 15.

Ansoff, H.I. (1968) *Corporate Strategy*, Harmondsworth: Penguin.

Archer, B. (1996) 'More of the same', *Financial Times* 11 December, Broadcast Media, p 3.

Armstrong, M. (1993) *A Handbook of Management Techniques* 2nd edn, London: Kogan Page.

Ashworth, J. (1997) 'Marketing offers head start', *The Times* 6 January.

Askham, D. (1992) 'Market research paved the way for specialist holidays in Cumbria', *The Times* 4 September, p 22.

Association of Market Survey Oganisations (1997) *Annual Report*, London: AMSO.

Atchley, K. (1993) 'Kato communications survey', *Financial Times* 4 November.

Atkinson, P.E. (1990) *Creating Culture Change: The Key to Successful Total Quality Management*, Bedford: IFS Publications.

Baker, M.J. (1979) *Marketing – An Introductory Text* 3rd edn, Basingstoke: Macmillan.

Baker, M. (1981) in Rines, M. (ed.), *Marketing Handbook* 2nd edn, Aldershot: Gower Publishing, pp 145–6.

Baker, M.J. (1991) *Marketing – An Introductory Text* 5th edn, Basingstoke: Macmillan.

Baker, M.J. (1996) *Marketing – An Introductory Text* 6th edn, Basingstoke: Macmillan.

Baxter, A. (1996) 'An attack of the vapours', *Financial Times* 5 November.

Beckett, M. (1997) 'Big fines to halt unfair trade', *Guardian* 8 August, p 21.

Bernoth, A. and Olins, R. (1996) 'Are you being served?' *Sunday Times*, Business Focus, 22 September.

Bickerton, R. 'Don't be afraid of the big bad Net', *Marketing Magazine* 27 June, Internet Guide.

Black, G. (1997) 'Case Study: Focus on PPP Healthcare', *Financial Times* 5 March, p FT-IT-17.

Blackstock, C. (1998) 'Jeans ads take bad taste to the limit', *Independent on Sunday* 1 February, News p 9.

Blois, K.J. (1987) 'Marketing for non-profit organizations', in Baker, M.J. (ed.), *The Marketing Book*, Oxford: Heinemann Professional Publishing.

Bogart, L. (1990) *Strategy in Advertising*, Chicago, IL: NTC Business Books.

Bolt, G. (1994) *Market and Sales Forecasting – A Total Approach* 3rd edn, London: Kogan Page.

Bonfield, Sir P. (1996) 'The key element is network management', *Financial Times* 6 March.

Boone, L.E. and Kurtz, D.L. (1980) *Contemporary Marketing* 3rd edn, Hinsdale, IL: Dryden Press.

Borden, N.H. (1969) 'The concept of the marketing mix', in Enis, B. and Cox, K. (eds), *Marketing Classics*, Boston: Allyn and Bacon.

Boulton, L. (1996) 'Energy efficiency – a business praying for "cultural revolution"', *Financial Times* survey, 11 November.

Boulton, L. (1997) 'Environmental achievement: green is the colour of money', *Financial Times* 21 April, p 20.

Bowersox, D.J. *et al.* (1980) *Management in Marketing Channels*, New York: McGraw-Hill.

Brassington, F. and Pettitt, S. (1997) *Principles of Marketing*, London: Pitman.

Bresnahan, T., Stern, S. and Trajtenberg, M. (n.d.) *Market Segmentation and the Sources of Rents from Innovation*, Cambridge, MA: National Bureau of Economic Research, Working Paper 5726.

Broadbent, S. (1979) *Spending Advertising Money* 3rd edn, London: Business Books.

Broadbent, S. (1984) *Spending Advertising Money* 4th edn, London: Business Books.

Burman, R. (1993) 'Customer-led machining/finishing', *Automotive Engineer* 18(4), August/September, pp 48ff.

Burnes, B. (1996) *Managing Change* 2nd edn, London: Pitman Publishing.

Burns, T. and Stalker, G.M. (1968) *The Management of Innovation* 2nd edn, London: Tavistock Publications.

Burt, T. (1996) 'T&N puts spark into German pistons group', *Financial Times* 5 March, p 22.

Campbell, K. (1997) 'Break out the fortress', *Financial Times* 28 January.

Cannon, T. (1980) *Basic Marketing – Principles and Practice*, London: Holt, Rinehart and Winston.

Cannon, T. (1997) 'From the top', *Guardian* 19 April, Management, p 25.

Carroll, A.B. (1987) 'In search of the moral manager', *Business Horizons* 30, March–April, pp 7–15.

Cassell, M. (1996) 'New look at innovation story', *Financial Times* 20 March, p 9.

Castells, M. (1996) *The Rise of the Network Society*, Oxford: Blackwell.

Caulkin, S. (1996a) 'The stake and the mistake', *Observer* 17 March.

Caulkin, S. (1996b) 'Reaping the profit of tomorrow's world', *Observer* 24 November.

Chambers Twentieth Century Dictionary (1982).

Champy, J. and Hammer, M. (1993) *Reengineering the Corporation*, London: Nicholas Brealey.

Chartered Institute of Marketing (n.d.) *Syllabus and Regulations, Certificates and Diploma in Marketing*, Cookham, Berks: Chartered Institute of Marketing.

Chisnall, P.M. (1986) *Marketing Research* 3rd edn, Maidenhead: McGraw-Hill.

Chisnall, P.M. (1987) 'Industrial Marketing', in Baker, M.J. (ed.), *The Marketing Book*, Oxford: Heinemann Professional Publishing, pp 352–3.

Chisnall, P.M. (1989) *Strategic Industrial Marketing* 2nd edn, Hemel Hempstead: Prentice-Hall International.

Christopher, M. and McDonald, M. (1991) *Marketing – An Introduction*, London: Pan Books.

Christopher, M. and McDonald, M. (1995) *Marketing – An Introductory Text*, Basingstoke: Macmillan.

Christopher, M., Walters, D. and Wills, G. (1978) *Introduction to Marketing* 3rd edn, Bradford: MCB Publications.

Clayton, G. (1997) 'Keeping a hand on the public purse', *The Times* 30 January, p 39.

Cobb, R. (1996) 'Prospecting for that research gold', *Marketing Magazine* 23 May.

Cole, G.A. (1994) *Strategic Management*, London: DP Publications.

Collins, M. (1986) 'Sampling', in Worcester, R.M. and Downham, J. (eds), *Consumer Market Research Handbook* 3rd edn, London: McGraw-Hill.

Cook, R. (1998) 'Time to make an exhibition of yourself', *Independent* 20 April, Media, p 11.

Corey, E. R. (1976) *Industrial Marketing: Cases and Concepts* 2nd edn, Englewood Cliffs, NJ: Prentice-Hall.

Couldwell, C. (1996) 'Tapping into the data revolution', *Marketing* 8 August, p 23.

Cowe, R. (1997) 'Food labels "misleading the public"', *Guardian* 10 November, Home News, p 9.

Cowe, R. (1998) 'When truth isn't part of the packet', *Guardian* 10 March, p 15.

Crainer, S. (1996) *Key Management Ideas*, London: Pitman Publishing.

Crosier, K. (1987) 'Promotion', in Baker, M.J. (ed.), *The Marketing Book*, Oxford: Heinemann Professional Publishing.

Culliton, J.W. (1948) 'The management of marketing costs', research bulletin, Boston: Division of Research, Graduate School of Business Administration, Harvard University.

Cunningham, S. (1996) 'High street heavyweights check out home shopping', *The Times* survey, 28 August, p 25.

Curzon, L.B. (1978) *Basic Law*, Plymouth: Macdonald & Evans.

Daft, R.L. *Management* 2nd edn, Orlando, FL: Dryden Press.

Dawson, J.A. (1979) *The Marketing Environment*, London: Croom Helm.

Dawson, S. (1992) *Analysing Organisations* 2nd edn, Basingstoke: Macmillan.

de Bono, E. (1990) *Lateral Thinking for Management*, London: Penguin Books.

Dearborn, C. and Simon, H. (1968) 'Selective perception: A note on departmental identification of executives', *Sociometry* 21.

Dell, M. (1996) 'Direct benefits pay off', *The Times* 27 March, Interface–Business special.

Department of Trade and Industry (1997) *Managing in the '90s*, Business & Consumer Services, DTI, 151 Buckingham Palace Road, London SW1 9SS or on Web site http://www.bnet.co.uk

Dibb, S., Simkin, L., Pride, W.M. and Ferrell, O.C. (1991) *Marketing Concepts and Strategies*, Boston: Houghton Mifflin Company.

Dolan, R.J. (1995) 'How do you know when the price is right?' *Harvard Business Review* September–October, pp 174–83.

Donegan, L. (1997) 'Car speed ads banned', *Guardian* 4 August, Home News, p 8.

Donkin, R. (1997) 'The poachers' progress', *Financial Times* 6 March, Management, p 23.

Douglas, T. (1985) *The Complete Guide to Advertising*, London: Guild Publishing.

Doyle, P. (1994) *Marketing Management and Strategy*, Hemel Hempstead: Prentice-Hall International.

Doyle, P. (1997) 'From the top', *Guardian* 12 April, Management, pp 19, 21.

Drucker, P. (1991a) 'The discipline of innovation', in Drucker, P. (ed.), *Innovation*, Boston, MA: Harvard Business Review Paperback No 90072.

Drucker, P. (1991) *The Coming of the New Organisation*, Boston, MA: Harvard Business Review Paperback No 90033.

Duncan, T. and Moriarty, S. (1998) *Driving Brand Value*, New York: McGraw-Hill.

Eadie, A. (1998) 'Taking the pain out of corporate change', *Sunday Telegraph* 1 March, p A.5.

Egan, C. (1995) *Creating Organizational Advantage*, Oxford: Butterworth-Heinemann.

Ehrenberg, A.S.C. (1991) *A Primer in Data Reduction*, Chichester: John Wiley & Sons.

Engel, J.F., Blackwell, R.D. and Kollat, D.T. (1978) *Consumer Behaviour* 3rd edn, Hinsdale, IL: Dryden Press.

Farbridge, V. (1982) 'The push-button problem solvers of a new society', *Campaign* 9 July, p 47.

Fennell, E. (1996) 'Human touch that counts', *The Times* 14 October, Investors in People feature, p 43.

Festinger, L. (1962) 'Cognitive Dissonance', *Scientific American* October, pp 93–102.

Financial Times (1992) World Economy and Business Review, 21 September.

Fisher, A. (1994) 'No frills approach', *Financial Times* 11 March.

Fitzroy, P.T. (1976) *Analytical Methods for Marketing Management*, London: McGraw-Hill.

Fletcher, W. (1996) 'Admen strive to embrace the appliance of science', *Financial Times* 16 December, p 15.

Fletcher, W. (1997) 'Trusty as underpants', *Guardian* 23 October, Comment, p 19.

Frain, J. (1990) *Principles and Practices of Marketing*, London: Pitman Publishing.

Frain, J. (1993) *The Changing Culture of a College*, London: The Falmer Press.

Francis, D. (1987) *Unblocking Organizational Communication*, Aldershot: Gower Publishing.

Furnham, A. (1997) 'Give trainers the sack', *Financial Times* 3 March, Management, p 12.

Galbraith, J.K. (1996) *The Good Society: The Human Agenda*, London: Sinclair-Stevenson.

Garner, C. (1997) 'Supermarkets prepare to charge more at prime time', *Independent* 8 December.

Garrett, A. (1996) 'Census sensibility on trial', *Observer*, 24 November, Business, p 2.

Gourlay, R. (1996) 'Franchising – demand is increasing', *Financial Times* 7 March, p 13.

Green, E.J. (1970) 'The concept of marketing planning', in Buel, V.P. (ed.) *Handbook of Modern Marketing*. New York: McGraw-Hill, pp 7–13.

Green, R.M. (1994) *The Ethical Manager*, Englewood Cliffs, NJ: Macmillan.

Greenhalgh, C. (1986) 'Research for new product development', in Worcester, R.M. and Downham, J. (eds), *Consumer Market Research Handbook* 3rd edn, London: McGraw-Hill.

Greenslade, R. (1992) 'Putting your brand on the British', *The Times* 29 June.

Guiltinan, J.P., Paul, G.W. and Madden, T.J. (1997) *Marketing Management – Strategies and Programs* 6th edn, London: McGraw-Hill.

Hague, P. and Harris, P. (1993) *Sampling and Statistics*, London: Kogan Page.

Haley, R.I. 'Benefit segmentation: a decision oriented research tool', *Journal of Marketing* July, pp 30–5.

Harrison, M. (1998) 'We looked in the mirror and didn't like what we saw', *Independent*, 22 April, Business, p 19.

Hibbert, E.P. (1989) *Marketing Strategy in International Business*, Maidenhead: McGraw-Hill.

Hobson, J. (1988) 'Advertising', in Lock, D. and Farrow, N (eds), *The Gower Handbook of Management*, Aldershot: Gower Publishing, pp 253–4.

Hobson, R. (1997) 'Getting the message: we value your custom', *The Times* 18 February, Communicating with your customer supplement, p 2.

Hollinger, P. (1997) 'UK Retailing', *Financial Times* survey, 13 March.

Houlder, V. (1996) 'A seal of approval', *Financial Times* 5 November, p 16.

Humble, J., Jackson, D. and Thompson, A. (1994) 'The strategic power of corporate values', *Long Range Planning*, 27(6), pp 28–42.

Hutt, M.D. and Speh, T.W. (1992) *Business Marketing Management* 4th edn, Orlando, FL: Dryden Press.

Jackson, T. (1997) 'A black belt in quality', *Financial Times* 24 February, p 11.

Jain, S.C. (1993) *Marketing Planning and Strategy* 4th edn, Cincinnati, OH: South-Western Publishing Co.

Jamieson, B. (1998) 'Who will be burned by the Russian inferno?' *Sunday Telegraph* 30 August. p B.5.

Jauch, L.R. and Glueck, W.F. (1988) *Business Policy and Strategic Management* 5th edn, New York: McGraw-Hill.

Jobber, D. (1995) *Principles and Practice of Marketing*, Maidenhead: McGraw-Hill.

Johnson, G. and Scholes, K. (1989) *Exploring Corporate Strategy*, Hemel Hempstead: Prentice-Hall.

Jolson, M.L. (1978) *Marketing Management*, London: Collier Macmillan.

Kaplan, R.S. and Norton, D.P. (1992) 'The balanced scorecard – measures that drive performance', *Harvard Business Review* January–February, pp 71–9.

Kashani, K. (1996) 'Why marketing still matters', Mastering Management Series, Part 1, *Financial Times*, pp 8–10.

Katz, E. and Lazarsfeld, P. (1955) *Personal Influence*, New York: Free Press.

Kay, J. (1996a) 'Driving in the stakes to bring new blood to British business', *Observer* 17 November.

Kay, J. (1996b) *The Business of Economics*, Oxford: Oxford University Press.

Kay, J. (1997) 'Lemon economics', *Financial Times* 14 March, p 16.

Keegan, W.J. (1989) *Global Marketing Management* 4th edn, Englewood Cliffs, NJ: Prentice-Hall.

Kehoe, L. (1997) 'Europe falling back in IT, US high-tech groups warn', *Financial Times* 27 January.

Kelly, J. (1996) 'A dangerous divide – highlighting the corporate information gap', *Financial Times* 14 November.

Kettering, C.F. (1989) 'Seed for Thought', in Keegan, W.J., *Global Marketing Management* 4th edn, Englewood Cliffs, NJ: Prentice Hall, p 703.

Kitson A. and Campbell, R. (1996) *The Ethical Organisation – Ethical Theory and Corporate Behaviour*, Basingstoke; Macmillan.

Koch, R. (1995) *The Financial Times Guide to Strategy*, London: FT Pitman Publishing.

Kotler, P. (1991) *Marketing Management* 7th edn, Hemel Hempstead: Prentice-Hall.

Kotler, P. (1994) *Marketing Management: Analysis, Planning, Implementation, and Control* 8th edn, Upper Saddle River, NJ: Prentice-Hall.

Kotler, P. (1997) *Marketing Management: Analysis, Planning, Implementation, and Control* 9th edn, Upper Saddle River, NJ: Prentice-Hall.

Kotler, P. and Armstrong, G. (1990) *Marketing – An Introduction* 2nd edn, Englewood Cliffs, NJ: Prentice-Hall International.

Krauschar, P. (1981) in Rines, M. (ed.), *Marketing Handbook* 2nd edn, Aldershot: Gower Publishing.

Kreitner, R. (1998) *Management* 7th edn, Boston, MA: Houghton Mifflin Company.

Lafferty, P. and Rowe, J. (eds) (1994) *The Hutchinson Dictionary of Science*, Oxford: Helicon Publishing.

Lancaster, G. and Massingham, L. (1993) *Essentials of Marketing* 2nd edn, Maidenhead: McGraw-Hill.

Lanigan, M. (1992) *Engineers in Business*, Wokingham: Addison-Wesley.

Lawler, E.E. (1973) *Motivation in Work Organizations*, Belmont, CA: Brooks/Cole.

Leadbeater, C. (1997) 'Flying with a clear view', *Financial Times* 1 April, p 17.

Lee, J. (1998) 'Professions take brand new approaach', *The Times* 24 March, Analysis, p 13.

Levitt, T. (1986) *The Marketing Imagination*, New York: Free Press.

Lewin, K. (1951) *Field Theory in Social Science*, Harper.

Little, J.D.C. (1979) 'Decision support systems for marketing managers', *Journal of Marketing* Summer, p 11.

Lock, D. and Farrow, N. (eds) (1988) *The Gower Handbook of Management* 2nd edn, Aldershot: Gower Publishing.

Lunn, J.A. (1968) 'Empirical techniques in consumer research', in Pym, D. (ed.), *Industrial Society – Social Sciences in Management*, Harmondsworth: Penguin.

Lupton, T. (1986) in Mayon-White, B. (ed.), *Planning and Managing Change*, London: Harper & Row.

McCann, P. (1998) 'Good for advertising but bad for the economy?' *Independent* 23 June, Tuesday Review, p 15.

McCarthy, E.J. (1978) *Basic Marketing – A Managerial Approach* 6th edn, Homewood, IL: Irwin.

McDaniel, C. Jnr and Gates, R. (1993) *Contemporary Marketing Research* 2nd edn, Minneapolis/ St Paul: West Publishing Company.

McDonald, M.H.B. (1999) *Marketing Plans – How to Prepare Them: How to Use Them* 4th edn, Oxford: Butterworth-Heinemann.

MacFie, C. (1998) 'You don't want to do that', *Independent on Sunday* 26 July, Smart Moves, p 3.

McGoldrick, P.J. (1990) *Retail Marketing*, Maidenhead: McGraw-Hill.

McPhee, N. (1996) 'Prospecting for that research gold', *Marketing Magazine* 23 May.

McRae, H. (1998) 'As big companies get bigger, consumers should think small', *Independent* 3 February, Business, p 27.

Maitland, A. (1997) 'Ban urged on healthy food claims', *Financial Times* 26 February, p 12.

Majaro, S. (1993) *The Essence of Marketing*, Hemel Hempstead: Prentice-Hall International.

Manners, D. (1993) 'Marketing issues a key to silicon boom year', *The Times* 27 October.

Market Research Society (n.d.) *Briefing a Research Agency*, London: MRS.

Marsh, P. (1996) 'Motor parts makers defy usual wisdom', *Financial Times* 7 November, p 13.

Martin, P. (1997) 'The weak link in the chain', *Financial Times* 6 March.

Martin, P. (1996) 'Branded by success', *Financial Times* 12 December, p 18.

Mangham, I. (1979) *The Politics of Organizational Change*, London: Associated Business Press.

Maugham, The Lord, (1977) in *The Law*, Newton Abbot: David & Charles.

Mercer, D. (1992) *Marketing*, Oxford: Blackwell.

Miles, R. and Snow, C. (1978) *Organizational Strategy, Structure and Process*, Maidenhead: McGraw-Hill.

Mintzberg, H. (1973) *The Nature of Managerial Work*, New York: Harper and Row.

Mintzberg, H. (1994) *The Rise and Fall of Strategic Planning*, Hemel Hempstead, Herts: Prentice-Hall International.

Mitchell, A. (1996) 'Stiff upper lips: sold out', *The Times*, 13 March, p 23.

Moir, C. (1996) 'The Franchisee', *Financial Times* survey, 7 March, p 15.

Morden, A.R. (1989) *Elements of Marketing*, London: DP Publications.

Morgan, G. (1986) *Images of Organization*, Beverley Hills, CA: Sage Publications.

Morris, M.H. (1992) *Industrial and Organizational Marketing*, London: Macmillan.

Morris, M.H. (1992) *Industrial and Organizational Marketing* 2nd edn, New York: Macmillan Publishing.

Morton-Williams, J. (1986) 'Questionnaire design', in Worcester, R.M. and Downham, J. (eds), *Consumer Market Research Handbook* 3rd edn, London: McGraw-Hill.

Mullins, L.J. (1989) *Management and Organizational Behaviour* 2nd edn, London: Pitman Publishing.

Murphy, J. (1996) 'Customer loyalty – the art of satisfaction', Mastering Management series, *Financial Times* 1 November.

Nadler, D.A. and Lawler, E.E., III (1979) 'Motivation: a diagnostic approach', in Steers, R.M. and Porter, L.W (eds), *Motivation and Work Behaviour*, New York: McGraw-Hill.

Nadler, D.A. and Tushman, M.L. (n.d.) 'Beyond the charismatic leader: leadership and organizational change', *California Management Review* 32(2).

Narus, J.A. and Anderson, J.C. (1996) Rethinking Distribution Adaptive Channels, Boston, MA: *Harvard Business Review*, July–August.

National Consumer Council (1996) Information Folder, Summer.

Nellis, J.G. and Parker, D. (1997) *The Essence of Business Economics* 2nd edn, London: Prentice-Hall Europe.

Norman, N.R. and Ramirez, R. (1993) 'From value chain to value constellation: designing interactive strategy', *Harvard Business Review* July–August, pp 65–77.

Nutting, J. (1996) 'The shape of tins to come', *Financial Times* 10 December, p 17.

Ohmae, K. (1982) *The Mind of the Strategist – The Art of Japanese Business*, New York: McGraw Hill Inc.

Ohmae, K. (1990) *The Borderless World – Power and Strategy in the Global Marketplace*, London: Fontana Press.

Oldfield, C. (1996) 'Sponsorship jazzes up the marketing of luxury goods', *Sunday Times* 10 November, Small Business, p 13.

Oliver, G. (1980) *Marketing Today*, Hemel Hempstead: Prentice-Hall.

Osgood, C.E. *et al.* (1957) *The Measurement of Meaning*, Urbana: University of Illinois Press.

O'Shaughnessy, J. (1988) *Competitive Marketing – A Strategic Approach*, 2nd edn, London: Unwin Hyman.

Paliwoda, S. (1993) *International Marketing* 2nd edn, Oxford: Butterworth-Heinemann.

Parkes, C. (1997) 'U.S. breathes more easily', *Financial Times* 17 April, Technology, p 25.

Pearce, F.T. (n.d.) *Parameters of Research*, Lichfield, Staffs: Industrial Marketing Research Association.

Pearson, A.E. (1991) 'Tough-minded ways to get innovative', in Drucker, P. (ed.), *Innovation*, Boston, MA: Harvard Business Review Paperback No 90072.

Perlick, W.W. and Lesikar, R.V. (1975) *Introduction to Business – A Societal Approach* rev edn, Dallas: Business Publications.

Perry, Sir M. (1996) 'Customer is ultimate stakeholder', *The Times* 26 January.

Peters, T.J. (1992) *Liberation Management: Necessary Disorganisation for the Nanosecond Nineties*, Basingstoke: Macmillan.

Pfeffer, J. (1998) *The Human Equation*, Boston, MA: Harvard Business School Press.

Piercy, N. (1992) *Market-Led Strategic Change*, Oxford: Butterworth-Heinemann.

Porter, M.E. (1985) *Competitive Advantage*, New York: The Free Press.

Porter, M.E. (1991) *Michael E. Porter on Competition and Strategy*, Boston, MA: Harvard Business Review Paperback No 90079.

Prahalad, C.K. and Hamel, G. (1990) 'The core competence of the corporation', *Harvard Business Review* May–June, pp 79–91.

Pratt, K. (1996) 'Insurers boost fringe benefits', *Sunday Times* 17 March, Money Section, p 9.

Pritchard, S. (1998) 'Learning the secrets of PR', *Independent* 23 July, Education, p 13.

Ritchie, L.D. (1991) *Information*, Newbury Park, CA: Sage Publications.

Robertson, I.T. and Cooper, C.L. (1983) *Human Behaviour in Organizations*, Plymouth: Macdonald & Evans.

Rogers, E.M. (1962) *Diffusion of Innovations*, New York: Free Press.

Rogers, E.M. and Shoemaker, F.F. (1971) *Communication of Innovations* 2nd edn, New York: Free Press.

Rose, D. (1965) 'The service element in added value', in Wilson, A. (ed.) *The Marketing of Industrial Products*, London: Hutchinson, p 128.

Sampson, P. (1986) 'Qualitative research and motivation research', in Worcester, R.M. and Downham, J. (eds), *Consumer Market Research Handbook* 3rd edn, London: McGraw-Hill.

Scase, R. (1998) 'Women drive the recovery', *Independent on Sunday* 5 March, Smart Moves, p 1.

Schmidt, R.A. and Wright, H. (1996) *Financial Aspects of Marketing*, Basingstoke: Macmillan Press.

Schwartz, D.J. (1981) *Marketing Today* 3rd edn, New York: Harcourt Brace Jovanovich.

Scott Poole, M. (1998) in Cooper, C.L. and Argyris, C. (eds), *Encyclopedia of Management* , Oxford: Blackwell Publishers, pp 85–7.

Segev, E. (1995) *Corporate Strategy – Portfolio Models*, London: International Thomson Publishing.

Semich, J.W. (1989) 'How Apple Computer buys for the 1990s', *Purchasing* 22 June, pp 43–7.

Seton, C. (1998) 'Communication for profit', *Sunday Telegraph Supplement* 29 March, p 4.

Sharpe, R. and Morgan, R. (1992) 'What a lot of wrap', *Independent on Sunday* 19 July, p 19.

Sheth, J.N. (1973) 'A model of industrial buyer behaviour', *Journal of Marketing* 37(4), pp 50–6.

Skapinker, M. (1997) 'Overdue departure', *Financial Times* 14 January.

Smith, A. (1997) 'Rebranded Credit Suisse thinks global', *Financial Times* 20 January.

Solomon, R.C. (1993) 'Business Ethics', in Singer, P. (ed.), *A Companion to Ethics*, Oxford; Blackwell.

Stanton, W.J. (1981) *Fundamentals of Marketing* 6th edn, New York: McGraw-Hill.

Steers, R.M. and Porter, L.W. (1979) *Motivation and Work Behaviour*, New York: McGraw-Hill.

Stelzer, I. (1996) 'Capitalism on fire', *Sunday Times* 17 March, American Account.

Sternberg, E. (1994) *Just Business – Business Ethics in Action*, London: Warner Books.

Sterne, J. (1995) *World Wide Web Marketing*, New York: John Wiley & Sons.

Stuttaford, R. (1997) 'Stress and the new wage slaves', *The Times* 16 January, Body and Mind, p 17.

Summers, D. (1996) 'Growth in number of people living alone', *Financial Times* 20 March, p 7.

Swartz, G. (1996) 'Elusive rules for finance', *Financial Times* 18 April, p 13.

Swindells, A.P.F. (1966) *Advertising Media and Campaign Planning*, London: Butterworth.

Tett, G. and Bowley, G. (1996) 'Number crunching turned upside down', *Financial Times* 6 March.

Thomas, M. (1980) 'Market segmentation', *Quarterly Review of Marketing* Autumn, p 26.

Thomas, W.H. (1979) *Pears Guide to the Law* (ed. Zander, M.), London: Pelham Books.

Thompson, A.A., Jr and Strickland, A.J., III (1996) *Strategic Management* 9th edn, Chicago: Richard D. Irwin.

Trapp, R. (1997) 'A brand new form of equity', *Independent on Sunday* 7 December, Inside Business, p 9.

Trapp, R. (1998a) "Sharp and simple' – tomorrow's annual report', *Independent on Sunday* 8 March.

Trapp, R. (1998b) 'The supply chain rattles and rolls', *Independent on Sunday* 26 July, Inside Business, p 6.

Trapp, R. (1998c) 'Integrity is not just an image', *Independent on Sunday*, 8 March, Inside Business, p 8.

Tull, D.S. and Hawkins, D.I. (1990) *Marketing Research – Measurement and Method* 5th edn, New York: Macmillan Publishing Co.

Turner, I. (1997) 'Strategy, complexity and uncertainty', Henley-on-Thames, Oxon: International Forum on Strategic Management, *Newsletter* 7.

Van Tassel, C.E. (1969) *Dimensions of Consumer Behaviour* (Paper No. 27), McNeal, J.U. (ed.), New York: Appleton-Century-Crofts.

Walker, D. (1996) 'More than mere messengers', *The Times* 21 March, p 26.

Waterman, R.H., Jr, Peters, T.J. and Phillips, J.R. (1991) 'The 7-S Framework', in Mintzberg, H. and Quinn, J.B., *The Strategy Process* 2nd edn, Englewood Cliffs, NJ: Prentice-Hall.

Waters, R. (1996) 'It's all in the timing for the Big Three', *Financial Times* 2 February, p 22.

Watson-Smyth, K. (1998) 'Ford forced to pull Full Monty ad', *Independent* 5 February, News, p 3.

Webb, J.R. (1992) *Understanding and Designing Marketing Research*, London: Academic Press.

Webster, F.E., Jr (1991) *Industrial Marketing Strategy* 3rd edn, New York: John Wiley & Sons.

Wheeler, D. and Silanpää, M. (1997) 'Let's nail ourselves to the stake', *Independent on Sunday* 13 April , Bloomberg, p 3.

Wentworth, F. (1981) *Handbook of Physical Distribution Management*, Centre for Physical Distribution Management, Farnborough: Gower Publishing.

Wille, E. (1992) *Quality: Achieving Excellence*, London: BCA (Sunday Times Business Skills series).

Williamson, R.J. (1979) *Marketing for Accountants and Managers*, London: Heinemann.

Willsmer, R.L. (1976) *The Basic Arts of Marketing*, London: Business Books.

Wilmshurst (1978) *The Fundamentals and Practice of Marketing*, London: Heinemann.

Wilson, A. (1973) *The Assessment of Industrial Markets*, London: Cassell/Associated Business Programmes.

Wolffe, R. (1996) 'The art of the possible', *Financial Times* 12 November.

Woodruffe, H. (1995) *Services Marketing*, London: M&E Pitman Publishing.

Worcester, R.M. and Downham, J. (eds) (1986) *Consumer Market Research Handbook* 3rd edn, London: McGraw-Hill.

Yankelovitch, D. *et al.* (1985) in Douglas, T., the *Complete Guide to Advertising*, London: Guild Publishing.

Yorke, D. (1998) in Cooper, C.L. and Argyris, C. (eds), *Encyclopedia of Management*, Oxford: Blackwell Publishers, p 16.

Zikmund, W.G. and d'Amico, M. (1993) *Marketing* 4th edn, West Publishing Company.

Index

INDEX

Above and below the line
    (communications) 317
ACCESS
    Face to Face omnibus 147
    by Telephone omnibus 147
    to Youth omnibus 147
*ACORN classification system 5
Activities, interests, opinions (AIO) 166–7
Action plan 420
Additional Panel Classifications (APCs) 343
Ad hoc data 138
Administrative error (sampling) 152
Adoption clasifications 188–90
Ad valorem tariffs 377
Advertising 325–31
Advertising Association, The 308
Advertising
    definition 307
    economics 308–10
    expenditure measurement 344
Advertising Standards Authority (ASA) 106–8
Affirmative action programmes 354
After-sales service 231–2
AIDA model 314, 325, 344
Aided recall 343
Airbus Industrie (European Airbus Project)
    41
Air miles 331–2
Alexander, G. 315
Alles, A. 333
Altman, W. 425
American Marketing Association (AMA)
    126–7, 194, 223
Ames, C.B. 371–2
Analytical model systems 129
Anderson, J.C. 277
Ansoff, H.I. 233
Ansoff matrix 233
Area Data service (CACI) 181
Argyl (Safeway) organization 293
Arithmetic mean 155–6
Armstrong, G. 241, 301
Armstrong, M. 266, 351, 361–2, 367, 368
Artificial intelligence 90
Ashworth, J. 425
Asset-based marketing 56
Association of British Marketing Research
    Companies (ABRMC) 130
Association for British Sponsorship of the Arts
    (ABSA) 340
Association of Market Survey Organizations
    (AMSO) 130–2, 149

Atkinson, P.E. 321
Attitude research/measurement 42
Audit Bureau of Circulation (ABC) 341
Audit
    external 412
    internal (marketing) 412
Automatic vending 301
Averages 155
Awareness, trial, reinforcement (ATR) model
    344

Baker, M. 27, 93, 175, 200
Balanced scorecard 71–2, 351
BARB TV audience surveys 322, 343
Bartolomé, F. 362
Benchmarking 69
Benefit analysis worksheet 196
Benefit ratio (product) 196
Benefit segmentation 184–5
Bickerton, R. 424
Binomial distribution 157–8
Blackstock, C. 310
Blackwell, R.D. 172
Bogart, L. 344
Boone, L.E. 163, 202
Bonfield, Sir P. 34
Borden, N.H. 61
Boston Consulting Group (BCG) matrix
    211–3
Boulton, L. 424
Boundary role 361
Brand
    connotations 225
    definitions 223, 226
    equity 224
    family 225
    identity 315
    image 58
    integrity 224, 227
    loyalty 227
    management 224–7
    switching 227
Brand/product structure 80–2
Branding technique 57
Brassington, F. 267
Break-even analysis 251–4
British Airways 331
British Broadcasting Corporation (BBC) 146
British Codes of Advertising and Sales
    Promotion 106–8
British Export Houses Association 275

British Franchise Association (BFA)   300–1
British Market Research Bureau (BMRB
    International)   136, 147, 205, 342
British Standards Institution (BSI)   103–4
Broadcasting Act 1950   108
BS 5750 standard   103
Budget
    finance   397
    marketing   397
    personnel   397
    production   397
    sales   397
Burnes, B.   367
Burson Marseller organization   391
Business Line omnibus   147
Business process re-engineering   354
Business strategy   53–61
Buyclasses   176
Buyer
    culture/sub-culture   165
    personal factors   166–7
    profile   165–71
    psychological factors   167–9
    social factors   165–6
BUYGRID model   176
Buyphases   176

Campaign budget (promotion)   323–5
    plan   321–5
    planning (promotion)   320–5
Campbell, R.   112–13
Cannon, T.   209, 351
Carroll, A.B.   351
Cause-related marketing   425
Caveat emptor   98
Census data (U.K.)   181, 190
Centralization strategy   77
Champy, J.   354
Chandler, A.   40
Change
    anticipatory   365
    incremental   366
    reactive   365
    strategic   366
Channel evolution   276–81
    leadership   289
    management   256, 268, 283–91
    policy (export)   381
    strategy   268, 278, 282–3
Channels of distribution   268–83
Chartered Institute of Marketing   109–10,
    325
Chief executive, responsibilities   54, 94
Chisnall, P.M.   145, 149, 374
Christopher, M.   196, 198, 227, 265, 267,
    288
Cinema (advertising medium)   330–1
Cinema and Video Industry Audience
    Research (CAVIAR)   342
Citizens' Advice Bureaux   104
Citizens' Charter   105
Closed systems   27
Cobb, R.   145
Code of ethics   114
    implementation of   116–7
Codes of practice   104–5, 106–11
Coefficient of elasticity   246
Cognitive dissonance   171, 173–4, 326
Cole, G.A.   94, 349, 352

Collaboration   41, 202
Committee of Advertising Practice (CAP)
    106–8
Communication   19, 311–4, 355–6
    function   312–4
Communications mix   316
Competitive advantage   55
    approaches (pricing)   248
    budding model   260
Completely knocked down (ckd)   378
Complexity theory   40
Composite forecast   409
Computer aided design (CAD)   30
    manufacturing (CAM)   30
    assisted personal interviewing (CAPI)   143
    assisted telephone interviewing (CATI)
        147
    integrated manufacturing   198
Concentrated marketing   56
Concept testing   202–4
Conditions (guarantee)   231
Confidence level (price)   254
Conjoint analysis   217–20, 249
Consumer   161–2
    Agreements Arbitration Act 1988   103
    Bill of Rights 1962   101–2
Consumer Credit Act 1974   99
    Credit (Advertisement) Regulations 1989
        100
    markets   127
    panels   146–7
    Protection Act 1987   100
Consumerism   101–11, 311
Consumers' Association, The   102–3
Cook, F.   366
Cook, R.   334
Cooper, C.L.   357, 425
Cooperative retail societies   298
Cooperative Wholesale Society (CWS)
    229–30, 298
Contract, law of   98
Contract manufacturing   384
Contingency plan   419
Contingency reserve   324–5
Continuous data   138–40
Core competences   51–2
Corey, E.R.   373
Cornhill Direct   73
Corporate centre strategy   24, 46–52
Corporate centre strategy, implementation of
    52–3
Corporate marketing   137, 388–91
Corporate plan   420
Corporate values   48–9
Corporate values programme   136
Correlation analysis   403
Correlation coefficient   403
Cost, insurance, freight (cif) price   379
Cost plus approach (pricing)   251
Cost:volume:profit relationships   234–5
Costs, production/distribution   271–4
Countertrading   386
Covered/open air markets   302
Cox Insurance company   73
Cowe, R.   229, 316
Crainer, S.   55, 364–5
Credit risk   378
Credit Suisse   41–3
Criterion group classification   189
Cross-elasticity of demand   259

Culliton, J.   61
Culture, organizational   93–7, 175
Curve of normal distribution   158–60
Curzon, L.   98
Customer   161–2
  buying behaviour   163–5
  care programmes   221
  loyalty   14
  retention   13
  satisfaction   14
Customer-led culture   368–70
Cyclical vartiation   400–1

Daft, R.L.   350–1, 356
DAGMAR model   344
d'Amico, M.   57–8, 264, 267–8
Data collection methods   142–9
Dawson, J.A.   186
Dawson, S.   76
Dealer's sales staff   339
de Bono, E.   141–2
Decision making process   174, 177–8
Decision making units (DMUs)   171–2,
  176–7
Decision support systems (DSS)   90, 128–9
Delegated legislation   32
Delivered, duty paid (DDP) price   379
Dell Computer Group   12
Delphi technique   409
Demographic classifications   179–80
Department of Trade and Industry (DTI)
  382
Department stores   297–8
Departmental conflict   95
Derived demand   174
Developmental systems   88
Design of research   149–54
Dibb, S. *et al.*   114, 208
Dichotomous questions   144
Differentiation strategy   59, 73
Digital Equipment Corporation (DEC)   12,
  27, 48
Direct mail   328–9
Direct Mail Information Service   329
Direct marketing/response selling   299–30
Direct Marketing Association   329
Direct marketing channel   268
Direct selling by correspondence   338
Director General of Fair Trading   99
Discount stores   293
Distribution – changing pattern   292–5
Distribution function   263–8
  power   291–5
Distributors' margin   285–6
Distributive partnerships, planning   288
Diversification   234
Do-It-All organization   91–2
Dolan, R.J.   241, 249–50
Donegan, L.   310
Donkin, R.   352
Door-to-door selling   302
Double loop learning   36–7
Downstream value chain   265
Doyle, P.   76, 199, 207, 265, 268, 337, 359,
  369, 425
Drucker, P.   201
Dual distribution   282–3, 286
Dual pricing   262
Dyson, J.   202

Eadie, A.   366
Eating Out of Home Monitor   146
Economic price   251
Economist Intelligence Unit (EIU)   125, 382,
  425–6
Edinburgh Health Care NHS Trust   215
Effectiveness   25
Efficiency   25
Egan, C.   34
Elasticity of demand   245–6
Electronic shopping   301
Electronic data interchange (EDI)   90,
  134
Engel, J.F.   172
Enlarged marketing mix   193
Entry limit pricing   244
Environment, external   25–35
Environmental health departments   104
Environmental influences
  collaboration   34
  competition   32–4
  economic   28
  legal   31–2
  political   28–9
  social   30–1
  technological   29–30
EPOS systems   139
Equilibrium price   241
Equity   98
Ethical audit   350
Ethical climate   350
Ethical dilemma   350
Ethical framework, the   349–51
Ethical ombudsman   350
Ethics of advertising   310–11
Ethics committee   350
Ethics, normative   111
Ethics of marketing   111–7
Ethnic/religious classifications   185–6
Euromonitor PLC   125
European Commission (EC)   228
European Union (EU)   21
EU legislation   106
European Toiletries and Cosmetics Database
  146
Exclusive distribution   282
Exhibitions   333–4
Expectancy/valance theory   357–8
Experience curve effect   70
Experimental marketing   208–11
Experimentation methods   142–3
Expert systems   90
Export marketing   376–83
Export payment methods   379
Export price   379–80
Extended Gabor Granger methods   248
External agencies   85–6
External data   137–8
Ex-works price   379

Face-to-face selling   337–8
Factor, services of   275
Fair Trading Act 1973   99
Family Food Panel   146
Family life-cycle   180–1
Feedback   27
Festinger, L.   171
Fiedler, F.E.   364–5
Field research (export)   382

Field sales force (management/motivation) 359–61
Financial Times 28, 224, 325
Fitzroy, P.T. 188
Fixed costs 250
Fletcher, W. 239, 309, 345
Focus group 145
Forecasting, and the computer 410
Forecasting
  methods 398–400
  process (steps) 394–7
  roles/responsibilities 398
  techniques:
    (qualitative 407_10
    quantitative) 400–7
Forecasts, types 397–8
Force-field theory 94
Forwarding agents 275, 380
Fractional factorial orthogonal array 218
Franchising 271, 300–1
Francis, D. 355–6
Free on board (f.o.b.) price 379
Functional organization 78
Functional strategy 24

Galbraith, J.K. 16
Gap analysis 63–5, 215–7
Garner, C. 262
Garrett, A. 190
Gates, R. 217
General Electric Company 70
General Electric/McKinsey model 213
Geodemographic classifications 182–4
Geogrpahical classifications 181
Geogrpahic division 83
Global structure 83
Globalization 387
Global marketing 386–8
'Glocal' strategy 388
Goal setting theory 358
Goetze Components 96–7
Gordon Simmons Research Group 137, 141
Gordon, W.P. 199
Green, E.J. 416
Greenhalgh, C. 201–2
Gross domestic product (GDP) 403
Group discussions 144–5
Group dynamics training 362
Guiltinan, J.P. 199

Haberman Company 201–2
Haley, R.I. 184
Hall tests 148
Hamel, G. 51
Hammer, M. 354
Harrison, M. 425
Hawkins, D.I. 218
Hibbert, E.P. 387
Hierarchy – pressures on 77
Hobson, J. 309
Hobson, R. 329
Hollinger, P. 296
Horizontal marketing systems 276–7
Human resource management 351–4
Human resource planning 352
Hutt, M.D. 196, 268
Hypermarkets 293

Ideas, marketing of 238–9
Imperial Chemical Industries (ICI) 390
Inbound logistics 265
Incentive and loyalty schemes 331–2
Incorporated Society of British Advertisers (ISBA) 334
'Incoterms' guide 379–80
Independent retailers 296
Independent Television Commission (ITC) 108, 310
Industrial Market Research Association (IMRA) 127–8
Industrial marketing 371–6
Industrial markets 127
Industrial markets – pricing 258–60
Industrial segmentation 187–8
Influences – buying behaviour 164–5
Information technology (IT) 89–91
Innovation 199
Institute of Personnel and Development 352
Institute of Practitioners in Advertising (IPA) 345
Institute of Public Relations (IPR) 336, 390–1
Institute of Sales Promotion (ISP) 331
Intensive distribution 282
Interaction system 129
Inter-Linked Economy (ILE) 28
Intermediaries 265, 270
  – assessment 288–90
  – motivation 285–8
  – selection 284–5
Internal data 137–8
Internal records system 121–3, 137
International Chamber of Commerce 379–80
International Institute for Management Development (IMD) 8
International marketing 383–6
International Monetary Fund (IMF) 423
International Standard Industrial Classification (ISIC) 188
ISO 9000 Standard 103
Internet 301–2
Inventory policy 303
Investment budget strategy 257

Jackson, T. 222
Jain, S.C. 33, 87, 88
Jamieson, B. 423
Jobber, D. 260, 284, 344
Johnson, G. 93
Johnson, H. & R. Tiles 116–7
Joint ventures 384–5
Jolson, M.L. 155
Just-in-time (JIT) 221, 266, 374

Kaplan, R.S. 71–2
Katz, E. 189
Kay, J. 16, 38, 51, 61
Keegan, W. 385–6
Keppel Corporation 52
Kettering, C.F. 423
Kitson, A. 112–3
Kleinwort Benson Investment Management 17–8
Koch, R. 22, 40, 66, 185, 387

Kollatt, D.T.   172
Kotler, P.   38, 120–1, 129, 163–4, 172, 223, 238, 241, 301, 368–9
Kreitner, R.   350, 354, 356–7, 362, 366

Labelling   229–30
Lancaster, G.   71
Lanigan, M.   163, 195–6
Laporte organization   116
Lawler, E.E.   357–8
Lazarsfeld, P.   189
Leadership   363–5
    contingency theory   364
    functional approach   363
    situational approach   363
    style   363
    traits approach   363
    transactional theory   365
    transformational theory   365
Lean media   356
Learning organization   36–7, 366
Learning, theory of   170
Leasing   375
Least squares method   405
Lee, J.   330
Levitt, T.   220
Lewin, K.   94
Licensing   375
Licensing and royalty agreements   383–4
Life-cycle   167
Life-style   166–7, 342
Limits of confidence   160
Linear relationship   405
Line of best fit   404
Locator model   137
Logical incrementalism   40
Logotype ('logo')   316
London Business School   325
Long-run welfare of society   311
Loss-leaders   257
Lunn, J.A.   189–90
Lupton, T.   369

MacFie, C.   365
Madden, T.J.   199
Magazines (Press)   327
Mail Order Protection Schemes Ltd (MOPS)   108–9
Mail order selling   299–30
Maitland, A.   333
Majaro, S.   200, 265
Managing
    change   365–8
    diversity approach   354
Management
    by objectives (MBO)   358
    contracting   384
    information system (MIS)   89–91, 120, 367
    role of   25
Margin remaining method   323
Market
    development   234
    -led organizational system   9
    penetration   233–4
    segmentation   56–7, 179–80
Market Research Society   110–1, 148–9, 151, 154

Marketing
    and strategy   7
    as philosophy and function   4
    communications   311–5
    communications strategy   314–5
    concept   4–5
    definition   7, 11
    function   3, 4
    information system (Mk IS)   120–9, 367
    intelligence system   123–6
    meanign of   3
    mix   58, 61–2, 193–4
    mix, enlarged   62–3, 193
    organization   78–86
    plan   420, 368
    plan, control and evaluation   417–8
    planning   411–21
    planning framework   411
    relationship   13
    research   126–8, 129–37
    societal concept   6, 38
    strategic and functional roles   4
Marketing department
    brand/product structure   80–2
    composite structure   83–4
    functional organization   78–80
    market structure   82–3
    task force structures   84–5
Marketing Science Institute   176
Martin, P.   267
Masiello, T.   96
Maslow's hierarchy   168–9, 357
Massingham, L.   71
McCann, P.   308
McDaniel, C. Jr.   217
McDonald, M.   196, 198, 227, 267, 288, 421
McGraw Hill Publishers   329
McKinsey Consultants   198
McRae, H.   424
MEAL service see Nielsen, A.C.
Means-end chain   416
Media
    atmosphere   320–1
    characteristics   320
    cost   321
    coverage   321
    richness   356
    weight tests   323–4
Median value   156
Mencap Organisation   223
Mercer, D.   235
Miles, L.D.   213
Mintel International Group Ltd   125, 190
Modal value   156
Monadic approaches   248
Monitoring and control systems   87–8
Monopolistic competition   244
Monopoly markets   244
Morden, A.R.   163
Morgan, G.   36
Morris, M.H.   27, 241, 260, 283, 289
Morton-Williams, J.   143
MOST acronym (Mission, Objectives Strategy, Tactics)   47
Motivation   357–61
    theories of   167–9
Moving averages   401–3
Mullins, L.J.   419

Multi-channel approach   269
Multiple choice questions   144
Multiple information cues   356
Multiple regression techniques   407
Multiples (retail)   296–7
Multinational corporations   385–6
Mystery shopping   148–9

Nadler, D.A.   358, 365
Narus, J.A.   277
National classifications   185
National Consumer Council   103, 333
National Exhibition Centre (NEC)   334
National newspapers   327
National Readership Survey (NRS)   180, 322,
    341–2
National Westminster Bank   229, 300–1
Nectar Manufacturing Ltd   382
Network analysis   416
Networking, computer   90
Neural networking software   129
New product planning   200–6
New Labour election campaign   239
Niche marketing   300
Nielsen, A.C. Organisation   125, 138–40,
    292
Nielsen, A.C. • MEAL service   344
Non-probability sample   153
Non-sampling error   152
Non-tariff barriers to trade   378
Normal distribution   158–60
Normann, R.   67
Normative moral relativism   311
North American Free Trade Agreement
    (NAFTA)   21, 376
Nutting, J.   228–9

Observation methods   142
Office of Fair Trading (OFT)   105–6,
    115–16
Office of National Statistics (ONS)   20, 121,
    124–5, 190–1
Ohmae, K.   28, 33, 185
'Okumaliuk' service   277
Oligopoly markets   245
Omnibus surveys   147
One-level channel   269
Open-ended questions   144
Open systems   27
Operational systems   87
Opportunities to see (OTS)   342
Options model (RI)   249
Organizational
    buying behaviour   174–8
    culture   10, 93–7, 175
    design   75–8
    management   75–8
    mission   47
    objectives   14–16
    structures   75–86
    systems   87–92
    vision   47
O'Shaughnessy, J.   175
Outdoor and transportation media   330
Outdoor Site Classification and Audience
    Research (OSCAR)   342
Out-of-town shopping centres   294
'Own-label' products   236–7

Pack   227
Packaging   227, 332–3
Paliwoda, S.   385
Pareto analysis ('80/20' rule)   66–7, 235
Parity pricing   257
Parkes, C.   424
Partially knocked down (pkd)   378
Participative management style   356
Party selling   302
Penetration pricing   257
Pepsi-Cola Corporation   315
'People' factor (export)   382
Perceived value approach (pricing)   254–5
Perception   169
Perception management   391
Perfect competition   244
Performance appraisal   420
Performance indicators   360
Personal care panel   146
Personal construct theory   216
Personal selling   337–9
    definition   307
Peters, T.J.   38, 40, 84, 87
Pettitt, S.   267
Pfeffer, J.   348, 357
Phillips, J.R.   38, 87
Physical distribution – export   380
Physical distribution management   302–6
Piercy, N.   75, 82, 96, 368, 396
PIMS database   70, 227
Place marketing   339
Point-of-sale display   332
Political risk   378
Porter, M.E.   33, 55, 67
    5 Forces concept   35
Portfolio models   211–3
Positioning strategy   57–61, 318–9
    avoidance (differentiation)   59, 60
    head-to-head (engagement)   59, 60
    map   58–9
PPP Healthcare   91
Prahalad, C.K.   51
Pre-Max technique   205
Press, U.K.   326–7
Press relations   334–6
Press release   335
Price
    and corporate policy   243
    and external constraints   246
    and marketing mix   243–4
    and product life cycle   246–7
    and product portfolio   247
    -demand relationships   244
    elasticity   245–6
    leader   245, 257
    lining   257
    maker   245
    sensitivity measurement (PSM)   248
    taker   245
Prices   241–50
Pricing
    objectives   242
    process   250–5
    strategy   241–50
Primary data   121, 382
Probability sample   152–3
Product
    /commodity markets   302
    costs   271–4
    definition   194–5

development/management techniques 206–20, 234
  failure 201
  life-cycle 206–8, 235–6
  localisation 387
  /market strategy 233–4
  -media survey 342
  mix 232
  new 199–200
  new, planning 200–6
  range extension 235
  range rationalisation 235
  strategy 232–3
Products
  consumer 194
  industrial 194–5
Production orientation 27
Profitability index (distributors') 289
Profit and loss statement 417
Profit maximisation 256–7
Promotion function 311–4
Promotional research 341–5
Proportional property (normal distribution) 159
Public relations 334–6
'Pull' strategy 162
'Push' strategy 162

Quality assurance systems 221
Qualitative data 141
Quality circles 221
Quantitative data 140–1
Quantity discounts 286–7
Queen's Awards for Environmental Achievement, 1997 116–7
Questionnaires, use of 143–4
Quick environmental scanning technique (QUEST) 25
Quota sample 153–4

Radio (advertising medium) 330
Radio Joint Audience Research (RAJAR) 342
Ramirez, R. 67
Random digit dialling 151
Random error 152
Random fluctuation 400–1
Rank Xerox Corporation 30
Rapid prototyping technology 49–50, 375
Ratio analysis 419
Reassurance advertising 171, 326
Reciprocal trading 375
Reference groups 165–6
Regional newspapers 327
Regression analysis 403–7
Regression line 405
Relationship marketing 13, 90
Repertory grid (Kelly) 215–6
Research brief 150–1
Research International (RI) 171
Research International – RI Specialist Units Ltd 136
Retailer 271
Retail Index (Nielsen) 138–9
Retail outlet – types 296–302
Retail parks 294
Ritchie, L.D. 311–2
Robertson, I.T. 357
'Roboshops' 295

Rogers, E.M. 188–9
Rolls Royce, Coventry 117
Rover Cars 52
Royal Dutch Shell 425
Royal Society of Arts (RSA) 17

Sainsbury, J. (Plc) 18, 293, 425
Sale of Goods (Implied Terms) Act 1973 100
Sales agents, brokers 274–5
Sales forecast – influence of 395
Sales forecasting 394–411
Salespeople (selection/training) 360
Sales promotion 331–3
  definition 307
Sampling
  error 152
  estimate 151
  frame 152
  process 151–2
Sampson, P. 215–6
Scalar methods 248
SCANTRACK service (Nielsen) 139
Scase, R. 354
Scattergraph 404
Schmidt, R.A. 420
Scholes, K. 93
Schwartz, D. 132–3, 394
Scientific method 131–3
Scott Poole, M. 312
Seasonality 401
Secondary data 121, 382
Secular trend 400–1
Seger, E. 211–3
Segmentation, market 56, 73, 178–90
  variables 57, 179
Selective distribution 282
  perception 169
Self-concept theory 166
Semantic differential 169–70
Semiconductor Manufacturers' Association (SMA) 12
Sensitivity analysis 324
Services, marketing of 237–8
Seton, C. 329
Settlement discounts 287
Seven-S Framework 38–9
Siebe, U.K. 198
Siemens of Germany 15, 20
Simple Gabor Granger methods 248
Simulated test marketing 209–11
Simultaneous engineering 198
Single loop learning 36
Single Person Households Survey 190–1
Situation analysis 412
'Six sigma' programme 222
'Skimming' technique 258
Small and medium sized enterprises (SMEs) 46
Smoothing constant 402–3
Social class 165
Society, long run welfare of 16
Solomon, R.C. 111–2
Span of control 79
Specialist panels 147
Speh, T.W. 196, 268
S.P. Engineering/Camber International 40–1
Sponsorship 339–41
Spreadsheets 410

Stakeholder concept   37–8, 389
Standard deviation   156–7
Standard error   158
Standard Industrial Classification (SIC)   187–8
Stanton, W.J.   200–1
Statistical packages   410
Statistical process control   221
Sternberg, E.   115
Strategic business unit (SBU)
  definition   23
  management   46, 211–3
  strategy   24, 412
Strategic cost analysis (value chain)   67–70
Strategic Planning Institute   70
Strategic management process   22–26
Strategic marketing process   58
  techniques   61–72
Strategy, organizational   21–43
Stratified random sample   154
Stickland, A.J. III   47, 69–70, 75–6
Structures, organizational   75–87
Struttaford, T.   354
Summers, D.   191
Supermarkets   293
Superstores   293
Supplier-customer interdependence   373–4
Supply of Goods and Services Act 1982   100
Surveys of buyer intentions   408
Surveys of sales force opinion   409
Swartz, G.   325
Swindells, A.P.F.   320
SWOT analysis   57, 413
Synergy   49–51
Systems (effective)   88–9
Systems thinking   10

Taguchi methodology   221
Target Group Index (TGI)   342
Target Group Ratings (TGRs)   343
Target profit pricing   252
Tariffs   377–8
Task force structures   84–5
Task method   324
Taylor Nelson AGB   146–7
Taylor Nelson Sofres   322
Team management   361–2
Technological forecasting   398
Television (advertising medium)   328
Telephone selling   338
Tesco organisation   293, 301–2
Test marketing   208–11
  choice of area   210
The Times newspaper   339
Thomas, M.   184
Thompson, A.A. Jr.   47, 69–70, 75–6
Three-level channel   269–70
Tied indicator   403
Time series analysis   400–3
Time scheduling   415
TLG Lighting, U.K.   86–7
Total distribution cost (TDC) analysis   304–6
Total oganizational commitment   18–9
Total product, the   223–32, 255, 258
Total quality management (TQM)   220–2, 368
Trade associations   104–5
Trade Descriptions Act 1968–72   98
Trading standards departments (TSDs)   104
Training and Enterprise Councils (TECs)   136

Transport, choice of   303
Trapp, R.   316
Trend extrapolation   402
Tull, D.S.   218
Two-factor theory (Herzberg)   167
Two-level channel   269

Undifferentiated marketing   56
Unfair Contract Terms Act 1977   99, 101
Unfair Contract Terms Unit (OFT)   115–6
Unilever organization   87
Unique selling proposition (USP)   315, 325
U.K. expenditure – advertising media   326
Unsolicited Good and Services Act 1971–75   100
Upstream value chain   265
User guarantees   230–1
Users' associations and consultative councils   105
Utilities of form   161
  place   161, 263–4
  time   161, 263–4

Value analysis/management   211–3
Value chain analysis   67–9
Value system   69–70
Values statement   350
Variable costs   250
Verdict Research Ltd   125
Vertical marketing systems (VMS)   276–7
Voluntary groups/chains   293

Walker, D.   391
Walkers Shortbread Ltd   378–9
Walters, D.   265–6
Warranties   231
Waterman, R.H. Jr.   38, 87
Watson-Smyth, K.   310
Weak signal approach   25
Webster, F.E.   57, 174, 179, 371–3, 375
Weighted factor approach (distributors)   289–90
Weighting (sample)   154
Weights and Measures Act 1985   100
Wheeler, D.   435
Which? magazine   102
Wholesaler – functions of   271
Wholly owned subsidiaries   385
Williamson, R.J.   274
Wills, G.   265–6
Willsmer, R.L.   394
Wilson, A.   397–8
Wolfensohn, J.   viii
Woodruffe, H.   238
World Trade Organization (WTO)   377
World Wide Web   30
Wright, H.   420

Xerox Corporation   69

Yorke, D.   314, 344

Zero channel   269
Zikmund, W.G.   57–8, 264, 267–8